BIBLICAL DOCTRINES

BIBLICAL DOCTRINES

Benjamin B. Warfield

THE BANNER OF TRUTH TRUST

THE BANNER OF TRUTH TRUST
3 Murrayfield Road, Edinburgh EH12 6EL
PO Box 621, Carlisle, Pennsylvania 17013, USA

*

First published 1929
First Banner of Truth edition 1988
ISBN 0 85151 534 7

*

Printed and bound in Great Britain at
The Camelot Press Ltd. Southampton

PREFATORY NOTE

REV. BENJAMIN BRECKINRIDGE WARFIELD, D.D., LL.D., Professor of Didactic and Polemic Theology in the Theological Seminary of the Presbyterian Church in the United States of America, at Princeton, New Jersey, provided in his will for the collection and publication of the numerous articles on theological subjects contained in encyclopaedias, reviews and other periodicals, and appointed a committee to edit and publish these papers. In pursuance of his instructions the first volume, entitled "Revelation and Inspiration," was published in 1927 by the Oxford University Press; this, the second volume, containing Dr. Warfield's articles on Biblical Doctrines, has been prepared under the editorial direction of this committee. In it the biblical references have been retained in the forms which were used in the several articles; but, while lacking in uniformity, it is believed that the abbreviations will readily be understood.

The generous permission to publish articles contained in this volume is gratefully acknowledged as follows: The Howard-Severance Co. for the articles taken from the "International Standard Encyclopaedia," Charles Scribner's Sons for the articles taken from "A Dictionary of the Bible," edited by James Hastings, and from "A Dictionary of Christ and the Gospels," edited by James Hastings.

The clerical preparation of this volume has been done by Miss Letitia N. Gosman, to whom the thanks of the committee are hereby expressed.

ETHELBERT D. WARFIELD
WILLIAM PARK ARMSTRONG
CASPAR WISTAR HODGE
Committee.

CONTENTS

I
PREDESTINATION

PREDESTINATION [1]

I. The Terms

THE words 'predestine,' 'predestinate,' 'predestination' seem not to have been domiciled in English literary use until the later period of Middle English (they are all three found in Chaucer: "Troylous and Cryseyde," 966; "Orisoune to the Holy Virgin," 69; translation of "Boëthius," b. 1, pr. 6, l. 3844; the Old English equivalent seems to have been 'forestihtian,' as in Ælfric's "Homilies," ii. 364, 366, in renderings of Rom. i. 4, viii. 30). 'Predestine,' 'predestination' were doubtless taken over from the French, while 'predestinate' probably owes its form directly to the Latin original of them all. The noun has never had a place in the English Bible, but the verb in the form 'predestinate' occurs in every one of its issues from Tindale to the Authorized Version. Its history in the English versions is a somewhat curious one. It goes back, of course, ultimately to the Latin '*prædestino*' (a good classical but not pre-Augustan word; while the noun '*prædestinatio*' seems to be of Patristic origin), which was adopted by the Vulgate as its regular rendering of the Greek προορίζω, and occurs, with the sole exception of Acts iv. 28 (Vulgate *decerno*), wherever the Latin translators found that verb in their text (Rom. i. 4, viii. 29, 30, I Cor. ii. 7, Eph. i. 5, 11). But the Wyclifite versions did not carry 'predestinate' over into English in a single instance, but rendered in every case by 'before ordain' (Acts iv. 28 'deemed'). It was thus left to Tindale to give the word a place in the English Bible. This he did, however, in only one passage, Eph. i. 11, doubtless under the influence of the Vulgate. His ordinary rendering of προορίζω is 'ordain before' (Rom. viii. 29, Eph. i. 5; cf. I Cor. ii. 7, where

[1] Article "Predestination," from *A Dictionary of the Bible*, ed. by James Hastings, v. 4, pp. 47–63. Pub. N. Y. 1909, by Charles Scribner's Sons.

3

the 'before' is omitted apparently only on account of the succeeding preposition into which it may be thought, therefore, to coalesce), varied in Rom. viii. 30 to 'appoint before'; while, reverting to the Greek, he has 'determined before' at Acts iv. 28 and, following the better reading, has 'declared' at Rom. i. 4. The succeeding English versions follow Tindale very closely, though the Genevan omits 'before' in Acts iv. 28 and, doubtless in order to assimilate it to the neighbouring Eph. i. 11, reads 'did predestinate' in Eph. i. 5. The larger use of the word was due to the Rhemish version, which naturally reverts to the Vulgate and reproduces its *prædestino* regularly in 'predestinate' (Rom. i. 4, viii. 29, 30, I Cor. ii. 7, Eph. i. 5, 11; but Acts iv. 28 'decreed'). Under this influence the Authorized Version adopted 'predestinate' as its ordinary rendering of προορίζω (Rom. viii. 29, 30, Eph. i. 5, 11), while continuing to follow Tindale at Acts iv. 28 'determined before,' I Cor. ii. 7 'ordained,' as well as at Rom. i. 4 'declared,' in margin 'Greek determined.' Thus the word, tentatively introduced into a single passage by Tindale, seemed to have intrenched itself as the stated English representative of an important Greek term. The Revised Version has, however, dismissed it altogether from the English Bible and adopted in its stead the hybrid compound 'foreordained' as its invariable representative of προορίζω (Acts iv. 28, Rom. viii. 29, 30, I Cor. ii. 7, Eph. i. 5, 11), — in this recurring substantially to the language of Wyclif and the preferred rendering of Tindale. None other than a literary interest, however, can attach to the change thus introduced: 'foreordain' and 'predestinate' are exact synonyms, the choice between which can be determined only by taste. The somewhat widespread notion that the seventeenth century theology distinguished between them, rests on a misapprehension of the evidently carefully-adjusted usage of them in the Westminster Confession, iii. 3 ff. This is not, however, the result of the attribution to the one word of a 'stronger' or to the other of a 'harsher' sense than that borne by its fellow, but a simple sequence of a current employment of 'predestination' as the precise synonym of 'election,' and a resultant hesitation to apply a term of such precious associations to the foreordination to death. Since then the tables have been quite turned, and it is questionable whether in popular speech the word 'predestinate' does not now bear an unpleasant suggestion.

That neither word occurs in the English Old Testament is due to the genius of the Hebrew language, which does not admit of such compound terms. Their place is taken in the Old Testament, therefore, by simple words expressive of purposing, determining, ordaining, with more or less contextual indication of previousness of action. These represent a variety of Hebrew words, the most explicit of which is perhaps יָצַר (Ps. cxxxix. 16, Isa. xxii. 11, xxxvii. 26, xlvi. 11), by the side of which must be placed, however, יָעַץ (Isa. xiv. 24, 26, 27, xix. 12, xix. 17, xxiii. 9, Jer. xlix. 20, l. 45), whose substantival derivative עֵצָה (Job xxxviii. 2, xlii. 3, Jer. xxiii. 19, Prov. xix. 21, Ps. xxxiii. 11, cvii. 11, Isa. xiv. 26, xlvi. 10, 11, Ps. cvi. 13, Isa. v. 19, xix. 17, Jer. xlix. 20, l. 45, Mic. iv. 12) is doubtless the most precise Hebrew term for the Divine plan or purpose, although there occurs along with it in much the same sense the term מַחֲשָׁבָה (Jer. xviii. 11, xxix. 11, xlix. 30, l. 45, Isa. lv. 8, Jer. li. 29, Mic. iv. 12, Ps. xcii. 6, a derivative of חָשַׁב (Gen. l. 20, Mic. ii. 3, Jer. xviii. 11, xxvi. 3, xxix. 11, xxxvi. 3, xlix. 50, l. 45, Lam. ii. 8). In the Aramaic portion of Daniel (iv. 14 (17), 21 (24) the common later Hebrew designation of the Divine decree (used especially in an evil sense) גְּזֵרָה occurs: and חק is occasionally used with much the same meaning (Ps. ii. 7, Zeph. ii. 2, Ps. cv. 10 = I Chron. xvi. 17, Job xxiii. 14). Other words of similar import are זָמַם (Jer. iv. 28, li. 12, Lam. ii. 19, Zec. i. 6, viii. 14, 15) with its substantive מְזִמָּה (Job xlii. 2, Jer. xxiii. 20, xxx. 24, li. 11); חָפֵץ (Ps. cxv. 3, cxxxv. 6, Prov. xxi. 1, Isa. lv. 11, Jon. i. 14, Judg. xiii. 23, Isa. ii. 25, Isa. liii. 10) with its substantive חֵפֶץ (Isa. xlvi. 10, xliv. 28, xlviii. 14, liii. 10); חָרַץ (Job xiv. 5, Isa. x. 22, 23, xxviii. 22, Dan. ix. 26, 27, xi. 36); חָתַךְ (Dan. ix. 24); הוֹאִיל (I Sam. xii. 22, I Chron. xvii. 27, II Sam. vii. 29). To express that special act of predestination which we know as 'election,' the Hebrews commonly utilized

the word בָּחַר (of Israel, Deut. iv. 37, vii. 6, 7, x. 15, xiv. 2, Isa.
xli. 8, 9, xliii. 10, 30, xliv. 1, 2, Jer. xxxiii. 24; and of the future,
Isa. xiv. 1, lxv. 9, 15, 22; of Jehovah's servant, xlii. 1, xlix. 7;
of Jerusalem, Deut. xii. 14, 18, 26, xiv. 25, xv. 20, xvi. 7, 15, 16,
xvii. 8, 10, xviii. 6, xxxi. 11, Jos. ix. 27, I Kings viii. 44, 48, xi.
13, 32, 36, xiv. 21, II Kings xxi. 7, xxiii. 27) with its substantive
בָּחִיר (exclusively used of Jehovah's 'elect,' II Sam. xxi. 6, I
Chron. xvi. 13, Ps. lxxxix. 4, cv. 6, 43, cvi. 5, 23, Isa. xlii. 1, xliii.
20, xlv. 4, lxv. 9, 15, 22), and occasionally the word יָדַע in a pregnant sense (Gen. xviii. 19, Amos. iii. 2, Hos. xiii. 5, cf. Ps. i. 6,
xxxi. 8(7), xxxvii. 18, Isa. lviii. 3); while it is rather the execution of this previous choice in an act of separation that is
expressed by הִבְדִּיל (Lev. xx. 24, xx. 26, I Kings viii. 53).

In the Greek of the New Testament the precise term
προορίζω (Acts iv. 28, I Cor. ii. 7, Rom. viii. 29, 30, Eph. i. 5,
11) is supplemented by a number of similar compounds, such
as προτάσσω (Acts xvii. 26); προτίθημι (Eph. i. 9) with its
more frequently occurring substantive, πρόθεσις (Rom. viii.
28, ix. 11, Eph. i. 11, iii. 11, II Tim. i. 9); προετοιμάζω (Rom.
ix. 23, Eph. ii. 10) and perhaps προβλέπω in a similar sense of
providential pre-arrangement (Heb. xi. 40), with which may
be compared also προεῖδον (Acts ii. 31, Gal. iii. 8); προγιγ-
νώσκω (Rom. viii. 29, xi. 2, I Pet. i. 20) and its substantive
πρόγνωσις (I Pet. i. 2, Acts ii. 23); προχειρίζω (Acts xxii. 14,
iii. 20) and προχειροτονέω (Acts iv. 41). Something of the same
idea is, moreover, also occasionally expressed by the simple
ὁρίζω (Luke xxii. 22, Acts xvii. 26, 31, ii. 23, Heb. iv. 7, Acts
x. 42), or through the medium of terms designating the will,
wish, or good-pleasure of God, such as βουλή (Luke vii. 30,
Acts ii. 23, iv. 28, xiii. 36, xx. 27, Eph. i. 11, Heb. vi. 17, cf.
βούλημα Rom. ix. 19 and βούλομαι Heb. vi. 17, Jas. i. 18, II
Pet. iii. 9), θέλημα (e. g., Eph. i. 5, 9, 11, Heb. x. 7, cf. θέλησις
Heb. ii. 4, θέλω, e. g., Rom. ix. 18, 22), εὐδοκία (Luke ii. 14,
Eph. i. 5, 9, Phil. ii. 13, cf. εὐδοκέω Luke xii. 32, Col. i. 19, Gal.
i. 15, I Cor. i. 21). The standing terms in the New Testament
for God's sovereign choice of His people are ἐκλέγεσθαι, in
which both the composition and voice are significant (Eph. i. 4,

Mark xiii. 20, John xv. 16 twice, 19, I Cor. i. 27 twice, Jas. ii. 5; of Israel, Acts xiii. 17; of Christ, Luke ix. 35; of the disciples, Luke vi. 13, John vi. 70, xiii. 18, Acts i. 2; of others, Acts i. 24, xv. 7), ἐκλεκτός (Matt. [xx. 16] xxii. 14, xxvi. 22, 24, 31, Mark xiii. 20, 22, 27, Luke xviii. 7, Rom. viii. 33, Col. iii. 12, II Tim. ii. 10, Tit. i. 1, I Pet. i. 1, [ii. 9], Rev. xvii. 14; of individuals, Rom. xvi. 13, II John i. 13; of Christ, Luke xxiii. 35, John xiii. 18; of angels, I Tim. v. 21), ἐκλογή (Acts ix. 15, Rom. ix. 11. xi. 5, 7, 28, I Thes. i. 4, II Pet. i. 10), — words which had been prepared for this New Testament use by their employment in the Septuagint — the two former to translate בָּחַר and בָּחִיר. In II Thes. ii. 13 αἱρέομαι is used similarly.

II. PREDESTINATION IN THE OLD TESTAMENT

No survey of the terms used to express it, however, can convey an adequate sense of the place occupied by the idea of predestination in the religious system of the Bible. It is not too much to say that it is fundamental to the whole religious consciousness of the Biblical writers, and is so involved in all their religious conceptions that to eradicate it would transform the entire scriptural representation. This is as true of the Old Testament as of the New Testament, as will become sufficiently manifest by attending briefly to the nature and implications of such formative elements in the Old Testament system as its doctrines of God, Providence, Faith, and the Kingdom of God.

Whencesoever Israel obtained it, it is quite certain that Israel entered upon its national existence with the most vivid consciousness of an almighty personal Creator and Governor of heaven and earth. Israel's own account of the clearness and the firmness of its apprehension of this mighty Author and Ruler of all that is, refers it to His own initiative: God chose to make Himself known to the fathers. At all events, throughout the whole of Old Testament literature, and for every period of history recorded in it, the fundamental conception of God remains the same, and the two most persistently emphasized elements in it are just those of might and personality: before everything else, the God of Israel is the Omnipotent Person. Possibly the keen sense of the exaltation and illimitable power of God which forms the very core of the Old Testament idea of God belongs rather to the general Semitic than to the specifically Israelitish element in its religion; certainly it was already prominent in the patriarchal God-consciousness, as is sufficiently evinced by the names of God current from the beginning of the Old Testament revelation, — *El, Eloah, Elohim, El Shaddai,* — and as is illustrated endlessly in the Biblical narrative. But it is equally clear that God was never conceived by the Old Testament saints as abstract power, but was ever thought of concretely as the all-powerful Person, and that, moreover, as clothed with all the attributes of moral personality, — pre-eminently with holiness, as the very summit of His exaltation, but along with holiness, also with all the characteristics that belong to spiritual personality as it exhibits itself familiarly in man. In a word, God is pictured in the Old Testament, and that from the beginning, purely after the pattern of human personality, — as an intelligent, feeling, willing Being, like the man who is created in His image in all in which the life of a free spirit consists. The anthropomorphisms to which this mode of conceiving God led were sometimes startling enough, and might have become grossly misleading had not the corrective lain ever at hand in the accompanying sense of the immeasurable exaltation of God, by which He was removed above all the weaknesses of humanity. The result accordingly was nothing other than a peculiarly pure form of Theism. The grosser anthropomorphisms were fully understood to be figurative, and the residuary conception was that of an infinite Spirit, not indeed expressed in abstract terms nor from the first fully brought out in all its implications, but certainly in all ages of the Old Testament development grasped in all its essential elements. (Cf. the art. GOD).

Such a God could not be thought of otherwise than as the free determiner of all that comes to pass in the world which is the product of His creative act; and the doctrine of Providence (פְּקֻדָּה) which is spread over the pages of the Old Testament

fully bears out this expectation. The almighty Maker of all
that is is represented equally as the irresistible Ruler of all
that He has made: Jehovah sits as King for ever (Ps. xxix. 10).
Even the common language of life was affected by this pervasive point of view, so that, for example, it is rare to meet
with such a phrase as 'it rains' (Amos iv. 7), and men by preference spoke of God sending rain (Ps. lxv. 9 f., Job xxxvi. 27,
xxxviii. 26). The vivid sense of dependence on God thus witnessed extended throughout every relation of life. Accident or
chance was excluded. If we read here and there of a מִקְרֶה it
is not thought of as happening apart from God's direction
(Ruth ii. 3, I Sam. vi. 9, xx. 26, Eccl. ii. 14, cf. I Kings
xxii. 34, II Chron. xviii. 33), and accordingly the lot was an
accepted means of obtaining the decision of God (Jos. vii. 16,
xiv. 2, xviii. 6, I Sam. x. 19, Jon. i. 7), and is didactically recognized as under His control (Prov. xvi. 33). All things without
exception, indeed, are disposed by Him, and His will is the
ultimate account of all that occurs. Heaven and earth and all
that is in them are the instruments through which He works
His ends. Nature, nations, and the fortunes of the individual
alike present in all their changes the transcript of His purpose.
The winds are His messengers, the flaming fire His servant:
every natural occurrence is His act: prosperity is His gift, and
if calamity falls upon man it is the Lord that has done it (Amos
iii. 5, 6, Lam. iii. 33–38, Isa. xlvii. 7, Eccl. vii. 14, Isa. liv. 16).
It is He that leads the feet of men, wit they whither or not;
He that raises up and casts down; opens and hardens the heart;
and creates the very thoughts and intents of the soul. So poignant is the sense of His activity in all that occurs, that an appearance is sometimes created as if everything that comes to
pass were so ascribed to His immediate production as to exclude the real activity of second causes. It is a grave mistake,
nevertheless, to suppose that He is conceived as an unseen
power, throwing up, in a quasi-Pantheistic sense, all changes
on the face of the world and history. The virile sense of the
free personality of God which dominates all the thought of the
Old Testament would alone have precluded such a conception.

Nor is there really any lack of recognition of 'second causes,' as we call them. They are certainly not conceived as independent of God: they are rather the mere expression of His stated will. But they are from the beginning fully recognized, both in nature — with respect to which Jehovah has made covenant (Gen. viii. 21, 22, Jer. xxxi. 35, 36, xxxiii. 20, 25, Ps. cxlviii. 6, cf. Jer. v. 22, Ps. civ. 9, Job xxxviii. 10, 33, xiv. 5), establishing its laws (חֻקּוֹת Job xxviii. 25, 28, Isa. xl. 12, Job xxxviii. 8–11, Prov. viii. 29, Jer. v. 22, Ps. civ. 9, xxxiii. 7, Isa. xl. 26) — and equally in the higher sphere of free spirits, who are ever conceived as the true authors of all their acts (hence God's proving of man, Gen. xxii. 1, Ex. xvi. 4, xx. 20, Deut. viii. 2, 16, xiii. 3, Judg. iii. 1, 4, II Chron. xxxii. 31). There is no question here of the substitution of Jehovah's operation for that of the proximate causes of events. There is only the liveliest perception of the governing hand of God behind the proximate causes, acting through them for the working out of His will in every detail. Such a conception obviously looks upon the universe teleologically: an almighty moral Person cannot be supposed to govern His universe, thus in every detail, either unconsciously or capriciously. In His government there is necessarily implied a plan; in the all-pervasiveness and perfection of His government is inevitably implied an all-inclusive and perfect plan: and this conception is not seldom explicitly developed.

It is abundantly clear on the face of it, of course, that this whole mode of thought is the natural expression of the deep religious consciousness of the Old Testament writers, though surely it is not therefore to be set aside as 'merely' the religious view of things, or as having no other rooting save in the imagination of religiously-minded men. In any event, however, it is altogether natural that in the more distinctive sphere of the religious life its informing principle of absolute dependence on God should be found to repeat itself. This appears particularly in the Old Testament doctrine of faith, in which there sounds the keynote of Old Testament piety, — for the religion of the Old Testament, so far from being, as Hegel, for example, would affirm, the religion of fear, is rather by way of eminence the religion of trust. Standing over against God, not merely as creatures, but as sinners, the Old Testament saints found no ground of hope save in the free initiative of the Divine love. At no period of the development of Old Testament religion was it permitted to be imagined that blessings might be wrung from the hands of an unwilling God, or gained in the strength of man's own arm. Rather it was ever inculcated that in this sphere, too, it is God alone that lifts up and makes rich, He alone that keeps the feet of His holy ones; while by strength, it is affirmed, no man shall prevail (I Sam. ii. 9). 'I am not worthy of the least of all thy mercies' is the constant refrain of the Old Testament saints (Gen. xxxii. 10); and from the very beginning, in narrative, precept and prophetic declaration alike, it is in trust in the unmerited love of Jehovah alone that the hearts of men are represented as finding peace. Self-sufficiency is the characteristic mark of the wicked, whose doom treads on his heels; while the mark of the righteous is that he lives by his faith (Hab. ii. 4). In the entire self-commitment to God, humble dependence on Him for all blessings, which is the very core of Old Testament religion, no element is more central than the profound conviction embodied in it of the free sovereignty of God, the God of the spirits of all flesh, in the distribution of His mercies. The whole training of Israel was directed to impressing upon it the great lesson enunciated to Zerubbabel, 'Not by might, nor by power, but by my Spirit, saith the Lord of hosts' (Zech. iv. 6) — that all that comes to man in the spiritual sphere, too, is the free gift of Jehovah.

Nowhere is this lesson more persistently emphasized than in the history of the establishment and development of the kingdom of God, which may well be called the cardinal theme of the Old Testament. For the kingdom of God is consistently represented, not as the product of man's efforts in seeking after God, but as the gracious creation of God Himself. Its inception and development are the crowning manifestation of the free grace of the Living God working in history in pursuance of His loving purpose to recover fallen man to Himself. To this end He preserves the race in existence after its sin, saves a seed from the destruction of the Flood, separates to Himself a family in Abraham, sifts it in Isaac and Jacob, nurses and trains it through the weakness of its infancy, and gradually moulds it to be the vehicle of His revelation of redemption, and the channel of Messianic blessings to the world. At every step it is God, and God alone, to whom is ascribed the initiative; and the most extreme care is taken to preserve the recipients of the blessings consequent on His choice from fancying that these blessings come as their due, or as reward for aught done by themselves, or to be found in themselves. They were rather in every respect emphatically not a people of their own making, but a people that God had formed that they might set forth His praise (Isa. xliii. 21). The strongest language, the most astonishing figures, were employed to emphasize the pure sovereignty of the Divine action at every stage. It was not because Israel was numerous, or strong, or righteous, that He chose it, but only because it pleased Him to make of it a people for Himself. He was as the potter, it as the clay which the potter moulds as he will; it was but as the helpless babe in its blood cast out to die, abhorred of man, which Jehovah strangely gathers to His bosom in unmerited love (Gen. xii. 1, 3, Deut. vii. 6–8, ix. 4–6, x. 15, 16, I Sam. xii. 22, Isa. xli. 8, 9, xliii. 20, xlviii. 9–11, Jer. xviii. 1 f., xxxi. 3, Hos. ii. 20, Mal. i. 2, 3). There was no element in the religious consciousness of Israel more poignantly realized, as there was no element in the instruction they had received more insisted on, than that they owed their separation from the peoples of the earth to be the Lord's inheritance, and all the blessings they had as such received from Jehovah, not to any claim upon Him which they could urge, but to His own gracious love faithfully persisted in in spite of every conceivable obstacle.

In one word, the sovereignty of the Divine will as the principle of all that comes to pass, is a primary postulate of the whole religious life, as well as of the entire world-view of the Old Testament. It is implicated in its very idea of God, its whole conception of the relation of God to the world and to the changes which take place, whether in nature or history, among the nations or in the life-fortunes of the individual; and also in its entire scheme of religion, whether national or personal. It lies at the basis of all the religious emotions, and lays the foundation of the specific type of religious character built up in Israel.

The specific teaching of the Old Testament as to predestination naturally revolves around the two foci of that idea which may be designated general and special, or, more properly, cosmical and soteriological predestination; or, in other words, around the doctrines of the Divine Decree and the Divine Election. The former, as was to be expected, is comparatively seldom adverted to — for the Old Testament is fundamentally a soteriological book, a revelation of the grace of God to sinners; and it is only at a somewhat late period that it is made the subject of speculative discussion. But as it is implied in the primordial idea of God as an Almighty Person, it is postulated from the beginning and continually finds more or less clear expression. Throughout the Old Testament, behind the processes of nature, the march of history and the fortunes of each individual life alike, there is steadily kept in view the governing hand of God working out His preconceived plan — a plan broad enough to embrace the whole universe of things, minute enough to concern itself with the smallest details, and actualizing itself with inevitable certainty in every event that comes to pass.

Naturally, there is in the narrative portions but little formal enunciation of this pervasive and all-controlling Divine teleology. But despite occasional anthropomorphisms of rather startling character (as, e.g., that which ascribes 'repentance' to God, Gen. vi. 6, Joel ii. 13, Jon. iv. 2, Jer. xviii. 8, 10, xxvi. 3, 13), or rather, let us say, just because of the strictly anthropomorphic mould in which the Old Testament conception of God is run, according to which He is ever thought of as a personal spirit, acting with purpose like other personal spirits, but with a wisdom and in a sovereignty unlike that of others because infinitely perfect, these narrative portions of the Old Testament also bear continual witness to the universal Old

Testament teleology. There is no explicit statement in the narrative of the creation, for example, that the mighty Maker of the world was in this process operating on a preconceived plan; but the teleology of creation lies latent in the orderly sequence of its parts, culminating in man for whose advent all that precedes is obviously a preparation, and is all but expressed in the Divine satisfaction at each of its stages, as a manifestation of His perfections (cf. Ps. civ. 31). Similarly, the whole narrative of the Book of Genesis is so ordered — in the succession of creation, fall, promise, and the several steps in the inauguration of the kingdom of God — as to throw into a very clear light the teleology of the whole world-history, here written from the Divine standpoint and made to centre around the developing Kingdom. In the detailed accounts of the lives of the patriarchs, in like manner, behind the external occurrences recorded there always lies a Divine ordering which provides the real plot of the story in its advance to the predetermined issue. It was not accident, for example, that brought Rebecca to the well to welcome Abraham's servant (Gen. xxiv), or that sent Joseph into Egypt (Gen. xlv. 8, l. 20; 'God meant [חשב] it for good'), or guided Pharaoh's daughter to the ark among the flags (Ex. ii), or that, later, directed the millstone that crushed Abimelech's head (Judg. ix. 53), or winged the arrow shot at a venture to smite the king in the joints of the harness (I Kings xxii. 34). Every historical event is rather treated as an item in the orderly carrying out of an underlying Divine purpose; and the historian is continually aware of the presence in history of Him who gives even to the lightning a charge to strike the mark (Job xxxvi. 32).

In the Psalmists and Prophets there emerges into view a more abstract statement of the government of all things according to the good-pleasure of God (Ps. xxxiii. 11, Jer. x. 12, li. 15). All that He wills He does (Ps. cxv. 3, cxxxv. 6), and all that comes to pass has pre-existed in His purpose from the indefinite past of eternity ('long ago' Isa. xxii. 11, 'of ancient times' Isa. xxxvii. 26 = II Kings xix. 25), and it is only because it so pre-existed in purpose that it now comes to pass (Isa. xiv.

24, 27, xlvi. 11, Zech. i. 6, Job xlii. 2, Jer. xxiii. 20, Jon. i. 14, Isa. xl. 10). Every day has its ordained events (Job xiv. 5, Ps. cxxxix. 16). The plan of God is universal in its reach, and orders all that takes place in the interests of Israel — the Old Testament counterpart to the New Testament declaration that all things work together for good to those that love God. Nor is it merely for the national good of Israel that God's plan has made provision; He exercises a special care over every one of His people (Job v. 15 f., Ps. xci, cxxi, lxv. 3, xxxvii, xxvii. 10, 11, cxxxix. 16, Jon. iii. 5, Isa. iv. 3, Dan. xii. 1). Isaiah especially is never weary of emphasizing the universal teleology of the Divine operations and the surety of the realization of His eternal purpose, despite the opposition of every foe (xiv. 24–27, xxxi. 2, xl. 13, lviii. 8–11) — whence he has justly earned the name of the prophet of the Divine sovereignty, and has been spoken of as the Paul, the Augustine, the Calvin of the Old Testament.

It is, however, especially in connexion with the Old Testament doctrine of the Wisdom (חָכְמָה) of God, the chief depository of which is the so-called *Ḥokhmah* literature, that the idea of the all-inclusive Divine purpose (עֵצָה and מַחֲשָׁבוֹת) in which lies predetermined the whole course of events — including every particular in the life of the world (Amos iii. 7) and in the life of every individual as well (Ps. cxxxix. 14–16, Judg. i. 2) — is speculatively wrought out. According to this developed conception, God, acting under the guidance of all His ethical perfections, has, by virtue of His eternal wisdom, which He 'possessed in the beginning of his way' (Prov. viii. 22), framed 'from everlasting, from the beginning,' an all-inclusive plan embracing all that is to come to pass; in accordance with which plan He now governs His universe, down to the least particular, so as to subserve His perfect and unchanging purpose. Everything that God has brought into being, therefore, He has made for its specific end (Prov. xvi. 4, cf. iii. 19, 20, Job xxviii. 23, xxxviii, xli, Isa. xl. 12 f., Jer. x. 12, 13); and He so governs it that it shall attain its end, — no chance can escape (Prov. xvi. 33), no might or subtlety defeat His direc-

tion (Prov. xxi. 30, 31, xix. 21, xvi. 9, cf. Isa. xiv. 24, 27,
Jer. x. 23), which leads straight to the goal appointed by God
from the beginning and kept steadily in view by Him, but often
hidden from the actors themselves (Prov. xx. 24, cf. iii. 6, xvi.
1–9, xix. 21, Job xxxviii. 2, xlii. 3, Jer. x. 23), who naturally
in their weakness cannot comprehend the sweep of the Divine
plan or understand the place within it of the details brought
to their observation — a fact in which the Old Testament
sages constantly find their theodicy. No different doctrine is
enunciated here from that which meets us in the Prophets and
Psalmists, — only it is approached from a philosophical-reli-
gious rather than from a national-religious view-point. To
prophet and sage alike the entire world — inanimate, animate,
moral — is embraced in a unitary teleological world-order (Ps.
xxxiii. 6, civ. 24, cxlviii. 8, Job ix. 4, xii. 13, xxxvii); and to
both alike the central place in this comprehensive world-order
is taken by God's redemptive purpose, of which Israel is at
once the object and the instrument, while the savour of its
saltness is the piety of the individual saint. The classical term
for this all-inclusive Divine purpose (עֵצָה) is accordingly found
in the usage alike of prophet, psalmist, and sage, — now used
absolutely of the universal plan on which the whole world is
ordered (Job xxxviii. 2, xlii. 3, cf. Delitzsch and Budde, *in loc.*),
now, with the addition of 'of Jehovah,' of the all-comprehending purpose, embracing all human actions (Prov. xix. 21 and
parallels; cf. Toy, *in loc.*), now with explicit mention of Israel
as the centre around which its provisions revolve (Ps. xxxiii. 11,
cvii. 11, cf. Delitzsch, *in loc.; Isa.* xiv. 26, xxv. 1, xlvi. 10, 11),
and anon with more immediate concern with some of the details (Ps. cvi. 13, Isa. v. 19, xix. 17, Jer. xlix. 20, l. 45, Mic.
iv. 12).

There seems no reason why a Platonizing colouring should
be given to this simple attributing to the eternal God of an
eternal plan in which is predetermined every event that comes
to pass. This used to be done, e. g., by Delitzsch (see, e. g., on
Job xxviii. 25–28, Isa. xxii. 11; "Biblical Psychology," I. ii.),
who was wont to attribute to the Biblical writers, especially of

the " Ḥokhmah " and the latter portion of Isaiah, a doctrine of
the pre-existence of all things in an ideal world, conceived as
standing eternally before God at least as a pattern if not even
as a quasi-objective mould imposing their forms on all His
creatures, which smacked more of the Greek Academics than
of the Hebrew sages. As a matter of course, the Divine mind was
conceived by the Hebrew sages as eternally contemplating all
possibilities, and we should not do them injustice in supposing
them to think of its 'ideas' as the *causa exemplaris* of all that
occurs, and of the Divine intellect as the *principium dirigens*
of every Divine operation. But it is more to the point to note
that the conceptions of the Old Testament writers in regard
to the Divine decree run rather into the moulds of 'purpose'
than of 'ideas,' and that the roots of their teaching are planted
not in an abstract idea of the Godhead, but in the purity of
their concrete theism. It is because they think of God as a person, like other persons purposeful in His acts, but unlike other
persons all-wise in His planning and all-powerful in His performing, that they think of Him as predetermining all that
shall come to pass in the universe, which is in all its elements
the product of His free activity, and which must in its form and
all its history, down to the least detail, correspond with His
purpose in making it. It is easy, on the other hand, to attribute
too little 'philosophy' to the Biblical writers. The conception
of God in His relation to the world which they develop is beyond question anthropomorphic; but it is no unreflecting an-
thropomorphism that they give us. Apart from all question of
revelation, they were not children prattling on subjects on
which they had expended no thought; and the world-view they
commend to us certainly does not lack in profundity. The sub-
tleties of language of a developed scholasticism were foreign to
their purposes and modes of composition, but they tell us as
clearly as, say, Spanheim himself (" Decad. Theol." vi. § 5), that
they are dealing with a purposing mind exalted so far above
ours that we can follow its movements only with halting steps,
— whose thoughts are not as our thoughts, and whose ways
are not as our ways (Isa. lv. 8; cf. xl. 13, 28, xxviii. 29, Job xi.

7 f., Ps. xcii. 5, cxxxix. 14 f., cxlvii. 5, Eccl. iii. 11). Least of all in such a theme as this were they liable to forget that infinite exaltation of God which constituted the basis on which their whole conception of God rested.

Nor may they be thought to have been indifferent to the relations of the high doctrine of the Divine purpose they were teaching. There is no scholastic determination here either; but certainly they write without embarrassment as men who have attained a firm grasp upon their fundamental thought and have pursued it with clearness of thinking, no less in its relations than in itself; nor need we go astray in apprehending the outlines of their construction. It is quite plain, for example, that they felt no confusion with respect to the relation of the Divine purpose to the Divine foreknowledge. The notion that the almighty and all-wise God, by whom all things were created, and through whose irresistible control all that occurs fulfils the appointment of His primal plan, could govern Himself according to a foreknowledge of things which — perhaps apart from His original purpose of present guidance — *might haply* come to pass, would have been quite contradictory to their most fundamental conception of God as the almighty and all-sovereign Ruler of the universe, and, indeed, also of the whole Old Testament idea of the Divine foreknowledge itself, which is ever thought of in its due relation of dependence on the Divine purpose. According to the Old Testament conception, God foreknows only because He has pre-determined, and it is therefore also that He brings it to pass; His foreknowledge, in other words, is at bottom a knowledge of His own will, and His works of providence are merely the execution of His all-embracing plan. This is the truth that underlies the somewhat incongruous form of statement of late becoming rather frequent, to the effect that God's foreknowledge is conceived in the Old Testament as 'productive.' Dillmann, for example, says ("Handbuch der alttestamentlichen Theologie," p. 251): 'His foreknowledge of the future is a productive one; of an otiose foreknowledge or of a *præscientia media* . . . there is no suggestion.' In the thought of the Old Testament writers, however, it is not God's foreknowledge that produces the events of the future; it is His irresistible providential government of the world He has created for Himself: and His foreknowledge of what is yet to be rests on His pre-arranged plan of government. His 'productive foreknowledge' is but a transcript of His will, which has already determined not only the general plan of the world, but every particular that enters into the whole course of its development (Amos iii. 7, Job xxviii. 26, 27), and every detail in the life of every individual that comes into being (Jer. i. 5, Ps. cxxxix. 14–16, Job xxiii. 13, 14).

That the acts of free agents are included in this 'productive foreknowledge,' or rather in this all-inclusive plan of the life of the universe, created for the Old Testament writers apparently not the least embarrassment. This is not because they did not believe man to be free, — throughout the whole Old Testament there is never the least doubt expressed of the freedom or moral responsibility of man, — but because they did believe God to be free, whether in His works of creation or of providence, and could not believe He was hampered or limited in the attainment of His ends by the creatures of His own hands. How God governs the acts of free agents in the pursuance of His plan there is little in the Old Testament to inform us; but that He governs them in even their most intimate thoughts and feelings and impulses is its unvarying assumption: He is not only the creator of the hearts of men in the first instance, and knows them altogether, but He fashions the hearts of all in all the changing circumstances of life (Ps. xxxiii. 15); forms the spirit of man within him in all its motions (Zech. xii. 1); keeps the hearts of men in His hands, turning them whithersoever He will (Prov. xxi. 1); so that it is even said that man knows what is in his own mind only as the Lord reveals it to him (Amos iv. 13). The discussion of any antinomy that may be thought to arise from such a joint assertion of the absolute rule of God in the sphere of the spirit and the freedom of the creaturely will, falls obviously under the topic of Providential Government rather than under that of the Decree: it requires to be adverted to here only that we may clearly note the fact that the Old Testament teachers, as they did not hesitate to affirm the absolute sway of God over the thoughts and intents of the human heart, could feel no embarrassment in the inclusion of the acts of free agents within the all-embracing plan of God, the outworking of which His providential government supplies. Nor does the moral quality of these acts present any apparent difficulty to the Old Testament construction. We are never permitted to imagine, to be sure, that God is the author of sin, either in the world at large or in any individual soul — that He is in any way implicated in the sinfulness of the acts performed by the perverse misuse of creaturely freedom. In all God's working He shows Himself pre-eminently the Holy One, and prosecutes His holy will, His righteous way, His all-wise plan: the blame for all sinful deeds rests exclusively on the creaturely actors (Ex. ix. 27, x. 16), who recognize their own guilt (II Sam. xxiv. 10, 17) and receive its punishment (Eccl. xi. 9 compared with xi. 5). But neither is God's relation to the sinful acts of His creatures ever represented as purely passive: the details of the doctrine of *concursus* were left, no doubt, to later ages speculatively to work out, but its assumption underlies the entire Old Testament representation of the Divine modes of working. That anything — good or evil — occurs in God's universe finds its account, according to the Old Testament conception, in His positive ordering and active concurrence; while the moral quality of the deed, considered in itself, is rooted in the moral character of the subordinate agent, acting in the circumstances and under the motives operative in each instance. It is certainly going beyond the Old Testament warrant to speak of the 'all-productivity of God,' as if He were the only efficient cause in nature and the sphere of the free spirit alike; it is the very delirium of misconception to say that in the Old Testament God and Satan are insufficiently discriminated, and deeds appropriate to the latter are assigned to the former. Nevertheless, it remains true that even the evil acts of the creature are so far carried back to God that they too are affirmed to be included in His all-embracing decree, and to be brought about, bounded and utilized in His providential government. It is He that hardens the heart of the sinner that persists in his sin (Ex. iv. 21, vii. 3, x. 1, 27, xiv. 4, 8, Deut. ii. 30, Jos. xi. 20, Isa. lxiii. 17); it is from Him that the evil spirits proceed that trouble sinners (I Sam. xvi. 14, Judg. ix. 23, I Kings xxii, Job i.); it is of Him that the evil impulses that rise in sinners' hearts take this or that specific form (II Sam. xxiv. 1). The philosophy that lies behind such representations, however, is not the pantheism which looks upon God as the immediate cause of all that comes to pass; much less the pandaimonism which admits no distinction between good and evil; there is not even involved a conception of God entangled in an undeveloped ethical discrimination. It is the philosophy that is expressed in Isa. xlv. 5 f., 'I am the LORD, and there is none else; beside me there is no God. . . . I am the LORD, and there is none else. I form the light and create darkness; I make peace and create evil; I am the LORD that doeth all these things'; it is the philosophy that is expressed in Prov. xvi. 4, 'The LORD hath made everything for its own end, yea, even the wicked for the day of evil.' Because, over against all dualistic conceptions, there is but one God, and He is indeed GOD; and because, over against all cosmotheistic conceptions, this God is a PERSON who acts purposefully; there is nothing that is, and nothing that comes to pass, that He has not first decreed and then brought to pass by His creation or providence. Thus all things find their unity in His eternal plan; and not their unity merely, but their justification as well; even the evil, though retaining its quality as evil and hateful to the holy God, and certain to be dealt with as hateful, yet does not occur apart from His provision or against His will, but appears in the world which He has made only as the instrument by means of which He works the higher good.

This sublime philosophy of the decree is immanent in every page of the Old Testament. Its metaphysics never come to explicit discussion, to be sure; but its elements are in a practical way postulated consistently throughout. The ultimate end in view in the Divine plan is ever represented as found in God alone: all that He has made He has made for Himself, to set forth His praise; the heavens themselves with all their splendid furniture exist but to illustrate His glory; the earth and all that is in it, and all that happens in it, to declare His majesty; the whole course of history is but the theatre of His self-manifestation, and the events of every individual life indicate His nature and perfections. Men may be unable to understand the place which the incidents, as they unroll themselves before their eyes, take in the developing plot of the great drama: they may, nay, must, therefore stand astonished and confounded before this or that which befalls them or befalls the world. Hence arise to them problems — the problem of the petty, the problem of the inexplicable, the problem of suffering, the problem of sin (e. g., Eccl. xi. 5). But, in the infinite wisdom of the Lord of all the earth, each event falls with exact precision into its proper place in the unfolding of His eternal plan; nothing, however small, however strange, occurs without His ordering, or without its peculiar fitness for its place in the working out of His purpose; and the end of all shall be the manifestation of His glory, and the accumulation of His praise. This is the Old Testament philosophy of the universe — a world-view which attains concrete unity in an absolute Divine teleology, in the compactness of an eternal decree, or purpose, or plan, of which all that comes to pass is the development in time.

Special or Soteriological Predestination finds a natural place in the Old Testament system as but a particular instance of the more general fact, and may be looked upon as only the general Old Testament doctrine of predestination applied to the specific case of the salvation of sinners. But as the Old Testament is a distinctively religious book, or, more precisely, a distinctively soteriological book, that is to say, a record of the gracious dealings and purposes of God with sinners, soteriological predestination naturally takes a more prominent place in it than the general doctrine itself, of which it is a particular application. Indeed, God's saving work is thrown out into such prominence, the Old Testament is so specially a record of the establishment of the kingdom of God in the world, that we easily get the impression in reading it that the core of God's general decree is His decree of salvation, and that His whole plan for the government of the universe is subordinated to His purpose to recover sinful man to Himself. Of course there is some slight illusion of perspective here, the materials for correcting which the Old Testament itself provides, not only in more or less specific declarations of the relative unimportance of what befalls man, whether the individual, or Israel, or the race at large, in comparison with the attainment of the Divine end; and of the wonder of the Divine grace concerning itself with the fortunes of man at all (Job xxii. 3 f., xxxv. 6 f., xxxviii, Ps. viii. 4): but also in the general disposition of the entire record, which places the complete history of sinful man, including alike his fall into sin and all the provisions for his recovery, within the larger history of the creative work of God, as but one incident in the greater whole, governed, of course, like all its other parts, by its general teleology. Relatively to the Old Testament record, nevertheless, as indeed to the Biblical record as a whole, which is concerned directly only with God's dealings with humanity, and that, especially, a sinful humanity (Gen. iii. 9, vi. 5, viii. 21, Lev. xviii. 24, Deut. ix. 4, I Kings viii. 46, Ps. xiv. 1, li. 5, cxxx. 3, cxliii. 2, Prov. xx. 9, Eccl. vii. 20, Isa. i. 4, Hos. iv. 1, Job xv. 14, xxv. 4, xiv. 4), soteriological predestination is the prime matter of importance; and the doctrine of election is accordingly thrown into relief, and the general doctrine of the decree more incidentally adverted to. It would be impossible, however, that the doctrine of election taught in the Old Testament should follow other lines than those laid down in the general doctrine of the decree, — or, in other words, that God should be conceived as working in the sphere of grace in a manner that would be out of accord with the fundamental conception entertained by these writers of the nature of God and His relations to the universe.

Accordingly, there is nothing concerning the Divine election more sharply or more steadily emphasized than its graciousness, in the highest sense of that word, or, in other terms, its absolute sovereignty. This is plainly enough exhibited even in the course of the patriarchal history, and that from the beginning. In the very hour of man's first sin, God intervenes *sua sponte* with a gratuitous promise of deliverance; and at every stage afterwards the sovereign initiation of the grace of God — the Lord of the whole earth (Ex. xix. 5) — is strongly marked, as God's universal counsel of salvation is more and more unfolded through the separation and training of a people for Himself, in whom the whole world should be blessed (Gen. xii. 3, xviii. 18, xxii. 18, xxvi. 4, xxviii. 14): for from the beginning it is plainly indicated that the whole history of the world is ordered with reference to the establishment of the kingdom of God (Deut. xxxii. 8, where the reference seems to be to Gen. xi). Already in the opposing lines of Seth and Cain (Gen. iv. 25, 26) a discrimination is made; Noah is selected as the head of a new race, and among his sons the preference is given to Shem (Gen. ix. 25), from whose line Abraham is taken. Every fancy that Abraham owed his calling to his own desert is carefully excluded, — he was 'known' of God only that in him God might establish His kingdom (Gen. xviii. 19); and the very acme of sovereignty is exhibited (as St. Paul points out) in the subsequent choice of Isaac and Jacob, and exclusion of Ishmael and Esau; while the whole Divine dealing with the patriarchs — their separation from their kindred, removal into a strange land, and the like — is evidently understood as intended to cast them back on the grace of God alone. Similarly, the covenant made with Israel (Ex. xix–xxiv) is constantly assigned to the sole initiative of Divine grace, and the fact of election is therefore appropriately set at the head of the Decalogue (Ex. xx. 2; cf. xxxiv. 6, 7); and Israel is repeatedly warned that there was nothing in it which moved or could move God to favour it (e. g., Deut. iv. 37, vii. 7, viii. 17, ix. 4, x. 11, Ezk. xvi. 1 f., Amos ix. 7). It has already been pointed out by what energetic figures this fundamental lesson was impressed on the Israelitish consciousness, and it is only true to say that no means are left unused to drive home the fact that God's gracious election of Israel is an absolutely sovereign one, founded solely in His unmerited love, and looking to nothing

ultimately but the gratification of His own holy and loving
impulses, and the manifestation of His grace through the formation of a heritage for Himself out of the mass of sinful men,
by means of whom His saving mercy should advance to the
whole world (Isa. xl, xlii, lx, Mic. iv. 1, Amos iv. 13, v. 8,
Jer. xxxi. 37, Ezk. xvii. 22, xxxvi. 21, Joel ii. 28). The simple
terms that are employed to express this Divine selection —
'know' (יָדַע), 'choose' (בָּחַר) — are either used in a pregnant
sense, or acquire a pregnant sense by their use in this connexion.
The deeper meaning of the former term is apparently not
specifically Hebrew, but more widely Semitic (it occurs also
in Assyrian; see the *Dictionaries* of Delitzsch and Muss-
Arnolt *sub. voc.*, and especially Haupt in "Beiträge zur Assyrio-
logie," i. 14, 15), and it can create no surprise, therefore, when
it meets us in such passages as Gen. xviii. 19 (cf. Ps. xxxvii. 18
and also i. 6, xxxi. 8; cf. Baethgen and Delitzsch *in loc.*), Hos.
xiii. 5 (cf. Wünsche *in loc.*) in something of the sense expressed
by the scholastic phrase, *nosse cum affectu et effectu;* while in
the great declaration of Amos iii. 2 (cf. Baur and Gunning *in
loc.*), 'You only have I known away from all the peoples of the
earth,' what is thrown prominently forward is clearly the elective love which has singled Israel out for special care. More
commonly, however, it is בָּחַר that is employed to express
God's sovereign election of Israel: the classical passage is, of
course, Deut. vii. 6, 7 (see Driver *in loc.*, as also, of the love
underlying the 'choice,' at iv. 37, vii. 8), where it is carefully
explained that it is in contrast with the treatment accorded to
all the other peoples of the earth that Israel has been honoured
with the Divine choice, and that the choice rests solely on the
unmerited love of God, and finds no foundation in Israel itself.
These declarations are elsewhere constantly enforced (e. g., iv.
37, x. 15, xiv. 2), with the effect of throwing the strongest
possible emphasis on the complete sovereignty of God's choice
of His people, who owe their 'separation' unto Jehovah (Lev.
xx. 24, 26, I Kings viii. 33) wholly to the wonderful love of
God, in which He has from the beginning taken knowledge of
and chosen them.

It is useless to seek to escape the profound meaning of this fundamental Old Testament teaching by recalling the undeveloped state of the doctrine of a future life in Israel, and the national scope of its election, — as if the sovereign choice which is so insisted on could thus be confined to the choice of a people as a whole to certain purely earthly blessings, without any reference whatever to the eternal destiny of the individuals concerned. We are here treading very close to the abyss of confusing progress in the delivery of doctrine with the reality of God's saving activities. The cardinal question, after all, does not concern the extent of the knowledge possessed by the Old Testament saints of the nature of the blessedness that belongs to the people of God; nor yet the relation borne by the election within the election, by the real Israel forming the heart of the Israel after the flesh, to the external Israel: it concerns the existence of a real kingdom of God in the Old Testament dispensation, and the methods by which God introduced man into it. It is true enough that the theocracy was an earthly kingdom, and that a prominent place was given to the promises of the life that now is in the blessings assured to Israel; and it is in this engrossment with earthly happiness and the close connexion of the friendship of God with the enjoyment of worldly goods that the undeveloped state of the Old Testament doctrine of salvation is especially apparent. But it should not be forgotten that the promise of earthly gain to the people of God is not entirely alien to the New Testament idea of salvation (Matt. vi. 37, I Tim. iv. 8), and that it is in no sense true that in the Old Testament teaching, in any of its stages, the blessings of the kingdom were summed up in worldly happiness. The covenant blessing is rather declared to be *life*, inclusive of all that that comprehensive word is fitted to convey (Deut. xxx. 15; cf. iv. 1, viii. 1, Prov. xii. 28, viii. 35); and it found its best expression in the high conception of 'the favour of God' (Lev. xxvi. 11, Ps. iv. 8, xvi. 2, 5, lxiii. 4); while it concerned itself with earthly prosperity only as and so far as that is a pledge of the Divine favour. It is no false testimony to the Old Testament saints when they are described as looking for the city that has the foundations and as enduring as seeing the Invisible One: if their hearts were not absorbed in the contemplation of the eternal future, they were absorbed in the contemplation of the Eternal Lord, which certainly is something even better; and the representation that they found their supreme blessedness in outward things runs so grossly athwart their own testimony that it fairly deserves Calvin's terrible invective, that thus the Israelitish people are thought of not otherwise than as a 'sort of herd of swine which (so, forsooth, it is pretended) the Lord was fattening in the pen of this world' ("Inst." II. x. 1). And, on the other hand, though Israel as a nation constituted the chosen people of God (I Chron. xvi. 13, Ps. lxxxix. 4, cv. 6, 13, cvi. 5), yet we must not lose from sight the fact that the nation as such was rather the symbolical than the real people of God, and was His people at all, indeed, only so far as it was, ideally or actually, identified with the inner body of the really 'chosen' — that people whom Jehovah formed for Himself that they might set forth His praise (Isa. xliii. 20, lxv. 9, 15, 22), and who constituted the real people of His choice, the 'remnant of Jacob' (Isa. vi. 13, Amos ix. 8–10, Mal. iii. 10; cf. I Kings xix. 18, Isa. viii. 18). Nor are we left in doubt as to how this inner core of actual people of God was constituted; we see the process in the call of Abraham, and the discrimination between Isaac and Ishmael, between Jacob and Esau, and it is no false testimony that it was ever a 'remnant according to the election of grace' that God preserved to Himself as the salt of His people Israel. In every aspect of it alike, it is the sovereignty of the Divine choice that is emphasized, — whether the reference be to the segregation of Israel as a nation to enjoy the earthly favour of God as a symbol of the true entrance into rest, or the choice of a remnant out of Israel to enter into that real communion with Him which was the joy of His saints, — of Enoch who walked with God (Gen. v. 22), of Abraham who found in Him his exceeding great reward (Gen. xv. 1), or of David who saw no good beyond Him, and sought in Him alone his inheritance and his cup. Later times may have enjoyed fuller knowledge of what the grace of God had in store for His saints — whether in this world or that which is to come; later times may have possessed a clearer apprehension of the distinction between the children of the flesh and the children of the promise: but no later teaching has a stronger emphasis for the central fact that it is of the free grace of God alone that any enter in any degree into the participation of His favour. The kingdom of God, according to the Old Testament, in every circle of its meaning, is above and before all else a stone cut out of the mountain 'without hands' (Dan. ii. 34, 44, 45).

III. Predestination among the Jews

The profound religious conception of the relation of God to the works of His hands that pervades the whole Old Testament was too deeply engraved on the Jewish consciousness to be easily erased, even after growing legalism had measurably corroded the religion of the people. As, however, the idea of law more and more absorbed the whole sphere of religious thought, and piety came to be conceived more and more as right conduct before God instead of living communion with God, men grew naturally to think of God more and more as abstract unapproachableness, and to think of themselves more and more as their own saviours. The post-canonical Jewish writings, while retaining fervent expressions of dependence on God as the Lord of all, by whose wise counsel all things exist and work out their ends, and over against whom the whole world, with every creature in it, is but the instrument of His will of good to Israel, nevertheless threw an entirely new emphasis on the autocracy of the human will. This emphasis increases until in the later Judaism the extremity of heathen self-sufficiency is reproduced, and the whole sphere of the moral life is expressly reserved from Divine determination. Meanwhile also heathen terminology was intruding into Jewish speech. The Platonic πρόνοια, προνοεῖν, for example, coming in doubtless through the medium of the Stoa, is found not only in Philo (περὶ προνοίας), but also in the Apocryphal books (Wis. vi. 7, xiv. 3, xvii. 2, III Mac. iv. 21, v. 30, IV Mac. ix. 24, xiii.

18, xvii. 22; cf. also Dan. vi. 18, Septuagint 19); the perhaps even more precise as well as earlier ἐφορᾶν occurs in Josephus (*BJ* ii. viii. 14), and indeed also in the Septuagint, though here doubtless in a weakened sense (II Mac. xii. 22, xv. 2, cf. III Mac. ii. 21, as also Job xxxiv. 24, xxviii. 24, xxii. 12, cf. xxi. 16; also Zech. ix. 1); while even the fatalistic term εἱμαρμένη is employed by Josephus (*BJ* ii. viii. 14; *Ant.* xiii. v. 9, xviii. i. 3) to describe Jewish views of predestination. With the terms there came in, doubtless, more or less of the conceptions connoted by them.

Whatever may have been the influences under which it was wrought, however, the tendency of post-canonical Judaism was towards setting aside the Biblical doctrine of predestination to a greater or less extent, or in a larger or smaller sphere, in order to make room for the autocracy of the human will, the רשות, as it was significantly called by the Rabbis (*Bereshith Rabba*, c. 22). This disintegrating process is little apparent perhaps in the Book of Wisdom, in which the sense of the almightiness of God comes to very strong expression (xi. 22, xii. 8–12). Or even in Philo, whose predestinarianism (*de Legg. Allegor.* i. 15, iii. 24, 27, 28) closely follows, while his assertion of human freedom (*Quod Deus sit immut.* 10) does not pass beyond that of the Bible: man is separated from the animals and assimilated to God by the gift of 'the power of voluntary motion' and suitable emancipation from necessity, and is accordingly properly praised or blamed for his intentional acts; but it is of the grace of God only that anything exists, and the creature is not giver but receiver in all things; especially does it belong to God alone to plant and build up virtues, and it is impious for the mind, therefore, to say 'I plant'; the call of Abraham, Isaac, Jacob was of pure grace without any merit, and God exercises the right to 'dispose excellently,' prior to all actual deeds. But the process is already apparent in so early a book as Sirach. The book at large is indeed distinctly predestinarian, and such passages as xvi. 26–30, xxiii. 20, xxxiii. 11–13, xxxix. 20, 21 echo the teachings of the canonical books on this subject. But, while this is its general character, another element is also pres-

ent: an assertion of human autocracy, for example, which is
without parallel in the canonical books, is introduced at xv.
11–20, which culminates in the precise declaration that 'man
has been committed to the hand of his own counsel' to choose
for himself life or death. The same phenomena meet us in the
Pharisaic Psalms of Solomon (b.c. 70–40). Here there is a general recognition of God as the great and mighty King (ii. 34,
36) who has appointed the course of nature (xviii. 12) and
directs the development of history (ii. 34, ix. 4, xvii. 4), ruling
over the whole and determining the lot of each (v. 6, 18), on
whom alone, therefore, can the hope of Israel be stayed (vii. 3,
xvii. 3), and to whom alone can the individual look for good.
But, alongside of this expression of general dependence on
God, there occurs the strongest assertion of the moral autocracy of the human will: 'O God, our works are in our own
souls' election and control, to do righteousness or iniquity in
the works of our hand' (ix. 7).

It is quite credible, therefore, when Josephus tells us that
the Jewish parties of his day were divided, as on other matters,
so on the question of the Divine predestination — the Essenes
affirming that fate (εἱμαρμένη, Josephus' affected Græcizing expression for predestination) is the mistress of all, and nothing
occurs to men which is not in accordance with its destination;
the Sadducees taking away 'fate' altogether, and considering
that there is no such thing, and that human affairs are not
directed according to it, but all actions are in our own power,
so that we are ourselves the causes of what is good, and receive
what is evil from our own folly; while the Pharisees, seeking a
middle ground, said that some actions, but not all, are the
work of 'fate,' and some are in our own power as to whether
they are done or not (*Ant.* xiii. v. 9). The distribution of the
several views among the parties follows the general lines of
what might have been anticipated — the Essenic system being
pre-eminently supranaturalistic, and the Sadducean rational-
istic, while there was retained among the Pharisees a deep
leaven of religious earnestness tempered, but not altogether
destroyed (except in the extremest circles), by their ingrained

legalism. The middle ground, moreover, which Josephus ascribes to the Pharisees in their attempt to distribute the control of human action between 'fate' and 'free will,' reflects not badly the state of opinion presupposed in the documents we have already quoted. In his remarks elsewhere (*BJ* II. viii. 14; *Ant.* XVIII. i. 3) he appears to ascribe to the Pharisees some kind of a doctrine of *concursus* also — a κρᾶσις between 'fate' and the human will by which both co-operate in the effect: but his language is obscure, and is coloured doubtless by reminiscences of Stoic teaching, with which philosophical sect he compares the Pharisees as he compares the Essenes with the Epicureans.

But whatever may have been the traditional belief of the Pharisees, in proportion as the legalistic spirit which constituted the nerve of the movement became prominent, the sense of dependence on God, which is the vital breath of the doctrine of predestination, gave way. The Jews possessed the Old Testament Scriptures in which the Divine lordship is a cardinal doctrine, and the trials of persecution cast them continually back upon God; they could not, therefore, wholly forget the Biblical doctrine of the Divine decree, and throughout their whole history we meet with its echoes on their lips. The laws of nature, the course of history, the varying fortunes of individuals, are ever attributed to the Divine predestination. Nevertheless, it was ever more and more sharply disallowed that man's moral actions fell under the same predetermination. Sometimes it was said that while the decrees of God were sure, they applied only so long as man remained in the condition in which he was contemplated when they were formed; he could escape all predetermined evil by a change in his moral character. Hence such sayings as, 'The righteous destroy what God decrees' (*Tanchuma* on דברים); 'Repentance, prayer, and charity ward off every evil decree' (*Rosh-hashana*). In any event, the entire domain of the moral life was more and more withdrawn from the intrusion of the decree; and Cicero's famous declaration, which Harnack says might be inscribed as a motto over Pelagianism, might with equal right be accepted as the working hypothesis of the later Judaism: 'For gold, land, and all the blessings of life we have to return thanks to God; but no one ever returned thanks to God for virtue' (*de Nat. Deorum*, iii. 36). We read that the Holy One determines prior to birth all that every one is to be — whether male or female, weak or strong, poor or rich, wise or silly; but one thing He does not determine — whether he is to be righteous or unrighteous; according to Deut. xxx. 15 this is committed to one's own hands. Accordingly, it is said that 'neither evil nor good comes from God; both are the results of our deeds' (*Midrash rab*, on ראה, and *Jalkut* there); and again, 'All is in the hands of God except the fear of God' (*Megilla* 25a); so that it is even somewhat cynically said, 'Man is led in the way in which he wishes to go' (*Maccoth* 10); 'If you teach him right, his God will make him know' (Isa. xxviii. 26; Jerusalem *Challah* i. 1). Thus the deep sense of dependence on God for all goods, and especially the goods of the soul, which forms the very core of the religious consciousness of the writers of the Old Testament, gradually vanished from the later Judaism, and was superseded by a self-assertiveness which hung all good on the self-determination of the human spirit, on which the purposes of God waited, or to which they were subservient.

IV. Predestination in the New Testament

The New Testament teaching starts from the plane of the Old Testament revelation, and in its doctrines of God, Providence, Faith, and the Kingdom of God repeats or develops in a right line the fundamental deliverances of the Old Testament, while in its doctrines of the Decree and of Election only such advance in statement is made as the progressive execution of the plan of salvation required.

In the teaching of our Lord, as recorded in the Synoptic Gospels, for example, though there is certainly a new emphasis thrown on the Fatherhood of God, this is by no means at the expense of His infinite majesty and might, but provides only a more profound revelation of the character of 'the great King'

(Matt. v. 35), the 'Lord of heaven and earth' (Matt. xi. 25, Luke x. 21), according to whose good pleasure all that is comes to pass. He is spoken of, therefore, specifically as the 'heavenly Father' (Matt. v. 48, vi. 14, 26, 32, xv. 13, xviii. 35, xxiii. 9, cf. v. 16, 45, vi. 1, 9, vii. 11, 21, x. 32, 33, xii. 50, xvi. 17, xviii. 14, 19, Mark xi. 25, 26, Luke xi. 13) whose throne is in the heavens (Matt. v. 34, xxiii. 22), while the earth is but the footstool under His feet. There is no limitation admitted to the reach of His power, whether on the score of difficulty in the task, or insignificance in the object: the category of the impossible has no existence to Him 'with whom all things are possible' (Matt. xix. 26, Mark x. 27, Luke xviii. 27, Matt. xxii. 29, Mark xii. 24, xiv. 36), and the minutest occurrences are as directly controlled by Him as the greatest (Matt. x. 29, 30, Luke xii. 7). It is from Him that the sunshine and rain come (Matt. v. 45); it is He that clothes with beauty the flowers of the field (Matt. vi. 28), and who feeds the birds of the air (Matt. vi. 26); not a sparrow falls to the ground without Him, and the very hairs of our heads are numbered, and not one of them is forgotten by God (Matt. x. 29, Luke xii. 6). There is, of course, no denial, nor neglect, of the mechanism of nature implied here; there is only clear perception of the providence of God guiding nature in all its operations, and not nature only, but the life of the free spirit as well (Matt. vi. 6, viii. 13, xxiv. 22, vii. 7, Mark xi. 23). Much less, however, is the care of God thought of as mechanical and purposeless. It was not simply of sparrows that out Lord was thinking when He adverted to the care of the heavenly Father for them, as it was not simply for oxen that God was caring when He forbade them to be muzzled as they trod out the corn (I Cor. ix. 9); it was that they who are of more value than sparrows might learn with what confidence they might depend on the Father's hand. Thus a hierarchy of providence is uncovered for us, circle rising above circle, — first the wide order of nature, next the moral order of the world, lastly the order of salvation or of the kingdom of God, — a preformation of the dogmatic, schema of *providentia generalis*, *specialis*, and *specialissima*. All these work together for the one end of advancing the whole world-fabric to its goal; for the care of the heavenly Father over the works of His hand is not merely to prevent the world that He has made from falling into pieces, and not merely to preserve His servants from oppression by the evil of this world, but to lead the whole world and all that is in it onwards to the end which He has appointed for it, — to that παλιγγενεσία of heaven and earth to which, under His guiding hand, the whole creation tends (Matt. xix. 28, Luke xx. 34).

In this divinely-led movement of 'this world' towards 'the world that is to come,' in which every element of the world's life has part, the central place is naturally taken by the spiritual preparation, or, in other words, by the development of the Kingdom of God which reaches its consummation in the 'regeneration.' This Kingdom, our Lord explains, is the heritage of those blessed ones for whom it has been prepared from the foundations of the world (Matt. xxv. 34, cf. xx. 23). It is built up on earth through a 'call' (Matt. ix. 13, Mark ii. 17, Luke v. 32), which, however, as mere invitation is inoperative (Matt. xxii. 2–14, Luke xiv. 16–23), and is made effective only by the exertion of a certain 'constraint' on God's part (Luke xiv. 23), — so that a distinction emerges between the merely 'called' and the really 'chosen' (Matt. xxii. 14). The author of this 'choice' is God (Mark xiii. 20), who has chosen His elect (Luke xviii.. 7, Matt. xxiv. 22, 24, 31, Mark xiii. 20–22) before the world, in accordance with His own pleasure, distributing as He will of what is His own (Matt. x. 14, 15); so that the effect of the call is already predetermined (Matt. xiii), all providence is ordered for the benefit of the elect (Matt. xxiv. 22), and they are guarded from falling away (Matt. xxiv. 24), and, at the last day, are separated to their inheritance prepared for them from all eternity (Matt. xxv. 34). That, in all this process, the initiative is at every point taken by God, and no question can be entertained of precedent merit on the part of the recipients of the blessings, results not less from the whole underlying conception of God in His relation to the course of providence than from the details of the teaching itself. Every means is utilized, however, to enhance the sense of the free sovereignty of God in the bestowment of His Kingdom; it is 'the lost' whom Jesus comes to seek (Luke xix. 10), and 'sinners' whom He came to call (Mark ii. 17); His truth is revealed only to 'babes' (Matt. xi. 25, Luke x. 21), and He gives His teaching a special form just that it may be veiled from them to whom it is not directed (Mark iv. 11), distributing His benefits, independently of merit (Matt. xx. 1–16), to those who had been chosen by God therefor (Mark xiii. 20).

In the discourses recorded by St. John the same essential spirit rules. Although, in accordance with the deeper theological apprehension of their reporter, the more metaphysical elements of Jesus' doctrine of God come here to fuller expression, it is nevertheless fundamentally the same doctrine of God that is displayed. Despite the even stronger emphasis thrown here on His Fatherhood, there is not the slightest obscuration of His infinite exaltation: Jesus lifts His eyes up when He would seek Him (xi. 41, xvii. 1); it is in heaven that His house is to be found (xiv. 2); and thence proceeds all that comes from Him (i. 51, iii. 13, vi. 31, 32, 33, 38, 41, 49, 50, 58); so that God and heaven come to be almost equivalent terms. Nor is there any obscuration of His ceaseless activity in governing the world (v. 17), although the stress is naturally thrown, in accordance with the whole character of this Gospel, on the moral and spiritual side of this government. But the very essence of the message of the Johannine Jesus is that the will ($\theta\acute{\epsilon}\lambda\eta\mu\alpha$) of the Father (iv. 34, v. 30, vi. 38, 39, 40, vii. 17, ix. 31, cf. iii. 8, v. 21, xvii. 24, xxi. 22, 23) is the principle of all things; and more especially, of course, of the introduction of eternal life into this world of darkness and death. The conception of the world as lying in the evil one and therefore judged already (iii. 18), so that upon those who are not removed from the evil of the world the wrath of God is not so much to be poured out as simply abides (iii. 36, cf. I John iii. 14), is fundamental to this whole presentation. It is therefore, on the one hand, that Jesus represents Himself as having come not to condemn the world, but to save the world (iii. 17, viii. 12, ix. 5, xii. 47, cf. iv. 42), and all that He does as having for its end the introduction of life into the world (vi. 33, 51); the already condemned world needed no further condemnation, it needed saving. And it is for the same reason, on the other hand, that He represents the wicked world as incapable of coming to Him that it might have life (viii. 43, 21, xiv. 17, x. 33), and as requiring first of all a 'drawing' from the Father to enable it to come (vi. 44, 65); so that only those hear or believe on Him who are 'of God' (viii. 47, cf. xv. 19, xvii. 14), who are 'of his sheep' (x. 26).

There is undoubtedly a strong emphasis thrown on the universality of Christ's mission of salvation; He has been sent into the world not merely to save some out of the world, but to save the world itself (iii. 16, vi. 51, xii. 47, xvii. 21, cf. i. 29, I John iv. 14, ii. 2). But this universality of destination and effect by which it is 'the world' that is saved, does not imply the salvation of each and every individual in the world, even in the earlier stages of the developing salvation. On the contrary, the saving work is a process (xvii. 20); and, meanwhile, the coming of the Son into the world introduces a crisis, a sifting by which those who, because they are 'of God,' 'of his sheep,' are in the world, but not of it (xv. 19, xvii. 14), are separated from those who are of the world, that is, of their father the devil (viii. 44), who is the Prince of this world (xii. 31, xiv. 30, xvi. 11). Obviously, the difference between men that is thus manifested is not thought of as inhering, after a dualistic or semi-Gnostic fashion, in their very natures as such, or as instituted by their own self-framed or accidentally received dispositions, much less by their own conduct in the world, which is rather the result of it, — but, as already pointed out, as the effect of an act of God. All goes back to the will of God, to accomplish which, the Son, as the Sent One, has come; and therefore also to the consentient will of the Son, who gives life, accordingly, to whom He will (v. 21). As no one can come to Him out of the evil world, except it be given him of the Father (vi. 65, cf. vi. 44), so all that the Father gives Him (vi. 37, 39) and only such (vi. 65), come to Him, being drawn thereunto by the Father (vi. 44). Thus the Son has 'his own in the world' (xiii. 1), His 'chosen ones' (xiii. 18, xv. 16, 19),

whom by His choice He has taken out of the world (xv. 19,
xvii. 6, 14, 16); and for these only is His high-priestly inter-
cession offered (xvii. 9), as to them only is eternal life communicated (x. 28, xvii. 2, also iii. 15, 36, v. 24, vi. 40, 54, viii. 12).
Thus, what the dogmatists call *gratia præveniens* is very strikingly taught; and especial point is given to this teaching in the
great declarations as to the new birth recorded in John iii,
from which we learn that the recreating Spirit comes, like the
wind, without observation, and as He lists (iii. 8), the mode of
action by which the Father 'draws' men being thus uncovered
for us. Of course this drawing is not to be thought of as proceeding in a manner out of accord with man's nature as a
psychic being; it naturally comes to its manifestation in an act
of voluntary choice on man's own part, and in this sense it is
'psychological' and not 'physical'; accordingly, though it be
God that 'draws,' it is man that 'comes' (iii. 21, vi. 35, 41,
xiv. 6). There is no occasion for stumbling therefore in the
ascription of 'will' and 'responsibility' to man, or for puzzling
over the designation of 'faith,' in which the 'coming' takes
effect, as a 'work' of man's (vi. 29). Man is, of course, conceived as acting humanly, after the fashion of an intelligent
and voluntary agent; but behind all his action there is ever
postulated the all-determining hand of God, to whose sovereign
operation even the blindness of the unbelieving is attributed
by the evangelist (xii. 39 f.), while the receptivity to the light
of those who believe is repeatedly in the most emphatic way
ascribed by Jesus Himself to God alone. Although with little
use of the terminology in which we have been accustomed to
expect to see the doctrines of the decree and of election expressed, the substance of these doctrines is here set out in the
most impressive way.

From the two sets of data provided by the Synoptists and
St. John, it is possible to attain quite a clear insight into the
conception of predestination as it lay in our Lord's teaching.
It is quite certain, for example, that there is no place in this
teaching for a 'predestination' that is carefully adjusted to the
foreseen performances of the creature; and as little for a 'de-

cree' which may be frustrated by creaturely action, or an 'election' which is given effect only by the creaturely choice: to our Lord the Father is the omnipotent Lord of heaven and earth, according to whose pleasure all things are ordered, and who gives the Kingdom to whom He will (Luke xii. 32, Mark xi. 26, Luke x. 21). Certainly it is the very heart of our Lord's teaching that the Father's good-pleasure is a *good* pleasure, ethically right, and the issue of infinite love; the very name of Father as the name of God by preference on His lips is full of this conception; but the very nerve of this teaching is, that the Father's will is all-embracing and omnipotent. It is only therefore that His children need be careful for nothing, that the little flock need not fear, that His elect may be assured that none of them shall be lost, but all that the Father has given Him shall be raised up at the last day. And if thus the elective purpose of the Father cannot fail of its end, neither is it possible to find this end in anything less than 'salvation' in the highest sense, than entrance into that eternal life to communicate which to dying men our Lord came into the world. There are elections to other ends, to be sure, spoken of: notably there is the election of the apostles to their office (Luke vi. 13, John vi. 70); and Christ Himself is conceived as especially God's elect one, because no one has the service to render which He has (Luke ix. 35, xxiii. 35). But the elect, by way of eminence; 'the elect whom God elected,' for whose sake He governs all history (Mark xiii. 20); the elect of whom it was the will of Him who sent the Son, that of all that He gave Him He should lose nothing, but should raise it up at the last day (John vi. 39); the elect whom the Son of Man shall at the last day gather from the four winds, from the uttermost parts of the earth to the uttermost part of heaven (Mark xiii. 27): it would be inadequate to suppose that these are elected merely to opportunities or the means of grace, on their free cultivation of which shall depend their undecided destiny; or merely to the service of their fellowmen, as agents in God's beneficent plan for the salvation of the race. Of course this election is to privileges and means of grace; and without these the great end of the election would not be attained: for the 'election' is given effect only by the 'call,' and manifests itself only in faith and the holy life. Equally of course the elect are 'the salt of the earth' and 'the light of the world,' the few through whom the many are blessed; the eternal life to which they are elected does not consist in or with the silence and coldness of death, but only in and with the intensest activities of the conquering people of God. But the prime end of their election does not lie in these things, and to place exclusive stress upon them is certainly to gather in the mint and anise and cummin of the doctrine. That to which God's elect are elected is, according to the teaching of Jesus, all that is included in the idea of the Kingdom of God, in the idea of eternal life, in the idea of fellowship with Christ, in the idea of participation in the glory which the Father has given His Son. Their choice, and the whole development of their history, according to our Lord's teaching, is the loving work of the Father: and in His keeping also is the consummation of their bliss. Their segregation, of course, leaves others not elected, to whom none of their privileges are granted; from whom none of their services are expected; with whom their glorious destiny is not shared. This, too, is of God. But this side of the matter, in accordance with Jesus' mission in the world as Saviour rather than as Judge, is less dwelt upon. In the case of neither class, that of the elect as little as that of those that are without, are the purposes of God wrought out without the co-operation of the activities of the subjects; but in neither case is the decisive factor supplied by these, but is discoverable solely in the will of God and the consonant will of the Son. The 'even so, Father; for so it seemed good in thy sight' (Matt. xi. 26, Luke x. 21), is to our Lord, at least, an all-sufficient theodicy in the face of all God's diverse dealings with men.

The disciples of Jesus continue His teaching in all its elements. We are conscious, for example, of entering no new atmosphere when we pass to the *Epistle of James*. St. James, too, finds his starting-point in a profound apprehension of the exaltation and perfection of God, — defining God's nature, indeed, with a phrase that merely repeats in other words the penetrating declaration that 'God is light' (I John i. 5), which, reflecting our Lord's teaching, sound the keynote of the beloved disciple's thought of God (Jas. i. 17), — and particularly in a keen sense of dependence on God (iv. 15, v. 7), to which it was an axiom that every good thing is a gift from Him (i. 17). Accordingly, salvation, the pre-eminent good, comes purely as His gift, and can be ascribed only to His will (i. 18); and its exclusively Divine origin is indicated by the choice that is made of those who receive it — not the rich and prosperous, who have somewhat perhaps which might command consideration, but the poor and miserable (ii. 5). So little does this Divine choice rest on even faith, that it is rather in order to faith (ii. 5), and introduces its recipients into the Kingdom as firstfruits of a great harvest to be reaped by God in the world (i. 18).

Similarly, in the *Book of Acts*, the whole stress in the matter of salvation is laid on the grace of God (xi. 23, xiii. 43, xiv. 3, 26, xv. 40, xviii. 27); and to it, in the most pointed way, the inception of faith itself is assigned (xviii. 27). It is only slightly varied language when the increase in the Church is ascribed to the hand of the Lord (xi. 21), or the direct act of God (xiv. 27, xviii. 10). The explicit declaration of ii. 47 presents, therefore, nothing peculiar, and we are fully prepared for the philosophy of the redemptive history expressed in xiii. 48, that only those 'ordained to eternal life' believed — the believing that comes by the grace of God (xviii. 27), to whom it belongs to open the heart to give heed to the gospel (xvi. 14), being thus referred to the counsel of eternity, of which the events of time are only the outworking.

The general philosophy of history thus suggested is implicit in the very idea of a promissory system, and in the recognition of a predictive element in prophecy, and is written large on the pages of the *historical books* of the New Testament. It is given expression in every declaration that this or that event came to pass 'that it might be fulfilled which was spoken by the prophets,' — a form of statement in which our Lord had Himself betrayed His teleological view of history, not only as respects details (John xv. 25, xvii. 12), but with the widest reference (Luke xxi. 22), and which was taken up cordially by His followers, particularly by Matthew (i. 22, ii. 15, 23, iv. 14, viii. 17, xii. 17, xiii. 35, xxi. 4, xxvi. 56, John xii. 38, xviii. 9, xix. 24, 28, 36). Alongside of this phrase occurs the equally significant 'δεῖ of the Divine decree,' as it has been appropriately called, by which is suggested the necessity which rules over historical sequences. It is used with a view now to Jesus' own plan of redemption (by Jesus Himself, Luke ii. 49, iv. 43, ix. 22, xiii. 33, xvii. 25, xxiv. 7, John iii. 14, x. 16, xii, 34; by the evangelist, Matt. xvi. 21), now to the underlying plan of God (by Jesus, Matt. xxiv. 6, Mark xiii. 7, 10, Luke xxi. 9; by the writer, Matt. xvii. 10, Mark ix. 11, Acts iii. 21, ix. 16), anon to the prophetic declaration as an indication of the underlying plan (by Jesus, Matt. xxvi. 56, Luke xxii. 37, xxiv. 26, 44; by the writer, John xx. 9, Acts i. 16, xvii. 3). This appeal, in either form, served an important apologetic purpose in the first proclamation of the gospel; but its fundamental significance is rooted, of course, in the conception of a Divine ordering of the whole course of history to the veriest detail.

Such a teleological conception of the history of the Kingdom is manifested strikingly in the speech of St. Stephen (Acts vii.), in which the developing plan of God is rapidly sketched. But it is in such declarations as those of St. Peter recorded in Acts ii. 23, iv. 28 that the wider philosophy of history comes to its clearest expression. In them everything that had befallen Jesus is represented as merely the emerging into fact of what had stood beforehand prepared for in 'the determinate counsel and foreknowledge of God,' so that nothing had been accomplished, by whatever agents, except what 'his hand and his counsel has foreordained to come to pass.' It would not be easy to frame language which should more explicitly proclaim the conception of an all-determining decree of God governing the entire sequence of events in time. Elsewhere in *the Petrine discourses* of Acts the speech is coloured by the same ideas: we note in the immediate context of these culminating passages the high terms in which the exaltation of God is expressed (iv. 24 f.), the sharpness with which His sovereignty in the 'call' (προσκαλέομαι) is declared (ii. 39), and elsewhere the repeated emergence of the idea of the necessary correspondence of the events of time with the predictions of Scripture (i. 16, ii. 24, iii. 21). The same doctrine of predestination meets us in the pages of *St. Peter's Epistles*. He does, indeed, speak of the members of the Christian community as God's elect (I i. 1, ii. 9, v. 13, II i. 10), in accordance with the apostolic habit of assuming the reality implied in the manifestation; but this is so far from importing that election hangs on the act of man that St. Peter refers it directly to the elective foreknowledge of God (I i. 2), and seeks its confirmation in sanctification (II i. 10), — even as the stumbling of the disobedient, on the other hand, is presented as a confirmation of their appointment to disbelief (I ii. 8). The pregnant use of the terms 'foreknow' (προγινώσκω) and 'foreknowledge' (πρόγνωσις) by St. Peter brought to our attention in these passages (Acts ii. 23, I Pet. i. 2, 20), where they certainly convey the sense of a loving, distinguishing regard which assimilates them to the idea of election, is worthy of note as another of the traits common to him and St. Paul (Rom. viii. 29, xi. 2, only in the New Testament). The usage might be explained, indeed, as the development of a purely Greek sense of the words, but it is much more probably rooted in a Semitic usage, which, as we have seen, is not without example in the Old Testament. A simple comparison of the passages will exhibit the impossibility of reading the terms of mere prevision (cf. Cremer *sub voc.*, and especially the full discussion in K. Müller's "Die Göttliche Zuvorersehung und Erwählung," etc. pp. 38 f., 81 f.; also Gennrich, "Theol. Studien und Kritiken," 1898, 382–395; Pfleiderer, "Urchristenthum," 289, "Paulinismus," 268; and Lorenz, "Lehrsystem," etc. 94).

The *teaching of St. John* in Gospel and Epistle is not distinguishable from that which he reports from his Master's lips, and need not here be reverted to afresh. The same fundamental view-points meet us also in the Apocalypse. The emphasis there placed on the omnipotence of God rises indeed to a climax. There only in the New Testament (except II Cor. vi. 18), for example, is the epithet παντοκράτωρ ascribed to Him (i. 8, iv. 8, xi. 17, xv. 3, xvi. 7, 14, xix. 6, 15, xxi. 22, cf. xv. 3, vi. 10); and the whole purport of the book is the portrayal of the Divine guidance of history, and the very essence of its message that, despite all surface appearances, it is the hand of God that really directs all occurrences, and all things are hastening to the end of His determining. Salvation is ascribed unvaryingly to the grace of God, and declared to be His work (xii. 10, xix. 1). The elect people of God are His by the Divine choice alone: their names are from the foundation of the world written in the Lamb's Book of Life (xiii. 8, xvii. 8, xx. 12–15, xxi. 27), which is certainly a symbol of Divine appointment to eternal life revealed in and realized through Christ; nor shall they ever be blotted out of it (iii. 5). It is difficult to doubt that the destination here asserted is to a complete salvation (xix. 9), that it is individual, and that it is but a single instance of the completeness of the Divine government to which the world is subject by the Lord of lords and King of kings, the Ruler of the earth and King of the nations, whose control of all the occurrences of time in accordance with His holy purposes it is the supreme object of this book to portray.

Perhaps less is directly said about the purpose of God in the *Epistle to the Hebrews* than in any other portion of the New Testament of equal length. The technical phraseology of the subject is conspicuously absent. Nevertheless, the conception of the Divine counsel and will underlying all that comes to pass (ii. 10), and especially the entire course of the purchase (vi. 17, cf. x. 5–10, ii. 9) and application (xi. 39, 31, ix. 15) of salvation, is fundamental to the whole thought of the Epistle; and echoes of the modes in which this conception is elsewhere expressed meet us on every hand. Thus we read of God's eternal counsel (βουλή, vi. 17) and of His precedent will (θέλημα, x. 10) as underlying His redemptive acts; of the enrolment of the names of His children in heaven (xii. 23); of the origin in the energy of God of all that is good in us (xiii. 21); and, above all, of a 'heavenly call' as the source of the whole renewed life of the Christian (iii. 1, cf. ix. 15).

When our Lord spoke of 'calling' (καλέω, Matt. ix. 13, Mark
ii. 17, Luke v. 32, and, parabolically, Matt. xxii. 3, 4, 8, 9, Luke
xiv. 8, 9, 10, 12, 13, 16, 17, 24; κλητός, Matt. xxii. 14 [xx. 16])
the term was used in the ordinary sense of 'invitation,' and refers therefore to a much broader circle than the 'elect' (Matt.
xxii. 14); and this fundamental sense of 'bidding' may continue
to cling to the term in the hands of the evangelists (Matt. iv. 21,
Mark i. 20, cf. Luke xiv. 7, John ii. 2), while the depth of meaning which might be attached to it, even in such a connotation,
may be revealed by such a passage as Rev. xix. 9 'Blessed are
they which are bidden to the marriage supper of the Lamb.' On
the lips of the apostolic writers, however, the term in its application to the call of God to salvation took on deeper meanings,
doubtless out of consideration of the author of the call, who
has but to speak and it is done (cf. Rom. iv. 17). It occurs in
these writers, when it occurs at all, as the synonym no longer
of 'invitation,' but rather of 'election' itself; or, more precisely,
as expressive of the temporal act of the Divine efficiency by
which effect is given to the electing decree. In this profounder
sense it is practically confined to the writings of St. Paul and
St. Peter and the *Epistle to the Hebrews,* occurring elsewhere
only in Jude 1, Rev. xvii. 14, where the children of God are
designated the 'called,' just as they are (in various collocations
of the term with the idea of election) in Rom. i. 6, 7, I Cor. i.
2, Rom. viii. 28, I Cor. i. 24 (cf. Rom. i. 1, I Cor. i. 1). Κλητός,
as used in these passages, does not occur in the *Epistle to the
Hebrews,* but in iii. 1 κλῆσις occurs in a sense indistinguishable
from that which it bears in St. Paul (Rom. xi. 29, I Cor. i. 26,
Eph. i. 18, iv. 1, 4, Phil. iii. 14, II Thes. i. 11, II Tim. i. 9) and
St. Peter (II Pet. i. 10); and in ix. 15 (cf. special applications
of the same general idea, v. 4, xi. 8), καλέω bears the same deep
sense expressed by it in St. Paul (Rom. viii. 30 twice, ix. 11, 24,
I Cor. i. 9, vii. 15, 17, 18 twice, 20, 21, 22 twice, 24, Gal. i. 6, 15,
v. 8, 13, Eph. iv. 1, 4, Col. iii. 15, I Thes. ii. 12, iv. 7, v. 24,
II Thes. ii. 14, II Tim. i. 9) and in St. Peter (I i. 15, ii. 9, 21,
iii. 9, v. 10, II i. 3, cf. προσκαλέω, Acts ii. 39, and in the language
of St. Luke, Acts xiii. 2, xvi. 10). The contrast into which the

'called' (iii. 1) are brought in this Epistle with the 'evangelized' (iv. 2, 6), repeating in other terms the contrast which our Saviour institutes between the 'elect' and 'called' (Matt. xxii. 14), exhibits the height of the meaning to which the idea of the 'call' has climbed. It no longer denotes the mere invitation, — that notion is now given in 'evangelize,' — but the actual ushering into salvation of the heirs of the promise, who are made partakers of the heavenly calling, and are called to the everlasting inheritance just because they have been destined thereunto by God (i. 14), and are enrolled in heaven as the children given to the Son of God (ii. 13).

It was reserved, however, to the Apostle Paul to give to the fact of predestination its fullest New Testament presentation. This was not because St. Paul exceeded his fellows in the strength or clearness of his convictions, but because, in the prosecution of the special task which was committed to him in the general work of establishing Christianity in the world, the complete expression of the common doctrine of predestination fell in his way, and became a necessity of his argument. With him, too, the roots of his doctrine of predestination were set in his general doctrine of God, and it was fundamentally because St. Paul was a theist of a clear and consistent type, living and thinking under the influence of the profound consciousness of a personal God who is the author of all that is and, as well, the upholder and powerful governor of all that He has made, according to whose will, therefore, all that comes to pass must be ordered, that he was a predestinarian; and more particularly he too was a predestinarian because of his general doctrine of salvation, in every step of which the initiative must be taken by God's unmerited grace, just because man is a sinner, and, as a sinner, rests under the Divine condemnation, with no right of so much as access to God, and without means to seek, much less to secure, His favour. But although possessing no other sense of the infinite majesty of the almighty Person in whose hands all things lie, or of the issue of all saving acts from His free grace, than his companion apostles, the course of the special work in which St. Paul was engaged, and the exigencies of the special controversies in which he was involved, forced him to a fuller expression of all that is implied in these convictions. As he cleared the whole field of Christian faith from the presence of any remaining confidence in human works; as he laid beneath the hope of Christians a righteousness not self-wrought but provided by God alone; as he consistently offered this God-provided righteousness to sinners of all classes without regard to anything in them by which they might fancy God could be moved to accept their persons, — he was inevitably driven to an especially pervasive reference of salvation in each of its elements to the free grace of God, and to an especially full exposition on the one hand of the course of Divine grace in the several acts which enter into the saving work, and on the other to the firm rooting of the whole process in the pure will of the God of grace. From the beginning to the end of his ministry, accordingly, St. Paul conceived himself, above everything else, as the bearer of a message of undeserved grace to lost sinners, not even directing his own footsteps to carry the glad tidings to whom he would (Rom. i. 10, I Cor. iv. 19, II Cor. ii. 12), but rather led by God in triumphal procession through the world, that through him might be made manifest the savour of the knowledge of Christ in every. place — a savour from life unto life in them that are saved, and from death unto death in them that are lost (II Cor. ii. 15, 16). By the 'word of the cross' proclaimed by him the essential character of his hearers was thus brought into manifestation, — to the lost it was foolishness, to the saved the power of God (I Cor. i. 18): not as if this essential character belonged to them by nature or was the product of their own activities, least of all of their choice at the moment of the proclamation, by which rather it ̄ was only revealed; but as finding an explanation only in an act of God, in accordance with the working of Him to whom all differences among men are to be ascribed (I Cor. iv. 7) — for God alone is the Lord of the harvest, and all the increase, however diligently man may plant and water, is to be accredited to Him alone (I Cor. iii. 5 f.).

It is naturally the soteriological interest that determines in the main St. Paul's allusions to the all-determining hand of God, — the letters that we have from him come from Paul the evangelist, — but it is not merely a soteriological conception that he is expressing in them, but the most fundamental postulate of his religious consciousness; and he is accordingly constantly correlating his doctrine of election with his general doctrine of the decree or counsel of God. No man ever had an intenser or more vital sense of God, — the eternal (Rom. xvi. 26) and incorruptible (i. 23) One, the only wise One (xvi. 27), who does all things according to His good-pleasure (I Cor. xv. 38, xii. 18, Col. i. 19), and whose ways are past tracing out (Rom. xi. 33); before whom men should therefore bow in the humility of absolute dependence, recognizing in Him the one moulding power as well in history as in the life of the individual (Rom. ix.). Of Him and through Him and unto Him, he fervently exclaims, are all things (Rom. xi. 36, cf. I Cor. viii. 6); He is over all and through all and in all (Eph. iv. 6, cf. Col. i. 16); He worketh all things according to the counsel of His will (Eph. i. 11): all that is, in a word, owes its existence and persistence and its action and issue to Him. The whole course of history is, therefore, of His ordering (Acts xiv. 16, xvii. 26, Rom. i. 18 f., iii. 25, ix–xi, Gal. iii. iv.), and every event that befalls is under His control, and must be estimated from the view-point of His purposes of good to His people (Rom. viii. 28, I Thes. v. 17, 18), for whose benefit the whole world is governed (Eph. i. 22, I Cor. ii. 7, Col. i. 18). The figure that is employed in Rom. ix. 22 with a somewhat narrower reference, would fairly express St. Paul's world-view in its relation to the Divine activity: God is the potter, and the whole world with all its contents but as the plastic clay which He moulds to His own ends; so that whatsoever comes into being, and whatsoever uses are served by the things that exist, are all alike of Him. In accordance with this world-view St. Paul's doctrine of salvation must necessarily be interpreted; and, in very fact, he gives it its accordant expression in every instance in which he speaks of it.

There are especially *three chief passages* in which the apostle so fully expounds his fundamental teaching as to the relation of salvation to the purpose of God, that they may fairly claim our primary attention.

(a) The first of these — Rom. viii. 29, 30 — emerges as part of the encouragement which the apostle offers to his readers in the sad state in which they find themselves in this world, afflicted with fears within and fightings without. He reminds them that they are not left to their weakness, but the Spirit comes to their aid: 'and we know,' adds the apostle, — it is no matter of conjecture, but of assured knowledge, — 'that with them that love God, God co-operates with respect to all things for good, since they are indeed the called according to [His] purpose.' The appeal is obviously primarily to the universal government of God: nothing takes place save by His direction, and even what seems to be grievous comes from the Father's hand. Secondarily, the appeal is to the assured position of his readers within the fatherly care of God: they have not come into this blessed relation with God accidentally or by the force of their own choice; they have been 'called' into it by Himself, and that by no thoughtless, inadvertent, meaningless, or changeable call; it was a call 'according to purpose,' — where the anarthrousness of the noun throws stress on the purposiveness of the call. What has been denominated 'the golden chain of salvation' that is attached to this declaration by the particle 'because' can therefore have no other end than more fully to develop and more firmly to ground the assurance thus quickened in the hearts of the readers: it accordingly enumerates the steps of the saving process in the purpose of God, and carries it thus successively through the stages of appropriating foreknowledge, — for 'foreknow' is undoubtedly used here in that pregnant sense we have already seen it to bear in similar connexions in the New Testament, — predestination to conformity with the image of God's Son, calling, justifying, glorifying; all of which are cast in the past tense of a purpose in principle executed when formed, and are bound together as mutually implicative, so that, where one is present, all are in principle present with it. It accordingly follows that, in St.

Paul's conception, glorification rests on justification, which in turn rests on vocation, while vocation comes only to those who had previously been predestinated to conformity with God's Son, and this predestination to character and destiny only to those afore chosen by God's loving regard. It is obviously a strict doctrine of predestination that is taught. This conclusion can be avoided only by assigning a sense to the 'foreknowing' that lies at the root of the whole process, which is certainly out of accord not merely with its ordinary import in similar connexions in the New Testament, nor merely with the context, but with the very purpose for which the declaration is made, namely, to enhearten the struggling saint by assuring him that he is not committed to his own power, or rather weakness, but is in the sure hands of the Almighty Father. It would seem little short of absurd to hang on the merely contemplative foresight of God a declaration adduced to support the assertion that the lovers of God are something deeper and finer than even lovers of God, namely, 'the called according to *purpose*,' and itself educing the joyful cry, 'If God is for us, who is against us?' and grounding a confident claim upon the gift of all things from His hands.

(*b*) The even more famous section, Rom. ix, x, xi, following closely upon this strong affirmation of the suspension of the whole saving process on the predetermination of God, offers, on the face of it, a yet sharper assertion of predestination, raising it, moreover, out of the circle of the merely individual salvation into the broader region of the historical development of the kingdom of God. The problem which St. Paul here faces grew so directly out of his fundamental doctrine of justification by faith alone, with complete disregard of all question of merit or vested privilege, that it must have often forced itself upon his attention, — himself a Jew with a high estimate of a Jew's privileges and a passionate love for his people. He could not but have pondered it frequently and deeply, and least of all could he have failed to give it treatment in an Epistle like this, which undertakes to provide a somewhat formal exposition of his whole doctrine of justification.

Having shown the necessity of such a method of salvation as he proclaimed, if sinful men were to be saved at all (i. 18–iii. 20), and then expounded its nature and evidence (iii. 21–v. 21), and afterwards discussed its intensive effects (vi. 1–viii. 39), he could not fail further to explain its extensive effects — especially when they appeared to be of so portentous a character as to imply a reversal of what was widely believed to have been God's mode of working heretofore, the rejection of His people whom He foreknew, and the substitution of the alien in their place. St. Paul's solution of the problem is, briefly, that the situation has been gravely misconceived by those who so represent it; that nothing of the sort thus described has happened or will happen; that what has happened is merely that in the constitution of that people whom He has chosen to Himself and is fashioning to His will, God has again exercised that sovereignty which He had previously often exercised, and which He had always expressly reserved to Himself and frequently proclaimed as the principle of His dealings with the people emphatically of His choice. In his exposition of this solution St. Paul first defends the propriety of God's action (ix. 6–24), then turns to stop the mouth of the objecting Jew by exposing the manifested unfitness of the Jewish people for the kingdom (ix. 30–x. 21), and finally expounds with great richness the ameliorating circumstances in the whole transaction (xi. 1–36). In the course of his defence of God's rejection of the mass of contemporary Israel, he sets forth the sovereignty of God in the whole matter of salvation — 'that the purpose of God according to election might stand, not of works, but of Him that calleth' — with a sharpness of assertion and a clearness of illustration which leave nothing to be added in order to throw it out in the full strength of its conception. We are pointed illustratively to the sovereign acceptance of Isaac and rejection of Ishmael, and to the choice of Jacob and not of Esau before their birth and therefore before either had done good or bad; we are explicitly told that in the matter of salvation it is not of him that wills, or of him that runs, but of God that shows mercy, and that has mercy on whom He wills, and whom He

wills He hardens; we are pointedly directed to behold in God
the potter who makes the vessels which proceed from His hand
each for an end of His appointment, that He may work out His
will upon them. It is safe to say that language cannot be chosen
better adapted to teach predestination at its height.

We are exhorted, indeed, not to read this language in isolation, but to remember that the ninth chapter must be interpreted in the light of the eleventh. Not to dwell on the equally
important consideration that the eleventh chapter must likewise be interpreted only in the light of the ninth, there seems
here to exhibit itself some forgetfulness of the inherent continuity of St. Paul's thought, and, indeed, some misconception
of the progress of the argument through the section, which is
a compact whole and must express a much pondered line of
thought, constantly present to the apostle's mind. We must
not permit to fall out of sight the fact that the whole extremity
of assertion of the ninth chapter is repeated in the eleventh
(xi. 4–10); so that there is no change of conception or lapse of
consecution observable as the argument develops, and we do
not escape from the doctrine of predestination of the ninth
chapter in fleeing to the eleventh. This is true even if we go at
once to the great closing declaration of xi. 32, to which we are
often directed as to the key of the whole section — which, indeed, it very much is: 'For God hath shut up all unto disobedience, that he might have mercy upon all.' On the face of
it there could not readily be framed a more explicit assertion
of the Divine control and the Divine initiative than this; it
is only another declaration that He has mercy on whom He
will have mercy, and after the manner and in the order that
He will. And it certainly is not possible to read it as a declaration of universal salvation, and thus reduce the whole preceding
exposition to a mere tracing of the varying pathways along
which the common Father leads each individual of the race
severally to the common goal. Needless to point out that thus
the whole argument would be stultified, and the apostle convicted of gross exaggeration in tone and language where otherwise we find only impressive solemnity, rising at times into

natural anguish. It is enough to observe that the verse cannot
bear this sense in its context. Nothing is clearer than that its
purpose is not to minimise but to magnify the sense of absolute
dependence on the Divine mercy, and to quicken apprehension
of the mystery of God's righteously loving ways; and nothing
is clearer than that the reference of the double ' all ' is exhausted
by the two classes discussed in the immediate context, — so
that they are not to be taken individualistically but, so to
speak, racially. The intrusion of the individualistic-universal-
istic sentiment, so dominant in the modern consciousness, into
the interpretation of this section, indeed, is to throw the whole
into inextricable confusion. Nothing could be further from the
nationalistic-universalistic point of view from which it was
written, and from which alone St. Paul can be understood when
he represents that in rejecting the mass of contemporary Jews
God has not cast off His people, but, acting only as He had
frequently done in former ages, is fulfilling His promise to the
kernel while shelling off the husk. Throughout the whole process of pruning and ingrafting which he traces in the dealings
of God with the olive-tree which He has once for all planted,
St. Paul sees God, in accordance with His promise, saving His
people. The continuity of its stream of life he perceives preserved throughout all its present experience of rejection (xi.
1–10); the gracious purpose of the present confinement of its
channel, he traces with eager hand (xi. 11–15); he predicts
with confidence the attainment in the end of the full breadth
of the promise (xi. 15–32), — all to the praise of the glory of
God's grace (xi. 33–36). There is undoubtedly a universalism
of salvation proclaimed here; but it is an eschatological, not
an individualistic universalism. The day is certainly to come
when the whole world — inclusive of all the Jews and Gentiles
alike, then dwelling on the globe — shall know and serve the
Lord; and God in all His strange work of distributing salvation
is leading the course of events to that great goal; but meanwhile the principle of His action is free, sovereign grace, to
which alone it is to be attributed that any who are saved in
the meantime enter into their inheritance, and through which

alone shall the final goal of the race itself be attained. The central thought of the whole discussion, in a word, is that Israel does not owe the promise to the fact that it is Israel, but conversely owes the fact that it is Israel to the promise, — that 'it is not the children of the flesh that are the children of God, but the children of the promise that are reckoned for a seed' (ix. 8). In these words we hold the real key to the whole section; and if we approach it with this key in hand we shall have little difficulty in apprehending that, from its beginning to its end, St. Paul has no higher object than to make clear that the inclusion of any individual within the kingdom of God finds its sole cause in the sovereign grace of the choosing God, and cannot in any way or degree depend upon his own merit, privilege, or act.

Neither, with this key in our hand, will it be possible to raise a question whether the election here expounded is to eternal life or not rather merely to prior privilege or higher service. These too, no doubt, are included. But by what right is this long section intruded here as a substantive part of this Epistle, busied as a whole with the exposition of 'the power of God unto salvation to every one that believeth, to the Jew first and also to the Greek,' if it has no direct concern with this salvation? By what chance has it attached itself to that noble grounding of a Christian's hope and assurance with which the eighth chapter closes? By what course of thought does it reach its own culmination in that burst of praise to God, on whom all things depend, with which it concludes? By what accident is it itself filled with the most unequivocal references to the saving grace of God 'which hath been poured out on the vessels of his mercy which he afore prepared for glory, even on us whom he also called, not from the Jews only, but also from the Gentiles'? If such language has no reference to salvation, there is no language in the New Testament that need be interpreted of final destiny. Beyond question this section does explain to us some of the grounds of the mode of God's action in gathering a people to Himself out of the world; and in doing this, it does reveal to us some of the ways in which the distribution of His electing grace serves the purposes of His kingdom on earth; reading it, we certainly do learn that God has many ends to serve in His gracious dealings with the children of men, and that we, in our ignorance of His multifarious purposes, are not fitted to be His counsellors. But by all this, the fact is in no wise obscured that it is primarily to salvation that He calls His elect, and that whatever other ends their election may subserve, this fundamental end will never fail; that in this, too, the gifts and calling of God are not repented of, and will surely lead on to their goal. The difficulty which is felt by some in following the apostle's argument here, we may suspect, has its roots in part in a shrinking from what appears to them an arbitrary assignment of men to diverse destinies without consideration of their desert. Certainly St. Paul as explicitly affirms the sovereignty of reprobation as of election, — if these twin ideas are, indeed, separable even in thought: if he represents God as sovereignly loving Jacob, he represents Him equally as sovereignly hating Esau; if he declares that He has mercy on whom He will, he equally declares that He hardens whom He will. Doubtless the difficulty often felt here is, in part, an outgrowth of an insufficient realization of St. Paul's basal conception of the state of men at large as condemned sinners before an angry God. It is with a world of lost sinners that he is representing God as dealing; and out of that world building up a Kingdom of Grace. Were not all men sinners, there might still be an election, as sovereign as now; and there being an election, there would still be as sovereign a rejection: but the rejection would not be a rejection to punishment, to destruction, to eternal death, but to some other destiny consonant to the state in which those passed by should be left. It is not indeed, then, because men are sinners that men are left unelected; election is free, and its obverse of rejection must be equally free: but it is solely because men are sinners that what they are left to is destruction. And it is in this universalism of ruin rather than in a universalism of salvation that St. Paul really roots his theodicy. When all deserve death it is a marvel of pure grace that any receive life; and who shall gain-

say the right of Him who shows this miraculous mercy, to have
mercy on whom He will, and whom He will to harden?

(c) In Eph. i. 1–12 there is, if possible, an even higher note
struck. Here, too, St. Paul is dealing primarily with the blessings bestowed on his readers, in Christ, all of which he ascribes
to the free grace of God; but he so speaks of these blessings as
to correlate the gracious purpose of God in salvation, not
merely with the plan of operation which He prosecutes in establishing and perfecting His kingdom on earth, but also with
the all-embracing decree that underlies His total cosmical
activity. In opening this circular letter, addressed to no particular community whose special circumstances might suggest
the theme of the thanksgiving with which he customarily
begins his letters, St. Paul is thrown back on what is common
to Christians; and it is probably to this circumstance that we
owe the magnificent description of the salvation in Christ with
which the Epistle opens, and in which this salvation is traced
consecutively in its preparation (vv. 4, 5), its execution (6, 7),
its publication (8–10), and its application (11–14), both to
Jews (11, 12) and to Gentiles (13, 14). Thus, at all events, we
have brought before us the whole ideal history of salvation in
Christ from eternity to eternity — from the eternal purpose as
it lay in the loving heart of the Father, to the eternal consummation, when all things in heaven and earth shall be summed
up in Christ. Even the incredible profusion of the blessings
which we receive in Christ, described with an accumulation of
phrases that almost defies exposition, is less noticeable here
than the emphasis and reiteration with which the apostle carries back their bestowment on us to that primal purpose of
God in which all things are afore prepared ere they are set in
the way of accomplishment. All this accumulation of blessings,
he tells his readers, has come to them and him only in fulfilment
of an eternal purpose — only because they had been chosen by
God out of the mass of sinful men, in Christ, before the foundation of the world, to be holy and blameless before Him, and had
been lovingly predestinated unto adoption through Jesus
Christ to Him, in accordance with the good-pleasure of His

will, to the praise of the glory of His grace. It is therefore, he further explains, that to them in the abundance of God's grace there has been brought the knowledge of the salvation in Christ, described here as the knowledge of the mystery of the Divine will, according to His good-pleasure, which He purposed in Himself with reference to the dispensation of the fulness of the times, to sum up all things in the universe in Christ, — by which phrases the plan of salvation is clearly exhibited as but one element in the cosmical purpose of God. And thus it is, the apostle proceeds to explain, only in pursuance of this all-embracing cosmical purpose that Christians, whether Jews or Gentiles, have been called into participation of these blessings, to the praise of the glory of God's grace, — and of the former class, he pauses to assert anew that their call rests on a predestination according to the purpose of Him that works all things according to the counsel of His will. Throughout this elevated passage, the resources of language are strained to the utmost to give utterance to the depth and fervour of St. Paul's conviction of the absoluteness of the dominion which the God, whom he describes as Him that works all things according to the counsel of His will, exercises over the entire universe, and of his sense of the all-inclusive perfection of the plan on which He is exercising His world-wide government — into which world-wide government His administration of His grace, in the salvation of Christ, works as one element. Thus there is kept steadily before our eyes the wheel within wheel of the all-comprehending decree of God: first of all, the inclusive cosmical purpose in accordance with which the universe is governed as it is led to its destined end; within this, the purpose relative to the kingdom of God, a substantive part, and, in some sort, the hinge of the world-purpose itself; and still within this, the purpose of grace relative to the individual, by virtue of which he is called into the Kingdom and made sharer in its blessings: the common element with them all being that they are and come to pass only in accordance with the good-pleasure of His will, according to His purposed good-pleasure, according to the purpose of Him who works all things in ac-

cordance with the counsel of His will; and therefore all alike
redound solely to His praise.

In these outstanding passages, however, there are only expounded, though with special richness, ideas which govern the
Pauline literature, and which come now and again to clear expression in each group of St. Paul's letters. The whole doctrine
of election, for instance, lies as truly in the declaration of II
Thes. ii. 13 or that of II Tim. i. 9 (cf. II Tim. ii. 19, Tit. iii. 5)
as in the passages we have considered from Romans (cf. I Cor. i.
26–31) and Ephesians (cf. Eph. ii. 10, Col. i. 27, iii. 12, 15, Phil.
iv. 3). It may be possible to trace minor distinctions through
the several groups of letters in forms of statement or modes of
relating the doctrine to other conceptions; but from the beginning to the end of St. Paul's activity as a Christian teacher his
fundamental teaching as to the Christian calling and life is
fairly summed up in the declaration that those that are saved
are God's 'workmanship created in Christ Jesus unto good
works, which God afore prepared that they should walk in
them' (Eph. ii. 10).

The most striking impression made upon us by a survey of
the whole material is probably the intensity of St. Paul's practical interest in the doctrine — a matter fairly illustrated by
the passage just quoted (Eph. ii. 10). Nothing is more noticeable than his zeal in enforcing its two chief practical contents
— the assurance it should bring to believers of their eternal
safety in the faithful hands of God, and the ethical energy it
should arouse within them to live worthily of their vocation.
It is one of St. Paul's most persistent exhortations, that believers should remember that their salvation is not committed
to their own weak hands, but rests securely on the faithfulness
of the God who has called them according to His purpose (e. g.,
I Thes. v. 24, I Cor. i. 8 f., x. 13, Phil. i. 6). Though the appropriation of their salvation begins in an act of faith on their
own part, which is consequent on the hearing of the gospel,
their appointment to salvation itself does not depend on this
act of faith, nor on any fitness discoverable in them on the foresight of which God's choice of them might be supposed to be

based, but (as I Thes. ii. 13 already indicates) both the preaching of the gospel and the exercise of faith consistently appear as steps in the carrying out of an election not conditioned on their occurrence, but embracing them as means to the end set by the free purpose of God. The case is precisely the same with all subsequent acts of the Christian life. So far is St. Paul from supposing that election to life should operate to enervate moral endeavour, that it is precisely from the fact that the willing and doing of man rest on an energizing willing and doing of God, which in turn rest on His eternal purpose, that the apostle derives his most powerful and most frequently urged motive for ethical action. That tremendous 'therefore,' with which at the opening of the twelfth chapter of Romans he passes from the doctrinal to the ethical part of the Epistle, — from a doctrinal exposition the very heart of which is salvation by pure grace apart from all works, and which has just closed with the fullest discussion of the effects of election to be found in all his writings, to the rich exhortations to high moral effort with which the closing chapters of this Epistle are filled, — may justly be taken as the normal illation of his whole ethical teaching. His Epistles, in fact, are sown (as indeed is the whole New Testament) with particular instances of the same appeal (e. g., I Thes. ii. 12, II Thes. ii. 13–15, Rom. vi, II Cor. v. 14, Col. i. 10, Phil. i. 21, ii. 12, 13, II Tim. ii. 19). In Phil. ii. 12, 13 it attains, perhaps, its sharpest expression: here the saint is exhorted to work out his own salvation with fear and trembling, just because it is God who is working in him both the willing and the doing because of His 'good-pleasure' — obviously but another way of saying, 'If God is for us, who can be against us?'

There is certainly presented in this a problem for those who wish to operate in this matter with an irreconcilable 'either, or,' and who can conceive of no freedom of man which is under the control of God. St. Paul's theism was, however, of too pure a quality to tolerate in the realm of creation any force beyond the sway of Him who, as he says, is over all, and through all, and in all (Eph. iv. 6), working all things according to the counsel of His will (Eph. i. 11). And it must be confessed that it is

more facile than satisfactory to set his theistic world-view summarily aside as a 'merely religious view,' which stands in conflict with a truly ethical conception of the world — perhaps
even with a repetition of Fritzsche's jibe that St. Paul would
have reasoned better on the high themes of 'fate, free-will, and
providence' had he sat at the feet of Aristotle rather than at
those of Gamaliel. Antiquity produced, however, no ethical
genius equal to St. Paul, and even as a teacher of the foundations of ethics Aristotle himself might well be content to sit
rather at his feet; and it does not at once appear why a so-
called 'religious' conception may not have as valid a ground
in human nature, and as valid a right to determine human conviction, as a so-called 'ethical' one. It can serve no good purpose even to proclaim an insoluble antinomy here: such an
antinomy St. Paul assuredly did not feel, as he urged the predestination of God not more as a ground of assurance of salvation than as the highest motive of moral effort; and it does
not seem impossible for even us weaker thinkers to follow him
some little way at least in looking upon those twin bases of
religion and morality — the ineradicable feelings of dependence and responsibility — not as antagonistic sentiments of
a hopelessly divided heart, but as fundamentally the same profound conviction operating in a double sphere. At all events,
St. Paul's pure theistic view-point, which conceived God as in
His providential *concursus* working all things according to the
counsel of His will (Eph. i. 11) in entire consistency with the
action of second causes, necessary and free, the proximate pro-
ducers of events, supplied him with a very real point of departure for his conception of the same God, in the operations of
His grace, working the willing and the doing of Christian men,
without the least infringement of the integrity of the free determination by which each grace is proximately attained. It
does not belong to our present task to expound the nature of
that Divine act by which St. Paul represents God as 'calling'
sinners 'into communion with his Son,' itself the first step in
the realization in their lives of that conformity to His image to
which they are predestinated in the counsels of eternity, and

of which the first manifestation is that faith in the Redeemer of God's elect out of which the whole Christian life unfolds. Let it only be observed in passing that he obviously conceives it as an act of God's almighty power, removing old inabilities and creating new abilities of living, loving action. It is enough for our present purpose to perceive that even in this act St. Paul did not conceive God as dehumanizing man, but rather as energizing man in a new direction of his powers; while in all his subsequent activities the analogy of the *concursus* of Providence is express. In his own view, his strenuous assertion of the predetermination in God's purpose of all the acts of saint and sinner alike in the matter of salvation, by which the discrimination of men into saved and lost is carried back to the free counsel of God's will, as little involves violence to the ethical spontaneity of their activities on the one side, as on the other it involves unrighteousness in God's dealings with His creatures. He does not speculatively discuss the methods of the Divine providence; but the fact of its universality — over all beings and actions alike — forms one of his most primary presuppositions; and naturally he finds no difficulty in postulating the inclusion in the prior intention of God of what is subsequently evolved in the course of His providential government.

V. The Bible Doctrine of Predestination

A survey of the whole material thus cursorily brought before us exhibits the existence of a consistent Bible doctrine of predestination, which, because rooted in, and indeed only a logical outcome of, the fundamental Biblical theism, is taught in all its essential elements from the beginning of the Biblical revelation, and is only more fully unfolded in detail as the more developed religious consciousness and the course of the history of redemption required.

The *subject* of the Decree is uniformly conceived as God in the fulness of His moral personality. It is not to chance, nor to necessity, nor yet to an abstract or arbitrary will, — to God acting inadvertently, inconsiderately, or by any necessity of nature, — but specifically to the almighty, all-wise, all-holy, all-righteous, faithful, loving God, to the Father of our Lord and Saviour Jesus Christ, that is ascribed the predetermination of the course of events. Naturally, the contemplation of the plan in accordance with which all events come to pass calls out primarily a sense of the unsearchable wisdom of Him who framed it, and of the illimitable power of Him who executes it; and these attributes are accordingly much dwelt upon when the Divine predestination is adverted to. But the moral attributes are no less emphasized, and the Biblical writers find their comfort continually in the assurance that it is the righteous, holy, faithful, loving God in whose hands rests the determination of the sequence of events and all their issues. Just because it is the determination of God, and represents Him in all His fulness, the decree is ever set forth further as in its *nature* eternal, absolute, and immutable. And it is only an explication of these qualities when it is further insisted upon, as it is throughout the Bible, that it is essentially one single composite purpose, into which are worked all the details included in it, each in its appropriate place; that it is the pure determination of the Divine will — that is, not to be confounded on the one hand with an act of the Divine intellect on which it rests, nor on the other with its execution by His power in the works of creation and providence; that it is free and unconditional — that is, not the product of compulsion from without nor of necessity of nature from within, nor based or conditioned on any occurrence outside itself, foreseen or unforeseen; and that it is certainly efficacious, or rather constitutes the unchanging norm according to which He who is the King over all administers His government over the universe. Nor is it to pass beyond the necessary implications of the fundamental idea when it is further taught, as it is always taught throughout the Scriptures, that the *object* of the decree is the whole universe of things and all their activities, so that nothing comes to pass, whether in the sphere of necessary or free causation, whether good or bad, save in accordance with the provisions of the primal plan, or more precisely save as the outworking in fact of what had lain in the Divine mind as purpose from all eternity, and is now only unfolded into actuality as the fulfilment of His all-determining will. Finally, it is equally unvaryingly represented that the *end* which the decreeing God had in view in framing His purpose is to be sought not without but within Himself, and may be shortly declared as His own praise, or, as we now commonly say, the glory of God. Since it antedates the existence of all things outside of God and provides for their coming into being, they all without exception must be ranked as means to its end, which can be discovered only in the glory of the Divine purposer Himself. The whole Bible doctrine of the decree revolves, in a word, around the simple idea of purpose. Since God is a Person, the very mark of His being is purpose. Since He is an infinite Person, His purpose is eternal and independent, all-inclusive and effective. Since He is a moral Person, His purpose is the perfect exposition of all His infinite moral perfections. Since He is the personal creator of all that exists, His purpose can find its final cause only in Himself.

Against this general doctrine of the decree, the Bible doctrine of ELECTION is thrown out into special prominence, being, as it is, only a particular application of the general doctrine of the decree to the matter of the dealings of God with a sinful race. In its fundamental characteristics it therefore partakes of all the elements of the general doctrine of the decree. It, too, is necessarily an act of God in His completeness as an infinite moral Person, and is therefore eternal, absolute, immutable — the independent, free, unconditional, effective determination by the Divine will of the objects of His saving operations. In the development of the idea, however, there are certain elements which receive a special stress. There is nothing that is more constantly emphasized than the absolute *sovereignty* of the elective choice. The very essence of the doctrine is made, indeed, to consist in the fact that, in the whole administration of His grace, God is moved by no consideration derived from the special recipients of His saving mercy, but the entire account of its distribution is to be found hidden in the free counsels of His own will. That it is not of him that runs, nor of him that wills, but of God that shows mercy, that the sinner obtains salvation, is the steadfast witness of the whole body of Scripture, urged with such reiteration and in such varied connexions as to exclude the possibility that there may lurk behind the act of election considerations of foreseen characters or acts or circumstances — all of which appear rather as results of election as wrought out in fact by the *providentia specialissima* of the electing God. It is with no less constancy of emphasis that the roots of the Divine election are planted in His unsearchable love, by which it appears as *the supreme act of grace*. Contemplation of the general plan of God, including in its provisions every event which comes to pass in the whole universe of being during all the ages, must redound in the first instance to the praise of the infinite wisdom which has devised it all; or as our appreciation of its provisions is deepened, of the glorious righteousness by which it is informed. Contemplation of the particular element in His purpose which provides for the rescue of lost sinners from the destruction due to their guilt, and their restoration to right and to God, on the other hand draws our thoughts at once to His inconceivable love, and must redound, as the Scriptures delight to phrase it, to the praise of His glorious grace. It is ever, therefore, specifically to the love of God that the Scriptures ascribe His elective decree, and they are never weary of raising our eyes from the act itself to its source in the Divine compassion. A similar emphasis is also everywhere cast on the *particularity* of the Divine election. So little is it the designation of a mere class to be filled up by undetermined individuals in the exercise of their own determination; or of mere conditions, or characters, or qualities, to be fulfilled or attained by the undetermined activities of individuals, foreseen or unforeseen; that the Biblical writers take special pains to carry home to the heart of each individual believer the assurance that he himself has been from all eternity the particular object of the Divine choice, and that he owes it to this Divine choice alone that he is a member of the class of the chosen ones, that he is able to fulfil the conditions of salvation, that he can hope to attain the character on which alone God can look with complacency, that he can look forward to an eternity of bliss as his own possession. It is the very nerve of the Biblical doctrine that each individual of that enormous multitude that constitutes the great host of the people of God, and that is illustrating the character of Christ in the new life now lived in the strength of the Son of God, has from all eternity been the particular object of the Divine regard, and is only now fulfilling the high destiny designed for him from the foundation of the world.

The Biblical writers are as far as possible from obscuring the doctrine of election because of any seemingly unpleasant corollaries that flow from it. On the contrary, they expressly draw the corollaries which have often been so designated, and make them a part of their explicit teaching. Their doctrine of election, they are free to tell us, for example, does certainly involve a corresponding *doctrine of preterition.* The very term adopted in the New Testament to express it — ἐκλέγομαι, which, as Meyer justly says (Eph. i. 4), '*always* has, and must *of logical necessity* have, a reference to *others* to whom the chosen would, without the ἐκλογή, still belong' — embodies a declaration of the fact that in their election others are passed by and left without the gift of salvation; the whole presentation of the doctrine is such as either to imply or openly to assert, on its every emergence, the removal of the elect by the pure grace of God, not merely from a state of condemnation, but out of the company of the condemned — a company on whom the grace of God has no saving effect, and who are therefore left without hope in their sins; and the positive just reprobation of the impenitent for their sins is repeatedly explicitly taught in sharp contrast with the gratuitous salvation of the elect despite their sins. But, on the other hand, it is ever taught that, as the body out of which believers are chosen by God's unsearchable grace is the mass of justly condemned sinners, so the destruction to which those that are passed by are left is the righteous recompense of their guilt. Thus the discrimination between men in the matter of eternal destiny is distinctly set forth as taking place in the interests of mercy and for the sake of salvation:

from the fate which justly hangs over all, God is represented as in His infinite compassion rescuing those chosen to this end in His inscrutable counsels of mercy to the praise of the glory of His grace; while those that are left in their sins perish most deservedly, as the justice of God demands. And as the broader lines of God's gracious dealings with the world lying in its iniquity are more and more fully drawn for us, we are enabled ultimately to perceive that the Father of spirits has not distributed His elective grace with niggard hand, but from the beginning has had in view the restoration to Himself of the whole world; and through whatever slow approaches (as men count slowness) He has made thereto — first in the segregation of the Jews for the keeping of the service of God alive in the midst of an evil world, and then in their rejection in order that the fulness of the Gentiles migh tbe gathered in, and finally through them Israel in turn may all be saved — has ever been conducting the world in His loving wisdom and His wise love to its destined goal of salvation, — now and again, indeed, shutting up this or that element of it unto disobedience, but never merely in order that it might fall, but that in the end He might have mercy upon all. Thus the Biblical writers bid us raise our eyes, not only from the justly condemned lost, that we may with deeper feeling contemplate the marvels of the Divine love in the saving of sinners not better than they and with no greater claims on the Divine mercy; but from the relatively insignificant body of the lost, as but the prunings gathered beneath the branches of the olive-tree planted by the Lord's own hand, to fix them on the thrifty stock itself and the crown of luxuriant leafage and ever more richly ripening fruit, as under the loving pruning and grafting of the great Husbandman it grows and flourishes and puts forth its boughs until it shall shade the whole earth. This, according to the Biblical writers, is the end of election; and this is nothing other than the salvation of the world. Though in the process of the ages the goal is not attained without prunings and fires of burning, — though all the wild-olive twigs are not throughout the centuries grafted in, — yet the goal of a saved world shall at the end be gloriously realized. Meanwhile, the hope of the world, the hope of the Church, and the hope of the individual alike, is cast solely on the mercy of a freely electing God, in whose hands are all things, and not least the care of the advance of His saving grace in the world. And it is undeniable that whenever, as the years have passed by, the currents of religious feeling have run deep, and the higher ascents of religious thinking have been scaled, it has ever been on the free might of Divine grace that Christians have been found to cast their hopes for the salvation alike of the world, the Church, and the individual; and whenever they have thus turned in trust to the pure grace of God, they have spontaneously given expression to their faith in terms of the Divine election.

LITERATURE. — The Biblical material can best be surveyed with the help of the Lexicons on the terms employed (especially Cremer), the commentaries on the passages, and the sections in the several treatises on Biblical Theology dealing with this and cognate themes; among these last, the works of Dillmann on the Old Testament, and Holtzmann on the New Testament, may be especially profitably consulted. The Pauline doctrine has, in particular, been made the subject of almost endless discussion, chiefly, it must be confessed, with the object of softening its outlines or of explaining it more or less away. Perhaps the following are the more important recent treatises: — Poelman, "de Jesu Apostolorumque, Pauli præsertim, doctrina de prædestinatione divina et morali hominis libertate," Gron. 1851; Weiss, "Predestinationslehre des Ap. Paul.," in "Jahrbb. f. D. Theol." 1857, p. 54 f.; Lamping, "Pauli de prædestinatione decretorum enarratio," Leov. 1858; Goens, "Le rôle de la liberté humaine dans la prédestination Paulinienne," Lausanne, 1884; Ménégoz, "La prédestination dans la théologie Paulinienne," Paris, 1885; Dalmer, "Zur Paulinischen Erwählungslehre," in "Greifswälder Studien," Gütersloh, 1895. The publication of Karl Müller's valuable treatise on "Die Göttliche Zuvorersehung und Erwählung," etc. (Halle, 1892), has called out a new literature on the section Rom. ix–xi,

the most important items in which are probably the reprint
of Beyschlag's "Die Paulinische Theodicee" (1896, first published in 1868), and Dalmer, "Die Erwählung Israels nach der
Heilsverkündigung des Ap. Paul." (Gütersloh, 1894), and
Kühl, "Zur Paulinischen Theodicee," in the "Theologische
Studien," presented to B. Weiss (Göttingen, 1897). But of
these only Goens recognizes the double predestination; even
Müller, whose treatise is otherwise of the first value, argues
against it, and so does Dalmer in his very interesting discussions; the others are still less in accordance with their text (cf.
the valuable critical note on the recent literature in Holtzmann's "N. T. Theologie," ii. 171–174).

Discussions of the doctrine of post-Canonical Judaism may
be found in Hamburger, "Real-Encyc." ii. 102 f., article "Be-
stimmung"; F. Weber, "Jüd. Theol." 148 ff., 205 ff.; Schürer,
HJP ii. ii. 14 f. (cf. p. 2 f., where the passages from Josephus
are collected); Edersheim, "Life and Times of Jesus," i. 316 ff.,
article "Philo" in Smith and Wace, 383 ª, and "Speak. Com."
on Ecclesiasticus, pp. 14, 16; Ryle and James, "Psalms of
Solomon" on ix. 7 and Introd.; Montet, "Origines des partis-
saducéen et pharisien," 258 f.; Holtzmann, "N. T. Theologie,"
i. 32, 55; P. J. Muller, "De Godsleer der middeleeuwische
Joden," Groningen, 1898; further literature is given in
Schürer. — For post-Canonical Christian discussion, see the
literature at the end of article ELECTION in the present work,
v. i. p. 681.

II

THE FORESIGHT OF JESUS

THE FORESIGHT OF JESUS [1]

THE interest of the student of the Gospels, and of the life of Jesus which forms their substance, in the topic of this article, is two-fold. Jesus is represented in the Gospels as at once the object and the subject of the most detailed foresight. The work which He came to do was a work ordained in the counsels of eternity, and in all its items prepared for beforehand with the most perfect prevision. In addressing Himself to the accomplishment of this work Jesus proceeded from the beginning in the fullest knowledge of the end, and with the most absolute adjustment of every step to its attainment. It is from this double view-point that each of the Evangelists depicts the course of our Lord's life on earth. They consentiently represent Him as having come to perform a specific task, all the elements of which were not only determined beforehand in the plan of God, but adumbrated, if somewhat sporadically, yet with sufficient fulness for the end in view, in the prophecies of the Old Testament. And they represent Him as coming to perform this task with a clear consciousness of its nature and a competent control of all the means for its discharge, so that His whole life was a conscientious fulfilment of a programme, and moved straight to its mark. The conception of foresight thus dominates the whole Evangelical narrative.

It is not necessary to dwell at length upon the Evangelists' conception of our Lord's life and work as *the fulfilment of a plan Divinely predetermined for Him.* It lies on the face of their narratives that the authors of the Gospels had no reservation with respect to the all-embracing predestination of God (cf. Hastings' *DB* iv. 54–56); and least of all could they exclude

[1] Article "Foresight" from *A Dictionary of Christ and the Gospels*, ed. by James Hastings, D.D., v. i, pp. 608–615. Pub. N. Y. 1908, by Charles Scribner's Sons.

from it this life and work which was to them the hinge upon
which all history turns. To them accordingly our Lord is by
way of eminence 'the man of destiny,' and His whole life
(Lk. ii. 49, iv. 43) was governed by 'the δεῖ of the Divine
counsel.' Every step of His pathway was a 'necessity' to Him,
in the fulfilment of the mission for which He had 'come forth'
(Mk. i. 38, cf. Swete), or as St. Luke (iv. 43) in quite Johannine wise (v. 23, 24, 30, 36, 38, vi. 29, 38, 39, 40 *et passim*) expresses it, 'was sent' (cf. Mt. x. 40, Mk. ix. 37, Lk. ix. 48, x.
16; Mt. xv. 24, xxi. 37, Mk. xii. 6, Lk. xx. 13, cf. Swete on Mk.
ix. 37). Especially was all that concerned His departure, the
accomplishment of which (Lk. ix. 31, cf. v. 51) was His particular task, under the government of this 'Divine necessity'
(Mt. xvi. 21, xxvi. 54, Mk. viii. 31, Lk. ix. 22, xvii. 25, xxii. 22,
37, xxiv. 7, 44, Jn. iii. 14, xx. 9, cf. Acts ii. 23, iii. 18, iv. 28, and
Westcott on Jn. xx. 9). His final journey to Jerusalem (Mt.
xvi. 21), His rejection by the rulers (Mk. viii. 31, Lk. ix. 22,
xvii. 25), His betrayal (Lk. xxiv. 7), arrest (Mt. xxvi. 54),
sufferings (Mt. xxvi. 54, Mk. viii. 31, Lk. ix. 22, xvii. 25), and
death (Mt. xvi. 21, Mk. viii. 31, Lk. ix. 22) by crucifixion (Lk.
xxiv. 7, Jn. iii. 14), His rising again (Jn. xx. 9) on the third
day (Mt. xvi. 21, Mk. viii. 31, Lk. ix. 22, xxiv. 7, 46) — each
item alike is declared to have been 'a matter of necessity in
pursuance of the Divine purpose' (Meyer, Mt. xxiv. 6), 'a
necessary part of the destiny assigned our Lord' (Meyer, Mt.
xxvi. 54). 'The death of our Lord' thus appears 'not as the
accidental work of hostile caprice, but (cf. Acts ii. 23, iii. 18)
the necessary result of the Divine predestination (Lk. xxii. 22),
to which Divine δεῖ (Lk. xxiv. 26) the personal free action of
man had to serve as an instrument' (Meyer, Acts iv. 28).

How far the several events which entered into this life had
been prophetically announced is obviously, in this view of it,
a mere matter of detail. All of them lay open before the eyes
of God; and the only limit to pre-announcement was the extent to which God had chosen to reveal what was to come to
pass, through His servants the prophets. In some instances,
however, the prophetic announcement is particularly adduced

as the ground on which recognition of the necessity of occurrence rests. The fulfilment of Scripture thus becomes regulative of the life of Jesus. Whatever stood written of Him in the
Law or the Prophets or the Psalms (Lk. xxiv. 44) must needs
(δεῖ) be accomplished (Mt. xxvi. 54, Lk. xxii. 37, xxiv. 26, Jn.
xx. 9). Or, in another form of statement, particularly frequent in Mt. (i. 22, ii. 15, 23, iv. 14, viii. 17, xii. 17, xiii. 35,
xxi. 4, xxvi. 56) and Jn. (xii. 38, xiii. 18, xv. 25, xvii. 12, xix.
24, 36), but found also in the other Evangelists (Mk. xiv. 49,
Lk. iv. 21), the several occurrences of His life fell out as they
did, 'in order that what was spoken by the Lord' through the
prophets or in Scripture, 'might be fulfilled' (cf. Mt. ii. 17,
xxvi. 54, xxvii. 9, Lk. xxiv. 44; in Jn. xviii. 9, 32, Lk. xxiv. 44
declarations of Jesus are treated precisely similarly). That is
to say, 'what was done stood . . . in the connexion of the
Divine necessity, as an actual fact, by which prophecy was
destined to be fulfilled. The Divine decree expressed in the
latter *must* be accomplished, and *to that end this . . . came to
pass*, and that, *according to the whole of its contents*' (Meyer,
Mt. i. 22). The meaning is, not that there lies in the Old Testament Scriptures a complete predictive account of all the details of the life of Jesus, which those skilled in the interpretation
of Scripture might read off from its pages at will. This programme in its detailed completeness lies only in the Divine
purpose; and in Scripture only so far forth as God has chosen
to place it there for the guidance or the assurance of His people.
The meaning is rather that all that stands written of Jesus in
the Old Testament Scriptures has its certain fulfilment in Him;
and that enough stands written of Him there to assure His followers that in the course of His life, and in its, to them, strange
and unexpected ending, He was not the prey of chance or the
victim of the hatred of men, to the marring of His work or perhaps even the defeat of His mission, but was following step
by step, straight to its goal, the predestined pathway marked
out for Him in the counsels of eternity, and sufficiently revealed
from of old in the Scriptures to enable all who were not 'foolish
and slow of heart to believe in all that the prophets have

spoken,' to perceive that the Christ must needs have lived just this life and fulfilled just this destiny.

That the whole course of the life of Jesus, and especially its culmination in the death which He died, was foreseen and afore-prepared by God, enters, thus, into the very substance of the Evangelical narrative. It enters equally into its very substance that *this life was from the beginning lived out by Jesus Himself in full view of its drift and its issue.* The Evangelists are as far from representing Jesus as driven blindly onwards by a Divine destiny unknown to Himself, along courses not of His own choosing, to an unanticipated end, as they are from representing Him as thwarted in His purposes, or limited in His achievement, or determined or modified in His aims or methods, by the conditions which from time to time emerged in His way. The very essence of their representation is that Jesus came into the world with a definite mission to execute, of the nature of which He was perfectly aware, and according to which He ordered the whole course of His life as it advanced under His competent control unswervingly to its preconceived mark. In their view His life was lived out, not in ignorance of its issues, or in the form of a series of trials and corrections, least of all in a more or less unavailing effort to wring success out of failure; but in complete knowledge of the counsels of God for Him, in perfect acquiescence in them, and in careful and voluntary fulfilment of them. The 'Divine δεῖ' which governed His life is represented as fully recognized by Himself (Mt. xvi. 21, Mk. viii. 31, Lk. iv. 43, ix. 22, xvii. 25, xxiv. 7, Jn. iii. 14, xii. 34), and the fulfilment of the intimations of prophecy in His life as accepted by Him as a rule for His voluntary action (Mt. xxvi. 54, Lk. xxii. 37, xxiv. 26, 44, Jn. xx. 9, Mk. xiv. 49, Lk. iv. 21, Jn. xiii. 18, xv. 25, xvii. 12; cf. Mt. xiii. 14, xv. 7, xxiv. 15, xxvi. 56, Mk. vii. 6). Determining all things, determined by none, the life He actually lived, leading up to the death He actually died, is in their view precisely the life which from the beginning He intended to live, ending in precisely the death in which, from the beginning, He intended this life to issue, undeflected by so much as a hair's-breadth

from the straight path He had from the start marked out for
Himself in the fullest prevision and provision of all the so-called
chances and changes which might befall Him. Not only were
there no surprises in life for Jesus and no compulsions; there
were not even 'influences,' as we speak of 'influences' in a
merely human career. The mark of this life, as the Evangelists depict it, is its calm and quiet superiority to all circumstance and condition, and to all the varied forces which sway
other lives; its prime characteristics are voluntariness and independence. Neither His mother, nor His brethren, nor His
disciples, nor the people He came to serve, nor His enemies
bent upon His destruction, nor Satan himself with his temptations, could move Him one step from His chosen path. When
men seemed to prevail over Him they were but working His
will; the great 'No one has taken my life away from me; I
have power to lay it down, and I have power to take it again'
(Jn. x. 18), is but the enunciation for the supreme act, of the
principle that governs all His movements. His own chosen
pathway ever lay fully displayed before His feet; on it His
feet fell quietly, but they found the way always unblocked.
What He did, He came to do; and He carried out His programme with unwavering purpose and indefectible certitude.
So at least the Evangelists represent Him. (Cf. the first half
of a striking article on "Die Selbständigkeit Jesu," by Trott,
in Luthardt's "Zeitschrift für kirchl. Wissenschaft u. kirchl.
Leben," 1883, iv. 233–241; in its latter half the article falls
away from its idea, and ends by making Jesus absolutely dependent on Scripture for His knowledge of God and Divine
things: 'We have no right whatever to maintain that Jesus
received revelations from the Father otherwise than through
the medium of the sacred Scriptures; that is a part of His complete humanity' (p. 238).)

The signature of this supernatural life which the Evangelists depict Jesus as living, lies thus in the perfection of the
foresight by which it was governed. Of the reality of this foresight they leave their readers in no doubt, nor yet of its completeness. They suggest it by the general picture they draw of

the self-directed life which Jesus lived in view of His mission. They record repeated instances in which He mentions beforehand events yet to occur, or foreshadows the end from the beginning. They connect these manifestations of foresight with the possession by Him of knowledge in general, in comprehension and penetration alike far beyond what is native to man. It may perhaps be natural to surmise in the first instance that they intend to convey merely the conviction that in Jesus was manifested a prophet of supreme greatness, in whom, as the culminating example of prophecy (cf. Acts iii. 22, 23), resided beyond precedent the gifts proper to prophets. There can be no question that to the writers of the Gospels Jesus was 'the incarnate ideal of the prophet, who, as such, forms a class by Himself, and is more than a prophet' (this is what Schwartz-kopff thinks Him, "The Prophecies of Jesus Christ," p. 7). They record with evident sympathy the impression made by Him at the outset of His ministry, that God had at last in Him visited His people (Mk. vi. 15, Lk. vii. 16, Jn. iv. 19, ix. 17); they trace the ripening of this impression into a well-settled belief in His prophetic character (Mt. xxi. 11, Lk. xxiv. 19, Mt. xxi. 46, Lk. vii. 39, Jn. vii. 40); and they remark upon the widespread suspicion which accompanied this belief, that He was something more than a prophet — possibly one of the old prophets returned, certainly a very special prophet charged with a very special mission for the introduction of the Messianic times (Mt. xvi. 14, Mk. vi. 15, viii. 28, Lk. ix. 8, 19, Jn. vi. 14, vii. 40). They represent Jesus as not only calling out and accepting this estimate of Him, but frankly assuming a prophet's place and title (Mt. xiii. 57, Mk. vi. 4, Lk. iv. 24, Jn. iv. 44, Lk. xiii. 33), exercising a prophet's functions, and delivering prophetic discourses, in which He unveils the future (Mt. xxiv. 21, Mk. xiii. 23, Jn. xiv. 29; cf. Mt. xxviii. 6, Lk. xxiv. 44, and such passages as Mt. xxvi. 32, 34, Mk. xvi. 7). Nevertheless it is very clear that in their allusions to the supernatural knowledge of Jesus, the Evangelists suppose themselves to be illustrating something very much greater than merely prophetic inspiration. The specific difference between Jesus and a prophet, in their view, was that while a prophet's human knowledge is increased by many things revealed to him by God (Amos. iii. 7), Jesus participated in all the fulness of the Divine knowledge (Mt. xi. 27, Lk. x. 22, Jn. xvi. 15, xviii. 4, xvi. 30, xxi. 17), so that all that is knowable lay open before Him (Jn. xvii. 10). The Evangelists, in a word, obviously intend to attribute Divine omniscience to Jesus, and in their adduction of instances of His supernatural knowledge, whether with respect to hidden things or to those yet buried in the future, are illustrating His possession of this Divine omniscience (cf. Muirhead, "The Eschatology of Jesus," p. 119, where, in partial correction of the more inadequate statement of p. 48, there is recognized in the Evangelists at least a 'tendency' to attribute to our Lord 'Divine dignity' and 'literal omniscience').

That this is the case with St. John's Gospel is very commonly recognized (for a plain statement of the evidence see Karl Müller, "Göttliches Wissen und göttliche Macht des johann. Christus," 1882, § 4, pp. 29–47: "Zeugnisse des vierten Evangeliums für Jesu göttliches Wissen"). It is not too much to say, indeed, that one of the chief objects which the author of that Gospel set before himself was to make clear to its readers the superhuman knowledge of Jesus, with especial reference, of course, to His own career. It therefore records direct ascriptions of omniscience to Jesus, and represents them as favourably received by Him (Jn. xvi. 30, xxi. 17; cf. Liddon, "The Divinity of our Lord," ed. 4, 1869, p. 466). It makes it almost the business of its opening chapters to exhibit this omniscience at work in the especially Divine form (Lk. xvi. 15, Acts i. 24, Heb. iv. 12, Ps. cxxxviii (cxxxix). 2, Jer. xvii. 10. xx. 12; cf. Swete on Mk. ii. 8) of immediate, universal, and complete knowledge of the thoughts and intents of the human heart (cf. Westcott on Jn. ii. 25), laying down the general thesis in ii. 24, 25 (cf. vi. 64, 70, xxi. 17), and illustrating it in detail in the cases of all with whom Jesus came into contact in the opening days of His ministry (cf. Westcott on Jn. i. 47), Peter (i. 42), Philip (i. 43), Nathanael (i. 47), Mary (ii. 4), Nicodemus (iii.), the woman of Samaria (iv.). In the especially striking case of the choice of Judas Iscariot as one of the Apostles, it expressly explains that this was due to no ignorance of Judas' character or of his future action (vi. 64, 70, xiii. 11), but was done as part of our Lord's voluntary execution of His own well-laid plans. It pictures Jesus with great explicitness as prosecuting His whole work in full knowledge of all the things that were coming upon Him (Jn. xviii. 4, cf. Westcott), and with a view to subjecting them all to His governing hand, so that His life from the beginning should run steadily onward on the lines of a thoroughly wrought-out plan (Jn. i. 47, ii. 19, 24, iii. 14, vi. 51, 64, 70, vii. 6, viii. 28, x. 15, 18, xii. 7, 23, xiii. 1, 11, 21, 38, xiv. 29, xvi. 5, 32, xviii. 4, 9).

It is difficult to see, however, why St. John's Gospel should be separated from its companions in this matter (Schenkel says frankly that it is only because there is no such passage in St. John's Gospel as Mk. xiii. 32, on which see below. Whatever else must be said of W. Wrede's "Das Messiasgeheimnis," etc., 1901, it must be admitted that it has broke down this artificial distinction between the Gospel of John and the Synoptics). If they do not, like St. John (xvi. 30, xxi. 17), record direct ascriptions of precise omniscience to Jesus by His followers, they do, like St. John, represent Him as Himself claiming to be the depository and distributer of the Father's knowledge (Mt. xi. 21–30, Lk. x. 22–24). Nor do they lag behind St. John in attributing to Jesus the Divine prerogative of reading the heart (Mt. ix. 4, Meyer; Mk. ii. 5, 8, viii. 17, xii. 15, 44, Swete, p. lxxxviii; Lk. v. 22, vii. 39) or the manifestation, in other forms, of God-like omniscience (Mt. xvii. 27, xxi. 2, Mk. xi. 2, xiv. 13, Lk. v. 4, xix. 30, xxii. 10; cf. O. Holtzmann, "War Jesus Ekstatiker?" p. 14 and p. 15, note). Least of all do they fall behind St. John in insisting upon the perfection of the foresight of Jesus in all matters connected with His own life and death (Mt. ix. 15, xii. 40, xvi. 21, xx. 18, 22, 28, xxvi. 2, 21, 34, 50, Mk. ii. 19, viii. 31, ix. 31, x. 33, 39, 45, xi. 2, xiv. 8, 13, 18, 30, Lk. v. 34, ix. 22, 44, 51, xii. 50, xiii. 35, xvii. 25, xviii. 31, xix. 30, xxii. 10, 21, 34, 37, xxiv. 44). Nothing could exceed the detailed precision of these announcements, — a

characteristic which has been turned, of course, to their discredit as genuine utterances of Jesus by writers who find difficulty with detailed prediction. 'The form and contents of these
texts,' remarks Wrede ('Messiasgeheimnis," etc. p. 88),
'speak a language which cannot be misunderstood. They are
nothing but a short summary of the Passion history — "cast,
of course, in the future tense." '"The Passion-history,"' he
proceeds, quoting Eichhorn, '"could certainly not be more
exactly related in few words."' In very fact, it is perfectly
clear — whether they did it by placing upon His lips predictions He never uttered and never could have uttered, is another question — that the Evangelists designed to represent
Jesus as endowed with the absolute and unlimited foresight
consonant with His Divine nature (see Liddon, "The Divinity
of our Lord," ed. 4, p. 464 ff.; and cf. A. J. Mason, "The conditions of our Lord's Life on Earth," pp. 155–194).

The force of this representation cannot be broken, of course,
by raising the question afresh whether the supernatural knowledge attributed by the Evangelists to our Lord may not, in
many of its items at least, if not in its whole extent, find its
analogues, after all, in human powers, or be explained as not
different in kind from that of the prophets (cf. e. g., Westcott,
"Additional Note on Jn. ii. 24"; A. J. Mason, "Conditions,"
etc. pp. 162–163). The question more immediately before us
does not concern our own view of the nature and origin of this
knowledge, but that of the Evangelists. If we will keep these
two questions separate we shall scarcely be able to doubt that
the Evangelists mean to present this knowledge as one of the
marks of our Lord's Divine dignity. In interpreting them we
are not entitled to parcel out the mass of the illustrations of
His supernormal knowledge which they record to differing
sources, as may fall in with our own conceptions of the inherent
possibilities of each case; finding indications in some instances
merely of His fine human instinct, in others of His prophetic
inspiration, while reserving others — if such others are left to
us in our analysis — as products of His Divine intuition. The
Evangelists suggest no such lines of cleavage in the mass; and

they must be interpreted from their own standpoint. This finds its centre in their expressed conviction that in Jesus Christ dwelt the fulness of the knowledge of God (Mt. xi. 27, Lk. x. 22, Jn. viii. 38, xvi. 15, xvii. 10). To them His knowledge of God and of Divine things, of Himself in His Person and mission, of the course of His life and the events which would befall Him in the prosecution of the work whereunto He had been sent, of the men around Him, — His followers and friends, the people and their rulers, — down to the most hidden depths of their natures and the most intimate processes of their secret thoughts, and of all the things forming the environment in which the drama He was enacting was cast, however widely that environment be conceived, or however minutely it be contemplated, — was but the manifestation, in the ever-widening circles of our human modes of conception, of the perfect apprehension and understanding that dwelt changelessly in His Divine intelligence. He who knew God perfectly, — it were little that He should know man and the world perfectly too; all that affected His own work and career, of course, and with it, equally of course, all that lay outside of this (cf. Mason, "Conditions," etc. p. 168): in a word, unlimitedly, all things. Even if nothing but the Law of Parsimony stood in the way, it might well be understood that the Evangelists would be deterred from seeking, in the case of such a Being, other sources of information besides His Divine intelligence to account for all His far-reaching and varied knowledge. At all events, it is clearly their conviction that all He knew — the scope of which was unbounded and its depth unfathomed, though their record suggests rather than fully illustrates it — found its explanation in the dignity of His person as God manifest in the flesh.

Nor can the effect of their representation of Jesus as the subject of this all-embracing Divine knowledge be destroyed by the discovery in their narratives of another line of representation in which our Lord is set forth as living His life out under the conditions which belong naturally to the humanity He had assumed. These representations are certainly to be neglected as little as those others in which His Divine omnis-

cience is suggested. They bring to our observation another side
of the complex personality that is depicted, which, if it cannot
be said to be as emphatically insisted upon by the Evangelists,
is nevertheless, perhaps, equally pervasively illustrated. This
is the true humanity of our Lord, within the scope of which He
willed to live out His life upon earth, that He might accomplish
the mission for which He had been sent. The suggestion that
He might break over the bounds of His mission, in order that
He might escape from the ruggedness of His chosen path, by
the exercise whether of His almighty power (Mt. iv. 3 f., Lk.
iv. 3 f.) or of His unerring foresight (Mt. xvi. 22 ||), He treated
first and last as a temptation of the Evil One — for 'how then
should the Scriptures be fulfilled that thus it must be' (Mt.
xxvi. 54 ||)? It is very easy, to be sure, to exaggerate the indi-
cations in the Evangelists of the confinement of our Lord's
activities within the limits of human powers. It is an exaggeration, for example, to speak as if the Evangelists represent
Him as frequently surprised by the events which befell Him:
they never predicate surprise of Him, and it is only by a very
precarious inference from the events recorded that they can
ever be supposed even to suggest or allow place for such an
emotion in our Lord. It is an exaggeration again to adduce our
Lord's questions as attempts to elicit information for His own
guidance: His questions are often plainly dialectical or rhetorical, or, like some of His actions, solely for the benefit of
those 'that stood around.' It is once more an exaggeration to
adduce the employment in many cases of the term γινώσκω,
when the Evangelists speak of our Lord's knowledge, as if it
were thereby implied that this knowledge was freshly born in
His mind: the assumed distinction, but faintly marked in
Greek literature, cannot be traced in the usage of the terms
γνῶναι and εἰδέναι in their application to our Lord's knowledge;
these terms even replace one another in parallel accounts of
the same instance (Mt. xxii. 18||Mk. xii. 15; [Mt. ix. 4]||Mk.
ii. 8, Lk. v. 22; cf. Mt. xii. 25, Lk. vi. 8, ix. 47, xi. 17, Jn. vi. 61);
γνῶναι is used of the undoubted Divine knowledge of our Lord
([Mt. xi. 25] Lk. x. 22, Jn. x. 15, xvii. 25, Mt. vii. 23; cf. Jn.

ii. 24, 25, v. 42, x. 14, 27); and indeed of the knowledge of God Himself (Lk. x. 22, xvi. 15, Jn. x. 15 [Mt. xi. 27]): and, in any event, there is a distinction which in such nice inquiries should not be neglected, between saying that the occurrence of an event, being perceived, was the occasion of an action, and saying that knowledge of the event, perceived as occurring, waited on its occurrence. Gravely vitiated by such exaggerations as most discussions of the subject are, enough remains, however, after all exaggeration is pruned away, to assure us, not indeed that our Lord's life on earth was, in the view of the Evangelists, an exclusively human one; or that, apart from the constant exercise of His will to make it such, it was controlled by the limitations of humanity; but certainly that it was, in their view, lived out, so far as was consistent with the fulfilment of the mission for which He came — and as an indispensable condition of the fulfilment of that mission — under the limitations belonging to a purely human life. The classical passages in this reference are those striking statements in the second chapter of Luke (ii. 40, 52) in which is summed up our Lord's growth from infancy to manhood, including, of course, His intellectual development and His own remarkable declaration recorded in Mt. xxiv. 36, Mk. xiii. 32, in which He affirms His ignorance of the day and hour of His return to earth. Supplemented by their general dramatization of His life within the range of the purely human, these passages are enough to assure us that in the view of the Evangelists there was in our Lord a purely human soul, which bore its own proper part in His life, and which, as human souls do, grew in knowledge as it grew in wisdom and grace, and remained to the end, as human souls must, ignorant of many things, — nay, which, because human souls are finite, must ever be ignorant of much embraced in the universal vision of the Divine Spirit. We may wonder why the 'day and hour' of His own return should remain among the things of which our Lord's human soul continued ignorant throughout His earthly life. But this is a matter about which surely we need not much concern ourselves. We can never do more than vaguely guess at the law which governs

the inclusions and exclusions which characterize the knowledge-
contents of any human mind, limited as human minds are not
only qualitatively but quantitatively; and least of all could we
hope to penetrate the principle of selection in the case of the
perfect human intelligence of our Lord; nor have the Evangelists hinted their view of the matter. We must just be content
to recognize that we are face to face here with the mystery of
the Two Natures, which, although they do not, of course, formally enunciate the doctrine in so many words, the Evangelists
yet effectively teach, since by it alone can consistency be induced between the two classes of facts which they present un-
hesitatingly in their narratives. Only, if we would do justice
to their presentation, we must take clear note of two of its
characteristics. They do not simply, in separated portions of
their narratives, adduce the facts which manifest our Lord's
Divine powers and His human characteristics, but interlace
them inextricably in the same sections of the narratives. And
they do not subject the Divine that is in Christ to the limitations of the human, but quite decisively present the Divine as
dominating all, and as giving play to the human only by a constant, voluntary withholding of its full manifestation in the
interests of the task undertaken. Observe the story, for example, in Jn. xi, which Dr. Mason ("Conditions," etc. p. 143)
justly speaks of as 'indeed a marvellous weaving together of
that which is natural and that which is above nature.' 'Jesus
learns from others that Lazarus is sick, but knows without any
further message that Lazarus is dead; He weeps and groans at
the sight of the sorrow which surrounds Him, yet calmly gives
thanks for the accomplishment of the miracle before it has
been accomplished.' This conjunction of the two elements is
typical of the whole Evangelical narrative. As portrayed in it
our Lord's life is distinctly duplex; and can be consistently construed only by the help of the conception of the Two Natures.
And just as distinctly is this life portrayed in these narratives
as receiving its determination not from the human, but from
the Divine side. If what John undertakes to depict is what was
said and done by the incarnated Word, no less what the Synop-

tics essay is to present the Gospel (as Mark puts it) of Jesus
Christ the Son of God. It is distinctly a supernatural life that
He is represented by them all as living; and the human aspect
of it is treated by each alike as an incident in something more
exalted, by which it is permitted, rather than on which it imposes itself. Though passed as far as was befitting within the
limits of humanity, this life remains at all times the life of God
manifest in the flesh, and, as depicted by the Evangelists, never
escapes beyond the boundaries set by what was suitable to it
as such.

The actual instances of our Lord's foresight which are recorded by the Evangelists are not very numerous outside of
those which concern the establishment of the Kingdom of God,
with which alone, of course, their narratives are particularly
engaged. Even the few instances of specific exhibitions of foreknowledge of what we may call trivial events owe their record
to some connexion with this great work. Examples are afforded
by the foresight that the casting of the nets at the exact time
and place indicated by our Lord would secure a draught of
fishes (Lk. v. 4, cf. Jn. xxi. 6); that the first fish that Peter
would take when he threw his hook into the sea would be one
which had swallowed a stater (Mt. xvii. 27); that on entering
a given village the disciples should find an ass tied, and a colt
with it, whose owners would be obedient to our Lord's request
(Mt. xxi. 2 ||); and that on entering Jerusalem to make ready
for the final passover-feast they should meet a man bearing a
pitcher, prepared to serve the Master's needs (Mk. xiv. 13).
In instances like these the interlacing of prevision and provision is very intimate, and doubt arises whether they illustrate
most distinctly our Lord's Divine foresight or His control of
events. In other instances the element of foresight comes, perhaps, more purely forward: such are possibly the predictions
of the offence of the disciples (Mt. xxvi. 31||), the denial of
Peter (xxvi. 34||), and the treachery of Judas (xxvi. 21||).
There may be added the whole series of utterances in which
our Lord shows a comprehensive foresight of the career of those
whom He called to His service (Mt. iv. 19, x. 17, 21, xx. 22,

xxiv. 9 f., Jn. xvi. 1 f.); and also that other series in which He
exhibits a like full foreknowledge of the entire history of the
Kingdom of God in the world (cf. especially the parables of the
Kingdom, and such passages as Mt. xvi. 18, xxiv. 5, 24, xxi. 43,
xxiv. 14, xxvi. 13, Lk. xix. 11, Jn. xiv. 18, 19). It is, however,
particularly with reference to His own work in establishing the
Kingdom, and in regard to the nature of that work, that stress
is particularly laid upon the completeness of His foreknowledge. His entire career, as we have seen, is represented by all
the Evangelists as lying plainly before Him from the beginning,
with every detail clearly marked and provided for. It is especially, however, with reference to the three great events in which
His work in establishing His Kingdom is summed up — His
death, His resurrection, His return — that the predictions become numerous, if we may not even say constant. Each of the
Evangelists represents Him, for example, as foreseeing His
death from the start (Jn. ii. 19, iii. 14, Mt. xii. 40, ix. 15, Mk.
ii. 19, Lk. xii. 49, v. 34; cf. Meyer on Mt. ix. 15, xvi. 21; Weiss
on Mk. viii. 31; Denney, "Death of Christ," p. 18; Wrede,
"Messiasgeheimnis," p. 19, etc.), and as so ordering His life as
to march steadfastly forward to it as its chosen climax (cf. e. g.,
Wrede, p. 84: 'It is accordingly the meaning of Mark that
Jesus journeys to Jerusalem because it is His will to die there').
He is represented, therefore, as avoiding all that could lead up
to it for a time, and then, when He was ready for it, as setting
Himself steadfastly to bring it about as He would; as speaking
of it only guardedly at first, and afterwards, when the time was
ripe for it, as setting about assiduously to prepare His disciples
for it. Similarly with respect to His resurrection, He is reported
as having it in mind, indeed, from the earliest days of His
ministry (Jn. ii. 19, Mt. xii. 40, xvi. 21, Mk. viii. 31, Lk. ix.
22), but adverting to it with pædagogical care, so as to prepare
rather than confuse the minds of His disciples. The same in
substance may be said with reference to His return (Mt. x.
23, xvi. 27, Mk. viii. 38, ix. 1, Lk. ix. 26, 27).

A survey in chronological order of the passages in which
He is reported as speaking of these three great events of the

future, cannot fail to leave a distinct impression on the mind
not only of the large space they occupy in the Evangelical narrative, but of the great place they take as foreseen, according
to that narrative, in the life and work of our Lord. In the following list the passages in which He adverts to His death stand
in the order given them in Robinson's "Harmony of the
Gospels": Jn. ii. 19, iii. 14, Mt. xii. 40 (cf. xvi. 4, Lk. xi. 32), Lk.
xii. 49, 50, Mt. ix. 15 (Mk. ii. 19, Lk. v. 34), Jn. vi. 51, vii. 6–8,
Mt. xvi. 21 (Mk. viii. 31, Lk. ix. 22), Lk. ix. 31, Mt. xvii. 17
(Mk. ix. 12), Mt. xvii. 22, 23 (Mk. ix. 31, Lk. ix. 44), Lk. ix.
51, Jn. vii. 34, viii. 21, 25, ix. 5, x. 11, 15, Lk. xiii. 32, xvii. 25,
Mt. xx. 18, 19 (Mk. x. 33, Lk. xviii. 31), Jn. xii. 28, Mt. xx. 22
(Mk. x. 38), Mt. xx. 28 (Mk. x. 45), Mt. xxi. 39 (Mk. xii. 8,
Lk. xx. 14), Jn. xii. 23, Mt. xxvi. 2, Jn. xiii. 1, 33, Mt. xxvi.
28 (Mk. xiv. 24, Lk. xxii. 20), Mt. xxvi. 31 (Mk. xiv. 27, Jn.
xiv. 28), Jn. xv. 13, xvi. 5, xvi. 16, xviii. 11, Mt. xxvi. 54 (Jn.
xviii. 11), Lk. xxiv. 26, 46.

The following allusions to His resurrection are in the same
order: Jn. ii. 19, Mt. xii. 40 (Lk. xi. 30), Mt. xvi. 21 (Mk. viii. 31,
Lk. ix. 22), Mt. xvii. 9 (Mk. ix. 9), Mt. xvii. 23 (Mk. ix. 31),
Jn. x. 18 [xvi. 16], Mt. xx. 19 (Mk. x. 34, Lk. xviii. 33), Mt.
xxvi. 32 (Mk. xiv. 28) [Mt. xxviii. 6‖Lk. xxiv. 8], Lk. xxiv. 46.

The following are, in like order, the allusions to His return:
Mt. x. 23, xvi. 27 (Mk. viii. 38, ix. 1, Lk. ix. 26, 27), Mk.
x. 40, Lk. xvii. 22, Mt. xix. 28, xxiii. 39, xxiv. 3 (Mk. xiii. 4,
Lk. xxi. 7), Mt. xxiv. 34–37 (Mk. xiii. 30, Lk. xxi. 32), Mt. xxiv.
44, xxv. 31, xxvi. 64 (Mk. xiv. 62, Lk. xxii. 69).

The most cursory examination of these series of passages
in their setting, and especially in their distribution through the
Evangelical narrative, will evince the cardinal place which the
eschatological element takes in the life of the Lord as depicted
in the Gospels. In particular, it will be impossible to escape the
conviction that it is distinctly the teaching of the Evangelists
that Jesus came into the world specifically to die, and ordered
His whole life wittingly to that end. As Dr. Denney puts it
(expounding Jn. x. 17, on which see also Westcott's note),
'Christ's death is not an incident of His life, it is the aim of it.'

The laying down of His life is not an accident in His career, it is His vocation; it is that in which the Divine purpose of His life is revealed.' 'If there was a period in His life during which He had other thoughts, it is antecedent to that at which we have any knowledge of Him' ("Death of Christ," pp. 259 and 18). Nothing could therefore be more at odds with the consentient and constant representations of the Evangelists than to speak of the 'shadow of the cross' as only somewhat late in His history beginning to fall athwart our Lord's pathway; of the idea that His earthly career should close in gloom as 'distinctly emerging in the teaching of Jesus only at a comparatively late period,' and as therefore presumably not earlier 'clear in His mind': unless, indeed, it be the accompanying more general judgment that 'there was nothing extraordinary or supernatural in Jesus' foreknowledge of His death,' and that 'His prophecy was but the expression of a mind which knew that it could not cease to be obedient while His enemies would not cease to be hostile' (A. M. Fairbairn, "The Expositor," 1897, i.; vol. iv. [1896] 283, 285). It is not less unwarranted to speak of Him as bowing to His fate only 'as the will of God, to which He yielded Himself up to the very end only with difficulty, and at best against His will' (Wernle, "Synopt. Frage," 200).

Such expressions as these, however, advise us that a very different conception from that presented by the Evangelists has found widespread acceptance among a class of modern scholars, whose efforts have been devoted to giving to our Lord's life on earth a character more normally human than it seems to possess as it lies on the pages of the Evangelists. The negative principle of the new constructions offered of the course and springs of our Lord's career being rejection of the account given by the Evangelists, these scholars are thrown back for guidance very much upon their own subjective estimate of probabilities. The Gospels are, however, the sole sources of information for the events of our Lord's life, and it is impossible to decline their aid altogether. Few, accordingly, have been able to discard entirely the general framework of the life of

Christ they present (for those who are inclined to represent Jesus as making no claim even to be the Messiah, see H. J. Holtzmann, "Lehrbuch der neutestamentlichen Theologie" i. 280, note; Meinhold as there referred to; and Wrede, "Das Messiasgeheimnis," especially Appendix vii.). Most have derived enough from the Gospels to assume that a crisis of some sort occurred at Cæsarea Philippi, where the Evangelists represent our Lord as beginning formally and frankly to prepare His disciples for His death (Mt. xvi. 21‖).

Great differences arise at once, however, over what this crisis was. Schenkel supposes that it was only at this point in His ministry that Jesus began to think Himself the Messiah; Strauss is willing to believe He suspected Himself to be the Messiah earlier, and supposes that He now first began to proclaim Himself such; P. W. Schmidt and Lobstein imagine that on this day He both put the Messianic crown upon His head and faced death looming in His path; Weizsäcker and Keim allow that He thought and proclaimed Himself the Messiah from the beginning, and suppose that what is new here is that only now did He come to see with clearness that His ministry would end in His death, — and as death for the Messiah means return, they add that here He begins His proclamation of His return in glory. To this Schenkel and Hase find difficulty in assenting, feeling it impossible that the Founder of a spiritual kingdom should look forward to its consummation in a physical one, and insisting, therefore, that though Jesus may well have predicted the destruction of His enemies, He can scarcely have foretold His own coming in glory. On the other hand, Strauss and Baur judge that a prediction of the destruction of Jerusalem too closely resembles what actually occurred not to be *post eventum*, but see no reason why Jesus should not have dreamed of coming back on the clouds of heaven. As to His death, Strauss thinks He began to anticipate it only shortly before His last journey to Jerusalem; while Holsten cannot believe that He realized what was before Him until He actually arrived at Jerusalem, and even then did not acquiesce in it (so Spitta). That He went to Jerusalem for the purpose of dying,

neither Weizsäcker, nor Brandt, nor H. Holtzmann, nor Schult-
zen will admit, though the two last named allow that He foresaw that the journey would end in His death; or at least that
it possibly would, adds Pünjer, since, of course, a possibility
of success lay open to Him (cf. H. J. Holtzmann, "Lehrb. der
neutestamentlichen Theologie," i, 285-286, note). As many
men, so many opinions. As the positive principle of construction in all these schemes of life for Jesus is desupernaturaliza-
tion, they differ, so far as the prophetic element in His teaching
as reported by the Evangelists is concerned, chiefly in the
measure in which they explain it as due more or less entirely
to the Evangelists carrying their own ideas, or the ideas of the
community in which they lived, back into Jesus' mouth; or
allow it more or less fully to Jesus, indeed, but only in a form
which can be thought of as not rising above the natural prog-
nostications of a man in His position. A few deny to Jesus the
entire series of predictions reported in the Gospels, and assign
them in mass to the thought of the later community (e. g., Eichhorn, Wrede). A few, on the other hand, allow the whole, or
nearly the whole, series to Jesus, and explain them all naturalis-
tically. Most take an intermediate position, determined by the
principle that all which seems to each critic incapable of naturalistic explanation as utterances of Jesus shall be assigned to
later origin. Accordingly, the concrete details in the alleged
predictions are quite generally denied to Jesus, and represented
as easily explicable modifications, in accordance with the actual
course of events, of what Jesus really said. The prediction of
resurrection on the third day, for example, is held by many
(e. g., Schwartzkopff) to be too precise a determination, and is
therefore excluded from the prophecy, or explained as only a
periphrasis for an indefinite short time, after the analogy of
Hos. vi. 2 (so even B. Weiss). To others a prediction of a resurrection at all seems incredible (Strauss, Schenkel, Weizsäcker,
Keim, Brandt), and it is transmuted into, at most, a premoni-
tion of future victory. By yet others (as Holsten) even the anticipation of death is doubted, and nothing of forecast is left
to Jesus except, possibly, a vague anticipation of difficulty and

suffering; while with others even this gives way, and Jesus is represented as passing either the greater part of His life (Fairbairn), or the whole of it, in joyful expectation of more or less unbroken success, or at least, however thickly the clouds gathered over His head, in inextinguishable hope in God and His interposition in His behalf (cf. the brief general sketch of opinions in Wrede, "Messiasgeheimnis," p. 85).

Thus, over-against the 'dogmatic' view of the life of Christ, set forth in the Evangelists, according to which Jesus came into the world to die, and which is dominated, therefore, by foresight, is set, in polar opposition to it, a new view, calling itself 'historical,' the principle of which is the denial to Jesus of any foresight whatever beyond the most limited human forecast. No pretence is ordinarily made that this new view is given support by the Evangelical records; it is put forward on *a priori* or general grounds — as, for example, the only psychologically possible view (e. g., Schwartzkopff, "Prophecies of Christ," p. 28; cf. Denney, "Death of Christ," p. 11, and especially the just strictures of Wrede, "Messiasgeheimnis," pp. 2, 3). It professes to find it incredible that Jesus entered upon His ministry with any other expectation than success. Contact with men, however, it allows, brought gradually the discovery of the hopelessness of drawing them to His spiritual ideals; the growing enmity of the rulers opened before Him the prospect of disaster; and thus there came to Him the slow recognition, first of the possibility, and then of the certainty, of failure; or, at least, since failure was impossible for the mission He had come to perform, of the necessity of passing through suffering to the ultimate success. So slowly was the readjustment to this new point of view made, that even at the end — as the prayer at Gethsemane shows — there remained a lingering hope that the extremity of death might be avoided. So far as a general sketch can be made of a view presented by its several adherents with great variety of detail, this is the essential fabric of the new view (cf. the general statements of Kähler, "Zur Lehre von der Versöhnung," 159; Denney, "Death of Christ," 11; Wrede, "Messiasgeheimnis," 86). Only such parts of the predictive element of the teaching attributed to Jesus in the Gospels as are thought capable of naturalistic interpretation are incorporated into this new construction. By those who wish to bring in as much as possible, it is said, for example, that our Lord was too firmly persuaded of His Messianic appointment and function, and was too clear that this function centred in the establishment of the Kingdom, to accept death itself as failure. When He perceived death impending, that meant to Him, therefore, return; and return to bring in the Messianic glory meant resurrection. When He thought and spoke of death, therefore, He necessarily thought and spoke also of resurrection and return; the three went inevitably together; and if He anticipated the one, He must have anticipated the others also. Under this general scheme all sorts of opinions are held as to when, how, and under what impulses Jesus formed and taught this eschatological programme. As notable a construction as any holds that He first became certain of His Messiahship in an ecstatic vision which accompanied His baptism; that the Messiah must suffer was already borne in upon His conviction in the course of His temptation; but it was not until the scene at Cæsarea Philippi that He attained the happy assurance that the Messianic glory lay behind the dreadful death impending over Him. This great conviction, attained in principle in the ecstasy of that moment, was, nevertheless, only gradually assimilated. When Jesus was labouring with His disciples, He was labouring also with Himself. In this particular construction (it is O. Holtzmann's) an element of 'ecstasy' is introduced; more commonly the advances Jesus is supposed to make in His anticipations are thought to rest on processes of formal reasoning. In either case, He is pictured as only slowly, under the stress of compelling circumstances, reaching convictions of what awaited Him in the future; and thus He is conceived distinctly as the victim rather than as the Lord of His destiny. So far from entering the world to die, and by His death to save the world, and in His own good time and way accomplishing this great mission, He enters life set upon living, and only yields step by step reluctantly to the hard fate which inexorably closes upon Him. That He clings through all to His conviction of His Messiahship, and adjusts His hope of accomplishing His Messianic mission to the overmastering pressure of circumstances, — is that not a pathetic trait of human nature? Do not all enthusiasts the like? Is it not precisely the mark of their fanaticism? The plain fact is, if we may express it in the brutal frankness of common speech, in this view of Jesus' career He miscalculated and failed; and then naturally sought (or His followers sought for Him) to save the failure (or the appearance of failure) by inventing a new *dénouement* for the career He had hoped for in vain, a new dénouement which — has it failed too? Most of our modern theorizers are impelled to recognize that it too has failed. When Jesus so painfully adjusted Himself to the hard destiny which more and more obtruded itself upon His recognition, He taught that death was but an incident in His career, and after death would come the victory. Can we believe that He foresaw that thousands of years would intervene between what He represented as but an apparent catastrophe and the glorious reversal to which He directed His own and His followers' eyes? On the contrary, He expected and He taught that He would come back soon — certainly before the generation which had witnessed His apparent defeat had passed away; and that He would then establish that Messianic Kingdom which from the beginning of His ministry He had unvaryingly taught was at hand. He did not do so. Is there any reason to believe that He ever will return? Can the 'foresight' which has repeatedly failed so miserably be trusted still, — for what we choose to separate out from the mass of His expectations as the core of the matter? On what grounds shall we adjust the discredited 'foresight' to the course of events, obviously unforeseen by Him, since His death? Where is the end of these 'adjustments'? Have we not already with 'adjustment' after 'adjustment' transformed beyond recognition the expectations of Jesus, even the latest and fullest to which He attained, and transmuted them into something fundamentally different, — passed, in a word, so far beyond Him, that we retain only an

artificial connexion with Him and His real teaching, a con-
nexion mediated by little more than a word? That in this modern construction we have the precise contradictory of the conception of Jesus and of the course of His
life on earth given us by the Evangelists, it needs no argument
to establish. In the Gospel presentation, foresight is made the
principlo of our Lord's caroor. In the modern view He is credited
with no foresight whatever. At best, He was possessed by a
fixed conviction of His Messianic mission, whether gained in
ecstatic vision (as, e. g., O. Holtzmann) or acquired in deep
religious experiences (as, e. g., Schwartzkopff); and He felt an
assurance, based on this ineradicable conviction, that in His
own good time and way God would work that mission out for
Him; and in this assurance He went faithfully onward fulfilling
His daily task, bungling meanwhile egregiously in His reading
of the scroll of destiny which was unrolling for Him. It is an
intensely, even an exaggeratedly, human Christ which is here
offered us: and He stands, therefore, in the strongest contrast
with the frankly Divine Christ which the Gospels present to
us. On what grounds can we be expected to substitute this for
that? Certainly not on grounds of historical record. We have
no historical record of the self-consciousness of Jesus except
that embodied in the Gospel dramatization of His life and the
Gospel report of His teaching; and that record expressly contradicts at every step this modern reconstruction of its contents
and development. The very principle of the modern construction is reversal of the Gospel delineation. Its peculiarity is that,
though it calls itself the 'historical' view, it has behind it no
single scrap of historical testimony; the entirety of historical
evidence contradicts it flatly. Are we to accept it, then, on the
general grounds of inherent probability and rational construction? It is historically impossible that the great religious movement which we call Christianity could have taken its origin and
derived its inspiration — an inspiration far from spent after
two thousand years — from such a figure as this Jesus. The
plain fact is that in these modern reconstructions we have
nothing but a sustained attempt to construct a naturalistic

Jesus; and their chief interest is that they bring before us with
unwonted clearness the kind of being the man must have been
who at that time and in those circumstances could have come
forward making the claims which Jesus made without supernatural nature, endowment, or aid to sustain Him. The value
of the speculation is that it makes superabundantly clear that
no such being could have occupied the place which the historical Jesus occupied; could have made the impression on His
followers which the historical Jesus made; could have become
the source of the stream of religious influence which we call
Christianity, as the historical Jesus became. The clear formulation of the naturalistic hypothesis, in the construction of a
naturalistic Jesus, in other words, throws us violently back
upon the Divine Jesus of the Evangelists as the only Jesus
that is historically possible. From this point of view, the la-
bours of the scholars who have with infinite pains built up this
construction of Jesus' life and development have not been in
vain.

What, then, is to be said of the predictions of Jesus, and
especially of the three great series of prophecies of His death,
resurrection, and return, with respect to their contents and
fulfilment? This is not the place to discuss the eschatology of
Jesus. But a few general remarks seem not uncalled for. The
topic has received of late much renewed attention with very
varied results, the number and variety of constructions proposed having been greatly increased above what the inherent
difficulty of the subject will account for, by the freedom with
which the Scripture data have been modified or set aside on so-
called critical grounds by the several investigators. Nevertheless, most of the new interpretations also may be classified under
the old categories of futuristic, preteristic, and spiritualistic.

The spiritualistic interpretation — whose method of dealing with our Lord's predictions readily falls in with a widespread theory that it is 'contrary to the spirit and manner of
genuine prophecy to predict actual circumstances like a sooth-
sayer' (Muirhead, "Eschatology of Jesus," p. 10; Schwartzkopff, "Prophecies of Jesus Christ," 78, 250, 258, 275, 312,

etc.) — has received a new impulse through its attractive presentation by Erich Haupt ("Eschatolog. Aussagen Jesu," etc., 1895). Christ's eschatology, says Haupt, is infinitely simple, and all that He predicts is to be accomplished in a heavenly way which passes our comprehension; there is no soothsaying in His utterances — 'nowhere any predictions of external occurrences, everywhere only great moral religious laws which must operate everywhere and always, while nothing is said of the form in which they must act' (p. 157). A considerable stir has been created also by the revival (Schleiermacher, Weisse) by Weiffenbach ("Der Wiederkunftsgedanke Jesu," 1873, "Die Frage der Wiederkunft Jesu," 1901) of the identification of the return of Christ with His resurrection, although this view has retained few adherents since its refutation by Schwartzkopff ("The Prophecies of Jesus Christ," 1895), whose own view is its exact contradictory, viz., that by His resurrection Jesus meant just His return. The general conception, however, that 'for Jesus the hope of resurrection and the thought of return fell together,' so that 'when Jesus spoke of His resurrection He was thinking of His return, and *vice versa*' (O. Holtzmann, "War Jesus Ekstatiker?" 67, note), is very widely held. The subsidiary hypothesis (first suggested by Colani) of the inclusion in the great eschatological discourse attributed by the Evangelists to our Lord of a 'little Apocalypse' of Jewish or Jewish Christian origin, by which Weiffenbach eased his task, has in more or less modified form received the widest acceptance (cf. H. J. Holtzmann, "Lehrbuch der neutestamentlichen Theologie," i. 327, note), but rests on no solid grounds (cf. Weiss, Beyschlag, Haupt, Clemen). Most adherents of the modern school are clear that Jesus expected and asserted that He would return in Messianic glory for the consummation of the Kingdom; and most of them are equally clear that in this expectation and assertion, Jesus was mistaken (cf. H. J. Holtzmann, "Lehrbuch der neutestamentlichen Theologie," i. 312 f.). 'In the expectation that the kingdom was soon to come,' says Oscar Holtzmann in a passage typical enough of this whole school of exposition ("War Jesus Ekstatiker?" p. 133), 'Jesus

erred in a human way'; and in such passages as Mk. ix. 1'
xiii. 30, Mt. x. 23 he considers that the error is obvious. He
adds, 'That such an error on the part of Jesus concerning not
a side-issue but a fundamental point of His faith, — His first
proclamation began, according to Mk. i. 15, with the πεπλή-
ρωται ὁ καιρὸς καὶ ἤγγικεν ἡ βασιλεία τοῦ θεοῦ, — does not facili-
tate faith in Jesus is self-evident; but this error of Jesus is for
His Church a highly instructive and therefore highly valuable
warning to distinguish between the temporary and the permanent in the work of Jesus.' Not every one even of this school
can go, however, quite this length. Even Schwartzkopff, while
allowing that Jesus erred in this matter, wishes on that very
account to think of the mere definition of times and seasons
as belonging to the form rather than to the essence of His
teaching ("The Prophecies of Jesus Christ," 1895, Eng. tr.
1897, p. 319; "Konnte Jesus irren?" 1896, p. 3); and in that
Baldensperger is in substantial agreement with him ("Selbst-
bewusstsein Jesu[1], p. 148, ed.[2], p. 205). From the other side, E.
Haupt ("Eschatolog. Aussagen Jesu," 1895, p. 138 f.) urges
that Jesus must be supposed to have been able to avoid all
errors, at least in the religious sphere, even if they concern
nothing but the form; while Weiffenbach ("Die Frage," etc.
p. 9) thinks we should hesitate to suppose Jesus could have
erred in too close a definition of the time of His advent, when
He expressly confesses that He was ignorant of its time (cf.
Muirhead, "Eschat. of Jesus," 48–50, and especially 117).
Probably Fritz Barth ("Die Hauptprobleme des Lebens Jesu,"
1899, pp. 167–170) stands alone in cutting the knot by appealing to the conditionality of all prophecy. According to him,
Jesus did, indeed, predict His return as coincident with the
destruction of Jerusalem; but all genuine prophecy is conditioned upon the conduct of the human agents involved —
'between prediction and fulfilment the conduct of man intrudes as a codetermining factor on which the fulfilment depends.' Thus this prediction has not failed, but its fulfilment
has only been postponed — in accordance, it must be confessed,
not with the will of God, but with that of man. It is difficult

to see how Jesus is thus shielded from the imputation of defective foresight; but at least Barth is able on this view still to look for a return of the Lord.

The difficulty which the passages in our Saviour's teaching under discussion present to the reverent expositor is, of course, not to be denied or minimized. But surely this difficulty would nood to be much more hopeless than it is before it could compel or justify the assumption of error 'in One who has never been convicted of error in anything else' (Sanday in Hastings' *DB* ii. 635 — the whole passage should be read). The problem that faces us in this matter, it is apparent, in the meantime, is not one which can find its solution as a corollary to a speculative general view of our Lord's self-consciousness, its contents, and development. It is distinctly a problem of exegesis. We should be very sure that we know fully and precisely all that our Lord has declared about His return — its what and how and when — before we venture to suggest, even to our most intimate thought, that He has committed so gross an error as to its what and how and when as is so often assumed; especially as He has in the most solemn manner declared concerning precisely the words under consideration that heaven and earth shall pass away, but not His words. It would be sad if the passage of time has shown this declaration also to be mistaken. Meanwhile, the perfect foresight of our Lord, asserted and illustrated by all the Evangelists, certainly cannot be set aside by the facile assumption of an error on His part in a matter in which it is so difficult to demonstrate an error, and in which assumptions of all sorts are so little justified. For the detailed discussion of our Lord's eschatology, including the determination of His meaning in these utterances, reference must, however, be made to works treating expressly of this subject.

III

THE SPIRIT OF GOD IN THE OLD TESTAMENT

THE SPIRIT OF GOD IN THE OLD TESTAMENT [1]

THE doctrine of the Spirit of God is an exclusively Biblical doctrine. Rückert tells us that the idea connoted by the term is entirely foreign to Hellenism, and first came into the world through Christianity.[2] And Kleinert, in quoting this remark, adds that what is peculiarly anti-heathenish in the conception is already present in the Old Testament.[3] It would seem, then, that what is most fundamental in the Biblical doctrine of the Spirit of God is common to both Testaments.

The name meets us in the very opening verses of the Old Testament, and it appears there as unannounced and unexplained as in the opening verses of the New Testament. It is plain that it was no more a novelty in the mouth of the author of Genesis than in the mouth of the author of Matthew. But though it is common to both Testaments, it is not equally common in all parts of the Bible. It does not occur as frequently in the Old Testament as in the New. It is found as often in the Epistles of Paul as in the whole Old Testament. It is not as pervasive in the Old Testament as in the New. It fails in no New Testament book, except the three brief personal letters Philemon and II and III John. On the other hand, in only some half of the thirty-nine Old Testament books is it clearly mentioned,[4] while in as many as sixteen all definite allusion to it seems to be lacking.[5] The principle which governs the use

---

[1] From *The Presbyterian and Reformed Review*, v. vi, 1895, pp. 665–687.

[2] " Korinthierbriefe " i, p. 80.

[3] Article, " Zur altest. Lehre vom Geiste Gottes," in the " Jahrbb. für deutsch. Theologie " for 1867, i, p. 9.

[4] These are Genesis, Exodus, Numbers, Judges, I and II Samuel, I and II Kings, II Chronicles, Nehemiah, Job, Psalms, Isaiah, Ezekiel, Joel, Micah, Haggai, Zechariah. Deuteronomy and I Chronicles may be added, although they do not contain the explicit phrase, "the Spirit of God" or "the Spirit of Jehovah."

[5] These are Leviticus, Joshua, Ruth, Ezra, Esther, Ecclesiastes, Song of Songs, Jeremiah, Lamentations, Hosea, Amos, Obadiah, Jonah, Nahum, Habakkuk and Zephaniah. Proverbs, Daniel and Malachi may, for one reason or another, remain unclassified.

or disuse of it does not lie on the surface. Sometimes it may, perhaps, be partly due to the nature of the subject treated. But if mention of the Spirit of God fails in Leviticus, it is made in Numbers; if it fails in Joshua and Ruth, it is made in Judges and Samuel; if it fails in Ezra, it is made in Nehemiah; if it fails in Jeremiah, it is made in Isaiah and Ezekiel; if it fails in seven or eight of the minor prophets, it is made in the remaining four or five. Whether it occurs in an Old Testament book seems to depend on a number of circumstances which have little or no bearing on the history of the doctrine. We need only note that the name "Spirit of God" meets us at the very opening of revelation, and it, or its equivalents, accompanies us sporadically throughout the volume. The Pentateuch and historical books provide us with the outline of the doctrine; its richest depositories among the prophets are Isaiah and Ezekiel, from each of which alone probably the whole doctrine could be derived.[6]

In passing from the Old Testament to the New, the reader is conscious of no violent discontinuity in the conception of the Spirit which he finds in the two volumes. He may note the increased frequency with which the name appears on the printed page. But he would note this much the same in passing from the earlier to the later chapters of the *Epistle to the Romans*. He may note an increased definiteness and fulness in the conception itself. But something similar to this he would note in passing from the Pentateuch to Isaiah, or from Matthew to John or Paul. The late Professor Smeaton may have overstated the matter in his interesting Cunningham Lectures on "The Doctrine of the Holy Spirit." "We find," he says, "that the doctrine of the Spirit taught by the Baptist, by Christ and by

---

[6] "There is one writer of the Old Testament, in whom all lines and rays of this development come together, and who so stood in the matter of time and of inner manner that they had to come together in this point of unity, if the Old Testament had otherwise found such. This is Ezekiel" (Kleinert, *op. cit.* p. 45). "Isaiah has scattered throughout his prophecies allusions to the Spirit so manifold and various in express descriptions and in brief turns of phrase, that it might not be difficult to put together from his words, the complete doctrine of the Spirit" (Smeaton, "Doctrine of the Holy Spirit," p. 35).

the Apostles, was in every respect the same as that with which
the Old Testament church was familiar. We nowhere find that
their Jewish hearers on any occasion took exception to it. The
teaching of our Lord and His Apostles never called forth a
question or an opposition from any quarter — a plain proof
that on this question nothing was taught by them which came
into collision with the sentiments and opinions which up to that
time had been accepted, and still continued to be current among
the Jews." Some such change in the conception of God doubtless needs to be recognized as that which Dr. Denney describes
in the following words: "The Apostles were all Jews, — men,
as it has been said, with monotheism as a passion in their
blood.[7] They did not cease to be monotheists when they became preachers of Christ, but they instinctively conceived God
in a way in which the old revelation had not taught them to
conceive him. . . . Distinctions were recognized in what had
once been the bare simplicity of the Divine nature. The distinction of Father and Son was the most obvious, and it was
enriched, on the basis of Christ's own teaching, and of the
actual experience of the Church, by the further distinction of
the Holy Spirit."[8] But if there be any fundamental difference
between the Old and the New Testament conceptions of the
Spirit of God, it escapes us in our ordinary reading of the Bible,
and we naturally and without conscious straining read our New
Testament conceptions into the Old Testament passages.

We are, indeed, bidden to do this by the New Testament
itself. The New Testament writers identify their "Holy Spirit"
with the "Spirit of God" of the older books. All that is attributed to the Spirit of God in the Old Testament, is attributed
by them to their personal Holy Ghost. It was their own Holy
Ghost who was Israel's guide and director and whom Israel re-
jected when they resisted the leading of God (Acts vii. 51). It
was in Him that Christ (doubtless in the person of Noah)
preached to the antediluvians (I Pet. iii. 18). It was He who
was the author of faith of old as well as now (II Cor. iv. 13).

[7] Fairbairn, "Christ in Modern Theology," p. 377.
[8] James Denney, "Studies in Theology," p. 70.

It was He who gave Israel its ritual service (Heb. ix. 8). It was
He who spoke in and through David and Isaiah and all the
prophets (Matt. xxii. 43, Mark xii. 36, Acts i. 16, xxviii. 25,
Heb. iii. 7, x. 15). If Zechariah (vii. 12) or Nehemiah (ix. 20)
tells us that Jehovah of Hosts sent His word by His Spirit by
the hands of the prophets, Peter tells us that these men from
God were moved by the Holy Ghost to speak these words
(II Pet. i. 21), and even that it was specifically the Spirit of
Christ that was in the prophets (I Pet. i. 11). We are assured
that it was in Jesus upon whom the Holy Ghost had visibly
descended, that Isaiah's predictions were fulfilled that Jehovah
would put His Spirit upon his righteous servant (Isa. xlii. 1) and
that (Isa. lxi. 1) the Spirit of the Lord Jehovah should be upon
Him (Matt. xii. 18, Luke iv. 18, 19). And Peter bids us look
upon the descent of the Holy Spirit at Pentecost as the accomplished promise of Joel that God would pour out His Spirit
upon all flesh (Joel ii. 27, 28, Acts ii. 16).[9] There can be no
doubt that the New Testament writers identify the Holy
Ghost of the New Testament with the Spirit of God of the Old.

This fact, of course, abundantly justifies the instinctive
Christian identification. We are sure, with the surety of a divine
revelation, that the Spirit of God of the Old Testament is the
personal Holy Spirit of the New. But this assurance does not
forestall the inquiry whether this personal Spirit was so fully
revealed in the Old Testament that those who were dependent
on that revelation alone, without the inspired commentary of
the New, were able to know Him as He is known to us who
enjoy the fuller light. The principle of the progressive delivery
of doctrine in the age-long process of God's self-revelation, is
not only a reasonable one in itself and one which is justified
by the results of investigation, but it is one which is assumed
in the Scriptures themselves as God's method of revealing Himself, and which received the practical endorsement of our Saviour
in His manner of communicating His saving truth to men. The
question is still an open one, therefore, how much of the doc-

---

[9] Cf. also the promise of Ezek. xxxvi. 27 and I Thes. iv. 8 (see Toy, "Quotations in the New Testament," p. 202). Cf. also Luke i. 17.

trine of the Holy Spirit as it lies in its completeness in the pages of the New Testament had already been made the property of the men of the old dispensation; in other words, what the Old Testament doctrine of the Spirit of God is. We may not find this inconsistent with the fuller New Testament teaching, but we may find it fall short of the whole truth revealed in the latter days in God's Son.

The deep unity between the New and Old Testament conceptions lies, in one broad circumstance, so upon the surface of the two Testaments that our attention is attracted to it at the outset of any investigation of the material. In both Testaments the Spirit of God appears distinctly as *the executive of the Godhead*. If in the New Testament God works all that He does by the Spirit, so in the Old Testament the Spirit is the name of God working. The Spirit of God is in the Old Testament the executive name of God — "the divine principle of activity everywhere at work in the world." [10] In this common conception lies doubtless the primary reason why we pass from one Testament to the other without sense of discontinuity in the doctrine of the Spirit. The further extent in which this unity may be traced will depend on the nature of the activities which are ascribed to the Spirit in both Testaments.

The Old Testament does not give us, of course, an exhaustive record of all God's activities. It is primarily an account of God's redemptive work prior to the coming of the Messiah — of the progress, in a word, so far, of the new creation of grace built upon the ruins of the first creation, a short account of which is prefixed as background and basis. In the nature of the case, we learn from the Old Testament of those activities of God only which naturally emerge in these accounts; and accordingly the doctrine of the Spirit of God as the divine principle of activity, as taught in the Old Testament, is necessarily confined to the course of divine activities in the first and the initial

---

[10] These words are C. F. Schmid's ("Biblical Theology of the New Testament,' Div. ii. § 24, p. 145, E. T.). Cf. Smeaton, *op. cit.* p. 36: "Events occurring in the moral government of God, are (in the Old Testament) also ascribed to the Spirit as the Executive of all the divine purposes."

stages of the second creation. In other words, it is subsumable under the two broad captions of God in the world, and God in His people. It is from this that the circumstance arises which has been frequently noted, that, after the entrance of sin into the world, the work of the Spirit of God on men's spirits is always set forth in the Old Testament in the interests and in the spirit of the kingdom of God.[11] The Old Testament is concerned after the sin of man only with the recovery of man; it traces the preparatory stages of the kingdom of God, as God laid its foundations in a chosen nation in whom all the nations of the earth were to be blessed. The segregation of Israel and the establishment of the theocracy thus mark the first steps in the new creation; and following this course of divine working, the doctrine of the Spirit in the new creation as taught in the Old Testament naturally concerns especially the activities of God in the establishment and development of the theocracy and in the preparation of a people to enjoy its blessings. In other words, it falls under the two captions of His national, or rather churchly, and of His individual work. Thus the Old Testament teaching concerning the Spirit, brings before us three spheres of His activity, which will correspond broadly to the conceptions of God in the world, God in the theocracy, and God in the soul.

Broadly speaking, these three spheres of the Spirit's activity appear successively in the pages of the Old Testament. In these pages the Spirit of God is introduced to us primarily in His cosmical, next in His theocratic, and lastly in His individual relations.[12] This is, of course, due chiefly to the natural

---

[11] Kleinert, *op. cit.*, p. 30: "The Old Testament everywhere knows only of an influence of the Divine Spirit upon the human Spirit in the interest and sphere of the Kingdom of God, which is in Israel and is to come through Israel." Hävernick, "Theologie des alten Testaments" p. 77: "Of a communication of the Spirit in the narrower sense, after the entrance of sin, there can be question only in the Theocracy." Oehler, "Biblical Theology of the Old Testament," § 65: "But the Spirit as רוּחַ יְהֹוָה, or to express it more definitely רוּחַ קֹדֶשׁ יְהֹוָה only acts within the sphere of revelation. It rules within the Theocracy."

[12] For example, in the Pentateuch His working is perhaps exclusively cosmical and theocratic-official, (Oehler, *op. cit.* § 65); while His ethical work in individuals, is throughout the Old Testament, more a matter of prophecy than of present enjoyment (Dale, "Christian Doctrine," p. 317).

correspondence of the aspects of His activity which are presented with the course of history, and is not to be taken so strictly as to imply that the revelations relative to each sphere of His working occur exclusively in a single portion of the Old Testament. It supplies us, however, not only with the broad outlines of the historical development of the doctrine of the Spirit in the Old Testament, but also with a logical order of presentation for the material. Perhaps we may also say, in passing, that it suggests a course of development of the doctrine of the Spirit which is at once most natural and, indeed, rationally inevitable, and, as Dr. Dale points out,[13] closely correspondent with what have come to be spoken of as the "traditional" dates attributed to the books of the Old Testament. These books, standing as they stand in this dating, are in the most natural order for the development of this doctrine.

THE COSMICAL SPIRIT

I. The Spirit of God is first brought before us in the Old Testament, then, in His relations to the first creation, or in what may be called his cosmical relations. In this connection He is represented as the source of all order, life and light in the universe. He is the divine principle of all movement, of all life and of all thought in the world. The basis of this conception is already firmly laid in the first passage in which the Spirit of God is mentioned (Gen. i. 2). In the beginning, we are told, God created the heavens and the earth. And then the process is detailed by which the created earth, at first waste and void, with darkness resting upon the face of the deep, was transformed by successive fiats into the ordered and populous world in which we live. As the ground of the whole process, we are informed that "the Spirit of God was brooding upon the face of the waters," as much as to say that the obedience, and the precedent power of obedience, of the waste of waters to the successive creative words — as God said, Let there be light; Let

---

[13] Dale, "Christian Doctrine," p. 318. A striking passage both for its presentation of this fact and for its unwillingness to accept its implications.

there be a firmament; Let the waters be gathered together; Let
the waters and the earth bring forth — depended upon the
fact that the Spirit of God was already brooding upon the formless void. To the voice of God in heaven saying, Let there be
light! the energy of the Spirit of God brooding upon the face
of the waters responded, and lo! there was light. Over against
the transcendent God, above creation, there seems to be postulated here God brooding upon creation, and the suggestion
seems to be that it is only by virtue of God brooding upon
creation that the created thing moves and acts and works out
the will of God. The Spirit of God, in a word, appears at the
very opening of the Bible as God immanent; and, as such, is
set over against God transcendent. And it is certainly very instructive to observe that God is conceived as immanent already
in what may be called the formless world-stuff which by His
immanence in it alone it constituted a stuff from which on the
divine command an ordered world may emerge.[14] The Spirit
of God thus appears from the outset of the Old Testament as
the principle of the very existence and persistence of all things,
and as the source and originating cause of all movement and
order and life. God's thought and will and word take effect in
the world, because God is not only over the world, thinking and
willing and commanding, but also in the world, as the principle
of all activity, *executing*: this seems the thought of the author
of the Biblical cosmogony.[15]

[14] Cf. Schultz, "Old Testament Theology," E. T. ii, 184: "Over the lifeless
and formless mass of the world-matter this Spirit broods like a bird on its nest,
and thus transmits to it the seeds of life, so that afterwards by the word of God
it can produce whatever God wills."

[15] Compare some very instructive words as to this account of creation, by
the Rev. John Robson, D.D. of Aberdeen (*The Expository Times*, July, 1894, vol.
v. No. 10, pp. 467, *sq*.): "The divine agents in creation are brought before us in
the opening of the Book of Genesis, and in the opening of the Gospel of John. The
object of John in his Gospel is to speak of Jesus Christ, the Word of God; and
so he refers only to His agency in the work of creation. The object of Moses in
Genesis is to tell the whole divine agency in that work; so in his narrative we
have the work of the Spirit recognized. But he does not ignore the Word of God;
he begins his account of each epoch or each day of creation with the words, 'And
God said.' We do not find in Genesis the theological fulness that we do in subsequent writers in the Bible; but we do find in it the elements of all that we subse-

A series of Old Testament passages range themselves under this conception and carry it forward. It is by the Spirit of God, says Job, that the heavens are garnished (xxvi. 13). Isaiah compares the coming of the God of vengeance, repaying fury to His adversaries and recompense to His enemies, to the bursting forth "of a pent-in stream which the Spirit of Jehovah driveth" (lix. 19); and represents the perishing of flesh as like the withering of the grass and the fading of the flower when "the Spirit of Jehovah bloweth upon it" (xl. 7). In such passages the Spirit appears as the principle of cosmical processes. He is also the source of all life, and, as such, the executor of Him with whom, as the Psalmist says, is the fountain of life (Ps. xxxvi. 10 [9]). The Psalmist accordingly ascribes the being of all creatures to Him: "Thou sendest forth thy Spirit, they are created" (Ps. civ. 30). "The Spirit of God hath made me," declares Job, "and the breath of the Almighty giveth me life" (xxxiii. 4). Accordingly he represents life to be due to the persistence of the Spirit of God in his nostrils (xxvii. 3), and therefore its continuance to be dependent upon the continuance of the Spirit with man: "If He set His heart upon man, if He gather unto Himself His Spirit and His breath all flesh shall perish together, and man shall turn again unto dust" (xxxiv. 14, 15, cf. xii. 10). He is also the source of all intellectual life. Elihu tells us that it is not greatness, nor years, but the Spirit of God that gives understanding: "There is a Spirit in man, and the breath of the Almighty giveth them understanding" (Job xxxii. 8) — a thought which is probably only expressed in another way in Prov. xx. 27, which declares that the spirit of man is "the lamp of the Lord, searching all the innermost parts of the belly." That the Spirit is the source also of all ethical life seems to follow from the obscure passage, Genesis vi. 3: "And the Lord said, My Spirit shall not strive with man for ever, for that he

quently learn or deduce regarding the divine agency in creation. . . . Two agents are mentioned: 'The Spirit of God brooding on the surface of the waters,' and at each new stage of creative development, the Word of God expressed in the words 'God said.' . . . There is thus the Spirit of God present as a constant energy, and there is the Word of God giving form to that energy, and at each new epoch calling new forms into being."

also is flesh." Apparently there is here either a direct threat from Jehovah to withdraw that Spirit by virtue of which alone morality could exist in the world, or else a threat that He will, on account of their sin, withdraw the Spirit whose presence gives life so that men may no longer be upheld in their wicked existence, but may sink back into nothingness. In either case ethical considerations come forward prominently, — the occasion of the destruction of mankind is an ethical one, and the gift of life appears as for ethical ends. This, however, is an element in the conception of the Spirit's work which comes to clear enunciation only in another connection.

It would not be easy to overestimate the importance of the early emergence of this doctrine of the immanent Spirit of God, side by side with the high doctrine of the transcendence of God which pervades the Old Testament. Whatever tendency the emphasis on the transcendence of God might engender towards Deistic conceptions would be corrected at once by such teaching as to the immanent Spirit; while in turn any tendencies to Pantheistic or Cosmotheistic conceptions which it might itself arouse would be corrected not only by the prevailing stress upon the divine transcendence, but also by the manner in which the immanence of God is itself presented. For we cannot sufficiently admire the perfection with which, in delivering the doctrine of the immanent Spirit, all possibility is excluded of conceiving of God as entangled in creation — as if the Spirit of God were merely the physical world-spirit, the proper ground rather than effecting cause of cosmical activities. In the very phraseology of Genesis i. 2, for example, the moving Spirit is kept separate from the matter to which He gives movement; He *broods over* rather than is merged in the waste of waters; He acts upon them and cannot be confounded with them as but another name for their own blind surging. So in the 104th Psalm (verses 29, 30) the creative Spirit is *sent forth* by God, and is not merely an alternative name for the unconscious life-ground of nature. It is a thing which is *given* by God and so produces life (Isa. xlii. 5). Though penetrating all things (Ps. cxxxix. 7) and the immanent source of all life-activities (Ps.

civ. 30), it is nevertheless always the *personal* cause of physical, psychical and ethical activities. It exercises choice. It is not merely the *general* ground of all such activities; it is the determiner as well of all the *differences* that exist among men. So, for example, Elihu appeals to the Spirit of understanding that is in him (Job xxxii. 8). It is not merely the ground of the *presence* of these powers; it is also to it that their *withdrawal* is to be ascribed (Isa. xl. 7, Gen. vi. 3). Nor are its manifestations confined altogether to what may be called *natural* modes of action; room is left among them for what we may call truly *supernatural* activity (I Kgs. xviii. 12, II Kgs. ii. 16, cf. II Kgs. xix. 7, Isa. xxxvii. 7). All nature worship is further excluded by the clearness of the identification of the Spirit of God with the God over all. Thus the unity of God was not only preserved but emphasized, and men were taught to look upon the emergence of divine powers and effects in nature as the work of His hands. "Whither shall I go," asks the Psalmist, "from thy Spirit? or whither shall I flee from thy presence" (Ps. cxxxix. 7)? Here the spiritual presence of God is obviously the presence of the God over all in His Spirit. "Who hath . . . meted out heaven with a span? . . . Who hath meted out the Spirit of Jehovah, or being his counsellor hath taught him?" asks Isaiah (xl. 12, 13) in the same spirit. Obviously the Spirit of God was not conceived as the impersonal ground of life and understanding, but as the personal source of all that was of being, life and light in the world, not as apart from but as one with the great God Almighty in the heavens. And yet, as immanent in the world, He is set over against God transcendent in a manner which prepares the way for His hypostatizing and so for the Christian doctrine of the Trinity.

It requires little consideration to realize how greatly the Old Testament conception of God is enriched by this teaching. In particular, it behooves us to note how, side by side with the emphasis that is laid upon God as the maker of all things, this doctrine lays an equal emphasis on God as the upholder and governor of all things. Side by side with the emphasis which is laid on the unapproachable majesty of God as the transcendent

Person, it lays an equal emphasis on God as the immanent agent in all world changes and all world movements. It thus lays firmly the foundation of the Christian doctrine of Providence — God in the world and in history, leading all things to their destined goal. If without God there was not anything made that has been made, so without God's Spirit there has not anything occurred that has occurred.

THE THEOCRATIC SPIRIT

II. All this is still further emphasized in the second and predominant aspect in which the Spirit of God is brought before us in the Old Testament, viz., in His relations to the second creation.

1. Here, primarily, He is presented as the source of all the supernatural powers and activities which are directed to the foundation and preservation and development of the kingdom of God in the midst of the wicked world. He is thus represented as the theocratic Spirit as pointedly as He is represented as the world-spirit. We are moving here in a distinctly supernatural atmosphere and the activities which come under review belong to an entirely supernatural order. There are a great variety of these activities, but they have this in common: they are all endowments of the theocratic organs with the gifts requisite for the fulfilment of their functions.[16]

There are, for example, the supernatural gifts of strength, resolution, energy, courage in battle which were awakened in chosen leaders for the service of God's people. Thus we are told that the Spirit of Jehovah came upon Othniel to fit him for his work as judge of Israel (Judg. iii. 10), and clothed itself

[16] Oehler, "Old Testament Theology," § 65: "But the Spirit as רוּחַ יְהוָֹה, or to express it more definitely רוּחַ קֹדֶשׁ יְהוָֹה, only acts within *the sphere of revelation*. It rules within the theocracy (Isa. lxiii. 11, Hag. ii. 5, Neh. ix. 20) but not as if all citizens of the Old Testament Theocracy as such participated in this Spirit, which Moses expresses as a wish (Num. xi. 29), but which is reserved for the future community of salvation (John iii. 1). In the Old Testament the Spirit's work in the divine kingdom is rather that of *endowing the organs of the theocracy with the gifts required for their calling*, and those gifts of office in the Old Testament are similar to the gifts of grace in the New Testament, I Cor. xii. ff."

with Gideon (vi. 34), and came upon Jephthah (xi. 29), and, most remarkably of all, came mightily upon and moved Samson, endowing him with superhuman strength (xiii. 25, xiv. 6, 19, xv. 14). Similarly the Spirit of God came mightily upon Saul (I Sam. xi. 6) and upon David (I Sam. xvi. 13), and clothed Amasai (I Chron. xii. 18). Then, there are the supernatural gifts of skill by which artificers were fitted to serve the kingdom of God in preparing a worthy sanctuary for the worship of the King. There were, for instance, those whom Jehovah had filled with the spirit of wisdom and who were, therefore, wise-hearted to make Aaron's sacred garments (Ex. xxviii. 3). And especially we are told that Jehovah had filled Bezalel "with the Spirit of God, in wisdom and in understanding, and in knowledge, and in all manner of workmanship, to devise cunning works, to work in gold, and in silver, and in brass, and in cutting of stones for setting, and in carving of wood, to work in all manner of workmanship" (Ex. xxxi. 3 f. cf. xxxv. 31): — and that he should therefore preside over the work of the wise-hearted, in whom the Lord had put wisdom, for the making of the tabernacle and its furniture. Similarly when the temple came to be built, the pattern of it, we are told, was given of Jehovah "by his Spirit" to David (I Chron. xxviii. 12). Quite near to these gifts, but on a higher plane, lies the supernatural gift of wisdom for the administration of judgment and government. Moses was so endowed. And, therefore, the seventy elders were also endowed with it, to fit them to share his cares: "And I will take of the Spirit which is upon thee," said Jehovah, "and will put it upon them; and they shall bear the burden of the people with thee" (Num. xi. 17, 25).[17] It is in this sense also, doubtless, that Joshua is said to have been full of the Spirit of wisdom (Num. xxvii. 18, Deut. xxxiv. 9).[18] In these aspects, the gift of the Spirit, appearing as it does as an endowment for office, is sometimes sacramentally con-

---

[17] The idea of communicating to others the Spirit already resting on one occurs again in II Kings ii. 9, 15, of the communication of Elijah's Spirit (of Prophecy) to Elisha.   Cf. Oehler, "Biblical Theology of the Old Testament," § 65.

[18] Cf. the prayer and endowment of Solomon, in I Kgs. iii.

nected with symbols of conference: in the case of Joshua with the laying on of hands (Deut. xxxiv. 9), in the cases of Saul and David with anointing (I Sam. x. 1, xvi. 13). Possibly its symbolical connection in Samson's case with Nazaritic length of hair may be classed in the same general category.

Prominent above all other theocratic gifts of the Spirit, however, are the gifts of supernatural knowledge and insight, culminating in the great gift of Prophecy. This greatest of gifts in the service of the Kingdom of God is sometimes very closely connected with the other gifts which have been mentioned. Thus the presence of the Spirit in the seventy elders in the wilderness, endowing them to share the burden of judgment with Moses, was manifested by prophetic utterance (Num. xi. 25). The descent of the Spirit upon Saul was likewise manifested by his prophesying (I Sam. x. 6, 10). Sometimes the Spirit's presence in the prophet even manifests itself in the production in others of what may be called sympathetic prophecy accompanied with ecstasy. Instances occur in the cases of the messengers sent by Saul and of Saul himself, when they went to apprehend David (I Sam. xix. 20, 23); and in these cases the phenomenon served the ulterior purpose of a protection for the prophets.[19] In the visions of Ezekiel the presence of the inspiring Spirit is manifested in physical as well as in mental effects (Ezek. iii. 12, 14, 24, viii. 3, xi. 1, 5, 24, xxxvii. 1). Thus clear it is that all these work one and the same Spirit.

In all cases, however, Prophecy is the free gift of the Spirit of God to special organs chosen for the purpose of the revelation of His will. It is so represented in the cases of Balaam (Num. xxiv. 2), of Saul (I Sam. x. 6), of David (I Sam. xvi. 13), of Azariah the son of Oded (II Chron. xv. 1), of Jahaziel the son of Zechariah (II Chron. xx. 14), of Zechariah the son of Jehoiada (II Chron. xxiv. 20). To Hosea, "the man that hath the Spirit" was a synonym for "prophet" (ix. 7). Isaiah (xlviii. 16) in a somewhat puzzling sentence declares, "The Lord God hath sent me and His Spirit," which seems to con-

---

[19] Compare the cases of the communication of the Spirit, in a different way, in Num. xi. 17, 25, 26 and II Kgs. ii. 9, 15 — already mentioned.

join the Spirit either with Jehovah as the source of the mission,
or else with the prophet as the bearer of the message; and, in
either case, refers the prophetic inspiration to the Spirit. A
very full insight into the nature of the Spirit's work in prophetic
inspiration is provided by the details which Ezekiel gives of
the Spirit's mode of dealing with him in communicating his
visions. While the richness of the prophetic endowment is indicated to us by Micah (iii. 8): "But I truly am full of power by
the Spirit of the Lord, and of judgment, and of might, to declare unto Jacob his transgression, and to Israel his sin." There
are, however, two passages that speak quite generally of the
whole body of prophets as Spirit-led men, which, in their brief
explicitness, deserve to be called the classical passages as to
prophetic inspiration. In one of these, — the great psalm-
prayer of the Levites recorded in the ninth chapter of Nehemiah, — God is first lauded for "giving His good Spirit to
instruct" His people, by the mouth of Moses; and then further
praised for enduring this people through so many years and
"testifying against them by His Spirit through His prophets"
(Neh. ix. 20, 30). Here the prophets are conceived as a body of
official messengers, through whom the Spirit of God made
known His will to His people through all the ages. In exactly
similar wise, Zechariah testifies that the Lord of Hosts had sent
His words "by His Spirit by the hand of the former prophets"
(Zech. vii. 12). These are quite comprehensive statements.
They include the whole series of the prophets, and they represent them as the official mouthpieces of the Spirit of God,
serving the people of God as His organs.[20]

It is sufficiently clear that an official character attaches to
all the manifestations of what we have called the theocratic
Spirit. The theocratic Spirit appears to be represented as the
executive of the Godhead within the sacred nation, the divine
power working in the nation for the protection, governing, instruction and leading of the people to its destined goal. The

---

[20] In such passages as Gen. xli. 38, Dan. iv. 8, ix. 18 and v. 11, 14, we have
"the Spirit of the Gods" as the equivalent of "the Spirit of God" on the lips of
heathen.

Levitic prayer in the ninth chapter of Nehemiah traces the history of God's people with great fulness; and all through this history represents God as not only looking down from heaven upon His people, leading them, but, as it were, working within them, inspiring organs for their government and instruction. — "clothing Himself with these" organs as the media of His working, as the expressive Hebrew sometimes suggests (Judges vi. 34, I Chron. xii. 18, II Chron. xxiv. 20). The aspect in which the theocratic Spirit seems to be conceived is as God in His people, manifesting Himself through inspired instruments in supernatural leading and teaching. Very illuminating as to the mode of His working are the instructions given to Zerubbabel through the prophets Zechariah and Haggai. He — and, with him, all the people of the land — is counseled to be strong and of good courage, "for I am with you, saith the Lord of Hosts, according to the word that I covenanted with you when you came out of Egypt, and my Spirit abideth among you: fear ye not" (Hag. ii. 5). "This is the word of the Lord unto Zerubbabel, saying, Not by might, nor by power, but by my Spirit, saith the Lord of Hosts" (Zech. iv. 6). The mountains of opposition are to be reduced to a plain; but not by armed force. The symbol of the source of strength is the seven lamps burning brightly by virtue of perennial supplies from the living olives growing by their side; thus, by a hidden, divine supply of deathless life, the Church of God lives and prospers in the world. Not indeed as if God so inhabited Israel, that all that the house of Israel does is of the Lord. "Shall it be said, O house of Israel, Is the Spirit of the Lord straitened? — are these his doings? Do not my words do good to him that walketh uprightly?" (Micah ii. 7). The gift of the Spirit is only for good. But there is very clearly brought before us here the fact and the mode of God's official inspiration. The theocratic Spirit represents, in a word, the presence of God with His people. And in the Old Testament teaching concerning it, is firmly laid the foundation of the Christian doctrine of God in the Church, leading and guiding it, and supplying it with all needed instruction, powers and graces for its preservation in the world.

We must not omit to observe that in this higher sphere of the theocratic Spirit, the freedom and, so to speak, detachment of the informing Spirit is even more thoroughly guarded than in the case of His cosmical relations. If in the lower sphere the Spirit hovered over rather than was submerged in matter, so here He acts upon His chosen organs in the same sense from without, so that it is impossible to confound His official gifts with their native powers, however exalted. The Spirit here, too, is given by God (Num. xi. 29, Isa. xlii. 1). God puts it on men or fills men with it (Num. xi. 25, Ex. xxviii. 3, xxxi. 3); or the Spirit comes (Jud. iii. 10, xi. 29), comes mightily (xiv. 6, 19, etc., I Sam. xi. 6) upon men, falls on them (Ezek. xi. 5), breaks in upon them, seizes them violently, as it were, and puts them on as a garment (Judg. vi. 34). And this is no less true of the prophets than of the other organs of the Spirit's theocratic work: they are all the instruments of a mighty power, which, though in one sense it is conceived as the endowment of the theocratic people, in another sense is conceived as seizing upon its organs from without and above. And "because it is thus fundamentally a power seizing man powerfully, often violently," it is often replaced by the locution, "the hand of Jehovah," [21] which is, in this usage, the equivalent of the Spirit of Jehovah (II Kgs. iii. 15, Ezek. i. 3, iii. 14, 22, xxxiii. 22, xxxvii. 1, xl. 1). The intermittent character of the theocratic gifts still further emphasized their gift by a personal Spirit working purposively. They were not permanent possessions of the theocratic organs, to be used according to their own will, but came and went according to the divine gift.[22] The theocratic gifts of the Spirit are, in a word, everywhere emphatically gifts *from* God as well as *of* God; and every tendency to conceive of them as formally the

[21] Cf. Orelli, "The Old Testament Prophecy," etc., E. T. p. 11, and also Oehler, "Biblical Theology of Old Testament," § 65 *ad fin.*

[22] Cf. A. B. Davidson, (*The Expositor*, July, 1895, p. 1): "The view that prevailed among the people — and it seems the view of the Old Testament writers themselves — appears to have been this: the prophet did not speak out of a general inspiration of Jehovah, bestowed upon him once for all, as, say, at his call; each particular word that he spoke, whether a prediction or a practical counsel, was due to a special inspiration, exerted on him for the occasion." The statement might well have been stronger.

result of a general inspiration of the nation instead of a special inspiration of the chosen organs is rebuked by every allusion to them. God working in and through man, by whatever variety of inspiration, works divinely and from above. He is no more merged in His church than in the creation, but is, in all His operations alike, the free, transcendent Spirit, dividing to each man severally as He will.

The representations concerning the official theocratic Spirit culminate in Isaiah's prophetic descriptions of the Spirit-endowed Messiah:

"And there shall come forth a shoot out of the stock of Jesse, and a branch out of his roots shall bear fruit: and the Spirit of the Lord shall rest upon him, the Spirit of wisdom and 'understanding, the Spirit of counsel and might, the Spirit of knowledge and of the fear of the Lord; and his delight shall be in the fear of the Lord: and he shall not judge after the sight of his eyes, neither reprove after the hearing of his ears: but with righteousness shall he judge the poor, and reprove with equity for the meek of the earth: and he shall smite the earth with the rod of his mouth, and with the breath of his lips shall he slay the wicked. And righteousness shall be the girdle of his loins, and faithfulness the girdle of his reins" (Isa. xi. 1 sq.).

"Behold my servant whom I uphold; my chosen in whom my soul delighteth: I have put my Spirit upon him; he shall bring forth judgment to the Gentiles. . . . He shall bring forth judgment in truth. He shall not fail nor be discouraged, till he have set judgment in the earth; and the isles shall wait for his law. Thus saith God the Lord, he that created the heavens, and stretched them forth; he that spread abroad the earth and that which cometh out of it; he that giveth breath unto the people upon it and Spirit to them that walk therein; I the Lord have called thee in righteousness, and will hold thine hand and will keep thee, and give thee for a covenant of the people, for a light of the Gentiles; to open the blind eyes, to bring out the prisoners from the dungeon, and them that sit in darkness out of the prison-house. I am the Lord: that is my name: and my glory will I not give to another, neither my praise unto graven images" (Isa. xlii. 1 sq.).

"The Spirit of the Lord God is upon me" — this is the response of the Messiah to such gracious promises — "because the Lord hath anointed me to preach good-tidings unto the meek; he hath sent me to bind up the broken hearted, to proclaim liberty to the captives, and the opening of the prison to them that are bound; to proclaim the acceptable year of the Lord, and the day of vengeance of our God; to comfort all that mourn; to appoint unto them that mourn in Zion, to give unto them a garland for ashes, the oil of gladness for mourning, the garment of praise for the spirit of heaviness; that they might be called trees of righteousness, the planting of the Lord, that he might be glorified" (Isa. lxi. 1 *sq.*).

No one will fail to observe in these beautiful descriptions of the endowments of the Messiah, how all the theocratic endowments which had been given separately to others unite upon Him; so that all previous organs of the Spirit appear but as partial types of Him to whom as we are told in the New Testament, God "giveth not the Spirit by measure" (John iii. 34). Here we perceive the difference between the Messiah and other recipients of the Spirit. To them the Spirit had been "meted out" (Isa. xl. 13), according to their place and function in the development of the kingdom of God; upon Him it was poured out without measure. By Him, accordingly, the kingdom of God is consummated. The descriptions of the spiritual endowments of the Messiah are descriptions also, as will no doubt have been noted, of the consummated kingdom of God. His endowment also was not for himself but for the kingdom; it, too, was official. Nevertheless, it was the source in Him of all personal graces also, the opulence and perfection of which are fully described. And thus He becomes the type not only of the theocratic work of the Spirit, but also of His work upon the individual soul, perfecting it after the image of God.

THE INDIVIDUAL SPIRIT

2. And this brings us naturally to the second aspect in which the Spirit is presented to us in relation to the new creation — His relation to the individual soul, working inwardly in the spirits of men, fitting the children of God for the kingdom of God, even as, working in the nation as such, He, as theocratic Spirit, was preparing God's kingdom for His people. In this

aspect He appears specifically as the Spirit of grace. As He is
the source of all cosmical life, and of all theocratic life, so is
He also the source of all spiritual life. He upholds the soul in
being and governs it as part of the great world He has created;
He makes it sharer in the theocratic blessings which He brings
to His people; but He deals with it, too, within, conforming it
to its ideal. In a word, the Spirit of God, in the Old Testament,
is not merely the immanent Spirit, the source of all the world's
life and all the world's movement; and not merely the inspiring
Spirit, the source of His church's strength and safety and of its
development in accordance with its special mission; He is as
well the indwelling Spirit of holiness in the hearts of God's
children. As Hermann Schultz puts it: "The mysterious impulses which enable a man to lead a life well-pleasing to God,
are not regarded as a development of human environment, but
are nothing else than 'the Spirit of God.' which is also called
as being the Spirit peculiarly God's — His Holy Spirit." [23]

We have already had occasion to note that these personal
effects of the Spirit's work are sometimes very closely connected
with others of His operations. Already as the immanent Spirit
of life, indeed, as we saw, there did not lack a connection of
His activity with ethical considerations (Gen. vi. 3). We will
remember, too, that Nehemiah recalls the goodness — *i.e.*, possibly the graciousness — of the Spirit, when He came to instruct Israel in the person of Moses in the wilderness: "Thou
gavest also thy good Spirit to instruct them" (Neh. ix. 20).[24]
When the Spirit came upon Saul, endowing him for his theocratic work, it is represented as having also a very far-reaching
personal effect upon him. "The Spirit of the Lord will come
mightly upon thee," says Samuel, "and thou shalt prophesy
with them, and shalt be turned into another man" (I Sam. x. 6).
"And it was so" adds the narrative, "that when he had turned
his back to go from Samuel, God gave him a new heart," or,

[23] *Op. cit.* ii, p. 203. The passage is cited for its main idea: we demur, of course,
to some of its implications.

[24] In Num. xiv. 24 we are told that Caleb followed the LORD fully, "because
he had another spirit in him," from that which animated his rebellious fellows.
Possibly the Spirit of the Lord may be intended.

as the Hebrew has it, "turned him a new heart." Possibly such revolutionary ethical consequences ordinarily attended the official gift of the Spirit, so that the gloss may be a true one which makes II Peter i. 21 declare that they were "holy men of God" who spake as they were moved by the Holy Ghost.[25]

At all events this conception of a thorough ethical change characterises the Old Testament idea of the inner work of the Spirit of Holiness, as He first comes to be called in the Psalms and Isaiah (Ps. li. 11; Isa. lxiii. 10, 11 only).[26] The classical passage in this connection is the Fifty-first Psalm — David's cry of penitence and prayer for mercy after Nathan's probing of his sin with Bathsheba. He prays for the creation within him of a new heart and the renewal of a right spirit within him; and he represents that all his hopes of continued power of new life rest on the continuance of God's holy Spirit, or of the Spirit of God's holiness, with him. Possibly the Spirit is here called holy, primarily, because He is one who cannot dwell in a wicked heart; but it seems also to be implicated that David looks upon Him as the author within him of that holiness without which he cannot hope to see the Lord. A like conception meets us in another Psalm ascribed to David, the One Hundred and Forty-third "Teach me to do thy will; for thou art my God: thy Spirit is good; lead me in the land of uprightness." The two conceptions of the divine grace and holiness are also combined by Isaiah in an account of how Israel had been, since the days of Moses, dealing ungratefully with God, and, by their rebellion, grieving "the Holy Spirit whom He had graciously put in

---

[25] Exceptions are found, of course; such as the cases of Balaam, Samson, etc. Cf. H. G. Mitchell, "Inspiration in the Old Testament," in *Christian Thought* for December 1893, p. 190.

[26] Cf. F. H. Woods, in *The Expository Times*, July, 1895, p. 462–463: "It may be extremely difficult to say what was the precise meaning which prophet or psalmist attached to the phrases, 'the Spirit of God' and 'the Spirit of Holiness.' But such language, at any rate, shows that they realised the divine character of that inward power which makes for holiness and truth. 'Cast me not away from Thy presence, and take not the Spirit of Thy holiness from me' (Ps. li. 11). 'And now the Lord God hath sent me, and His Spirit' (Isa. xlviii. 16). 'Not by might, nor by power, but by My Spirit, saith Jehovah of Hosts' (Zech. iv. 6). In such passages as these we can see the germ of the fuller Christian thought."

the midst of them" (Isa. lxiii. 10, 11).[27] The conception may primarily be that the Spirit given to guide Israel was a Spirit of holiness in the sense that He could not brook sin in those with whom He dealt, but the conception that He would guide them in ways of holiness underlies that.

This aspect of the work of the Spirit of God is most richly developed, however, in prophecies of the future. In the Messianic times, Isaiah tells us, the Spirit shall be poured out from on high with the effect that judgment shall dwell in the wilderness and righteousness shall abide in the peaceful field (Isa. xxxii. 15). It is in such descriptions of the Messianic era as a time of the reign of the Spirit in the hearts of the people, that the opulence of His saving influences is developed. It is He who shall gather the children of God into the kingdom, so that no one shall be missing (Isa. xxxiv. 16). It is He who, as the source of all blessings, shall be poured out on the seed with the result that it shall spring up in the luxuriant growth and bear such rich fruitage that one shall cry 'I am the Lord's,' and another shall call himself by the name of Jacob, and another shall write on his hand, 'Unto the Lord,' and shall surname himself by the name of Israel (Isa. xliv. 3 *sq.*). It is His abiding presence which constitutes the preëminent blessing of the new covenant which Jehovah makes with His people in the day of redemption: "And as for me, this is my covenant with them, saith the Lord: my Spirit that is upon thee, and my words which I have put in thy mouth, shall not depart out of thy mouth, nor out of the mouth of thy seed, nor out of the mouth of thy seed's seed, saith the Lord, from henceforth and for ever" (Isa. lix. 21). The gift of the Spirit as an abiding presence in the heart of the individual is the crowning Messianic blessing. To precisely the same effect is the teaching of Ezekiel. The new heart and new spirit is one of the burdens of his message (xi. 19, xviii. 31, xxxvi. 26): and these are the Messianic gifts of God to His people through the Spirit. God's people are dead; but He will open their graves and cause them to come up out of their graves: "And I will put my Spirit in you, and ye

[27] Cf. Psalm cvi. 13.

shall live" (xxxvii. 14). They are in captivity; he will bring
them out of captivity: "Neither will I hide my face any more
from them: for I have poured out my Spirit upon the house of
Israel, saith the Lord God" (xxxix. 29). Like promises appear
in Zechariah: "And I will pour upon the house of David, and
upon the inhabitants of Jerusalem, the Spirit of grace and
supplication; and they shall look upon me whom they have
pierced" (xii. 10). It is the converting Spirit of God that is
spoken of. One thing only is left to complete the picture, — the
clear declaration that, in these coming days of blessing, the
Spirit hitherto given only to Israel shall be poured out upon
the whole world. This Joel gives us in that wonderful passage
which is applied by Peter to the out-pouring begun at Pentecost: "And it shall come to pass afterward," says the Lord
God through His prophet, "that I will pour out my Spirit upon
all flesh; . . . and also upon the servants and upon the hand-
maids in those days will I pour out my Spirit. . . . And it
shall come to pass, that whosoever shall call on the name of
the Lord shall be delivered" (ii. 28–32).

In this series of passages, the indwelling Spirit of the New
Testament is obviously brought before us — the indwelling
God, author of all holiness and of all salvation. Thus there are
firmly laid by them the foundations of the Christian doctrine
of Regeneration and Sanctification, — of God in the soul quickening its powers of spiritual life and developing it in holiness.
Nor can it be a ground of wonder that this aspect of His work
is less frequently dwelt upon than His theocratic activities; nor
that it is chiefly in prophecies of the future that the richer
references to it occur.[28] This was the time of theocratic development; the old dispensation was a time of preparation for the
fulness of spiritual graces. It is rather a ground of wonder that
even in few and scattered hints and in prophecies of the times
of the Spirit yet to come, such a deep and thorough grasp upon
His individual work should be exhibited.

By its presentation of this work of the Spirit in the heart,

[28] See such wonder, nevertheless, expressed by Dr. Dale, in a striking passage
in his "Christian Doctrine," p. 317.

the Old Testament completes its conception of the Spirit of God — the great conception of the immanent, inspiring, indwelling God. In it the three great ideas are thrown prominently forward, of God in the world, God in the Church, God in the soul: the God of Providence, the immanent source of all that comes to pass, the director and governor of the world of matter and spirit alike; the God of the Church, the inspiring source of all Church life and of all Church gifts, through which the Church is instructed, governed, preserved and extended; and the God of grace, the indwelling source of all holiness and of all religious aspirations, emotions and activities. Attention has already been called to the great enrichment which was brought to the general conception of God by this doctrine of the Spirit of God in its first aspect. The additional aspects in which He is presented in the pages of the Old Testament of course still further enrich and elevate the conception. By throwing a still stronger emphasis on the personality of the Spirit they made even wider the great gulf that already yawned between all Pantheising notions and the Biblical doctrine of the Personal God, the immanent source of all that comes to pass. And they bring out with great force and clearness the conceptions of grace and holiness as inherent in the idea of God working, and thus operate to deepen the ethical conception of the Divine Being. It is only as a personal, choosing, gracious and holy God, who bears His people on His heart for good, and who seeks to conform them in life and character to His own holiness — that we can conceive the God of the Old Testament, if we will attend to its doctrine of the Spirit. Thus the fundamental unity of the conception with that of the Holy Ghost of the New Testament grows ever more obvious, the more attentively it is considered. The Spirit of God of the Old Testament performs all the functions which are ascribed to the Holy Ghost of the New Testament, and bears all the same characteristics. They are conceived alike both in their nature and in their operations. We cannot help identifying them.

Such an identification need not involve, however, the assertion that the Spirit of God was conceived in the Old Testament as the Holy Ghost is in the New, as a distinct hypostasis in the divine nature. Whether this be so, or, if so in some measure, how far it may be true, is a matter for separate investigation. The Spirit of God certainly acts as a person and is presented to us as a person, throughout the Old Testament. In no passage is He conceived otherwise than personally — as a free, willing, intelligent being. This is, however, in itself only the pervasive testimony of the Scriptures to the personality of God. For it is equally true that the Spirit of God is everywhere in the Old Testament identified with God. This is only its pervasive testimony to the divine unity. The question for examination is, how far the one personal God was conceived of as embracing in His unity hypostatical distinctions. This question is a very complicated one and needs very delicate treatment. There are, indeed, three questions included in the general one, which for the sake of clearness we ought to keep apart. We may ask, May the Christian properly see in the Spirit of God of the Old Testament the personal Holy Spirit of the New? This we may answer at once in the affirmative. We may ask again, Are there any hints in the Old Testament anticipating and adumbrating the revelation of the hypostatic Spirit of the New? This also, it seems, we ought to answer in the affirmative. We may ask again, Are these hints of such clearness as actually to reveal this doctrine, apart from the revelation of the New Testament? This should be doubtless answered in the negative. There are hints, and they serve for points of attachment for the fuller New Testament teaching. But they are only hints, and, apart from the New Testament teaching, would be readily explained as personifications or ideal objectivations of the power of God. Undoubtedly, side by side with the stress put upon the unity of God and the identity of the Spirit with the God who gives it, there is a distinction recognized between God and His Spirit — in the sense at least of a discrimination between God over all and God in all, between the Giver and the Given, between the Source and the Executor of the moral law. This distinction already emerges in Genesis i. 2; and it does not grow less observable as we advance through the Old

Testament. It is prominent in the standing phrases by which, on the one hand, God is spoken of as sending, putting, placing, pouring, emptying His Spirit upon man, and on the other the Spirit is spoken of as coming, resting, falling, springing upon man. There is a sort of objectifying of the Spirit over against God in both cases; in the former case, by sending Him from Himself God, as it were, separates Him from Himself; in the latter, He appears almost as a distinct person, acting *sua sponte*. Schultz does not hesitate to speak of the Spirit even in Genesis i. 2 as appearing "as very independent, just like a hypostasis or person." [29] Kleinert finds in this passage at least a tendency towards hypostatizing — though he thinks this tendency was not subsequently worked out.[30] Perhaps we are warranted in saying as much as this — that there is observable in the Old Testament, not, indeed, an hypostatizing of the Spirit of God, but a tendency towards it — that, in Hofmann's cautious language, the Spirit appears in the Old Testament "as somewhat distinct from the 'I' of God which God makes the principle of life in the world." [31] A preparation, at least, for the full revelation of the Trinity in the New Testament is observable; [32] points of connection with it are discoverable; and so Christians are able to read the Old Testament without offence, and to find without confusion their own Holy Spirit in its Spirit of God.[33]

[29] *Op. cit.* ii. p. 184.

[30] *Op. cit.* pp. 55–56.

[31] "Schriftbeweis," i. p. 187.

[32] Cf. Oehler, *op. cit.* § 65, note 5. He looks on Isa. xliii. 16 as implying personality and reminds us that the Old Testament prepared the way for the œconomic Trinity of the new. Cf. also Dale, "Christian Doctrine," p. 317.

[33] Cf. Dr. Hodge's admirable summary statement: "Even in the first chapter of Genesis, the Spirit of God is represented as the source of all intelligence, order and life in the created universe; and in the following books of the Old Testament He is represented as inspiring the prophets, giving wisdom, strength and goodness to statesmen and warriors, and to the people of God. This Spirit is not an agency but an agent, who teaches and selects; who can be sinned against and grieved; and who in the New Testament is unmistakably revealed as a distinct person. When John the Baptist appeared, we find him speaking of the Holy Spirit as of a person with whom his countrymen were familiar, as an object of Divine worship and the giver of saving blessings. Our divine Lord also takes this truth for granted,

More than this could scarcely be looked for. The elements in the doctrine of God which above all others needed emphasis in Old Testament times were naturally His unity and His personality. The great thing to be taught the ancient people of God was that the God of all the earth is one person. Over against the varying idolatries about them, this was the truth of truths for which Israel was primarily to stand; and not until this great truth was ineffaceably stamped upon their souls could the personal distinctions in the Triune-God be safely made known to them. A premature revelation of the Spirit as a distinct hypostasis could have wrought nothing but harm to the people of God. We shall all no doubt agree with Kleinert [34] that it is pragmatic in Isidore of Pelusium to say that Moses knew the doctrine of the Trinity well enough, but concealed it through fear that Polytheism would profit by it. But we may safely affirm this of God the Revealer, in the gradual delivery of the truth concerning Himself to men. He reveals the whole truth, but in divers portions and in divers manners: and it was incident to the progressive delivery of doctrine that the unity of the Godhead should first be made the firm possession of men, and the Trinity in that unity should be unveiled to them only afterwards, when the times were ripe for it. What we need wonder over is not that the hypostatical distinctness of the Spirit is not more clearly revealed in the Old Testament but that the approaches to it are laid so skillfully that the doctrine of the hypostatical Holy Spirit of the New Testament finds so many and such striking points of attachment in the Old Testament, and yet no Israelite had ever been disturbed in repeating with hearty faith his great Sch'ma, "Hear O Israel, the Lord our God is one Lord" (Deut. vi. 4). Not until the whole doctrine of the Trinity was ready to be manifested in

and promised to send the Spirit as a Paraclete, to take his place, to instruct, comfort and strengthen them; whom they were to receive and obey. Thus, without any violent transition, the earliest revelations of this mystery were gradually unfolded, until the triune God, Father, Son and Spirit, appears in the New Testament as the universally recognized God of all believers" (Charles Hodge, "Systematic Theology," i. p. 447).

[34] *Op. cit.* p. 56.

such visible form as at the baptism of Christ — God in heaven, God on earth and God descending from heaven to earth — could any part of the mystery be safely uncovered.

There yet remains an important query which we cannot pàss wholly by. We have seen the rich development of the doctrine of the Spirit in the Old Testament. We have seen the testimony the Old Testament bears to the activity of the Spirit of God throughout the old dispensation. What then is meant by calling the new dispensation the dispensation of the Spirit? What does John (vii. 39) mean by saying that the Spirit was not yet given because Jesus was not yet glorified? What our Lord Himself, when he promised the Comforter, by saying that the Comforter would not come until He went away and sent Him (John xvi. 7); and by breathing on His disciples, saying, "Receive ye the Holy Spirit" (John xx. 22)? What did the descent of the Spirit at Pentecost mean, when He came to inaugurate the dispensation of the Spirit? It cannot be meant that the Spirit was not active in the old dispensation. We have already seen that the New Testament writers themselves represent Him to have been active in the old dispensation in all the varieties of activity with which He is active in the new. Such passages seem to have diverse references. Some of them may refer to the specifically miraculous endowments which characterized the apostles and the churches which they founded.[35] Others refer to the world-wide mission of the Spirit, promised, indeed, in the Old Testament, but only now to be realized. But there is a more fundamental idea to be reckoned with still. This is the idea of the preparatory nature of the Old Testament dispensation. The old dispensation was a preparatory one and must be strictly conceived as such. What spiritual blessings came to it were by way of prelibation.[36] They were

[35] Cf. Redford, "Vox. Dei.," p. 236.

[36] Smeaton (*Op. cit.* p. 49) comments on John vii. 37 *sq.* thus: "But the apostle adds that 'the Spirit was not yet' because Christ's glorification had not yet arrived. He does not mean that the Spirit did not yet exist — for all Scripture attests His eternal preëxistence — nor that His regenerative efficacy was still unknown — for countless millions had been regenerated by His power since the first promise in Eden — but that these operations of the Spirit had been but an

many and various. The Spirit worked in Providence no less universally then than now. He abode in the Church not less really then than now. He wrought in the hearts of God's people not less prevalently then than now. All the good that was in the world was then as now due to Him. All the hope of God's Church then as now depended on Him. Every grace of the godly life then as now was a fruit of His working. But the object of the whole dispensation was only to prepare for the outpouring of the Spirit upon all flesh. He kept the remnant safe and pure; but it was primarily only in order that the seed might be preserved. This was the fundamental end of His activity, then. The dispensation of the Spirit, properly so-called, did not dawn until the period of preparation was over and the day of outpouring had come. The mustard seed had been preserved through all the ages only by the Spirit's brooding care. Now it is planted, and it is by His operation that it is growing up into a great tree which shades the whole earth, and to the branches of which all the fowls of heaven come for shelter. It is not that His work is more real in the new dispensation than in the old. It is not merely that it is more universal. It is that it is directed to a different end — that it is no longer for the mere preserving of the seed unto the day of planting, but for the perfecting of the fruitage and the gathering of the harvest. The Church, to use a figure of Isaiah's, was then like a pent-in stream; it is now like that pent-in stream with the barriers broken down and the Spirit of the Lord driving it. It was He who preserved it in being when it was pent in. It is He who is now driving on its gathered floods till it shall cover the earth as the waters cover the sea. In one word, that was a day in which the Spirit restrained His power. Now the great day of the Spirit is come.

anticipation of the atoning gift of Christ rather than a GIVING. The apostle speaks comparatively, not absolutely." Compare further the eloquent words on page 53 with the quotation there from Goodwin.

IV

THE BIBLICAL DOCTRINE OF
THE TRINITY

THE BIBLICAL DOCTRINE OF THE TRINITY [1]

THE term "Trinity" is not a Biblical term, and we are not using Biblical language when we define what is expressed by it as the doctrine that there is one only and true God, but in the unity of the Godhead there are three coeternal and coequal Persons, the same in substance but distinct in subsistence. A doctrine so defined can be spoken of as a Biblical doctrine only on the principle that the sense of Scripture is Scripture. And the definition of a Biblical doctrine in such un-Biblical language can be justified only on the principle that it is better to preserve the truth of Scripture than the words of Scripture. The doctrine of the Trinity lies in Scripture in solution; when it is crystallized from its solvent it does not cease to be Scriptural, but only comes into clearer view. Or, to speak without figure, the doctrine of the Trinity is given to us in Scripture, not in formulated definition, but in fragmentary allusions; when we assembled the *disjecta membra* into their organic unity, we are not passing from Scripture, but entering more thoroughly into the meaning of Scripture. We may state the doctrine in technical terms, supplied by philosophical reflection; but the doctrine stated is a genuinely Scriptural doctrine.

In point of fact, the doctrine of the Trinity is purely a revealed doctrine. That is to say, it embodies a truth which has never been discovered, and is indiscoverable, by natural reason. With all his searching, man has not been able to find out for himself the deepest things of God. Accordingly, ethnic thought has never attained a Trinitarian conception of God, nor does any ethnic religion present in its representations of the Divine Being any analogy to the doctrine of the Trinity.

[1] Article "Trinity" from *The International Standard Bible Encyclopaedia*, James Orr, General editor, v. v, pp. 3012–3022. Pub. Chicago, The Howard-Severance Co. 1915.

Triads of divinities, no doubt, occur in nearly all polytheistic religions, formed under very various influences. Sometimes, as in the Egyptian triad of Osiris, Isis and Horus, it is the analogy of the human family with its father, mother and son which lies at their basis. Sometimes they are the effect of mere syncretism, three deities worshipped in different localities being brought together in the common worship of all. Sometimes, as in the Hindu triad of Brahma, Vishnu and Shiva, they represent the cyclic movement of a pantheistic evolution, and symbolize the three stages of Being, Becoming and Dissolution. Sometimes they are the result apparently of nothing more than an odd human tendency to think in threes, which has given the number three widespread standing as a sacred number (so H. Usener). It is no more than was to be anticipated, that one or another of these triads should now and again be pointed to as the replica (or even the original) of the Christian doctrine of the Trinity. Gladstone found the Trinity in the Homeric mythology, the trident of Poseidon being its symbol. Hegel very naturally found it in the Hindu Trimurti, which indeed is very like his pantheizing notion of what the Trinity is. Others have perceived it in the Buddhist Triratna (Söderblom); or (despite their crass dualism) in some speculations of Parseeism; or, more frequently, in the notional triad of Platonism (e. g., Knapp); while Jules Martin is quite sure that it is present in Philo's neo-Stoical doctrine of the "powers," especially when applied to the explanation of Abraham's three visitors. Of late years, eyes have been turned rather to Babylonia; and H. Zimmern finds a possible forerunner of the Trinity in a Father, Son, and Intercessor, which he discovers in its mythology. It should be needless to say that none of these triads has the slightest resemblance to the Christian doctrine of the Trinity. The Christian doctrine of the Trinity embodies much more than the notion of "threeness," and beyond their "threeness" these triads have nothing in common with it.

As the doctrine of the Trinity is indiscoverable by reason, so it is incapable of proof from reason. There are no analogies to it in Nature, not even in the spiritual nature of man, who is made in the image of God. In His trinitarian mode of being, God is unique; and, as there is nothing in the universe like Him in this respect, so there is nothing which can help us to comprehend Him. Many attempts have, nevertheless, been made to construct a rational proof of the Trinity of the Godhead. Among these there are two which are particularly attractive, and have therefore been put forward again and again by speculative thinkers through all the Christian ages. These are derived from the implications, in the one case, of self-consciousness; in the other, of love. Both self-consciousness and love, it is said, demand for their very existence an object over against which the self stands as subject. If we conceive of God as self-conscious and loving, therefore, we cannot help conceiving of Him as embracing in His unity some form of plurality. From this general position both arguments have been elaborated, however, by various thinkers in very varied forms.

The former of them, for example, is developed by a great seventeenth century theologian — Bartholomew Keckermann (1614) — as follows: God is self-conscious thought: and God's thought must have a perfect object, existing eternally before it; this object to be perfect must be itself God; and as God is one, this object which is God must be the God that is one. It is essentially the same argument which is popularized in a famous paragraph (§ 73) of Lessing's "The Education of the Human Race." Must not God have an absolutely perfect representation of Himself — that is, a representation in which everything that is in Him is found? And would everything that is in God be found in this representation if His necessary reality were not found in it? If everything, everything without exception, that is in God is to be found in this representation, it cannot, therefore, remain a mere empty image, but must be an actual duplication of God. It is obvious that arguments like this prove too much. If God's representation of Himself, to be perfect, must possess the same kind of reality that He Himself possesses, it does not seem easy to deny that His representations of everything else must possess objective reality. And this would be as much as to say that the eternal objective coexistence of all that God can conceive is given in the very idea of God; and that is open pantheism. The logical flaw lies in including in the perfection of a representation qualities which are not proper to representations, however perfect. A perfect representation must, of course, have all the reality proper to a representation; but objective reality is so little proper to a representation that a representation acquiring it would cease to be a representation. This fatal flaw is not transcended, but only covered up, when the argument is compressed, as it is in most of its modern presentations, in effect to the mere assertion that the condition of self-consciousness is a real distinction between the thinking subject and the thought object, which, in God's case, would be between the subject ego and the object ego. Why, however, we should deny to God the power of self-contemplation enjoyed by every finite spirit, save at the cost of the distinct hypostatizing of the contemplant and the contemplated self, it is hard to understand. Nor is it always clear that what we get is a distinct hypostatization rather than a distinct substantializing of the contemplant and contemplated ego: not two persons in the Godhead so much as two Gods. The discovery of the third hypostasis — the Holy Spirit — remains meanwhile, to all these attempts rationally to construct a Trinity in the Divine Being, a standing puzzle which finds only a very artificial solution.

The case is much the same with the argument derived from the nature of love. Our sympathies go out to that old Valentinian writer — possibly it was Valentinus himself — who reasoned — perhaps he was the first so to reason — that "God is all love," "but love is not love unless there be an object of love." And they go out more richly still to Augustine, when, seeking a basis, not for a theory of emanations, but for the doctrine of the Trinity, he analyzes this love which God is into the triple implication of "the lover," "the loved" and "the love itself," and sees in this trinary of love an analogue of the Triune God. It requires, however, only that the argument thus broadly suggested should be developed into its details for its artificiality to become apparent. Richard of St. Victor works it out as follows: It belongs to the nature of *amor* that it should turn to another as *caritas*. This other, in God's case, cannot be the world; since such love of the world would be inordinate. It can only be a person; and a person who is God's equal in eternity, power and wisdom. Since, however, there cannot be two Divine substances, these two Divine persons must form one and the same substance. The best love cannot, however, confine itself to these two persons; it must become *condilectio* by the desire that a third should be equally loved as they love one another. Thus love, when perfectly conceived, leads necessarily to the Trinity, and since God is all He can be, this Trinity must be real. Modern writers (Sartorius, Schöberlein, J. Müller, Liebner, most lately R. H. Grützmacher) do not seem to have essentially improved upon such a statement as this. And after all is said, it does not appear clear that God's own all-perfect Being could not supply a satisfying object of His all-perfect love. To say that in its very nature love is self-communicative, and therefore implies an object other than self, seems an abuse of figurative language.

Perhaps the ontological proof of the Trinity is nowhere more attractively put than by Jonathan Edwards. The peculiarity of his presentation of it lies in an attempt to add plausibility to it by a doctrine of the nature of spiritual ideas or ideas of spiritual things, such as thought, love, fear, in general. Ideas of such things, he urges, are just repetitions of them, so that he who has an idea of any act of love, fear, anger or any other act or motion of the mind, simply so far repeats the motion in question; and if the idea be perfect and complete, the original motion of the mind is absolutely reduplicated. Edwards presses this so far that he is ready to contend that if a man could have an absolutely perfect idea of all that was in his mind at any past moment, he would really, to all intents and purposes, be over again what he was at that moment. And if he could perfectly contemplate all that is in his mind at any given moment, as it is and at the same time that it is there in its first and direct existence, he would really be two at that time, he would be twice at once: "The idea he has of himself would be himself again." This now is the case with the Divine Being. "God's idea of Himself is absolutely perfect, and therefore is an express and perfect image of Him, exactly like Him in every respect. . . . But that which is the express, perfect image of God and in every respect like Him is God, to all intents and purposes, because there is nothing wanting: there is nothing in the Deity that renders it the Deity but what has something exactly answering to it in this image, which will therefore also render that the Deity." The Second Person of the Trinity being thus attained, the argument advances. "The Godhead being thus begotten of God's loving [having?] an idea of Himself and showing forth in a distinct Subsistence or Person in that idea, there proceeds a most pure act, and an infinitely holy and sacred energy arises between the Father and the Son in mutually loving and delighting in each other. . . . The Deity becomes all act, the Divine essence itself flows out and is as it were breathed forth in love and joy. So that the Godhead therein stands forth in yet another manner of Subsistence, and there proceeds the Third Person in the Trinity, the Holy Spirit, viz., the Deity in act, for there is no other act but the act of the will." The inconclusiveness of the reasoning lies on the surface. The mind does not consist in its states, and the repetition of its states would not, therefore, duplicate or triplicate it. If it did, we should have a plurality of Beings, not of Persons in one Being. Neither God's perfect idea of Himself nor His perfect love of Himself reproduces Himself. He differs from His idea and His love of Himself precisely by that which distinguishes His Being from His acts. When it is said, then, that there is nothing in the Deity which renders it the Deity but what has something answering to it in its image of itself, it is enough to respond — except the Deity itself. What is wanting to the image to make it a second Deity is just objective reality.

Inconclusive as all such reasoning is, however, considered as rational demonstration of the reality of the Trinity, it is very far from possessing no value. It carries home to us in a very suggestive way the superiority of the Trinitarian conception of God to the conception of Him as an abstract monad, and thus brings important rational support to the doctrine of the Trinity, when once that doctrine has been given us by revelation. If it is not quite possible to say that we cannot conceive of God as eternal self-consciousness and eternal love, without conceiving Him as a Trinity, it does seem quite necessary to say that when we conceive Him as a Trinity, new fulness, richness, force are given to our conception of Him as a self-conscious, loving Being, and therefore we conceive Him more adequately than as a monad, and no one who has ever once conceived Him as a Trinity can ever again satisfy himself with a monadistic conception of God. Reason thus not only performs the important negative service to faith in the Trinity, of showing the self-consistency of the doctrine and its consistency with other known truth, but brings this positive rational support to it of discovering in it the only adequate conception of God as self-conscious spirit and living love. Difficult, therefore, as the idea of the Trinity in itself is, it does not come to us as an added burden upon our intelligence; it brings us rather the solution of the deepest and most persistent difficulties in our conception of God as infinite moral Being, and illuminates, enriches and elevates all our thought of God. It has accordingly become a commonplace to say that Christian theism is the only stable theism. That is as much as to say that theism requires the enriching conception of the Trinity to give it a permanent hold upon the human mind — the mind finds it difficult to rest in the idea of an abstract unity for its God; and that the human heart cries out for the living God in whose Being there is that fulness of life for which the conception of the Trinity alone provides.

So strongly is it felt in wide circles that a Trinitarian conception is essential to a worthy idea of God, that there is abroad a deep-seated unwillingness to allow that God could ever have made Himself known otherwise than as a Trinity. From this point of view it is inconceivable that the Old Testament revelation should know nothing of the Trinity. Accordingly, I. A. Dorner, for example, reasons thus: "If, however — and this is the faith of universal Christendom — a living idea of God must be thought in some way after a Trinitarian fashion, it must be antecedently probable that traces of the Trinity cannot be lacking in the Old Testament, since its idea of God is a living or historical one." Whether there really exist traces of the idea of the Trinity in the Old Testament, however, is a nice question. Certainly we cannot speak broadly of the revelation of the doctrine of the Trinity in the Old Testament. It is a plain matter of fact that none who have depended on the revelation embodied in the Old Testament alone have ever attained to the doctrine of the Trinity. It is another question, however, whether there may not exist in the pages of the Old Testament turns of expression or records of occurrences in which one already acquainted with the doctrine of the Trinity may fairly see indications of an underlying implication of it. The older writers discovered intimations of the Trinity in such phenomena as the plural form of the Divine name *Ĕlōhīm*, the occasional employment with reference to God of plural pronouns ("Let us make man in our image," Gen. i. 26; iii. 22; xi. 7; Isa. vi. 8), or of plural verbs (Gen. xx. 13; xxxv. 7), certain repetitions of the name of God which seem to distinguish between God and God (Ps. xlv. 6, 7; cx. 1; Hos. i. 7), threefold liturgical formulas Num. vi. 24, 26; Isa. vi. 3), a certain tendency to hypostatize the conception of Wisdom (Prov. viii.), and especially the remarkable phenomena connected with the appearances of the Angel of Jehovah (Gen. xvi. 2–13, xxii. 11. 16; xxxi. 11, 13; xlviii. 15, 16; Ex. iii. 2, 4, 5; Jgs. xiii. 20–22). The tendency of more recent authors is to appeal, not so much to specific texts of the Old Testament, as to the very "organism of revelation" in the Old Testament in which there is perceived an underlying suggestion "that all things owe their existence and persistence to a threefold cause," both with reference to the first creation, and, more plainly, with reference to the second creation. Passages like Ps. xxxiii. 6; Isa. lxi. 1; lxiii. 9–12; Hag. ii. 5, 6, in which God and His Word and His Spirit are brought together, co-causes of effects, are adduced. A tendency is pointed out to hypostatize the Word of God on the one hand (e. g., Gen. i. 3; Ps. xxxiii. 6; cvii. 20; cxlvii. 15–18; Isa.

lv. 11); and, especially in Ezek. and the later Prophets, the
Spirit of God, on the other (e. g., Gen. i. 2; Isa. xlviii. 16; lxiii.
10; Ezek. ii. 2; viii. 3; Zec. vii. 12). Suggestions — in Isa. for
instance (vii. 14; ix. 6) — of the Deity of the Messiah are appealed to. And if the occasional occurrence of plural verbs and
pronouns referring to God, and the plural form of the name
Elohim, are not insisted upon as in themselves evidence of a
multiplicity in the Godhead, yet a certain weight is lent them
as witnesses that "the God of revelation is no abstract unity,
but the living, true God, who in the fulness of His life embraces
the highest variety" (Bavinck). The upshot of it all is that it
is very generally felt that, somehow, in the Old Testament
development of the idea of God there is a suggestion that the
Deity is not a simple monad, and that thus a preparation is
made for the revelation of the Trinity yet to come. It would
seem clear that we must recognize in the Old Testament doctrine of the relation of God to His revelation by the creative
Word and the Spirit, at least the germ of the distinctions in
the Godhead afterward fully made known in the Christian
revelation. And we can scarcely stop there. After all is said, in
the light of the later revelation, the Trinitarian interpretation
remains the most natural one of the phenomena which the older
writers frankly interpreted as intimations of the Trinity; especially of those connected with the descriptions of the Angel
of Jehovah no doubt, but also even of such a form of expression
as meets us in the "Let us make man in our image" of Gen. i.
26 — for surely verse 27: "And God created man in his own
image," does not encourage us to take the preceding verse as
announcing that man was to be created in the image of the
angels. This is not an illegitimate reading of New Testament
ideas back into the text of the Old Testament; it is only reading the text of the Old Testament under the illumination of
the New Testament revelation. The Old Testament may be
likened to a chamber richly furnished but dimly lighted; the
introduction of light brings into it nothing which was not in it
before; but it brings out into clearer view much of what is in
it but was only dimly or even not at all perceived before. The

mystery of the Trinity is not revealed in the Old Testament; but the mystery of the Trinity underlies the Old Testament revelation, and here and there almost comes into view. Thus the Old Testament revelation of God is not corrected by the fuller revelation which follows it, but only perfected, extended and enlarged.

It is an old saying that what becomes patent in the New Testament was latent in the Old Testament. And it is important that the continuity of the revelation of God contained in the two Testaments should not be overlooked or obscured. If we find some difficulty in perceiving for ourselves, in the Old Testament, definite points of attachment for the revelation of the Trinity, we cannot help perceiving with great clearness in the New Testament abundant evidence that its writers felt no incongruity whatever between their doctrine of the Trinity and the Old Testament conception of God. The New Testament writers certainly were not conscious of being "setters forth of strange gods." To their own apprehension they worshipped and proclaimed just the God of Israel; and they laid no less stress than the Old Testament itself upon His unity (Jn. xvii. 3; I Cor. viii. 4; I Tim. ii. 5). They do not, then, place two new gods by the side of Jehovah as alike with Him to be served and worshipped; they conceive Jehovah as Himself at once Father, Son and Spirit. In presenting this one Jehovah as Father, Son and Spirit, they do not even betray any lurking feeling that they are making innovations. Without apparent misgiving they take over Old Testament passages and apply them to Father, Son and Spirit indifferently. Obviously they understand themselves, and wish to be understood, as setting forth in the Father, Son and Spirit just the one God that the God of the Old Testament revelation is; and they are as far as possible from recognizing any breach between themselves and the Fathers in presenting their enlarged conception of the Divine Being. This may not amount to saying that they saw the doctrine of the Trinity everywhere taught in the Old Testament. It certainly amounts to saying that they saw the Triune God whom they worshipped in the God of the Old

Testament revelation, and felt no incongruity in speaking of their Triune God in the terms of the Old Testament revelation. The God of the Old Testament was their God, and their God was a Trinity, and their sense of the identity of the two was so complete that no question as to it was raised in their minds.

The simplicity and assurance with which the New Testament writers speak of God as a Trinity have, however, a further implication. If they betray no sense of novelty in so speaking of Him, this is undoubtedly in part because it was no longer a novelty so to speak of Him. It is clear, in other words, that, as we read the New Testament, we are not witnessing the birth of a new conception of God. What we meet with in its pages is a firmly established conception of God underlying and giving its tone to the whole fabric. It is not in a text here and there that the New Testament bears its testimony to the doctrine of the Trinity. The whole book is Trinitarian to the core; all its teaching is built on the assumption of the Trinity; and its allusions to the Trinity are frequent, cursory, easy and confident. It is with a view to the cursoriness of the allusions to it in the New Testament that it has been remarked that "the doctrine of the Trinity is not so much heard as overheard in the statements of Scripture." It would be more exact to say that it is not so much inculcated as presupposed. The doctrine of the Trinity does not appear in the New Testament in the making, but as already made. It takes its place in its pages, as Gunkel phrases it, with an air almost of complaint, already "in full completeness" (*völlig fertig*), leaving no trace of its growth. "There is nothing more wonderful in the history of human thought," says Sanday, with his eye on the appearance of the doctrine of the Trinity in the New Testament, "than the silent and imperceptible way in which this doctrine, to us so difficult, took its place without struggle — and without controversy — among accepted Christian truths." The explanation of this remarkable phenomenon is, however, simple. Our New Testament is not a record of the development of the doctrine or of its assimilation. It everywhere presupposes the doctrine as the fixed possession of the Christian community; and the process by which it became the possession of the Christian community lies behind the New Testament.

We cannot speak of the doctrine of the Trinity, therefore, if we study exactness of speech, as revealed in the New Testament, any more than we can speak of it as revealed in the Old Testament. The Old Testament was written before its revelation; the New Testament after it. The revelation itself was made not in word but in deed. It was made in the incarnation of God the Son, and the outpouring of God the Holy Spirit. The relation of the two Testaments to this revelation is in the one case that of preparation for it, and in the other that of product of it. The revelation itself is embodied just in Christ and the Holy Spirit. This is as much as to say that the revelation of the Trinity was incidental to, and the inevitable effect of, the accomplishment of redemption. It was in the coming of the Son of God in the likeness of sinful flesh to offer Himself a sacrifice for sin; and in the coming of the Holy Spirit to convict the world of sin, of righteousness and of judgment, that the Trinity of Persons in the Unity of the Godhead was once for all revealed to men. Those who knew God the Father, who loved them and gave His own Son to die for them; and the Lord Jesus Christ, who loved them and delivered Himself up an offering and sacrifice for them; and the Spirit of Grace, who loved them and dwelt within them a power not themselves, making for righteousness, knew the Triune God and could not think or speak of God otherwise than as triune. The doctrine of the Trinity, in other words, is simply the modification wrought in the conception of the one only God by His complete revelation of Himself in the redemptive process. It necessarily waited, therefore, upon the completion of the redemptive process for its revelation, and its revelation, as necessarily, lay complete in the redemptive process.

From this central fact we may understand more fully several circumstances connected with the revelation of the Trinity to which allusion has been made. We may from it understand, for example, why the Trinity was not revealed in the Old Testament. It may carry us a little way to remark, as it has been customary to remark since the time of Gregory of Nazianzus, that it was the task of the Old Testament revelation to fix firmly in the minds and hearts of the people of God the great fundamental truth of the unity of the Godhead; and it would have been dangerous to speak to them of the plurality within this unity until this task had been fully accomplished. The real reason for the delay in the revelation of the Trinity, however, is grounded in the secular development of the redemptive purpose of God: the times were not ripe for the revelation of the Trinity in the unity of the Godhead until the fulness of the time had come for God to send forth His Son unto redemption, and His Spirit unto sanctification. The revelation in word must needs wait upon the revelation in fact, to which it brings its necessary explanation, no doubt, but from which also it derives its own entire significance and value. The revelation of a Trinity in the Divine unity as a mere abstract truth without relation to manifested fact, and without significance to the development of the kingdom of God, would have been foreign to the whole method of the Divine procedure as it lies exposed to us in the pages of Scripture. Here the working-out of the Divine purpose supplies the fundamental principle to which all else, even the progressive stages of revelation itself, is subsidiary; and advances in revelation are ever closely connected with the advancing accomplishment of the redemptive purpose. We may understand also, however, from the same central fact, why it is that the doctrine of the Trinity lies in the New Testament rather in the form of allusions than in express teaching, why it is rather everywhere presupposed, coming only here and there into incidental expression, than formally inculcated. It is because the revelation, having been made in the actual occurrences of redemption, was already the common property of all Christian hearts. In speaking and writing to one another, Christians, therefore, rather spoke out of their common Trinitarian consciousness, and reminded one another of their common fund of belief, than instructed one another in what was already the common property of all. We are to look for, and we shall find, in the New Testament allusions to the Trinity, rather evidence of how the Trinity, believed in by all, was conceived by the authoritative teachers of the church, than formal attempts, on their part, by authoritative declarations, to bring the church into the understanding that God is a Trinity.

The fundamental proof that God is a Trinity is supplied thus by the fundamental revelation of the Trinity in fact: that is to say, in the incarnation of God the Son and the outpouring of God the Holy Spirit. In a word, Jesus Christ and the Holy Spirit are the fundamental proof of the doctrine of the Trinity. This is as much as to say that all the evidence of whatever kind, and from whatever source derived, that Jesus Christ is God manifested in the flesh, and that the Holy Spirit is a Divine Person, is just so much evidence for the doctrine of the Trinity; and that when we go to the New Testament for evidence of the Trinity we are to seek it, not merely in the scattered allusions to the Trinity as such, numerous and instructive as they are, but primarily in the whole mass of evidence which the New Testament provides of the Deity of Christ and the Divine personality of the Holy Spirit. When we have said this, we have said in effect that the whole mass of the New Testament is evidence for the Trinity. For the New Testament is saturated with evidence of the Deity of Christ and the Divine personality of the Holy Spirit. Precisely what the New Testament is, is the documentation of the religion of the incarnate Son and of the outpoured Spirit, that is to say, of the religion of the Trinity, and what we mean by the doctrine of the Trinity is nothing but the formulation in exact language of the conception of God presupposed in the religion of the incarnate Son and outpoured Spirit. We may analyze this conception and adduce proof for every constituent element of it from the New Testament declarations. We may show that the New Testament everywhere insists on the unity of the Godhead; that it constantly recognizes the Father as God, the Son as God and the Spirit as God; and that it cursorily presents these three to us as distinct Persons. It is not necessary, however, to enlarge here on facts so obvious. We may content ourselves with simply observing that to the New Testament there is but one only living and true God; but that to it Jesus Christ and the Holy Spirit are each God in the fullest sense of the term; and yet Father, Son and Spirit stand over against each other as I, and Thou, and He. In this composite fact the New Testament gives us the doctrine of the Trinity. For the doctrine of the Trinity is but the statement in well-guarded language of this composite fact. Throughout the whole course of the many efforts to formulate the doctrine exactly, which have followed one another during the entire history of the church, indeed, the principle which has ever determined the result has always been determination to do justice in conceiving the relations of God the Father, God the Son and God the Spirit, on the one hand to the unity of God, and, on the other, to the true Deity of the Son and Spirit and their distinct personalities. When we have said these three things, then — that there is but one God, that the Father and the Son and the Spirit is each God, that the Father and the Son and the Spirit is each a distinct person — we have enunciated the doctrine of the Trinity in its completeness.

That this doctrine underlies the whole New Testament as its constant presupposition and determines everywhere its forms of expression is the primary fact to be noted. We must not omit explicitly to note, however, that it now and again also, as occasion arises for its incidental enunciation, comes itself to expression in more or less completeness of statement. The passages in which the three Persons of the Trinity are brought together are much more numerous than, perhaps, is generally supposed; but it should be recognized that the formal collocation of the elements of the doctrine naturally is relatively rare in writings which are occasional in their origin and practical rather than doctrinal in their immediate purpose. The three Persons already come into view as Divine Persons in the annunciation of the birth of Our Lord: 'The Holy Ghost shall come upon thee,' said the angel to Mary, 'and the power of the Most High shall overshadow thee: wherefore also the holy thing which is to be born shall be called the Son

of God; (Lk. i. 35 m; cf. Mt. i. 18 ff.). Here the Holy Ghost is
the active agent in the production of an effect which is also
ascribed to the power of the Most High, and the child thus
brought into the world is given the great designation of "Son
of God." The three Persons are just as clearly brought before
us in the account of Mt. (i. 18 ff.), though the allusions to them
are dispersed through a longer stretch of narrative, in the course
of which the Deity of the child is twice intimated (ver. 21:
'It is He that shall save *His* people from their sins'; ver. 23:
'They shall call His name Immanuel; which is, being interpreted, *God-with-us*'). In the baptismal scene which finds record by all the evangelists at the opening of Jesus' ministry
(Mt. iii. 16, 17; Mk. i. 10, 11; Lk. iii. 21, 22; Jn. i. 32–34), the
three Persons are thrown up to sight in a dramatic picture in
which the Deity of each is strongly emphasized. From the
open heavens the Spirit descends in visible form, and 'a voice
came out of the heavens, Thou art my Son, the Beloved, in
whom I am well pleased.' Thus care seems to have been taken
to make the advent of the Son of God into the world the revelation also of the Triune God, that the minds of men might as
smoothly as possible adjust themselves to the preconditions of
the Divine redemption which was in process of being wrought
out.

With this as a starting-point, the teaching of Jesus is Trini-
tarianly conditioned throughout. He has much to say of God
His Father, from whom as His Son He is in some true sense
distinct, and with whom He is in some equally true sense one.
And He has much to say of the Spirit, who represents Him as
He represents the Father, and by whom He works as the Father
works by Him. It is not merely in the Gospel of John that
such representations occur in the teaching of Jesus. In the Synoptics, too, Jesus claims a Sonship to God which is unique (Mt.
xi. 27; xxiv. 36; Mk. xiii. 32; Lk. x. 22; in the following passages the title of "Son of God" is attributed to Him and accepted by Him: Mt. iv. 6; viii. 29; xiv. 33; xxvii. 40, 43, 54;
Mk. iii. 11; xv. 39; Lk. iv. 41; xxii. 70; cf. Jn. i. 34, 49; ix. 35;
xi. 27), and which involves an absolute community between

the two in knowledge, say, and power: both Mt. (xi. 27) and Lk. (x. 22) record His great declaration that He knows the Father and the Father knows Him with perfect mutual knowledge: "No one knoweth the Son, save the Father; neither doth any know the Father, save the Son." In the Synoptics, too, Jesus speaks of employing the Spirit of God Himself for the performance of His works, as if the activities of God were at His disposal: "I by the Spirit of God" — or as Luke has it, "by the finger of God" — "cast out demons" (Mt. xii. 28; Lk. xi. 20; cf. the promise of the Spirit in Mk. xiii. 11; Lk. xii. 12).

It is in the discourses recorded in John, however, that Jesus most copiously refers to the unity of Himself, as the Son, with the Father, and to the mission of the Spirit from Himself as the dispenser of the Divine activities. Here He not only with great directness declares that He and the Father are one (x. 30; cf. xvii. 11, 21, 22, 25) with a unity of interpenetration ("The Father is in me, and I in the Father," x. 38; cf. xvi. 10, 11), so that to have seen Him was to have seen the Father (xiv. 9; cf. xv. 21); but He removes all doubt as to the essential nature of His oneness with the Father by explicitly asserting His eternity ("Before Abraham was born, I am," Jn. viii. 58), His co-eternity with God ("had with thee before the world was," xvii. 5; cf. xvii. 18; vi. 62), His eternal participation in the Divine glory itself ("the glory which I had with thee," in fellowship, community with Thee "before the world was," xvii. 5). So clear is it that in speaking currently of Himself as God's Son (v. 25; ix. 35; xi. 4; cf. x. 36), He meant, in accordance with the underlying significance of the idea of sonship in Semitic speech (founded on the natural implication that whatever the father is that the son is also; cf. xvi. 15; xvii. 10), to make Himself, as the Jews with exact appreciation of His meaning perceived, "equal with God" (v. 18), or, to put it brusquely, just "God" (x. 33). How He, being thus equal or rather identical with God, was in the world, He explains as involving a coming forth (ἐξῆλθον, exélthon) on His part, not merely from the presence of God (ἀπό, apó, xvi. 30; cf. xiii. 3)

or from fellowship with God (παρά, *pará*, xvi. 27; xvii. 8), but
from out of God Himself (ἐκ, *ek*, viii. 42; xvi. 28). And in the
very act of thus asserting that His eternal home is in the depths
of the Divine Being, He throws up, into as strong an emphasis
as stressed pronouns can convey, His personal distinctness from
the Father. 'If God were your Father,' says He (viii. 42), 'ye
would love *me:* for *I* came forth and am come out of God; for
neither have I come of *myself*, but it was *He* that sent *me*.'
Again, He says (xvi. 26, 27): 'In that day ye shall ask in my
name: and I say not unto you that *I* will make request of the
Father for you; for *the Father Himself* loveth you, because ye
have loved *me*, and have believed that it was *from fellowship
with the Father* that *I* came forth; I came from out of the Father,
and have come into the world.' Less pointedly, but still distinctly, He says again (xvii. 8): 'They know of a truth that it
was *from fellowship with Thee* that I came forth, and they believed that it was Thou that didst send me.' It is not necessary
to illustrate more at large a form of expression so characteristic
of the discourses of Our Lord recorded by John that it meets us
on every page: a form of expression which combines a clear implication of a unity of Father and Son which is identity of Being,
and an equally clear implication of a distinction of Person between them such as allows not merely for the play of emotions
between them, as, for instance, of love (xvii. 24; cf. xv. 9 [iii.
35]; xiv. 31), but also of an action and reaction upon one another which argues a high measure, if not of exteriority, yet
certainly of exteriorization. Thus, to instance only one of the
most outstanding facts of Our Lord's discourses (not indeed
confined to those in John's Gospel, but found also in His say-
ings recorded in the Synoptists, as e. g., Lk. iv. 43 [cf. || Mk. i.
38]; ix. 48; x. 16; iv. 34; v. 32; vii. 19; xix. 10), He continually
represents Himself as on the one hand sent by God, and as, on
the other, having come forth from the Father (e. g., Jn. viii.
42; x. 36; xvii. 3; v. 23, *et saepe*).

It is more important to point out that these phenomena of
interrelationship are not confined to the Father and Son, but
are extended also to the Spirit. Thus, for example, in a context

in which Our Lord had emphasized in the strongest manner
His own essential unity and continued interpenetration with
the Father ("If ye had known me, ye would have known my
Father also"; "He that hath seen me hath seen the Father";
"I am in the Father, and the Father in me"; "The Father
abiding in me doeth his works," Jn. xiv. 7, 9, 10), we read as
follows (Jn. xiv. 16–26): 'And *I* will make request of the
Father, and He shall give you *another* [thus sharply distinguished from Our Lord as a distinct Person] Advocate, that
He may be with you forever, the Spirit of Truth . . . He
abideth with you and shall be in you. I will not leave you orphans; I come unto you. . . . In that day ye shall know
that I am in the Father. . . . If a man love me, he will
keep my word; and my Father will love him and we [that is,
both Father and Son] will come unto him and make our abode
with him. . . . These things have I spoken unto you while
abiding with you. But the Advocate, the Holy Spirit, whom
the Father will send in my name, *He* shall teach you all things,
and bring to your remembrance all that *I* said unto you.' It
would be impossible to speak more distinctly of three who were
yet one. The Father, Son and Spirit are constantly distinguished from one another — the Son makes request of the
Father, and the Father in response to this request gives an
Advocate, "another" than the Son, who is sent in the Son's
name. And yet the oneness of these three is so kept in sight
that the coming of this "another Advocate" is spoken of without embarrassment as the coming of the Son Himself (vs. 18,
19, 20, 21), and indeed as the coming of the Father and the
Son (ver. 23). There is a sense, then, in which, when Christ
goes away, the Spirit comes in His stead; there is also a sense
in which, when the Spirit comes, Christ comes in Him; and
with Christ's coming the Father comes too. There is a distinction between the Persons brought into view; and with it an
identity among them; for both of which allowance must be
made. The same phenomena meet us in other passages. Thus,
we read again (xv. 26): 'But when there is come the Advocate
whom *I* will send unto you from [fellowship with] the Father,

the Spirit of Truth, which goeth forth from [fellowship with] the Father, *He* shall bear witness of *me.*' In the compass of this single verse, it is intimated that the Spirit is personally distinct from the Son, and yet, like Him, has His eternal home (in fellowship) with the Father, from whom He, like the Son, comes forth for His saving work, being sent thereunto, however, not in this instance by the Father, but by the Son.

This last feature is even more strongly emphasized in yet another passage in which the work of the Spirit in relation to the Son is presented as closely parallel with the work of the Son in relation to the Father (xvi. 5 ff.). 'But now I go unto Him that sent me. . . . Nevertheless *I* tell you the truth: it is expedient for you that *I* go away; for, if I go not away the Advocate will not come unto you; but if I go I will send Him unto you. And *He*, after He is come, will convict the world . . . of righteousness because I go to the Father and ye behold me no more. . . . I have yet many things to say unto you, but ye cannot bear them now. Howbeit when *He*, the Spirit of truth is come, He shall guide you into all the truth; for He shall not speak from Himself; but what things soever He shall hear, He shall speak, and He shall declare unto you the things that are to come. *He* shall glorify *me:* for He shall take of mine and shall show it unto you. All things whatsoever *the Father* hath are *mine:* therefore said I that He taketh of mine, and shall declare it unto you.' Here the Spirit is sent by the Son, and comes in order to complete and apply the Son's work, receiving His whole commission from the Son — not, however, in derogation of the Father, because when we speak of the things of the Son, that is to speak of the things of the Father.

It is not to be said, of course, that the doctrine of the Trinity is formulated in passages like these, with which the whole mass of Our Lord's discourses in John are strewn; but it certainly is presupposed in them, and that is, considered from the point of view of their probative force, even better. As we read we are kept in continual contact with three Persons who act, each as a distinct person, and yet who are in a deep, underlying sense, one. There is but one God — there is never any question of that — and yet this Son who has been sent into the world by God not only represents God but is God, and this Spirit whom the Son has in turn sent unto the world is also Himself God. Nothing could be clearer than that the Son and Spirit are distinct Persons, unless indeed it be that the Son of God is just God the Son and the Spirit of God just God the Spirit.

Meanwhile, the nearest approach to a formal announcement of the doctrine of the Trinity which is recorded from Our Lord's lips, or, perhaps we may say, which is to be found in the whole compass of the New Testament, has been preserved for us, not by John, but by one of the synoptists. It too, however, is only incidentally introduced, and has for its main object something very different from formulating the doctrine of the Trinity. It is embodied in the great commission which the resurrected Lord gave His disciples to be their "marching orders" "even unto the end of the world": "Go ye therefore, and make disciples of all the nations, baptizing them into the name of the Father and of the Son and of the Holy Spirit" (Mt. xxviii. 19). In seeking to estimate the significance of this great declaration, we must bear in mind the high solemnity of the utterance, by which we are required to give its full value to every word of it. Its phrasing is in any event, however, remarkable. It does not say, "In the names [plural] of the Father and of the Son and of the Holy Ghost"; nor yet (what might be taken to be equivalent to that), "In the name of the Father, and in the name of the Son, and in the name of the Holy Ghost," as if we had to deal with three separate Beings. Nor, on the other hand, does it say, "In the name of the Father, Son and Holy Ghost," as if "the Father, Son and Holy Ghost" might be taken as merely three designations of a single person. With stately impressiveness it asserts the unity of the three by combining them all within the bounds of the single Name; and then throws up into emphasis the distinctness of each by introducing them in turn with the repeated article: "In the name of the Father, and of the Son, and of the Holy Ghost" (Authorized Version). These three, the Father, and the Son, and the Holy Ghost, each stand in some clear sense over against the others in distinct personality: these three, the Father, and the Son, and the Holy Ghost, all unite in some profound sense in the common participation of the one Name. Fully to comprehend the implication of this mode of statement, we must bear in mind, further, the significance of the term, "the name," and the associations laden with which it came to the recipients of this commission. For the Hebrew did not think of the name, as we are accustomed to do, as a mere external symbol; but rather as the adequate expression of the innermost being of its bearer. In His name the Being of God finds expression; and the Name of God — "this glorious and fearful name, Jehovah thy God" (Deut. xxviii. 58) — was accordingly a most sacred thing, being indeed virtually equivalent to God Himself. It is no solecism, therefore, when we read (Isa. xxx. 27), "Behold, the name of Jehovah cometh"; and the parallelisms are most instructive when we read (Isa. lix. 19): 'So shall they fear the Name of Jehovah from the west, and His glory from the rising of the sun; for He shall come as a stream pent in which the Spirit of Jehovah driveth.' So pregnant was the implication of the Name, that it was possible for the term to stand absolutely, without adjunction of the name itself, as the sufficient representative of the majesty of Jehovah: it was a terrible thing to 'blaspheme the Name' (Lev. xxiv. 11). All those over whom Jehovah's Name was called were His, His possession to whom He owed protection. It is for His Name's sake, therefore, that afflicted Judah cries to the Hope of Israel, the Saviour thereof in time of trouble: 'O Jehovah, Thou art in the midst of us, and Thy Name is called upon us; leave us not' (Jer. xiv. 9); and His people find the appropriate expression of their deepest shame in the lament, 'We have become as they over whom Thou never barest rule; as they upon whom Thy Name was not called' (Isa. lxiii. 19); while the height of joy is attained in the cry, 'Thy Name, Jehovah, God of Hosts, is called upon me' (Jer. xv. 16; cf. II Chron. vii. 14; Dan. ix. 18, 19). When, therefore, Our Lord commanded His disciples to baptize those whom they brought to His obedience "into the name of . . . ," He was using language charged to them with high meaning. He could not have been understood otherwise than as substituting for the Name of Jehovah this other Name "of the Father, and of the Son, and of the Holy Ghost"; and this could not possibly have meant to His disciples anything else than that Jehovah was now to be known to them by the new Name, of the Father, and the Son, and the Holy Ghost. The only alternative would have been that, for the community which He was founding, Jesus was supplanting Jehovah by a new God; and this alternative is no less than monstrous. There is no alternative, therefore, to understanding Jesus here to be giving for His community a new Name to Jehovah and that new Name to be the threefold Name of "the Father, and the Son, and the Holy Ghost." Nor is there room for doubt that by "the Son" in this threefold Name, He meant just Himself with all the implications of distinct personality which this carries with it; and, of course, that further carries with it the equally distinct personality of "the Father" and "the Holy Ghost," with whom "the Son" is here associated, and from whom alike "the Son" is here distinguished. This is a direct ascription to Jehovah the God of Israel, of a threefold personality, and is therewith the direct enunciation of the doctrine of the Trinity. We are not witnessing here the birth of the doctrine of the Trinity; that is presupposed. What we are witnessing is the authoritative announcement of the Trinity as the God of Christianity by its Founder, in one of the most solemn of His recorded declarations. Israel had worshipped the one only true God under the Name of Jehovah; Christians are to worship the same one only and true God under the Name of "the Father, and the Son, and the Holy Ghost." This is the distinguishing characteristic of Christians; and that is as much as to say that the doctrine of the Trinity is, according to Our Lord's own apprehension of it, the distinctive mark of the religion which He founded.

A passage of such range of implication has, of course, not escaped criticism and challenge. An attempt which cannot be characterized as other than frivolous has even been made to dismiss it from the text of Matthew's Gospel. Against this, the whole body of external evidence cries out; and the internal evidence is of itself not less decisive to the same effect. When the "universalism," "ecclesiasticism," and "high theology" of the passage are pleaded against its genuineness, it is forgotten that to the Jesus of Matthew there are attributed not only such parables as those of the Leaven and the Mustard Seed, but such declarations as those contained in viii. 11, 12; xxi. 43; xxiv. 14; that in this Gospel alone is Jesus recorded as speaking familiarly about His church (xvi. 18; xviii. 17); and that, after the great declaration of xi. 27 ff., nothing remained in lofty attribution to be assigned to Him. When these same objections are urged against recognizing the passage as an authentic saying of Jesus' own, it is quite obvious that the Jesus of the evangelists cannot be in mind. The declaration here recorded is quite in character with the Jesus of Matthew's Gospel, as has just been intimated; and no less with the Jesus of the whole New Testament transmission. It will scarcely do, first to construct a priori a Jesus to our own liking, and then to discard as "unhistorical" all in the New Testament transmission which would be unnatural to such a Jesus. It is not these discarded passages but our a priori Jesus which is unhistorical. In the present instance, moreover, the historicity of the assailed saying is protected by an important historical relation in which it stands. It is not merely Jesus who speaks out of a Trinitarian consciousness, but all the New Testament writers as well. The universal possession by His followers of so firm a hold on such a doctrine requires the assumption that some such teaching as is here attributed to Him was actually contained in Jesus' instructions to His followers. Even had it not been attributed to Him in so many words by the record, we should have had to assume that some such declaration had been made by Him. In these circumstances, there can be no good reason to doubt that it was made by Him, when it is expressly attributed to Him by the record.

When we turn from the discourses of Jesus to the writings

of His followers with a view to observing how the assumption
of the doctrine of the Trinity underlies their whole fabric also,
we naturally go first of all to the letters of Paul. Their very
mass is impressive; and the definiteness with which their composition within a generation of the death of Jesus may be fixed
adds importance to them as historical witnesses. Certainly they
leave nothing to be desired in the richness of their testimony
to the Trinitarian conception of God which underlies them.
Throughout the whole series, from I Thess., which comes from
about 52 A.D., to II Tim., which was written about 68 A.D., the
redemption, which it is their one business to proclaim and commend, and all the blessings which enter into it or accompany
it are referred consistently to a threefold Divine causation.
Everywhere, throughout their pages, God the Father, the Lord
Jesus Christ, and the Holy Spirit appear as the joint objects
of all religious adoration, and the conjunct source of all Divine
operations. In the freedom of the allusions which are made to
them, now and again one alone of the three is thrown up into
prominent view; but more often two of them are conjoined in
thanksgiving or prayer; and not infrequently all three are
brought together as the apostle strives to give some adequate
expression to his sense of indebtedness to the Divine source of
all good for blessings received, or to his longing on behalf of
himself or of his readers for further communion with the God
of grace. It is regular for him to begin his Epistles with a prayer
for "grace and peace" for his readers, "from God our Father,
and the Lord Jesus Christ," as the joint source of these Divine
blessings by way of eminence (Rom. i. 7; I Cor. i. 3; II Cor. i.
2; Gal. i. 3; Eph. i. 2; Phil. i. 2; II Thess. i. 2; I Tim. i. 2; II Tim.
i. 2; Philem. ver. 3; cf. I Thess. i. 1). It is obviously no departure from this habit in the essence of the matter, but only in
relative fulness of expression, when in the opening words of
the Epistle to the Colossians the clause "and the Lord Jesus
Christ" is omitted, and we read merely: "Grace to you and
peace from God our Father." So also it would have been no
departure from it in the essence of the matter, but only in
relative fulness of expression, if in any instance the name of

the Holy Spirit had chanced to be adjoined to the other two, as in the single instance of II Cor. xiii. 14 it is adjoined to them in the closing prayer for grace with which Paul ends his letters, and which ordinarily takes the simple form of, "the grace of our Lord Jesus Christ be with you" (Rom. xvi. 20; I Cor. xvi. 23; Gal. vi. 18; Phil. iv, 23; I Thess. v. 28; II Thess. iii. 18; Philem. ver. 25; more expanded form, Eph. vi. 23, 24; more compressed, Col. iv. 18; I Tim. vi. 21; II Tim. iv. 22; Tit. iii. 15). Between these opening and closing passages the allusions to God the Father, the Lord Jesus Christ, and the Holy Spirit are constant and most intricately interlaced. Paul's mono-theism is intense: the first premise of all his thought on Divine things is the unity of God (Rom. iii. 30; I Cor. viii. 4; Gal iii. 20; Eph. iv. 6; I Tim. ii. 5; cf. Rom. xvi. 22; I Tim. i. 17). Yet to him God the Father is no more God than the Lord Jesus Christ is God, or the Holy Spirit is God. The Spirit of God is to him related to God as the spirit of man is to man (I Cor. ii. 11), and therefore if the Spirit of God dwells in us, that is God dwelling in us (Rom. viii. 10 ff.), and we are by that fact con-stituted temples of God (I Cor. iii. 16). And no expression is too strong for him to use in order to assert the Godhead of Christ: He is "our great God" (Tit. ii. 13); He is "God over all" (Rom. ix. 5); and indeed it is expressly declared of Him that the "fulness of the Godhead," that is, everything that enters into Godhead and constitutes it Godhead, dwells in Him. In the very act of asserting his monotheism Paul takes Our Lord up into this unique Godhead. "There is no God but one," he roundly asserts, and then illustrates and proves this assertion by remarking that the heathen may have "gods many, and lords many," but "to us there is one God, the Father, of whom are all things, and we unto him; and one Lord, Jesus Christ, through whom are all things, and we through him" (I Cor. viii. 6). Obviously, this "one God, the Father," and "one Lord, Jesus Christ," are embraced together in the one God who alone is. Paul's conception of the one God, whom alone he worships, includes, in other words, a recogni-tion that within the unity of His Being, there exists such a distinction of Persons as is given us in the "one God, the Father" and the "one Lord, Jesus Christ."

In numerous passages scattered through Paul's Epistles, from the earliest of them (I Thess. i. 2–5; II Thess. ii. 13, 14) to the latest (Tit. iii. 4–6; II Tim. i. 3, 13, 14), all three Persons, God the Father, the Lord Jesus Christ and the Holy Spirit, are brought together, in the most incidental manner, as co-sources of all the saving blessings which come to believers in Christ. A typical series of such passages may be found in Eph. ii. 18; iii. 2–5, 14, 17; iv. 4–6; v. 18–20. But the most interesting instances are offered to us perhaps by the Epistles to the Corinthians. In I Cor. xii. 4–6 Paul presents the abounding spiritual gifts with which the church was blessed in a threefold aspect, and connects these aspects with the three Divine Persons. "Now there are diversities of gifts, but the same Spirit. And there are diversities of ministrations, and the same Lord. And there are diversities of workings, but the same God, who worketh all things in all." It may be thought that there is a measure of what might almost be called artificiality in assigning the endowments of the church, as they are graces to the Spirit, as they are services to Christ, and as they are energizings to God. But thus there is only the more strikingly revealed the underlying Trinitarian conception as dominating the structure of the clauses: Paul clearly so writes, not because "gifts," "workings," "operations" stand out in his thought as greatly diverse things, but because God, the Lord, and the Spirit lie in the back of his mind constantly suggesting a threefold causality behind every manifestation of grace. The Trinity is alluded to rather than asserted; but it is so alluded to as to show that it constitutes the determining basis of all Paul's thought of the God of redemption. Even more instructive is II Cor. xiii. 14, which has passed into general liturgical use in the churches as a benediction: "The grace of the Lord Jesus Christ, and the love of God, and the communion of the Holy Spirit, be with you all." Here the three highest redemptive blessings are brought together, and attached distributively to the three Persons of the Triune God. There is again no formal teaching

of the doctrine of the Trinity; there is only another instance of
natural speaking out of a Trinitarian consciousness. Paul is
simply thinking of the Divine source of these great blessings;
but he habitually thinks of this Divine source of redemptive
blessings after a trinal fashion. He therefore does not say, as
he might just as well have said, "The grace and love and communion of God be with you all," but "The grace of the Lord
Jesus Christ, and the love of God, and the communion of the
Holy Spirit, be with you all." Thus he bears, almost unconsciously but most richly, witness to the trinal composition of
the Godhead as conceived by Him.

The phenomena of Paul's Epistles are repeated in the other
writings of the New Testament. In these other writings also it
is everywhere assumed that the redemptive activities of God
rest on a threefold source in God the Father, the Lord Jesus
Christ, and the Holy Spirit; and these three Persons repeatedly
come forward together in the expressions of Christian hope or
the aspirations of Christian devotion (e. g., Heb. ii. 3, 4; vi.
4–6; x. 29–31; I Pet. i. 2; ii. 3–12; iv. 13–19; I Jn. v. 4–8; Jude
vs. 20, 21; Rev. i. 4–6). Perhaps as typical instances as any are
supplied by the two following: "According to the foreknowledge of God the Father, in sanctification of the Spirit, unto
obedience and sprinkling of the blood of Jesus Christ" (I Pet.
i. 2); "Praying in the Holy Spirit, keep yourselves in the love
of God, looking for the mercy of our Lord Jesus Christ unto
eternal life" (Jude vs. 20, 21). To these may be added the
highly symbolical instance from the Apocalypse: 'Grace to
you and peace from Him which is and was and which is to come;
and from the Seven Spirits which are before His throne; and
from Jesus Christ, who is the faithful witness, the firstborn of
the dead, and the ruler of the kings of the earth' (Rev. i. 4, 5).
Clearly these writers, too, write out of a fixed Trinitarian consciousness and bear their testimony to the universal understanding current in apostolical circles. Everywhere and by all
it was fully understood that the one God whom Christians
worshipped and from whom alone they expected redemption
and all that redemption brought with it, included within His

undiminished unity the three: God the Father, the Lord Jesus Christ, and the Holy Spirit, whose activities relatively to one another are conceived as distinctly personal. This is the uniform and pervasive testimony of the New Testament, and it is the more impressive that it is given with such unstudied naturalness and simplicity, with no effort to distinguish between what have come to be called the ontological and the economical aspects of the Trinitarian distinctions, and indeed without apparent consciousness of the existence of such a distinction of aspects. Whether God is thought of in Himself or in His operations, the underlying conception runs unaffectedly into trinal forms.

It will not have escaped observation that the Trinitarian terminology of Paul and the other writers of the New Testament is not precisely identical with that of Our Lord as recorded for us in His discourses. Paul, for example — and the same is true of the other New Testament writers (except John) — does not speak, as Our Lord is recorded as speaking, of the Father, the Son, and the Holy Spirit, so much as of God, the Lord Jesus Christ, and the Holy Spirit. This difference of terminology finds its account in large measure in the different relations in which the speakers stand to the Trinity. Our Lord could not naturally speak of Himself, as one of the Trinitarian Persons, by the designation of "the Lord," while the designation of "the Son," expressing as it does His consciousness of close relation, and indeed of exact similarity, to God, came naturally to His lips. But He was Paul's Lord; and Paul naturally thought and spoke of Him as such. In point of fact, "Lord" is one of Paul's favorite designations of Christ, and indeed has become with him practically a proper name for Christ, and in point of fact, his Divine Name for Christ. It is naturally, therefore, his Trinitarian name for Christ. Because when he thinks of Christ as Divine he calls Him "Lord," he naturally, when he thinks of the three Persons together as the Triune God, sets Him as "Lord" by the side of God — Paul's constant name for "the Father" — and the Holy Spirit. Question may no doubt be raised whether it would have been possible for Paul to have done this, especially with the constancy with which he has done it, if, in his conception of it, the very essence of the Trinity were enshrined in the terms "Father" and "Son." Paul is thinking of the Trinity, to be sure, from the point of view of a worshipper, rather than from that of a systematizer. He designates the Persons of the Trinity therefore rather from his relations to them than from their relations to one another. He sees in the Trinity his God, his Lord, and the Holy Spirit who dwells in him; and naturally he so speaks currently of the three Persons. It remains remarkable, nevertheless, if the very essence of the Trinity were thought of by him as resident in the terms "Father," "Son," that in his numerous allusions to the Trinity in the Godhead, he never betrays any sense of this. It is noticeable also that in their allusions to the Trinity, there is preserved, neither in Paul nor in the other writers of the New Testament, the order of the names as they stand in Our Lord's great declaration (Mt. xxviii. 19). The reverse order occurs, indeed, occasionally, as, for example, in I Cor. xii. 4–6 (cf. Eph. iv. 4–6); and this may be understood as a climactic arrangement and so far a testimony to the order of Mt. xxviii. 19. But the order is very variable; and in the most formal enumeration of the three Persons, that of II Cor. xiii. 14, it stands thus: Lord, God, Spirit. The question naturally suggests itself whether the order Father, Son, Spirit was especially significant to Paul and his fellow-writers of the New Testament. If in their conviction the very essence of the doctrine of the Trinity was embodied in this order, should we not anticipate that there should appear in their numerous allusions to the Trinity some suggestion of this conviction?

Such facts as these have a bearing upon the testimony of the New Testament to the interrelations of the Persons of the Trinity. To the fact of the Trinity — to the fact, that is, that in the unity of the Godhead there subsist three Persons, each of whom has his particular part in the working out of salvation — the New Testament testimony is clear, consistent, pervasive and conclusive. There is included in this testimony constant and decisive witness to the complete and undiminished

Deity of each of these Persons; no language is too exalted to apply to each of them in turn in the effort to give expression to the writer's sense of His Deity: the name that is given to each is fully understood to be "the name that is above every name." When we attempt to press the inquiry behind the broad fact, however, with a view to ascertaining exactly how the New Testament writers conceive the three Persons to be related, the one to the other, we meet with great difficulties. Nothing could seem more natural, for example, than to assume that the mutual relations of the Persons of the Trinity are revealed in the designations, "the Father, the Son, and the Holy Spirit," which are given them by Our Lord in the solemn formula of Mt. xxviii. 19. Our confidence in this assumption is somewhat shaken, however, when we observe, as we have just observed, that these designations are not carefully preserved in their allusions to the Trinity by the writers of the New Testament at large, but are characteristic only of Our Lord's allusions and those of John, whose modes of speech in general very closely resemble those of Our Lord. Our confidence is still further shaken when we observe that the implications with respect to the mutual relations of the Trinitarian Persons, which are ordinarily derived from these designations, do not so certainly lie in them as is commonly supposed.

It may be very natural to see in the designation "Son" an intimation of subordination and derivation of Being, and it may not be difficult to ascribe a similar connotation to the term "Spirit." But it is quite certain that this was not the denotation of either term in the Semitic consciousness, which underlies the phraseology of Scripture; and it may even be thought doubtful whether it was included even in their remoter suggestions. What underlies the conception of sonship in Scriptural speech is just "likeness"; whatever the father is that the son is also. The emphatic application of the term "Son" to one of the Trinitarian Persons, accordingly, asserts rather His equality with the Father than His subordination to the Father; and if there is any implication of derivation in it, it would appear to be very distant. The adjunction of the adjective "only begot-

ten" (Jn. i. 14; iii. 16–18; I Jn. iv. 9) need add only the idea
of uniqueness, not of derivation (Ps. xxii. 20; xxv. 16; xxxv. 17;
Wisd. vii. 22 m.); and even such a phrase as "God only begotten" (Jn. i. 18 m.) may contain no implication of derivation,
but only of absolutely unique consubstantiality; as also such
a phrase as "the first-begotten of all creation" (Col. i. 15) may
convey no intimation of coming into being, but merely assert
priority of existence. In like manner, the designation "Spirit
of God" or "Spirit of Jehovah," which meets us frequently in
the Old Testament, certainly does not convey the idea there
either of derivation or of subordination, but is just the executive name of God — the designation of God from the point of
view of His activity — and imports accordingly identity with
God; and there is no reason to suppose that, in passing from
the Old Testament to the New Testament, the term has taken
on an essentially different meaning. It happens, oddly enough,
moreover, that we have in the New Testament itself what
amounts almost to formal definitions of the two terms "Son"
and "Spirit," and in both cases the stress is laid on the notion
of equality or sameness. In Jn. v. 18 we read: 'On this account,
therefore, the Jews sought the more to kill him, because, not
only did he break the Sabbath, but also called God his own
Father, making himself equal to God.' The point lies, of course,
in the adjective "own." Jesus was, rightly, understood to call
God "his *own* Father," that is, to use the terms "Father" and
"Son" not in a merely figurative sense, as when Israel was
called God's son, but in the real sense. And this was understood
to be claiming to be all that God is. To be the Son of God in any
sense was to be like God in that sense; to be God's *own* Son was
to be exactly like God, to be "equal with God." Similarly, we
read in I Cor. ii. 10, 11: 'For the Spirit searcheth all things,
yea, the deep things of God. For who of men knoweth the things
of a man, save the spirit of man which is in him? Even so the
things of God none knoweth, save the Spirit of God.' Here the
Spirit appears as the substrate of the Divine self-consciousness,
the principle of God's knowledge of Himself: He is, in a word,
just God Himself in the innermost essence of His Being. As

the spirit of man is the seat of human life, the very life of
man itself, so the Spirit of God is His very life-element. How
can He be supposed, then, to be subordinate to God, or to derive His Being from God? If, however, the subordination of the
Son and Spirit to the Father in modes of subsistence and their
derivation from the Father are not implicates of their designation as Son and Spirit, it will be hard to find in the New
Testament compelling evidence of their subordination and
derivation.

There is, of course, no question that in "modes of operation," as it is technically called — that is to say, in the functions
ascribed to the several Persons of the Trinity in the redemptive
process, and, more broadly, in the entire dealing of God with
the world — the principle of subordination is clearly expressed. The Father is first, the Son is second, and the Spirit
is third, in the operations of God as revealed to us in general,
and very especially in those operations by which redemption
is accomplished. Whatever the Father does, He does through
the Son (Rom. ii. 16; iii. 22; v. 1, 11, 17, 21; Eph. i. 5; I Thess.
v. 9; Tit. iii. v) by the Spirit. The Son is sent by the Father
and does His Father's will (Jn. vi. 38); the Spirit is sent by the
Son and does not speak from Himself, but only takes of
Christ's and shows it unto His people (Jn. xvii. 7 ff.); and we
have Our Lord's own word for it that 'one that is sent is not
greater than he that sent him' (Jn. xiii. 16). In crisp decisive-
ness, Our Lord even declares, indeed: 'My Father is greater
than I' (Jn. xiv. 28); and Paul tells us that Christ is God's,
even as we are Christ's (I Cor. iii. 23), and that as Christ is
"the head of every man," so God is "the head of Christ" (I
Cor. xi. 3). But it is not so clear that the principle of subordination rules also in "modes of subsistence," as it is technically
phrased; that is to say, in the necessary relation of the Persons
of the Trinity to one another. The very richness and variety
of the expression of their subordination, the one to the other,
in modes of operation, create a difficulty in attaining certainty
whether they are represented as also subordinate the one to
the other in modes of subsistence. Question is raised in each

case of apparent intimation of subordination in modes of subsistence, whether it may not, after all, be explicable as only another expression of subordination in modes of operation. It may be natural to assume that a subordination in modes of operation rests on a subordination in modes of subsistence; that the reason why it is the Father that sends the Son and the Son that sends the Spirit is that the Son is subordinate to the Father, and the Spirit to the Son. But we are bound to bear in mind that these relations of subordination in modes of operation may just as well be due to a convention, an agreement, between the Persons of the Trinity — a "Covenant" as it is technically called — by virtue of which a distinct function in the work of redemption is voluntarily assumed by each. It is eminently desirable, therefore, at the least, that some definite evidence of subordination in modes of subsistence should be discoverable before it is assumed. In the case of the relation of the Son to the Father, there is the added difficulty of the incarnation, in which the Son, by the assumption of a creaturely nature into union with Himself, enters into new relations with the Father of a definitely subordinate character. Question has even been raised whether the very designations of Father and Son may not be expressive of these new relations, and therefore without significance with respect to the eternal relations of the Persons so designated. This question must certainly be answered in the negative. Although, no doubt, in many of the instances in which the terms "Father" and "Son" occur, it would be possible to take them of merely economical relations, there ever remain some which are intractable to this treatment, and we may be sure that "Father" and "Son" are applied to their eternal and necessary relations. But these terms, as we have seen, do not appear to imply relations of first and second, superiority and subordination, in modes of subsistence; and the fact of the humiliation of the Son of God for His earthly work does introduce a factor into the interpretation of the passages which import His subordination to the Father, which throws doubt upon the inference from them of an eternal relation of subordination in the Trinity itself. It must at least be

said that in the presence of the great New Testament doctrines
of the Covenant of Redemption on the one hand, and of the
Humiliation of the Son of God for His work's sake and of the
Two Natures in the constitution of His Person as incarnated,
on the other, the difficulty of interpreting subordinationist
passages of eternal relations between the Father and Son becomes extreme. The question continually obtrudes itself,
whether they do not rather find their full explanation in the
facts embodied in the doctrines of the Covenant, the Humiliation of Christ, and the Two Natures of His incarnated Person.
Certainly in such circumstances it were thoroughly illegitimate
to press such passages to suggest any subordination for the
Son or the Spirit which would in any manner impair that complete identity with the Father in Being and that complete
equality with the Father in powers which are constantly presupposed, and frequently emphatically, though only incidentally, asserted for them throughout the whole fabric of the New
Testament.

The Trinity of the Persons of the Godhead, shown in the
incarnation and the redemptive work of God the Son, and the
descent and saving work of God the Spirit, is thus everywhere
assumed in the New Testament, and comes to repeated fragmentary but none the less emphatic and illuminating expression in its pages. As the roots of its revelation are set in the
threefold Divine causality of the saving process, it naturally
finds an echo also in the consciousness of everyone who has
experienced this salvation. Every redeemed soul, knowing himself reconciled with God through His Son, and quickened into
newness of life by His Spirit, turns alike to Father, Son and
Spirit with the exclamation of reverent gratitude upon his lips,
"My Lord and my God!" If he could not construct the doctrine of the Trinity out of his consciousness of salvation, yet
the elements of his consciousness of salvation are interpreted
to him and reduced to order only by the doctrine of the Trinity
which he finds underlying and giving their significance and consistency to the teaching of the Scriptures as to the processes
of salvation. By means of this doctrine he is able to think

clearly and consequently of his threefold relation to the saving
God, experienced by Him as Fatherly love sending a Redeemer,
as redeeming love executing redemption, as saving love applying redemption: all manifestations in distinct methods and by
distinct agencies of the one seeking and saving love of God.
Without the doctrine of the Trinity, his conscious Christian
life would be thrown into confusion and left in disorganization
if not, indeed, given an air of unreality; with the doctrine of
the Trinity, order, significance and reality are brought to every
element of it. Accordingly, the doctrine of the Trinity and the
doctrine of redemption, historically, stand or fall together. A
Unitarian theology is commonly associated with a Pelagian
anthropology and a Socinian soteriology. It is a striking testimony which is borne by F. E. Koenig ("Offenbarungsbegriff
des AT," 1882, I, 125): "I have learned that many cast off
the whole history of redemption for no other reason than because they have not attained to a conception of the Triune
God." It is in this intimacy of relation between the doctrines
of the Trinity and redemption that the ultimate reason lies
why the Christian church could not rest until it had attained
a definite and well-compacted doctrine of the Trinity. Nothing
else could be accepted as an adequate foundation for the experience of the Christian salvation. Neither the Sabellian nor
the Arian construction could meet and satisfy the data of the
consciousness of salvation, any more than either could meet
and satisfy the data of the Scriptural revelation. The data of
the Scriptural revelation might, to be sure, have been left un-
satisfied: men might have found a *modus vivendi* with neglected,
or even with perverted Scriptural teaching. But perverted or
neglected elements of Christian experience are more clamant
in their demands for attention and correction. The dissatisfied
Christian consciousness necessarily searched the Scriptures, on
the emergence of every new attempt to state the doctrine of
the nature and relations of God, to see whether these things
were true, and never reached contentment until the Scriptural
data were given their consistent formulation in a valid doctrine
of the Trinity. Here too the heart of man was restless until it

found its rest in the Triune God, the author, procurer and applier of salvation.

The determining impulse to the formulation of the doctrine of the Trinity in the church was the church's profound conviction of the absolute Deity of Christ, on which as on a pivot the whole Christian conception of God from the first origins of Christianity turned. The guiding principle in the formulation of the doctrine was supplied by the Baptismal Formula announced by Jesus (Mt. xxviii. 19), from which was derived the ground-plan of the baptismal confessions and "rules of faith" which very soon began to be framed all over the church. It was by these two fundamental *principia* — the true Deity of Christ and the Baptismal Formula — that all attempts to formulate the Christian doctrine of God were tested, and by their molding power that the church at length found itself in possession of a form of statement which did full justice to the data of the redemptive revelation as reflected in the New Testament and the demands of the Christian heart under the experience of salvation.

In the nature of the case the formulated doctrine was of slow attainment. The influence of inherited conceptions and of current philosophies inevitably showed itself in the efforts to construe to the intellect the immanent faith of Christians. In the second century the dominant neo-Stoic and neo-Platonic ideas deflected Christian thought into subordinationist channels, and produced what is known as the Logos-Christology, which looks upon the Son as a prolation of Deity reduced to such dimensions as comported with relations with a world of time and space; meanwhile, to a great extent, the Spirit was neglected altogether. A reaction which, under the name of Monarchianism, identified the Father, Son, and Spirit so completely that they were thought of only as different aspects or different moments in the life of the one Divine Person, called now Father, now Son, now Spirit, as His several activities came successively into view, almost succeeded in establishing itself in the third century as the doctrine of the church at large. In the conflict between these two opposite tendencies the church gradually found its way, under the guidance of the Baptismal Formula elaborated into a "Rule of Faith," to a better and more well-balanced conception, until a real doctrine of the Trinity at length came to expression, particularly in the West, through the brilliant dialectic of Tertullian. It was thus ready at hand, when, in the early years of the fourth century, the Logos-Christology, in opposition to dominant Sabellian tendencies, ran to seed in what is known as Arianism, to which the Son was a creature, though exalted above all other creatures as their Creator and Lord; and the church was thus prepared to assert its settled faith in a Triune God, one in being, but in whose unity there subsisted three consubstantial Persons. Under the leadership of Athanasius this doctrine was proclaimed as the faith of the church at the Council of Nice in 325 A.D., and by his strenuous labors and those of "the three great Cappadocians," the two Gregories and Basil, it gradually won its way to the actual acceptance of the entire church. It was at the hands of Augustine, however, a century later, that the doctrine thus become the church doctrine in fact as well as in theory, received its most complete elaboration and most carefully grounded statement. In the form which he gave it, and which is embodied in that "battle-hymn of the early church," the so-called Athanasian Creed, it has retained its place as the fit expression of the faith of the church as to the nature of its God until today. The language in which it is couched, even in this final declaration, still retains elements of speech which owe their origin to the modes of thought characteristic of the Logos-Christology of the second century, fixed in the nomenclature of the church by the Nicene Creed of 325 A.D., though carefully guarded there against the subordinationism inherent in the Logos-Christology, and made the vehicle rather of the Nicene doctrines of the eternal generation of the Son and procession of the Spirit, with the consequent subordination of the Son and Spirit to the Father in modes of subsistence as well as of operation. In the Athanasian Creed, however, the principle of the equalization of the three Persons, which was already the dominant motive of the Nicene Creed — the *homooúsia* — is so strongly emphasized as practically to push out of sight, if not quite out of existence, these remanent suggestions of derivation and subordination. It has been found necessary, nevertheless, from time to time, vigorously to reassert the principle of equalization, over against a tendency unduly to emphasize the elements of subordinationism which still hold a place thus in the traditional language in which the church states its doctrine of the Trinity. In particular, it fell to Calvin, in the interests of the true Deity of Christ — the constant motive of the whole body of Trinitarian thought — to reassert and make good the attribute of self-existence (*autotheotōs*) for the Son. Thus Calvin takes his place, alongside of Tertullian, Athanasius and Augustine, as one of the chief contributors to the exact and vital statement of the Christian doctrine of the Triune God.

LITERATURE. — F. C. Baur, "Die christliche Lehre von der Dreieinigkeit Gottes," 3 vols., Tübingen, 1841–1843; Dionysius Petavius, "De Trinitate (vol. ii, of "De Theologicis Dogmaticis," Paris, 1647); G. Bull, "A Defence of the Nicene Creed" (1685), 2 vols., Oxford, 1851; G. S. Faber, "The Apostolicity of Trinitarianism," 2 vols., 1832; Augustine, "On the Holy Trinity" (vol. iii of "Nicene and Post-Nicene Fathers of the Christian Church," 1–228), New York, 1887; Calvin, "Institutes of the Christian Religion," I, ch. xiii; C. Hodge, "Systematic Theology and Index," I, New York, 1873, 442–482; H. Bavinck, "Gereformeerde Dogmatiek²," II, Kampen, 1908, 260–347 (gives excellent references to literature); S. Harris, "God, the Creator, and Lord of All," New York, 1896; R. Rocholl, "Der christliche Gottesbegriff," Göttingen, 1900; W. F. Adeney, "The Christian Conception of God," London, 1909, 215–246; J. Lebreton, "Les origines du dogme de la Trinité," Paris, 1910; J. C. K. Hofmann, "Der Schriftbeweis²," Nördlingen, 1857–1860, I, 85–111; J. L. S. Lutz, "Biblische Dogmatik," Pforzheim, 1847, 319–394; R. W. Landis, "A Plea for the Catholic Doctrine of the Trinity," Philadelphia, 1832; E. H. Bickersteth, "The Rock of Ages," etc., London, 1860, New York, 1861; E. Riggenbach, "Der trinitarische Taufbefehl,

Mt. xxviii. 19" (in Schlatter and Cremer, "Beiträge zur För-
derung christlicher Theologie," 1903, VII; also 1904, VIII);
F. J. Hall, "The Trinity," London and New York, 1910, 100–
141; J. Pearson, "An Exposition of the Creed," ed. Chevallier
and Sinker, Cambridge, 1899; J. Howe, "Calm Discourse on
the Trinity," in "Works," ed. Hunt, London, 1810–1822; J.
Owen, "Vindication of the Doctrine of the Holy Trinity,"
and "Saint's Fellowship with the Trinity," in "Works,"
Gould's ed., London, 1850–1855; J. Edwards, "Observations
concerning the Scripture Economy of the Trinity," etc., New
York, 1880, also "An Unpublished Essay on the Trinity," New
York, 1903; J. R. Illingworth, "The Doctrine of the Trinity
Apologetically Considered," London and New York, 1907;
A. F. W. Ingram, "The Love of the Trinity," New York, 1908.

[NOTE. — In this article the author has usually given his own
renderings of original passages, and not those of any particular
VS. — EDITORS.]

V

THE PERSON OF CHRIST

THE PERSON OF CHRIST [1]

I<small>T</small> is the purpose of this article to make as clear as possible the conception of the Person of Christ, in the technical sense of that term, which lies on — or, if we prefer to say so, beneath — the pages of the New Testament. Were it its purpose to trace out the process by which this great mystery has been revealed to men, a beginning would need to be taken from the intimations as to the nature of the person of the Messiah in Old Testament prophecy, and an attempt would require to be made to discriminate the exact contribution of each organ of revelation to our knowledge. And were there added to this a desire to ascertain the progress of the apprehension of this mystery by men, there would be demanded a further inquiry into the exact degree of understanding which was brought to the truth revealed at each stage of its revelation. The magnitudes with which such investigations deal, however, are very minute; and the profit to be derived from them is not, in a case like the present, very great. It is, of course, of importance to know how the person of the Messiah was represented in the predictions of the Old Testament; and it is a matter at least of interest to note, for example, the difficulty experienced by Our Lord's immediate disciples in comprehending all that was involved in His manifestation. But, after all, the constitution of Our Lord's person is a matter of revelation, not of human thought; and it is pre-eminently a revelation of the New Testament, not of the Old Testament. And the New Testament is all the product of a single movement, at a single stage of its development, and therefore presents in its fundamental teaching a common character. The whole of the New Testament was written within the limits of about half a century; or,

[1] Article "Person of Christ" from *The International Standard Bible Encyclopaedia*, James Orr, General editor, v. 4, pp. 2338–2348. Pub. Chicago, 1915, by Howard–Severance Co.

if we except the writings of John, within the narrow bounds of
a couple of decades; and the entire body of writings which enter
into it are so much of a piece that it may be plausibly represented that they all bear the stamp of a single mind. In its
fundamental teaching, the New Testament lends itself, therefore, more readily to what is called dogmatic than to what is
called genetic treatment; and we shall penetrate most surely
into its essential meaning if we take our start from its clearest
and fullest statements, and permit their light to be thrown upon its more incidental allusions. This is peculiarly the case with
such a matter as the person of Christ, which is dealt with chiefly
incidentally, as a thing already understood by all, and needing
only to be alluded to rather than formally expounded. That we
may interpret these allusions aright, it is requisite that we
should recover from the first the common conception which
underlies them all.

I. The Teaching of Paul

We begin, then, with the most didactic of the New Testament writers, the apostle Paul, and with one of the passages in
which he most fully intimates his conception of the person of
his Lord, Phil. ii. 5–9. Even here, however, Paul is not formally
expounding the doctrine of the Person of Christ; he is only alluding to certain facts concerning His person and action perfectly well known to his readers, in order that he may give
point to an adduction of Christ's example. He is exhorting his
readers to unselfishness, such unselfishness as esteems others
better than ourselves, and looks not only on our own things
but also on those of others. Precisely this unselfishness, he declares, was exemplified by Our Lord. He did not look upon His
own things but the things of others; that is to say, He did not
stand upon His rights, but was willing to forego all that He
might justly have claimed for Himself for the good of others.
For, says Paul, though, as we all know, in His intrinsic nature
He was nothing other than God, yet He did not, as we all
know right well, look greedily on His condition of equality

with God, but made no account of Himself, taking the form of a servant, being made in the likeness of men; and, being found in fashion as a man, humbled Himself, becoming obedient up to death itself, and that, the death of the cross. The statement is thrown into historical form; it tells the story of Christ's life on earth. But it presents His life on earth as a life in all its elements alien to His intrinsic nature, and assumed only in the performance of an unselfish purpose. On earth He lived as a man, and subjected Himself to the common lot of men. But He was not by nature a man, nor was He in His own nature subject to the fortunes of human life. By nature He was God; and He would have naturally lived as became God — 'on an equality with God.' He became man by a voluntary act, 'taking no account of Himself,' and, having become man, He voluntarily lived out His human life under the conditions which the fulfilment of His unselfish purpose imposed on Him.

The terms in which these great affirmations are made deserve the most careful attention. The language in which Our Lord's intrinsic Deity is expressed, for example, is probably as strong as any that could be devised. Paul does not say simply, "He was God." He says, "He was in the form of God," employing a turn of speech which throws emphasis upon Our Lord's possession of the specific quality of God. "Form" is a term which expresses the sum of those characterizing qualities which make a thing the precise thing that it is. Thus, the "form" of a sword (in this case mostly matters of external configuration) is all that makes a given piece of metal specifically a sword, rather than, say, a spade. And "the form of God" is the sum of the characteristics which make the being we call "God," specifically God, rather than some other being — an angel, say, or a man. When Our Lord is said to be in "the form of God," therefore, He is declared, in the most express manner possible, to be all that God is, to possess the whole fulness of attributes which make God God. Paul chooses this manner of expressing himself here instinctively, because, in adducing Our Lord as our example of self-abnegation, his mind is naturally resting, not on the bare fact that He is God, but on the richness and fulness of His being as God. He was all this, yet He did not look on His own things but on those of others.

It should be carefully observed also that in making this great affirmation concerning Our Lord, Paul does not throw it distinctively into the past, as if he were describing a mode of being formerly Our Lord's, indeed, but no longer His because of the action by which He became our example of unselfishness. Our Lord, he says, "being," "existing," "subsisting" "in the form of God" — as it is variously rendered. The rendering proposed by the Revised Version margin, "being originally," while right in substance, is somewhat misleading. The verb employed means "strictly 'to be beforehand,' 'to be already' so and so" (Blass, "Grammar of NT Greek," English translation, 244), "to be there and ready," and intimates the existing circumstances, disposition of mind, or, as here, mode of subsistence in which the action to be described takes place. It contains no intimation, however, of the cessation of these circumstances or disposition, or mode of subsistence; and that, the less in a case like the present, where it is cast in a tense (the imperfect) which in no way suggests that the mode of subsistence intimated came to an end in the action described by the succeeding verb (cf. the parallels, Lk. xvi. 14, 23; xxiii. 50; Acts ii. 30; iii. 2; II Cor. viii. 17; xii. 16; Gal. i. 14). Paul is not telling us here, then, what Our Lord was once, but rather what He already was, or, better, what in His intrinsic nature He is; he is not describing a past mode of existence of Our Lord, before the action he is adducing as an example took place — although the mode of existence he describes was Our Lord's mode of existence before this action — so much as painting in the background upon which the action adduced may be thrown up into prominence. He is telling us who and what He is who did these things for us, that we may appreciate how great the things He did for us are.

And here it is important to observe that the whole of the action adduced is thrown up thus against this background — not only its negative description to the effect that Our Lord (although all that God is) did not look greedily on His (conse-quent) being on an equality with God; but its positive de-scription as well, introduced by the "but . . . ." and that in both of its elements, not merely that to the effect (ver. 7) that 'he took no account of himself' (rendered not badly by the Au-thorized Version, He "made himself of no reputation"; but quite misleading by the Revised Version, He "emptied himself"), but equally that to the effect (ver. 8) that "he humbled him-self." It is the whole of what Our Lord is described as doing in vs. 6–8, that He is described as doing despite His "subsistence in the form of God." So far is Paul from intimating, therefore, that Our Lord laid aside His Deity in entering upon His life on earth, that he rather asserts that He retained His Deity throughout His life on earth, and in the whole course of His humiliation, up to death itself, was consciously ever exercising self-abnegation, living a life which did not by nature belong to Him, which stood in fact in direct contradiction to the life which was naturally His. It is this underlying implication which determines the whole choice of the language in which Our Lord's earthly life is described. It is because it is kept in mind that He still was "in the form of God," that is, that He still had in possession all that body of characterizing qualities by which God is made God, for example, that He is said to have been made, not man, but "in the likeness of man," to have been found, not man, but "in fashion as a man"; and that the wonder of His servanthood and obedience, the mark of servant-hood, is thought of as so great. Though He was truly man, He was much more than man; and Paul would not have his readers imagine that He had become merely man. In other words, Paul does not teach that Our Lord was once God but had become instead man; he teaches that though He was God, He had be-come also man.

An impression that Paul means to imply, that in entering upon His earthly life Our Lord had laid aside His Deity, may be created by a very prevalent misinterpretation of the central clause of his statement — a misinterpretation unfortunately given currency by the rendering of the English Revised Version:

"counted it not a prize to be on an equality with God, but emptied himself," varied without improvement in the American Revised Version to: "counted not the being on an equality with God a thing to be grasped, but emptied himself." The former (negative) member of this clause means just: He did not look greedily upon His being on an equality with God; did not "set supreme store" by it (see Lightfoot on the clause). The latter (positive) member of it, however, cannot mean in antithesis to this, that He therefore "emptied himself," divested Himself of this, His being on an equality with God, much less that He "emptied himself," divested Himself of His Deity ("form of God") itself, of which His being on an equality with God is the manifested consequence. The verb here rendered "emptied" is in constant use in a metaphorical sense (so only in the New Testament: Rom. iv. 14; I Cor. i. 17; ix. 15; II Cor. ix. 3) and cannot here be taken literally. This is already apparent from the definition of the manner in which the "emptying" is said to have been accomplished, supplied by the modal clause which is at once attached: by "taking the form of a servant." You cannot "empty" by "taking" — *adding*. It is equally apparent, however, from the strength of the emphasis which, by its position, is thrown upon the "himself." We may speak of Our Lord as "*emptying* Himself" of something else, but scarcely, with this strength of emphasis, of His "emptying *Himself*" of something else. This emphatic "Himself," interposed between the preceding clause and the verb rendered "emptied," builds a barrier over which we cannot climb backward in search of that of which Our Lord emptied Himself. The whole thought is necessarily contained in the two words, "emptied *Himself*," in which the word "emptied" must therefore be taken in a sense analogous to that which it bears in the other passages in the New Testament where it occurs. Paul, in a word, says here nothing more than that Our Lord, who did not look with greedy eyes upon His estate of equality with God, emptied Himself, if the language may be pardoned, of Himself; that is to say, in precise accordance with the exhortation for the enhancement of which His example is adduced, that He did not look on His own things. 'He made no account of Himself,' we may fairly paraphrase the clause; and thus all question of what He emptied Himself of falls away. What Our Lord actually did, according to Paul, is expressed in the following clauses; those now before us express more the moral character of His act. He took "the form of a servant," and so was "made in the likeness of men." But His doing this showed that He did not set overweening store by His state of equality with God, and did not account Himself the sufficient object of all the efforts. He was not self-regarding: He had regard for others. Thus He becomes our supreme example of self-abnegating conduct.

The language in which the act by which Our Lord showed that He was self-abnegating is described, requires to be taken in its complete meaning. He took "the form of a servant, being made in the likeness of men," says Paul. The term "form" here, of course, bears the same full meaning as in the preceding instance of its occurrence in the phrase "the form of God." It imparts the specific quality, the whole body of characteristics, by which a servant is made what we know as a servant. Our Lord assumed, then, according to Paul, not the mere state or condition or outward appearance of a servant, but the reality; He became an actual "servant" in the world. The act by which He did this is described as a "taking," or, as it has become customary from this description of it to phrase it, as an "assumption." What is meant is that Our Lord took up into His personality a human nature; and therefore it is immediately explained that He took the form of a servant by "being made in the likeness of men." That the apostle does not say, shortly, that He assumed a human nature, is due to the engagement of his mind with the contrast which he wishes to bring out forcibly for the enhancement of his appeal to Our Lord's example, between what Our Lord is by nature and what He was willing to become, not looking on His own things but also on the things of others. This contrast is, no doubt, embodied in the simple opposition of God and man; it is much more pungently expressed in the qualificative terms, "form of God" and "form of a servant." The Lord of the world became a servant in the world; He whose right it was to rule took obedience as His life-characteristic. Naturally therefore Paul employs here a word of quality rather than a word of mere nature; and then defines his meaning in this word of quality by a further epexegetical clause. This further clause — "being made in the likeness of men" — does not throw doubt on the reality of the human nature that was assumed, in contradiction to the emphasis on its reality in the phrase "the form of a servant." It, along with the succeeding clause — "and being found in fashion as a man" — owes its peculiar form, as has already been pointed out, to the vividness of the apostle's consciousness, that he is speaking of one who, though really man, possessing all that makes a man a man, is yet, at the same time, infinitely more than a man, no less than God Himself, in possession of all that makes God God. Christ Jesus is in his view, therefore (as in the view of his readers, for he is not instructing his readers here as to the nature of Christ's person, but reminding them of certain elements in it for the purposes of his exhortation), both God and man, God who has "assumed" man into personal union with Himself, and has in this His assumed manhood lived out a human life on earth.

The elements of Paul's conception of the person of Christ are brought before us in this suggestive passage with unwonted fulness. But they all receive endless illustration from his occasional allusions to them, one or another, throughout his Epistles. The leading motive of this passage, for example, reappears quite perfectly in II Cor. viii. 9, where we are exhorted to imitate the graciousness of Our Lord Jesus Christ, who became for our sakes (emphatic) poor — He who was (again an imperfect participle, and therefore without suggestion of the cessation of the condition described) rich — that we might by His (very emphatic) poverty be made rich. Here the change in Our Lord's condition at a point of time perfectly understood between the writer and his readers is adverted to and assigned to its motive, but no further definition is given of the nature of either condition referred to. We are brought closer to the precise nature of the act by which the change was wrought by such a passage as Gal. iv. 4. We read that "When the fulness of the time came, God sent forth his Son, born of a woman, born under the law, that he might redeem them that were under the law." The whole transaction is referred to the Father in fulfilment of His eternal plan of redemption, and it is described specifically as an incarnation: the Son of God is born of a woman — He who is in His own nature the Son of God, abiding with God, is sent forth from God in such a manner as to be born a human being, subject to law. The primary implications are that this was not the beginning of His being; but that before this He was neither a man nor subject to law. But there is no suggestion that on becoming man and subject to law, He ceased to be the Son of God or lost anything intimated by that high designation. The uniqueness of His relation to God as His Son is emphasized in a kindred passage (Rom. viii. 3) by the heightening of the designation to that of God's "own Son," and His distinction from other men is intimated in the same passage by the declaration that God sent Him, not in sinful flesh, but only "in the likeness of sinful flesh." The reality of Our Lord's flesh is not thrown into doubt by this turn of speech, but His freedom from the sin which is associated with flesh as it exists in lost humanity is asserted (cf. II Cor. v. 21). Though true man, therefore (I Cor. xv. 21; Rom. v. 21; Acts xvii. 31), He is not without differences from other men; and these differences do not concern merely the condition (as sinful) in which men presently find themselves; but also their very origin: they are from below, He from above — 'the first man is from the earth, earthy; the second man is from heaven' (I Cor. xv. 47). This is His peculiarity: He was born of a woman like other men; yet He descended from Heaven (cf. Eph. iv. 9; Jn. iii. 13). It is not meant, of course, that already in heaven He was a man; what is meant is that even though man He derives His origin in an exceptional sense from heaven. Paul describes what He was in heaven (but not alone in heaven) — that is to say before He was sent in the likeness of sinful flesh (though not alone before this) — in the great terms of "God's Son," "God's own Son," "the form of God," or yet again in words whose import cannot be mistaken, 'God over all' (Rom. ix. 5). In the last cited passage, together with its parallel earlier in the same epistle (Rom. i. 3), the two sides or elements of Our Lord's person are brought into collocation after a fashion that can leave no doubt of Paul's conception of His twofold nature. In the earlier of these passages he tells us that Jesus Christ was born, indeed, of the seed of David according to the flesh, that is, so far as the human side of His being is concerned, but was powerfully marked out as the Son of God according to the Spirit of Holiness, that is, with respect to His higher nature, by the resurrection of the dead, which in a true sense began in His own rising from the dead. In the later of them, he tells us that Christ sprang indeed, as concerns the flesh, that is on the human side of His being, from Israel, but that, despite this earthly origin of His human nature, He yet is and abides (present participle) nothing less than the Supreme God, "God over all [emphatic], blessed forever." Thus Paul teaches us that by His coming forth from God to be born of woman, Our Lord, assuming a human nature to Himself, has, while remaining the Supreme God, become also true and perfect man. Accordingly, in a context in which the resources of language are strained to the utmost to make the exaltation of Our Lord's being clear — in which He is described as the image of the invisible God, whose being antedates all that is created, in whom, through whom and to whom all things have been created, and in whom they all subsist — we are told not only that (naturally) in Him all the fulness dwells (Col. i. 19), but, with complete explication, that 'all the fulness of the Godhead dwells in him bodily' (Col. ii. 9); that is to say, the very Deity of God, that which makes God God, in all its completeness, has its permanent home in Our Lord, and that in a "bodily fashion," that is, it is in Him clothed with a body. He who looks upon Jesus Christ sees, no doubt, a body and a man; but as he sees the man clothed with the body, so he sees God Himself, in all the fulness of His Deity, clothed with the humanity. Jesus Christ is therefore God "manifested in the flesh" (I Tim. iii. 16), and His appearance on earth is an "epiphany" (II Tim. i. 10), which is the technical term for manifestations on earth of a God. Though truly man, He is nevertheless also our "great God" (Tit. ii. 13).

II. TEACHING OF THE EPISTLE TO THE HEBREWS

The conception of the person of Christ which underlies and finds expression in the Epistle to the Hebrews is indistinguishable from that which governs all the allusions to Our Lord in the Epistles of Paul. To the author of this epistle Our Lord is above all else the Son of God in the most eminent sense of that word; and it is the Divine dignity and majesty belonging to Him from His very nature which forms the fundamental feature of the image of Christ which stands before his mind. And yet it is this author who, perhaps above all others of the New Testament writers, emphasizes the truth of the humanity of Christ, and dwells with most particularity upon the elements of His human nature and experience.

The great Christological passage which fills chap. ii of the Epistle to the Hebrews rivals in its richness and fulness of detail, and its breadth of implication, that of Phil. ii. It is thrown up against the background of the remarkable exposition of the Divine dignity of the Son which occupies chap. i (notice the "therefore" of ii. 1). There the Son had been declared to be "the effulgence of his (God's) glory, and the very image of his substance, through whom the universe has been created and by the word of whose power all things are held in being; and His exaltation above the angels, by means of whom the Old Covenant had been inaugurated, is measured by the difference between the designations "ministering spirits" proper to the one, and the Son of God, nay, God itself (i. 8, 9), proper to the other. The purpose of the succeeding statement is to enhance in the thought of the Jewish readers of the epistle the value of the salvation wrought by this Divine Saviour, by removing from their minds the offence they were in danger of taking at His lowly life and shameful death on earth. This earthly humiliation finds its abundant justification, we are told, in the greatness of the end which it sought and attained. By it Our Lord has, with His strong feet, broken out a pathway along which, in Him, sinful man may at length climb up to the high destiny which was promised him when it was declared he should have dominion over all creation. Jesus Christ stooped only to conquer, and He stooped to conquer not for Himself (for He was in His own person no less than God), but for us.

The language in which the humiliation of the Son of God is in the first instance described is derived from the context. The establishment of His Divine majesty in chap. i had taken the form of an exposition of His infinite exaltation above the angels, the highest of all creatures. His humiliation is described here therefore as being "made a little lower than the angels" (ii. 9). What is meant is simply that He became man; the phraseology is derived from Ps. viii., Authorized Version, from which had just been cited the declaration that God has made man (despite his insignificance) "but a little lower than the angels," thus crowning him with glory and honor. The adoption of the language of the psalm to describe Our Lord's humiliation has the secondary effect, accordingly, of greatly enlarging the reader's sense of the immensity of the humiliation of the Son of God in becoming man: He descended an infinite distance to reach man's highest conceivable exaltation. As, however, the primary purpose of the adoption of the language is merely to declare that the Son of God became man, so it is shortly afterward explained (ii. 14) as an entering into participation in the blood and flesh which are common to men: "Since then the children are sharers in flesh and blood, he also himself in like manner partook of the same." The voluntariness, the reality, the completeness of the assumption of humanity by the Son of God, are all here emphasized.

The proximate end of Our Lord's assumption of humanity is declared to be that He might die; He was "made a little lower than the angels . . . because of the suffering of death" (ii. 9); He took part in blood and flesh in order "that through death . . ." (ii. 14). The Son of God as such could not die; to Him belongs by nature an "indissoluble life" (vii. 16 m.).

If he was to die, therefore, He must take to Himself another
nature to which the experience of death were not impossible
(ii. 17). Of course it is not meant that death was desired by
Him for its own sake. The purpose of our passage is to save its
Jewish readers from the offence of the death of Christ. What
they are bidden to observe is, therefore, Jesus, who was made
a little lower than the angels because of the suffering of death,
'crowned with glory and honor, that by the grace of God the
bitterness of death which he tasted might redound to the benefit of every man' (ii. 9), and the argument is immediately
pressed home that it was eminently suitable for God Almighty,
in bringing many sons into glory, to make the Captain of their
salvation perfect (as a Saviour) by means of suffering. The
meaning is that it was only through suffering that these men,
being sinners, could be brought into glory. And therefore in
the plainer statement of verse 14 we read that Our Lord took
part in flesh and blood in order "that through death he might
bring to nought him that has the power of death, that is, the
devil; and might deliver all them who through fear of death
were all their lifetime subject to bondage"; and in the still
plainer statement of verse 17 that the ultimate object of His
assimilation to men was that He might "make propitiation
for the sins of the people." It is for the salvation of sinners
that Our Lord has come into the world; but, as that salvation
can be wrought only by suffering and death, the proximate end
of His assumption of humanity remains that He might die;
whatever is more than this gathers around this.

The completeness of Our Lord's assumption of humanity
and of His identification of Himself with it receives strong
emphasis in this passage. He took part in the flesh and blood
which is the common heritage of men, after the same fashion
that other men participate in it (ii. 14); and, having thus become a man among men, He shared with other men the ordinary circumstances and fortunes of life, "in all things" (ii.
17). The stress is laid on trials, sufferings, death; but this is
due to the actual course in which His life ran — and that it
might run in which He became man — and is not exclusive of

other human experiences. What is intended is that He became
truly a man, and lived a truly human life, subject to all the
experiences natural to a man in the particular circumstances
in which He lived.

It is not implied, however, that during this human life —
"the days of his flesh" (v. 7) — He had ceased to be God, or
to have at His disposal the attributes which belonged to Him
as God. That is already excluded by the representations of
chap. i. The glory of this dispensation consists precisely in the
bringing of its revelations directly by the Divine Son rather
than by mere prophets (i. 1), and it was as the effulgence of
God's glory and the express image of His substance, upholding
the universe by the word of His power, that this Son made
purification of sins (i. 3). Indeed, we are expressly told that
even in the days of the flesh, He continued still a Son (v. 8),
and that it was precisely in this that the wonder lay: that
though He was and remained (imperfect participle) a Son, He
yet learned the obedience He had set Himself to (cf. Phil. ii. 8)
by the things which He suffered. Similarly, we are told not only
that, though an Israelite of the tribe of Judah, He possessed
"the power of an indissoluble life" (vii. 16 m.), but, describing
that higher nature which gave Him this power as an "eternal
Spirit" (cf. "spirit of holiness," Rom. i. 4), that it was through
this eternal Spirit that He could offer Himself without blemish
unto God, a real and sufficing sacrifice, in contrast with the
shadows of the Old Covenant (ix. 14). Though a man, therefore, and truly man, sprung out of Judah (vii. 14), touched
with the feeling of human infirmities (iv. 15), and tempted like
as we are, He was not altogether like other men. For one thing,
He was "without sin" (iv. 15; vii. 26), and, by this characteristic, He was, in every sense of the words, separated from sinners. Despite the completeness of His identification with men,
He remained, therefore, even in the days of His flesh different
from them and above them.

III. Teaching of Other Epistles

It is only as we carry this conception of the person of Our Lord with us — the conception of Him as at once our Supreme Lord, to whom our adoration is due, and our fellow in the experiences of a human life — that unity is induced in the multiform allusions to Him throughout, whether the Epistles of Paul or the Epistle to the Hebrews, or, indeed, the other epistolary literature of the New Testament. For in this matter there is no difference between those and these. There are no doubt a few passages in these other letters in which a plurality of the elements of the person of Christ are brought together and given detailed mention. In I Pet. iii. 18, for instance, the two constitutive elements of His person are spoken of in the contrast, familiar from Paul, of the "flesh" and the "spirit." But ordinarily we meet only with references to this or that element separately. Everywhere Our Lord is spoken of as having lived out His life as a man; but everywhere also He is spoken of with the supreme reverence which is due to God alone, and the very name of God is not withheld from Him. In I Pet. i. 11 His preëxistence is taken for granted; in Jas. ii. 1 He is identified with the Shekinah, the manifested Jehovah — 'our Lord Jesus Christ, the Glory'; in Jude verse 4 He is "our only Master [Despot] and Lord"; over and over again He is the Divine Lord who is Jehovah (e. g., I Pet. ii. 3, 13; II Pet. iii. 2, 18); in II Pet. i. 1, He is roundly called "our God and Saviour." There is nowhere formal inculcation of the entire doctrine of the person of Christ. But everywhere its elements, now one and now another, are presupposed as the common property of writer and readers. It is only in the Epistles of John that this easy and unstudied presupposition of them gives way to pointed insistence upon them.

IV. Teaching of John

In the circumstances in which he wrote, John found it necessary to insist upon the elements of the person of Our

Lord — His true Deity, His true humanity and the unity of His person — in a manner which is more didactic in form than anything we find in the other writings of the New Testament. The great depository of his teaching on the subject is, of course, the prologue to his Gospel. But it is not merely in this prologue, nor in the Gospel to which it forms a fitting introduction, that these didactic statements are found. The full emphasis of John's witness to the twofold nature of the Lord is brought out, indeed, only by combining what he says in the Gospel and in the Epistles. "In the Gospel," remarks Westcott (on Jn. xx. 31), "the evangelist shows step by step that the historic Jesus was the Christ, the Son of God (opposed to mere 'flesh'); in the Epistle he re-affirms that the Christ, the Son of God, was true man (opposed to mere 'spirit'; I Jn. iv. 2)." What John is concerned to show throughout is that it was "the true God" (I Jn. v. 20) who was "made flesh" (Jn. i. 14); and that this 'only God' (Jn. i. 18, Revised Version, margin "God only begotten") has truly come "in . . . flesh" (I Jn. iv. 2). In all the universe there is no other being of whom it can be said that He is God come in flesh (cf. II Jn. ver. 7, He that "cometh in the flesh," whose characteristic this is). And of all the marvels which have ever occurred in the marvelous history of the universe, this is the greatest — that 'what was from the beginning' (I Jn. ii. 13, 14) has been heard and gazed upon, seen and handled by men (I Jn. i. 1).

From the point of view from which we now approach it, the prologue to the Gospel of John may be said to fall into three parts. In the first of these, the nature of the Being who became incarnate in the person we know as Jesus Christ is described; in the second, the general nature of the act we call the incarnation; and in the third, the nature of the incarnated person.

John here calls the person who became incarnate by a name peculiar to himself in the New Testament — the "Logos" or "Word." According to the predicates which he here applies to Him, he can mean by the "Word" nothing else but God Himself, "considered in His creative, operative, self-revealing, and communicating character," the sum total of what is Divine

(C. F. Schmid). In three crisp sentences he declares at the outset His eternal subsistence, His eternal intercommunion with
God, His eternal identity with God: 'In the beginning the Word
was; and the Word was with God; and the Word was God'
(Jn. i. 1). "In the beginning," at that point of time when things
first began to be (Gen. i. 1), the Word already "was." He antedates the beginning of all things. And He not merely antedates
them, but it is immediately added that He is Himself the creator of all that is: 'All things were made by him, and apart from
him was not made one thing that hath been made' (i. 3). Thus
He is taken out of the category of creatures altogether. Accordingly, what is said of Him is not that He was the first of exist-
ences to come into being — that 'in the beginning He already
had come into being' — but that 'in the beginning, when
things began to come into being, He already *was*.' It is express
eternity of being that is asserted: "the imperfect tense of the
original suggests in this relation, as far as human language can
do so, the notion of absolute, supra-temporal existence" (Westcott). This, His eternal subsistence, was not, however, in isolation: "And the Word was with God." The language is pregnant. It is not merely coexistence with God that is asserted, as
of two beings standing side by side, united in a local relation, or
even in a common conception. What is suggested is an active
relation of intercourse. The distinct personality of the Word is
therefore not obscurely intimated. From all eternity the Word
has been with God as a fellow: He who in the very beginning
already "was," "was" also in communion with God. Though
He was thus in some sense a second along with God, He was
nevertheless not a separate being from God: "And the Word
was" — still the eternal "was" — "God." In some sense distinguishable from God, He was in an equally true sense identical with God. There is but one eternal God; this eternal God,
the Word is; in whatever sense we may distinguish Him from
the God whom He is "with," He is yet not another than this
God, but Himself is this God. The predicate "God" occupies
the position of emphasis in this great declaration, and is so
placed in the sentence as to be thrown up in sharp contrast

with the phrase "with God," as if to prevent inadequate inferences as to the nature of the Word being drawn even momentarily from that phrase. John would have us realize that what the Word was in eternity was not merely God's coeternal fellow, but the eternal God's self.

Now, John tells us that it was this Word, eternal in His subsistence, God's eternal fellow, the eternal God's self, that, as "come in the flesh," was Jesus Christ (I Jn. iv. 2). "And the Word became flesh" (Jn. i. 14), he says. The terms he employs here are not terms of substance, but of personality. The meaning is not that the substance of God was transmuted into that substance which we call "flesh." "The Word" is a personal name of the eternal God; "flesh" is an appropriate designation of humanity in its entirety, with the implications of dependence and weakness. The meaning, then, is simply that He who had just been described as the eternal God became, by a voluntary act in time, a man. The exact nature of the act by which He "became" man lies outside the statement; it was matter of common knowledge between the writer and the reader. The language employed intimates merely that it was a definite act, and that it involved a change in the life-history of the eternal God, here designated "the Word." The whole emphasis falls on the nature of this change in His life-history. He became *flesh*. That is to say, He entered upon a mode of existence in which the experiences that belong to human beings would also be His. The dependence, the weakness, which constitute the very idea of flesh, in contrast with God, would now enter into His personal experience. And it is precisely because these are the connotations of the term "flesh" that John chooses that term here, instead of the more simply denotative term "man." What he means is merely that the eternal God became man. But he elects to say this in the language which throws best up to view what it is to become man. The contrast between the Word as the eternal God and the human nature which He assumed as flesh, is the hinge of the statement. Had the evangelist said (as he does in I Jn. iv. 2) that the Word 'came in flesh,' it would have been the continuity throug the change which would have been most emphasized. When he says rather that the Word became flesh, while the continuity of the personal subject is, of course, intimated, it is the reality and the completeness of the humanity assumed which is made most prominent.

That in becoming flesh the Word did not cease to be what He was before entering upon this new sphere of experiences, the evangelist does not leave, however, to mere suggestion. The glory of the Word was so far from quenched, in his view, by His becoming flesh, that he gives us at once to understand that it was rather as "trailing clouds of glory" that He came. "And the Word became flesh," he says, and immediately adds: "and dwelt among us (and we beheld his glory, glory as of the only begotten from the Father), full of grace and truth" (i. 14). The language is colored by reminiscences from the Tabernacle, in which the Glory of God, the Shekinah, dwelt. The flesh of Our Lord became, on its assumption by the Word, the Temple of God on earth (cf. Jn. ii. 19), and the glory of the Lord filled the house of the Lord. John tells us expressly that this glory was visible, that it was precisely what was appropriate to the Son of God as such. "And we beheld his glory," he says; not divined it, or inferred it, but perceived it. It was open to sight, and the actual object of observation. Jesus Christ was obviously more than man; He was obviously God. His actually observed glory, John tells us further, was a "glory as of the only begotten from the Father." It was unique; nothing like it was ever seen in another. And its uniqueness consisted precisely in its consonance with what the unique Son of God, sent forth from the Father, would naturally have; men recognized and could not but recognize in Jesus Christ the unique Son of God. When this unique Son of God is further described as "full of grace and truth," the elements of His manifested glory are not to be supposed to be exhausted by this description (cf. ii. 11). Certain items of it only are singled out for particular mention. The visible glory of the incarnated Word was such a glory as the unique Son of God, sent forth from the Father, who was full of grace and truth, would naturally manifest.

That nothing should be lacking to the declaration of the continuity of all that belongs to the Word as such into this new sphere of existence, and its full manifestation through the veil of His flesh, John adds at the close of his exposition the remarkable sentence: 'As for God, no one has even yet seen him; God only begotten, who is in the bosom of the Father — He hath declared him' (i. 18 m.). It is the incarnate Word which is here called 'only begotten God.' The absence of the article with this designation is doubtless due to its parallelism with the word "God" which stands at the head of the corresponding clause. The effect of its absence is to throw up into emphasis the quality rather than the mere individuality of the person so designated. The adjective "only begotten" conveys the idea, not of derivation and subordination, but of uniqueness and consubstantiality: Jesus is all that God is, and He alone is this. Of this 'only begotten God' it is now declared that He "is" — not "was," the state is not one which has been left behind at the incarnation, but one which continues uninterrupted and unmodified — "into" — not merely "in" — "the bosom of the Father" — that is to say, He continues in the most intimate and complete communion with the Father. Though now incarnate, He is still "with God" in the full sense of the external relation intimated in i. 1. This being true, He has much more than seen God, and is fully able to "interpret" God to men. Though no one has ever yet seen God, yet he who has seen Jesus Christ, "God only begotten," has seen the Father (cf. xiv. 9; xii. 45). In this remarkable sentence there is asserted in the most direct manner the full Deity of the incarnate Word, and the continuity of His life as such in His incarnate life; thus He is fitted to be the absolute revelation of God to man.

This condensed statement of the whole doctrine of the incarnation is only the prologue to a historical treatise. The historical treatise which it introduces, naturally, is written from the point of view of its prologue. Its object is to present Jesus Christ in His historical manifestation, as obviously the Son of God in flesh. "These are written," the Gospel testi-

fies, "that ye may believe that Jesus is the Christ, the Son
of God" (xx. 31); that Jesus who came as a man (i. 30) was
thoroughly known in His human origin (vii. 27), confessed
Himself man (viii. 40), and died as a man dies (xix. 5), was,
nevertheless, not only the Messiah, the Sent of God, the fulfiller of all the Divine promises of redemption, but also the
very Son of God, that God only begotten, who, abiding in the
bosom of the Father, is His sole adequate interpreter. From
the beginning of the Gospel onward, this purpose is pursued:
Jesus is pictured as ever, while truly man, yet manifesting Himself as equally truly God, until the veil which covered the eyes
of His followers was wholly lifted, and He is greeted as both
Lord and God (xx. 28). But though it is the prime purpose of
this Gospel to exhibit the Divinity of the man Jesus, no obscuration of His manhood is involved. It is the Deity of the man
Jesus which is insisted on, but the true manhood of Jesus is as
prominent in the representation as in any other portion of the
New Testament. Nor is any effacement of the humiliation of
His earthly life involved. For the Son of man to come from
heaven was a descent (iii. 13), and the mission which He came
to fulfil was a mission of contest and conflict, of suffering and
death. He brought His glory with Him (i. 14), but the glory
that was His on earth (xvii. 22) was not all the glory which He
had had with the Father before the world was, and to which,
after His work was done, He should return (xvii. 5). Here too
the glory of the celestial is one and the glory of the terrestrial
is another. In any event, John has no difficulty in presenting
the life of Our Lord on earth as the life of God in flesh, and in
insisting at once on the glory that belongs to Him as God and
on the humiliation which is brought to Him by the flesh. It is
distinctly a duplex life which he ascribes to Christ, and he attributes to Him without embarrassment all the powers and
modes of activity appropriate on the one hand to Deity and
on the other to sinless (Jn. viii. 46; cf. xiv. 30; I Jn. iii. 5)
human nature. In a true sense his portrait of Our Lord is a
dramatization of the God-man which he presents to our contemplation in his prologue.

V. TEACHING OF THE SYNOPTIC GOSPELS

The same may be said of the other Gospels. They are all dramatizations of the God-man set forth in thetical exposition in the prologue to John's Gospel. The Gospel of Luke, written by a known companion of Paul, gives us in a living narrative the same Jesus who is presupposed in all Paul's allusions to Him. That of Mark, who was also a companion of Paul, as also of Peter, is, as truly as the Gospel of John itself, a presentation of facts in the life of Jesus with a view to making it plain that this was the life of no mere man, human as it was, but of the Son of God Himself. Matthew's Gospel differs from its fellows mainly in the greater richness of Jesus' own testimony to His Deity which it records. What is characteristic of all three is the inextricable interlacing in their narratives of the human and Divine traits which alike marked the life they are depicting. It is possible, by neglecting one series of their representations and attending only to the other, to sift out from them at will the portrait of either a purely Divine or a purely human Jesus. It is impossible to derive from them the portrait of any other than a Divine-human Jesus if we surrender ourselves to their guidance and take off of their pages the portrait they have endeavored to draw. As in their narratives they cursorily suggest now the fulness of His Deity and now the completeness of His humanity and everywhere the unity of His person, they present as real and as forcible a testimony to the constitution of Our Lord's person as uniting in one personal life a truly Divine and a truly human nature, as if they announced this fact in analytical statement. Only on the assumption of this conception of Our Lord's person as underlying and determining their presentation, can unity be given to their representations; while, on this supposition, all their representations fall into their places as elements in one consistent whole. Within the limits of their common presupposition, each Gospel has no doubt its own peculiarities in the distribution of its emphasis. Mark lays particular stress on the Divine power of the man Jesus, as evidence of His supernatural being; and on the irresistible impres-

sion of a veritable Son of God, a Divine being walking the earth
as a man, which He made upon all with whom He came into
contact. Luke places his Gospel by the side of the Epistle to
the Hebrews in the prominence it gives to the human development of the Divine being whose life on earth it is depicting and
to the range of temptation to which He was subjected. Matthew's Gospel is notable chiefly for the heights of the Divine
self-consciousness which it uncovers in its report of the words
of Him whom it represents as nevertheless the Son of David,
the Son of Abraham; heights of Divine self-consciousness which
fall in nothing short of those attained in the great utterances
preserved for us by John. But amid whatever variety there
may exist in the aspects on which each lays his particular emphasis, it is the same Jesus Christ which all three bring before
us, a Jesus Christ who is at once God and man and one individual person. If that be not recognized, the whole narrative of
the Synoptic Gospels is thrown into confusion; their portrait of
Christ becomes an insoluble puzzle; and the mass of details
which they present of His life-experiences is transmuted into
a mere set of crass contradictions.

VI. TEACHING OF JESUS

1. The Johannine Jesus. — The Gospel narratives not only
present us, however, with dramatizations of the God-man, according to their authors' conception of His composite person.
They preserve for us also a considerable body of the utterances
of Jesus Himself, and this enables us to observe the conception
of His person which underlay and found expression in Our
Lord's own teaching. The discourses of Our Lord which have
been selected for record by John have been chosen (among
other reasons) expressly for the reason that they bear witness
to His essential Deity. They are accordingly peculiarly rich in
material for forming a judgment of Our Lord's conception of
His higher nature. This conception, it is needless to say, is precisely that which John, taught by it, has announced in the prologue to his Gospel, and has illustrated by his Gospel itself,

compacted as it is of these discourses. It will not be necessary to present the evidence for this in its fulness. It will be enough to point to a few characteristic passages, in which Our Lord's conception of His higher nature finds especially clear expression.

That He was of higher than earthly origin and nature, He repeatedly asserts. "Ye are from beneath," he says to the Jews (viii. 23), "I am from above: ye are of this world; I am not of this world" (cf. xvii. 16). Therefore, He taught that He, the Son of Man, had "descended out of heaven" (iii. 13), where was His true abode. This carried with it, of course, an assertion of preëxistence; and this preëxistence is explicitly affirmed: "What then," He asks, "if ye should behold the Son of man ascending where he was before?" (vi. 62). It is not merely preëxistence, however, but eternal preëxistence which He claims for Himself: "And now, Father," He prays (xvii. 5), "glorify thou me with thine own self with the glory which I had with thee before the world was" (cf. ver. 24); and again, as the most impressive language possible, He declares (viii. 58 A.V.): "Verily, verily, I say unto you, Before Abraham was, I am," where He claims for Himself the timeless present of eternity as His mode of existence. In the former of these two last-cited passages, the character of His preëxistent life is intimated; in it He shared the Father's glory from all eternity ("before the world was"); He stood by the Father's side as a companion in His glory. He came forth, when He descended to earth, therefore, not from heaven only, but from the very side of God (viii. 42; xvii. 8). Even this, however, does not express the whole truth; He came forth not only from the Father's side where He had shared in the Father's glory; He came forth out of the Father's very being — "I came out from the Father, and am come into the world" (xvi. 28; cf. viii. 42). "The connection described is internal and essential, and not that of presence or external fellowship" (Westcott). This prepares us for the great assertion: "I and the Father are one" (x. 30), from which it is a mere corollary that "He that hath seen me hath seen the Father" (xiv. 9; cf. viii. 19; xii. 45).

In all these declarations the subject of the affirmation is the actual person speaking: it is of Himself who stood before men and spoke to them that Our Lord makes these immense assertions. Accordingly, when He majestically declared, "I and the Father are" (plurality of persons) "one" (neuter singular, and accordingly singleness of being), the Jews naturally understood Him to be making Himself, the person then speaking to them, God (x. 33; cf. v. 18; xix. 7). The continued sameness of the person who has been, from all eternity down to this hour, one with God, is therefore fully safeguarded. His earthly life is, however, distinctly represented as a humiliation. Though even on earth He is one with the Father, yet He "descended" to earth; He had come out from the Father and out of God; a glory had been left behind which was yet to be returned to, and His sojourn on earth was therefore to that extent an obscuration of His proper glory. There was a sense, then, in which, because He had "descended," He was no longer equal with the Father. It was in order to justify an assertion of equality with the Father in power (x. 25, 29) that He was led to declare: "I and my Father are one" (x. 30). But He can also declare "The Father is greater than I" (xiv. 28). Obviously this means that there was a sense in which He had ceased to be equal with the Father, because of the humiliation of His present condition, and in so far as this humiliation involved entrance into a status lower than that which belonged to Him by nature. Precisely in what this humiliation consisted can be gathered only from the general implication of many statements. In it He was a "man": 'a man who hath told you the truth, which I have heard from God' (viii. 40), where the contrast with "God" throws the assertion of humanity into emphasis (cf. x. 33). The truth of His human nature is, however, everywhere assumed and endlessly illustrated, rather than explicitly asserted. He possessed a human soul (xii. 27) and bodily parts (flesh and blood, vi. 53 ff.; hands and side, xx. 27); and was subject alike to physical affections (weariness, iv. 6, and thirst, xix. 28, suffering and death), and to all the common human emotions — not merely the love of compassion (xiii. 34; xiv. 21; xv. 8–13), but the love of simple affection which we pour out on "friends" (xi. 11; cf.

xv. 14, 15), indignation (xi. 33, 38) and joy (xv. 11; xvii. 13). He felt the perturbation produced by strong excitement (xi. 33; xii. 27; xiii. 21), the sympathy with suffering which shows itself in tears (xi. 35), the thankfulness which fills the grateful heart (vi. 11, 23; xi. 41. Only one human characteristic was alien to Him: He was without sin: "the prince of the world," He declared, "hath nothing in me" (xiv. 30; cf. viii. 46). Clearly Our Lord, as reported by John, knew Himself to be true God and true man in one indivisible person, the common subject of the qualities which belong to each.

2. The Synoptic Jesus. — (a) Mk. xiii. 32: The same is true of His self-consciousness as revealed in His sayings recorded by the synoptists. Perhaps no more striking illustration of this could be adduced than the remarkable declaration recorded in Mk. xiii. 32 (cf. Mt. xxiv. 36): 'But of that day or that hour knoweth no one, not even the angels in heaven, nor yet the Son, but the Father.' Here Jesus places Himself, in an ascending scale of being, above "the angels in heaven," that is to say, the highest of all creatures, significantly marked here as supramundane. Accordingly, He presents Himself elsewhere as the Lord of the angels, whose behests they obey: "The Son of man shall send forth his angels, and they shall gather out of his kingdom all things that cause stumbling, and them that do iniquity" (Mt. xiii. 41), "And he shall send forth his angels with a great sound of a trumpet, and they shall gather together his elect from the four winds, from one end of heaven to the other" (Mt. xxiv. 31; cf. xiii. 49; xxv. 31; Mk. viii. 38). Thus the "angels of God" (Lk. xii. 8, 9; xv. 10) Christ designates as His angels, the "kingdom of God" (Mt. xii. 28; xix. 24; xxi. 31, 43; Mk. and Lk. often) as His Kingdom, the "elect of God" (Mk. xiii. 20; Lk. xviii. 7; cf. Rom. viii. 33; Col. iii. 12; Tit. i. 1) as His elect. He is obviously speaking in Mk. xiii. 22 out of a Divine self-consciousness: "Only a Divine being can be exalted above angels" (B. Weiss). He therefore designates Himself by His Divine name, "the Son," that is to say, the unique Son of God (ix. 7; i. 11), to claim to be whom would for a man be blasphemy (Mk. xiv. 61, 64). But though He desig-

nates Himself by this Divine name, He is not speaking of what He once was, but of what at the moment of speaking He is: the action of the verb is present, "knoweth." He is claiming, in other words, the supreme designation of "the Son," with all that is involved in it, for His present self, as He moved among men: He is, not merely was, "the Son." Nevertheless, what He affirms of Himself cannot be affirmed of Himself distinctively as "the Son." For what He affirms of Himself is ignorance — "not even the Son" knows it; and ignorance does not belong to the Divine nature which the term "the Son" connotes. An extreme appearance of contradiction accordingly arises from the use of this terminology, just as it arises when Paul says that the Jews "crucified the Lord of glory" (I Cor. ii. 8), or exhorts the Ephesian elders to "feed the church of God which he purchased with his own blood" (Acts xx. 28 m.); or John Keble praises Our Lord for "the blood of souls by Thee redeemed." It was not the Lord of Glory as such who was nailed to the tree, nor have either "God" or "souls" blood to shed.

We know how this apparently contradictory mode of speech has arisen in Keble's case. He is speaking of men who are composite beings, consisting of souls and bodies, and these men come to be designated from one element of their composite personalities, though what is affirmed by them belongs rather to the other; we may speak, therefore, of the "blood of souls" meaning that these "souls," while not having blood as such, yet designate persons who have bodies and therefore blood. We know equally how to account for Paul's apparent contradictions. We know that he conceived of Our Lord as a composite person, uniting in Himself a Divine and a human nature. In Paul's view, therefore, though God as such has no blood, yet Jesus Christ who is God has blood because He is also man. He can justly speak, therefore, when speaking of Jesus Christ, of His blood as the blood of God. When precisely the same phenomenon meets us in Our Lord's speech of Himself, we must presume that it is the outgrowth of precisely the same state of things. When He speaks of "the Son" (who is God) as ignorant, we must understand that He is designating Himself as "the

Son" because of His higher nature, and yet has in mind the
ignorance of His lower nature; what He means is that the person properly designated "the Son" is ignorant, that is to say
with respect to the human nature which is as intimate an
element of His personality as is His Deity.

When Our Lord says, then, that "the Son knows not," He
becomes as express a witness to the two natures which constitute His person as Paul is when he speaks of the blood of God,
or as Keble is a witness to the twofold constitution of a human
being when he speaks of souls shedding blood. In this short
sentence, thus, Our Lord bears witness to His Divine nature
with its supremacy above all creatures, to His human nature
with its creaturely limitations, and to the unity of the subject
possessed of these two natures.

(b) Other passages: Son of Man and Son of God: All these
elements of His personality find severally repeated assertions
in other utterances of Our Lord recorded in the Synoptics.
There is no need to insist here on the elevation of Himself
above the kings and prophets of the Old Covenant (Mt. xii.
41 ff.), above the temple itself (Mt. xii. 6), and the ordinances
of the Divine Law (Mt. xii. 8); or on His accent of authority
in both His teaching and action, His great "I say unto you"
(Mt. v. 21, 22), 'I will; be cleansed' (Mk. i. 41; ii. 5; Lk. vii.
14); or on His separation of Himself from men in His relation
to God, never including them with Himself in an "Our Father,"
but consistently speaking distinctively of "my Father" (e. g.,
Lk. xxiv. 49) and "your Father" (e. g., Mt. v. 16); or on His
intimation that He is not merely David's Son but David's
Lord, and that a Lord sitting on the right hand of God (Mt.
xxii. 44); or on His parabolic discrimination of Himself a Son
and Heir from all "servants" (Mt. xxi. 33 ff.); or even on His
ascription to Himself of the purely Divine functions of the forgiveness of sins (Mk. ii. 8) and judgment of the world (Mt. xxv.
31), or of the purely Divine powers of reading the heart (Mk.
ii. 8; Lk. ix. 47), omnipotence (Mt. xxiv. 30; Mk. xiv. 62) and
omnipresence (Mt. xviii. 20; xxviii. 10). These things illustrate
His constant assumption of the possession of Divine dignity

and attributes; the claim itself is more directly made in the two great designations which He currently gave Himself, the Son of Man and the Son of God. The former of these is His favorite self-designation. Derived from Dan. vii. 13, 14, it intimates on every occasion of its employment Our Lord's consciousness of being a supramundane being, who has entered into a sphere of earthly life on a high mission, on the accomplishment of which He is to return to His heavenly sphere, whence He shall in due season come back to earth, now, however, in His proper majesty, to gather up the fruits of His work and consummate all things. It is a designation, thus, which implies at once a heavenly preëxistence, a present humiliation, and a future glory; and He proclaims Himself in this future glory no less than the universal King seated on the throne of judgment for quick and dead (Mk. viii. 31; Mt. xxv. 31). The implication of Deity imbedded in the designation, Son of Man, is perhaps more plainly spoken out in the companion designation, Son of God, which Our Lord not only accepts at the hands of others, accepting with it the implication of blasphemy in permitting its application to Himself (Mt. xxvi. 63, 65; Mk. xiv. 61, 64; Lk. xxii. 29, 30), but persistently claims for Himself both, in His constant designation of God as His Father in a distinctive sense, and in His less frequent but more pregnant designation of Himself as, by way of eminence, "the Son." That His consciousness of the peculiar relation to God expressed by this designation was not an attainment of His mature spiritual development, but was part of His most intimate consciousness from the beginning, is suggested by the sole glimpse which is given us into His mind as a child (Lk. ii. 49). The high significance which the designation bore to Him is revealed to us in two remarkable utterances preserved, the one by both Matthew (xi. 27 ff.) and Luke (x. 22 ff.), and the other by Matthew (xxviii. 19).

(c) Mt. xi. 27; xxviii. 19: In the former of these utterances, Our Lord, speaking in the most solemn manner, not only presents Himself, as the Son, as the sole source of knowledge of God and of blessedness for men, but places Himself in a position, not of equality merely, but of absolute reciprocity and interpenetration of knowledge with the Father. "No one," He says, "knoweth the Son, save the Father; neither doth any know the Father, save the Son . . ." varied in Luke so as to read: "No one knoweth who the Son is, save the Father; and who the Father is, save the Son . . ." as if the being of the Son were so immense that only God could know it thoroughly; and the knowledge of the Son was so unlimited that He could know God to perfection. The peculiarly pregnant employment here of the terms "Son" and "Father" over against one another is explained to us in the other utterance (Mt. xxviii. 19). It is the resurrected Lord's commission to His disciples. Claiming for Himself all authority in heaven and on earth — whieh implies the possession of omnipotence — and promising to be with His followers 'alway, even to the end of the world '— which adds the implications of omnipresence and omniscience — He commands them to baptize their converts 'in the name of the Father and of the Son and of the Holy Ghost.' The precise form of the formula must be carefully observed. It does not read: 'In the names' (plural) — as if there were three beings enumerated, each with its distinguishing name. Nor yet: 'In the name of the Father, Son and Holy Ghost,' as if there were one person, going by a threefold name. It reads: 'In the name [singular] of the Father, and of the [article repeated] Son, and of the [article repeated] Holy Ghost,' carefully distinguishing three persons, though uniting them all under one name. The name of God was to the Jews Jehovah, and to name the name of Jehovah upon them was to make them His. What Jesus did in this great injunction was to command His followers to name the name of God upon their converts, and to announce the name of God which is to be named on their converts in the threefold enumeration of "the Father" and "the Son" and "the Holy Ghost." As it is unquestionable that He intended Himself by "the Son," He here places Himself by the side of the Father and the Spirit, as together with them constituting the one God. It is, of course, the Trinity which He is describing; and that is as much as to say that He announces Himself as one of the persons of the Trinity. This is what Jesus, as reported by the Synoptics, understood Himself to be.

In announcing Himself to be God, however, Jesus does not deny that He is man also. If all His speech of Himself rests on His consciousness of a Divine nature, no less does all His speech manifest His consciousness of a human nature. He easily identifies Himself with men (Mt. iv. 1; Lk. iv. 1), and receives without protest the imputation of humanity (Mt. xi. 19; Lk. vii. 34). He speaks familiarly of His body (Mt. xxvi. 12, 26; Mk. xiv. 8; xiv. 22; Lk. xxii. 19), and of His bodily parts — His feet and hands (Lk. xxiv. 39), His head and feet (Lk. vii. 44–46), His flesh and bones (Lk. xxiv. 39), His blood (Mt. xxvi. 28, Mk. xiv. 24; Lk. xxii. 20). We chance to be given indeed a very express affirmation on His part of the reality of His bodily nature; when His disciples were terrified at His appearing before them after His resurrection, supposing Him to be a spirit, He reassures them with the direct declaration: "See my hands and my feet, that it is I myself: handle me, and see; for a spirit hath not flesh and bones, as ye behold me having" (Lk. xxiv. 39). His testimony to His human soul is just as express: "My soul," says He, "is exceeding sorrowful, even unto death" (Mt. xxvi. 38; Mk. xiv. 34). He speaks of the human dread with which He looked forward to His approaching death (Lk. xii. 50), and expresses in a poignant cry His sense of desolation on the cross (Mt. xxvii. 46; Mk. xv. 34). He speaks also of His pity for the weary and hungering people (Mt. xv. 32; Mk. viii. 2), and of a strong human desire which He felt (Lk. xxii. 15). Nothing that is human is alien to Him except sin. He never ascribes imperfection to Himself and never betrays consciousness of sin. He recognizes the evil of those about Him (Lk. xi. 13; Mt. vii. 11; xii. 34, 39; Lk. xi. 29), but never identifies Himself with it. It is those who do the will of God with whom He feels kinship (Mt. xii. 50), and He offers Himself to the morally sick as a physician (Mt. ix. 12). He proposes Himself as an example of the highest virtues (Mt. xi. 28 ff.) and pronounces him blessed who shall find no occasion of stumbling in Him (Mt. xi. 6).

These manifestations of a human and Divine consciousness

simply stand side by side in the records of Our Lord's self-expression. Neither is suppressed or even qualified by the other. If we attend only to the one class we might suppose Him to proclaim Himself wholly Divine; if only to the other we might equally easily imagine Him to be representing Himself as wholly human. With both together before us we perceive Him alternately speaking out of a Divine and out of a human consciousness; manifesting Himself as all that God is and as all that man is; yet with the most marked unity of consciousness. He, the one Jesus Christ, was to His own apprehension true God and complete man in a unitary personal life.

VII. The Two Natures Everywhere Presupposed

There underlies, thus, the entire literature of the New Testament a single, unvarying conception of the constitution of Our Lord's person. From Matthew where He is presented as one of the persons of the Holy Trinity (xxviii. 19) — or if we prefer the chronological order of books, from the Epistle of James where He is spoken of as the Glory of God, the Shekinah (ii. 1) — to the Apocalypse where He is represented as declaring that He is the Alpha and the Omega, the First and the Last, the Beginning and the End (i. 8, 17; xxii. 13), He is consistently thought of as in His fundamental being just God. At the same time from the Synoptic Gospels, in which He is dramatized as a man walking among men, His human descent carefully recorded, and His sense of dependence on God so emphasized that prayer becomes almost His most characteristic action, to the Epistles of John in which it is made the note of a Christian that He confesses that Jesus Christ has come in flesh (I Jn. iv. 2) and the Apocalypse in which His birth in the tribe of Judah and the house of David (v. 5; xxii. 16), His exemplary life of conflict and victory (iii. 21), His death on the cross (xi. 8) are noted, He is equally consistently thought of as true man. Nevertheless, from the beginning to the end of the whole series of books, while first one and then the other of His two natures comes into repeated prominence, there is never a question of conflict between the two, never any confusion in their relations, never any schism in His unitary personal action; but He is obviously considered and presented as one, composite indeed, but undivided personality. In this state of the case not only may evidence of the constitution of Our Lord's person properly be drawn indifferently from every part of the New Testament, and passage justly be cited to support and explain passage without reference to the portion of the New Testament in which it is found, but we should be without justification if we did not employ this common presupposition of the whole body of this literature to illustrate and explain the varied representations which meet us cursorily in its pages, representations which might easily be made to appear mutually contradictory were they not brought into harmony by their relation as natural component parts of this one unitary conception which underlies and gives consistency to them all. There can scarcely be imagined a better proof of the truth of a doctrine than its power completely to harmonize a multitude of statements which without it would present to our view only a mass of confused inconsistencies. A key which perfectly fits a lock of very complicated wards can scarcely fail to be the true key.

VIII. FORMULATION OF THE DOCTRINE

Meanwhile the wards remain complicated. Even in the case of our own composite structure, of soul and body, familiar as we are with it from our daily experience, the mutual relations of elements so disparate in a single personality remain an unplumbed mystery, and give rise to paradoxical modes of speech, which would be misleading, were not their source in our duplex nature well understood. We may read, in careful writers, of souls being left dead on battlefields, and of everybody's immortality. The mysteries of the relations in which the constituent elements in the more complex personality of Our Lord stand to one another are immeasurably greater than in our simpler case. We can never hope to comprehend how the infinite God and a finite humanity can be united in a single person; and it is very easy to go fatally astray in attempting to explain the interactions in the unitary person of natures so diverse from one another. It is not surprising, therefore, that so soon as serious efforts began to be made to give systematic explanations of the Biblical facts as to Our Lord's person, many one-sided and incomplete statements were formulated which required correction and complementing before at length a mode of statement was devised which did full justice to the Biblical data. It was accordingly only after more than a century of controversy, during which nearly every conceivable method of construing and misconstruing the Biblical facts had been proposed and tested, that a formula was framed which successfully guarded the essential data supplied by the Scriptures from destructive misconception. This formula, put together by the Council of Chalcedon, 451 A.D., declares it to have always been the doctrine of the church, derived from the Scriptures and Our Lord Himself, that Our Lord Jesus Christ is "truly God and truly man, of a reasonable soul and body; consubstantial with the Father according to the Godhead, and consubstantial with us according to the manhood; in all things like unto us, without sin; begotten before all ages of the Father according to the Godhead, and in these latter days, for us and for our salvation, born of the Virgin Mary, the Mother of God, according to the manhood; one and the same Christ, Son, Lord, Only-begotten, to be acknowledged in two natures inconfusedly, unchangeably, indivisibly, inseparably; the distinction of natures being by no means taken away by the union, but rather the property of each nature being preserved, and concurring in one Person and one subsistence, not parted or divided into two persons, but one and the same Son, and Only-begotten, God, the Word, the Lord Jesus Christ." There is nothing here but a careful statement in systematic form of the pure teaching of the Scriptures; and therefore this statement has stood ever since as the norm of thought and teaching as to the person of the Lord. As such, it has been incorporated, in one form or another, into the creeds of all the great branches of the church; it underlies and gives their form to all the allusions to Christ in the great mass of preaching and song which has accumulated during the centuries; and it has supplied the background of the devotions of the untold multitudes who through the Christian ages have been worshippers of Christ.

LITERATURE. — The appropriate sections in the treatises on the Biblical theology of the New Testament; also A. B. Bruce, "The Humiliation of Christ," 2d ed., Edinburgh, 1881; R. L. Ottley, "The Doctrine of the Incarnation," London, 1896; H. C. Powell, "The Principle of the Incarnation," London, 1896; Francis J. Hall, "The Kenotic Theory," New York, 1898; C. A. Briggs, "The Incarnation of the Lord," New York, 1902; G. S. Streatfeild, "The Self-Interpretation of Jesus Christ," London, 1906; B. B. Warfield, "The Lord of Glory," New York, 1907; James Denney, "Jesus and the Gospel," London, 1908; M. Lepin, "Christ and the Gospel: or, Jesus the Messiah and Son of God," Philadelphia, 1910; James Stalker, "The Christology of Jesus," New York, 1899; D. Somerville, "St. Paul's Conception of Christ," Edinburgh, 1897; E. H. Gifford, "The Incarnation: a Study of Phil. ii. 5–11," London, 1897; S. N. Rostron, "The Christology of St. Paul," London, 1912; E. Digges La Touche, "The Person of Christ in Modern Thought," London, 1912.

[NOTE. — In this article the author has usually given his own translation of quotations from Scripture, and not that of any particular VS.]

VI

"GOD OUR FATHER AND THE LORD JESUS CHRIST"

"GOD OUR FATHER AND THE LORD JESUS CHRIST"[1]

In the opening sentence of the very first of Paul's letters which have come down to us — and that is as much as to say, in the very first sentence which, so far as we know, he ever wrote, — he makes use of a phrase in speaking of the Christians' God, which at once attracts our interested attention. According to the generous way he had of thinking and speaking of his readers at the height of their professions, he describes the church at Thessalonica as living and moving and having its being in God. But, as it was a Christian church which he was addressing, he does not content himself, in this description, with the simple term "God." He uses the compound phrase, "God the Father and the Lord Jesus Christ." The Thessalonians, he says, because they were Christians, lived and moved and had their being "in God the Father and the Lord Jesus Christ."

It is quite clear that this compound phrase was not new on Paul's lips, coined for this occasion. It bears on its face the evidence of a long and familiar use, by which it had been worn down to its bare bones. All the articles have been rubbed off, and with them all other accessories; and it stands out in its baldest elements as just "God Father and Lord Jesus Christ." Plainly we have here a mode of speaking of the Christians' God which was customary with Paul.

We are not surprised, therefore, to find this phrase repeated in precisely the same connection in the opening verses of the next letter which Paul wrote — II Thessalonians — with only the slight variation that an "our" is inserted with "God the Father," — "in God our Father and the Lord Jesus Christ." The significance of this variation is, probably, that, although it is a customary formula which is being employed, it has not hardened into a mechanically repeated series of mere words.

[1] From *The Princeton Theological Review*, v. xv, 1917, pp. 1–20.

It is used with lively consciousness of its full meaning, and with such slight variations of wording from time to time as the circumstances of each case, or perhaps the mere emotional movement of the moment, suggested.

This free handling of what is, nevertheless, clearly in essence a fixed formula, is sharply illustrated by a third instance of its occurrence. Paul uses it again in the opening sentence of the third letter which he wrote, — that to the Galatians. Here it is turned, however, end to end, while yet preserving all its essential elements; and is set in such a context as to throw its fundamental meaning into very strong emphasis. Paul was called upon to defend to the Galatians the validity of his apostleship, and he characteristically takes occasion to assert, in the very first words which he wrote to them, that he received it from no human source, — no, nor even through any human intermediation, — but directly from God. The way he does this is to announce himself as "an apostle not from men, neither through man, but through Jesus Christ and God the Father" — "who," he adds, "raised Him from the dead." The effect of the addition of these last words is to throw the whole emphasis of the clause on "Jesus Christ"; even "God the Father" is defined in relation to Him. Yet the whole purpose of the sentence is to assert the divine origin of Paul's apostleship in strong contrast with any possible human derivation of it. Clearly, the phrase "Jesus Christ and God the Father" denotes something purely Divine. It is in effect a Christian periphrasis for "God." And in this Christian periphrasis for "God" the name of Jesus Christ takes no subordinate place.

It will conduce to our better apprehension of the nature and implications of this Christian periphrasis for "God" which Paul employs in the opening words of each of the first three of his epistles, if we will set side by side the actual words in which it is phrased in these three instances.

I Thess. i. 1: ἐν θεῷ πατρὶ καὶ κυρίῳ Ἰησοῦ Χριστῷ.

II Thess. i. 1: ἐν θεῷ πατρὶ ἡμῶν καὶ κυρίῳ Ἰησοῦ Χριστῷ.

Gal. i. 1: διὰ Ἰησοῦ Χριστοῦ καὶ θεοῦ πατρὸς τοῦ ἐγείραντος αὐτὸν ἐκ νεκρῶν.

It is not, however, merely or chiefly in these three instances that Paul uses this Christian periphrasis for God. It is the apostle's custom to bring the address which he prefixes to each of his letters to a close in a formal prayer that the fundamental Christian blessings of grace and peace (or, in the letters to Timothy, grace, mercy and peace) may be granted to his readers. In this prayer he regularly employs this periphrasis to designate the Divine Being to whom the prayer is offered. It fails to appear in this opening prayer in two only of his thirteen letters; and its failure to appear in these two is useful in fixing its meaning in the other eleven. It is quite clear that Paul intends to say the same thing in all thirteen instances: they differ only in the fulness with which he expresses his identical meaning. When he says in I Thess. i. 1 only "Grace to you and peace," he is not expressing a mere wish; he is invoking the Divine Being in prayer; and his mind is as fully on Him as if he had formally named Him. And when he names this Divine Being whom he is invoking in this prayer, in Col. i. 2, "God our Father," — "Grace to you and peace from God our Father" — his meaning is precisely the same as when he names Him in the companion letter, Eph. i. 2, "God our Father and the Lord Jesus Christ" — "Grace to you and peace from God our Father and the Lord Jesus Christ" — or in a similar prayer at the end of the same letter, Eph. vi. 23, "God the Father and the Lord Jesus Christ" — "Peace to the brethren and love along with faith from God the Father and the Lord Jesus Christ." In every instance Paul is invoking the Divine Being and only the Divine Being. Once he leaves that to be understood from the nature of the case. Once he names this Being simply "God the Father." In the other eleven instances he gives Him the conjunct name, which ordinarily takes the form of "God our Father and the Lord Jesus Christ," — obviously employing a formula which had become habitual with him in such formal prayers.

That we may see at a glance how clear it is that Paul is making use here of a fixed formula in his designation of the Christians' God, and may observe at the same time the amount of freedom which he allows himself in repeating it in these very formal prayers, we bring together the series of these opening prayers, in the chronological order of the epistles in which they occur.

I Thess. i. 1: χάρις ὑμῖν καὶ εἰρήνη.

II Thess. i. 2: χάρις ὑμῖν καὶ εἰρήνη ἀπὸ θεοῦ πατρὸς καὶ κυρίου Ἰησοῦ Χριστοῦ.

Gal. i. 3: χάρις ὑμῖν καὶ εἰρήνη ἀπὸ θεοῦ πατρὸς ἡμῶν καὶ κυρίου Ἰησοῦ Χριστοῦ.

I Cor. i. 3: χάρις ὑμῖν καὶ εἰρήνη ἀπὸ θεοῦ πατρὸς ἡμῶν καὶ κυρίου Ἰησοῦ Χριστοῦ.

II Cor. i. 2: χάρις ὑμῖν καὶ εἰρήνη ἀπὸ Θεοῦ πατρὸς ἡμῶν καὶ κυρίου Ἰησοῦ Χριστοῦ.

Rom. i. 7: χάρις ὑμῖν καὶ εἰρήνη ἀπὸ θεοῦ πατρὸς ἡμῶν καὶ κυρίου Ἰησοῦ Χριστοῦ.

Eph. i. 2: χάρις ὑμῖν καὶ εἰρήνη ἀπὸ θεοῦ πατρὸς ἡμῶν καὶ κυρίου Ἰησοῦ Χριστοῦ.

[Eph. vi. 23: εἰρήνη τοῖς ἀδελφοῖς καὶ ἀγάπη μετὰ πίστεως ἀπὸ θεοῦ πατρὸς καὶ κυρίου Ἰησοῦ Χριστοῦ.]

Col. i. 2: χάρις ὑμῖν καὶ εἰρήνη ἀπὸ θεοῦ πατρὸς ἡμῶν.

Phile. 3: χάρις ὑμῖν καὶ εἰρήνη ἀπὸ θεοῦ πατρὸς ἡμῶν καὶ κυρίου Ἰησοῦ Χριστοῦ.

Phil. i. 2: χάρις ὑμῖν καὶ εἰρήνη ἀπὸ θεοῦ πατρὸς ἡμῶν καὶ κυρίου Ἰησοῦ Χριστοῦ.

I Tim. i. 2: χάρις ἔλεος εἰρήνη ἀπὸ θεοῦ πατρὸς καὶ Χριστοῦ Ἰησοῦ τοῦ κυρίου ἡμῶν.

Tit. i. 4: χάρις καὶ εἰρήνη ἀπὸ θεοῦ πατρὸς καὶ Χριστοῦ Ἰησοῦ τοῦ σωτῆρος ἡμῶν.

II Tim. i. 2: χάρις ἔλεος εἰρήνη ἀπὸ θεοῦ πατρὸς καὶ Χριστοῦ Ἰησοῦ τοῦ κυρίου ἡμῶν.

Alfred Seeberg, seeking evidence of the survival of old Christian formulas in the literature of the New Testament, very naturally fixes on these passages, and argues that we have here a combination of the names of God the Father and the Lord Jesus Christ in prayer which Paul found already in use in the Christian community when he attached himself to it, and which

he took over from it. It is a hard saying when Ernst von Dobschütz professes himself ready to concede that Paul received
this combination of names from his predecessors, but sharply
denies that he received it as a "fixed formula." One would
have supposed it to lie on the face of Paul's use of it that he
was repeating a formula; while it might be disputed whether
it was a formula of his own making or he had adopted it from
others. It goes to show that it was not invented by Paul, that it
is found not only in other connections in Paul's writings, as we
have seen, but also in other New Testament books besides his.

Jas. i. 1: θεοῦ καὶ κυρίου 'Ιησοῦ Χριστοῦ δοῦλος.

II Pet. i. 2: ἐν ἐπιγνώσει τοῦ θεοῦ καὶ 'Ιησοῦ τοῦ κυρίου ἡμῶν.

II Jno. 3: ἔσται μεθ' ἡμῶν χάρις ἔλεος εἰρήνη παρὰ θεοῦ πατρὸς καὶ παρὰ 'Ιησοῦ Χριστοῦ τοῦ υἱοῦ τοῦ πατρός.

In the presence of these passages it is difficult to deny that we
have in the closely knit conjunction of these two Divine names
part of the established phraseology of primitive Christian religious speech.

It would not be easy to exaggerate the closeness with which
the two names are knit together in this formula. The two persons brought together are not, to be sure, absolutely identified.
They remain two persons, to each of whom severally there
may be ascribed activities in which the other does not share.
In Gal i. 1 we read of "Jesus Christ and God the Father who
raised Him from the dead." In Gal. i. 3, we read of "God the
Father and our Lord Jesus Christ who gave Himself for our
sins." The epithets by which they are described, moreover, are
distinctive, — the Father, our Father, the Lord, our Lord, our
Saviour. There is no obscuration, then, of the peculiarities of
the personalities brought together. But their equalization is
absolute. And short of thoroughgoing identification of persons
the unity expressed by their conjunction seems to be complete.

How complete this unity is may be illustrated by another
series of passages. J. B. Lightfoot has called attention to the
symmetrical structure of the two Epistles to the Thessalonians.
Each is divided into two parts ("the first part being chiefly

narrative and explanatory, and the second hortatory"), and
each of these parts closes with a prayer introduced by αὐτὸς δέ
followed by the Divine name, — a construction not found elsewhere in these epistles. Clearly there is formal art at work here;
and it will repay us to bring together the opening words of the
four prayers, including the designations by which God is invoked in each.

I Thess. iii. 11: αὐτὸς δὲ ὁ θεὸς καὶ πατὴρ ἡμῶν καὶ ὁ κύριος
    ἡμῶν ᾽Ιησοῦς.

I Thess. v. 23: αὐτὸς δὲ ὁ θεὸς τῆς εἰρήνης.

II Thess. ii. 16: αὐτὸς δὲ ὁ κύριος ἡμῶν ᾽Ιησοῦς Χριστὸς καὶ
    ὁ θεὸς ὁ πατὴρ ἡμῶν ὁ ἀγαπήσας ἡμᾶς καὶ δοὺς παρά-
    κλησιν αἰωνίαν καὶ ἐλπίδα ἀγαθὴν ἐν χάριτι.

II Thess. iii. 16: αὐτὸς δὲ ὁ κύριος τῆς εἰρήνης.

It is remarkable how illuminating the mere conjunction of
these passages is. Taking I Thess. iii. 11 in isolation, we might
wonder whether we ought to read it, "God Himself, even our
Father and our Lord Jesus," or "Our God and Father Himself,
and our Lord Jesus," or "Our God and Father and our Lord
Jesus, Himself." So, taking it in isolation, we might hesitate
whether we should construe II Thess. ii. 16, "Our Lord Jesus
Christ Himself, and God our Father," or "Our Lord Jesus
Christ and God our Father, Himself." The commentators accordingly divide themselves among these views, each urging
reasons which scarcely seem convincing for his choice. But so
soon as we bring the passages together it becomes clear that the
αὐτός is to be construed with the whole subject following it in
every case, and thus a solid foundation is put beneath the opinion arrived at on other grounds by Martin Dibelius, Ernst von
Dobschütz and J. E. Frame, that in I Thess. iii. 11 and II
Thess. ii. 16, the αὐτός binds together the two subjects, God
and the Lord, as the conjunct object of Paul's prayer.

The four prayers are in every sense of the word parallel.
The petition is substantially the same in all. It cannot be
imagined that the Being to whom the several prayers are addressed was consciously envisaged as different. Paul is in every

case simply bringing his heart's desire for his converts before his God. Yet, in describing the God before whom he lays his petition, he fairly exhausts the possibilities of variety of designation which the case affords. As a result, God the Father and the Lord Jesus Christ could not be more indissolubly knit together as essentially one. Both are mentioned in two of the addresses, but the order in which they are mentioned is reversed from one to the other, and all the predicates in both instances are cast in the singular number. In the other two addresses only one is named, but it is a different one in each case, although an identical epithet is attributed to them both. We learn thus not only that Paul prays indifferently to God and to the Lord — in precisely the same way, for precisely the same things, and with precisely the same attitude of mind and heart, expressed in identical epithets, — but also that he prays thus indifferently to God or the Lord separately and to God and the Lord together. And when he prays to the two together, he does all that it is humanly possible to do to make it clear that he is thinking of them not as two but as one. Interchanging the names, so that they stand indifferently in the order "God and the Lord," or "the Lord and God," he binds them together in a single "self"; and then, proceeding with his prayer, he construes this double subject, thus bound together in a single "self," in both cases alike with a singular verb, — "Now our Lord Jesus Christ and God our Father who loved us . . . Himself," he prays, "may He comfort your hearts and establish them in every good work and word." "Now our God and Father and our Lord Jesus, Himself," he prays again, "may He direct our way unto you": and then he proceeds immediately, continuing the prayer, but now with only one name, though obviously with no change in the Being addressed, — "and may the Lord make you to increase and abound in love toward one another and toward all men." If it was with any difference of consciousness that Paul addressed God or the Lord, or God and the Lord together, in his prayers, he certainly has taken great pains to obscure that fact. If he had intended to show plainly that to him God and the Lord were so one that

God and the Lord conjoined were still one to his consciousness, he could scarcely have found more effective means of doing so. There is probably no instance in all Paul's epistles where God and the Lord are mentioned together, that they are construed with a plural adjective or verb.

We should not pass without notice that it is in the passages from II Thessalonians that ὁ κύριος is given relative prominence. In the two passages from I Thessalonians ὁ θεός comes forward, while in those from II Thessalonians it is ὁ κύριος. That is in accordance with the general character of II Thessalonians, which is distinctively a κύριος epistle. Proportionately to the lengths of the two epistles, while θεός occurs about equally often in each, κύριος occurs about twice as often in the second as in the first. We do not pause to inquire into the causes of this superior prominence of κύριος in II Thessalonians, although it may be worth remarking in passing that in both epistles it is relatively prominent in the hortatory portions. Whatever, however, may have been the particular causes which brought about the result in this case, the result is in itself one which could not have been brought about if θεός and κύριος had not stood in the consciousness of Paul in virtual equality as designations of Deity. For the phenomenon amounts at its apex, — as we see in the four passages more particularly before us — to the simple replacement of θεός by κύριος as the designation of Deity. And that means at bottom that Paul knows no difference between θεός and κύριος in point of rank; they are both to him designations of Deity and the discrimination by which the one is applied to the Father and the other to Christ is (so far) merely a convention by which two that are God are supplied with differentiating appellations by means of which they may be intelligibly spoken of severally. With respect to the substance of the matter there seems no reason why the Father might not just as well be called κύριος and Christ θεός.

Whether the convention by which the two appellations are assigned respectively to the Father as θεός and to Christ as κύριος is ever broken by Paul, is a question of little intrinsic importance, but nevertheless of some natural interest. It is probable that Paul never, — not only in these epistles to the Thessalonians, but throughout his epistles, — employs κύριος of the Father. The term seems to appear uniformly in his writings, except in a few (not all) quotations from the Old Testament, as a designation of Christ. Thus the Old Testament divine name κύριος (Jehovah) is appropriated exclusively to Christ; and that in repeated instances even when the language of the Old Testament is adduced, — which Paul carries over to and applies to Christ as the Lord there spoken of. The question whether Paul ever applies the term θεός to Christ is brought sharply before us by the form in which the formula, the use of which we are particularly investigating, occurs in II Thess. i. 12. There we read of Paul's constant prayer that "our God" should count his readers worthy of their calling and fulfil with reference to them every good pleasure of goodness and work of faith with power, to the end that "the name of our Lord Jesus" might be glorified in them, and they in Him, κατὰ τήν χάριν τοῦ θεοῦ ἡμῶν καὶ κυρίου ᾿Ιησοῦ Χριστοῦ.

It will probably be allowed that in strictness of grammatical rule, rigidly applied, this should mean, "according to the grace of our God and Lord Jesus Christ," or, if we choose so to phrase it, "according to the grace of our God, even the Lord Jesus Christ." All sorts of reasons are advanced, however, why the strict grammatical rule should not be rigidly applied here. Most of them are ineffective enough and testify only to the reluctance of expositors to acknowledge that Paul can speak of Christ as "God." This reluctance is ordinarily given expression either in the simple empirical remark that it is not in accordance with the usage of Paul to call Christ God, or in the more far-reaching assertion that it is contrary to Paul's doctrinal system to represent Christ as God. Thus, for example, W. Bornemann comments briefly: "In themselves, these words might be so taken as to call Jesus here both God and Lord. That is, however, improbable, according to the Pauline usage elsewhere." This mild statement is particularly interesting as a recession from the strong ground taken by G. Lünemann, whose commentary on the Thessalonian epistles in the Meyer series

Bornemann's superseded. Lünemann argues the question at some length and one might almost say with some heat. "According to Hofmann and Riggenbach," he writes, "Christ is here named both our God and our Lord, — an interpretation which, indeed, grammatically is no less allowable than the interpretation of the doxology ὁ ὢν ἐπὶ πάντων θεὸς εὐλογητὸς εἰς τοὺς αἰῶνας, Rom. ix. 5, as an apposition to Χριστός; but is equally inadmissible as it would contain an un-Pauline thought: on account of which also Hilgenfeld, "Zeitschr.f.d. wiss. Theol.," Halle, 1862, p. 264, in the interest of the supposed spuriousness of the Epistle, has forthwith appropriated to himself this discovery of Hofmann." Ernst von Dobschütz, who has superseded Bornemann as Bornemann superseded Lünemann, is as sure as Lünemann that it is un-Pauline to call Christ God; but as he is equally sure that this passage does call Christ God, he has no alternative but to deny the passage to Paul, — though he prefers to deny to him only this passage and not, like Hilgenfeld, the whole Epistle. "But an entirely un-Pauline trait meets us here," he writes, "that to τοῦ θεοῦ ἡμῶν there is added καὶ κυρίου Ἰησοῦ Χριστοῦ· Not that the combination, God our Father and the Lord Jesus Christ, is not original-Pauline (see on I Thess. i. 1), but that what stands here must be translated, 'Of our God and Lord Jesus Christ' as Hofmann and Wohlenberg rightly maintain. This, however, is in very fact in the highest degree un-Pauline (Lünemann) in spite of Rom. ix. 5, and has its parallel only in Tit. ii. 13, 'Of our Great God and Saviour, Christ Jesus,' or II Pet. i. 1, 11, 'Of our God (Lord) and Saviour, Jesus Christ.'" H. J. Holtzmann, as is his wont, sums up the whole contention crisply: "In the entire compass of the Pauline literature, only II Thess. i. 12 and Tit. ii. 13 supply two equally exegetically uncertain parallels" to Rom. ix. 5 "while, in Eph. iv. 6, God the Father is ὁ ἐπὶ πάντων."

It is manifest that reasoning of this sort runs great risk of merely begging the question. The precise point under discussion is whether Paul does ever, or could ever, speak of Christ as God. This passage is offered in evidence that he both can and does. It is admitted that there are other passages which may be adduced in the same sense. There is Rom. ix. 5 which everybody allows to be Paul's own. There is Tit. ii. 13 which occurs in confessedly distinctively "Pauline literature." There is Acts xx. 28, credibly attributed to Paul by one of his pupils. There is II Pet. i. 1 to show that the usage was not unknown to other of the New Testament letter-writers. It is scarcely satisfactory to say that all these passages are as "exegetically uncertain" as II Thess. i. 12 itself. This "exegetical uncertainty" is in each case imposed upon the passage by reluctance to take it in the sense which it most naturally bears, and which is exegetically immediately given. It is as exegetically certain, for example, as any thing can be purely exegetically certain, that in Rom. ix. 5 Paul calls Christ roundly "God over all." It is scarcely to be doubted that this would be universally recognized if Romans could with any plausibility be denied to Paul, or even could be assigned to a date subsequent to that of, say, Colossians. The equivalent may be said of each of the other passages *mutatis mutandis*. The reasoning is distinctly circular which denies to each of these passages in turn its natural meaning on the ground of lack of supporting usage, when this lack of supporting usage is created by a similar denial on the same ground of its natural meaning to each of the other passages. The ground of the denial in each case is merely the denial in the other cases. Meanwhile the usage is there, and is not thus to be denied away. If it may be, any usage whatever may be destroyed in the same manner.

In these circumstances there seems no reason why the ordinary laws of grammar should not determine our understanding of II Thess. i. 12. We may set it down here, therefore, with its parallels in Tit. ii. 13 and II Pet. i. 1 in which the same general phrasing even more clearly carries this sense.

II Thess. i. 12: τὴν χάριν τοῦ θεοῦ ἡμῶν καὶ κυρίου Ἰησοῦ Χριστοῦ.

Tit. ii. 13: καὶ ἐπιφάνειαν τῆς δόξης τοῦ μεγάλου θεοῦ καὶ σωτῆρος ἡμῶν Χριστοῦ Ἰησοῦ.

II Pet. i. 1: πίστιν ἐν δικαιοσύνῃ τοῦ θεοῦ ἡμῶν καὶ σωτῆρος Ἰησοῦ Χριστοῦ.

In these passages the conjunction, in which God and Christ are brought together in the general formula which we are investigating, reaches its culmination in an express identification of them. We have seen that the two are not only united in this formula on terms of complete equality, but are treated as in some sense one. Grammatically at least, they constitute one "self" ($a\dot{v}\tau\delta s$); and they are presented in nearly every phraseology possible as the common source of Christian blessing and the unitary object of Christian prayer. Their formal identification would seem after this to be a matter of course, and we may be a little surprised that the recognition of it should be so strenuously resisted. The explanation is no doubt to be sought in the consideration that so long as this formal identification is not acknowledged to be expressly made, those who find difficulty in believing that Christ is included by Paul in the actual Godhead may feel the way more or less open to explain away by one expedient or another the identity of the two, manifoldly implied in the general representation indeed, but not formally announced.

Expositor after expositor, at any rate, may be observed introducing into his reproduction of Paul's simple equalization, or rather, unification, of God and the Lord, qualifying phrases of his own which tend to adjust them to his personal way of thinking of the relations subsisting between the two. C. J. Ellicott already found occasion to rebuke this practice in G. Lünemann and A. Koch. The former explains that Paul conjoins Christ with God in his prayers, because, according to Paul's conception — "see Usteri, "Lehrb." ii. 2. 4, p. 315" — Christ, as sitting at the right hand of God, has a part in the government of the world. The latter, going further, asserts that Paul brings the two together only because he regards Christ "as the wisdom and power of God." Few expositors entirely escape the temptation to go thus beyond what is written. It is most common, perhaps, to follow the path in which Lünemann walks, and to declare that Paul unites the two persons because Christ by His exaltation has been made for the time co-regnant with God over the universe, or perhaps only over the Church. Quite frequently, however, it is asserted, more like Koch, that the unity instituted between them amounts merely to a unity of will, or even only to a harmony of operation. At the best it is explained that our Lord is placed by the side of God only because it is through Him as intermediary that the blessings which have their source in God are received or are to be sought. An especially flagrant example of the substitution of quite alien phraseology for Paul's, in a professed restatement of his conception, is afforded by David Somerville in his Cunningham Lectures on "St. Paul's Conception of Christ." He tells us that Paul's "conjunction of God and Christ in his stated greetings to the churches indicated his belief that a co-partnership of Divine power and honor was included in the exaltation of Christ to be Lord." It obviously smacks, however, less of Paul than of Socinus to speak of the relation of Christ to God as a "co-partnership of Divine power and honor," and of this co-partnership of Divine power and honor between them as resulting from Christ becoming Lord by His exaltation.

Benjamin Jowett, with that fine condescension frequently exhibited by the "emancipated," remarks on Chrysostom's comment on Gal. i. 3: "This is the mind not of the Apostolic but of the Nicene age." He does not stay to consider that the mind of his own age and coterie may in such a matter be as much further removed than that of the Nicene age from the mind of the Apostolic age in substance as it is in time. Nevertheless it may be admitted that even the Nicene commentators were prone to read their own conceptions of the relations of Christ to God explanatorily into Paul's simple equalization of them. Athanasius appeals, — as he was thoroughly entitled to do, — to Paul's conjunction of God the Father and the Lord Jesus Christ as the common source of grace and the common object of prayer, against the Arian contention that the Father and the Son are concordant, indeed, in will but not one in being. In the eleventh section of the third of his Orations against the Arians he gives expression to this appeal thus: "Therefore also, as we said just now, when the Father gives grace and peace, the Son also gives it, as Paul signifies in every epistle, writing,

'Grace to you and peace, from God our Father and the Lord Jesus Christ.' For one and the same grace is from the Father in the Son, as the light of the sun and of the radiance is one, and as the sun's illumination is effective through the radiance; and so, when he prays for the Thessalonians, in saying, 'Now God even the Father and the Lord Jesus Christ Himself, may He direct our way unto you,' he has guarded the unity of the Father and of the Son. For he has not said, 'May they direct,' as of a double grace given from two, from This and That, but, 'May he direct,' to show that the Father gives it through the Son.'' This is not to emphasize the unity of the Father and the Son more strongly than Paul does: it is only to repeat Paul's testimony to their unity. But Athanasius cannot repeat Paul's testimony to their unity without interpolating his own conception of the manner in which this unity is to be conceived. One and the same grace comes to us from the Father and the Son, he gives us to understand, because the grace of the Father comes to us in the Son; one and the same prayer is addressed to the Father and the Son, because whatever the Father gives He gives through the Son. This explanation is interpolated into Paul's language. Paul places God and the Lord absolutely side by side, as joint source of the blessings he seeks for his readers; addresses his prayers for benefits he desires for his readers to them in common; treats them, in a word, as one. Athanasius' explanations are, of course, not as gross interpolations into the text as Arius'; but they are no less real interpolations. The outstanding fact governing Paul's collocation of God and the Lord, is that he makes no discrimination between them whatever, but treats them as a unity.

This is well brought out in the remarks of Chrysostom on which Jowett had his eye when he accused him of intruding a Nicene meaning on the text. These remarks are on the prepositions in Gal. i. 1 and Rom. i. 7. Had Paul written in the former of these passages, says Chrysostom, either "through Jesus Christ," or "through God the Father," alone, the Arians would have had their explanation of his having done so, in the interests of some essential distinction between the Father and the Son. But Paul "leaves no opening for such a cavil, by mentioning at once both the Son and the Father, and making the language apply to both." "This he does," he adds, "not as referring the acts of the Son to the Father, but to show that the expression implies no distinction of essence." On Rom. i. 7 he remarks similarly on the use of "from" with both the Father and the Son. "For he did not say, 'Grace be unto you and peace, from God the Father, through the Lord Jesus Christ,' but 'from God the Father and the Lord Jesus Christ.'" There is no imposing of a Nicene sense on Paul's language here. There is a simple reflection, as in a clear mirror, of the exact sense of the texts in hand, with an emphasis on their underlying implication of oneness between God and our Lord.

We are constantly pointed to I Cor. viii. 6, to be sure, as in some way supplying a warrant for supposing an unexpressed subordinationism to be hidden beneath the surface of all of Paul's equalizations of God the Father and the Lord Jesus Christ. It is exceedingly difficult, however, to see how this passage can be made to supply such a warrant. It lies open to the sight of all, of course, that in it the one God the Father and the one Lord Jesus Christ, — who are included in the one only God that, it is understood by all, alone exists, — are differentiated by the particular relations in which the first and the second creations alike are said to stand to them severally. All things are said to be "of" God the Father and "through" the Lord Jesus Christ; Christians are said to be "unto" the one and "by means of" the other. These characterizations are of course, not made at random; and it is right to seek diligently for their significance. It would doubtless be easy, however, to press such prepositional distinctions too far, as such passages as Rom. xi. 36 and Col. i. 16 may advise us. Perhaps it would not be wrong to say that they are to be taken rather eminently than exclusively. What it is at the moment especially important that we observe, however, is that they concern the relations of God the Father and the Lord Jesus Christ *ad extra* and say nothing whatever of their relations to one another. With respect to their relations to one another, what the passage tells

us is that they are both embraced in that one God which, it is
declared with great emphasis, alone exists. We must not permit to fall out of sight that the whole passage is dominated by
the clear-cut assertion that "there is no God but one" (verse
4, at the end). Of this assertion the words now particularly before us (verse 6b) are the positive side of an explication and
proof (verse 5, γάρ). And the thing for us distinctly to note is
that Paul explicates the assertion that there is no God but one
by declaring, as if that was quite *ad rem*, that Christians know
but one God the Father and one Lord Jesus Christ. There
meets us here again, we perceive, — as underlying and giving
its force to this assertion, — the precise formula we have been
having under consideration. And it meets us after a fashion
which brings very strikingly to our attention once more that,
when Paul says "God the Father and the Lord Jesus Christ,"
he has in mind not two Gods, much less two beings of unequal
dignity, a God and a Demi-god, or a God and a mere creature,
— but just one God. Though Christians have one God the
Father and one Lord Jesus Christ, they know but one only
God.

The essential meaning of the passage is wholly unaffected
by the question whether in the words, "There is no God but
one" at the end of verse 4, we have Paul's own language or
that of his Corinthian correspondents repeated by him. We
may read the verse, if we choose, — perhaps we ought to, —
"Concerning the meats offered to idols, then, we are perfectly
well aware that, as you say, there is no idol in the world, and
there is no God but one." Still, the assertion that there is no
God but one rules the succeeding verses, which, introduced as
its justification, become in effect a reiteration of it. "There is
no God but one, *for* — for, although there are indeed so-called
Gods, whether in heaven or on earth, — as there are Gods a-
plenty and Lords a-plenty! — yet for us there is one God the
Father . . . and one Lord Jesus Christ. . . ." Obviously
this can mean nothing else than that the "one God the Father
and one Lord Jesus Christ" of the Christians is just the one
only God which exists. To attempt to make it mean anything

else is to stultify the whole argument. You cannot prove that only one God exists by pointing out that you yourself have two.

We are referred, it is true, to the declaration that the heathen have not only many Gods, but also many Lords, and we are bidden to see in their one God the Father and one Lord Jesus Christ a parallel among the Christians to this state of affairs among the heathen. And then we are further instructed that it is only fair to suppose that Paul felt some difference in grade between the Gods and the Lords of the heathen and, in paralleling the two objects of Christian worship with them respectively, intended to intimate a discrimination in rank between God the Father and the Lord Jesus Christ. On this ground, we are then asked to conclude that Paul does not range the Lord Jesus Christ here along with God the Father within the Godhead, but adjoins Him to God the Father as an additional and inferior object of reverence, placed distinctly as "Lord" outside the category of "God." This whole construction, however, is purely artificial and has no standing ground in the world of realities. There is no evidence that the heathen discriminated between the designations "God" and "Lord" in point of dignity to the disadvantage of the latter; this, at the end of the day, has to be admitted by both Johannes Weiss and W. Bousset, who yet urge that Paul must be supposed to presuppose such a distinction here. Paul, however, intimates in no way at all that he felt any such distinction on his part; on the contrary he includes the "Gods many" and "Lords many" of the heathen without question in their "so-called Gods" on equal terms. Least of all is it possible to separate off "one God the Father" from its fellow "one Lord Jesus Christ," linked to it immediately by the simple "and," and make the former alone refer back to the "There is no God but one." Paul obviously includes both "God the Father" and "the Lord Jesus Christ" within this one only God whom alone he and his readers alike recognize as existing. It would void his whole argument if Jesus Christ were conceived of as a second and inferior object of worship outside the limits of the one only

God. The thing which above all others the passage says plainly, is that the acknowledgment by Christians of "one God the Father and one Lord Jesus Christ" accords with the fundamental postulate that "there is no God but one." And that can mean nothing else than that God the Father and the Lord Jesus Christ together make but one God. So far from this passage throwing itself athwart the implications of the repeated employment by Paul, as by others of the writers of the New Testament, of the formula in which God the Father and the Lord Jesus Christ are conjoined as the one object of Christian prayer and source of Christian blessings, it brings a notable support to them. It supplies what is in effect an explicit assertion of the fact on which this formula implicitly proceeds. It declares that the one God of the Christians includes in His Being both "God the Father" and "the Lord Jesus Christ." Christians acknowledge but one God; and these are the one God which Christians acknowledge.

Something of the same thing that Paul expresses by this conjunction of God the Father and the Lord Jesus Christ, John expresses in his own phraseology by the conjunction of the Father and the Son, — as in I Jno. ii. 24: "If what you heard from the beginning abide in you, you also shall abide in the Son and the Father"; or II Jno. 9, in the reverse order: "He that abideth in the teaching, the same hath the Father and the Son"; as well as in II Jno. 3, already quoted: "Grace, mercy, peace shall be with us, from God the Father, and from Jesus Christ, the Son of the Father." It is true, but not adequate, to say that John never thinks of Christ apart from God and never thinks of God apart from Christ. With him, to have the Son is to have the Father also, and to have the Father is to have the Son also. The two are as inseparable in fact as in thought. The terminology is different, but the idea is the same as that which underlies Paul's unification of God the Father and the Lord Jesus Christ.

Clearly the suggestions of this formula carry us into the midst not only of Paul's Christology but of his conception of God — which obviously is not simple. Short of this, they bring

us face to face with two matters of great preliminary importance to the correct apprehension of Paul's doctrines of Christ
and of God, which have been much discussed of late, not always very illuminatingly. We mean the matters of the significance of the title "Lord" which is so richly applied to Christ
in the New Testament writings, and of the meaning of the
adoration of Christ which is everywhere reflected in these writings. We must deny ourselves the pleasure of following out these
suggestions here. It must content us for the moment to have
pointed out a line of approach to the correct understanding of
these great matters which, surely, cannot be neglected in any
earnest attempt to reach the truth concerning them, and which,
if not neglected, will certainly conduct us to very high conclu-
sions in regard to them.

VII

THE CHRIST THAT PAUL PREACHED

THE CHRIST THAT PAUL PREACHED [1]

"THE monumental Introduction of the Epistle to the Romans" — it is thus that W. Bousset speaks of the seven opening verses of the Epistle — is, from the formal point of view, merely the Address of the Epistle. In primary purpose and fundamental structure it does not differ from the Addresses of Paul's other Epistles. But even in the Addresses of his Epistles Paul does not confine himself to the simple repetition of a formula. Here too he writes at his ease and shows himself very much the master of his form.

It is Paul's custom to expand one or another of the essential elements of the Address of his Epistles as circumstances suggested, and thus to impart to it in each several instance a specific character. The Address of the Epistle to the Romans is the extreme example of this expansion. Paul is approaching in it a church which he had not visited, and to which he apparently felt himself somewhat of a stranger. He naturally begins with some words adapted to justify his writing to it, especially as an authoritative teacher of Christian truth. In doing this he is led to describe briefly the Gospel which had been committed to him, and that particularly with regard to its contents.

There is very strikingly illustrated here a peculiarity of Paul's style, which has been called "going off at a word." His particular purpose is to represent himself as one authoritatively appointed to teach the Gospel of God. But he is more interested in the Gospel than he is in himself; and he no sooner mentions the Gospel than off he goes on a tangent to describe it. In describing it, he naturally tells us particularly what its contents are. Its contents, however, were for him summed up in Christ. No sooner does he mention Christ than off he goes

[1] From *The Expositor*, 8th ser., v. xv, 1918, pp. 90–110.

again on a tangent to describe Christ. Thus it comes about
that this passage, formally only the Address of the Epistle,
becomes actually a great Christological deliverance, one of
the chief sources of our knowledge of Paul's conception of
Christ. It presents itself to our view like one of those nests
of Chinese boxes; the outer encasement is the Address of the
Epistle; within that fits neatly Paul's justification of his addressing the Romans as an authoritative teacher of the Gospel;
within that a description of the Gospel committed to him; and
within that a great declaration of who and what Jesus Christ
is, as the contents of this Gospel.

The manner in which Paul approaches this great declaration concerning Christ lends it a very special interest. What
we are given is not merely how Paul thought of Christ, but how
Paul preached Christ. It is the content of "the Gospel of God,"
the Gospel to which he as "a called apostle" had been "separated," which he outlines in these pregnant words. This is how
Paul preached Christ to the faith of men as he went up and
down the world "serving God in his spirit in the Gospel of His
Son." We have no abstract theologoumena here, categories of
speculative thought appropriate only to the closet. We have
the great facts about Jesus which made the Gospel that Paul
preached the power of God unto salvation to every one that
believed. Nowhere else do we get a more direct description of
specifically the Christ that Paul preached.

The direct description of the Christ that Paul preached is
given us, of course, in the third and fourth verses. But the
wider setting in which these verses are embedded cannot be
neglected in seeking to get at their significance. In this wider
setting the particular aspect in which Christ is presented is
that of "Lord." It is as "Lord" that Paul is thinking of Jesus
when he describes himself in the opening words of the Address
— in the very first item of his commendation of himself to the
Romans — as "the slave of Christ Jesus." "Slave" is the correlate of "Lord," and the relation must be taken at its height.
When Paul calls himself the slave of Christ Jesus, he is calling
Christ Jesus his Lord in the most complete sense which can be

ascribed to that word (cf. Rom. i. 1, Col. iii. 4). He is declaring
that he recognises in Christ Jesus one over against whom he
has no rights, whose property he is, body and soul, to be disposed of as He will. This is not because he abases himself. It is
because he exalts Christ. It is because Christ is thought of by
him as one whose right it is to rule, and to rule with no limit
to His right.

How Paul thought of Christ as Lord comes out, however,
with most startling clearness in the closing words of the Address. There he couples "the Lord Jesus Christ" with "God
our Father" as the common source from which he seeks in
prayer the divine gifts of grace and peace for the Romans.
We must renounce enervating glossing here too. Paul is not
thinking of the Lord Jesus Christ as only the channel through
which grace and peace come from God our Father to men; nor
is he thinking of the Lord Jesus Christ as only the channel
through which his prayer finds its way to God our Father. His
prayer for these blessings for the Romans is offered up to God
our Father and the Lord Jesus Christ together, as the conjoint
object addressed in his petition. So far as this Bousset's remark
is just: "Prayer to God in Christ is for Pauline Christianity, too,
a false formula; adoration of the Kyrios stands in the Pauline
communities side by side with adoration of God in unrecon-
ciled reality."

Only, we must go further. Paul couples God our Father
and the Lord Jesus Christ in his prayer on a complete equality.
They are, for the purposes of the prayer, for the purposes of
the bestowment of grace and peace, one to him. Christ is so
highly exalted in his sight that, looking up to Him through the
immense stretches which separate Him from the plane of human life, "the forms of God and Christ," as Bousset puts it,
"are brought to the eye of faith into close conjunction." He
should have said that they completely coalesce. It is only half
the truth — though it is half the truth — to say that, with Paul,
"the object of religious faith, as of religious worship, presents
itself in a singular, thoroughgoing dualism." The other half
of the truth is that this dualism resolves itself into a complete

unity. The two, God our Father and the Lord Jesus Christ, are steadily recognized as two, and are statedly spoken of by the distinguishing designations of "God" and "Lord." But they are equally steadily envisaged as one, and are statedly combined as the common object of every religious aspiration and the common source of every spiritual blessing. It is no accident that they are united in our present passage under the government of the single preposition, "from," — "Grace to you and peace from God our Father and the Lord Jesus Christ." This is normal with Paul. God our Father and the Lord Jesus Christ are not to him two objects of worship, two sources of blessing, but one object of worship, one source of blessing. Does he not tell us plainly that we who have one God the Father and one Lord Jesus Christ yet know perfectly well that there is no God but one (I Cor. viii. 4, 6)?

Paul is writing the Address of his Epistle to the Romans, then, with his mind fixed on the divine dignity of Christ. It is this divine Christ who, he must be understood to be telling his readers, constitutes the substance of his Gospel-proclamation. He does not leave us, however, merely to infer this. He openly declares it. The Gospel he preaches, he says, concerns precisely "the Son of God . . . Jesus Christ our Lord." He expressly says, then, that he presents Christ in his preaching as "our Lord." It was the divine Christ that he preached, the Christ that the eye of faith could not distinguish from God, who was addressed in common with God in prayer, and was looked to in common with God as the source of all spiritual blessings. Paul does not speak of Christ here, however, merely as "our Lord." He gives Him the two designations: "the Son of God . . . Jesus Christ our Lord." The second designation obviously is explanatory of the first. Not as if it were the more current or the more intelligible designation. It may, or it may not, have been both the one and the other; but that is not the point here. The point here is that it is the more intimate, the more appealing designation. It is the designation which tells what Christ is to us. He is our Lord, He to whom we go in prayer, He to whom we look for blessings, He to whom all our religious emotions turn, on whom all our hopes are set — for this life and for that to come. Paul tells the Romans that this is the Christ that he preaches, their and his Lord whom both they and he reverence and worship and love and trust in. This is, of course, what he mainly wishes to say to them; and it is up to this that all else that he says of the Christ that he preaches leads.

The other designation — "the Son of God" — which Paul prefixes to this in his fundamental declaration concerning the Christ that he preached, supplies the basis for this. It does not tell us what Christ is to us, but what Christ is in Himself. In Himself He is the Son of God; and it is only because He is the Son of God in Himself, that He can be and is our Lord. The Lordship of Christ is rooted by Paul, in other words, not in any adventitious circumstances connected with His historical manifestation; not in any powers or dignities conferred on Him or acquired by Him; but fundamentally in His metaphysical nature. The designation "Son of God" is a metaphysical designation and tells us what He is in His being of being. And what it tells us that Christ is in His being of being is that He is just what God is. It is undeniable — and Bousset, for example, does not deny it, — that, from the earliest days of Christianity on, (in Bousset's words) "Son of God was equivalent simply to equal with God" (Mark xiv. 61–63; John x. 31–39).

That Paul meant scarcely so much as this, Bousset to be sure would fain have us believe. He does not dream, of course, of supposing Paul to mean nothing more than that Jesus had been elevated into the relation of Sonship to God because of His moral uniqueness, or of His community of will with God. He is compelled to allow that "the Son of God appears in Paul as a supramundane Being standing in close metaphysical relation with God." But he would have us understand that, however close He stands to God, He is not, in Paul's view, quite equal with God. Paul, he suggests, has seized on this term to help him through the frightful problem of conceiving of this second Divine Being consistently with his monotheism. Christ is not quite God to him, but only the Son of God. Of such refinements, however, Paul knows nothing. With him too the

maxim rules that whatever the father is, that the son is also:
every father begets his son in his own likeness. The Son of God
is necessarily to him just God, and he does not scruple to declare this Son of God all that God is (Phil. ii. 6; Col. ii. 9) and
even to give him the supreme name of "God over all" (Rom.
ix. 5).

This is fundamentally, then, how Paul preached Christ —
as the Son of God in this supereminent sense, and therefore
our divine Lord on whom we absolutely depend and to whom
we owe absolute obedience. But this was not all that he was
accustomed to preach concerning Christ. Paul preached the
historical Jesus as well as the eternal Son of God. And between
these two designations — Son of God, our Lord Jesus Christ —
he inserts two clauses which tell us how he preached the historical Jesus. All that he taught about Christ was thrown up
against the background of His deity: He is the Son of God, our
Lord. But who is this that is thus so fervently declared to be
the Son of God and our Lord? It is in the two clauses which
are now to occupy our attention that Paul tells us.

If we reduce what he tells us to its lowest terms it amounts
just to this: Paul preached the historical Christ as the promised
Messiah and as the very Son of God. But he declares Christ
to be the promised Messiah and the very Son of God in language so pregnant, so packed with implications, as to carry us
into the heart of the great problem of the two-natured person
of Christ. The exact terms in which he describes Christ as the
promised Messiah and the very Son of God are these: "Who
became of the seed of David according to the flesh, who was
marked out as the Son of God in power according to the Spirit
of holiness by the resurrection of the dead." This in brief is the
account which Paul gives of the historical Christ whom he
preached.

Of course there is a temporal succession suggested in the
declarations of the two clauses. They so far give us not only a
description of the historical Christ, but the life-history of the
Christ that Paul preached. Jesus Christ became of the seed of
David at His birth and by His birth. He was marked out as

the Son of God in power only at His resurrection and by His resurrection. But it was not to indicate this temporal succession that Paul sets the two declarations side by side. It emerges merely as the incidental, or we may say even the accidental, result of their collocation. The relation in which Paul sets the two declarations to one another is a logical rather than a temporal one: it is the relation of climax. His purpose is to exalt Jesus Christ. He wishes to say the great things about Him. And the two greatest things he has to say about Him in His historical manifestation are these — that He became of the seed of David according to the flesh, that He was marked out as the Son of God in power according to the Spirit of holiness by the resurrection of the dead.

Both of these declarations, we say, are made for the purpose of extolling Christ: the former just as truly as the latter. That Christ came as the Messiah belongs to His glory: and the particular terms in which His Messiahship is intimated are chosen in order to enhance His glory. The word "came," "became" is correlated with the "promised afore" of the preceding verse. This is He, Paul says, whom all the prophets did before signify, and who at length came — even as they signified — of the seed of David. There is doubtless an intimation of the preëxistence of Christ here also, as J. B. Lightfoot properly instructs us: He who was always the Son of God now "became" of the seed of David. But this lies somewhat apart from the main current of thought. The heart of the declaration resides in the great words, "Of the seed of David." For these are great words. In declaring the Messiahship of Jesus Paul adduces His royal dignity. And he adduces it because he is thinking of the majesty of the Messiahship. We must beware, then, of reading this clause depreciatingly, as if Paul were making a concession in it: "He came, no doubt, . . . He came, indeed, . . . of the seed of David, but . . ." Paul never for an instant thought of the Messiahship of Jesus as a thing to be apologised for. The relation of the second clause to the first is not that of opposition, but of climax; and it contains only so much of contrast as is intrinsic in a climax. The connection would be better expressed

by an "and" than by a "but"; or, if by a "but," not by an
"indeed . . . but," but by a "not only . . . but." Even the
Messiahship, inexpressibly glorious as it is, does not exhaust
the glory of Christ. He had a glory greater than even this.
This was but the beginning of His glory. But it was the begin-
ning of His glory. He came into the world as the promised
Messiah, and He went out of the world as the demonstrated
Son of God. In these two things is summed up the majesty of
His historical manifestation.

It is not intended to say that when He went out of the
world, He left His Messiahship behind Him. The relation of
the second clause to the first is not that of supersession but
that of superposition. Paul passes from one glory to another,
but he is as far as possible from suggesting that the one glory
extinguished the other. The resurrection of Christ had no tendency to abolish His Messiahship, and the exalted Christ remains "of the seed of David." There is no reason to doubt that
Paul would have exhorted his readers when he wrote these
words with all the fervour with which he did later to "remember Jesus Christ, risen from the dead, of the seed of David"
(II Tim. ii. 8). "According to my Gospel," he adds there, as an
intimation that it was as "of the seed of David" that he was
accustomed to preach Jesus Christ, whether as on earth as here,
or as in heaven as there. It is the exalted Jesus that proclaims
Himself in the Apocalypse "the root and the offspring of
David" (Rev. xxii. 16, v. 5), and in whose hands "the key of
David" is found (iii. 7).

And as it is not intimated that Christ ceased to be "of the
seed of David" when He rose from the dead, neither is it intimated that He then first became the Son of God. He was
already the Son of God when and before He became of the seed
of David: and He did not cease to be the Son of God on and
by becoming of the seed of David. It was rather just because
He was the Son of God that He became of the seed of David,
to become which, in the great sense of the prophetic announcements and of His own accomplishment, He was qualified only
by being the Son of God. Therefore Paul does not say He was

made the Son of God by the resurrection of the dead. He says he was defined, marked out, as the Son of God by the resurrection of the dead. His resurrection from the dead was well adapted to mark Him out as the Son of God: scarcely to make Him the Son of God. Consider but what the Son of God in Paul's usage means; and precisely what the resurrection was and did. It was a thing which was quite appropriate to happen to the Son of God; and, happening, could bear strong witness to Him as such: but how could it make one the Son of God?

We might possibly say, no doubt, with a tolerable meaning, that Christ was installed, even constituted, "Son of God in power" by the resurrection of the dead — if we could see our way to construe the words "in power" thus directly with "the Son of God." That too would imply that He was already the Son of God before He rose from the dead, — only then in weakness; what He had been all along in weakness He now was constituted in power. This construction, however, though not impossible, is hardly natural. And it imposes a sense on the preceding clause of which it itself gives no suggestion, and which it is reluctant to receive. To say, "of the seed of David" is not to say weakness; it is to say majesty. It is quite certain, indeed, that the assertion "who was made of the seed of David" cannot be read concessively, preparing the way for the celebration of Christ's glory in the succeeding clause. It stands rather in parallelism with the clause that follows it, asserting with it the supreme glory of Christ.

In any case the two clauses do not express two essentially different modes of being through which Christ successively passed. We could think at most only of two successive stages of manifestation of the Son of God. At most we could see in it a declaration that He who always was and continues always to be the Son of God was manifested to men first as the Son of David, and then, after His resurrection, as also the exalted Lord. He always was in the essence of His being the Son of God; this Son of God became of the seed of David and was installed as — what He always was — the Son of God, though now in His proper power, by the resurrection of the dead. It is assuredly wrong, however, to press even so far the idea of temporal succession. Temporal succession was not what it was in Paul's mind to emphasize, and is not the ruling idea of his assertion. The ruling idea of his assertion is the celebration of the glory of Christ. We think of temporal succession only because of the mention of the resurrection, which, in point of fact, cuts our Lord's life-manifestation into two sections. But Paul is not adducing the resurrection because it cuts our Lord's life-manifestation into two sections; but because of the demonstration it brought of the dignity of His person. It is quite indifferent to his declaration when the resurrection took place. He is not adducing it as the producing cause of a change in our Lord's mode of being. In point of fact it did not produce a change in our Lord's mode of being, although it stood at the opening of a new stage of His life-history. What it did, and what Paul adduces it here as doing, was that it brought out into plain view who and what Christ really was. This, says Paul, is the Christ I preach — He who came of the seed of David, He who was marked out in power as the Son of God, by the resurrection of the dead. His thought of Christ runs in the two molds — His Messiahship, His resurrection. But he is not particularly concerned here with the temporal relations of these two facts.

Paul does not, however, say of Christ merely that He became of the seed of David and was marked out as the Son of God in power by the resurrection of the dead. He introduces a qualifying phrase into each clause. He says that He became of the seed of David "according to the flesh," and that He was marked out as the Son of God in power "according to the Spirit of holiness" by the resurrection of the dead. What is the nature of the qualifications made by these phrases?

It is obvious at once that they are not temporal qualifications. Paul does not mean to say, in effect, that our Lord was Messiah only during His earthly manifestation, and became the Son of God only on and by means of His resurrection. It has already appeared that Paul did not think of the Messiahship of our Lord only in connection with His earthly manifestation, or of His Sonship to God only in connection with His post-resurrection existence. And the qualifying phrases themselves are ill-adapted to express this temporal distinction. Even if we could twist the phrase "according to the flesh" into meaning "according to His human manifestation" and violently make that do duty as a temporal definition, the parallel phrase "according to the Spirit of holiness" utterly refuses to yield to any treatment which could make it mean, "according to His heavenly manifestation." And nothing could be more monstrous than to represent precisely the resurrection as in the case of Christ the producing cause of — the source out of which proceeds — a condition of existence which could be properly characterised as distinctively "spiritual." Exactly what the resurrection did was to bring it about that His subsequent mode of existence should continue to be, like the precedent, "fleshly"; to assimilate His post-resurrection to His pre-resurrection mode of existence in the matter of the constitution of His person. And if we fall back on the ethical contrast of the terms, that could only mean that Christ should be supposed to be represented as imperfectly holy in His earthly stage of existence, and as only on His resurrection attaining to complete holiness (cf. I Cor. xv. 44, 46). It is very certain that Paul did not mean that (II Cor. v. 21).

It is clear enough, then, that Paul cannot by any possibility have intended to represent Christ as in His pre-resurrection and His post-resurrection modes of being differing in any way which can be naturally expressed by the contrasting terms "flesh" and "spirit." Least of all can he be supposed to have intended this distinction in the sense of the ethical contrast between these terms. But a further word may be pardoned as to this. That it is precisely this ethical contrast that Paul intends has been insisted on under cover of the adjunct "of holiness" attached here to "spirit." The contrast, it is said, is not between "flesh" and "spirit," but between "flesh" and "spirit of holiness"; and what is intended is to represent Christ, who on earth was merely "Christ according to the flesh" — the "flesh of sin" of course, it is added, that is "the flesh which was in the grasp of sin" — to have been, "after and in consequence of the resurrection," "set free from 'the likeness of (weak and sinful) flesh.'" Through the resurrection, in other words, Christ has for the first time become the holy Son of God, free from entanglement with sin-cursed flesh; and, having thus saved Himself, is qualified, we suppose, now to save others, by bringing them through the same experience of resurrection to the same holiness. We have obviously wandered here sufficiently far from the declarations of the Apostle; and we have landed in a *reductio ad absurdum* of this whole system of interpretation. Paul is not here distinguishing times and contrasting two successive modes of our Lord's being. He is distinguishing elements in the constitution of our Lord's person, by virtue of which He is at one and the same time both the Messiah and the Son of God. He became of the seed of David with respect to the flesh, and by the resurrection of the dead was mightily proven to be also the Son of God with respect to the Spirit of holiness.

It ought to go without saying that by these two elements in the constitution of our Lord's person, the flesh and the spirit of holiness, by virtue of which He is at once of the seed of David and the Son of God, are not intended the two constituent elements, flesh and spirit, which go to make up common humanity. It is impossible that Paul should have represented our Lord as the Messiah only by virtue of His bodily nature; and it is absurd to suppose him to suggest that His Sonship to God was proved by His resurrection to reside in His mental nature or even in His ethical purity — to say nothing now of supposing him to assert that He was made by the resurrection into the Son of God, or into "the Son of God in power" with respect to His mental nature here described as holy. How the resurrection — which was in itself just the resumption of the body — of all things, could be thought of as constituting our Lord's mental nature the Son of God passes imagination; and if it be conceivable that it might at least prove that He was the Son of God, it remains hidden how it could be so emphatically asserted that it was only with reference to His mental nature, in sharp contrast with His bodily, thus recovered to Him, that this was proved concerning Him precisely by His resurrection. Is Paul's real purpose here to guard men from supposing that our Lord's bodily nature, though recovered to Him in this great act, the resurrection, entered into His Sonship to God? There is no reason discoverable in the context why this distinction between our Lord's bodily and mental natures should be so strongly stressed here. It is clearly an artificial distinction imposed on the passage.

When Paul tells us of the Christ which he preached that He was made of the seed of David "according to the flesh," he quite certainly has the whole of His humanity in mind. And in introducing this limitation, "according to the flesh," into his declaration that Christ was "made of the seed of David," he intimates not obscurely that there was another side — not aspect but element — of His being besides His humanity, in which He was not made of the seed of David, but was something other and higher. If he had said nothing more than just these words: "He was made of the seed of David according to the flesh," this intimation would still have been express; though we might have been left to speculation to determine what other element could have entered into His being, and what He must have been according to that element. He has not left us, however, to this speculation, but has plainly told us that the Christ he preached was not merely made of the seed of David according to the flesh, but was also marked out as the Son of God, in power, according to the Spirit of holiness by the resurrection of the dead. Since the "according to the flesh" includes all His humanity, the "according to the Spirit of holiness" which is set in contrast with it, and according to which He is declared to be the Son of God, must be sought outside of His humanity. What the nature of this element of His being in which He is superior to humanity is, is already clear from the fact that according to it He is the Son of God. "Son of God" is, as we have already seen, a metaphysical designation asserting equality with God. It is a divine name. To say that Christ is, according to the Spirit of holiness, the Son of God, is to say that the Spirit of holiness is a designation of His divine nature.

Paul's whole assertion therefore amounts to saying that, in one element of His being, the Christ that he preached was man, in another God. Looked at from the point of view of His human nature He was the Messiah — "of the seed of David." Looked at from the point of view of His divine nature, He was the Son of God. Looked at in His composite personality, He was both the Messiah and the Son of God, because in Him were united both He that came of the seed of David according to the flesh and He who was marked out as the Son of God in power according to the Spirit of holiness by the resurrection of the dead.

We may be somewhat puzzled by the designation of the divine nature of Christ as "the Spirit of holiness." But not only is it plain from its relation to its contrast, "the flesh," and to its correlate, "the Son of God," that it is His divine nature which is so designated, but this is made superabundantly clear from the closely parallel passage, Rom. ix. 5. There, in enumerating the glories of Israel, the Apostle comes to his climax in this great declaration, — that from Israel Christ came. But there, no more than here, will he allow that it was the whole Christ who came — as said there from the stock of Israel, as said here from the seed of David. He adds there too at once the limitation, "as concerns the flesh," — just as he adds it here. Thus he intimates with emphasis that something more is to be said, if we are to give a complete account of Christ's being; there was something about Him in which He did not come from Israel, and in which He is more than "flesh." What this something is, Paul adds in the great words, "God over all." He who was from Israel according to the flesh is, on the other side of His being, in which He is not from Israel and not "flesh," nothing other than "God over all." In our present passage, the phrase, "Spirit of holiness" takes the place of "God over all" in the other. Clearly Paul means the same thing by them both.

This being very clear, what interests us most is the emphasis which Paul throws on holiness in his designation of the divine nature of Christ. The simple word "Spirit" might have been ambiguous: when "the Spirit of holiness" is spoken of, the divine nature is expressly named. No doubt, Paul might have used the adjective, "holy," instead of the genitive of the substantive, "of holiness"; and have said "the Holy Spirit." Had he done so, he would have as expressly intimated deity as in his actual phrase. But he would have left open the possibility of being misunderstood as speaking of that distinct Holy Spirit to which this designation is commonly applied. The relation in which the divine nature which he attributes to Christ stands to the Holy Spirit was in Paul's mind no doubt very close; as close as the relation between "God" and "Lord" whom he constantly treats as, though two, yet also one. Not only does he identify the activities of the two (e. g., Rom. viii. 9 ff.); but also, in some high sense, he identifies them themselves. He can make use, for example, of such a startling expression as "the Lord is the Spirit" (II Cor. iii. 17). Nevertheless it is perfectly clear that "the Lord" and "the Spirit" are not one person to Paul, and the distinguishing employment of the designations "the Spirit," "the Holy Spirit" is spread broadcast over his pages. Even in immediate connection with his declaration that "the Lord is the Spirit," he can speak with the utmost naturalness not only of "the Spirit of the Lord," but also of "the Lord of the Spirit" (II Cor. iii. 17 f.). What is of especial importance to note in our present connection is that he is not speaking of an endowment of Christ either from or with the Holy Spirit; although he would be the last to doubt that He who was made of the seed of David according to the flesh was plenarily endowed both from and with the Spirit. He is speaking of that divine Spirit which is the complement in the constitution of Christ's person of the human nature according to which He was the Messiah, and by virtue of which He was not merely the Messiah, but also the very Son of God. This Spirit he calls distinguishingly the Spirit of holiness, the Spirit the very characteristic of which is holiness. He is speaking not of an acquired holiness but of an intrinsic holiness; not, then, of a holiness which had been conferred at the time of or attained by means of the resurrection from the dead; but of a holiness which had always been the very quality of Christ's being. He is not representing Christ as having first been after a fleshly fashion the son of David and afterwards becoming by or at the resurrection from the dead, after a spiritual fashion, the holy Son of God. He is representing Him as being in his very nature essentially and therefore always and in every mode of His manifestation holy. Bousset is quite right when he declares that there is no reference in the phrase "Spirit of holiness" to the preservation of His holiness by Christ in His earthly manifestation, but that it is a metaphysical designation describing according to its intrinsic quality an element in the constitution of Christ's person from the beginning. This is the characteristic of the Christ Paul preached; as truly His characteristic as that He was the Messiah. Evidently in Paul's thought of deity holiness held a prominent place. When he wishes to distinguish Spirit from spirit, it is enough for him that he may designate Spirit as divine, to define it as that Spirit the fundamental characteristic of which is that it is holy.

It belongs to the very essence of the conception of Christ as Paul preached Him, therefore, that He was of two natures, human and divine. He could not preach Him at once as of the seed of David and as the Son of God without so preaching Him. It never entered Paul's mind that the Son of God could become a mere man, or that a mere man could become the Son of God. We may say that the conception of the two natures is unthinkable to us. That is our own concern. That a single nature could be at once or successively God and man, man and God, was what was unthinkable to Paul. In his view, when we say God and man we say two natures; when we put a hyphen between them and say God-man, we do not merge them one in the other but join the two together. That this was Paul's mode of thinking of Jesus, Bousset, for example, does not dream of denying. What Bousset is unwilling to admit is that the divine element in his two-natured Christ was conceived by Paul as completely divine. Two metaphysical entities, he says, combined themselves for Paul in the person of Christ: one of these was a human, the other a divine nature: and Paul, along with the whole Christian community of his day, worshipped this two-natured Christ, though he (not they) ranked Him in his thought of His higher nature below the God over all.

The trouble with this construction is that Paul himself gives a different account of the matter. The point of Paul's designation of Christ as the Son of God is, not to subordinate Him to God, as Bousset affirms, but to equalize Him with God. He knows no difference in dignity between his God and his Lord; to both alike, or rather to both in common, he offers his prayers; from both alike and both together he expects all spiritual blessings (Rom. i. 7). He roundly calls Christ, by virtue of His higher nature, by the supreme name of "God over all" (Rom. ix. 5). These things cannot be obscured by pointing to expressions in which he ascribes to the Divine-human Christ a relation of subordination to God in His saving work. Paul does not fail to distinguish between what Christ is in the higher element of His being, and what He became when, becoming poor that we might be made rich, He assumed for His work's sake the position of a servant in the world. Nor does he permit the one set of facts to crowd the other out of his mind. It is no accident that all that he says about the historical two-natured Christ in our present passage is inserted between His two divine designations of the Son of God and Lord; that the Christ that he preached he describes precisely as "the Son of God — who was made of the seed of David according to the flesh, who was marked out as the Son of God in power according to the Spirit of holiness by the resurrection of the dead — Jesus Christ our Lord." He who is defined as on the human side of David, on the divine side the Son of God, this two-natured person, is declared to be from the point of view of God, His own Son, and — as all sons are — like Him in essential nature; from the point of view of man, our supreme Lord, whose we are and whom we obey. Ascription of proper deity could not be made more complete; whether we look at Him from the point of view of God or from the point of view of man, He is God. But what Paul preached concerning this divine Being belonged to His earthly manifestation; He was made of the seed of David, He was marked out as God's Son. The conception of the two natures is not with Paul a negligible speculation attached to his Gospel. He preached Jesus. And he preached of Jesus that He was the Messiah. But the Messiah that he preached was no merely human Messiah. He was the Son of God who was made of the seed of David. And He was demonstrated to be what He really was by His resurrection from the dead.

This was the Jesus that Paul preached: this and none other.

VIII

JESUS' MISSION, ACCORDING TO HIS OWN TESTIMONY

JESUS' MISSION, ACCORDING TO HIS OWN TESTIMONY [1]

(Synoptics)

Under the title of "'*I came*': *the express self-testimony of Jesus to the purpose of His sending and His coming*," Adolf Harnack has published a study of the sayings of Jesus reported in the Synoptic Gospels, which are introduced by the words "I came" or, exceptionally, "I was sent," or their equivalents.[2] These, says he, are "programmatic" sayings, and deserve as such a separate and comprehensive study, such as has not heretofore been given to them. In his examination of them, he pursues the method of, first, gathering the relevant sayings together and subjecting them severally to a critical and exegetical scrutiny; and, then, drawing out from the whole body of them in combination Jesus' own testimony to His mission.

It goes without saying that, in his critical scrutiny of the passages, Harnack proceeds on the same presuppositions which govern his dealing with the Synoptic tradition in general; that is to say, on the presuppositions of the "Liberal" criticism, which he applies, however, here as elsewhere, with a certain independence. It goes without saying also, therefore, that the passages emerge from his hands in a very mauled condition; brought as far as it is possible to bring them, even with violence, into line with the "Liberal" view of what the mission of Jesus ought to have been. It is reassuring, however, to observe that, even so, they cannot be despoiled of their central testimony. That Jesus proclaimed Himself to have come — to have been sent — on a mission of salvation, of salvation of the lost, Harnack is constrained to present as their primary content. By the side of this, it is true, he places a second purpose — to ful-

---

[1] From *The Princeton Theological Review*, v. xiii, 1915, pp. 513-586.

[2] *Zeitschrift für Theologie und Kirche*, 1912, xxii, pp. 1-30.

fil the law, that is, to fill it out, to complete it. Accordingly, he says, Jesus' self-testimony is to the effect that "the purpose of His coming, and therewith His significance, are given in this — that He is at once Saviour and Lawgiver." Behind both lies, no doubt, love, as the propulsive cause — "I came to minister" — and yet Jesus is perfectly aware that His purpose is not to be attained without turmoil and strife — "I came to cast fire upon the land and to bring a sword." These sayings, he remarks in conclusion, contain very few words; and yet is not really everything said in them? Shall we call it an accident that "under the superscription 'I came,' the purpose, the task, the manner of Jesus' work, all seem to be really exhaustively stated, and even the note of a bitter and plaintive longing is not lacking"?

It seems to be well worth while to follow Harnack's example and to make this series of sayings in which our Lord's testimony to the nature of His mission has been preserved for us in the Synoptic record, the object of a somewhat careful examination. Approaching them free from the "Liberal" presuppositions which condition Harnack's dealing with them, we may hope to obtain from them a more objective understanding than he has been able to attain of how Jesus really thought of His mission.

I

Our differences with Harnack begin with even so simple a matter as the collection of the passages. He discovers eight, as follows: Mt. x. 34 ff. = Lk. xii. 51, 53; Mk. ii. 17 = Mt. ix. 13 = Lk. v. 32; Mk. x. 45 = Mt. xx. 28; Lk. xii. 49; Lk. xix. 10; Lk. ix. 56; Mt. v. 17, Mt. xv. 24. This list, however, seems to us to require a certain amount of correction.

(1) We are compelled to omit from it Lk. ix. 56, as, despite the vigorous defence of its genuineness by Theodor Zahn,[3] certainly spurious.

---

[3] "Das Evangelium des Lucas" ausgelegt von Theodor Zahn, 1913, pp. 400 ff., 765 ff. The grounds on which the omission of the passage is justified are sufficiently stated by F. J. A. Hort, "The New Testament in the Original Greek." [ii], Appendix, 1881, pp. 59 ff.

Harnack's argument in its favor suffers somewhat from a confusion of it with some neighboring interpolations. Because he supposes himself to discover certain Lucan characteristics in these, he concludes that this too is Lucan in origin. Because some of them appear to have stood in Marcion's Gospel he assumes that this also stood in that Gospel. It is a matter of complete indifference, meanwhile, whether it stood in Marcion's Gospel or not. It may be urged, to be sure, that it is easier to suppose that it was stricken out of Luke because of Marcion's misuse of it, than that it was taken over into Luke from the Gospel of that "first-born of Satan." Meanwhile, there is no decisive evidence that it stood in Marcion's Gospel;[4] and, if it had a place there, there is no reason to suppose that it was taken over thence into Luke. It was, on the contrary, already current in certain Lucan texts before Marcion.[5]

The method of criticism which is employed by Harnack here, — a method with which Hilgenfeld used to vex us and of which Harnack and Bousset and Conybeare seem to have served themselves especially heirs [6] — is, let us say it frankly, thoroughly vicious. Its one effort is at all costs to get behind the total formal transmission, and in the attempt to do this it is tempted to prefer to the direct evidence, however great in mass and conclusive in effect, any small item of indirect evidence which may be unearthed, however weak in its probative force or ambiguous in its bearing. The fundamental principle of this method of criticism naturally does not commend itself to those who have made the criticism of texts their business. Even an Eduard Norden sounds a salutary warning against

[4] Cf. Zahn, as cited, p. 767: "On the other hand we do not as yet know whether Marcion had this third questionable passage also (verse 56ᵃ: ὁ γὰρ υἱὸς . . . σῶσαι in his Gospel. Tertullian, however, had precisely this passage in his text. . . ."

[5] The character of its attestation implies as much. Accordingly Tischendorf remarks ad loc.: "It is unquestionable from the witnesses, especially the Latin and Syriac, that the whole of this interpolation was current in MSS. already in the second century."

[6] This vicious critical method is thetically asserted by H. J. Holtzmann, "Einleitung," § 49, ed. 2, p. 49. It has been recently defended in principle by G. Kittel, *TSK*, 1912, 85, pp. 367–373.

it,[7] and the professional critics of the New Testament text reject it with instructive unanimity.[8] Nobody doubts that wrong readings were current in the second century and it goes but a little way towards showing that a reading is right to show that it was current in the second century. Many of the most serious corruptions which the text of the New Testament has suffered had already entered it in the first half of that century. The matter of importance is not to discover which of the various readings at any given passage chances to appear earliest, by a few years, in the citations of that passage which have happened to be preserved to us in extant writings. It is to determine which of them is a genuine part of the text as it came from its author's hands. For the determination of this question Harnack's method of criticism advances us directly not a single step, and indirectly (through, that is, the better ascertainment of the history of the transmission of the text) but a little way.

When, now Harnack deserts the textual question and suggests that it is of little importance whether the passage be a genuine portion of the Gospel of Luke or not, since in any event it comes from an ancient source, he completely misses the state of the case. This professed saying of Jesus has no independent existence. It exists only as transmitted in Luke's Gospel. If it is spurious there, we have no evidence whatever that it was spoken by Jesus. It comes to us as a saying of Jesus' only on the faith of its genuineness in Luke. Falling out of Luke it falls out of existence. There is no reason to suppose that it owes its origin to anything else than the brooding mind of some devout scribe — or, if we take the whole series of interpolations in verses 54–56 together, we may say to the brooding minds of a series of scribes, supplementing the work one of another —

---

[7] "Agnostos Theos," 1913, p. 301: "The philologist knows from experience that the manuscript transmission must be given a higher value than the indirect."

[8] Cf. C. R. Gregory, "Prolegomena" to the eighth edition of Tischendorf's New Testament, "Pars Ultima," 1894, p. 1138; "Textkritik des Neuen Testaments," ii, 1902, p. 754; "Canon and Text of the New Testament," 1907, p. 422; E. Miller in Scriverner's "Introduction," etc., ed. 4, ii, pp. 188–189; Hammond, "Outlines," etc., ed. 2, p. 66. On the general subject, see Ll. J. M. Bebb, in the Oxford "Studia Biblica," ii, 1890, p. 221.

whose pen — or pens — filled out more or less unconsciously the suggestions of the text which was in process of copying. The manuscripts are crowded with such complementary inter-polations, — E. S. Buchanan, for example, has culled many instructive examples from Latin manuscripts[9] — and none could bear more clearly on its face the characteristic marks of the class than those now before us. "And when His disciples James and John saw, they said, Lord, wilt Thou that we bid fire to come down from heaven and consume them [as [also] Elias did]? But He turned and rebuked them and said, ye know not what manner of spirit ye are of. [[For] the Son of Man came not to destroy [men's] lives, but to save them]."

(2) As an offset to the omission of Lk. ix. 56 we should insert into the list Mk. i. 38 = Lk. iv. 43.

This passage Harnack rejects on the ground that no refer-ence is made to the mission of Jesus in Mark's "for to this end came I out," His coming forth from Capernaum alone being meant; while Luke's specific, "for therefore was I sent" is due merely to a misunderstanding on Luke's part of Mark's state-ment. The major premiss of the conclusion thus reached is obvi-ously a particular hypothesis of the composition of the Synoptic Gospels and especially of the relation of Luke to Mark. On this hypothesis, Mark is the original "Narrative-Source," and the matter common to Luke and Mark is derived directly by Luke from Mark. We cannot share this hypothesis: the matter presented by both Luke and Mark seems to us rather to be derived by both alike from a common source (call it the "Primi-

---

[9] In his "Sacred Latin Texts" (i, 1912; ii, 1914, iii, 1914) Buchanan is accustomed to give lists of striking readings occurring in the manuscript he is editing. Here are a few from the Irish codex, Harl., 1023: Lk. i. 57, And she brought forth *according to the word of God* a son; viii. 12, Take heed how ye hear *the word of God;* xi. 3, Give us today for bread, *the word of God from heaven;* xv. 29, But as soon as this *son of the devil came;* Jno. vi. 44, No man can come unto me except the Father which sent me *and the Holy Spirit* draw him; viii. 12, He that followeth me shall not walk in darkness, but shall have the *eternal* light of the life *of God.* See also "The Records Unrolled," 1911. The parallel is made more striking by Buchanan's tendency to think such readings more original than those of the criti-cal texts. The lengths he would go in this contention may be observed in his pam-phlet: "The Search for the Original Words of the Gospel," 1914.

tive Mark" — *Urmarkus* — if you like) underlying both. But assuredly no hypothesis could be more infelicitous as an explanation of the relation of Luke to Mark in our present passage. If Luke is here drawing directly on Mark, he certainly uses a very free hand. The same general sense could scarcely be conveyed by two independent writers more diversely. This is apparent even to the reader of the English version, for the difference extends to the whole literary manner, the very conception and presentation of the incident. It is much more striking in the Greek, for the difference permeates so thoroughly the language employed by the two writers as to approach the limit of the possible. In the verse which particularly concerns us, for example, it is literally true that except at most the two words, translated diversely in the English version, in Mark "to this end," in Luke "therefore," [10] no single word is the same in the two accounts. If there is anything clear from the literary standpoint, it is clear that Luke is not here drawing upon Mark but is giving an independent account. In that case, Luke's report of what our Lord said cannot be summarily set aside as a mere misunderstanding of Mark.

It may still be said, of course, that what Luke gives us is a deliberate alteration of Mark. Something like this appears to be the meaning of C. G. Montefiore, who writes: "Luke's 'I was sent' (i. e. by God) is a grandiose and inaccurate interpretation of Mark's 'I came forth' (from the city)." Alfred Loisy traces at length what he conceives to be the transformation of the simple record of facts given by Mark into the announcement of a principle by Luke. "The difference between the historical tradition and the theological point of view," he remarks, "appears very clearly in the words of Christ; '*Let us go elsewhere* . . . it is for this *that I came out*'; and '*It must needs be that I proclaim* to other towns *the kingdom of God* — I was sent for that.'" It is the same general conception that underlies H. A. W. Meyer's explanation that Mark's "expression is original, but had already acquired in the tradition that Luke

---

[10] We give to εἰς τοῦτο the benefit of the doubt in Lk. iv. 43. Probably the right reading is ἐπὶ τοῦτο.

here follows a doctrinal development with a higher meaning."
And the step from this is not a long one to H. J. Holtzmann's
representation of Luke's "I was sent" as a transition-step to
the doctrinal language of John. Luke's language, however,
bears no appearance of being a correction, conscious or unconscious, either of Mark's or anybody else's statement: it looks
rather very much like an independent account of a well-trans-
mitted saying of Jesus'. And we are moving ever further from
the actual state of the case, in proportion as we introduce into
our explanation the principle of a developing tradition with its
implication of lapse of time. There is no decisive reason for
supposing that Luke wrote later than Mark. And it is no less
unjustified to describe his point of view than his Gospel as
later than Mark's. The two Gospels were written near the
same time, — Mark's being probably, indeed, a few years the
younger.[11] They came out of the same circle, the missionary
circle of Paul. And they reflect the same tradition in the same
stage of development, if we may speak of stages of development
regarding a tradition in which we can trace no growth whatever. If the element of time be eliminated, and we speak merely
of differing temperaments, there might be more propriety in
attributing a more theological tendency to the one than to the
other. When a matter of historical accuracy is involved, however, Luke surely is not a historian who can be lightly set aside
in his statements of fact. His representation that Jesus spoke
here of His divine mission and not merely of His purpose in
leaving the city that morning, makes on purely historical
grounds as strong a claim upon our credence as any contradictory representation which may be supposed to be found in
Mark, especially as it was confessedly no unwonted thing for
Jesus to speak of His divine mission.

In point of fact, however, there is no difference of repre-

[11] A. Plummer's dating of Mark ("The Gospel According to St. Mark,"
1914), between 65 and 70 A. D., probably nearer the latter than the former date
(we should say about A. D. 68), seems to us the only reasonable one: cf. Johannes
Weiss, "Die Schriften des Neuen Testaments," I¹, 1906, p. 32 (cf. also p. 35):
"about the year 70, probably somewhat earlier." On the other hand Harnack's
later view of the date of Luke as prior to A. D. 63 seems to be not improbable.

sentation between Luke and Mark. Mark too reports Jesus as speaking of His divine mission. The possibility that he does so is allowed by Harnack himself, when he writes: "The probability is altogether preponderant that in the words of Jesus (Mark i. 38), 'Let us go elsewhere into the next towns that I may preach there also; for to this end came I forth,' the 'came I forth' (ἐξῆλθον) has no deeper sense, but takes up again the 'went out' (ἐξῆλθεν) of verse 35: 'And in the morning, a great while before day, He rose up and went out [from Capernaum] and departed.'" Others, making the same general contention, open the door to this possibility still wider. C. G. Montefiore comments: "'I came out' — i. e., from the city. But the phrase is odd. Does it mean 'from heaven'? In that case it would be a late 'theological' reading." In similar doubt Johannes Weiss writes: "It is not altogether clear whether He means 'For this purpose I left the house so early,' or 'For this purpose I have come out from God — come into the world' (it is thus that Luke understood the text)." Mark's meaning is, then, not so clearly that Jesus referred merely to His coming out from Capernaum, nor indeed is it quite so simple, as it is sometimes assumed to be.

Harnack is scarcely right in any event in making the "I came out" of verse 38 both refer to Jesus' leaving Capernaum and resume the "He went out" of verse 35. It is not at all likely that the "He went out" of verse 35 refers to His leaving Capernaum. The statements as to Jesus' movements in verse 35 are remarkably circumstantial: they tell us that Jesus, having got up [12] before dawn, went out and went forth to a desert place. It is not the "went out" (ἐξῆλθεν) but the "went forth" (ἀπῆλθεν) which refers to His departure from Capernaum: the "went out" means that He "went out of doors," "out of the house." This is very generally recognized. It is recognized, for example by both Loisy and Montefiore, as well as by Holtzmann before them, all of whom understand the "going out" of verse 38 of "leaving the town." It is recognized also by

---

[12] Cf. Holtzmann's note: "ἀναστάς is to be taken here literally, therefore not merely as = וַיָּקָם." Cf. also G. Wohlenberg's note.

Johannes Weiss, who saves the back reference to it of verse 38
by making the "I came out" of that verse too mean "from the
house." Surely, however, it would be too trivial to make Jesus
say: "It was for this reason that I left the house so early this
morning — that I might preach also in the neighboring towns."
Was He to visit all those towns that day, and therefore needed
to make an early start? Mark apparently means us to understand, on the contrary, that the reason of His leaving the house
so early was that He might find retirement for prayer. The
"coming out" of verse 38 is then, in any case, not a resumption
of that of verse 35, but a new "coming out" not previously
mentioned. What reason is there for referring it back to the
"going forth" ($\dot{a}\pi\hat{\eta}\lambda\theta\epsilon\nu$, "departed") from Capernaum of verse
35? Would it be much less trivial to make Jesus say that He
came out from Capernaum so early that morning to preach
throughout Galilee than that He came out of the house for
that purpose? The solemn declaration, "For to this end came
I out" must have a deeper meaning than this. In point of fact
He did "come" in this deeper meaning to preach; and He did
fulfil this purpose and preached throughout Galilee as Mark
had just duly recorded (i. 14). Is it not much more natural
that He should have said this here, and that His biographer
should have recorded that He said it, than that He should have
said and been recorded as saying that He came out of Capernaum that morning early with this purpose in view? We cannot but think G. Wohlenberg right in pronouncing such an
understanding of the declaration "superficial." Jesus seems
clearly to be making here a solemn reference to His divine
mission.[13]

(3) There is another passage with Harnack's dealing with
which we cannot agree. This is Luke xii. 49–53.

Harnack rends this closely knit paragraph into fragments;
discards two of its five constituent sentences altogether; and,
separating the other three into two independent sayings, identifies one of these (verses 51, 53) with Mt. x. 34 ff. and leaves

[13] So J. A. Alexander, J. J. Van Oosterzee, E. Klostermann, H. B. Swete, A.
Plummer, et al. Mayer ad loc. gives older names.

the other (verses 49, 50) off to itself. This drastic treatment of
the passage seems to have been suggested to him by the comment on it of Julius Wellhausen.[14] This comment runs as
follows:

The three first verses do not square with one another. The fire
which Jesus longs for is an abiding, universal effect, the baptism of
death a passing personal experience, the prospect of which he dreads.
What stands here is not: My death is the necessary precondition of
my great historical effect. Rather, the declarations of verse 49 and
verse 50 are presented as parallel, although they are not so. Just as
little is verse 50 homogeneous with verse 51. But neither do verses
49 and 51 agree together; the wished-for fire can have nothing to do
with the terrible division of families. The whole of verse 50 and the
second half of verse 49 are lacking in Marcion. In their absence, a
connection would no doubt be instituted; the fire would be the inward
war, and Luke would be reduced to Matthew (x. 34, 35). I have,
however, no confidence whatever in this reading of Marcion's, but
rather believe that Luke has brought together wholly disparate things
according to some sort of association of ideas.

This slashing criticism Harnack reproduces in its main features,
as follows:

Luke would undoubtedly have these two verses [49 and 50] considered as fellows: they are bound together by δέ, are framed similarly, and close even with a rhyme. But their contents are so diverse
as to interpose a veto on their conjunction. It has been in vain, moreover, that the expositors have tried to build a bridge between the two
verses. Every bridge is wrecked on the consideration that the first
verse refers to the action of Jesus, the second to something which
threatens Him; for it is impossible to think in the second verse of
baptism in general (Jesus' own baptism of suffering is meant, see Mk.
x. 39), since the words, "How am I straitened, etc.," would then be
wholly unintelligible or would have to be explained in a very artificial
manner. The contention also that the eschatological idea connects
the two verses is wrong; for the futures which the two verses contem-

---

[14] A. Loisy appears not unwilling also to make a discreet use of Wellhausen's
disintegrating criticism in his attempt to show how Luke concocted his narrative.
Montefiore after reporting Wellhausen's criticism, expresses doubt regarding it,
and then slips off into the lines of his favorite mentor, Loisy.

plate are different. Add that the "fire" of the first verse has nothing
to do with the "baptism with fire"; for Jesus could not say of that
fire that He came "to cast" it upon the earth. It is therefore to be
held that Luke who often follows external associations of ideas, has
been led to put the two verses transmitted to him together by the
similarity of their structure, and because some connection between
fire and baptism hovered before his mind. He has similarly again
made an arbitrary connection in the case of the next verse, when he
adjoins the saying about peace and sword of which we have already
spoken. This saying too can scarcely have been spoken in the same
breath with ours, precisely because it exhibits a certain relationship
with it but is differently oriented.

The superficiality of this criticism is flagrant. It owes whatever plausibility it may possess to the care which is taken not
to go below the surface. So soon as we abstract ourselves from
the mere vocables and attend to the thought the logical unity
of the paragraph becomes even striking. Even in form of statement, however, the passage is clearly a unity. Harnack himself calls attention to the structure of verses 49 and 50 as a
plain intimation that they form a pair in their author's intention, and the bridge which he desiderates to connect them he
himself indicates in the "but" by which the author, before the
expositors busied themselves with the matter, expressly joins
them. When Jesus had given expression to the pleasure that
it would give Him to see the fire He had come to cast into the
world already kindled, it was altogether natural that He should
add an intimation of what it was that held this back — He
must die first. And nothing could be more natural than that
He should proceed then to speak further of the disturbance
which His coming should create. It would be difficult to find
a series of five verses more inseparately knit together. That
such rents should exist between them as are asserted, and they
be invisible to H. J. Holtzmann, say, or Johannes Weiss, neither
of whom is commonly either unable or unwilling to see flaws
in the evangelical reports of Jesus' sayings is, to say the least,
very remarkable; and a unitary understanding of the passage
which commends itself in its general features alike to these ex-

positors and, say, Theodor Zahn, can scarcely be summarily
cast aside as impossible. It is quite instructive to observe that
the lack of harmony between verses 49 and 50, which is the
hinge of the disintegrating criticism of the passage, is so little
obvious to, say, Johannes Weiss, that it is precisely to the combination of these two verses that he directs us to attend if we
wish really to understand Jesus' state of mind with reference
to His death. "The parallelism of the fire and baptism, preserved only by Luke," he urges, "is one of Jesus' most important sayings, because we can perceive from it how Jesus thought
of His end." "How Jesus really thought of His future," he says
in another place, "a declaration like Luke xii. 49 f., perhaps
shows." [15]

Looking, thus, upon Lk. xii. 49–53 as a closely knit unit, it
would be difficult for us to accept Harnack's identification of
Lk. xii. 51, 53, torn from its context, with Mt. x. 34–36, also
removed from its context; and the assignment of the "saying,"
thus preserved by both Matthew and Luke, to the hypothetical "Discourse-Source," which it is now fashionable to cite by
the symbol "Q." Even apart from this difficulty, however, the
equation of the two passages would not commend itself to us.
The phraseology in which they are severally cast is distinctly
different. The decisive matter, however, is the difference in
the settings into which they are severally put by the two evangelists. Both of the sections in which they severally occur,
confessedly present difficulties to the harmonist, and the dispositions which harmonists have made of them in their arrangement of the evangelical material vary greatly.[16] It seems to be
reasonably clear, however, that in the tenth chapter of Mat-

[15] "Die Schriften," etc.[1], i, pp. 438 and 138. Weiss even speaks of Mk. x. 38
as "no doubt an echo of Lk. xii. 50" (p. 160), but it is not perfectly clear what he
means by this (it is retained in the second edition).

[16] For example, Edward Robinson, having placed Mt. x. 34 ff. in its natural
position in his § 62, preposits Lk. xii. 49 ff. to his § 52. John H. Kerr, on the contrary, retaining the same natural position for Mt. x. 34 ff. (at his § 50), more
correctly places Lk. xii. 49 ff. at his § 90. C. W. Hodge, Sr., "Syllabus of Lectures
on the Gospel History," 1888, p. 73, very properly speaks of Robinson's "dislo-
cation" of the material of Luke as "the principal blot on his harmony": "he
breaks up the connection just where commentators find a striking unity."

thew and the twelfth chapter of Luke we are dealing with two quite distinct masses of material, spoken by our Lord on separate occasions. We may be sorry to forego any advantage which may be thought to accrue from the assignment of one of the sayings of Jesus in which He speaks of His mission to the hypothetical "Discourse-Source." [17] But we cannot admit that there is involved any loss of authenticity for the two sayings in question. We see no reason to suppose that the source or sources, from which the two evangelists drew severally the sayings they have reported to us, compared unfavorably, in point of trustworthiness as vehicles of the tradition of Jesus' sayings, with the hypothetical "Discourse-Source," from which they both sometimes draw in common. On the whole the certainty that Jesus said what is here attributed to Him is increased by His being credibly reported to have said it twice in very similar language and to entirely the same effect.

We therefore amend Harnack's list at this point also, and instead of listing the two sayings as Mt. x. 34–36 = Lk. xii. 51, 53, and Lk. xii. 49, 50, give them as Mt. x. 34–36 and Lk. xii. 49–53.

As the result of this survey of the material, we find ourselves, like Harnack, with eight "sayings" at our disposal, although these eight are not precisely the same as those which he lists. Arranged, as nearly as the chronological order can be made out, in the order in which they were spoken, they are as follows: Mk. i. 38 = Lk. iv. 43; Mt. v. 17; Mk. ii. 17 = Mt. ix. 13 = Lk. v. 32; Mt. x. 34 f.; Mt. xv. 24; Lk. xii. 49 ff.; Mk. x. 45 = Mt. xx. 28; Lk. xix. 10.[18] Five of these sayings are

[17] Willoughby C. Allen and A. Plummer deny that Mt. x. 34 ff. and Lk. xii. 51 ff. come from Q. "Phraseology and context alike differ," says Allen. "The two evangelists draw from different sources."

[18] Along with these there are certain other sayings which come illustratively into consideration. Primary among them is Mt. xi. 3 ff. = Lk. vii. 20 ff. which Harnack (p. 23) is tempted to include in the list itself as a ninth saying. Others are: Mk. xi. 9, 10 = Mt. xxi. 9 = Lk. xix. 38 = Jno. xii. 13; Mt. xxiii. 39; Mt. xi. 18, 19 = Lk. vii. 33, 34. Cf. also Mt. x. 40; Mk. ix. 37 = Lk. ix. 48; Lk. x. 16. There may be added [Mk. ix. 11 = Mt. xvii. 13; Mt. iii. 11 = Lk. iii. 16]. We have made some remarks on the general subject in "The Lord of Glory," pp. 39 f., 76 f., 126 f., 190 f.

found in Matthew; four in Luke; and three in Mark. As no one of them is found only in Matthew and Luke we need not insist that any of them is derived from the hypothetical "Discourse-Source" (Q), to which are commonly assigned the portions of the Synoptics found in Matthew and Luke but lacking in Mark. As all of these sayings are found in either Matthew or in Luke (and one in both) there seems to be no good reason, however, why some (or all) of them may not possibly have had a place in a document from which both Matthew and Luke are supposed to draw.[19] One is found in all three Gospels, one in Mark and Matthew, and one in Mark and Luke. These three at least, two of them very confidently in the form in which we have them, and the third (Mk. i. 38 = Lk. iv. 43) very possibly in one of the forms in which it has come to us, may be thought to have stood in the hypothetical "Narrative-Source" (*Urmarkus*). And it is possible that all the others may have stood in it too, since all the Gospels draw from it. Three are found in Matthew alone and two in Luke alone. These are at no disadvantage in point of trustworthiness in comparison with their companions which occur in more than one Gospel. Apart from the fact that they may have stood in any source from which their companions were drawn but did not chance to be taken from it by more than one evangelist, the determination that some of the sources used by the evangelists were drawn upon by more than one of them has no tendency to depreciate the value of those which were drawn upon by only one. No doubt the hypothetical "Narration-Source" which lies behind all three of the Synoptics is a very old document and is very highly commended to us by the confident dependence of them all upon it. There is no sound reason for assigning any of these Gospels to a date later than the sixties, and Luke and Matthew may easily have come from a considerably earlier date. A document underlying them all must have existed in

---

[19] We may quote here, say, Johannes Weiss, who says ("Die Schriften[1]," i, p. 33): "Possibly there belongs to it yet many another [passage] which is found only in Matthew, or only in Luke." As we ourselves believe that Mark also knew the "Discourse-Source," we might add also "or only in Mark."

the fifties and may be carried back almost to any date subsequent to the facts it records. But much the same may be said of a document underlying any one of the Synoptics: a document drawn on by one of them only may be just as old and just as authoritative as one drawn on by all of them. The matter of primary importance does not concern the particular hypothetical document — they are all hypothetical — from which it may be supposed that our Gospels have derived this saying or that. The disentangling of the hypothetical sources from which they may be supposed to have derived the several items of their narratives is a mere literary matter. We know nothing of these sources after we have disentangled them except that they all are earlier than the Gospels which used them; and that when the contents of each are gathered together and scrutinized, the contents of them all prove to be, from the historical point of view, all of a piece. This is the fundamental fact concerning them which requires recognition. The tradition of Jesus' sayings and doings, gathered out of earlier sources (written or oral) and preserved by the Synoptic Gospels, is a homogeneous tradition, and the original tradition. Behind it there lies nothing but the facts. Whether written down in the fifties or the forties or the thirties: whether some short interval separates its writing from the facts it records — say ten or twenty years — or no interval at all; no trace whatever exists of any earlier tradition of any kind behind it. It is for us at least the absolute beginning. In these circumstances we are justified in holding with confidence to all the sayings of Jesus transmitted to us in these Gospels. It is not that we cannot get behind these Gospels: it is that we can get behind them and find behind them nothing but what is in them.[20]

The term used by our Lord in these passages to express the fact of His mission is normally the simple "I came" ($\tilde{\eta}\lambda\theta o\nu$, Mk. ii. 17, Mt. v. 17, ix. 13, Mt. x. 34, Lk. xii. 49; cf. $\tilde{\eta}\lambda\theta\epsilon\nu$, Mk. x. 45, Mt. xx. 28). But variations from this "technical term" occur. Once, after it has been once employed, it is varied on

[20] See the state of the case as presented in the *Princeton Theological Review*, 1913, xi, 2, pp. 195–269.

repetition to "the more elegant" (as Harnack calls it) term for public manifestation, "I came forth" (παρεγενόμην, Lk. xii. 49, 51). Once, in a parallel, the tense is changed to "I have come" (ἐλήλυθα, Lk. v. 32). Once the compound "I came out" (ἐξῆλθον, Mk. i. 38) is used. And in two passages, "I was sent" (Lk. iv. 43, Mt. xv. 24; cf. Mk. ix. 37 = Lk. ix. 48, Mt. x. 40, Lk. x. 16) takes the place of "I came." In the majority of cases our Lord speaks directly of Himself as the one whose mission He is describing, in the first person: "I came," "I was sent," "I came out." In a few instances, however, He speaks of Himself in the third person under the designation of "the Son of Man" — "the Son of Man came" (Mk. x. 45 = Mt. xx. 28, Lk. xix. 10). There is a difference also in the nature and, so to say, the profundity of the reference to His mission. Sometimes He is speaking only of His personal ministry in "the days of His flesh," and the manner of its performance (Mk. i. 38 = Lk. iv. 43, Mt. xv. 24, cf. Lk. xix. 10). Sometimes His mind is on the circumstantial effects of the execution of His mission (Mt. x. 34 ff., Lk. xii. 49 ff.). Sometimes the horizon widens and the ultimate ethical result of His work is indicated (Mt. v. 17). Sometimes the declaration cuts to the bottom and the fundamental purpose of His mission is announced with respect both to the object sought and the means of its accomplishment (Mk. ii. 17 = Mt. ix. 13 = Lk. v. 32; Lk. xix. 10; Mk. x. 45 = Mt. xx. 28): "I came not to call the righteous but sinners"; "The Son of Man came to seek and to save that which was lost"; "The Son of Man came not to be ministered unto but to minister, and to give His life a ransom for many." It should not pass without notice that it is in these last instances only that our Lord deserts the simple form of statement with the personal pronoun, "I came," and substitutes for it the solemn declaration, "the Son of Man came."

II

In investigating the meaning of these sayings severally it is not necessary to follow carefully the chronological order of their utterance. In a broad sense they increase in richness of contents as our Lord's ministry develops itself. It was not until late in His ministry, for example, that our Lord spoke insistently of His death and His allusions to His mission in His later ministry reflect this change. Nevertheless these sayings do not grow uniformly in richness as time goes on, and it will be more convenient to arrange them arbitrarily in order of relative richness of content than strictly to follow the chronological sequence. The order to be pursued has been suggested at the close of the immediately preceding paragraph.

1

| Mk. i. 38: And He saith unto them, Let us go elsewhere into the next towns, that I may preach there also; for to this end came I out. | Lk. iv. 43: But He said unto them, I must preach the good tidings of the kingdom of God to the other cities also; for to this end was I sent. |

As reported by Mark, in this saying Jesus declares His mission in the briefest and simplest terms possible. It was just to preach. "For to this end came I out," He says; namely "to preach." [21] The context intimates, it is true, that this preaching was to be done in the first instance in the immediately neighboring towns: "Let us go elsewhere into the next towns that I may preach there also." It lay in the nature of the case that any preaching intended to extend over the land should begin with the nearest towns, and that these therefore should be particularly in mind in the announcement. But that the preaching was not intended to be limited to these "next" towns [22] is clear enough in itself, and is made quite plain (so far as the understanding of the reporter, at least, is concerned) by the next verse, which tells us what Jesus did by way of fulfilling the mission which He here announces: "And He went

[21] Cf. G. Wohlenberg *in loc.*: "The εἰς τοῦτο, verse 38, means just the κηρύσσειν in general, not especially the κἀκεῖ κηρύσσειν."

[22] In the parallel, Luke says simply, "to the other cities," which suggests no other limitation than what Th. Zahn (p. 247) calls "the self-evident one" of "the other Jewish cities of Palestine."

into their synagogues throughout all Galilee,[23] preaching and casting out devils." Luke in the parallel, extends the boundaries even further. "And He was preaching in the synagogues of Judaea," he says, — but without prefixing the emphatic "all." By "Judaea" he means "Palestine as a whole,"[24] but, as the omission of the "all" already advises us, he does not intend to assert that there was no part of Palestine to which Jesus did not carry His Gospel, so much as that His mission was distinctively to Palestine.[25] In a word, Jesus announces His mission here as a mission to the Jewish people: He came out, was sent, to preach to the Jews.

The emphasis thus laid on preaching as the substance of Jesus' mission does not, however, so set preaching in contrast, say, to the working of miracles as to exclude the latter from any place in His mission. It has become fashionable in one school of expositors to see in the accounts which the evangelists give here a more or less complete misunderstanding of Jesus' motives in leaving Capernaum, although these are supposed nevertheless to shimmer through the narrative sufficiently to guide "the seeing eye." [26] When Jesus is represented as moved by a desire to preach in other places, less than half the truth, it is said, is told. What really determined His action was a desire to get away from Capernaum. And the reason for His desire to get away from Capernaum was that a thaumaturgical function had been thrust upon Him there. He fled from this in the night (Mk. i. 35). What He really announced in the words here misleadingly reported, was that His mission

[23] Cf. Mt. iv. 23: "And He went about in all Galilee, teaching in their synagogues, and preaching the good tidings of the Kingdom, and healing all manner of disease, and all manner of sickness among the people." The emphasis in both Mark and Matthew is on the completeness with which Galilee was covered by this itinerant preaching.

[24] See especially Th. Zahn, p. 248, and pp. 61 f. Cf. A. Loisy, i, p. 462: "Luke has chosen a general term in order to signify that the mission of Jesus was for the whole country, conformably to what was said in verse 43 (B. Weiss, "Einleitung," pp. 307–308)." Also, B. Weiss, C. F. Keil, Johannes Weiss *in loc.* Wellhausen: "Judaea (verse 44) includes Galilee in it: cf. i. 5; vi. 17; vii. 17, and D. xxiii. 5." Godet rejects the reading "Judaea" as "absurd."

[25] We are following Th. Zahn here (p. 248).

[26] So, e. g., H. J. Holtzmann, A. Loisy, J. Weiss. C. G. Montefiore draws back.

was to preach, not to work miracles. So far from permitting this to shimmer through them however, the narratives of the evangelists flatly contradict it. Mark, for example, tells us that in leaving Capernaum Jesus did not leave His miracles behind Him: "And He went into their synagogues throughout all Galilee, preaching, and casting out devils." The parallel in Matthew (iv. 23) enlarges on this: "And He went about in all Galilee, teaching in their synagogues and preaching the Gospel of the kingdom, and healing all manner of disease and all manner of sickness among the people." It may be easy to say, as Johannes Weiss for example does say, that such statements do not correspond with what really happened, and that Luke in his parallel account (iv. 44) has done well to omit them. But it is not so easy thus lightly to erase, not a couple of remarks merely, but the entire presentation of Jesus' work by the evangelists. According to their account, not merely at Capernaum in the beginning, but throughout His whole ministry, "mighty works" were as characteristic a feature of Jesus' ministry as His mighty word itself.[27] There is not the least justification in the narratives themselves, moreover, for the attempted re-reading of their implications. There is no suggestion in them that Jesus was "betrayed into thaumaturgical works" at Capernaum. There is no hint that He was shocked or troubled by His abounding miracles there, or that He looked upon them as a scattering of His energies, or a diversion of Him from His proper task or as making a draft upon His strength. They are represented rather as His crown of glory. He is not represented as fleeing from them and as endeavoring to confine Himself to activities of a different nature. He is represented rather as looking upon them as the seal of His mission and His incitement to its full accomplishment. "I must needs preach in *the other* towns": "that I may preach there *also*." Not a contrast with His work at Capernaum, but a repetition of it, is what He hopes for elsewhere. The whole contrast lies between Capernaum and the rest of the land: between a local and an itinerant

[27] Cf. the conjunction of the two in Jesus' instructions to the Twelve, Mt. x. 5–8, and His reply to the Baptist's question, Mt. xi. 4–5.

ministry. What He had done in Capernaum, He felt the divine necessity of His mission driving Him to do also in the other cities. And therefore "He went into their synagogues throughout all Galilee preaching, and casting out devils." The ground of Jesus' leaving Capernaum lay, shortly, as Holtzmann recognizes it to be Luke's purpose to intimate, solely in "the universality of His mission." [28]

What Jesus came out to preach in fulfilment of His mission Mark's statement does not tell us. It says simply, "I came out to preach." But this is not to leave it in doubt. It was too well understood to require statement. Mark had just told his readers summarily that "after John was delivered up, Jesus came into Galilee, preaching the glad-tidings of God, and saying, The time is fulfilled and the kingdom of God is at hand: repent ye and believe in the glad-tidings" (cf. Mt. iv. 17). When he tells them now that Jesus announced His mission to be to preach, it is perfectly evident that it is just this preaching which he has in mind. The parallel in Luke declares this in so many words. "I must needs," Jesus is there reported as saying, "proclaim the glad-tidings of the kingdom of God, for to this end was I sent." The accent of necessity is here sounded. It were impossible that Jesus should do anything other than preach just this Gospel of the kingdom of God. His mission to this end lays a compulsion upon Him: He was sent to do precisely this, and needs must do it. [29] Jesus' mission is to preach a Gospel, the Gospel of the kingdom of God.

For Jesus so to describe His mission, clearly was to lay claim to the Messianic function. Preaching the glad-tidings of the kingdom of God is the Messianic proclamation. The accompanying miracles are the signs of the Messiah. Accordingly when the Baptist sent to Jesus inquiring, "Art thou He that Cometh or look we for another?" Jesus replied by pointing to these things: "the blind receive their sight, and the lame walk, the lepers are cleansed, and the deaf hear, and the dead are

[28] P. 333: "The ground of His flight, verse 43 finds in the universality of His mission."

[29] On the accent of "necessity" in Jesus' life, see Hastings' "Dictionary of Christ and the Gospels," article "Foresight," at the beginning.

raised up, and the poor have the glad-tidings preached to them." [30] "He that Cometh" is a Messianic title, and therefore, as Harnack reminds us, those who heard Jesus say, "For I say unto you, ye shall not see me henceforth, till ye shall say, Blessed is He that cometh in the name of the Lord," understood Him to be speaking of the Messiah, and would have understood that just the same if the words "in the name of the Lord" had been wanting.[31] The question lies near at hand, accordingly, whether Jesus merely by speaking of "coming," "being sent," does not lay claim to Messianic dignity. In that case those terms would be used pregnantly. The Baptist "came," neither eating nor drinking, as truly as Jesus "came" eating and drinking (Mt. xi. 18; cf. xxi. 32). The prophet is "sent" as truly as the Messiah (Lk. iv. 26; Mt. xiii. 37 = Lk. xiii. 34; Jno. i. 6, 8, iii. 28). What the words openly declare is a consciousness of divine mission; and the two modes of expression differ according as the emphasis falls on the divine source of the mission ("I was sent") or on its voluntary performance ("I came").[32] Something more needs to be added, therefore, to mark the mission which they assume, plainly as Messianic. That something more is added in the present passage by the purpose which is declared to be subserved by the mission. That purpose is the Messianic proclamation. He who came to preach the glad-tidings of the kingdom of God and who could point to the signs of the Messiah accompanying His preaching, has come as the Messiah.

Jesus, however, does not here say merely "I came." He says, "I came *out*," and the preposition should not be neglected. At the least it must refer to Jesus' coming publicly forward

[30] Mt. xi. 3 ff. = Lk. vii. 20 ff. Harnack (p. 23) says: "The question whether the miracles which are enumerated are to be understood spiritually is to be answered in the negative for Matthew and Luke, and probably also for Jesus Himself." But that places Harnack in a quandary: "But that Jesus should have spoken here literally of raising the dead is nevertheless not easy to acknowledge."

[31] P. 1: Mt. xxiii. 39 = Lk. xiii. 35.

[32] Cf. Th. Zahn's words "Das Evangelium des Matthäus³," p. 610, distinguishing between "the execution of a commission laid on Him by God (Mt. x. 40, ὁ ἀποστείλας με, xv. 24; xxi. 37)" and "the purpose and meaning of His life comprehended by Himself (ἦλθεν)."

and entering upon the task of public teacher. J. J. van Oosterzee insists upon this sense: "The Saviour speaks simply of the
purpose for which He now appeared publicly as a teacher."[33]
That, however, in this Messianic context, appears scarcely adequate. We seem to be compelled to see in this term a reference
to Jesus' manifestation as Messiah with whatever that may
carry with it. This is apparently what C. F. Keil and G. Wohlenberg have in mind. According to the former, the phrase "I
came out" is used here absolutely in the sense of coming into
publicity, coming into the world; and if, he adds, we wish to
supply anything we may add in thought $\pi\alpha\rho\dot{\alpha}$ or $\dot{\alpha}\pi\dot{o}$ $\tau o\hat{v}$ $\theta\epsilon o\hat{v}$ —
as we may find in Jno. xiii. 3; xvi. 27, 30. Similarly the latter
considers the reference to be to Jesus' entrance upon His Messianic calling, and adds that it is not surprising if the expression
tempts us to find in it an allusion to the coming forth from the
Father such as John speaks of at xiii. 3; xvi. 27, 30; xvii. 8.
Even if we follow this path to its end and say simply, with J.
A. Alexander, F. Godet, A. Plummer, H. B. Swete and others,
that when He says, "I came out" Jesus means, "I came out
from God" or "from heaven" we are not going beyond the
implications of the Messianic reference. If Jesus thought Himself the Messiah there is no reason why He may not be supposed
to have thought of Himself as that transcendent Messiah
which was "in the air" in "the days of His flesh." That He
did think of Himself as the transcendent Messiah is indeed
already evident from His favorite self-designation of the Son
of Man, — as reported by Mark as by the other evangelists.
The Son of Man carries with it the idea of preëxistence. When
then Mark records that He spoke of His mission as a "coming
out," the phrase may very well come before us as the vehicle
of Jesus' consciousness of His preëxistence; and F. Godet is
speaking no less critically than theologically when he remarks
that "Mark's term appears to allude to the incarnation, Luke's
only refers to the mission of Jesus." [34]

[33] On Lk. iv. 43.

[34] It is less obvious that the simple "I came" presupposes preëxistence as
many commentators insist (e. g., A. Plummer, "Matthew," p. 156, note 2, cf.
A. M. McNeille on Mt. x. 40).   But on this see below pp. 568, 581 ff.

When we say Messiah we say Israel. We naturally revert
here, then, to Jesus' testimony that His mission was to preach
the Gospel of the Kingdom of God to the cities of Judaea. He
is obviously speaking not of the utmost reach of His mission,
but of the limits of His personal ministry. His personal ministry,
however, He describes as distinctively to the Jews. He "came
out," He "was sent," to proclaim the glad-tidings of the im-
minence of that Kingdom to the people of God to whom the
Kingdom had been promised. This was, in its external aspects,
His mission.

2

Mt. xv. 24: And He answered and said, I was not sent but unto
the lost sheep of the house of Israel.

What in the former saying is given a perhaps somewhat
unarresting positive expression is in this saying asserted in a
strong, almost startling, negative form. Jesus declares that His
mission was not only to the Jews, but to them only. Denying
a request from His disciples that He should exercise His miraculous powers for the healing of a heathen girl who was suffering from possession, He justifies the denial by explaining
that His mission was not to the heathen but solely to the Jews:
"I was not sent but to the lost sheep of the house of Israel."
The language in which He clothes this explanation had been
employed by Him on a previous occasion. When He was sending His disciples on their first mission He laid, first of all, this
charge upon them: "Go not into any way of the Gentiles, and
enter not into any city of the Samaritans; but go rather to the
lost sheep of the house of Israel" (Mt. x. 5–6). The circumstantial negative clauses act as definitions of the language of
the positive clause. This language is just as sharply definite in
our present saying. Jesus declares that He has no mission to
the heathen. His mission is distinctively to the Jews.

It may be possible to exaggerate, however, the exclusive-
ness of this declaration. After all, it has a context. And it
should not be overlooked that despite the emphasis of His assertion that He had no mission to the heathen, Jesus healed

this heathen girl. Nor can it quite be said that He healed her by way of exception; overpersuaded, perhaps, by the touching plea of her mother, or even, perhaps, instructed by her shrewd common-sense to a wider apprehension of the scope of His mission than He had before attained. When He threw Himself back on His mission, He invoked in His justification the authority of God.[35] And therefore, in adducing His mission, He employs the phrase "I was sent" rather than "I came." By that phrase He appeals to Him with whose commission He was charged, and transfers the responsibility for the terms of His mission to Him.[36] After this it can scarcely be supposed that He overstepped the terms of His mission, as He understood them, in healing the heathen child. In other words, when He declares, "I was not sent but unto the lost sheep of the house of Israel," He is not to be understood as declaring that His mission was so exclusively to the Jews that the heathen had no part in it whatever.

The whole drift of the incident as recorded whether by Mark or by Matthew bears out this conclusion. The precise point which is stressed in both accounts alike is, not that the Jews have the exclusive right to the benefits of Jesus' mission, but that the preference belongs to them. This is given open expression in Jesus' words as reported by Mark, "Let the children *first* be fed; it is not meet to take the children's bread and cast it to the dogs." But it is equally the implication of Mat-

[35] Montefiore is quite right in saying: "The explanation is that God had ordered this limitation."

[36] In only two of the sayings in which Jesus expounds His mission (Lk. iv. 43, Mt. xv. 24) is the form "I was sent" employed. It is perhaps not without significance that in the only one of these which has a parallel (Lk. iv. 43), it is not the simple "I came" which stands in this parallel (Mk. i. 38), but a form which more pointedly refers to the source of the mission in God ("I came out"). The "I was sent" is reflected in its active equivalent in the "Johannine" (Jno. xiii. 20) phrase of Mt. x. 40; Mk. ix. 37 = Lk. ix. 48; Lk. x. 16, in which the unity of the sent and sender is suggested. Note the emphasis placed on Jesus' employment of "I was sent" in our present passage by F. L. Steinmeyer, "The Miracles of Our Lord," pp. 140 ff., and J. Laidlaw, "The Miracles of Our Lord," p. 252. Th. Zahn remarks that here for the first time in Matthew is Jesus presented as the ἀπόστολος of God, and adds: "cf. xv. 24; xxi. 37 as correlate of the ἦλθον of v. 17; ix. 13; x. 34. Apart from John cf. Heb. iii. 1, Clem., I Cor. xl, 1."

thew's account.[37] Jesus does not suggest that the dogs [38] shall
have nothing; but that they shall have only the dogs' portion.
What the portion of the dogs is, is not here indicated. It is only
intimated that they have a portion. The children have the
preference, of course: but there is something also for the dogs.
Jesus' whole conversation in this incident is certainly peda-
gogically determined. He employed the application of this
heathen woman to Him in order to teach His disciples the real
scope of His mission. There is no contradiction between His
declaration to them that He was sent distinctively to Israel
and His subsequent healing of the heathen child. He heals the
child not in defiance of the terms of His mission, but because
it fell within its terms; and He commends the mother because
she had found the right way: "And He said unto her, *For this
saying*, go thy way: the devil is gone out of thy daughter."
A comment of Alfred Edersheim's sums up not badly the teaching of the incident: "when He breaks the bread to the children,
in the breaking of it the crumbs must fall all around." [39]

Obviously what Jesus tells us here is very much what Paul
tells us, when, summing up his Gospel ringingly as the power
of God unto salvation to every one that believes, he adds, "To
the Jew first and also to the Greek" (Rom. i. 16, cf. ii. 10).
Many "Liberal" expositors therefore represent Mark as corrupting the record of Jesus' conversation when he puts on
Jesus' lips a sharp assertion of this principle: "Let the children
first be filled." [40] "If the Jews have only the *first* right," comments Johannes Weiss, for example, "it follows that the hea-

---

[37] This is solidly shown by Th. Zahn.

[38] It has been often pointed out that the use of the diminutive here softens
the apparent harshness of the language. Shall we say "doglings"?

[39] "Life and Times of Jesus the Messiah¹," ii, 1883, p. 41.

[40] H. J. Holtzmann (p. 184): "*Let first* (πρῶτον = prius, maxim from Rom.
i. 16; ii. 9, 10) *the children* (Israelites) *be filled*"; this explanation, which still
leaves room for the satisfaction of the mother, is simply lacking in Mt. xv. 26,
and therefore the conclusion is commonly drawn that in the narrative of Mark
we have a deliberate mitigation, a dependence upon the later, Pauline mission,
and therefore secondary work (so Hilgenfeld, last in *ZWTh*, 1889, p. 497; B. and J.
Weiss, Jülicher, "Gleichnisreden," ii, p. 256 f., even Wittichen p. 188, and with
more reserve, Wernle, p. 133)."

then too have a right. This is an echo from the Epistle to the Romans, i. 16, — the Jew first, then the Greek!" [41] It is not, however, merely in this sharp assertion of it that this principle is given expression in the narrative of the incident. It is present as truly in the account of Matthew as in that of Mark. The whole drift of both accounts alike — the climax of which is found not in any word of Jesus' but in a marvellous word of His petitioner's — is that there is something left for the dogs after the children are filled: "Even the dogs under the table eat of the crumbs of the children"; "even the dogs eat of the crumbs that fall from the table of their masters." Had there been no provision for the Gentiles, indeed, Jesus could scarcely have expected His disciples to recognize Him as that "One to Come" with whose mission there had from the beginning been connected blessings for the Gentiles also. The evangelists are not drawing from Paul when they represent Jesus as teaching that His mission was to Israel and yet extends in its beneficial effects to the world (cf. especially Mt. viii. 11; xxviii. 19). [42] Paul on the contrary is reflecting the teaching of Jesus as reported by the evangelists when, as Jesus proclaimed Himself to have been sent only to Israel, he declares Him to have been made a minister of the circumcision; [43] and when, as Jesus suggests that nevertheless there is in His mission a blessing for Gentiles also, he declares that by His ministry to the circumcision not only is the truth of God exalted and the promises unto the fathers confirmed, but mercy is brought to the Gentiles also (Rom. xv. 8 ff.).

How His mission could be distinctively for Israel and yet contain in it a blessing for the Gentiles also Jesus does not here explain to His disciples. He is content to fix the fact in their

[41] "Schriften," etc.[1], i, 1906, p. 128.

[42] Wellhausen represents Mark as free from such universalizing utterances. Nowhere does it put such a statement as Mt. viii. 11 f. on Jesus' lips; and only in the eschatological discourse, Mk. xiii. 10, do we find a prediction of the extension of the preaching of the Gospel to the heathen attributed to Jesus. Montefiore adds xiv. 9. The implication is, of course, that neither of these passages is authentic.

[43] "Christ has become minister of the circumcised," comments H. A. W. Meyer; "for to devote His activity to the welfare of the Jewish nation was, according to promise, the duty of His Messianic office, cf. Mt. xx. 28, xv. 24."

minds by the awakening object-lesson of this memorable miracle in which His saving power goes out of Himself and effects its beneficent result across the borders of a strange land.[44] We can scarcely go astray, however, if we distinguish here, as in the case of Mark i. 38 = Lk. iv. 43, between His personal ministry and the wider working of His mission. When He says, "I was not sent but to the lost sheep of the house of Israel," He has His personal ministry in mind. It will hardly be doubted that this was the understanding of the evangelist. C. G. Montefiore, for example, paraphrases thus: "His disciples shall convert the world; He Himself is sent only to Israel." "Jesus says that He has been sent to the lost sheep of Israel only. This looks like a 'narrow' tradition. But it is not. It is intended to explain the undoubted but perplexing fact that Jesus the universal Saviour and Mediator, did actually confine Himself to the Jews. The explanation is that God had ordered this limitation. After His resurrection, He will send His disciples to all the world." [45] Did Jesus Himself have no anticipation of this course of events, or purpose with reference to it? It should go without saying that, just because He conceived His mission as Messianic, He necessarily conceived it both as immediately directed to Israel, and as in its effects extending also to the Gentiles. That was how the mission of the Messiah had been set forth in those prophecies on which He fed. We cannot be surprised, then, that it is customary to recognize that it is to His personal ministry alone that Jesus refers when He declares that He "was not sent but to the lost sheep of the house of Israel."[46]

The Messianic character of His mission is already implied

[44] "It has been remarked," says Wellhausen ("Das Ev. Marci," 1903, p. 60), "that this is up to now the only example in Mark in which Jesus heals from a distance, by His mere word." "This is the second example of a miracle wrought from a distance," says Loisy (i, p. 977). "The first was wrought on the centurion's son." Then he cites Augustine's remarks in "Quaest. Ev.," i, 18.

[45] Vol. ii, pp. 657, 658.

[46] So from Augustine and Jerome down. H. A. W. Meyer expresses the general opinion when he says: "It was not intended that Christ should come to the *Gentiles* in the days of His flesh, but that He should do so at the subsequent period (xxviii. 19) in the person of the Spirit acting through the medium of the Apostolic preaching (Jno. x. 16, Eph. ii. 17)." Cf. Th. Zahn: "His personal and

in the terms in which He here describes it. When He speaks of
"the lost sheep of the house of Israel," His mind is on the great
messianic passage, Ezek. xxxiii., xxxiv., in which Jehovah
promises that He Himself will feed His sheep, "and seek that
which was lost"; and that He will "set up one shepherd over
them, and he shall feed them, even my servant David; he shall
feed them and he shall be their shepherd." [47] When, with His
mind on this prophecy, Jesus spoke of His mission as to "the
lost sheep of the house of Israel" it may admit of question
whether the genitive is epexegetical or partitive, — whether
He conceives His mission to be directed to Israel as a whole,
conceived as having wandered from God, or to that portion
of Israel which had strayed [48] — but it can admit of no question
that He conceived of those to whom His mission was directed
as "lost." He thought of His mission, therefore, as distinctively
a saving mission, and He might just as well have said, "I was
sent to save the lost sheep of the house of Israel." Harnack is
quite right, therefore, when, after calling attention to the adoption of the language of Ezek. xxxiv. 15, 16, he adds: "And the
mission to the lost sheep contains implicitly the 'to seek and
to save.'" How He is to accomplish the saving of the lost sheep
of the house of Israel, Jesus does not in this utterance tell us.
He tells us only that He has come, as the promised Messiah,
with this mission entrusted to Him, — to save these lost sheep.

immediate vocation." Also, R. C. Trench, "Notes on the Miracles of Our Lord,"
second American ed., 1852, p. 274; J. Laidlaw, "The Miracles of Our Lord,"
1890, p. 252; A. Edersheim, "Life and Times," etc.[1], 1883, ii, p. 40.

[47] Observe the address of the petitioner in our passage (Mt. xv. 22), "O
Lord, Son of David," which is not repelled by Jesus. "Spoken by a heathen,"
remarks Edersheim (ii, p. 39), "these words were an appeal, not to the Messiah
of Israel, but to an Israelitish Messiah." They supply the starting point for a
conversation, however, in which the Messiah of Israel brings relief to the heathen.

[48] That in Mt. x. 6, "the lost sheep of the house of Israel," the genitive is
not partitive seems to be shown by the contrast of verse 5: the disciples are to go,
not to Gentiles or the Samaritans, but to Israel, described here as "lost sheep."
Cf. H. A. W. Meyer *in loc.*: "Such sheep (ix. 36) were *all*, seeing that they were
without faith in Him, the heaven-sent Shepherd." The same phrase in Mt. xv.
24, in a similar contrast (with the Canaanitish woman), might naturally be held
to be used in the same broad sense. Israel as a whole in that case would be the
"lost sheep."

3

Mt. x. 34 ff.: Think not that I came to cast peace on the earth; I came not to cast peace but a sword. For I came to set a man at variance against his father, and the daughter against her mother, and the daughter-in-law against her mother-in-law: and a man's foes shall be they of his own household.

In this context Jesus is preparing His disciples for the persecutions which awaited them. They must not think their case singular: their Teacher and Lord had Himself suffered before them. Nor must they imagine that they are deserted: the Father has not forgotten them. And after all, such things belong in their day's work. They have not been called to ease but to struggle. Strife then is their immediate portion; but after the strife comes the reward.

When Jesus introduces what He has to say with the words, "Think not," He intimates that He is correcting a false impression, prevalent among His hearers (cf. v. 17).[49] His reference can only be to expectations of a kingdom of peace founded on Old Testament prophecy.[50] Since these expectations are focussed upon His own person He is obviously speaking out of a Messianic consciousness; and is assuming for Himself the rôle of the Messiah, come to introduce the promised kingdom.[51] Of course He does not mean to deny that the Messianic kingdom which He has come to introduce is the eternal kingdom of peace promised in the prophets. He is only warning His followers that the Messianic peace must be conquered before it is

[49] Cf. B. Weiss (Meyer, 9, 1898) and A. Plummer *in loc.*, and A. Loisy, i, p. 891.

[50] G. S. Goodspeed, "Israel's Messianic Hope," 1900, p. 123: "All the seers of Israel look forward out of their present, whether gloomy or bright, to a golden age of peace." W. A. Brown, Hastings' "Dictionary of the Bible," iii, p. 733[a]: "Among the blessings to which Israel looks forward in the Messianic times, none is more emphasized than peace." Cf. A. Loisy, i, p. 891.

[51] Neglecting this, Harnack speaks inadequately when he writes: "This discourse is not Messianic in the literal sense — even John the Baptist could, it would appear, have said it — but in the burden of the discourse and in the saying, 'I came for this purpose,' there lies a claim which soars above the prophets and the Baptist. For Jesus implicitly demands here that the severest sacrifices be made and the enmity of the nearest kindred be incurred, *for the sake of His person* "

enjoyed. As His mind at the moment is on the individual, He describes the strife which awaits His followers in terms of the individual's experience. The language in which He does this is derived from an Old Testament passage (Micah vii. 6) in which the terrible disintegration of natural relationships incident to a time of deep moral corruption is described. The dissolution of social ties which His followers shall have to face will be like this. Let them gird themselves to meet the strain upon them loyally. For, as the succeeding verses show, it is distinctly a question of personal loyalty that is at issue.[52]

It should be observed that Jesus does not say merely, "Think not that I came to *send* (or *bring*) peace upon the earth," as our English versions have it. He says, "Think not that I came to *cast* peace upon the earth." The energy of the expression should not be evaporated (cf. vii. 6). What Jesus denies is that He has come to fling peace suddenly and immediately upon the earth,[53] so that all the evils of life should at once and perfectly give way to the unsullied blessedness of the consummated kingdom. Such seems to have been the expectation of His followers. He undeceives them by telling them plainly that He came on the contrary to cast a sword. Strife and struggle lie immediately before them, and the peace to which they look forward is postponed. The pathway upon which they have adventured in attaching themselves to Him leads indeed to peace, but it leads through strife.

When Jesus says that He came to cast a sword upon the earth and to set men at variance with one another, the declaration of purpose must not be weakened into a mere prediction of result.[54] He is speaking out of the fundamental presupposi-

---

[52] Cf. the excellent remarks of Th. Zahn, p. 415.

[53] So B. Weiss, "Das Matthaeusevangelium und seine Lucas-Parallelen," 1876, p. 281, also in Meyer, 9th ed., 1898, and in "Die Vier Evangelien," etc., 1900, *in loc.* So also H. J. Holtzmann, "Die Synoptiker³," 1901, p. 235, who remarks: "Thus Jesus strikes out of the picture of the Messianic age, at least for the immediately following transitional period, the joy and peace predicted in Micah. iv. 3, v. iv, Zech. ix. 9, 10, and brings war into prospect in its stead, in reminiscence of Ex. xxxii. 27, Ezek. vi. 3, xiv. 17, xxi. 12."

[54] It is often so weakened. Thus e. g., A. Loisy: "The appearance of the Christ has therefore, for consequence — not for end, but the Biblical language does not

tion of the universal government of God, which had just found
expression in the assertion that not even a sparrow, or indeed
a hair of our heads, falls to the ground "apart from our Father"
(verses 29–31). The essence of the declaration lies in the assurance that nothing is to befall His followers by chance or the
hard necessity of things, but all that comes to them comes
from Him.[55] Not merely the ultimate end, but all the means
which lead up to this end — in a linked chain of means and
ends — are of His appointment and belong to the arrange-
ments which He has made for His people. They are to face the
strife which lies before them, therefore, as a part of the service
they owe to Him (verses 37 ff.), their Master and Lord (verses
24 f.). This strife is not indeed all that Jesus came to bring,
but this too He came to bring; and when He casts it upon the
earth, He is fulfilling so far His mission. He "came," "was
sent" (verse 40) to "cast a sword."

In this saying, too, we perceive, Jesus is dealing with what
we may without impropriety speak of as a subordinate element
of His mission. He does not mean that the sole or the chief
purpose of His coming was to stir up strife. He means that the
strife which His coming causes has its part to play in securing
the end for which He came. When He said in Mk. i. 38 = Lk.
iv. 43, "I came to preach," He was looking through the preaching, as means, to the end which it was to subserve. When He
said in Mt. xv. 24 that He was not sent but to the lost sheep of
the house of Israel, He did not forget the wider end of which
His ministry to Israel should be the means. So, when He says,
"I came to cast a sword upon the earth," He is thinking of the
strife which He thus takes up unto His plan not for itself but
as an instrument by which His ultimate purpose should be
reached. He tells us nothing of how long this strife is to last,

make a sharp distinction between the two — the division signified by the sword."
Also, B. Weiss (Meyer, 9th ed., 1898): "What is the immediate, inevitable conse-
quence of His coming, Jesus announces as its purpose." Cf. A. H. McNeille on
Mt. x. 34.

[55] Cf. B. Weiss, "Das Matthaeusevangelium," etc., 1876, p. 281: "It does
not come like an unavoidable evil which is connected with the sought-for good,
but it is foreseen and intended by Him."

or through what steps and stages it is to pass into the peace
which waits behind it. Is He speaking only of the turmoil
which must accompany the acceptance of Him as Messiah by
His own people, involving as it does adjustment to the revised
Messianic ideal which He brought? [56] Is He speaking in a
"springing sense" of the ineradicable conflict of His Gospel
with worldly ideals, through age after age, until at last "the
end shall come"? [57] Or is He speaking of the "growing pains"
which must accompany the steady upward evolution through
all the ages of the religion which He founded? [58] The passage
itself tells us nothing more than that Jesus came to cast a
sword upon the earth; that there were to result from His coming strife and strain; and that only through this strife and strain
is the full purpose for which He came attainable. For what is
more than this we must go elsewhere. Only let us bear well in
mind that the note of the saying is not discouragement but
confidence. There rings through it the "Fear not!" of verse 31.

[56] This appears to be A. Loisy's idea: "Because the proclamation of the kingdom has as its immediate effect (had not the Saviour found this Himself in His
own home?) to cause discord in families — one accepting the faith, another rejecting it, and this discord placing believers and unbelievers at odds." See also
C. G. Montefiore: "The sword does not mean war between nations, but dissension between families, of which one member remains a Jew, while another becomes
a Christian."

[57] This appears to be A. Plummer's meaning: "So long as men's wills are
opposed to the Gospel there can be no peace. . . . Once more Christ guards His
disciples against being under any illusions. They have entered the narrow way,
and it leads to tribulation, before leading to eternal life."

[58] Something like this seems to be Johannes Weiss' meaning: "This saying
belongs to the most characteristic and the most authentic sayings of Jesus concerning Himself: 'I came not to bring peace on the earth but a sword.' Jesus must
have felt deeply how utterly His proclamation stood in contradiction with what
men were accustomed to hear and wished to hear. And what He Himself in His
parental home seems to have experienced, that he foresees as a universal phenomenon which He portrays by means of words derived from Micah: a cleft is to
go through families; and indeed it is to be the young generation which shall op-
pose the old ('three against two and two against three' says Luke: the wife of
the son lives in the house of her parents-in-law). Jesus does not reprehend this,
and offers no exhortation against loss of piety. He simply posits it as an inevitable
fact. Thus it has always been a thousand times over; and it may be to the elders
a warning and to the children a consolation, that even the Gospel of Jesus must
create so painful a division."

There underlies it the "I too will confess him before my Father in heaven" of verse 32. And it passes unobserved into the "He who loses His life for my sake shall find it" of verse 39, and the "whosoever shall give to drink to one of these little ones a cup of cold water only in the name of a disciple, verily I say unto you, he shall not lose his reward" of verse 42. Jesus warns His followers of the stress and strain before them. But He does this as one who buckles their armor on them and sends them forth to victory. The word on which the discussion closes is "Reward."

4

Lk. xii. 49–53: I came to cast fire upon the earth; and how I wish that it was already kindled! But I have a baptism to be baptized with; and how am I straitened until it be accomplished! Think ye that I am come to give peace in the earth? I tell you, Nay; but rather division: for there shall be from henceforth five in one house divided, three against two and two against three. They shall be divided, father against son, and son against father; mother against daughter, and daughter against her mother; mother-in-law against her daughter-in-law, and daughter-in-law against her mother-in-law.

To some of the questions started by Mt. x. 34 ff., answers are suggested by the present saying. Here too Jesus is protecting His followers against the false expectation which they had been misled into forming, that He, the Messiah, would at once introduce the promised reign of peace.[59] In repelling this expectation, His own claim to the Messianic dignity and function is given express intimation. He corrects, not their estimate of His person or vocation, but their conception of the nature of the Messianic work. The language in which He makes this correction is very strong: "Ye think that it is peace that I am come to give in the earth. Not at all, I tell you; nothing but division."[60] The emphasis which, by its position, falls on the word "fire" in the first clause, corresponds with this strength

[59] Cf. Hahn's note *in loc.*

[60] A. Plummer: "I came not to send *any other thing than* division." Th. Zahn: "Think ye that I am come to give peace on earth? No, I say to you, nothing else than division." Cf. II Cor. i. 13.

of language and prepares the way for it: "It is fire that I came to cast upon the earth." [61] It is clear that the two sentences belong together and constitute together but a single statement. The "fire" of the one is, then, taken up and explained by the "division" of the other, just as the "came" ($\mathring{\eta}\lambda\theta\sigma\nu$) of the one is repeated in the "am come" ($\pi\alpha\rho\epsilon\gamma\epsilon\nu\acute{o}\mu\eta\nu$) of the other, and the "cast" ($\beta\alpha\lambda\epsilon\hat{\imath}\nu$) of the one by the "give" ($\delta\sigma\hat{\nu}\nu\alpha\iota$) of the other. The greater energy of the language in the former declaration is due to its being the immediate expression of Jesus' own thought and feeling: "It is fire that I came to cast upon the earth"; whereas in its repetition it is the thought of His followers to which He gives expression: "Ye think that it is peace that I am here [62] to give." What it is of chief importance for us to observe is that by the "fire" which He has come to cast upon the earth, Jesus means just the "division" [63] which He describes in the subsequent clauses in much the same language in which He had spoken of it in Mt. x. 34 ff. That is to say, He has in mind, here as there, a great disarrangement of social relationships which He speaks of as the proximate result of the introduction of the Kingdom of God into the world.

No more here than there does Jesus mean to represent this discord which He declares He came to give in the earth, as the proper purpose or the ultimate result of His coming.[64] The

[61] Cf. Plummer's note.

[62] $\pi\alpha\rho\alpha\gamma\acute{\imath}\nu\omega\mu\alpha\iota$ "to come to the side of," is, says Harnack, a "more elegant" word than $\mathring{\epsilon}\rho\chi\omega\mu\alpha\iota$, and Luke has varied the $\mathring{\eta}\lambda\theta\sigma\nu$ of verse 49 to the $\pi\alpha\rho\epsilon\gamma\epsilon\nu\acute{o}\mu\eta\nu$ of verse 51 for the sake of better literary form. If Luke was really the author of all the nice touches with which he is credited, he would need to be recognized as one of the most "exquisite" writers of literary history. The variations of language between the parallel statements of verses 49 and 51 are grounded in the nature of the case and reflect the truth of life. It is better to explain $\pi\alpha\rho\epsilon\gamma\epsilon\nu\acute{o}\mu\eta\nu$ as the natural phrase to express the disciples' thought of Jesus' "coming" relatively to themselves, than to give it with Thayer-Grimm the sense of "coming forth," "making one's public appearance" (Mt. iii. 1, Heb. ix. 11).

[63] Cf. Loisy, p. 892: "In view of the expressions chosen and of the progress of the discourse, the fire is nothing else than the discord introduced into the world by the preaching of the Gospel, or, better still perhaps the movement excited for or against the religion of Jesus by the Apostolic preaching, from which the discord arose."

[64] Cf. Zahn, p. 516: "That the ultimate purpose of His life and work is to bring peace upon the earth, Jesus of course does not here deny" [cf. to the con-

strength of the language in which He declares it to be His purpose in coming to produce this dissension, shuts off, indeed, all view beyond. When He says, "Ye think it is peace that I am here to give on the earth. Not at all, I tell you: nothing but division," He is thinking, of course, only of the immediate results, and, absorbed in them, leaving what lies beyond for the time out of sight. The absoluteness of the language is like the absoluteness of the, "I was not sent but to the lost sheep of the house of Israel." But something does lie beyond. This not only belongs to the nature of the case, but is already intimated in the last clause of the first sentence (verse 49): "It is fire that I came to cast on the earth, and how I wish that it was already kindled." Clearly Jesus did not long for the kindling of the fire for the fire's own sake; but for the sake of what would come out of the fire.

What this clause particularly teaches us, however, is that the fire which Jesus came to cast on the earth was not yet kindled. The clause is of recognized difficulty and has been variously rendered. Most of these renderings yield, however, the same general sense; and it is reasonably clear that the meaning is represented with sufficient accuracy by, "And how I wish that it was already kindled." [65] For even the fire which He came to cast upon the world, Jesus thus points to the future. Not even it has yet been kindled. The peace which His followers were expecting lies yet beyond it. He was not to give peace in the world but nothing but division: yet even the division was not yet come — for even that His followers were to look forward. He is, then, not accounting to His followers for the trials they were enduring: He is warning them of trials yet to come. He is saying to them in effect, "In the world ye shall have

---

trary, Acts x. 36, Lk. i. 79, Isa. ix. 6, Eph. ii. 14–17], "but only that the intended and immediate consequence of His coming and manifestation is a universal condition of peace upon earth, — a thing which even the angels on the night of His birth did not proclaim. . . ."

[65] So Kuinoel, Olshausen, De Wette, Bleek, Meyer, B. Weiss, Holtzmann, Zahn. On this use of the τί see A. T. Robertson, "A Grammar of the Greek of the New Testament," 1914, on Lk. xii. 49 as per Index, and Zahn *in loc.* p. 514, note 54. On the εἰ ἤδη ἀνήφθη see Zahn *in loc.* and note 53.

tribulation"; but the subaudition also is present, "But be of good cheer; I have overcome the world." These things He was speaking to them, therefore, that despite the impending tribulation, they might have the peace which they were expecting — at least in sure prospect.

From the strong wish which Jesus expresses that the fire which He came to cast upon the earth had already been kindled, Harnack takes occasion to represent Him as a disappointed man. Harnack explains the fire which Jesus says He came to cast upon the earth as "an inflammation and refining agitation of spirits," and discovers an immense pathos in Jesus' inability to see that it had as yet been kindled.

Jesus moved with pain, acknowledges that the fire does not yet burn . . . What Jesus wishes, yes, what He speaks of as the purpose of His coming, He does not yet see fulfilled — the great trying and refining agitation of spirits in which the old is consumed and the new is kindled. That "men of violence" ($\beta\alpha\sigma\tau\alpha\iota$) are necessary that the kingdom of God may be taken, He says at Mt. xi. 12. To become such a man of violence ($\beta\alpha\sigma\tau\eta s$) one must be kindled from the fire. This fire He fain would bring, He has brought; but it will not yet burn; hence His pained exclamation. Elsewhere, only in the saying about Jerusalem (Mt. xxiii. 37) does this pained complaint of the failure of results come to such sharp expression.

It is needless to point out that this whole representation is in direct contradiction with the context. Harnack has prepared the way for it by cutting off the context and taking the single sentence of verse 49 in complete isolation. In so doing, he has rendered it impossible, however, confidently to assign any particular meaning to that, in that case, perfectly insulated saying. It is in this state equally patient to a dozen hypothetical meanings. The sense which Harnack puts upon it is simply imposed upon it from his own subjectivity: he merely ascribes to Jesus the feelings which, from his general conception of His person and work, he supposes He would naturally express in such an exclamation. Fortunately, the context interposes a decisive negative to the ascription. We have here not the weak wail of disappointment, but a strong assertion of conscious control.

That, indeed, is sufficiently clear from the declaration itself. When Jesus asserts, "It is to cast fire upon the earth that I came" it is anything but the consciousness of impotence that is suggested to us. And the note of power vibrating in the assertion is not abolished by the adjoined expression of a wish that this fire was already kindled. No doubt there is an acknowledgment that the end for which He came was not yet fully accomplished: He had not finished His work which He came to do. But this does not involve confession either of disappointment at the slowness of its accomplishment, or fear that it may never be accomplished. The very form of the acknowledgment suggests confidence in the accomplishment. When Jesus says, "Would that it was already kindled"! He expresses no uncertainty that it will in due time be kindled. And even the time, He does not put outside of His power. He even tells us why it has not already been kindled. And the reason proves to lie in the orderly prosecution of His task. "How I wish," He exclaims, "that it was already kindled! But . . ." He himself is postponing the kindling: "But I have a baptism to be baptized with." The fire cannot be kindled until He has undergone His baptism.[66] Its kindling is contingent upon that. No doubt He looks forward to this baptism with apprehension: "And how am I straitened till it be accomplished"! But with no starting back. It is to be accomplished: and His face is set to its accomplishment. The entire course of events lies clearly in His view, and fully within His power. He has come to cast fire on the earth; but one of the means through which this fire is to be cast on the earth is a baptism with which He is to be baptized. This baptism is a dreadful experience which oppresses His soul as He looks forward to it. He could wish it were all well over. But He has no thought of doubting its accomplishment or of shrinking from His part in it. It is a veritable pre-Gethsemane which is revealed to us here.[67] But as in the actual Gethsemane, with the "Let this cup pass from me," there is conjoined the, "Nevertheless not my will but thine be done."

[66] So Holtzmann (p. 374), and Zahn (p. 515).
[67] Cf. "Princeton Biblical and Theological Studies," 1912, pp. 71 f.

That the baptism with which Jesus declares that He is to be baptized (cf. Mk. x. 38) is His death is unquestionable and is unquestioned. What we learn, then, is that the kindling of the fire which He came to cast upon the earth is in some way consequent upon His death.[68] Of the manner of His death He tells us nothing, save what we may infer from the oppression of spirit which its prospect causes Him. Of the nature of its connection with the kindling of the fire which He came to cast upon the earth He tells us as little. We may be sure, indeed, that the relation of the two events is not a merely chronological one of precedence and subsequence. The relation between such events cannot be merely chronological; the order of time which is imperative in the development of Jesus' mission can never be a purely arbitrary temporal order. We must assume that the death of Jesus stands in some causal relation to the kindling of the fire He came to cast on the earth. What this causal relation is He does not, however, tell us here. Can we think of His death as needed to prepare Him to execute His task of casting fire upon the earth? Shall we think of His death giving impressiveness to His teaching and example and so creating in all hearts that crisis which issues in the decision by which there is produced the division with which the fire is identified? Or are we to think of His death entering in some yet more intimate manner into the production of this crisis, lying in some yet more fundamental manner at the basis of His efficient activity in the world? Jesus is silent. He tells us only that His death has a part to play in the kindling of the fire which He came to cast upon the earth; and that before it — and that means with-

---

[68] The "from henceforth" of verse 52 introduces no difficulty; cf. H. A. W. Meyer's comment: "Jesus already realizes His approaching death." "The lighting up of this fire," he remarks at an earlier point, "which by means of His teaching and work He had already prepared, was to be effected by His death (see ἀπὸ τοῦ νῦν verse 52) which became the subject of offense, as, on the other hand, of His divine courage of faith and life (cf. ii. 35)." A. Loisy is altogether unreasonable when he writes (p. 893): "In making Jesus say that the divisions will exist henceforth, 'from now,' the evangelist appears to forget that, according to him, the fire of discord should be kindled only later, when the Saviour had been baptized in death; but with him the time when Jesus spoke and that of His death were almost confounded together."

out it — that fire cannot be kindled. He tells us that His death is indispensable to His work; but He does not explain how it is indispensable.

Meanwhile we are advanced greatly in our understanding of what Jesus means by the "fire," the "sword," the "division" which, according to His statement in Mt. x. 34 ff., Lk. xii. 49 ff., He came to cast on the earth. And our sense of His control over the events by which His mission is accomplished is greatly deepened. What He came to do, He will do; even though in order to do it, He must die: even though He die — nay, just because He dies — He will do it. He came to set the world on fire. He came to die that He might set the world on fire. He wishes that the conflagration was already kindled: He is oppressed by the prospect before Him as He walks the path to death. But let no man mistake Him or His progress in the performance of His mission. His death, He will accomplish: the fire He will kindle. Men may fancy that He is come to give peace: not at all: nothing but division. That primarily. We shall see the whole world turned up-side-down (Acts xvii. 6). After that, no doubt, we shall see what we shall see. But the implication is express that, in whatever we shall see, will be included at least that peace which, after all said, lies at the end of the sequence.

5

Mt. v. 17, 18: Think not that I came to destroy the law or the prophets: I came not to destroy, but to fulfil. For, verily I say unto you, Till heaven and earth pass away, one jot or one tittle shall in no wise pass away from the law, till all things be accomplished.

"Think not," says Jesus to His disciples, "that I came to destroy the law or the prophets." That is as much as to say that they were thinking it, or at least were in danger of thinking it.[69] And that is as much as to say that He was recognized

[69] It is unreasonable for Johannes Weiss (p. 246) to say: "The error that Jesus came to destroy the law and the prophets was no doubt current in the time of the evangelist in certain circles, but cannot be proved for the life-time of Jesus, at least in the case of His disciples." Harnack refutes Weiss on his own ground (pp. 19 f.): but no refutation is needed beyond the words themselves.

by them as the Messiah, and that He was speaking to them on
the presupposition of His Messiahship, and of His Messianic
mission. On the basis of such a prophecy as that on the New
Covenant in Jer. xxxi. 31 ff.[70] it was not unnatural to think
of the Messiah as a new law-giver under whom "the old law
should be annulled and a new spiritual law given in its stead."[71]
This point of view, we know, existed among the later Jews,[72]
and could hardly fail to have its part to play in the Messianic
conceptions of Jesus' time. That Jesus needed to guard His
disciples against it was, thus, a matter of course,[73] and it was
most natural that He should take opportunity to do so after
the great words in which He greeted them as the salt of the
earth and the light of the world, and exhorted them to let their
light so shine before men that their good works should be seen
and their Father in heaven be glorified. In guarding them
against it He declares, almost expressly following out the
thought of Jeremiah's prediction with respect to the writing
of the law on the heart (Jer. xxxi. 33), that He came not to
abrogate but to perfect. Thus, in the most striking way possible, Jesus lays claim to the Messianic dignity.

Richness and force is given to Jesus' declaration, "I came
not to destroy but to fulfil," by the absence of an expressed
object. The object naturally taken over from the preceding

[70] Cf. F. Giesebrecht, "Com. on Jer.," 1894, *in loc.*: "For Jeremiah, to whom
it was a matter of course that the old covenant would not last forever, there can
therefore lie in the future only a new covenant, as with Isa. lv. 3; lix. 21, lx. 20,
lxi. 8, and Ezek. xxxiv. 25, xxxvii, 26. The old covenant had proved its insufficiency by the people's not keeping it and not being able to keep it. And since
every good and perfect gift comes from above, God must for the future give the
strength which the people lack for keeping the law, or else no stable, abiding
relation between God and the people is ever possible. The requirement envisag-
ing the people now in external letters must become one with the mind and will
of man. . . . He has not yet attained to the conception of a 'new heart,' Ezek. xi.
19, xxx. 2 ff.; Ps. li. 12, although he thinks of an inward influencing of the heart
by divine power, so that it acquires a new attitude towards the content of the
law."

[71] These words are quoted from A. F. Gfrörer, "Das Jahrhundert des Heils,"
1838, ii, p. 341.

[72] See Gfrörer as cited, and especially the citation (p. 342) from the book
Siphra on Levit. xxvi. 9.

[73] H. A. W. Meyer states the matter excellently with respect to our passage.

clause is a double one, "the law or the prophets." The development in the subsequent verses deals only with the law. The statement itself stands in majestic generality. Jesus declares that His mission was not a destroying but a fulfilling one. In making this declaration, His mind was particularly engaged with the law, as the course of the subsequent discussion suggests; or rather with the Scriptures of the Old Covenant as a whole, thought of at the moment from the point of view of the righteousness which they inculcate, as the collocation of the "law" and the "prophets" in the preceding clause suggests. But His mind is engaged with the law as an application [74] of the general principle asserted, rather than as exhausting its whole content. He presents Himself quite generally as not an abrogator but a perfecter.

The commentators are at odds with one another as to the exact meaning which should be assigned to the word "fulfil." Some insist that, in its application to the law, it means nothing but to do what the law commands: Theodor Zahn, for example, employing a lucid figure, describes the law — or more broadly the written Word — as an empty vessel which is fulfilled when it receives the content appropriate to it, — law in obedience, prophecy in occurrence.[75] Others urge that "to fulfil the law" means to fill the law out, to bring it to its full and perfect formulation: [76] Theophylact beautifully illustrates this idea by likening Jesus' action to that of a painter who does not abrogate the sketch which he completes into a picture. The generality of the expression surely requires us to assign to it its most inclusive meaning, and we do not see that Th. Keim can be far wrong when he expounds "to fulfil" as "to teach the law, to do it, and to impose it." It is clear enough from the subsequent context that when Jesus applied to the law His broad declaration that He had come not as an abrogator but as a fulfiller, He had in mind both the perfecting and the keeping of the law. In point of fact, He presents Himself both as the legislator developing the law into its fullest implications (verses 21 ff.),

[74] See Zahn's discussion here.   [75] P. 213 f.
[76] So H. A. W. Meyer, and A. H. McNeille.

and as the administrator, securing full obedience to the law (verses 18–20). The two functions are fairly included in the one act spoken of by Jeremiah — whose prophecy we have seen reason to suppose underlay Jesus' remark — as writing the law on the heart. To write the law on the heart is at once to perfect it — to give it its most inclusive and most searching meaning — and to secure for it spontaneous and therefore perfect obedience. It is to obtain these two ends that Jesus declares that He came, when He represents His mission to be that of "fulfiller" with reference to the law.

Harnack, nevertheless, lays all the stress on the single element of legislation.[77] Jesus, he supposes, presents Himself here as lawgiver; and what He declares, he paraphrases thus: "I came not to break, that is, to dissolve the law together with the prophets: I came not in general to dissolve but to consummate, that is, to make complete." He explains:

The exact opposite to καταλύσαι is to "establish," to "ratify." But Jesus intends to say something more than this. He is not satisfied, as Wellhausen finely remarks, with the positive but chooses the superlative. Not to ratify, that is to say, to establish (see Rom. iii. 31), is His intention, but to consummate. That could be done, with reference to the law, in a twofold manner, either by strengthening its authority, or by completing its contents. Since, however, the former cannot be thought of — because the law possesses divine authority — only the latter can be meant; and it is precisely this to which expression is given in verses 21–48. In this discourse the law is completed thus — that what "was said to them of old time" remains indeed in existence (οὐ καταλύω) but is completed by deeper and stricter commands which go to the bottom and direct themselves to the disposition, through which moreover it comes about that many definitions are supplanted by others. Those that are replaced do not appear, however, to be abrogated because the legislative intention of Jesus does not look upon the previous legislation as false but as incomplete, and completes it.

What is said here is not without its importance. Jesus does present Himself as a lawgiver come to perfect the law, by un-

---

[77] So also Wellhausen.

covering the depths of its meaning, and thus extending its
manifest reach. How He, thus, as legislator brings the law to
its perfection He shows in the specimen instances brought together in verses 21–48. But, saying this, we have said only half
of what must be said. What Jesus is primarily concerned for
here, is not the completer formulation of the law but its better
keeping. And what He proclaims His mission fundamentally
to be is less the perfecting of the law as a "doctrine" as Harnack puts it — "our verses [17–19] too are spoken by Him as
legislator, that is, they contain a doctrine" — (although this
too enters into His mission) than the perfecting of His disciples
as righteous men (a thing which could not be done without the
perfecting of the law as a "doctrine"). The immediately succeeding context of His proclamation of His mission as not one
of destruction but of fulfilment, deals not with the formulation
of the law but with its observance (verses 18–20).

"I came not," says Jesus, "to destroy but to fulfil, — *for*
. . ." And, then, with this "for," He immediately grounds
His assertion in the further one that the whole law in all its
details, down to its smallest minutiae, remains permanently
in force and shall be obeyed. "For, verily I say unto you, until
heaven and earth pass away, not one jot or one tittle shall
pass away from the law until all [of them] be accomplished."
This assertion is made with the utmost solemnity: "Verily, I
say unto you"; and there are two elements in it neither of which
should be allowed to obscure the other. On the one hand it is
asserted with an emphasis which could not easily be made
stronger, that the law in its smallest details remains in undiminished authority so long as the world lasts. Jesus has not
come to abrogate the law — on the contrary the law will never
be abrogated, not even in the slightest of its particulars — the
dotting of an "i" or the crossing of a "t" — so long as the world
endured. But Jesus does not content Himself with this "canoniz-
ing of the letter" as H. J. Holtzmann calls it, certainly without
exaggeration. The law, remaining in all its details in undiminished authority, is, on the other hand, to be perfectly observed. Jesus declares that while the world lasts no jot or tittle

of the law shall pass away — until they all, all the law's merest jots and tittles, shall be accomplished. He means to say not merely that they should be accomplished, but that they shall be accomplished. The words are very emphatic. The "all," standing in correlation with the "one" of the "one jot" and "one tittle," declares that all the jots and all the tittles of the law shall be accomplished. Not one shall fail. The expression itself is equivalent to a declaration that a time shall come when in this detailed perfection, the law shall be observed. This amounts to a promise that the day shall surely come for which we pray when, in accordance with Jesus' instruction we ask, "Thy Kingdom come, Thy will be done as in heaven so on earth." So far from coming to abrogate the law, He comes then to get the law kept; not merely to republish it, in all its reach, whether of the jots and tittles of its former publication, or of its most deeply cutting and widely reaching interpretation, but to reproduce it in actual lives, to write it on the hearts of men and in their actual living. "Therefore," He proceeds to tell His disciples (verses 19–20), the "breaking" [78] of one of the least of these — these jots and tittles of — commandments, and the teaching of men so, is no small matter for them. Their place in the kingdom of heaven depends on their faithfulness to the least of them; and unless their righteousness far surpasses that of the Scribes and Pharisees with all their, no doubt misplaced, strictness, they shall have no place in that kingdom at all.

In a word, we do not understand the nature of the mission which Jesus here ascribes to Himself until we clearly see that it finds its end in the perfecting of men. His purpose in coming is not accomplished in merely completing the law: it finds its fulfilment in bringing men completely to keep the completed law. If we speak of Him as legislator, then, we mean that He claims plenary authority with respect to the law. The law is His, and He uses it as an instrument in the accomplishment of His great end, the making of men righteous. He knows what is in the law, and He brings all its content out, with the most

---

[78] That λύσῃ, verse 19, is "break," not "abrogate," the parallel ποιήσῃ sufficiently shows.

searching analysis. But this is but the beginning. He came to make this law, thus nobly expounded, the actual law of human lives. Abrogate it? Nothing could be further from His purpose. He came rather to fulfil it, to work it out into its most wide-reaching applications, and to work it, thus worked-out, into men's lives. Those who are His disciples will not be behind the Scribes and Pharisees themselves in the perfection of their obedience to its very jots and tittles. But their righteousness will not be the righteousness of the Scribes and Pharisees. The difference will be that their obedience will not be confined to these jots and tittles. In their lives there will be "accomplished" the whole law of God in its highest and profoundest meaning. Their lives will be a perfect transcript in act of the law of God, a perfect reflection of the will of God in life. It is for this that Jesus says that He "came." When this complete moralization of His disciples shall be accomplished; how, by what means, in what stages this perfect righteousness is to be made theirs; He does not tell us here. He tells us merely that He "came" to do this thing: so that His disciples shall be truly the salt of the earth which has not lost its savor, the light of the world which cannot be hid.

6

| Mk. ii. 17: And when Jesus heard it, He saith unto them, They that are whole have no need of a physician, but they that are sick: I came not to call the righteous but sinners. | Mat. ix. 12–13: But when He heard it, He said, They that are whole have no need of a physician, but they that are sick. But go ye and learn what this meaneth, I desire mercy and not sacrifice: for I came not to call the righteous, but sinners. | Lk. v. 31: And Jesus answering said unto them, They that are whole have no need of a physician but they that are sick. I am not come to call the righteous but sinners to repentance. |

In the immediately preceding saying (Mt. v. 17), Jesus tells us that He came to make men righteous. In this He tells us

what manner of men they are whom He came to make righteous. They are sinners. "I came not to call righteous but
sinners." The anarthrous terms throw the qualities of the opposing classes into strong relief. Of course Jesus means by these
terms the really righteous and really sinful. This Harnack perceives. "The righteous," he rightly remarks, "are really, apart
from all irony, the righteous; and the sinners are really the
sinners; and Jesus says that His life-calling is not to call the
one but the other." Here, says Harnack, is an immense paradox. "It is one of the greatest milestones in the history of religion," he declares; "for Jesus puts His call in contrast with
all that had hitherto been considered the presupposition of
religion." So Celsus, he adds, already saw; and that is the reason
of his passion when he writes: [79]

Those who invite to the solemnization of other mysteries make
proclamation as follows: "He who has clean hands and an understanding tongue, come hither," or "He who is pure from all fault,
and who is conscious in his soul of no sin, and who has led a noble
and righteous life, come hither." This is what is proclaimed by those
who promise expiation of sins! Let us hear, on the other hand, what
kind of people the Christians invite: "Him who is a sinner, a fool, a
simpleton, in a word an unfortunate — him will the Kingdom of God
receive. By the sinner they mean the unjust, the thief, the burglar,
the poisoner, the sacrilegious, the grave-robber. If one wished to re-
cruit a robber band, it would be such people that he would collect.

The contrast here is very arresting and very instructive.
But we can scarcely call it paradoxical to invite sinners to
salvation — as Origen did not fail to remind Celsus. Paradox
is already expressly excluded when Luke, in his record, adds
the words, "to repentance." There is no paradox in calling not
righteous but sinners — to repentance. Harnack, no doubt,
asserts that this addition is "inappropriate." So little inappropriate is it, however, that it would necessarily be understood
even if it were not expressed, and it is understood in the records
of Matthew and Mark where it is not expressed. There can be
no doubt that Jesus came preaching precisely repentance (Mk.

[79] Origen, "Contra Celsum," iii. 59.

i. 15, Mt. iv. 17): and when He says that He came to call not
righteous but sinners, it is clear that this was just because He
was calling to repentance. All paradox, moreover, is already
excluded by the preceding "parable" of which this declaration
is the plain explanation: "They that are strong," says Jesus,
"have no need of a physician, but they that are sick: I came not
to call righteous but sinners." If Jesus' mission is like that of
a physician and its end is healing, how could it be directed to
the strong? Just because He came to save, He came to call
only sinners. "But," says Harnack, "we have no certainty
that this saying stood originally in this context (see Wellhausen
on the passage), nor that the saying of Jesus originally combined both clauses." And if it did (he contends), — it would
not yield the idea of calling to repentance. For in that case, sin
would be likened to sickness, and sickness requires healing, not
repentance. It is best, then, to take the simple words, "I came
not to call righteous but sinners" by themselves. They need
no presupposition to be supplied by the preceding "parable":
"they stand on their own feet with equal surety." This is
obviously special pleading. Harnack does not desire the qualifications provided by the context, and therefore will have no
context. Meanwhile, it is clear that Jesus who came preaching
the Gospel of God, and crying Repent! (Mk. i. 15, Mt. iv. 17)
— to preach which Gospel He declares that He "was sent,"
(Lk. iv. 43) — very naturally represents that His mission is
not to righteous but sinners; and equally naturally likens His
work to that of a physician who deals not with well people but
with the sick. He does not mean by this to say that sin is merely
a sickness and that sinners must therefore be dealt with in the
unmixed tenderness of a healer of diseases; but that the terms
of His mission like those of a physician cast His lot with the
derelicts of the world. He has come to call sinners, and where
would men expect to find Him except with sinners?

When Jesus declares, "I came not to call righteous but
sinners," then, He uses the words "righteous" and "sinners"
in all seriousness, in their literal senses. By "righteous," He
does not mean the Pharisees; nor by "sinners" the publicans.

Nevertheless it is clear that He so far takes His start from the
Pharisaic point of view that He accepts its estimate of His
table-companions as sinners. He does not deny that those with
whom He ate were sinners.[80] His defence is not that they were
miscalled sinners, but that His place was with sinners, whom
He came to call.[81] Similarly His employment of the term "righteous" may not be free from a slight infusion of ironic reference
to the Pharisees, who, by their question, contrasted themselves
with the others and thus certainly ranked themselves with
those "which trusted in themselves that they were righteous
and set the rest at nought" (Lk. xviii. 9). His saying would at
least raise in their own minds the question where they came
in; and thus would act as a probe to enable them to "come to
themselves" and to form a juster estimate of themselves. That
such a probing of their consciences was within the intention
of Jesus, is made clear by a clause in His declaration, preserved
only by Matthew, interposed between the "parable" of the
physician and the plain statement of the nature of His mission:
"But go and learn what this meaneth, I desire mercy and not
sacrifice" (Mt. ix. 13).[82] He is as far as possible from implying,
therefore, that the Pharisees were well and had no need of His
curative ministrations. He rather subtly suggests to them (and
perhaps with Hos. vi. 6 in mind we would better not say so
subtly either) that they deceived themselves if they fancied
that to be the case. In thus intimating that the Pharisees were
themselves sinners, He intimates that there were none righteous.
A. Jülicher, it is true, vigorously asserts the contrary,[83] and in-

[80] Cf. H. A. W. Meyer on Mt. ix. 10: "Observe that Jesus Himself by no
means denies the πονηρὸν εἶναι in regard to those associated with Him at table,
ver. 12 f. They were truly diseased ones," sinners.

[81] Cf. Johannes Weiss (p. 167): "The answer which He gives to the criticism
of the Scribes neither provides a complete analysis of His motives nor wholly
reveals what He holds as to the publicans and sinners. He justifies His conduct
only by an immediately obvious reason against which there is nothing to adduce:
'The strong have no need of a physician, but the sick' . . . He goes to those
who need help and where He can help."

[82] Cf. H. A. W. Meyer in loc.: "Through that quotation from the Scriptures
. . . it is intended to make the Pharisees understand how much they too were
sinners."

[83] "Die Gleichnisreden Jesu," ii, pp. 175, 322.

sists that the "righteous" must be as actually existing a class of men as "sinners": and A. Loisy follows him in this. Jesus, looking out upon mankind, saw that some were righteous and some sinners. With the righteous, He had nothing to do; they needed no saving. It was to the sinners only that He had a mission; and His mission to them was, as Luke is perfectly right in adding, to call them to repentance. There were many who needed no repentance (Lk. xv. 2), but no sinner can be saved without repentance, and Luke's motive in adding "to repentance" is to make this clear and thus to guard against Jesus' call of sinners being taken in too broad, not to say too loose, a sense. This, however, is quite inconsistent with the whole drift of the narrative. Jesus is not separating mankind into two classes and declaring that His mission is confined to one of these classes. He is contemplating men from two points of view and declaring that His mission presupposes the one point of view rather than the other. Reprobation of Him had been expressed, because He associated with publicans and sinners. He does not pursue the question of the justice of the concrete contrast — though, as we have seen, not failing to drop hints even of it. He responds simply, "That is natural, I came on a mission not to righteous men but to sinners." The question whether any righteous men actually existed is not raised.[84] The point is that His mission is to sinners, and that it ought to occasion no surprise, therefore, that He is found with sinners.[85]

What Jesus does in this saying, therefore, is to present Himself as the Saviour of sinners.[86] He came to call sinners; He is

[84] So far rightly, H. H. Wendt, "The Teaching of Jesus," E. T., vol. ii, p. 51: "In these words He left quite untouched the question whether any were truly righteous in His sense."

[85] Cf. J. A. Alexander: "The distinction which He draws is not between two classes of men, but between two characters or conditions of the whole race."

[86] J. Weiss will not allow that Jesus spoke more than the "parable" of the physician; but he recognizes that the Evangelist, by the main saying he puts into Jesus' mouth reflects the belief of the community that Jesus is the Saviour of sinners: "All those called into the community, felt themselves saved sinners, and in the retrospect of the whole work of Jesus, He appears as the savior of sinners. Cf. Lk. xix. 10."

the physician who brings healing to sick souls. He does not tell us how He saves sinners. He speaks only of "calling them," of calling them "to repentance." From this we may learn that an awakened sense of wrong-doing, and a "change of heart," issuing in a changed life, enter into the effects of their "calling," — that, in a word, it issues in a transformed mind and life. But nothing is told us of the forces brought to bear on sinners to bring about these results. Meanwhile Jesus declares explicitly that His mission in the world was to "call sinners." That was no doubt implicit in all the definitions of this mission which have heretofore come before us. It is here openly proclaimed. Harnack says this saying is not Messianic, "because," he explains, "it has nothing to do with the Judgment or the Kingdom." When He who came to announce the Kingdom of God, calling on men to repent, called sinners to repentance, — had that nothing to do with the Kingdom? A "call to repentance" — has that not the Judgment in view? Who in any case is the Saviour of Sinners if not the Messiah? And who but the Messiah could proclaim with majestic brevity, "I came not to call righteous but sinners"?

7

Lk. xix. 10: — For the Son of Man came to seek and to save that which was lost.

This saying is very much a repetition of the immediately preceding one in more searching language. Harnack himself points out the closeness of their relation. "This saying," says he, "in the best way completes that one, with which it is intimately connected; the 'sinners' are the 'lost,' but in being 'called' they are 'saved.'" The expressive language of the present saying is derived from the great Messianic prophecy of Ezek. xxxiv. 11 ff., which Jesus has taken up and applies to Himself and His mission. Harnack is thoroughly justified, therefore, in saying: "What is most important about this saying, along with its contents, is that Jesus claims for Himself the work which God proclaimed through the prophets as His own future work." The whole figurative background of the saying, and its peculiarities of language as well, are taken from Ezekiel. "Thus saith the Lord Jehovah," we read there: "Behold I myself, even I, will search for my sheep, and will seek them out. As a shepherd seeketh out his flock in the day that he is among his sheep that are scattered abroad, so will I seek out my sheep and I will deliver them . . . I will seek that which was lost, and will bring again that which was driven away, and will bind up all that which was broken, and will strengthen that which was sick. . . ." Jesus obviously means to say that He came like this shepherd, with the particular task laid upon Him to seek and to save what was lost. Because the statement is introduced as the reason, we might almost say the justification, of His saving that "sinful man," Zacchaeus, the word "came" is put prominently forward,[87] with the effect of declaring with great emphasis that it was the very purpose of Jesus' "coming" "to seek and to save that which is lost." Here too Harnack's observations are just:

'Ηλθεν is given the first place here with emphasis. Thus it is made very clear that the salvation of what is lost (see Mt. x. 6, xv. 24; Lk. xv. 6, 9, 32) is the main purpose of Jesus' coming. What appears often in the parables and in separate sayings, is here collected into a general declaration, which elevates the saving activity of Jesus above all that is accidental. He Himself testifies that it is His proper work.

The term "lost" here is a neuter singular, used collectively.[88] It is simply taken over in this form from Ezek. xxxiv. 16, where Jehovah declares: "I will seek that which was lost."[89] In explaining His saving of Zacchaeus, Jesus assigns him to the class to seek and save which He declares to be His particular mission. Precisely what He meant by speaking of the objects of His saving actively as "lost" has been made the subject of some

---

[87] Cf. H. A. W. Meyer: "ἦλθε: emphatically placed first."

[88] Cf. the similar use of the collective neuter in Jno. vi. 37, xvii. 2, 24.

[89] Harnack therefore remarks that Wellhausen rightly supplies "sheep," translating: "For the Son of man came to seek and save das verlorene Schaf." Is the employment of the singular, "Schaf," here accurate? Wellhausen can scarcely intend it to apply to Zacchaeus as the example of a class.

discussion. Hermann Cremer, for example, wishes us to bear in mind that "lost sheep" may always be found again; that they exist, so to speak for the purpose of being found. And A. B. Bruce, taking up this notion, even reduces the idea of "the lost" to that of "the neglected," and invites us to think of Jesus' mission as directed to "the neglected classes." [90] Such minimizing interpretations are not only wholly without support in the usage of the terms, and in the demands of the passages in which they occur. They are derogatory to the mission which Jesus declares that He came to execute. He speaks of His mission in tones of great impressiveness, as involving supremely great accomplishments. Obviously "the lost" which He declares that He came to seek and to save were not merely neglected people but veritably lost people, lost beyond retrieval save only as He not merely sought them but in some great sense saved them. The solemnity with which Jesus speaks of having come as the Saviour of "the lost" will not permit us to think lightly of their condition, which necessarily carries with it thinking lightly also of His mission and achievement.

The solemnity of this declaration is much enhanced by Jesus' designation of Himself in it by the great title of "the Son of Man." He does not say here simply, as in the sayings we have heretofore had before us, "I came," or "I was sent," but, speaking of Himself in the third person, "The Son of Man came." By thus designating Himself He does far more than explicitly declare Himself the Messiah and His mission the Messianic mission, thus justifying His adoption of Ezekiel's language to describe it. He declares Himself the transcendent Messiah, and in so doing declares His mission, to put it shortly, a divine work, not merely in the sense that it was prosecuted under the divine appointment, but in the further sense that it

---

[90] "The Kingdom of God," p. 136. Bruce allows that the middle voice of the verb ἀπόλλυμι sometimes imports "irretrievable perdition," but he will allow no such connotation to "the neuter participle τὸ ἀπολωλός ." The neuter participle τὸ ἀπολωλός is found in the absolute sense of the "the lost," however, only in Lk. xix. 10. The participle occurs, however, as a qualifier of substantives in Lk. xv. 4, 6, 24, 32, Mt. x. 6, xv. 24. These are all the passages which Bruce has to go on: they obviously do not sustain his contention.

was executed by a divine agent. Great pregnancy is at once imparted to the simple verb "came" by giving it the transcendent Son of Man for its subject. To say "I came" may mean nothing more than a claim to divine appointment. But to say, "the Son of Man came" transports the mind back into the pretemporal, heavenly existence of the Son of Man and conveys the idea of His voluntary descent to earth. We recall here the language of Mk. i. 38, and see that intimation that Jesus thought of His work on earth as a mission of a visitant from a higher sphere, raised into the position of an explicit assertion. We perceive that Jesus is employing a high solemnity of utterance which necessarily imparts to every word of His declaration its deepest significance. The terms "lost," "saved" must be read in their most pregnant sense. Jesus represents those whom He came to seek and save as "lost"; but He declares that the Son of Man who came from heaven for the purpose has power to "save" them. The stress lies on the greatness of the agent, which carries with it the greatness of the achievement, and that in turn carries with it the hopelessness, apart from this achievement by this agent, of the condition of the "lost." It is with the fullest meaning that Jesus represents Himself here as the Saviour of the lost.

If Jesus represents Himself here as the Saviour of the lost, however, does He not represent Himself as the Saviour of the lost of Israel only? We have heard Him in a previous saying, with the same passage from Ezekiel lying in the background, declaring, "I was not sent but to the lost sheep of the house of Israel" (Mt. xv. 24). Is not salvation here similarly declared to have been brought by Him to Zacchaeus' house only because Zacchaeus too was a son of Abraham? [91] Jesus is speaking, primarily, of course, of His own personal ministry, which was strictly confined to Israel.[92] It was in the prosecution of His

[91] Cf. the language of Lk. xiii. 16. We cannot take the words in a spiritual sense, even with the modification suggested by Holtzmann and Plummer who combine the two senses.

[92] Cf. Zahn p. 623, note 73: "According to the whole evangelical tradition, Jesus repeatedly indeed visited localities with a preponderant heathen population, and even worked some healings there (cf. Lk. viii. 27–39, Mt. xv. 26–28, xv.

personal ministry to Israel that He came to Zacchaeus' house, bringing salvation. When He justifies doing this by appealing to the terms of His mission as the Saviour of the lost, He naturally has primary reference to the salvation of Zacchaeus, that Son of Abraham, and may be said by the "lost" to mean, in the first instance, such as he. Must we understand Him as having the lost specifically of Israel therefore exclusively in view? The evangelist who has recorded these words for us certainly did not so understand them. They are in themselves quite general. The Gentiles too are sinners, and are comprehended too under the word "lost." However they may have lain outside the scope of Jesus' personal ministry, they did not lie beyond the horizon of His saving purpose.[93] If we cannot quite say that He tells us here that His mission of salvation extends to them also, we need not contend that He tells us that it does not. The declaration has, in point of fact, nothing to say of the extension of His mission. It absorbs itself in the definition of its intensive nature. It is a mission of salvation. It is a mission to the "lost." Jesus in it declares that the explicit purpose of His coming was to save the lost. This is the great message which this saying brings us.

8

| Mk. x. 45: For verily the Son of Man came not to be ministered unto, but to minister, and to give His life a ransom for many. | Mt. xx. 28: Even as the Son of Man came not to be ministered unto, but to minister, and to give His life a ransom for many. |

Although Harnack too includes this saying among Jesus' testimonies to the purpose of His "coming," he nevertheless, expresses grave doubt of its authenticity; and this doubt passes,

29–39, and see "Commentary on Matthew³," pp. 531 ff.), but He never preached to the heathen or even once entered a heathen's house (cf. Lk. vii. 2–10, Jno. vii. 35, xix. 20–32, and see "Commentary on John³," pp. 391 f. 511, 518)."

[93] Cf. in Luke, iii. 5, 6; iv. 24 ff.; xiii. 18–21, 29; xiv. 22 f.; xx. 16; xxiv. 47. See above in Mt. xv. 24. On the universalism of Luke, cf. Hastings' "Dictionary of the Bible," vol. iii, pp. 172 f. On the universalism of Jesus, cf. F. Spitta, "Jesus und die Heidenmission," 1909, and the article "Missions" in Hastings' "Dictionary of Christ and the Gospels."

with respect to the latter member of it, into decisive rejection.
The grounds on which he bases this doubt and rejection are
three.[94] The saying is not recorded in Lk. xxii. 24–34, a passage
which Harnack chooses to consider another and older form of
the tradition reproduced in Mt. xx. 20–28 = Mk. x. 35–45.
The transition from "ministering" to "giving the life as a
ransom," Harnack represents as, although not unendurable,
yet unexpected and hard: "ministry" is the act of a servant
and no servant is in a position to ransom others. Nowhere else,
except in the words spoken at the Last Supper, is there preserved in the oldest tradition an announcement by Jesus that
He was to give His life instead of others.[95] As these reasons bear
chiefly upon the latter portion of the saying, Harnack contents
himself with rejecting it, and allows to Jesus the former half,
which commends itself to him, moreover, by its paradoxical
form and the pithiness of its contents. The statement of these
grounds of doubt is their sufficient refutation. There is no reason
to suppose that the incident recorded in Lk. xxii. 24–36 is the
same as that recorded in Mt. xx. 20–28 = Mk. x. 35–45. The
differences are decisive.[96] Jesus does not represent the giving
of one's life as a ransom for others as a servant's function, or

[94] In these criticisms Harnack pretty closely follows Wellhausen, "Das
Evangelium Marci," 1903, p. 91: "The ἀπολύτρωσις through the death of
Jesus intrudes into the Gospel only here: immediately before, He did not die *for*
others and in their stead, but He died *before* them that they might die afterwards.
The words καὶ δοῦναι κτλ. are lacking in Lk. xxii. 27. They do not in fact fit in
with διακονῆσαι, for that means 'wait at table' as the third and fourth evangelists
rightly understand. The passage from serving to giving life as a ransom is a μετά-
βασις εἰς ἀλλὸ γένος. It is explained by the service at the Lord's Supper, where
Jesus administers His flesh and blood with bread and wine." Wellhausen is an
adept at this sort of carping, surface verbal criticism.

[95] Johannes Weiss, "Die Schriften," etc.[1],i. p. 161, tells us that the grounds
on which recent criticism denies the saying to Jesus are these three — which may
be compared with Harnack's: "First, the entire life-activity of the Lord is here
reviewed ('He came'); secondly, the term 'ransom' and the whole series of conceptions opened up by it, do not occur elsewhere in Jesus' preaching; and thirdly,
the parallel declaration from the Discourse-Source, Lk. xxii. 27, contains nothing
of the redemptive death." That is to say, in brief, Jesus cannot have said what He
is here reported to have said, because He is not reported to have said it often.

[96] Cf. G. Hollmann, "Die Bedeutung des Todes Jesu" and Runze as there
quoted.

even ascribe the act to a servant. He represents the giving of one's life as a ransom for others as a supreme act of service for one, not Himself a servant, to render when He gave Himself to service to the uttermost. Harnack himself allows that in one other saying, at least, Jesus does represent His death as offered for others, and, indeed, in a subsequent passage, himself extracts all the probative force from this objection, by pointing out that no presumption can lie against Jesus' expressing Himself concerning His death as He is here reported as doing (p. 26):

Whether Jesus Himself expressly included in the service which He performed, the giving of His life as a ransom for many, we must leave an open question; but the matter is not of so much importance as is commonly supposed. If His eye was always fixed upon His death (and the zealous effort to throw this into doubt is, considering the situation in which He ordinarily stood, simply whimsical) and knew Himself as the good shepherd, John has only said the most natural thing in the world when he puts on Jesus' lips the declaration that the good shepherd gives his life for the sheep. Whether Jesus really said it, whether He, in another turn of phrase, represented His life as a thing of value for the ransoming of others, is not to be certainly determined; but if He designated His life in general as "service" then His death is properly included in it, for the highest service is — so it has been and so it will remain — the giving of the life.[97]

The case being so; it is surely unreasonable to deny to Jesus words credibly reported from His lips in which He declares that His ministry culminated in the giving of His life for others,

[97] Somewhat similarly, Johannes Weiss, who denies Mk. x. 45, Mk. xx. 28, to Jesus but allows to Him Lk. xxii. 27, writes ("Die Schriften[1]," vol. i, pp. 161–162): "It is, however, of course not inconceivable that Jesus should have included also His approaching death in this work of service and love. It is even probable that He was of the conviction that His death would somehow accrue to the advantage of the men for whom He had labored in word and deed. But whether He thought directly of a sacrificial death, or of a vicarious punishment, such as is described by Isaiah in the Fifty-third chapter, — that must remain doubtful, cf. xiv. 24." Why — when He certainly knew Isaiah liii, certainly applied it to Himself, and is credibly reported to have spoken of His death as a sacrificial offering (Mk. xiv. 24) and as a vicarious punishment (Mk. x. 45)? The discussion by H. J. Holtzmann, "Synopt[3].," p. 160 is notable from the same point of view.

merely because He is not reported as having frequently made
this great declaration.[98]

There is the less reason for doubting that we have before
us here an authentic saying of Jesus', because it was eminently
natural and to be expected that Jesus, at this stage of His
ministry, when describing the nature of His mission, should
not pause until He had intimated the place of His death in it.
According to the representation of all the evangelists, it was
characteristic of this period of His ministry that He spoke
much and very insistently of the death which He should accomplish at Jerusalem, and of the indispensableness of this
death for the fulfilment of His task. "From that time," says
Matthew, marking the beginning of a period, "began Jesus to
show unto His disciples, how that He must go unto Jerusalem
. . . and be killed." [99] His insistence upon this teaching during
this period is marked by all the evangelists again and again,[100]
and it was immediately after the third of these insistences
which have been recorded for us that the incident is introduced
by Matthew and Mark which occasioned the declaration before us. Jesus' preoccupation with His death is strikingly betrayed by His allusion to it even in His response to the ambitious request of James and John, and that in such a manner as
to show that it held, in His view, an indispensable place in
His work.[101] It would have been unnatural, if when, in the
sequel to this incident, He came to reveal to His disciples the
innermost nature of His mission as one of self-sacrificing devotion, He had made no allusion whatever to the death in which
it culminated, and the indispensableness of which to its accomplishment He was at the time earnestly engaged in impressing
upon them.

[98] It is purely arbitrary for Harnack to add in a note: "If the declaration,"
as to giving His life as a ransom, "comes from Jesus, we have at least no guaranty
that it was spoken in connection with the διακονεῖν and was introduced by
ἦλθον." There is no justification in any legitimate method of criticism for thus
rending unitary sayings into fragments and dealing with each clause as a separate
entity.   [99] Mt. xvi. 21; cf. Mk. viii. 31; Lk. ix. 22.
[100] Mt. xvii. 22 f., Mk. ix. 30 f., Lk. ix. 43 ff.: Mt. xx. 17 ff., Mk. x. 32 ff.,
Lk. xviii., 31 ff.   [101] Mt. xx. 22, Mk. x. 38.

The naturalness, not to say inevitableness, of an allusion to His death in this saying has not prevented some expositors, it is true, from attempting violently to explain away the open allusion which is made to it.[102] Thus, for example, Ernest D. Burton [103] wishes us to believe that "to give His life" means not "to die" but "to live," — "to devote His life-energies" — and that Jesus here without direct reference to His death is only exhorting His followers to devote their lives without reserve to the service of their fellows. In support of this desperate contention, he urges that he has not been able to find elsewhere the exact phrase, "to give life," used as a synonym of "to die." [104] It does not seem very difficult to find; [105] but in any event Burton might have remembered that this phrase is not so much used here as the synonym of "to die," as the wider phrase "to give His life a ransom for" is used as a synonym for "to die instead of." [106] In other words, the employment of the term "to give" is determined here by the idea of a ransom — which is a thing given, whether it be money or

[102] Not Harnack, whose phrase: "The announcement that Jesus gave His life as a λύτρον for others, that is to say, was to die for all" . . . indicates his conception of the meaning of the words.

[103] "Biblical Ideas of Atonement," 1909, pp. 114 ff.

[104] He finds the phrase "give your lives" in the exhortations of Mattathias to his sons, I Macc. ii. 50 f.; but he supposes it to mean there, "to devote your life energies," an interpretation which did not suggest itself to Josephus, "Antt." xii. 6. 3, Niese iii. pp. 120f. (cf. Sirach xxix. 15, and, with παραδίδωμι, Acts xv. 26, Hermas, "Sim.," ix. 28.2; Just. "Apol." i, 50 from Isa. 53, 12).

[105] See preceding note, and also cf. Ex. xxi. 23: δώσει ψυχὴν ἀντὶ ψυχῆς. A. Seeberg, "Der Tod Christi," etc., 1895, p. 350, says: "The words δοῦναι τὴν ψυχήν refer in any case to death, for this formula which corresponds to the Hebrew נֶפֶשׁ נָתַן occurs frequently in the sense of the surrender of the life in death." In a note he cites Ex. xxi. 23, I Macc. ii. 55, Sr. xxix. 15, with other less close parallels. There can be no doubt that "to give His life" means to Clement of Alexandria, for instance, "Paed." I, ix, somewhat past the middle, simply to die.

[106] Cf. Th. Zahn, "Das Ev. d. Matthaeus¹," 1903, p. 604, ed. 3, 1910, p. 611: "The greatest service, however, will be done by Him only in the gift of His life. No doubt this is not said clearly by δοῦναι τὴν ψυχὴν αὐτοῦ by itself; δοῦναι rather finds its necessary supplement only in the object-predicate λύτρον ἀντὶ πολλῶν. But just this action described so figuratively, can take place only in a voluntary endurance of death; for no one can give a purchase-price for another without in doing so depriving himself of it."

blood — and not by the idea of dying. [107] Its employment
carries with it, indeed, the implication that Jesus' death was
a voluntary act — He gave it; but the thought is not completed
until the purpose for which He gave it is declared — He gave
it as a ransom.

In this context, the saying occurs as an enforcement of
Jesus' exhortation to His disciples to seek their greatness in
service. He adduces His own example. "For even the Son of
Man," He says, "came not to be ministered unto but to minister, and to give His life a ransom for many." To enhance His
example He designates Himself by the transcendent title, "The
Son of Man." [108] If any, the Son of Man might expect "to be
ministered unto" in His sojourn on earth. In His sojourn on
earth — for, when we say "Son of Man" we intimate that His
earthly life is a sojourn. The eye fixes itself at once on a heavenly origin and a heavenly issue; and we necessarily think of
pomp and glory. If even the Son of Man "came" not to be
ministered unto but to minister, what shall we say of the proper
life-ideal for others? Jesus is not speaking of the manner of His
daily life on earth when He speaks here of "coming" to serve.
The manner of His daily life on earth was not that of a servant.
He lived among His followers as their Master and Lord, claiming their obedience and receiving their reverence. [109] He did
not scruple to accept from others or to apply to Himself titles
of the highest, even of superhuman, dignity. In this very saying
He speaks of Himself by a title which assigns to Him a transcendent being. It was not the manner of His earthly life but

---

[107] Cf. H. A. W. Meyer, on Mt. xx. 28 (E. T., ii, p. 51): "δοῦναι is made
choice of, because the ψυχή (*the soul*, as the principle of the life of the body) is
conceived of as a λύτρον (a ransom)." Note Josephus, "Antt." xiv. 7.1: λύτρον ἀντὶ
πάντων ἔδοκεν, and cf. LXX Ex. xxi. 30, xxx. 12.

[108] Cf. Harnack (p. 10): "That Jesus says here, not 'I' but 'the Son of
Man' is explained from the contents of the saying, which acquires force from
Jesus' laying claim at the same time to the (future) Messianic dignity." This is
saying too little and its says it with a wrong implication, but it allows the main
matter. Jesus' use of "the Son of Man" here plays the same part that Paul's
phrase "being in the form of God" plays in Phil. ii. 6.

[109] Cf. the striking presentation of the facts here by Zahn, "Matthew¹,"
p. 603.

the mere fact of this earthly life for Him, which He speaks of as a servile mission. That He was on earth at all; that He, the heavenly one, demeaned Himself to a life in the world; this was what required explanation. And the explanation was, service.

This was not news to His followers. He is not informing them of something hitherto unimagined by them. He is reminding them of a great fact concerning Himself which, He intimates, it were well for them to bear in mind. He "came," not to exercise the lordship which belongs naturally to a great one like Himself, but to perform a service. What the service which He came to perform was, and how He performs it He tells us by mentioning a single item, but that single item one lying so much at the center that it is in effect the whole story. "To minister *and* to give His life a ransom" are not presented as two separate things. They are one thing presented in general and in particular. The "and" is not merely copulative; it is intensive,[110] and may almost be read epexegetically: "The Son of Man came to minister, *namely* to give His life a ransom.[111] It is in "to give His life a ransom" that the declaration culminates; on it that it rests; through it that it conveys its real meaning. For this is the wonderful thing of which Jesus reminds His followers, to compose their ambitious rivalries — that He, the Son of Man, came unto the world to die. Dying was the service by way of eminence which He came to perform. Dying in the stead of others who themselves deserved to die [112] — that they need not die. We do not catch the drift of this great saying until we perceive that all its emphasis gathers itself up upon the declaration that Jesus came into the world just to die as a ransom.

The mode in which the service which Jesus came to render

[110] Cf. H. A. W. Meyer: "intensive: adding on the *highest act*, the culminating point in the διακονῆσαι."

[111] Cf. Seeberg, p. 348: "Jesus became man, in order as Messiah, to give His life in death, for of course the words δοῦναι τὴν ψυχήν give the content of διακονῆσαι."

[112] Whoever the "many" are, they certainly include the "sinners" whom He "came to call" (Mk. ii. 17, Mt. ix. 13, Lk. v. 32) and "the lost" whom "He came to seek and save" (Lk. xix. 10). For these "sinners" and "lost" He came to give His life a ransom. This is the way He saves them.

to others is performed is described here, then, in the phrase, "to give His life a ransom for many." It would be difficult to make the language more precise. Jesus declares that He came to die; to die voluntarily; to die voluntarily in order that His death may serve a particular purpose. This particular purpose He describes as a "ransom"; and the idea of a "ransom" is explicated by adding that, in thus giving His life as a ransom, His given life, His death, is set over against others in a relation of equivalence, takes their place and serves their need and so releases them.[113]

It is always possible to assign to each word in turn in a statement like this the least definite or the most attenuated meaning which is ever attached to it in its varied literary applications, and thus to reduce the statement as a whole literally to insignificance. Thus Jesus' strong and precise assertion that He came into the world in order to give His life as a ransom-price for the deliverance of many has been transmuted into the expression of a dawning recognition by Him that His death had became inevitable and of a more or less strong hope, or expectation, that it might not be quite a fatal blow to His wish to be of use, but might in some way or to some extent prove of advantage to His followers.[114] According to H. H.

[113] Cf. H. A. W. Meyer on Mt. xx. 28: "ἀντί denotes *substitution*. That which is given as a *ransom* takes the *place* (is given *instead*) of those who are to be set free in consideration thereof." The "meaning is strictly and specifically defined by λύτρον (כֹּפֶר) according to which ἀντί can only be understood in the sense of *substitution*, the act of which the ransom is presented as an equivalent to secure the deliverance of those on whose behalf it is paid." In the κοινή, ἀντί seems to be going out of use. Instead of it ὑπέρ is employed (L. Rademacher, "N. T. Grammatik," 1911, pp. 115–116). It must therefore be held to be fully intended when used.

[114] Cf. C. G. Montefiore, vol. i, p. 260: "Moreover Jesus may just conceivably have realized that His death would be to the advantage of many; that many would enter the Kingdom as the effect of His death. Menzies takes this view. He thinks 'Jesus became reconciled to the prospect of death when He saw that He was to die for the benefit of others.' This is a possible view, though I think it an unlikely one. It is rebutted by Pfleiderer, "Urchristentum," i, p. 372. Holtzmann thinks that λύτρον here is a translation of an Aramaic word which may merely mean 'deliverance.' Jesus 'delivered' people by causing them to repent . . ." "Holtzmann" at the end of this extract is a misprint for "Hollmann": see G. Hollmann, "Die Bedeutung des Todes Jesu," 1901, pp. 124 f.: "The following is

Wendt,[115] for example, Jesus makes no reference whatever here to the "ransoming" of individual souls from the guilt and punishment of sin: "it is more correct to say that Jesus meant the bringing about of the salvation of the Messianic end-time in a wholly general sense."

Because He now, as death threatened Him for His works' sake, was determined rather to give His life up than be untrue to the vocation imposed on Him by God (Jno. x. 11–18); and because in strong trust in God, He was assured that His death would work out not for the destruction but for the furthering of His work; He could designate His yielding up of His life a "ransom," that is a means for bringing about the Messianic "liberation" for all those who would permit themselves to be led by Him to the Messianic salvation.

According to Friedrich Niebergall,[116] on the other hand, there is no objective reference in the allusion to a ransom: "the figure is doubtless here only an expression for the religious impression that by Christ's death we are liberated from evil Powers." In a similar vein Johannes Weiss says: [117]

When Mark wrote this declaration it was immediately intelligible to all his readers. For their religious life was governed by the fundamental feeling that they were liberated from the dominion of the devil and the demons (cf. I Cor. xii. 2, Gal. iv. 8) and therewith delivered from the terrible destruction which impended over the kingdom of sin at the end of the ages.

Questions, such as have been raised by the dogmaticians, as to the meaning of the saying "will no longer occupy us," says Weiss, "if we keep the main idea in mind, that the immediate

then to be summarily derived from our passage: (1) that Jesus' death stands on the same plane with Jesus' life-work; (2) (negatively) that it prevents many souls from falling into destruction; (3) (positively) that it brings many hitherto unbelieving to salvation. There can be added as most probable that (4) their salvation lies in the operation of μετανοια."

[115] "System der Christl. Lehre," pp. 308 ff., 323.

[116] Lietzmann's "Handbuch zum N. T.," v, 1909, pp. 102 f.

[117] "Die Schriften," etc[1]. v. i, p. 161. He speaks of the statement as Mark's, not Jesus'.

liberation from the dominion of demonic tyrants which was felt directly by the ancient Christians was a mark of the ministering love of the Christ who gave His life for them."

Comments like these merely lead away from the simple, penetrating declaration of Jesus, the meaning of which is perfectly clear in itself,[118] and is further fixed by the testimony of His followers. For Jesus' declaration did not fall fruitless to the ground: it finds an echo in the teaching of His followers, and in this echo we can hear His own tones sounding.[119] It marks the very extremity of perverseness, when an attempt is made to reverse the relation of this key-declaration and its echoes in the apostolical writings, explaining it as rather an echo of them. How this is managed may be read briefly in, say, H. J. Holtzmann's comment on Mk. x. 45.

The thought of the Discourse-Source, Lk. xxii. 27, is so expressed here in Paulinizing form (cf. Rom. xv. 3) that Jesus also is represented as having found His vocation only in service (Phil. ii. 7, I Cor. ix. 19), and as having yielded up His life in that service (Phil. ii. 8). . . . While, however, the disciple can only "lose" his life in the service of his Lord (Mk. viii. 35 = Mt. x. 39, xvi. 25 = Lk. ix. 24, xvii. 33), it is the part of the Lord to give it voluntarily, according to Gal. i. 4, ii. 20. Especially, however, the "give His life a ransom for many" corresponds to the "who gave Himself a ransom for all" of I Tim. ii. 6 and the "He gave Himself for us that He might ransom us" of Titus ii. 14, that is, the idea of Jesus is glossed by a reminiscence of the Pauline doctrine of redemption.

Perverse as this is, it at least fixes the sense of Jesus' declaration. The attempt to represent it as a reminiscence of the Pauline doctrine of redemption shows at any rate that it is identical with the Pauline doctrine of redemption.

It lies in the nature of the case that a brief saying, consisting of only two short clauses, made, moreover, not for itself but in

---

[118] We content ourselves with referring here to the excellent remarks of James Denney, "The Death of Christ[3]," 1903, pp. 36 ff., cap. pp. 42 ff.

[119] Cf. Zahn, p. 605, note 90: "The conception of the redemption (*redemptio*) wrought by Jesus and especially by His death, would not recur everywhere in the New Testament, if it did not go back to Jesus Himself." Zahn then cites the details.

order to enforce an exhortation to conduct becoming in followers of Jesus, should not tell us all we should like to know of the great matter which it thus allusively brings before us. Many questions arise for guidance on which we must look elsewhere. Fortunately answers to some of them are supplied by the sayings which have already engaged our attention. We can scarcely refuse to correlate Jesus' testimony in them, for example, that He came "to call sinners," that He came "to save the lost" with His testimony here that He came to do many a service, — above all, this service, by His death to ransom them. Undoubtedly the giving of His life as a ransom is the manner in which He saves the lost. And undoubtedly by the "lost" are meant just "sinners," and by "sinners" in turn are meant those who are not "righteous," that is to say the guilt-laden.[120] What we have here, then, is a declaration by Jesus that He came to save lost sinners by giving His life a ransom for them. The effect, called in a former saying "salvation," is clearly in the first instance relief from the penalties due to their sin: He purchases lost sinners out of the obligations which they have incurred by their sin, by giving His life a ransom for them. That is as far perhaps as our particular saying will carry us. Others of the sayings which have come before us, however, carry us further. They tell us that Jesus secures for lost sinners also perfected righteousness of life — and perhaps something like that is after all suggested in this saying also, for it too has to do with conduct. His disciples are exhorted to follow Jesus' example, and it is implied that His example is a perfect one. The ransom-paying certainly lies at the bottom of all and of that alone is there explicit mention. But there is a call to perfection of life too: and not a call to it merely, but a provision for it. In a word there is a complete "salvation" hinted at here: relief from sin both in its curse and its power. Say that it is in this its completeness only hinted at. That is to say that it *is* hinted at.

---

[120] Cf. Harnack (p. 24): "The 'lost' and the 'sinners' are, however, still more closely characterized by the contrast 'not the righteous,' — they are really the dying and guilt-laden, who must perish without Him."

III

We shall only in the briefest possible manner sum up the results of this survey of the eight sayings in which, according to the report of the Synoptics, Jesus declared the purpose of His mission. In doing so we may take our start from the remarks with which Harnack opens the summary of the results of his survey of practically the same series of sayings. "The eight sayings from the Synoptics which we have collected and studied," says he, "contain very few words, but how much is said in them! On investigation they compose a unity which is equally important for the characterization of Jesus, and for the compass and range of His work." We shall wish to say a word each on both of these matters.

First of all, we note, then, that these sayings are not without their teaching as to Jesus' person. The simple phrases, "I came," "I was sent," naturally, do not of themselves testify to more than Jesus' consciousness of a divine mission. It is quite clear, however, that this divine mission of which He thus expresses consciousness, stands in His mind as that of the Messiah. He speaks in all these sayings out of the Messianic consciousness and assumes in them all Messianic functions. Even that, however, does not exhaust their implications.[121] There is a certain pregnancy of speech in them, a certain majesty of tone, a certain presupposition of voluntariness in the action expressed by the "I came," — of active acquiescence lying behind the "I was sent" — which have constantly led expositors to feel in them a claim greater than that to the Messianic dignity itself. Harnack will not admit that even the specifically Messianic consciousness speaks through them, and yet is constrained to exclaim (p. 28):

Who, then is this "I" that here "came". . . Undoubtedly there lies in that "I came," no matter who is meant, something

---

[121] A. Seeberg, "Der Tod Christi," etc., 1895, p. 348, is quite right when he says: "All the passages in which a coming of Jesus into the world is spoken of (Mk. ii. 17, Mt. v. 17, ix. 13, Lk. v. 32, xii. 49, xix. 10) fix their eyes upon a nearer or more distant purpose of His Messianic vocation."

authoritative and final. There lies in it the consciousness of a divine mission, as indeed it is interchanged with the expression "I was sent." The finality, however, is given by the definitions of purpose. He who came to perfect the law, He who was sent to recover the lost sheep, that is, to fulfil the prediction of the coming of God Himself, He who came with fire and sword — He comes as the final and ultimate one.

To others, even this seems inadequate; and they are right. Justice may be done by it to the impression which the reader receives from these sayings of the majesty of the speaker; scarcely to the impression which they equally make on him of the speaker's sense of complete control over all the circumstances of His mission, including the mission itself. It is this strong impression which expresses itself in the constant tendency of expositors to see in the "I came," "I was sent" a testimony by Jesus not merely to His divine mission but to His heavenly origin. "In the coming of Jesus," expounds A. Seeberg, for example,[122] "it is not some kind of an appearance (*Auftreten*) of Jesus in the world that is spoken of, but His entrance (*Eintritt*) into the world, such as is unmistakably spoken of in Jno. xvi. 28, where the coming into the world corresponds to the going away to the Father."

Unquestionably in some of these sayings Jesus speaks out of a consciousness of preëxistence. That is not merely suggested by the appearance in one of them, instead of the simple "I came" of a more significant "I came out" (Mk. i. 38), which is scarcely completely satisfied by any other supplement than "from heaven" or "from the Father." It is clearly presupposed in two of them by the employment, instead of the personal pronoun, of the descriptive periphrasis, "the Son of Man," the particular Messianic designation which especially emphasizes preëxistence (Lk. xix. 10, Mk. x. 45 = Mt. xx. 28). The declaration of Mk. x. 45 = Mt. xx. 28 runs most strikingly on the same lines with Phil. ii. 5 ff., and bears similar testimony to the preëxistent glory of the great exemplar of humility, whom both passages hold up to view. The whole force of the example presented turns on the immense incongruity of the Son of Man

[122] As cited.

appearing in the rôle of a servant; this force would be much decreased, if not destroyed, if the Son of Man had never been anything but a servant, was in His own nature a servant, and was fitted only for a servant's rôle. That three out of eight of these sayings thus imply the preëxistence of Jesus, and take their coloring from this implication, perhaps sufficiently accounts for the tendency of commentators to read the whole of them from this point of sight. We know at least that He who says in them, "I came," "I was sent," was conscious of having come from heaven to perform the mission which He ascribes to Himself.

In this implication of a preëxistence in glory, distinct in some of these sayings, possibly to be assumed in them all, they range themselves by the side of the more numerous similar sayings of Jesus recorded in the Gospel of John.[123] "The not infrequent addition, 'into the world,'" remarks Harnack, in commenting on these, "shows a new horizon, alien to Jesus Himself." Not so. The difference in this as in other things, between the Synoptic and the Johannine record, is rather quantitative than qualitative. This Johannine feature too is found in the Synoptic record; but in fewer instances.

It is not, however, of the person of Jesus, but, as was to be expected — for do they not speak of His mission? — of His work, that we learn most from these sayings. According to their teaching Jesus' work may be fairly summed up in the one word, "salvation." He came to call "sinners"; He came to seek and save "the lost"; He came to give His life a "ransom" for many. Everything else which Jesus testifies that He came to do takes a place subordinate and subsidiary to "salvation." Even the "fulfilling" of the law. Harnack is wrong in attempting to coördinate the two functions of Saviour and Lawgiver in Jesus' testimony to His mission. "According to His self testimony, the purpose of His coming and thus His significance is given in this — that He is at once Saviour and Lawgiver.

---

[123] The Johannine passages are adverted to by Harnack twice, pp. 2 and 22. For a synoptical view of them see B. F. Westcott in the "additional note" on Jno. xx. 21.

. . . Redeemer and Lawgiver: all that constitutes the significance of His coming is exhausted in that collocation . . . Programmatic in the strict sense are only these two sayings: 'I came to save' and 'I came to fulfil the law.'" [124] Jesus does declare that He came to fulfil the law, and by this He means also "to fill it out," to complete and perfect it, so that it shall be a faultless transcript of the will of God, the Righteous One. But not this only, or even mainly. He means more fundamentally that He came to get the law observed, so that it shall be perfectly expressed in righteous lives. His mind is more on the transforming of law-breakers into law-keepers, than on the perfecting of the codex itself. That is to say, He is thinking of salvation; of salvation in its ultimate effects. And what could be more poignant than to declare side by side, "I came not to call righteous but sinners," "I came to make human lives the perfect reflection of the law of God"?

Those whom Jesus came to call, He describes as sinners and as lost, that is to say as lost sinners; as those who can lay claim to no righteousness of their own and who have no power to obtain any, that is to say as helpless dependents on Him the Saviour. To them He comes to preach the Gospel of the Kingdom; He calls them to repentance; He seeks them out and saves them; He gives His life a ransom for them; He writes the law of God upon their hearts. This is the process of His "salvation." Their own energies are enlisted: He preaches the Gospel of the Kingdom to them and calls them to repentance. Their hearts are changed: He writes the law of God upon their hearts and sets them spontaneously to fulfil it. But beneath all this, there lies something deeper still which attracts to itself especially His greatest word: "I came to save." He gives His life a ransom for them. And it is only as He thus ransoms them by the gift of Himself that they cease to be "lost"; and having thus ceased to lie under the curse, can cease also to lie under the power of sin.

Harnack pushes this greatest declaration, "I came to give my life a ransom for many" into the background. It makes

[124] Pp. 25–26.

little difference, he hints, whether Jesus ever said it or not.
Jesus certainly died. And if all His work in the world was comprehended — as He witnesses that it was — in the category
of ministry, then of course His death was included in this ministry. We may even say it was the culmination of His ministry,
since the gift of one's life is the highest ministry which he can
render. But the main matter is that Jesus declares that He
came into the world to minister — whether by living or dying.
"What it has meant in history that Jesus expressly said that
He did not come to be ministered unto but to 'minister' —
that cannot be expressed in words! All the advance in ethics,
in these nineteen centuries which have flowed by, has had its
most powerful lever in this." [125]

Imitatio Christi! It certainly is the most powerful lever to
move men to endeavor which has ever entered the world; it
has revolutionized all conceptions of values; it has transformed
the whole spirit of conduct and changed the entire aspect of
life. But it has one indispensable precondition. Only living
things can imitate anything. Dead things must be brought to
life. Lost things must be found. Sinners must be saved. Even
the heathen knew that he may see the good and yet pursue
the bad. The awakened soul cries out, O wretched man that I
am who shall deliver me out of this body of death? Jesus has
done for us something far greater than set us a good example,
and summon us to its imitation: something without which there
could have been no imitation of His example; no transformed
ethics; no transfigured lives. He has undoubtedly set before
our eyes in living example the perfect law of love. But He has
done more than that. He has written it on our hearts. He has
given us new ideals. And He has given us something even above
that. He has given us the power to realize these ideals. In one
word, He has brought to us newness of life. And He has obtained
for us this newness of life by His own blood.

It is this that Jesus declares when He says, "I came to give
my life a ransom for many." And therefore this is the greatest
declaration of all. In it He shows us not how He has become our

[125] P. 26.

supreme example merely, but how He has become our Saviour. He has set us a perfect example. He has given us a new ideal. But He has also given us His life. And in giving us His life, He has given us life. For "He gave His life a ransom instead of many."

IX

THE NEW TESTAMENT TERMINOLOGY
OF "REDEMPTION"

THE NEW TESTAMENT TERMINOLOGY
OF "REDEMPTION"[1]

The most direct, but not the exclusive,[2] vehicle in the Greek of the New Testament of the idea which we commonly express in our current speech by the term "redeem" and its derivatives, is provided by a group of words built up upon the Greek term λύτρον, "ransom."[3] The exact implications of this group of words as employed by the writers of the New Testament have been brought into dispute.[4] It seems desirable therefore to look afresh into their origin and usage sufficiently to become clear as to the matter, and the inquiry may perhaps be thought to possess enough intrinsic interest to justify going a little farther afield in it, and entering somewhat more into details, than would be necessary for the immediate purpose in hand.

[1] From *The Princeton Theological Review*, v. xv, 1917, pp. 201–249.

[2] Compare for example, the use of ἀγοράζω I Cor. vi. 20, vii. 23, II Pet. ii. 1, Rev. v. 9, xiv. 3, 4; ἐξαγοράζω Gal. iii. 13, iv. 5; περιποιέομαι Acts xx. 28.

[3] λύτρον Mt. xx. 28, Mk x. 45; ἀντίλυτρον I Tim. ii. 6; λυτροῦσθαι Lk. xxiv. 21, Tit. ii. 14, I Pet. i. 18; λύτρωσις Lk. i. 68, ii. 38, Heb. ix. 12; ἀπολύτρωσις Lk. xxi. 28, Rom. iii. 24, viii. 23, I Cor. i. 30, Eph. 1, 7, 14, iv. 30, Col. i. 14, Heb. ix. 15, xi. 35; [λυτρωτής] Acts vii. 35.

[4] Cf. what Johannes Weiss says in his comment on I Cor. i. 30b (Meyer series): "Whereas heretofore the notion of ἀπολύτρωσις has been carefully investigated with reference to its shade of meaning (whether it is to be taken simply generally as = 'Deliverance,' or — because of the λυτρ — as = 'Ransoming') and also with reference to the particular relations of the notion (Who was the former owner? What is the ransom price? Who pays it? Why is it of so great value?), the tendency of the day is to push all these questions aside as wrongly put: Paul uses here a common *terminus technicus*, as a piece of current coin, with regard to which he reckons on a ready understanding; it is approximately = σωτηρία; accordingly it is translated simply 'Deliverance,' and no questions are asked with respect to a more exact explanation. This is generally right. . . ." Weiss himself conceives the term to be used primarily of the eschatological salvation, but to have received (like others of the kind) a certain predating and not to have lost entirely the idea of ransoming, though laying the stress on the effects rather than the means.

I

To begin at the beginning, at any rate, the ultimate base to which this group of words goes back seems to be represented by the Sanscrit Lû, which bears the meaning of "to cut," or "to clip"; hence it is inferred that the earliest implication of the general Indo-European root LU was to set free by cutting a bond. The Greek primitive of this base, λύειν, has the general meaning of "to loose," which is applied and extended in a great variety of ways. When applied to men, its common meaning is "'to loose, release, set free,' especially from bonds or prison, and so, generally, from difficulty, or danger." It developed a particular usage with reference to prisoners,[5] which is of interest to us. In this usage, it means, in the active voice, "to release on receipt of ransom," "to hold to ransom"; and in the middle voice, "to secure release by payment of ransom," "to ransom" in the common sense of that word,[6] passing on to a broader

[5] See Liddell and Scott, *Sub voc.* I. 2. c.

[6] This distinctive usage of the active and middle may be excellently observed in the First and Twenty Fourth Books of the "Iliad." In the opening lines of Book I we are told that Chryses came to the ships of the Achæans to ransom (λυσόμενος, line 13) his daughter, bearing a boundless ransom (ἄποινα); and that accordingly he supplicated the Achæans to ransom (λῦσαι [λύσατε], line 20) her to him and accept the ransom (ἄποινα). Agamemnon, however, declared roundly that he would not ransom (λύσω, line 29) her, and this was brought home to him in the subsequent council by Chalcas who charged him with not having ransomed (ἀπέλυσε) her and accepted the ransom (ἄποινα), and required him now (lines 95 ff.) no longer to look for ransom but to give (δόμεναι) the maiden to her father unbought (ἀπριάτην) and unransomed (ἀνάποινον). Similarly, early in Book xxiv we read that Here despatched Thetis to Achilles (lines 115–116) to chide him for holding Hector's body and not ransoming (ἀπέλυσεν) it, and to see to it, that, respecting her, he now ransomed (λύση) it; and added that she will send Iris to Priam bidding him go and ransom (λύσασθαι) his son bearing gifts to Achilles. Accordingly Thetis goes and chides Achilles (line 135) for holding Hector's body and not ransoming (ἀπέλυσας) it, and bids him ransom (λῦσαι) it, accepting the ransom (ἄποινα) offered for the corpse: while Iris goes to Troy and urges Priam to go (line 144) to the ships and ransom (λύσασθαι) his son, carrying gifts to Achilles. Stephanus, "Thesaurus," *sub voc.* observes that the French word *Delivrer* has the same two senses; "for *Delivrer un prisonnier* is said both concerning him who redeems him and concerning him who releases him to a redeemer." The same is true of the English word, "to deliver" and also, indeed, of the English word "to ransom."

usage of simply "to redeem" (in which it is applied not merely to prisoners but to animals and landed property [7]) and even "to buy." [8] It also acquired the sense of paying debts, and, when used with reference to wrong-doings, a sense of "undoing" or "making up for," which is not far removed from that of making atonement for, them.[9]

Naturally, the usual derivatives and compounds are formed from λύειν. Among the former the abstract active substantive, λύσις, is especially interesting to us because among its various senses it reflects both of the usages of its primitive to which we have just called attention. It is used of a release, deliverance, effected by the payment of a ransom — a "ransoming." [10] And it is used of a cleansing from guilt by means of an expiation — an "atonement." [11] Little less interesting, however, are the nouns of agent, of which several are formed, bearing the general sense of "deliverer" — λύσιος (λύσειος), λυτήρ (λύτειρα), λύτωρ. Λύσιος was used in the Dionysiac myth as an epithet of Diony-sus,[12] and in the Orphics a great part was played by the θεοὶ λύσιοι.[13] In the Second Book of the "Republic," [14] Plato makes Adeimantos, performing the office of *advocatus diaboli*, urge in favor of being wicked and reaping its gains, that the penalties

---

[7] Liddell and Scott adduce ἵππον Xen. "An." 7. 8. 6; τὸ χωρίον Dem. 1215.20.

[8] Liddell and Scott adduce "to buy from a pimp," Ar. "Vesp." 1353.

[9] Cf. the usages classified by Liddell and Scott under IV, V = e.g. "to atone for, make up for, like Latin *luere, rependere*," as "to atone for sins," "to pay wages in full, to quit oneself of them," in the sense of "loosing" an obligation. According to the Greek conception wrong-doing was inevitably followed by punishment. "On the other hand, the punishment itself was sometimes regarded as an expiation of the guilt. So the death of Laius' murderer was to 'loose' *i.e.*, undo, the effect of the original deed (Sophocles, "Oed. Tyr." 100 f.); so the chorus pray that Orestes' deed, a just manslaughter, may 'loose' the blood of long past murders (Æsch. "Choeph." 803 f.; cf. Eurip. "Her. Fur." 40)" — Arthur Fairbanks, Hastings' *ERE*, v, p. 653a.

[10] E. g., Homer, "Il." xxiv. 655: "And there might be delay in the ransoming of the corpse (ἀνάβλησις λύσιος νεκροῖο)."

[11] E. g., Plato, "Rep." 364 E. where it is said that λύσεις καὶ καθαρμοὶ τῶν ἀδικη-μάτων — "expiations and atonements for sin" (Jowett) — are made by the Orphics both for the living and the dead. Cf. E. Rohde, "Psyche²," 1898, ii, p. 127 f.

[12] See E. Rohde, as cited, p. 50, note 2; and Roscher, "Ausführrlices Lexikon der Griechischen und Römischen Mythologie," vol. ii, col. 2212.

[13] Cf. Rohde, as cited, p. 124.   [14] P. 366. AB: Jowett, ii, p. 187.

of wickedness may very easily be escaped: the gods can be
propitiated, and so we can sin and pray, and then sin and pray
some more, — and if you talk of a dread hereafter, why, are
there not mysteries and λύσιοι θεοί to whom we can look for
deliverance? The form λυτήρ obtained sufficient currency to
render it possible for the Christian poet Nonnus, the paraphrast
of John, to employ it as a designation of our Lord, whom he
calls "the Deliverer of the whole human race (ὅλης Λυτῆρα
γενέθλης)." [15] But Nonnus was somewhat precious in his choice
of words.

The prepositional compounds are numerous and appear to
have been in wide use to express the many modifications which
the general notion of "loosing" was capable of receiving from
them.[16] We are naturally most interested in those of them which
are employed of releasing men from chains or bondage, or
broadly from other evils. Among these the special implication
of ἀναλύειν is that the release effected is a restoration. In ἐκλύειν
— the exact etymological equivalent of the German *Auslösung*
(or its doublet *Erlösung*, which has become the standing German designation of the Christian Redemption) — the emphasis
falls on the deliverance which is wrought by the release in
question, and this form tends to be employed when the idea
of relief is prominent. It is, however, with ἀπολύειν — in itself
a close synonym of ἐκλύειν — that we are most nearly concerned.
It is employed alternatively with the simple λύειν, and like that
term developed a discriminating use of the active and middle
voices to express respectively releasing on the receipt or releasing
by the payment of a ransom. Thus, like λύειν, it came to mean
not merely releasing but distinctively ransoming, and is used
in that sense of the action of both of the parties involved.[17]

[15] On Jno. xvii. 21: Migne, xliii, col. 888. Nonnus is ordinarily assigned to
the end of the fourth or beginning of the fifth century.

[16] Ἀναλύειν, ἀνάλυσις, ἀναλυτήρ, ἀναλύτης; ἀπολύειν, ἀπόλυσις; διαλύειν, διάλυσις,
διαλυτής, διάλυτος, διαλυτικός; ἐκλύειν, ἔκλυσις, ἐκλυτήριος, τὸ ἐκλυτήριον, ἔκλυτος;
ἐπιλύειν, ἐπίλυσις, ἐπιλυτέον, ἐπιλυτικός; καταλύειν, κατάλυσις, κατάλυμα, καταλυτή-
ριον, καταλύτης, καταλυτής, καταλύσιμος, καταλυτέος, καταλυτικός; παραλύειν, παράλυσις,
παραλυτέον, παραλυτικός; προλύειν, προλύται; ὑπολύειν, ὑπόλυσις.

[17] See Liddell and Scott, *sub voc.*, II. "In 'Iliad' always = ἀπολυτρόω [*to
set at liberty*], to let go free *on receipt of ransom*, . . . 24, 115, al.: Med. *to set free*

The particular derivative of λύειν with which we are at the moment directly concerned — λύτρον — belongs to that class of derivatives usually spoken of as "instrumental," which denote the instrument or means by which the action of the verb is accomplished.[18] The particular actions expressed by the verb λύειν for the performance of which λύτρον denotes the instrument are those to which we have called especial attention above, — ransoming and atoning — the former regularly and the latter by way of exception. It commonly means just a ransom; infrequently, however, it means an expiation;[19] and very rarely it passes over into the general sense of a recompense.[20] "Λύτρον 'means of deliverance' (Lösemittel)," says Franz Steinleitner[21] quite accurately, "is employed by the old writers almost universally (mostly in the plural) in the sense of the ransom (Lösegeld) paid or to be paid for prisoners, in accordance with the use of λύειν for the liberation (Auslösung) of prisoners, especially by ransoming (Loskauf)." It is only a special application of this general sense when the word is found in use in inscriptions and papyri as the technical term for the manu-

by payment of ransom, to ransom, redeem, χαλκοῦ τε χρυσοῦ τ' ἀπολυσόμεθ' at a price of . . ., 'Il.' 22.50; so too in 'Att.,' ἀπολύεσθαι πολλῶν χρημάτων Xen. 'Hell.' 4.8, 21." Th. Zahn ("Römerbrief," p. 179, note 50) has a note illustrating this double usage of ἀπολύειν active and middle. Cf. above note 5.

[18] Cf. W. E. Jelf, "A Grammar of the Greek Language[4]," 1866, vol. i, p. 338 (§ 335, e): "Instrumental: (signifying the instrument or means by which a certain end is obtained) in τρον and τρα (contracted from τήριον, τήρια), as σεῖστρον, a rattle, δίδακτρον, schooling-money, λοῦτρον, bathing-water, bath." Cf. G. Hollmann, "Die Bedeutung des Todes Jesu," 1901, p. 104, note 2: "That λύτρον is derived from λύω is certain. From λύτρον is λυτρόω then formed like μετρέω from μέτρον. Compare further χύω, χύτρα, ἰάομαι, ἰατρός etc., Brugmann, "Griech. Gramm." 1900, p. 192 f. Numerous examples are given in Kühner-Blass, "Ausführl. Gramm. der griech. Sprache," 1892, iv. p. 271."

[19] Cf. H. Cremer, "Biblisch-theologisches Wörterbuch[3]," 1883 (cf. E. T., p. 408), sub voc.: "Meanwhile it should be taken into consideration that λύτρον in profane Greek denotes also the means of expiation with reference to the intended result as in Æsch. "Choeph." 48, λύτρον αἵματος, following λύειν, in the sense of expiatory acts."

[20] Liddell and Scott, sub voc.: "3. generally, a recompense, λύτρον καμάτων Pind. I. 8 (7). 1."

[21] "Die Beicht in Zusammenhange mit der sakralen Rechtspflege, in der Antike," 1913, p. 37.

mission-price of slaves.[22] Its occurrence on two late inscriptions
of a piacular character found near Könes in Lydia, on the other
hand, illustrates its less common use of a means, an instrument,
of expiation.[23] Both of these are, however, only special applications serving rather to illustrate than to qualify the essential
meaning of the term as just the price paid as a ransom in order
to secure release.[24]

The formation of λύτρον was not due to any serious need of
a term of its significance. It has synonyms enough.[25] Its forma-

[22] "The same word," continues Steinleitner, "in the plural, is employed
in three documents of the first century after Christ, from Oxyrhynchus, in which
slaves are emancipated; and stands in the same sense in the singular as well as
in the plural in the Thessalian stone-records of slave-manumissions." He refers
for the papyri to the "Oxyrhynchus Papyri," Part I, ed. by Grenfell-Hunt (London 1898) p. 105, no. XLVIII, . . . no. XLIX; Part IV (London 1904) p. 199, no.
722, line 24 f., line 29/30 . . . line 39/40; and also to L. Mitteis, "Papyri aus Oxy-
rhynchos," in "Hermes," vol. xxxiv (1899) p. 103 f. For the inscriptions he refers
to Gualterus Rensch, "De Manumissionum titulis apud Thessalos," Dissert.-
"Inaugural. Philologica," Halis Sax., 1908. Cf. also A. Deissmann, "Light from
the Ancient East," (1910) pp. 324 ff., especially 331 ff.: he gives the literature.

[23] They are described and expounded by Steinleitner, as cited. The longer
of the two inscriptions reads: " "Ετους σκς. Artemidorus, the son of Diodotus and
Amia, together with his six kinsmen, witting and unwitting, λύτρον according to
the command of Mem Tyrannos and Zeus Ogmenos and the Gods with him."
Steinleitner explains: "They liberate Artemidorus and his kindred from the God
to whom they have become indebted through a transgression, which had occurred
partly wittingly and partly unwittingly, by means of a λύτρον to which the God
had himself given the injunction through a dream-image or the mouth of the
priest. This λύτρον consists in this case certainly not of money, but of the confession
of guilt (Schuld) and the erection of the public expiatory monument." It is quite
unnecessary, however, to labor to derive this expiatory usage of λύτρον from its use
as the price of the manumission of slaves. The expiatory use was current from the
days of Pindar and Aeschylus. What these inscriptions show is that λύτρον was
in use not only of the emancipation price of slaves but also of the expiatory offering for guilt, until after the Christian era. Cf. also Deissmann, op.cit., p. 332,
note 2.

[24] Stephanus' definition very fairly describes its fundamental significance:
"Redemptorium, Redemptionis Pretium, Pretium redempti, sine adjectione,
quod Bud. ex Livio affert; Quod pro redemptione dependitur, Pretium quo
captivi redimuntur; ab ea sc. verbi λύεσθαι signif. qua ponitur pro Redimo."

[25] ἄλλαγμα, ἀντάλλαγμα, τιμή, ποινή, ἄποινα, ζωάγρια, ἀντίψυχον. "Αποινα
is regularly used in the "Iliad" in the sense of λύτρον, λύτρα; perhaps also in that
of ζωάγρια; the verb ἀποινάω formed from it and used in the active of demanding
the fine from the murderer, is in the middle the synonym of λυτροῦν to hold to
ransom.

tion must be traced to the natural influence of its primitive, λύειν, dominating the mind when the idea of ransoming occupied it, and leading to the framing from it of derived vocables expressive of that idea. It "came natural" to a Greek, in other words, when he wished to say ransom, to say λύτρον, because when he thought of ransoming he thought in terms of λύειν. This is an indication of the strength of the association of the idea of ransoming with λύειν; but, after all, the idea of ransoming was connected with λύειν only by association. It was not the intrinsic sense of that verb but only a signification which had — however firmly — been attached to it by usage. Accordingly the process of word-formation which began with λύτρον did not stop with it. It went on and built upon it a new verb with the distinctive meaning of just ransoming, — λυτροῦν, λυτροῦσθαι, — which meant and could mean nothing but to release for or by a ransom.[26] If λύειν, by a convention of speech, had come to express the idea of ransoming, this remained a mere convention of speech: the word intrinsically meant nothing more than to loose, to release, and was used in this wider sense side by side with its employment in the sense of ransoming. But λυτροῦν meant intrinsically just to ransom and nothing else, and could lose, not the suggestion merely, but the open assertion of specifically ransoming as the mode of deliverance of which it spoke, only by suffering such a decay of its native sense as to lose its very heart. He who said λυτροῦν, λυτροῦσθαι said λύτρον, and he who said λύτρον not merely intimated but asserted ransom. The only reason for the existence of this verb was to set by the side of the ambiguous λύειν (ἀπολύειν) an unambiguous term which would convey with surety, and without aid from the context or from the general understanding ruling its use, the express sense of ransoming. We are not surprised to observe therefore that throughout the whole history of profane Greek literature λυτροῦν, λυτροῦσθαι

---

[26] Jelf, "Grammar," as cited, vol. i, p. 332 (§ 330, c): "Verbs in όω mostly from substantives and adjectives of the II. decl.; . . . have all a factitive meaning, *making to be* that which the primitive expresses, as πυρόω, *I set on fire* from πῦρ; χρυσόω, *I gild*, from χρυσός; δηλόω, *I make known* from δῆλος."

maintained this sense unbrokenly. Its one meaning is just "to ransom"; in the active voice in the sense of to release on receipt of a ransom, and in the middle voice in the sense of to release by the payment of a ransom. We could ask no better proof of this than that neither H. Oltramare [27] nor Th. Zahn,[28] both of whom have sought diligently, has been able to discover an instance to the contrary.

Of course the derivatives and compounds of λυτροῦν, λυτροῦσθαι continue to convey the idea of ransoming. Impulse for forming them could arise only from a feeling out for unambiguous terms to express this idea. For the wider notion of deliverance the derivatives and compounds of the primitive, λύειν, λύεσθαι lay at hand. Not many derivatives and compounds of λυτροῦν, λυτροῦσθαι seem, it is true, to have been formed, and those that were formed appear to occur only sparsely in profane Greek literature. Of the derivatives [29] we

---

[27] "Commentaire sur l'Épitre aux Romains," 1881, i, p. 308.

[28] "Römerbrief[1]," p. 179. Zahn remarks that the regular meaning of the active λυτροῦν, ἀπολυτροῦν is *dimittere*, and of the middle λυτροῦσθαι, ἀπολυτροῦσθαι is *redimere*, the λύτρον being supposed in both cases. It is his view, however, that in the middle sense, "to ransom," the λύτρον may be neglected and the verb come to mean merely "to deliver." When he comes to give vouchers, however, (p. 181, note 52), he fails to find any in profane Greek for this loose sense. He cites indeed only three passages from profane Greek: Plato, "Theat.," 165. E; Polyb. 18 (al. 17), 16, 1; Plutarch, "Cimon," 9; all of which expressly intimate a ransom-price as paid. Plato,"Theat." 165. E (Jowett iii, p. 368): "He will have got you into his net, out of which you will not escape, until you have come to an understanding about the sum which is to be paid for your release." Polybius, 18 (al. 17), 16, 1 (Shuckburgh ii. 216): "King Attalus had for some time past been held in extraordinary honor by the Sicyonians, ever since the time that he ransomed the sacred land of Apollo for them at the cost of a large sum of money." Plutarch, "Cimon," 9 (Perrin ii. 432–433): "But a little time after the friends and kinsmen of the captives came home from Phrygia and Lydia and ransomed every one of them at a great price, so that Cimon had four months' pay and rations for his fleet, and besides that, much gold from the ransom (λύτρον) left over for the city."

[29] The Lexicons record no other uncompounded derivative as occurring in profane Greek except λυτρωτέον, Aristot. "Eth. Nic.," 9.2.4 (see next note). Other derivatives, for which no vouchers from profane Greek are given, include: λύτρωμα, from a Christian hymn — "the precious redemption of our Jesus"; λυτρώσιμος, Photius and Suidas, "redemmable"; λυτρωτήριος, "Chron. Pasch.," "redeeming"; λυτρωτής, LXX. and Acts, "redeemer"; λυτρωτικός, Theodorus Prodromus, "of or for ransoming."

need concern ourselves only with λύτρωσις; of the compounds [30] only with ἀπολυτροῦν, ἀπολυτροῦσθαι and its derivative, ἀπολύτρωσις.

Λύτρωσις is so rare in profane Greek that it appears to have turned up heretofore only in a single passage, Plutarch, "Aratus" XI. There we read of Aratus that "having a present of five and twenty talents sent him from the king, he took them, it is true, but gave them all to his fellow-citizens who wanted money, among other purposes for the ransoming of those who had been taken prisoners (εἴς τε τἆλλα καὶ λύτρωσιν αἰχμαλώτων)."

Ἀπολυτροῦν (active voice) occurs somewhat more frequently, but ἀπολυτροῦσθαι (middle voice) and ἀπολύτρωσις are again very rare. How the active, ἀπολυτροῦν is employed, may

---

[30] The Lexicons record such compound derivatives as the following: Ἀντιλυτρωτέον Aristot. "Eth. Nic.," 9.2.4: "But perhaps this is not always the case: for instance, must a person who has been ransomed (λυτρωθέντι) from robbers, ransom in return (ἀντιλυτρωτέον) him who ransomed (λυσάμενον) him, whoever he may be? Or should he repay him who has not been taken prisoner, but demands payment as a debt? Or should he ransom (λυτρωτέον) his father rather than the other? For it would seem that he ought to ransom his father even in preference to himself." Διαλύτρωσις, Polyb. 6.58.11: "But they frustrated the calculations of Hannibal and the hopes he had formed of the ransoming of the men" (there is no suggestion of mutual ransoming — "exchange of prisoners" we should say: on the contrary, it is a distinctly one-sided transaction, — the Romans were to pay three minae for each man); 27.11.2 (al. 14): "Just about the time when Perseus retired for the winter from the Roman war, Antenor arrived at Rhodes from him to negotiate for the ransom of Diophanes and those who were on board with him. Thereupon there arose a great dispute among the statesmen as to what course they ought to take. Philophenax, Theatetus and their party were against entering into such an arrangement upon any terms, Deinon and Polyaratus were for doing so. Finally they did enter upon an arrangement for their redemption." Ἐκλυτροῦσθαι, Scholium on Homer. "Odyss.," IV. 33: When princely Telemachus and the proud son of Nestor arrived at Menelaus' palace, Eteoneus asks whether they are to be received or sent about their business. Menelaus replies that of course they are to be received: they had themselves often had to depend on the courtesy of strangers, "and we must look to Zeus henceforth to keep us safe from harm." The Scholium explains this as meaning that they would have to hope, "that after these things he (Zeus) may deliver (ἐκλυτρώσηται) us from the impending distress." There is no obvious implication of ransoming here, but Liddell and Scott quite naturally define the word, with this sole voucher, "to redeem by payment of ransom." Ἐπίλυτρος, set at liberty for ransom, Strabo, ii, p. 496: Ἃ δ'ἂν λάβωσιν ἐπίλυτρα ποιοῦνται ῥᾳδίως. Παραλυτρούμενος is given by Athenaeus Grammaticus, p. 368, as the name of a comedy by Sotades.

be seen from the following examples, which are all that the lexicographers adduce. Plato, "Laws," XI, § 919 A (Jowett, iv, p. 430): He "treats them as enemies and captives who are at his mercy, and will not release (ἀπολυτρώσῃ) them until they have paid the highest, most exorbitant and base price." The Epistle of Philip to the Athenians in Demosthenes 159, 15: "He put Amphilochus to ransom (ἀπολύτρωσε) for nine talents." Polybius 2.6.6: "They made a truce with the inhabitants to deliver up all freemen and the city of Phoenice for a fixed ransom (ἀπολυτρώσαντες)." Polybius 22.21.8: "On a large sum of gold being agreed to be paid for the woman, he led her off to put her to ransom (ἀπολυτρώσαν)." Stephanus adds that Lucian somewhere says of Achilles that "he ransomed (ἀπολύτρωσας) the body of Hector for a small sum."

For the middle, ἀπολυτροῦσθαι, only late passages are cited. Th. Zahn, however, remarks very properly,[31] that while "the middle ἀπολυτροῦσθαι is very rare, and is not to be found in the Bible," it nevertheless "lies in essentially the same sense as the middle λυτροῦσθαι at the basis of the use of the passive in Zeph. iii. 1 (iii. 3),[32] and in Plutarch, 'Pompey,' 24." In this passage of Plutarch [33] we read that Helo who had been taken captive by pirates "was ransomed (ἀπελυτρώθη) with a great sum." In these passages ἀπολυτροῦσθαι is the passive of the middle, not of the active, sense. The lexicographers cite only two passages in which the middle is actually found. Polyaenus, a Macedonian rhetorician of the time of Marcus Aurelius and Lucius Verus, relates how Aristocrates the Athenian, entering a Spartan port in a ship disguised as peaceful, was able by this ruse to slay some and to abduct others as prisoners, which last, he adds, "Aristocles ransomed with a great sum (οὓς πολλῶν χρημάτων Ἀριστοκλῆς ἀπολυτρώσατο)."[34] That is the manuscript

---

[31] "Römerbrief¹⁺²," p. 181, note 52.

[32] The LXX here reads, ὦ ἡ ἐπιφανὴς καὶ ἀπολελυτρωμένη πόλις — "Alas, the glorious and ransomed city." Oltramare (on Rom. 3.24) wishes to render, "relaxed, licentious." Morison supports Zahn quite properly in insisting on the sense of ransomed.   [33] Reiske, p. 775.

[34] "Strategemata," v. 40: Ed. Mursinna, Berlin, 1756, p. 326. In a note it is said: "Read, Ἀριστοκράτης. For ἀπολυτρώσατο is not redemit, but pro redemptione

reading. Nevertheless the modern editors, adopting an emendation of Casaubon's, print 'Αριστοκράτης for 'Αριστοκλῆς. By this correction the meaning of ἀπολυτρώσατο is transformed, and we are made to read it, "Extorted a great sum for their ransom": that is to say, the middle is given the active sense. This result is unacceptable in view of the regular middle sense preserved in λύεσθαι, ἀπολύεσθαι, λυτροῦσθαι implied for ἀπολυτροῦσθαι in the passive use noted above, and actually appearing in the middle ἀπολυτροῦσθαι elsewhere. It must be held questionable, therefore, whether the text of the passage has been rightly settled by the editors: we need a different subject or else a different voice for the verb. There can be no question that in the only remaining passage in which it is cited, the Emperor Julian uses ἀπολυτροῦσθαι in its expected middle sense, and as the general equivalent of λυτροῦσθαι. "Whom, then," he says,[35] "are we to regard as a slave? Shall it be him whom we buy for so many silver drachmas, for two minae, or for ten staters of gold? Probably you will say that such a man is truly a slave. And why? Is it because we have paid down money for him to the seller? But in that case the prisoners of war whom we ransom (λυτρούμεθα) would be slaves. And yet the law on the one hand grants these their freedom when they have come safe home, and we on the other hand ransom (ἀπολυτρούμεθα) them not that they may become slaves, but that they may be free. Do you see then that in order to make a ransomed man (λυτρωθέντα) a slave it is not enough to pay down a sum of money . . .?"[36]

exegit. Casaubon." Accordingly the Teubner Ed. 1877, edited by Melber, p. 270, prints 'Αριστοκράτης in the text with the note, "'Αριστοκράτης Casaubon; 'Αριστοκλῆς F." "F" is the archetype from which all extant MSS. are descended. It reads 'Αριστοκλῆς which Casaubon in the editio princeps (Lugdunum Batavorum 1589) already suggested should be changed to 'Αριστοκράτης on the ground reported above. Whatever may be the true reading, the reason assigned for the proposed emendation is a bad one. For not only does the middle ἀπολυτροῦσθαι but the middle of the simple λυτροῦσθαι and the middles λύεσθαι and ἀπολύεσθαι before them, all mean distinctly not put to ransom but ransom.

[35] "Sixth Oration, to the Uneducated Cynics": "Works," ed. by W. C. Wright, 1913, vol. ii. p. 44; ed. Teubner, 1875. vol. i. p. 253.

[36] Stephanus cites also the late Christian writer Nicetas, "Paraphrasis [carm. arcan.] S. Gregorii Naz," ed. Dronk, pp. 26. 221; i.e., Migne, "Patr. Graec." 38.

The noun ἀπολύτρωσις might express the action of either the active or the middle of the verb from which it is formed.[37] Zahn remarks:[38] "For the corresponding use of ἀπολύτρωσις" — that is to say for the use of it in a sense corresponding to the middle sense of the verb, "to secure release by paying ransom" — "it seems that undoubted examples are lacking. Polybius, 6.58.11; 27.11.3, uses διαλύτρωσις in its stead, and most writers content themselves with λύτρωσις." This is already to say that the use of ἀπολύτρωσις in this sense has the support of its cognates; and certainly there is nothing in its own very rare usage to object. The lexicons give, it is true, only a single instance of the word's occurrence — Plutarch, "Pompey," 24 [39] — and in this instance it expresses the action of the active voice of the verb.[40] "Music," we read, "and dancing and banquets all along the shore, and seizings of officers and ransomings of captured cities (καὶ πόλεων αἰχμαλώτων ἀπολυτρῶσεις) were a reproach to the Roman supremacy." [41] Another instance, however, has turned up in an inscription from Kos of the first or second Christian century, in which the word expresses the action

705. Nicetas simply speaks of what Christ did that he might redeem (ἀπολυτρώσηται) men.

[37] Zahn, "Römerbrief ¹," pp. 179–181 says: "We must bear in mind that according as we take our start from the regular sense of the active λυτροῦν, ἀπολυτροῦν (dimittere) or from that of the middle, λυτροῦσθαι, ἀπολυτροῦσθαι (redimere), the derived substantive will designate either the action of him who discharges or releases from duress" (there should be added: "on receipt of a ransom") "him that is in duress to him, or the action of him who by means of the payment of a ransom, or else without such a payment" (there is no justification in profane Greek for this last clause) "secures the release of one in duress to another, be it person or thing." [38] P. 181. Note 52. [39] Reiske, p. 754.

[40] So it is rightly taken both by Zahn (p. 181, note 52) and Oltramare (i. 310).

[41] Liddell and Scott refer also to Philo, 2. 463 [Mangey], that is to say to "Quod Omn. Prob. Liber," § 17. med.: "He judged a violent death preferable to the life that was before him, and despairing of ransoming (ἀπολύτρωσιν), he cheerfully slew himself." Here ἀπολύτρωσις expresses distinctly the action of the middle voice of the verb. In the account given by Aristeas in the earlier portion of his letter to Philocrates (cf., also Josephus, "Antt." XII. ii. 2 ff.) of the liberation of the Jews by Ptolemy Philadelphus, the changes are rung on ἀπολύειν, ἀπόλυσις, ἀπολυτροῦν (20), ἀπολύτρωσις (12, 33) in the sense of securing release by payment of a ransom. The transaction was not a mere liberation, but involved the payment of a ransom — twenty drachmas for each (20 and 22), — the whole sum amount-

of the middle voice. The inscription is speaking of that form of manumission of slaves, very widely current after the period of the Diadochi and illustrated by a great number of inscriptions at Delphi, in which the slave really purchased his own liberty, but did so through the intermediation of priests so as ostensibly to be purchased by a god. The purchase money deposited in the temple for the purpose is called the λύτρον or λύτρα. In the inscription in question, those who perform the ἀπελευθέρωσις are instructed "not to make formal record of the ἀπολύτρωσις until the priests have reported that the necessary sacrifice has been made." [42] Both Deissmann and Zahn apparently suppose that the paralleling of ἀπολύτρωσις here with ἀπελευθέρωσις empties it of its specific meaning. This is obviously unjustified: the transaction was a manumission (ἀπελευθέρωσις) which took place by means of a payment (λύτρον, λύτρα) and was therefore, more exactly described, a ransoming (ἀπολύτρωσις). We are clearly to interpret: those who make the manumission are not to record the sale until the whole transaction is actually completed; and the two terms are respectively in their right places.[43]

---

ing to more than 400 talents (20): "More than 400 talents τῆς ἀπολυτρώσεως" that is to say "of redemption money," says Josephus (Niese III. 77, line 11). Cf. § 27 with Josephus XII. ii. 2 *ad fin.*

[42] A. Deissmann, "Light from the Ancient East," p. 331, note 4; cf., Th. Zahn, "Römerbrief[1]," p. 180, note 51. Both Deissmann and Zahn give the fundamental references.

[43] Naturally the details of the transactions in which slaves purchased their freedom varied endlessly. There are instances on record in which the money is paid down, but the manumission is to take effect only at some future time, say at the master's death. There are others in which the manumission is so far only partial that the slave remains bound to certain specified services. On the other hand there are instances in which the manumission is accomplished on credit, that is to say, it is enjoyed on sufferance until the price is paid in. This class of freedmen appears to have been known as πάλαι ἐλεύθεροι. "To such a suspended freedom," writes L. Mitteis ("Reichsrecht und Volksrecht," etc., 1891, p. 388), "must be reckoned the remission of the purchase money (*Lösegeld*) in the will of the master, as in the testament of Lyko ("Diog. Laert.," v. 61–64), where we read: Δημητρίῳ μὲν ἐλευθέρῳ πάλαι ὄντι ἀφίημι τὰ λύτρα [to Demetrius who is a πάλαι ἐλεύθερος I remit the purchase-money]; E. Curtius has already correctly recognized that a πάλαι ἐλεύθερος who is still in debt for his purchase money, is certainly no real freeman, but only a *statu liber* ("Anecdot.," p. 11)."

Throughout the whole history of the profane usage of the derivatives of λύτρον, we perceive, the intrinsic significance of λύτρον continuously determines their meaning.[44] This was to be expected. The case is not similar to that of such a word as, say, "dilapidated" in English which readily loses in figurative usages all suggestion of its underlying reference to stones; or even to that of such a word as "redeem" itself in English, which easily rubs off its edges and comes to mean merely to buy out and even simply to release. The bases of these words are foreign to English speech and do not inevitably obtrude themselves on the consciousness of every one who employs them. Λύτρον was a distinctively Greek word, formed from a Greek primitive in everyday use, according to instinctively working Greek methods of word-formation, carrying with them regular modifications of sense. No Greek lips could frame it, no Greek ear could hear it, in any of its derivatives, without consciousness of its intrinsic meaning. This is, of course, not to say that the word could not conceivably lose its distinctive sense. But in words of this kind the processes of such decay are difficult, and illustrations of it are comparatively rare; especially when as in this instance, the terms in question stand out on a background of a far more widely current use of their primitive in the broader sense. A Greek might well be tempted to use λύειν and its derivatives in the sense of λυτροῦν and its derivatives; and in point of fact he did so use them copiously. But it would not be natural for him to reverse the process and use λυτροῦν and its derivatives in the sense of λύειν. It may be natural for us, standing at a sales-counter, to say "I will take that," meaning to "buy"; but it would never be natural for us to say, "I will buy that," meaning merely to "take." In the group of words built up around λύτρον the Greek language offered to the New Testament a series of terms which distinctly said "ransom"; and just in proportion as we think of the writers of the New Testament as using Greek naturally we must think of them as feeling the intrinsic significance of these words as they used

---

[44] The only apparent exception which we have noted is the use of ἐκλυτροῦσθαι in a scholium on Homer, "Odyss.," IV. 35; see above, note 30.

them, and as using them only when they intended to give expression to this their intrinsic significance. It is safe to say that no Greek, to the manner born, could write down any word, the center of which was λύτρον, without consciousness of ransoming as the mode of deliverance of which he was speaking.

The fact is not to be obscured, of course, that the writers of the New Testament were not in the strict sense Greeks. At the most Luke enjoys that unique distinction; and even he may have been in the wide sense a Hellenist rather than in the strict sense a Hellene. The rest were Jews: even Paul, coming out of the Diaspora, yet was able to speak in Aramaic; and apart from him and the author of the Epistle to the Hebrews, they were all of immediate Palestinian origin and traditions. Moreover they all had in their hands the Septuagint version of the Old Testament and may be thought to have derived their Greek religious terminology from it. We must, therefore, ascertain, we are told, how the group of words built up on λύτρον are employed in the Septuagint before we can venture to pass upon the sense in which they are used in the New Testament. And in turning to the Septuagint, it must be confessed, a surprising thing confronts us. Words of this group are certainly employed in the Septuagint without clear intimation of ransoming. This remarkable phenomenon is worthy of our careful and discriminating attention.

II

A considerable number of words of this group occur in the Septuagint — λύτρον, [ἀντιλύτρον], λυτροῦσθαι, λύτρωσις, λυτρωτής, λυτρωτός, ἀπολυτροῦν, ἀπολύτρωσις, ἐκλύτρωσις. Some of these, however, occur very seldom, and only one, λυτροῦσθαι, is copiously employed.

'Αντιλύτρον was printed in some of the early editions at Ps. xlviii. (xlix.) 9, but has been eliminated in the modern critical texts.

Λύτρον occurs nineteen times and always, of course, in the quite simple sense of a ransom-price. H. Oltramare gives a very good account of its usage.[45] "Λύτρον, usually in the plural λύτρα, (= כפר, פדיון, גאלה) [46] designates an indemnification, a pecuniary compensation, given in exchange for a cessation of rights over a person or even a thing, *ransom*. It is used for the money given to redeem a field, Lev. xxv. 24 — the life of an ox about to be killed, Ex. xxi. 30 — one's own life in arrest of judicial proceedings, Num. xxxv. 31, 32, or of vengeance, Prov. vi. 35, — the first-born over whom God had claims, Num. iii. 46, 48, 51, Lev. xviii. 15, etc. It is ordinarily used of the ransom given for redemption from captivity or slavery, Lev. xix. 20, Isa. xlv. 13, etc."

The adjective λυτρωτός occurs only twice, in a single connection (Lev. xxv. 31, 32), in which we are told that the houses in unwalled villages and in the Levitical cities were alike at all times redeemable (λυτρωταὶ διαπαντὸς ἔσονται: representing גאלא).

The compound active noun, ἐκλύτρωσις, occurs only a single time (Num. iii. 49): "And for τὰ λύτρα . . . thou shalt take five shekels apiece . . . and thou shalt give the money to Aaron and to his sons as λύτρα of the supernumerary among them; . . . and Moses took the money, τὰ λύτρα of the supernumerary, for the ἐκλύτρωσις of the Levites . . . and Moses gave τὰ λύτρα of the supernumeraries to Aaron and his sons."

The compound verb, ἀπολυτροῦν occurs twice, once in the active voice (Ex. xxi. 8 [47] for the Hiphil of פדה) and once in

---

[45] "Comm. sur L'Épitre aux Romains," 1881, i. p. 308.

[46] כפר six times: Ex. xxi. 30, xxx. 12, Num. xxxv. 31, 32, Prov. vi. 35, xiii. 8; פדיון seven times: Num. iii. 46, 48, 51; Ex. xxi. 30; Num. iii. 49, Lev. xix. 20, Num. xviii. 15; גאלה five times, Lev. xxv. 24, 26, 51, 52; xxvii. 31; also מהיר once, Isa. xlv. 13. Cf. G. Hollmann, "Die Bedeutung des Todes Jesu," 1901, p. 102. Hollmann notes that λύτρα occurs in the same sentence as the rendering both of כפר and פדיון in Ex. xxi. 30, "If there be laid on him a כפר he shall give for the פדיון of his life whatever is laid on him."

[47] A. Seeberg, "Der Tod Christi," p. 218 says that in this passage "the master to whom the Israelitish maiden bought by him does not prove to be pleasing, is required והפדה, which the LXX translate ἀπολυτρώσει αὐτήν, and that of course cannot mean, 'he shall buy her free' but only 'he shall free her.'" But verse 11 opposes her going out for nothing, "without money," to the disposal of her required in verse 8, — which therefore must be for money. Undoubtedly the E. V. renders rightly: "Then shall he let her be redeemed," in accordance with

the passive voice (Zeph. iii. 1 (3) for the Niphal of נאל). In both instances the idea of ransoming is express; and, as Th. Zahn points out, the sense in which the passive is used in Zeph. iii. 1 (3) presupposes the middle, ἀπολυτροῦσθαι, in the sense of "to deliver by the payment of a ransom." Thus this verb bears the distinctive active and middle senses in the Septuagint which it and its congeners bear in profane Greek.

So far the Septuagint usage shows no modification of that of profane Greek. No modification can be assumed even with reference to ἀπολύτρωσις, the active substantive derived from ἀπολυτροῦν, ἀπολυτροῦσθαι. This term occurs only in Dan. iv. 32 (29 or 30) LXX in a context which at first sight might mislead us into giving it the undifferentiated signification of just "deliverance." "And at the end of the seven years," we read, "the time of my ἀπολυτρώσεως came, and my sins and my ignorance were fulfilled in the sight of the God of heaven." The "deliverance" here spoken of, however, must be held to be defined by the preceding context as resting on a "ransoming." There is a manifest reference back from this verse to iv. 24 where the king is exhorted to pray God concerning his sins and "to redeem (λύτρωσαι) all his iniquities with almsgiving." [48] No doubt the emphasis is thrown on the result of the ransoming, on the deliverance in which it has at last issued. This is doubtless the reason why the compound term is used here — ἀπολύτρωσις, — the ἀπό in which, signifying "away from," shifting the emphasis from the process to the effects. The two terms, λυτροῦσθαι, verse 24, and ἀπολύτρωσις, verse 32, are respectively in their right places.

When we turn to the verb λυτροῦσθαι itself and its two sub-

---

the proper sense of the active voice of the verb — "to release for a ransom." Joseph Wirtz, "Die Lehre von der Apolytrosis," 1906, p. 2 and p. 3, note 2 has the right interpretation.

[48] Cf. Dan. iv. 24, Theod.: "Therefore, O King, let my counsel be acceptable to thee and λύτρωσαι thy sins with almsgivings and thine iniquities with mercies to the poor." The Aramaic word rendered by λύτρωσαι here is p'rak — to take away: λύτρωσαι accordingly represents a term which does not specifically express a ransoming (cf. S. R. Driver in loc.); cf. note 56. Nevertheless the purchase price is expressed and therefore λύτρωσαι is appropriate.

stantival derivatives, λύτρωσις and λυτρωτής, we find ourselves in deeper water.

Λύτρωσις occurs eight times,[49] representing the Hebrew bases נאל and פדה, each four times. In four of its occurrences, it is employed in the simple literal sense of ransoming or redeeming (Lev. xxv. 29, 29, 48; Num. xviii. 16); and in yet another (Ps. xlviii. (xlix.) 8), — "the price of the redemption of his soul" — it is used equally of ransoming by a price, although now in the higher, spiritual sphere. In the remaining three instances an implication of a ransom-price is less clear: Ps. cx. (cxi), 9, "He sent redemption to His people; He commanded His covenant forever"; Ps. cxxix (cxxx), 7, "For with the Lord is mercy, and with Him is plenteous redemption"; Isa. lxiii. 4, "For the day of recompense (ἀνταποδόσεως) is upon them, and the year of redemption is at hand." Passages like these will naturally receive their precise interpretation from the implication of the usage of their more copiously employed primitive, λυτροῦσθαι.

Similarly the noun of agent, λυτρωτής, which occurs only twice (Ps. xviii (xix), 14; lxxvii (lxxviii), 35, representing נאל) — in both instances as an epithet of God, "our Redeemer" — will necessarily receive its exact shade of meaning from the general usage of its primitive, λυτροῦσθαι.

This verb, λυτροῦσθαι, occurs some hundred and five times. It usually has at its base either נאל (about forty-two times) or פדה (about forty times),[50] and rarely פרק (five times). Sometimes, of course, there is no Hebrew base (Sir. xlviii. 20, xlix. 10, l. 24, li. 2, 3; Zech. iii. 15; I Macc. iv. 11). It is employed in more than one shade of meaning.

First, it is used quite literally to express the redeeming of a thing by the payment for it of a ransom price. Thus, for example: Ex. xiii. 13, "Every one of an ass that openeth the womb, thou shalt exchange for a sheep; but if thou wilt not exchange, thou shalt *redeem* it; every firstborn of a man of thy sons, thou shalt *redeem*"; Levit. xix. 20, "If any one lie carnally

---

[49] We do not concern ourselves with Judges i. 15.

[50] For the Hebrew synonyms פדה and נאל, see R. D. Wilson, *PTR* July 1919, p. 431.

with a woman, and she is a house-slave, kept for a man, and she has not been *redeemed* with a ransom (λύτροις) and freedom has not been given to her, . . . they shall not be put to death, because she was not set free"; Num. xviii. 15–17, "And everything which openeth the womb of all flesh, whatsoever they offer unto the Lord, from man unto beast, shall be thine; nevertheless the firstborn of men *shall be redeemed* with a ransom (λύτροις), and the firstborn of unclean beasts thou shalt *redeem*. And its redemption (λύτρωσις) is from a month old; the valuation (συντίμησις) is five sheckels, according to the sacred sheckel — there are twenty obols." In this simple literal usage the word occurs about twenty-seven times; but it seems to be confined to Exodus (six times), Leviticus (eighteen times) and Numbers (three times).[51]

Sharply differentiated from this literal usage is a parallel one in which λυτροῦσθαι is applied to the deliverance from Egypt. Here there is at least no emphasis placed on the deliverance being in mode a ransoming. The stress is thrown rather on the power exerted in it and the mind is focussed on the mightiness of the transaction. This is so marked that B. F. Westcott is led by it to declare,[52] too broadly, of the use of λυτροῦσθαι and its derivatives in the Septuagint, that "the idea of the exertion of a mighty force, the idea that the 'redemption' costs much, is everywhere present." It is at least clear that the idea that the redemption from Egypt was the effect of a great expenditure of the divine power and in that sense cost much, is prominent in the allusions to it, and seems to constitute the central idea sought to be conveyed. The earliest passage in which this usage occurs is typical of the whole series: Ex. vi. 6, "Go, speak to the sons of Israel, saying, I am the Lord, and I will lead you forth from the tyranny of the Egyptians, and deliver (ῥύσομαι) you from your bondage and *redeem* (λυτρώσομαι) you with a high hand and a great judgment; and I will take you to myself for my people, and I will be to you a God and ye shall

---

[51] Ex. xiii. 13 bis, 15, xxxiv. 20 bis; Lev. xix. 20, xxv. 25, 30, 33, 48, 49 bis, 54, xxvii. 13, 15, 19, 20 bis, 27, 28, 29, 31, 33; Num. xviii. 15 bis, 17. Cf. Dan. iv. 24.

[52] "Hebrews³," p. 298, med.

know that I am the Lord your God which bringeth you out from the oppression of the Egyptians." Other examples are: Deut. ix. 26, "And I prayed to God and said, O Lord, king of the Gods, destroy not thy people and thy portion which thou didst *redeem*, and didst lead forth out of Egypt by thy great might and by thy strong hand and by thy high hand"; Neh. i. 10, "And these are thy children and thy people, whom thou didst *redeem* by thy great power and by thy strong hand"; Ps. lxxvi (lxxvii) 15, 16, "Thou art the God that doest wonders, thou didst make known among the peoples thy power, thou didst *redeem* with thine arm thy people, the sons of Jacob and Joseph." This usage of the deliverance out of Egypt in might lies in the Pentateuch side by side with the former, occurring in Exodus (three times), and Deuteronomy (six times), and occurs on occasion in the later books.[53]

Similarly to its employment to express the fundamental national deliverance from Egypt in the divine might, λυτροῦσθαι is used of other great national deliverances in which the power of Jehovah was manifested. In "the praise of famous men and of our fathers which begat us," that fills the later chapters of Sirach, the word is employed repeatedly in this sense: (xlviii. 20), "But they called upon the Lord which is merciful and stretched out their hands towards him; and immediately the Holy One heard them out of heaven, and *delivered* them by the ministry of Esay"; (xlix. 10), "And of the twelve prophets let the memorial be blessed, and let their bones flourish again out of their place; for they comforted Jacob, and *delivered* them by assured hope"; (l. 22, 24), "Now, then bless ye the God of all, which only doeth wondrous things everywhere. . . . That he would confirm his mercy with us and *deliver* us at his time." The general point of view finds clear expression in I Macc. iv. 10, 11, "Now, therefore, let us cry unto heaven, if peradventure the Lord will have mercy upon us, and remember the covenant

---

[53] Ex. vi. 6, xv. 13, 16; Deut. vii. 8, ix. 26, xiii. 5 (6), xv. 15, xxi. 8, xxiv. 18; II Sam. vii. 23 bis; I Chron. xvii. 21 bis, Neh. i. 10, Esther iv. 16, (9); Ps. lxxvi. (lxxvii.) 15, cv. (cvi.) 10, cvi. (cvii.) 2 bis; cxxxv. (cxxxvi.) 24; Mic. vi. 4 (Isa. lxiii. 9?).

of our fathers, and destroy this host before our face this day: that so all the heathen may know that there is one that *delivereth* and saveth (σώζειν) Israel."

Among these great deliverances wrought for Israel, the chief place is taken, of course, by its second great cardinal emancipation — that from the Babylonian captivity. The employment of λυτροῦσθαι to express this deliverance is naturally comparatively frequent, and as naturally it shades insensibly into the expression of the Messianic deliverance of which this liberation (along with that from Egypt) is treated as the standing type. We may find the key-note struck, perhaps, in Jer. xxvii. (l.) 33, 34: "Thus saith the Lord, Oppressed have been the children of Israel and the children of Judah: all they that have taken them captive, together oppress them because they refuse to let them go. And *their redeemer* is strong, the Lord Almighty is his name; he shall judge judgment with his adversary, that he may destroy the land and disquiet the inhabitants of Babylon. A sword is upon the Chaldeans and upon the inhabitants of Babylon! . . ." How close the eschatological application lies may be illustrated by Isa. li. 11–13 (9–11): "Awake, awake Jerusalem and put on the strength of thine arm; awake as in the beginning of day, as the generation of eternity. Art thou not she that dried the sea, the deep waters of the abyss? that madest the depths of the sea a way for the delivered (ῥυομένοις) and the *redeemed* to pass through? For by the Lord shall they return, and shall come into Zion with joy and eternal exultation." And we seem fairly on eschatological ground in Isa. xxxv. 9–10: "And there shall be no lion there, neither shall any of the evil beasts go up upon it, nor be found there, but the *redeemed* and the gathered on account of the Lord shall walk in it, and they shall return and come into Zion with joy and everlasting joy shall be over their heads." [54]

Not essentially different is the employment of the word to

[54] In this general class there may be counted such passages as Isa. xli. 14, xliii.14, xliv. 22, 23, 24, lxii. 12, lxiii. 9, Jer. xv. 21, xxxviii. (xxxi.) 11, Hos. vii. 13, xiii. 14, Mic. iv. 10, Zeph. (iii. 1) iii. 15, Zech. x. 8 and perhaps Ps. xxiv. (xxv.) 22, xliii. (xliv.) 26, lxxiii. (lxiv.) 2, cxxix. (cxxx.) 8.

express the intervention of God for the deliverance of an individual either from some great specific evil or from evil in general — the term rising in the latter case fully into the spiritual region. A couple of very instructive instances occur in the Septuagint: Daniel iii. 88, "Bless ye the Lord, Ananias, Adzarias and Misael, hymn and exalt him forever; because he liberated (ἐξείλατο) us from hades, and saved (ἔσωσεν) us from the bonds of death, and delivered (ἐρρύσατο) us from the midst of the burning flame, and redeemed (ἐλυτρώσατο) us from the fire"; vi. 27, "I, Darius, will worship and serve him all my days, for the idols made with hands cannot save (σῶσαι) as the God of Daniel redeemed Daniel." Quite similarly we read in II Sam. iv. 9 (and I Kings i. 29): "And David answered Rechab and Baanah his brother, . . . and said unto them, As the Lord liveth, who hath redeemed my soul out of all adversity"; and in Ps. cxliii. (cxliv.) 9–10: "O God, I will sing a new song to thee, . . . who giveth salvation unto kings, who redeemeth David his servant from the hurtful sword" (cf. vii. 2–3). "I will thank thee, O Lord King," says the son of Sirach in his concluding prayer (li. 1 ff.), "and I will praise thee, O God my Savior (σωτῆρα), I give thanks to thy name, because thou hast become my defender and helper, and hast redeemed my body from destruction, and from the snare of the slanderous tongue, from the lips that forge a falsehood, and hast become my helper against my adversaries and hast redeemed me, according to the multitude of thy mercies and name, from the teeth of them that were ready to devour me, from the hand of those that seek my life, from the manifold afflictions which I had. . . ." [55] The Psalms afford a number of examples in which this individual redemption in the region of the spirit is spoken of. The note that sounds through them is struck in Ps. xxxiii. (xxxiv.), 23: "The Lord will redeem the souls of his servants, and none of them that hope in him shall go wrong." [56]

[55] Cf. Ps. lviii. (lix.) 1, lxviii. (lxix.) 18, cxviii. (cxix.) 134.

[56] Cf. Ps. xxv. (xxvi.) 11, xxx. (xxxi.) 5, xxxi. (xxxii.) 7, xlviii. (xlix.) 15, liv. (lv.) 18, lxx. (lxxi.) 23, lxxi. (lxxii.) 14, cii. (ciii.) 4, cxviii. (cxix.) 154; cf. Lam. iii. 58.

The redeeming power in all this range of applications of
λυτροῦσθαι is uniformly conceived as divine. It is to God, the
Lord God Almighty, alone that redemption is ascribed, whether
it be the redemption of Israel or of the individual, or whether
it be physical or spiritual. God and God alone is the Redeemer
alike of Israel and of the individual, in every case of deliverance of whatever order. We hear in Sirach, it is true, of the Holy
One redeeming Israel by the hand of Isaiah (xlviii. 20); and indeed, in a somewhat confused sentence, of the twelve prophets,
or of their bones, redeeming Jacob (xlix. 10) — or are we to
assume that God is understood as the nominative of the verbs
and read: "But God comforted Israel and redeemed them by
the faith of hope"? There are besides two negative statements
which may seem to imply the possibility of a human redeemer.
The one is found in Ps. vii. 2–3, and the other, — a very instructive passage — in Lam. v. 8.[57] In Ps. vii. 2–3 David prays:
"O Lord, my God, in thee do I put my hope, save (σῶσον) me
from all that persecute me, and deliver (ῥῦσαι) me; let him not
seize my soul, like a lion, while there is none to redeem (λυτρουμένου) or to save (σώζοντος)." In Lam. v. 8 we read: "Slaves,
have ruled over us: there is none to redeem (λυτροῦμενος) out
of their hand." In neither instance is it intimated, however,
that a human redeemer could be found: despair is rather expressed, and the cry is for the only Redeemer that can suffice.
It is only in Dan. iv. 24 that we find a clear reference to a human
redeemer. "Entreat him concerning thy sins and redeem thine
iniquities with alms" (LXX); "redeem thy sins with alms"
(Theod.). Here the king is exhorted to ransom his own soul by
his good works. This conception, however, cuts athwart the
whole current of the usage of λυτροῦσθαι in the Septuagint elsewhere when it is a matter of spiritual redemption. How little
such a point of view accords with that elsewhere connected
with λυτροῦσθαι may be learned from Ps. xlviii. (xlix.) 8–10:

[57] In both cases the Hebrew word rendered by λυτροῦσθαι is פרק, as it is
also in Ps. cxxxv (cxxxvi), 24; cf. the corresponding Aramaic in Dan. iv. 24 (and
Driver's note on it). On this word see Giesebrecht, *ZATW*, 1881, p. 285 and the
note of Baethgen on Ps. vii. 3. It is literally "to snatch away," "to rescue"; cf.
Brown-Driver *in loc.* Cf. note 48.

"A brother redeemeth (λυτροῦται) not: shall a man redeem (λυτρώσεται)? He shall not give to God an expiation (ἐξίλασμα) for himself or the price of the redemption (τὴν τιμὴν τῆς λυτρώσεως) of his soul though he labor forever and live to the end, so that he should not see corruption." The sense of ὁ λυτρούμενος in Prov. xxiii. 10–11: "Remove not the ancient landmarks and enter not into the possession of orphans, for he that redeemeth them is a powerful Lord, and judgeth thy judgment with thee," may be open to some question. It is probably the intention of the Septuagint translators to intimate that the poor are under the especial protection of the God who is the "redeemer" by way of eminence of the needy.

The emphasis put upon the power of God manifested in redemption which accompanies the entire usage of λυτροῦσθαι except in its literal sense, may tempt us to suppose that the notion of ransoming has been altogether lost in this usage. This is in point of fact widely taken for granted. B. F. West-cott, for example, writes:[58] "It will be obvious from the usage of the LXX. that the idea of a ransom received by the power from which the captive is delivered is practically lost in λυτροῦσθαι &c." Such a statement is in any case fatally defective. It takes no account of the large use of λυτροῦσθαι in the Pentateuch in the purely literal sense· (cf. Dan. iv. 24). It is doubtful, however, whether it can be fully sustained even with respect to the use of λυτροῦσθαι of the divine deliverance. No doubt, as has already been pointed out, the sense of the power of God exerted in the deliverances wrought by Him comes so forcibly forward as to obscure the implication of ransoming. This is pushed so far into the background as to pass out of sight; and not infrequently it seems to be pushed not only out of sight but out of existence. In a passage like Dan. iii. 88 LXX, for example, there seems no place left for ransom-paying; and the same may appear to be true of such passages as Dan. vi. 27 LXX, Lam. v. 8, Ps. vii. 2. Nor does the synonymy in which the word sometimes stands encourage seeking for it such an underlying idea: Ex. vi. 6, ῥύσομαι, λυτρώσομαι; Ps. vii. 2–3,

[58] "Hebrews³," p. 298.

σῶσον, ῥῦσαι, λυτρουμένου, σώζοντος; Ps. lviii. (lix.) 2–3, ἐξελοῦ, λύτρωσαι, ῥῦσαι; Ps. cv. (cvi.) 10, ἔσωσεν, ἐλυτρώσατο; Hos. xiii. 14, ῥύσομαι, λυτρώσομαι; Dan. iii. 88 LXX, ἐξείλετο, ἔσωσεν, ἐρρύσατο, ἐλυτρώσατο; Dan. vi. 27 LXX, σῶσαι, ἐλυτρώσατο; I Macc. iv. 10, 11, λυτρούμενος, σώζων.

Nevertheless, as Westcott himself perceives, there is an abiding implication that the redemption has cost something: "the idea that the redemption costs much," says he, "is everywhere present." Perhaps we may say that, in this underlying suggestion, the conception of price-paying intrinsic in λυτροῦσθαι is preserved, and in this the reason may be found why it appears to be employed only when the mind is filled with the feeling that the redemption wrought has entailed the expenditure of almighty power.

It is going too far, in any case, however, to say that the idea of ransoming "is practically lost in λυτροῦσθαι, &c." in their Septuagint usage — as, to be sure the insertion of the word "practically" may show that Westcott himself felt. Whatever may be the implications of λυτροῦσθαι when used to designate the intervention of God in His almighty power for the deliverance of His people, there is evidence enough to show that the feeling of ransoming as the underlying sense of the word remained ever alive in the minds of the writers. That could not in any event fail to be the fact, because of the parallel use of λυτροῦσθαι in its literal sense; we must not permit to fall out of memory that λυτροῦσθαι is employed in its literal sense in more than a fourth of all its occurrences in the Septuagint. Every now and then moreover the consciousness of the underlying sense of ransoming is thrown up to observation. This may be the case in a passage like Ps. lxxiii. (lxxiv.) 2: "Remember thy synagogue which thou didst acquire (ἐκτήσω = purchase) of old; thou didst redeem (ἐλυτρώσω) the rod of thine inheritance." It is more clearly the case in a passage like Isa. lii. 3: "Ye were sold for nought (δωρεάν) and ye shall not be redeemed (λυτρωθήσεσθε) with money." There is an intimation here that no ransom price (in the sense intended) is to be paid for Israel; its redemption is to be wrought by the might of

Jehovah. But it is equally intimated that a redemption without a price paid is as anomalous a transaction as a sale without money passing. That is to say, here is an unexceptionable testimony that the term λυτροῦσθαι in itself was felt to imply a ransom price. Another passage in point is provided by Ps. xlviii. (xlix.) 8: "A brother redeemeth (λυτροῦται) not: shall a man redeem (λυτρώσεται)? He shall not give to God an expiation (ἐξίλασμα) for himself, and the price of the redemption (τὴν τιμὴν τῆς λυτρώσεως) of his soul, though he labor forever." To redeem is distinctly set forth here as the giving of a price which operates as an expiation: and the inability of a man to redeem a man out of the hand of God turns precisely on his inability to pay the price. Perhaps the most instructive passage, however, will be found in Isa. xliii. 1 ff.: "Fear not," Jehovah here says to His people, "because I have redeemed (ἐλυτρωσάμην) thee. . . . I have made Egypt thy price (ἄλλαγμα) and Ethiopia and Soene in thy stead (ὑπέρ σοῦ) . . . . And I will give men for thee (ὑπέρ σοῦ) and rulers for thy head." Such passages as these, it surely does not require to be said, could not have been written by and to men in whose minds the underlying implication of ransoming had faded out of the terms employed. They bear witness to a living consciousness of this implication, and testify that, though λυτροῦσθαι and its derivatives may be employed to describe a redemption wrought in the almighty power of God, that was not in forgetfulness that redemption was properly a transaction which implies paying a price.

III

The broader use of λυτροῦσθαι (λύτρωσις, λυτρωτής) by the Septuagint of God's deliverance of His people, may not unfairly be said to throw the emphasis so strongly on the almightiness of the power manifested as to obscure, if not to obliterate, intimation of its mode as a ransoming. The assumption is frequently made that this usage is simply projected into the New Testament and determines the sense of all the terms of this group which are found in the New Testament.

This assumption is met, however, by the initial difficulty that the usage of the New Testament is not even formally a continuation of that of the Septuagint. The usage of the Septuagint in question is distinctly a usage of λυτροῦσθαι, and affects only it and, to a limited extent, its two immediate derivatives, λύτρωσις (Ps. cx. (cxi.) 9, cxxix. (cxxx.) 7, Isa. lxiii. 4) and λυτρωτής (Ps. xviii. (xix.) 15, lxxvii. (lxxviii.) 35), which could not fail to be drawn somewhat into the current of any extended usage of λυτροῦσθαι. The more proper usage of other members of the group, and indeed even of these members of it in a large section of their employment, remains untouched. On the other hand, the usage of the New Testament is characteristically a usage of ἀπολύτρωσις, an otherwise rare form, which appears never to occur — itself or its primitive, ἀπολυτροῦν, ἀπολυτροῦσθαι, — whether in profane Greek,[59] or in the Septuagint,[60] or in writers directly dependent on the Septuagint,[61] in any other than its intrinsic sense of ransoming. It would be plausible to suggest that the Septuagint usage in question is continued in the λύτρωσις of Luke i. 68, ii. 38 and λυτροῦσθαι of Luke xxiv. 21 where redemption is spoken of on the plane of Old Testament expectation. But the suggestion loses all plausibility when extended beyond this. It would be more plausible to argue that the form ἀπολύτρωσις was selected by the New Testament writers in part purposely to avoid the ambiguities which might arise from the Septuagint associations clinging to λυτροῦσθαι. The simple fact, however, is that the characteristic terminology in the two sets of writings is different.

This formal difference in the usages of the two sets of writers is immensely reinforced by a material difference in the presuppositions underlying what they severally wrote. Whatever may have been the nature of the expectations which the Old Testament saints cherished as to the mode of the divine deliverance

[59] Plato, "Laws," 919. A; Demosthenes 159, 15; Polybius 2.6.6, 22.21.8; Lucian; Plutarch, "Pompey," 24; Polyaenus, "Strat.," V. 40; Julian Imp., "Orat., vi," Teubner I. 253; Inscription from Kos. The passages are given above.

[60] Ex. xxi. 8, Zeph. iii. 1 (3), Dan. LXX. iv. 24.

[61] Philo, Mangey, ii. 463; Josephus, Niese, III. 77. 11; Aristeas, Wendland, 4.12; 7.19; 12.8.

to which they looked forward, the New Testament writers wrote of it, as a fact lying in the past, under the impression of a revolutionary experience of it as the expiatory death of the Son of God. It would have been unnatural to the verge of impossibility for them to speak of it colorlessly as to this central circumstance, especially when using phraseology with respect to it which in its intrinsic connotation emphasized precisely this circumstance. We must not obscure the fact that something had happened between the writing of the Old Testament and the New, something which radically affected the whole conception of the mode of the divine deliverance, and which set the development of Jewish and Christian ideas and expressions concerning it moving thenceforward on widely divergent pathways. It may sound specious when the Jewish eschatological conceptions are represented as supplying an analogy, according to which the New Testament phraseology may be understood. We may be momentarily impressed when it is explained that, as the Jews have set the Messiah as the great Deliverer (גואל) by the side of Moses, the first Deliverer (גואל.הראשון), and expect him, as Moses led Israel out of Egypt, to achieve the final Deliverance (גאלה) and bring Israel home, without any interruption by an expiatory suffering and death, and merely by the power of his own personal righteousness,[62] — so we must understand the New Testament writers, borrowing their language from the Jewish eschatology, to ascribe to Christ merely the Messianic deliverance, without any implication that it is wrought by an act of ransoming. But we can be only momentarily impressed by such representations. Between the Jewish and the New Testament conceptions of the Messianic deliverance there is less an analogy than a fundamental contradiction. There had taken place, first of all, on the part of the Christians what it is fashionable to speak of as a "predating" of the Messianic expectations: the redemption of God's people does not wait, with them, for the end-time, but has already been in principle wrought and awaits only its full realization in all its

---

[62] Cf. F. Weber, "Jüdische Theologie auf Grund des Talmud und verwandter Schriften²," 1897, p. 359 f. (§ 79.2); also p. 361.

effects, in the end-time. And precisely what has already been wrought, contributing the very hinge on which the whole conception of the Messianic deliverance turns, is just that act of expiation which is wholly absent from the Jewish representation. If, in other words, the Jews looked only for a Deliverance, wrought by sheer power, the Christians put their trust precisely in a Redemption wrought in the blood of Christ. Of course so fundamental a difference could not fail to reflect itself in the language employed to give expression to the divergent conceptions. And that, again, may be, in part, the account to give of the adoption by the New Testament writers of the rare form ἀπολύτρωσις instead of the more current λυτροῦσθαι colored by Septuagint conceptions, to describe the redemption in Christ. That they conceived this redemption in terms of ransoming is made clear in any event by repeated contextual intimations to that effect.[63]

[63] Even Johannes Weiss is constrained to allow that it is probable that the idea of ransoming was felt in the New Testament usage, as appears from his very instructive comment on I Cor. i. 30: "The σωτηρία, the ζωή, is the benefit which is obtained for us by the ἀπολύτρωσις. How far the conception of *ransom* is still felt in this is not to be debated here. Paul thinks in our passage more of the *effect* than of the *means* of the deliverance. But it is very probable (from passages like Gal. iii. 13, I Pet. 1. 18) that this shade is still felt." How impossible it is to eliminate the idea of purchase from the conceptions of the New Testament writers is illustrated by the admission by writers who argue for the wider notion of ἀπολύτρωσις that it lies expressed in other language by the side of the general notion of deliverance expressed by ἀπολύτρωσις. This is done, for example, by A. Ritschl. It is done also by H. Oltramare (on Rom. iii. 24): "That the idea of *ransom* is Scriptural," he says, "is incontestable; but who proves to us that ἀπολύτρωσις is the equivalent of these expressions?" — that is to say, such as are found in Mt. xx. 28, I Tim. ii. 6, I Pet. i. 18, I Cor. vi. 20, Gal. iii. 13. Similarly B. F. Westcott ("Hebrews [3]," pp. 298–299), after arguing that the idea of ransom has faded from "λυτροῦσθαι etc." in the LXX and its place has been taken by that of power, is disinclined to confine the expenditure which God makes in the New Testament conception to that of might alone. Love or self-sacrifice, he suggests, may be the thing expended. He therefore remarks that in "the spiritual order" the idea of deliverance must be supplemented by that of purchase; and he adduces the passages in which that is expressed. He concludes with the dictum: "The Christian, it appears, is bought at the price of Christ's Blood for God." Like Ritschl he is only concerned to show that the idea is not intrinsic in the term λυτροῦσθαι (ἀπολύτρωσις): it is a fact that we are bought to God by the blood of Christ, but this fact is not expressed by this term. The ingenuity required to validate this position (see especially Ritschl here) is its sufficient refutation.

The attempts which have been made to construe the terms
derived from λυτροῦσθαι, employed by the writers of the New
Testament [64] of the deliverance wrought by Christ, as inexpressive of their intrinsic implication that the deliverance intimated was in the mode of a ransoming, were foreordained to
failure in the presence of general considerations like this. H.
Oltramare's extended discussion in his comments on Rom. iii.
24 is often referred to as a typical instance of these attempts.[65]
This, however, is rather unfair to them. Oltramare's argument
is vitiated from the beginning by failure to discriminate between the differing usages of the active and middle voices of
the whole series of verbs, λύειν, ἀπολύειν, λυτροῦν, ἀπολυτροῦν
by which the active means "to put to ransom" and the middle
"to ransom." It loses itself speedily accordingly in mere para-
doxes. Of course he cites no passages from the Greek authors
in which any of these terms is employed without intimation of
a ransom-paying: to all appearance such passages do not exist.
He is compelled to rely entirely therefore on the Septuagint
usage of λυτροῦσθαι mechanically treated. He allows, of course,
that λυτροῦσθαι (with which he confounds also λυτροῦν) "signifies properly and etymologically to release, to liberate an object by giving to its holder or to one who has rights in it, a sum
in return for which he desists from his possession, or from
his rights, to *ransom*, to *redeem*." He very strangely, because
it thus signifies "to secure a release by paying a ransom," sets
it in contrast with ἀπολυτροῦν which he represents as meaning
"to put to ransom," without observing that he has thus set the
purely middle use of the one over against the purely active use
of the other. Thus he parcels out between the two verbs the

[64] We remind ourselves that these include a somewhat rare use of λυτροῦσθαι
itself (Luke xxiv. 21; Tit. ii. 14, I Pet. i. 18) and its derivative λύτρωσις (Luke i.
68, ii. 38, Heb. ix. 12), with a relatively large use of ἀπολύτρωσις (Luke xxi. 28;
Rom. iii. 24, viii. 23, I Cor. i. 30; Eph. i. 7, 14; Col. i. 14, Heb. ix. 15, xi. 35). Λυτρωτής
occurs Acts vii. 35, but of Moses, not of Christ. Λύτρον occurs at Mt. xx. 28,
Mark x. 45, and ἀντίλυτρον at I Tim. ii. 6.

[65] E.g. by Sanday-Headlam, on Rom. iii. 24, whose own conclusion is that
"the idea of the λύτρον retains its full force, that it is identical with the τιμή, and
that both are ways of describing the Death of Christ. The emphasis is on the *cost*
of man's redemption."

distinctive usages which obtain between the active and middle of each of them. "'Απολυτρόω," he says, "does not have the sense of the simple verb, 'to ransom' = redimere: we do not know a single example of it. The prefix ἀπό (as in ἀπολύω, ἀφίημι) so emphasizes the idea of liberating, delivering, that in profane authors, ἀπολυτροῦν signifies properly to *release* for a ransom, to hold to ransom." Even this is not all. For he now proceeds to conclude that "ἀπολύτρωσις designates therefore the action of releasing for a demanded ransom." "Its meaning is such," he continues gravely, "that if we absolutely insist on giving to ἀπολύτρωσις the sense of 'deliverance for ransom,' the expression διὰ τῆς ἀπολυτρώσεως τῆς ἐν Χριστῷ 'Ιησοῦ signifies 'by the *release*, the *ransom-taking* which is found in Jesus Christ' — that is to say that Jesus delivers us by demanding a ransom of us, far from by paying it for us." He sees but one way of escape from this conclusion. "Very happily," he concludes, "ἀπολύτρωσις is also used in the sense of *deliverance*, liberation, without any accessory idea of ransoming. All that it seems to have preserved of the radical is that it speaks principally of releasing from that which binds, confines, impedes, or shuts up." He has no evidence to present for this cardinal assertion, however, except the fact that Schleusner cites from the Old Testament the passage "χρόνος τῆς ἀπολυτρώσεως ἦλθε." As we know, this passage comes from Dan. iv. 32 LXX, where the context suggests that the deliverance had been purchased by almsgiving. To it Oltramare can add only certain New Testament passages in which he finds no accessory idea of ransoming notified. This is all quite incompetent.

Th. Zahn's discussion, distributed through his notes on the same passage, is free, of course, from such eccentricities, and constitutes in its several parts a careful presentation of all the evidence which can possibly be brought together for taking ἀπολύτρωσις in Rom. iii. 24 in the undifferentiated sense of deliverance. No evidence, of course, for this sense of the term is adduced from the usage of any derivative of λύτρον by a profane author: and no decisive instance is adduced from any quarter of the use of the term itself in this undifferentiated sense.[66] The force of the argument is dependent wholly on the cumulative effect of the discussion of the several terms λυτ-ροῦσθαι, λύτρωσις, ἀπολυτροῦν, ἀπολύτρωσις successively. In these discussions the more utilizable passages from the Septuagint are skilfully marshalled; certain New Testament passages in which there is no express intimation in the context that the deliverance in question is a ransoming (as if the form of the word itself and its appropriate usage elsewhere counted for nothing!) are added; and a few Patristic passages are subjoined. Despite the thoroughness of the research and the exhaustive adduction of the material, the whole discussion remains unconvincing. The reader rises from it with the conviction that an unnatural meaning is being thrust upon the term on insufficient grounds, and that, after all is said, "redemption" continues to mean redemption.

Much more formidable than either Oltramare's or Zahn's argument is that which is developed with his usual comprehensiveness and vigor by Albrecht Ritschl in the second volume of his great work on "Justification and Reconciliation."[67] Ritschl begins by speaking of the use of λυτροῦν and its derivatives by the Septuagint to render the Hebrew stems נאל and פדה. These stems, he remarks, had originally, like the Greek terms, the sense of delivering specifically by means of purchase. This im-

---

[66] The only vouchers cited (pp. 179–180, note 51) are Rom. viii. 23, Eph. i. 14, iv. 30, and Clem. Alex. "Strom." VII. 56, to which Dan. iv. 30 Theod: ὁ χρόνος τῆς ἀπολυτρώσεως is added p. 179, note 49. Clement, "Strom." VII. 10 (56) looks forward to a time when we shall live "with gods according to the will of God," "after we shall have been redeemed (ἀπολυθέντων) from all chastisement and punishment which we shall have had to endure as salutary chastening in consequence of our sins." "After which redemption (ἀπολύτρωσιν)," he continues, "the rewards and honors are assigned to those who have become perfect, when they have got done with purification, and ceased from all service, though it be holy service, and among saints." They enter into eternal contemplation and receive the name of Gods and live with other Gods who have before been elevated to this condition by the Savior. Here the ἀπολύτρωσις is conceived as a release from punishment and the moment of thought is fixed on the final removal of the soul to its rest. It is an instance of the so-called "eschatological sense" of the term, and "deliverance" would convey the main thought. But it does not follow that the idea of ransoming is eliminated, or that the term ἀπολύτρωσις is not employed because this "deliverance" is felt to rest at bottom on a ransoming.

[67] Edition 3, 1899, pp. 222 ff.

plication of purchase had been lost, however, in usage. Their etymological implication was similarly lost, of course, by the Greek terms which were employed to render them, through an assimilation to the Hebrew terms which they rendered. These Greek terms came to the New Testament writers, therefore, with this broadened sense; and the New Testament writers naturally continued to employ them in it. If they are sometimes used by the New Testament writers in connections in which the original sense of purchasing might seem to be intimated, it is nevertheless not to be assumed that their original sense has reasserted itself. It is more natural to read them in these passages too in the broadened sense in which they have been inherited from the Septuagint. Paul, for example, must be supposed to have had the Hebrew in mind when he cited from the Septuagint, and to have taken from it his religious phraseology. This would hold him, when he used the Greek words, to the sense which they have as renderings of the broadened Hebrew terms. Of course, it may be argued that the Apostolic use of these words is rather controlled by our Lord's declaration that He came into the world to give His life as a ransom for many (Mark x. 45). But there is really no proof that this saying was known to Paul, to say nothing of its having determined the sense in which he employed terms only remotely related to the word used. The impression is left on the mind, rather, that Paul has chosen the compound term ἀπολύτρωσις instead of the simple λύτρωσις of the Septuagint, because by it the idea of separation from, or liberation, is thrown into great emphasis: he wishes, in a word, to say not ransoming but deliverance.

The steps in this argument are the successive assertions that: (1) The Hebrew words נאל and פדה had lost their original connotation of purchase; (2) The Greek words used to translate them must as a consequence have lost theirs; (3) The Septuagint usage of these Greek words must have extended itself into the New Testament; (4) The ordinary usage of these terms in the New Testament is in point of fact of this undifferentiated sort; (5) The instances of their use which do not seem of this sort must be nevertheless interpreted in harmony with this usage.

No one of these propositions is, however, unqualifiedly true. (1) Though the original senses of נאל and פדה — to redeem and to ransom [68] — are sometimes submerged in their figurative use, they are so far from being wholly obliterated that the words are copiously employed quite literally, and it is repeatedly made clear that even in the most extreme extension of their figurative use their etymological significance does not wholly cease to be felt. (2) The Greek terms fitted to these Hebrew terms seem to have been selected to render them because they were their closest Greek representatives in their literal sense. The use of these Greek terms to render the Hebrew is evidence therefore that they retained their fundamental meaning of redemption, ransoming; and though they naturally acquired from the Hebrew terms their figurative meanings when they were used to express them, there is no evidence that they ever really lost their native implications. It is misleading to speak of "the Septuagint usage" of these Greek terms, as if this "extended" usage were the only usage they have in the Septuagint. Λυτροῦσθαι, the most important of the Septuagint terms, is used in twenty-seven out of the one hundred and five instances in which it occurs in its literal sense of ransoming, redeeming; λύτρωσις is used in five out of its eight occurrences in the sense of redemption, ransoming; all the compounds derived from λυτροῦν are used solely in this sense. (3) In point of fact, the New Testament usage is not a "projection" of the Septuagint usage. The terminology of the New Testament is different from that of the Septuagint, and therefore the terminology of the New Testament was very certainly not derived from that of the Septuagint. Are we to suppose that the New Testament writers carried over the senses of the Septuagint terms without carrying over the terms which were the vehicles of those senses? The fundamental assumption, moreover, that the New Testament writers derived their whole phraseology from the Septuagint — Ritschl even speaks of Paul's "Greek

[68] Cf. Driver, on Deut. vii. 8.

speech, formed from the Septuagint" — cannot be justified. The Greek speech of the New Testament writers is the common speech of their day and generation and their terminology more naturally reflects a popular usage of the time. (4) It is not the fact that the ordinary usage of the derivatives of λύτρον in the New Testament is without modal implications. The contextual implications rather show ordinarily that the modal implications are present. (5) There is not only no reason why a broadened sense should be made normative for these derivatives and imposed upon them in defiance of their natural implication to the contrary, but in several instances they are so recalcitrant to it that it cannot be imposed upon them without intolerable violence.

A brief survey of the New Testament passages seems to be desirable in order to justify the last two of these remarks.[69]

Despite Ritschl's protest we must take our starting-point from our Lord's own description of His mission on earth as to give His life a ransom for many (Mt. xx. 28, Mark x. 45). This could not fail to determine for His followers their whole conception of the nature of His redemptive work.[70] We cannot be surprised, therefore, to find one of them, echoing His very words, describing His work as a giving of Himself as a ransom (ἀντίλυτρον) for all (I Tim. ii. 6). Nor can we profess to be doubtful of his meaning when the same writer, writing at nearly the same time, but using now the verbal form, tells us that "our great God and Savior gave Himself for us that He might redeem (λυτροῦσθαι) us from all iniquity and purify unto Himself a people for His own possession, zealous of good works" (Tit. i. 14); or when another of the New Testament writers, closely affiliated with this one, and writing at about the same time, reminds the Christians that they "were redeemed (λυτροῦσθαι), not with corruptible things, with silver or gold, from their vain manner of life handed down from their fathers, but with precious blood, as of a lamb without blemish and without spot,

---

[69] For a fuller discussion of the implications of the New Testament usage, see the Article, "Redemption" in Hastings' "Dictionary of the Apostolic Church."

[70] Cf. A. Deissmann, "Light from the Ancient East," p. 331 and note 6.

even the blood of Christ" (I Pet. i. 18). There is in these passages an express intimation that the deliverance described by the verb λυτροῦσθαι as wrought by our Lord, was wrought in the mode of a ransoming. He gave Himself in working it. He gave His blood, as a lamb's blood is given at the altar. We cannot fail to hear here the echoes of His own declaration, that He came to give His life a ransom for many, or to perceive that the verb λυτροῦσθαι is employed in its native etymological sense of a deliverance by means of a price paid. It is not less clear that the noun λύτρωσις is used in the same natural sense in Heb. ix. 12, where, as in I Pet. i. 18, the blood of Jesus is compared with less precious things — here with the blood of goats and calves — and He is asserted, by means of this His own blood, to have "procured eternal redemption." No subtlety of interpretation can rid such passages of their implication of ransoming.

The specialty of the New Testament usage lies, however, not in these simple forms, but in the large use made of the rare compound substantive, ἀπολύτρωσις. This unusual form occurs seven times in the Epistles of Paul, twice in the Epistle to the Hebrews and once in the Gospel of Luke.[71] The preposition ἀπό ("away from") with which it is compounded, no doubt, calls especial attention to the deliverance wrought by the ransoming intimated; and we are prepared, therefore, to see this form used when the mind is directed rather to the effects than to the process of the ransoming.[72] That does not justify us, however, in supposing the term to declare the effects alone, with a total neglect of the process, namely ransoming, by which they are

[71] "This rare word," exclaims Deissmann (p. 331, note 2) "occurs seven times in St. Paul!"

[72] This is what Chrysostom means, in his comment on Rom. iii. 24, when he says: "And he said not simply, λύτρωσις (ransoming) but ἀπολύτρωσις (ransoming away), so that we come not again into the same bondage." Our ransoming *removed* us from the bondage under which we had suffered so that we were in no danger of falling back into it. Cf., R. C. Trench, "Synonyms of the N. T.," 1871, p. 273; A. Deissmann, "Light from the Ancient East," p. 331, note 3. This is probably also all that Theophylact means when he defines ἀπολύτρωσις as "recall (ἐπανάκλητις) from captivity," not intending to deny that a ransoming is intimated (as Trench and Deissmann suppose) but emphasizing the reference to the effects of the transaction.

attained. In point of fact, in a number of instances the deliverance declared is in one way or another distinctly defined by the context as having been obtained by the payment of a price. Thus, in Heb. ix. 15, we are told that this deliverance was wrought by a death; in Eph. i. 7 by the blood of Christ; in Rom. iii. 24 by His being offered as a propitiatory sacrifice.

The implications of the term being fixed by its usage in such passages, it is necessarily interpreted in accordance with them on the other occasions where it occurs. Some of these are so closely connected with these normative passages, indeed, as to be inevitably carried on with them in the same sense. Thus Eph. i. 14 must be read in connection with Eph. i. 7; and Col. i. 14 but repeats Eph. i. 14 and cannot bear a different meaning. From these passages, however, we learn that the effects of the ransoming intimated by ἀπολύτρωσις stretch into the far future and are not all reaped until the end itself. Thus the key is given us for the understanding of it in its "eschatological" application, as it occurs in Luke xxi. 28, Rom. viii. 33, Eph. iv. 30.[73] In such passages the ultimate effects of the ransoming wrought by Jesus in His death are spoken of, not some new and different deliverance, unconnected with that ransoming or with any ransoming, and most certainly not some ransoming distinct from that. The mind of the writer is on the death of Christ as the procuring cause of the deliverance which he is representing by his employment of this term as obtained only at such a cost.

No doubt there are a couple of passages in which there is

---

[73] Cf. J. B. Lightfoot's comment on Eph. 1. 7: — "The ἀπολύτρωσις may be two-fold: (1) it may be *initial* and *immediate*, the liberation from the consequences of past sin and the inauguration of a new and independent life, as here: so Rom. iii. 24, I Cor. i. 30, Col. i. 14, Heb. ix. 15; or (2) *future* and *final*, the ultimate emancipation from the power of evil in all its forms, as in Luke xxi. 28. . . . Rom. viii. 23; comp. Heb. xi. 35. In the latter sense it is used below, ver. 14, and iv. 30. . . ." The point to be emphasized is that the only difference between these two classes of passages concerns the particular effects of the one "ransoming" by the blood of Christ which are for the moment engaging the mind of the writer as he thinks of what Christ has ransomed us *away from*. There is no specifically "eschatological sense" of ἀπολύτρωσις; there is only an eschatological application of the ransoming which has been wrought by Christ's gift of Himself.

less to go upon. There is nothing in I Cor. i. 30, for example,[74] which would independently fix the sense of the term as there used. But it is unnecessary that there should be, in the presence of so firmly established a significance for it. We must, of course, read it here in accordance with its etymological implications supported by its usage elsewhere: particularly in a writer like Paul whose whole thought of "redemption" is coloured through and through with the blood of Christ.[75] And there is certainly no reason why we should not conceive the deliverance spoken of in Heb. xi. 35 as one to be purchased by some price which the victims were unwilling to pay. That is indeed implied in the declaration that they would not accept deliverance, because they were looking for a better resurrection. Does it not mean that they would not accept deliverance, on the terms, say, apostasy, on which alone it could be had? It is quite clear in sum that ἀπολύτρωσις in the New Testament is conceived, in accordance with its native connotation, and its usage elsewhere, distinctly as a ransoming; and that that implication must be read in it on every occasion of its occurrence.

There remain, to be sure, three or four instances of the occurrence of the simple forms — λυτροῦσθαι Luke xxiv. 21, λύτρωσις Luke i. 68, ii. 38, λυτρωτής Acts vii. 35 — all in writings of Luke — which have the peculiarity of standing on the plane of the Old Testament dispensation, and of being consequently unaffected in their suggestions by the new revelation which had come in the ransoming death of Christ. When Zacharias blessed the Lord, the God of Israel, because in the promise to him of a son, He had "visited and brought redemption for His people" (Luke i. 68); when Anna spoke of God "to all those that were looking for the redemption of Jerusalem" (Luke ii. 38); when the two disciples, on their journey to Emmaus, bewailed to one another the death of Jesus, because they had

---

[74] Cf. Johannes Weiss' comment on this passage.

[75] G. P. Wetter, "Charis," 1913, p. 21, says strikingly: "Something great, something not to be understood, has happened to all men. And this great thing is an act of God, an ἀπολύτρωσις, a ransoming, of course out of the earlier condition of wrath and condemnation, and that means with Paul that it happened on the cross."

hoped that "it was He that should redeem Israel" — it is clear enough that we are still on Old Testament ground. The redemptive "death which Jesus was to accomplish at Jerusalem" is not in sight to illuminate and give precision to the ideas which inform the language. In these passages, belonging to the dawn of the new dispensation, the usage of the Septuagint may not unnaturally be thought to prolong itself. And this point of view may, no doubt, not unnaturally be extended to such a passage as Acts vii. 35, where Moses, thought of as a type of Christ, is called a "redeemer." Even this is not to say, however, that λυτροῦσθαι, λύτρωσις, λυτρωτής stand in these passages wholly without implication of ransoming. As they were written down by Luke, they doubtless were written down with Calvary read into their heart. As they were originally spoken they were doubtless informed with longings which though surer of the deliverance promised than instructed in the precise manner in which it should be wrought, were not without some premonitions, vague and unformed, perhaps, that it would be costly. Those who spoke these words were not mere Jews (as we might say); they were the "quiet in the land" whose hearts were instructed above their fellows. After all, the main fact is that in the Old Testament, and in these few echoes of the Old Testament usage "in the beginnings of the Gospel," before the light of the cross had shined upon the world, the great deliverance which was longed for from God, was spoken of, not in the use of terms which expressed merely deliverance — of which plenty to choose from lay at hand — but in the use of terms which enshrined in their heart the conception of ransoming.

Whatever we may think, however, of these few phrases preserved by Luke from the speech of men still only looking forward to the Gospel, they obviously stand apart from the general New Testament usage. That usage, whether of λυτροῦσθαι (Tit. ii. 14, I Pet. i. 18), λύτρωσις (Heb. ix. 12), or of ἀπολύτρωσις (Luke xxi. Rom. iii. 24, viii. 23, I Cor. i. 30, Eph. i. 7, 14, iv. 30, Col. i. 14, Heb. ix. 15, xi. 35), is very distinctly a usage in which the native sense of this group of words — the express sense of ransoming — is clearly preserved. We shall not do justice to the New Testament use of these terms unless we read them in every instance of their occurrence as intimating that the deliverance which they assert has been accomplished, in accordance with the native sense of the words in which it is expressed, by means of a ransom-paying.

IV

It is not of large importance, but it is not without an interest of its own to observe how this group of terms is used in the earliest Patristic literature. Three currents of inheritance unite here, and the effect is naturally to impart to the resultant usage a certain lack of consistency and sureness. There was the general Greek tradition, which gave to all the members of the group the uniform connotation of ransoming. There was the Septuagint modification of the simple terms, which wrought the more powerfully because the Septuagint supplied a rich body of quotable passages that were everywhere employed as vehicles of Christian faith and hope. And there was the New Testament usage in which the deliverance wrought by Christ is distinctly presented as a ransoming, but in which also a certain tendency is manifested to throw the emphasis on the effects of this ransoming and especially on its ultimate effect in delivering us from the wrath of God at the end-time. We can observe the influence of all these currents at work.

In the first age, to be sure, there is no very copious use made of this group of terms. Only λύτρον, λυτροῦσθαι and λύτρωσις occur, for example, in the Apostolic Fathers; and they only sparingly.

Λύτρον occurs twice and in both instances, of course, in its natural sense of "ransom." "Thou shalt work with thy hands," says Barnabas (xix. 10), commanding diligence in business, "for a ransom for thy sins." And in the Epistle to Diognetus, the greatness and power of God in our salvation is beautifully praised because "in pity He took upon Himself our sins and Himself parted with His own Son as a ransom for us, the holy for the lawless, the guiltless for the evil, the just for the unjust, the incorruptible for the corruptible, the immortal for the mortal."

Λυτροῦσθαι occurs nine times. In some of these occurrences, it has reference to human rather than divine acts. One of these is I Clem. lv. "Many among ourselves have delivered themselves to bondage that they might ransom others." The native notion of ransoming intrinsic to the verb is here expressed very purely. This note is less clearly struck in Hermas, "Mand.," viii. 10. Hermas is giving a catalogue of Christian duties. "Hear now what follow upon these," he says: "To minister to widows, to visit the orphans and the needy, to ransom the servants of God from their afflictions, to be hospitable." And the note of ransoming appears to have sunk into silence in another passage of Hermas ("Vis.," iv. 1, 7). Pursued by a dreadful beast, he says, "And I began to cry and to beseech the Lord that He would deliver me from him." Dependence appears to be put on the might of God.

In none of these instances is there reference to the great normal deliverance which the redemption of God is. This is spoken of, however, in Ignatius' Christ-like prayer for the persecutors of his friends (Phil. ii. 1): "May those who treated them with dishonor be redeemed through the grace of Jesus Christ." And it is spoken of also in Barnabas' exhortation (xix. 2): "Thou shalt glorify Him that redeemed thee from death." Neither passage gives clear intimation of how the redemption spoken of is supposed to be wrought. Nor indeed does the earlier passage in Barnabas (xiv. 4–8) in which, within the space of a few lines, he uses λυτροῦσθαι of the saving work of our Lord no less than four times. We quote Lightfoot's version with its odd variations in the rendering of the term: "Even the Lord Jesus, who was prepared beforehand hereunto, that, appearing in person, He might *redeem* out of darkness our hearts which had already been paid over unto death. . . . For it is written how the Father chargeth Him to *deliver* us from darkness. . . . We perceive, then, whence we are *ransomed*. Again the prophet saith, . . . 'Thus saith the Lord that *ransomed* thee, even God.'" The citation at the end is from Isa.

xlix. 6 ff. where the Septuagint has ὁ ῥυσαμένος. Why Barnabas substitutes ὁ λυτρωσαμένος is a matter of conjecture. Possibly it was inadvertent. Possibly it was due to his having already written λυτροῦσθαι three times, and he adjusts his text to the language of the passage into which he brings it. Possibly he substitutes a term which more exactly describes what Christ actually did — Christianizes Isaiah's language, in a word. In the only remaining passage in which λυτροῦσθαι occurs in the Apostolic Fathers, II Clem. xvii. 4, it is used in the so-called "eschatological sense," illustrated in the New Testament by Luke xxi. 28, Rom. viii. 23, Eph. i. 14, iv. 30, Col. i. 14: "The Lord said, 'I will come to gather together all the peoples, tribes and tongues.' And He means by this the day of His epiphany, when, coming, He shall redeem us, each according to his works."

The only other form which occurs in the Apostolic Fathers is λύτρωσις and it occurs only twice (I Clem. xii. 7, Did. iv. 6, cf. Barn. xix. 10 as v.r. for λύτρον). In Did. iv. 6, the Christians are being exhorted to almsgiving, and quite after the Jewish fashion (cf. Dan. iv. 24 Theod.) the exhortation takes the form: "If thou hast aught passing through thy hands, thou shalt give a ransom for thy sins." Almsgiving is a means of securing deliverance: it is the purchase-price paid for immunity from deserved punishment. In I Clem. xii. 7, the scarlet thread which Rahab hung out of the window is declared to have showed beforehand that "through the blood of the Lord there shall be redemption unto all them that believe and hope in God." Here also the sense is distinctly that of ransoming, and the price paid for redemption is noted as Christ's blood.

This is rather a meagre showing for the currency of the language of redemption in the first age of the Church. The Apostolic Fathers are notable, however, for poverty of doctrinal content: perhaps it is only natural that this doctrine too finds only occasional allusion in them. We receive no impression that λυτροῦσθαι and its derivatives are employed as technical terms, as established vehicles of a definite doctrine. They appear to be cursorily used in the several senses and applications in which they would naturally suggest themselves to writers

of the varied inheritance of these first Christians. The term
which comes nearest to a technical term in the New Testament
— Paul's ἀπολύτρωσις — does not occur here at all. And the
terms that do occur are dealt with freely and librate in their
suggestion between the two extremes of a strict ransoming and
an undifferentiated deliverance — with the balance falling, as
was natural, in the direction of the stricter signification.

When we advance to the next age — the age of the Apologists — we meet with similar phenomena, though for a different reason. Apologies are no more natural receptacles of
doctrinal terms than practical letters. No single term of our
group of words occurs in a single Apology of this epoch. The
whole period would be barren of these terms were it not that
the Dialogue between Justin and Trypho happens to have been
written in it. It this Dialogue, λυτροῦσθαι appears seven times,
and λύτρωσις, λυτρωτής and ἀπολύτρωσις each once. Here it will
be observed, first in Christian literature, is our Lord called
"Redeemer" (λυτρωτής). And here first in uninspired Christian
literature does Paul's ἀπολύτρωσις reappear — and it does not
appear here of Christ's redemption of His people to which usage Paul had consecrated it, but only of the redemption of
Israel through Moses.

It is clear that the mind of this writer is not on these terms
as technical terms for the Christian salvation, described in its
mode. Of the ten passages in which they occur six are citations
from the Old Testament: xix. 6 (Ez. xx. 12, 20), "That ye may
know that I am God who redeemed you" (LXX: "who sancti-
fieth you"); xxvi. 3 (Isa. lxii. 12), "And he shall call it a holy
nation, redeemed by the Lord"; xxxiv. 5 (Ps. lxxii. 14); "He
shall redeem their souls from usury and injustice"; cxix. 3 (Isa.
lxii. 12), "And they shall call them the holy people, redeemed
of the Lord"; xxvi. 4 (Isa. lxiii. 4), "For the day of retribution
has come upon them, and the year of redemption (λύτρωσις) is
present"; xxx. 3 (Ps. xviii. (xix.) 15), "For we call him Helper
and Redeemer (λυτρωτής)." In two more of them the allusion
is not to the Christian redemption but to the Deliverance of
Israel from Egypt: cxxxi. 3, "Ye who were redeemed from

Egypt with a high hand and a visitation of great glory, when
the sea was parted for you"; lxxxvi. 1, "Moses was sent with
a rod to effect the redemption (ἀπολύτρωσις) of the people; and
with this in his hands at the head of the people he divided the
sea."

Only two passages remain in which Justin uses λυτροῦσθαι
at his own instance of the Christian redemption.

The first of these is lxxxiii. 3. Here Justin is commenting on
the Jewish attempt to interpret Ps. cx. 1 ff. of Hezekiah: "The
Lord saith to my Lord, Sit at my right hand, till I make thine
enemies my footstool. He shall send forth a rod of power over
Jerusalem, and it shall rule in the midst of thine enemies. In
the splendor of the saints before the morning star have I begotten thee. The Lord hath sworn and will not repent, Thou art
a priest forever after the order of Melchizedek." He asks scorn-
fully, "Who does not admit then, that Hezekiah is no priest
after the order of Melchizedek? And who does not know that
he is not the redeemer (λυτρούμενος) of Jerusalem? And who does
not know that he neither sent a rod of power over Jerusalem,
nor ruled in the midst of her enemies; but that it was God who
averted from him the enemies after he mourned and was
afflicted? But our Jesus. . . ." The reference to Jesus here is
only indirect and the exact nature of the redemption spoken
of is not clear.

The other passage, lxxxvi. 6, is clearer. It runs: "Our Christ
by being crucified on the tree, and by purifying us with water,
has redeemed us, though plunged in the direst offences which
we have committed, and has made us a house of prayer and
adoration." Here it is from sin that we are said to have been
redeemed, both from its guilt and from its pollution. The redeeming act is seen in the crucifixion; while the cleansing by
baptism is associated with that as co-cause of the effect. The
whole process of salvation is thus included in what is called
redemption; the impetration and application of salvation alike.
There is a price paid; and there is a work wrought. So broadly
does Justin conceive of the scope of λυτροῦσθαι.

We need not pursue the matter further. With Justin we are

already a hundred years later than the New Testament usage. We perceive that, under the varied influences moulding its usage, the idea of redemption in the early fathers is at once very deep and very broad. It has not lost the implication of ransoming with which it began, but it embraces the whole process of salvation, which, beginning with our ransoming by the precious blood of Jesus, proceeds with our purification from sin, to end only with our deliverance from the final destruction and our ushering into the eternal glory. The breadth of the reference is interestingly illustrated in the opening words of the beautiful letter of the Churches of Lyons and Vienne in Gaul. It is the New Testament word ἀπολύτρωσις which is used here. "The servants of Christ residing at Vienne and Lyons in Gaul," the letter begins, "to the brethren throughout Asia and Phrygia who hold with us the same faith and hope of redemption, peace and grace and glory from God the Father and Christ Jesus our Lord." [76] "Who have the same faith and hope in the redemption that we have" — οἱ αὐτὴν τῆς ἀπολυτρώσεως ἡμῖν πίστιν καὶ ἐλπίδα ἔχοντες.

Adolf Harnack [77] warns us against supposing that the terms σωτηρία, ἀπολύτρωσις and the like refer always — or regularly — to deliverance from sin. "In the superscription of the Epistle from Lyons, for example," he says, "it is manifestly the future redemption that is to be understood by ἀπολύτρωσις." Harnack's fault lies in introducing an illicit alternative. It is not a matter of *either* the redemption from sin *or* the future deliverance from wrath. Both are embraced. The writers of the letter speak not only of the common hope of redemption, but before that of the common faith in redemption: "to all that have the same *faith and hope* in redemption that we have." It is a redemption that has taken place in the past and that extends in its effects into the farthest future, of which they speak.

It was just this comprehensiveness of redemption, meeting all our needs here and hereafter, that filled the hearts of the fathers with adoring gratitude. They did not think of eliminat-

[76] Eusebius, H. E., V. 1. 3.
[77] "History of Dogma," E. T., i. p. 202 note (German ed., i. p. 145 note).

ing the fundamental ransoming in which it consisted on the one side, because their outlook on its effects extended on the other to the final deliverance from the wrath of God. There is therefore a marked tendency among the fathers to speak of Christ's work as double, past and future. Christ came, says Origen,[78] "in order that λυτρωθῶμεν καὶ ῥυσθῶμεν from the enemy" — not for the one or the other, but for both. "Christ endured death for our sakes," says Eusebius,[79] "giving Himself as a λύτρον καὶ ἀντίψυχον for those who are to be saved by Him." He died as a ransom certainly: but the salvation purchased by this ransom-price works itself out steadily in its successive stages unto the very end. This is the key to the "broad" use of λυτροῦσθαι and its derivatives of the redemption that is in Christ Jesus.[80]

[78] "Hom. XIV on Jer.," Ed. Klostermann, III. 116.1.
[79] Fragment on "The Theophany," Migne, xxiv. 633 B.
[80] We have no concern here with the Patristic doctrine of the ransoming from Satan; see J. Wirtz, "Die Lehre von der Apolytrosis," 1906, on the early history of that.

X

"REDEEMER" AND "REDEMPTION"

"REDEEMER" AND "REDEMPTION" [1]

There is no one of the titles of Christ which is more precious
to Christian hearts than "Redeemer." There are others, it is
true, which are more often on the lips of Christians. The acknowledgment of our submission to Christ as our Lord, the
recognition of what we owe to Him as our Saviour, — these
things, naturally, are most frequently expressed in the names
we call Him by. "Redeemer," however, is a title of more intimate revelation than either "Lord" or "Saviour." It gives
expression not merely to our sense that we have received salvation from Him, but also to our appreciation of what it cost
Him to procure this salvation for us. It is the name specifically
of the Christ of the cross. Whenever we pronounce it, the cross
is placarded before our eyes and our hearts are filled with loving remembrance not only that Christ has given us salvation,
but that He paid a mighty price for it.

It is a name, therefore, which is charged with deep emotion,
and is to be found particularly in the language of devotion.
Christian song is vocal with it. How it appears in Christian
song, we may see at once from old William Dunbar's invocation,
"My King, my Lord, and my Redeemer sweit." Or even from
Shakespeare's description of a lost loved-one as "The precious
image of our dear Redeemer." Or from Christina Rossetti's,

> "Up Thy Hill of Sorrows
> Thou all alone,
> Jesus, man's Redeemer,
> Climbing to a Throne."

Best of all perhaps from Henry Vaughan's ode which he in-
scribes "To my most merciful, my most loving, and dearly-

[1] From *The Princeton Theological Review*, vol. xiv, 1916, pp. 177–201. Opening
Address, delivered in Miller Chapel, Princeton Theological Seminary, September
17, 1915. Some references and explanatory notes have been added.

loved REDEEMER; the ever blessed, the only HOLY and JUST
ONE, JESUS CHRIST, *The Son of the living God, and the Sacred
Virgin Mary,*" and in which he sings to

"My dear Redeemer, the world's light,
    And life too, and my heart's delight."

Terms of affection gather to it. Look into your hymns. Fully
eight and twenty of those in our own "Hymnal" celebrate our
Lord under the name of "Redeemer." [2]

Let our whole soul an offering be
    To our Redeemer's Name;
While we pray for pardoning grace,
    Through our Redeemer's Name;
Almighty Son, Incarnate Word,
    Our Prophet, Priest, Redeemer, Lord;
To that dear Redeemer's praise
    Who the covenant sealed with blood;
O for a thousand tongues to sing
    My dear Redeemer's praise;
To our Redeemer's glorious Name
    Awake the sacred song;
Intercessor, Friend of sinners,
    Earth's Redeemer, plead for me;
All hail, Redeemer, hail,
    For Thou hast died for me;
Let us learn the wondrous story
    Of our great Redeemer's birth;
Guide where our infant Redeemer is laid;
    My dear Redeemer and my Lord;
All glory, laud and honor
    To Thee Redeemer, King;
Your Redeemer's conflict see;

---

[2] The references are (by Hymns and Verses): 52. 3; 54. 2; 59. 2; 73. 3; 147. 1;
148. 1; 150. 3; 162. 4; 172. 6; 190. 1,5; 197. 1; 216. 1; 218. 1; 239. 3; 276. 1; 293. 3;
300. 1; 311.2; 331. 3; 401. 4; 445. 3; 454. 3; 476. 5; 555. 1; 569. 3; 593. 2; 649. 2;
651. 1.

Maker and Redeemer,
   Life and Health of all;
Our blest Redeemer, ere He breathed
   His tender, last farewell;
Here the Redeemer's welcome voice
   Spreads heavenly peace around;
The church our blest Redeemer saved
   With His own precious blood;
The slain, the risen Son,
   Redeemer, Lord alone;
The path our dear Redeemer trod
   May we, rejoicing, tread;
Till o'er our ransomed nature
   The Lamb for sinners slain,
Redeemer, King, Creator,
   In bliss returns to reign;
O the sweet wonders of that cross
   Where my Redeemer loved and died;
Once, the world's Redeemer, dying,
   Bore our sins upon the Tree;
Redeemer, come: I open wide
   My heart to thee;
I know that my Redeemer lives;
For, every good
   In the Redeemer came;
A heart resigned, submissive, meek,
   My great Redeemer's throne;
Jesus, merciful Redeemer;
Father, and Redeemer, hear.

From our earliest childhood the preciousness of this title has been impressed upon us. In "The Shorter Catechism," as the most precise and significant designation of Christ, from the point of view of what He has done for us, it takes the place of the more usual "Saviour," which never occurs in that document. Thus there is permanently imprinted on the hearts of us all, the great fact that "the only Redeemer of God's elect is the

Lord Jesus Christ"; through whom, in the execution of His offices of a Prophet, of a Priest, and of a King, God delivers us out of the estate of sin and misery and brings us into an estate of salvation.[3] The same service is performed for our sister, Episcopalian, communion by its "Book of Common Prayer." The title "Redeemer" is applied in it to Christ about a dozen times:[4]

> O God the Son, Redeemer of the world;
> Our blessed Saviour and Redeemer;
> Joyfully receive Him for our Redeemer;
> Jesus Christ, our Mediator and Redeemer;
> The merits of our Saviour and Redeemer;
> O Lord, our Saviour and Redeemer;
> Jesus Christ, our only Saviour and Redeemer;
> Our Redeemer and the author of everlasting life;
> Our Redeemer and the author of everlasting life;
> O Lord our strength and our Redeemer;
> Only Mediator and Redeemer.

This constant pregnant use of the title "Redeemer" to express our sense of what we owe to Christ, has prevailed in the Church for, say, a millennium and a half. It comes with a little shock of surprise to learn that it has not always prevailed. In the first age of the Church, however, the usage had not become so characteristic of Christians as to stamp itself upon their literary remains. So far as appears, the first occurrence of the epithet "Redeemer" as applied to Christ in extant Christian literature is in Justin Martyr's "Dialogue with Trypho the Jew," which was written about the middle of the second century.[5] And it does not seem to occur frequently for a couple of centuries more. This is not to say that it was not in use among

---

[3] Questions, 20 and 21.

[4] According to the concordance of the (American) "Book of Common Prayer," published by the Rev. J. Courtney Jones, 1898. The actual number, as will be seen, is eleven.

[5] "Dial.," 30. 3: "For we call Him Helper (Βοηθόν) and Redeemer (Λυτρωτήν), the power of whose name even the Demons do fear"; cf. 83.3 Justin is applying to Christ the language of Ps. xviii. 14 (LXX: E. V. xix. 14). Λυτρωτής occurs in the LXX only at Ps. xviii. 14 and Ps. lxxvii. (lxxviii) 35.

Christians during this early period. When Eusebius opens the
tenth Book of his "Church History" with the words, "Thanks
for all things be given unto God the omnipotent Ruler and King
of the universe, and the greatest thanks to Jesus Christ, the
Saviour and Redeemer of our souls," it is quite clear that he is
not describing Christ by an unwonted name. Even more clear
is it that Justin is not inventing a new name for Christ when he
tells Trypho that Christians depend upon Jesus Christ to preserve them from the demons which they had served in the time
of their heathenism, "for we call Him Helper and Redeemer,
the power of whose name even the demons do fear." Indeed, he
explicitly tells us that the Christians were accustomed to employ this name of Christ: "*we call Him Redeemer*" he says.
Nevertheless it seems hardly likely that so little trace of the
use of this designation would have been left in the extant literature of the day, if it had occupied then quite the place it has
occupied in later ages. This applies also to the New Testament.
For, despite the prominence in the New Testament of the idea
of redemption wrought by Christ, the designation "Redeemer"
is not once applied to Christ in the New Testament. The word
"Redeemer" occurs, indeed, only a single time in the New
Testament, and then as a title of Moses, not of Christ, — although it is applied to Moses only as a type of Christ and presupposes its employment of Christ.[6]

The comparative rarity of the use of this title of Christ in
the first age of the Church is probably due, in part at least, to
the intense concreteness of the Greek term ($\Lambda\upsilon\tau\rho\omega\tau\dot{\eta}s$) which
our "Redeemer" represents, and the definiteness with which
it imputes a particular function to our Lord, as Saviour. This
gave it a sharply analytical character, which, perhaps, militated
against its adoption into wide devotional use until the analytical edges had been softened a little by habit. A parallel may
perhaps be found in the prevalence in the New Testament of
the locution, "He died in our behalf" over the more analyti-

[6] Acts vii. 35; cf. H. A. W. Meyer and J. A. Alexander *in loc*. Christ is called
"Deliverer" only once in the New Testament (Rom. xi. 26) and then by an
adaptation of an Old Testament passage.

cally exact, "He died in our stead." The latter occurs; occurs frequently enough to show that it expresses the fact as it lay in the minds of the New Testament writers. But these writers expressed themselves instinctively rather in the former mode because it was a more direct expression of the sense of benefit received, which was the overpowering sentiment which filled their hearts. That Christ died instead of them was the exact truth, analytically stated; that He died for their sake was the broad fact which suffused their hearts with loving emotion.

The word "Redeemer" is of course of Latin origin, and we owe it, together with its cognates "redemption," "redeem," "redeemed," to the nomenclature of Latin theology, and ultimately to the Latin Bible. These Latin words, however, do not, at their best, exactly reproduce the group of Greek words which they represent in the New Testament, although they are underlaid by the same fundamental idea of purchase. Etymologically, redimo, 'redeem,' means to buy back, while the Greek term which it renders in the New Testament (λυτροῦσθαι) means rather to buy out, or, to employ its exact equivalent, to ransom. Our English word "ransom" is, of course, philologically speaking, only a doublet of "redemption." But, in losing the significant form of that word, it has more completely than that word lost also the suggestion that the purchase which it intimates is a re-purchase. It might have been better, therefore, if, instead of "redemption," "to redeem," "redeemed," "redeemer," we had employed as the representatives of the Greek terms (λυτροῦσθαι, λύτρωσις, ἀπολύτρωσις, λυτρωτής) "ransom," "to ransom," "ransomed," "ransomer."

Of these, only the noun, "ransom" has actually a place in the English New Testament, — in the great passage in which our Lord Himself declares that He "came, not to be ministered unto but to minister, and to give His life a ransom for many" (Mt. xx. 28 = Mk. x. 45), and in its echo in the scarcely less great declaration of Paul that the one mediator between God and men, Himself man, Christ Jesus, "gave Himself a ransom for all" (I Tim. ii. 6). Nevertheless these terms, emphatically defining, like the Greek terms which they represent, the work of Christ in terms of ransoming, have made a place for themselves in the language of Christian devotion only a little inferior to that of those which somewhat less exactly define it in terms of redeeming. The noun of agent, "Ransomer," is used, it is true, comparatively rarely; although its use, as a designation of Christ, seems actually to have preceded in English literature that of "Redeemer," or even of its forerunner, the now obsolete "Redemptor." The earliest citation for "Redeemer" given by the "Oxford Dictionary," at all events, comes from the middle of the fifteenth century [7] — of "Redemptor" from the late fourteenth [8] — while "Ransomer" is cited from the "Cursor Mundi," some half a century earlier: "Christ and king and ranscorner . . ." "Ransomer" is found side by side with "Redeemer" in William Dunbar's verses at the opening of the sixteenth century: "Thy Ransonner with woundis fyve"; and is placed literally by its side by John Foxe in the "Book of Martyrs" in the middle of that century, apparently as more closely defining the nature of the saving act of Him whom Foxe calls "the onlie sauior, redeemer and raunsomer of them which were lost in Adam our forefather."

The other forms have, however, been more widely used in all ages of English literature. The character of their earlier use may be illustrated again from William Dunbar who tells us that "the heaven's king is clad in our nature, Us from the death with ransom to redress"; or from a couple of very similar instances from even earlier verses. In one, Christ is described as Him "that deyid up on the rood, To raunsoun synfull creature." [9] In the other He is made Himself to say

> "Vpon a crosse nayled I was for the,
> Soffred deth to pay the rawnison." [10]

Milton, our theological poet by way of eminence, not only speaks of Christ as, in rising, raising with Himself, "His breth-

---

[7] "1432–1450, tr. *Higden* (Rolls) viii, 201: 'A man . . . havynge woundes in his body lyke to the woundes of Criste, seyenge that he was redemer of man.'"

[8] "1377, Langland: 'And after his resurrecioun Redemptor was his name.'"

[9] "Oxford Dictionary," *sub voc.*: "1414, Brampton, *Penit. Ps.* (Percy Society), 28."   [10] "Political Poems," etc. (ed. Furnivale), p. 111.

ren, ransom'd with His own dear life," but discriminatingly
describes Him as "man's friend, his mediator, his design'd
both ransom and redeemer voluntarie." "We learn with wonder," says Cowper, almost in Milton's manner, "how this world
began, who made, who marr'd, and who has ransom'd man."
Or, coming at once to our own days Tennyson can put upon the
lips of a penitent sinner, the desire to minister (as he expresses
it) "to poor sick people, richer in His eyes who ransom'd us,
and haler too, than I." Let us appeal, however, again to our
hymns.

Surprisingly few instances appear, in the hymns gathered in
our own "Hymnal" at least, of the use of the noun "ransom,"
for which direct warrant is given in the text of our English
New Testament. Only, it appears, these three: [11]

> Father of heaven, whose love profound
> A ransom for our souls hath found;
> I'd sing the precious blood He spilt
> My ransom from the dreadful guilt
> Of sin and wrath divine;
> Jesus, all our ransom paid,
> All Thy Father's will obeyed,
> Hear us, Holy Jesus.

But as over against the dozen times that the word "redeemed"
occurs [12] in this "Hymnal" we have counted no fewer than
twenty-two times in which the word "ransomed" occurs. In a
couple of these instances, the two words stand together: [13]

> He crowns thy life with love,
> When ransomed from the grave;
> He that redeemed my soul from hell,
> Hath sovereign power to save.

[11] 59. 1; 159. 2; 227. vi, 1. The verb "ransom," of course, also occurs (e. g.
141. 6); see below, note 14, for the form "ransomed."

[12] Redeemed, 55. 5; 88. 2; 130. 4; 150. 4; 172. 3; 236. 4; 336. 1; 383. 5; 396. 2;
453. 5; 546. 1; 642. 1. Consult, however, the following also: Redeeming, 81.1;
179. 3; 223. 5; 332. 2; 402. 2; 441. 4; 470. 2; 609. 1; Redemption, 141. 4; 152. 2;
258. 4; 259. 1; 264. 1; 265. 4; 394. 1; 395. 1; 406. 2; 435. 4.

[13] 130. 4; 453. 5.

And when, redeemed from sin and hell,
With all the ransomed throng I dwell.

The others run as follows:[14]

Then be His love in Christ proclaimed
    With all our ransomed powers;
Ransomed, healed, restored, forgiven,
    Who like me His praise should sing;
Sing on your heavenly way,
    Ye ransomed sinners, sing;
Ye ransomed from the fall,
    Hail Him who saves you by His grace;
Bring our ransomed souls at last
    Where they need no star to guide;
One, the light of God's own presence
    O'er His ransomed people shed;
A wretched sinner, lost to God,
    But ransomed by Emanuel's blood;
Thy ransomed host in glory;
My ransomed soul shall be
    Through all eternity
        Offered to thee;
Our ransomed spirits rise to Thee;
Let none whom He hath ransomed fail to greet Him;
    When we, a ransomed nation,
        Thy scepter shall obey;
Till o'er our ransomed nature
    The Lamb for sinners slain,
Redeemer, King, Creator,
    In bliss returns to reign;
Till all the ransomed number
    Fall down before the throne;
Blessed are the sons of God,
They are bought with Christ's own blood,
They are ransomed from the grave;

[14] 132. 4; 134. 1; 154. 4; 157. 4; 189. 4; 303. 2; 325. 2; 354. 4; 375. 4; 390. 4; 395. 5; 399. 2; 401. 4; 420. 3; 421. 1; 441. 3; 444. 1; 512. 2; 636. 4.

Till all the ransomed church of God
   Be saved to sin no more;
Thy blood, O Lord, was shed
   That I might ransomed be;
Where streams of living water flow
   My ransomed soul He leadeth;
His laud and benediction
   Thy ransomed people raise.

It does not appear, then, that Christian emotion would have found any more difficulty in gathering about the term "ransom" and its derivatives, and consecrating them as the channel of its expression, than it has found in gathering around and consecrating "redeem" and its derivatives. Had these terms taken their proper place in our English New Testament as the exact renderings of the Greek terms now less precisely rendered by "redeem" and its derivatives, and had they from the English New Testament entered into our familiar Christian speech, there is no reason to doubt that "Christ our Ransomer" would now be as precious to the Christian heart as "Christ our Redeemer" is. There is certainly no one who will not judge with old John Brown that "a Ransomer," especially one who has ransomed us "at such a rate," "will be most tender" of His ransomed ones;[15] and His ransomed ones, realizing what His ransoming of them involved, may be trusted — if we may take the language of our hymns as indications — to speak of Him with the deepest gratitude and love. Nor should we consider it a small gain that then the sense of the New Testament representations would have been conveyed to us more precisely and with their shades of meaning and stresses of emphasis more clearly and sharply presented. After all is said, the New Testament does not set forth the saving work of Christ as a redemption, but as a ransoming; and does not present Him to us therefore so much as our Redeemer as our Ransomer; and

[15] John Brown, "Life of Faith in Time of Trial and Affliction," etc., 1678 (ed. 1726, p. 161; ed. 1824, p. 129): "And sure a Ransomer who hath purchased many persons to himself, at such a Rate, will be most tender of them, and will not take it well, that any wrong them."

it is a pity that we have been diverted by the channels through which we have historically received our religious phraseology from the adoption and use in our familiar speech of the more exact terminology.

One of the gains which would have accrued to us had this more exact terminology become our current mode of speech concerning our Lord's saving action, is that we should then have been measurably preserved from a danger which has accompanied the use of "redeem" and its derivatives to describe it — a danger which has nowadays become very acute — of dissipating in our thought of it all that is distinctive in our Lord's saving action. We are not saying, of course, that "ransom," any more than other terms, is immune from that disease of language by which, in the widening application of terms, they suffer a progressive loss of their distinctive meaning. But "ransom" has, in point of fact, retained with very great constancy its intrinsic connotation of purchase. It may possibly be that, in an extreme extension of its application, it is occasionally employed in the loose sense of merely "to rescue." The "Standard Dictionary" gives that as one of its definitions, marking it as "archaic"; though the "Oxford Dictionary" supplies no citations supporting it. At all events, the word does not readily lend itself to evacuating extensions of application; and when we say "to ransom" our minds naturally fix themselves on a price paid as the means of the deliverance intimated. The word is essentially a modal word; it emphasizes the means by which the effect it intimates is accomplished, and does not exhaust itself merely in declaring the effect. The same, of course, may be said in principle of "redeem." But this word has suffered far more from attrition of meaning than "ransom," and indeed had already lost the power inevitably to suggest purchase before it was adopted into specifically Christian use. We shall not forget, of course, what we have just noted, that "ransom" and "redeem" are at bottom one word; that they are merely two English forms of the Latin *redimo*. It is, no doubt, inexact, therefore, to speak of the usage of the Latin *redimo* and its derivatives as if it belonged to the early history of "redeem" more than to that of "ransom." Nevertheless it is convenient and not really misleading to do so, when we have particularly in mind the use of the two words in Christian devotional speech. "To redeem" has come into our English New Testament and our English religious usage in direct and continuous descent from its previous usage in Latin religious speech and the Latin Bible; while "to ransom" has come in from without, bringing with it its own set of implications, fixed through a separate history. And what needs to be said is that "to ransom" has quite firmly retained its fixed sense of securing a release by the payment of a price, while "to redeem" had already largely lost this sense when it was first applied in the Latin New Testament to render Greek terms, the very soul of which was this intimation of the payment of a price, and needed to reacquire this emphasis through the influence of these terms shining through it; and that it moreover continues to be employed in general usage today in very wide and undistinctive senses which naturally react more or less injuriously upon the particular meaning which it is employed in Christian usage to convey.[16]

The Latin verb *redimo* already in its classical usage was employed not only, in accordance with its composition, in the sense of "to buy back," and not merely more broadly in the sense of "to buy," — whether to "buy off" or "to buy up"; but, also in more extended applications still, in the senses simply of "to release" or "rescue," "to acquire" or "obtain," or even "to obviate" or "avert." It had acquired, indeed, a special sense of "to undertake," "to contract," "to hire" or "to farm." In accordance with this special sense, its derivative, *redemptor*, in all periods of the language, was used, as the synonym of the less common *conductor*, of a contractor, undertaker, purveyor, farmer, — as when Cicero speaks of the *redemptor* who had contracted to build a certain column, or Pliny of the *redemptor* who farmed the tolls of a bridge. When Christ was

---

[16] When R. C. Trench, "The Study of Words," ed. 15, 1874, p. 312, counsels the school-teacher to insist both on the idea of *purchase*, and on that of purchasing *back*, in all usages of Redemption, he is indulging in an etymological purism which the general use of the word will not sustain.

called the *Redemptor*, then, there was some danger that the
notion conveyed to Latin ears might be nearer that which is
conveyed to us by a Sponsor or a Surety (the seventeenth
century divines spoke freely of Christ as our "Undertaker")
than that of a Ransomer; and this danger was obviated only
by the implication of the Greek terms which this and its companion Latin terms represented and by which, and the contexts
natural to them, they were held to their more native significance, not, indeed, of buying back, but of buying off. The persistence of the secular use of these terms, parallel with the
religious, but with a more or less complete neglect of their original implication of purchase — through the whole period of their
use in Latin, and later of the use of their descendants in English — has constituted a perpetual danger that they would, by
assimilation, lose their specific implication of purchase in their
religious usage also. Obviously in these circumstances they cannot throw up an effective barrier against the elimination from
them of the idea of purchase even in their religious applications,
on the setting in of any strong current of thought and feeling in
that direction. Men who have ceased to think of the work of
Christ in terms of purchasing, and to whom the whole conception of His giving His life for us as a ransom, or of His pouring
out His blood as a price paid for our sins, has become abhorrent,
feel little difficulty, therefore, in still speaking of Him as our
Redeemer, and of His work as a Redemption, and of the Christianity which He founded as a Redemptive Religion. The ideas
connected with purchase are not so inseparably attached to
these terms in their instinctive thought that the linguistic feeling is intolerably shocked by the employment of them with no
implication of this set of ideas. Such an evacuation of these
great words, the vehicles thus far of the fundamental Christian
confession, of their whole content as such, is now actually going
on about us. And the time may be looked forward to in the
near future when the words "Redeemer" "redemption" "redeem" shall have ceased altogether to convey the ideas which
it has been thus far their whole function in our religious terminology to convey.

What has thus been going on among us has been going on at a much more rapid pace in Germany, and the process has reached a much more advanced stage there than here. German speech was much less strongly fortified against it than ours. It has been the misfortune of the religious terminology of Germany, that the words employed by it to represent the great ransoming language of the New Testament are wholly without native implication of purchase. Redeem, redemption, Redeemer, at least in their fundamental etymological suggestion, say purchase as emphatically as the Greek terms, built up around the notion of ransom, which they represent; and they preserve this implication in a large section of their usage. The German *erlösen*, *Erlösung*, *Erlöser*, on the contrary, contain no native suggestion of purchase whatever; and are without any large secular usage in which such an implication is distinctly conveyed.[17] They mean in themselves just deliver, deliverance, Deliverer, and they are employed nowhere, apart from their religious application, with any constant involvement of the mode in which the deliverance is effected. One of their characteristic usages, we are told by Jacob Grimm, is as the standing expression in the *Märchen* for the act of disenchanting (equivalent to *entzaubern*); in such phrases, for example, as "the princess is now *erlöst*," "the serpent can be *erlöst* by a kiss," "at twelve o'clock they were all *erlöst*."[18] If you will turn over the pages of the brother Grimm's "Kinder-

---

[17] Kluge, in his etymological dictionary of the German language, under "er-," tells us it is the new-high-German equivalent of the old-high-German "ir-," "ar-," "ur-," and refers us to the emphasized "ur-" for information. Under that form, he tells us that "er-" is the unemphasized form of the prefix, and adds: "The prefix means *aus*, *ursprünglich*, *anfänglich*." Thus it appears that *erlösen* is a weaker way of saying *auslösen;* and the usage bears that out, *auslösen* tending to suggest "extirpation," *erlösen*, "deliverance." By this feeling, apparently, G. Hollmann, "Die Bedeutung des Todes Jesu," 1901, pp. 108–109, is led to parallel *Auslösung* with *Loskaufung* as strong terms in contrast with *Erlösung* paralleled with *Befreiung*. The Greek equivalents of *erlösen* and *auslösen* are ἀπολύειν and ἐκλύειν, both of which are found in the New Testament, but elsewhere in senses more significant for our purposes. In the Iliad ἀπολύειν (like the simple λύειν) bears even the acquired sense of "to ransom." It is interesting to note that in Job xix. 25, for "my Redeemer" (גֹּאֲלִי), the LXX reads ὁ ἐκλύειν με.

[18] "Deutsches Wörterbuch," iii, 1862, *sub voc.*

und Haus-Märchen," you will come about the middle of the
book upon the tale of "The King of the Golden Mountain,"
and may read in it of how a young merchant's son comes one day
to a magnificent castle and finds in it nothing but a serpent.
"The serpent, however," we read on, "was a bewitched maiden,
who rejoiced when she saw him and said to him, 'Art thou
come, my *Erlöser?* I have already waited twelve years for thee,
this kingdom is bewitched and thou must *erlösen* it.'" A still
more instructive passage may be met with a few pages earlier, in
the tale of "The Lark." There, when the traveller found himself in the clutches of a lion, he begged to be permitted to ransom (*loskaufen*) himself with a great sum, and so to save (*retten*)
himself; but the lion himself, who was, of course, an enchanted
prince, was — at the proper time and by the proper means —
neither ransomed nor saved, but simply *erlöst. Erlösen, Erlösung, Erlöser* of themselves awaken in the consciousness of
the hearer no other idea than that of deliverance; and although,
in religious language, they may have acquired suggestions of
purchase by association — through their employment as the
representatives of the Greek terms of ransoming and the contexts of thought into which they have thus been brought, —
these do not belong to them intrinsically and fall away at
once when external supports are removed.

We cannot feel surprise accordingly, when we meet in recent German theological discussion — as we repeatedly do —
an express distinction drawn between *Loskaufung,* "ransoming," as a narrow term intimating the manner in which a given
deliverance is effected, and *Erlösung,* "deliverance," as a broad
term, declaring merely the fact of deliverance, with no intimation whatever of the mode by which it is effected. Thus, for
example, Paul Ewald commenting on Eph. i. 7, remarks [19]
that there is no reason why ἀπολύτρωσις should be taken there
as meaning, "ransoming" (*Loskaufung*), rather than "in the
more general sense of *Erlösung,*" that is to say, of "deliver-

[19] "Kommentar zum N. T. herausgegeben von T. Zahn," x, 1905, p. 7 note.
So also Zahn himself in vol. vi¹⁻², p. 181, note 52 (cf. also p. 179, note 50): "Accordingly, λύτρωσις, *Loskaufung,* Lev. xxv. 48, Plut. "Aratus," 11; in the wider sense,
'deliverance,' *Erlösung,* Ps. cx. (cxi.) 9, Lk. i. 68, ii. 38, Heb. ix. 12; I Clem. xii. 7."

ance." Similarly A. Seeberg speaks [20] of ἀπυλύτρωσις as having lost in the New Testament its etymological significance, and come to mean, as he says, "nothing more than *Erlösung*," that is, "deliverance." And again G. Hollmann declares [21] that the Hebrew verb פָּדָה while meaning literally "to ransom" (*loskaufen*), yet, in the majority of the passages in which it occurs, means simply "to liberate," "to deliver" (*befreien, erlösen*); that is to say, "to free," "to liberate," and not "to ransom," are in his mind synonymous with *erlösen*. We are not concerned for the moment with the rightness, or the wrongness, of the opinions expressed by these writers with respect to the meaning of the Biblical terms which they are discussing. What concerns us now is only that, in endeavoring to fix their meaning, these writers expressly discriminate the term *erlösen* from *loskaufen*, and expressly assign to it the wide meaning "to deliver," and thus bring it into exact synonymy with such other non-modal words as "to free," "to liberate." We may speculate as to what might have been the effect on the course of German religious thought if, from the beginning, some exact reproductions of the Greek words built up around the idea of ransom — such as say *loskaufen, Loskaufung, Loskaufer,* — had been adopted as their representatives in the pages of the German New Testament, and, consequent upon that, in the natural expression of the religious thought and feeling of German Christians. But we can scarcely doubt that it has been gravely injurious to it, that, in point of fact, a loose terminology, importing merely deliverance, has taken the place of the more exact Greek terms, in the expression of religious thought and feeling; and thus German Christians have been habituated to express their conceptions of Christ's saving act in language which left wholly unnoted the central fact that it was an act of purchase.

The way to the reversion which has thus taken place of late in German religious speech, from the narrower significance which had long been attached in Christian usage to the word *Erlösung*, "ransoming," to its wider, native sense, "deliver-

[20] "Der Tod Christi," etc., 1905, p. 218.
[21] "Die Bedeutung des Todes Jesu," etc., 1901, pp. 102, 108–109.

ance," was led — like the way to so many other things which have acted disintegratingly upon Christian conceptions — by Schleiermacher. So, at least, Julius Kaftan tells us. "Schleiermacher," says he,[22] "explained the peculiar nature of Christianity by means of the notion of *Erlösung*. Christianity is the religion in which every thing is related to the *Erlösung* accomplished by Jesus of Nazareth. It dates from this that the word is employed by us in a comprehensive sense. We say of the Lord that He is our *Erlöser*. We sum up what He has brought us in this word, *Erlösung*." Kaftan himself is of the opinion that justice is scarcely done to the definition of Christianity when it is thus identified with *Erlösung*, deliverance, taken in the wide, undifferentiated sense given it by Schleiermacher, and after him by the so-called "Liberal theology." A closer definition, he thinks, is needed. But it is very significant that he seeks this closer definition by emphasizing not the mode in which the deliverance is wrought, but rather the thing from which the deliverance is effected. "The word *Erlösung*," he says, "is of a *formal* nature. That it may have its full sense, there must be added *that from which* we are *erlöst*." This he declares is, in the Christian, the New Testament conception, the world. And so, he goes on to assert with great emphasis, "The fundamental idea of Christianity is *Erlösung* from the world."

We are not concerned here with the justice of the opinion thus expressed. We are not even concerned for the moment with the assimilation which results from this opinion of Christianity with certain other religions, the fundamental idea of which is deliverance from the world. We pause only in passing to note that Kaftan explicitly admits that it was "the history of religion which opened his eyes to the fact that in Christianity as in other religions of deliverance (*Erlösungsreligionen*) *Erlösung* from the world is the chief and fundamental conception." What we are for the moment interested in is the clearness with which Kaftan ascribes to the word *Erlösung* the wide sense of "deliverance," with no implication whatever of "ran-

[22] *Zeitschrift für Theologie und Kirche*, 1908, 18, p. 238.

soming." Christianity, it is said, like other religions of high grade, is an *Erlösungsreligion*, a religion of deliverance. "We have today," we read,[23] "attained a wider survey of the religious life of humanity, a wider one, I mean, than that of the older teachers. We have learned that even outside of Christianity, whether really or supposedly, there is something like *Erlösung* (deliverance.) From this the arrangement has resulted, in the classification of religions, that we designate the highest stage of the religious life, that of the spiritual religions, also that of the *Erlösungsreligionen* (religions of deliverance)." That is to say, there is a class of religions, — no doubt, it embraces only the highest, the spiritual, religions, — which may justly be called *Erlösungsreligionen*, religions of deliverance, and Christianity belongs to this class. When we speak of *Erlösung* with reference to Christianity, we mean the same kind of a thing which we mean when we speak of it with reference to these other religions. As one of the *Erlösungsreligionen* (religions of deliverance) Christianity like the rest offers man deliverance. In point of fact, the deliverance which Christianity offers, according to Kaftan, is just a subjective change of mind and heart; he can write currently such a phrase as "*Erlösung oder Wiedergeburt*" (deliverance or regeneration.[24]) *Erlösung* (deliverance) in other words, as applied to describe the benefits conferred by Christianity, has come to mean for him just the better ethical life of Christians.

The classification of religions of which Kaftan avails himself in this discussion is derived ultimately from Hermann Siebeck, whose "Hand-book of the Philosophy of Religion" enjoys great vogue among Germans of Ritschlian tendency. This classification has not, however, commended itself universally. Many, like C. P. Tiele for example, strongly object to the distinguishing of a class of *Erlösungsreligionen* (religions of deliverance), which is placed at the apex of the series of religions. In reality, they say, all religions are *Erlösungsreligionen* (religions of deliverance). Precisely what religion is, always and everywhere, is a means of deliverance from some evil or other,

[23] P. 239.   [24] "Dogmatik[3-4]," p. 459.

felt as such. Does not the proverb say, *not lehrt beten* — a sense of need is the mother of all religion? [25] The designation *Erlösungsreligionen* (religions of deliverance) has, however, evidently come to stay, whether it be taken discriminatingly as the designation of a particular class of religions, or merely descriptively as a declaration of the essential nature of all religions. And it is rapidly becoming the accepted way of speaking of Christianity to call it an *Erlösungsreligion* — a religion of deliverance, — whether it is meant thereby to assign it to a class or merely to indicate its nature. The point to be noted is that *Erlösung* is employed in these phrases in its looser native sense of deliverance, not in its narrower, acquired sense of ransoming. When Christianity is declared to be an *Erlösungsreligion* all that is meant is that it offers like all other religions, or very eminently like some other religions, a deliverance of some kind or other to men.

What gives this importance for us, is that these phrases have passed over from German into English, partly through the translation into English of the German books which employ them, partly by the adoption of the phrases themselves by native English writers for use in their own discussions. And in passing over into English, these phrases have not been exactly rendered with a care to reproducing their precise sense

[25] According to Rudolf Eucken, "Christianity and the New Idealism," E. T., 1909, p. 115, "That which drives men to religion is the break with the world of their experience, the failure to find satisfaction in what this world offers or is able to offer." It is probably something like this that Henry Osborn Taylor, "Deliverance," 1915, p. 5, means when he says: "Evidently every 'religion' is a means of adjustment or deliverance." According to this all religions represent efforts of men to adjust themselves "to the fears and hopes of their natures," thus attaining peace or even "freedom of action in which they accomplish their lives." This "adjustment," Taylor speaks of as a "deliverance," that is to say, no doubt, deliverance from the discomfort of non-adjustment with its clogging effects on life. In this view religion is deliverance from conscious maladjustment of life. The implication is, apparently, that all men are to this extent conscious of being out of joint, in one way or another, with themselves or the universe in which they live, and struggle after adjustment. Thus religion arises, or rather the various religions, since they differ much both in the maladjustments they feel and their methods of correcting them. And there are even modes of adjustment which have been tried that cannot be called "religions."

in unambiguous English, but have been mechanically transferred into what are supposed to be the corresponding conventional English equivalents for the terms used.[26] Thus we have learned in these last days to speak very freely of "redemptive religions" or "religions of redemption," and it has become the fashion to describe Christianity as a "redemptive religion" or a "religion of redemption," — while yet the conception which lies in the mind is not that of redemption in the precise sense, but that of deliverance in its broadest connotation. This loose German usage has thus infected our own, and is coöperating with the native influences at work in the same direction, to break down the proper implications of our English redemptive terminology.[27]

You see, that what we are doing today as we look out upon our current religious modes of speech, is assisting at the death bed of a word. It is sad to witness the death of any worthy thing, — even of a worthy word. And worthy words do die, like any other worthy thing — if we do not take good care of them. How many worthy words have already died under our

[26] Thus, for example, Paul Wernle writes, "Die Anfänge unserer Religion[1]," p. 106, of Paul's view of Christianity: "Es war ihm ganz Erlösungsreligion"; "Jesus Erlöser, nicht Gesetzgeber, das war seine Parole." W. M. Macgregor, "Christian Freedom," 1914, p. 85, knowing what he is about, rightly translates: "To Paul Christianity was altogether a religion of deliverance." But the English translation of Wernle's book ("The Beginnings of Christianity," 1903, i, p. 176) renders: "Christianity was entirely a religion of redemption for him": " Jesus the Redeemer, not the lawgiver, was his watchword." This is, of course, a truer description of Paul's actual point of view; but it is not what Wernle means to say of him. Similarly Rudolf Eucken constantly speaks of Christianity as an "ethical" or "moral" "Erlösungsreligion" and of the particular "Erlösungstat" to which, as such, it points us (e. g. "Hauptprobleme der Religionsphilosophie der Gegenwart[4-5]," 1912, pp. 124, 126, 129). His translators ("Christianity and the New Idealism," 1909, pp. 114, 117, 119, 120) render as constantly "the religion of moral redemption," "act of redemption," although Eucken has no proper "redemption" whatever in mind, — as indeed the adjective "ethical," "moral" shows sufficiently clearly. An ethical revolution may be a deliverance but it is not properly a "redemption."

[27] For example, on the basis of this note: "Beyschlag ('N. T. Theol.' II. 157) frankly takes ἀπολυτροῦν, ἐλευθεροῦν, ἐξαιρεῖν (Gal. i. 4), ἀγοράζειν as synonymous," W. M. Macgregor, "Christian Freedom," 1914, p. 276. He retires into the background of all of them, all other notion than that of "Emancipation," that is, the notion of the weakest and least modal of them all.

very eyes, because we did not take care of them! Tennyson
calls our attention to one of them. "The grand old name of
gentleman," he sings, "defamed by every charlatan, and soil'd
with all ignoble use." If you persist in calling people who are
not gentlemen by the name of gentleman, you do not make
them gentlemen by so calling them, but you end by making
the word gentleman mean that kind of people. The religious
terrain is full of the graves of good words which have died from
lack of care — they stand as close in it as do the graves today
in the flats of Flanders or among the hills of northern France.
And these good words are still dying all around us. There is
that good word "Evangelical." It is certainly moribund, if not
already dead. Nobody any longer seems to know what it
means. Even our Dictionaries no longer know. Certainly there
never was a more blundering, floundering attempt ever made to
define a word than "The Standard Dictionary's" attempt to
define this word; and the "Century Dictionary" does little
better. Adolf Harnack begins one of his essays with some para-
graphs animadverting on the varied and confused senses in
which the word "Evangelical" is used in Germany.[28] But he
betrays no understanding whatever of the real source of a great
part of this confusion. It is that the official name of the Protestant Church in a large part of Germany is "The Evangelical
Church." When this name was first acquired by that church
it had a perfectly defined meaning, and described the church
as that kind of a church. But having been once identified with
that church, it has drifted with it into the bog. The habit of
calling "Evangelical" everything which was from time to time
characteristic of that church or which any strong party in that
church wished to make characteristic of it — has ended in
robbing the term of all meaning. Along a somewhat different
pathway we have arrived at the same state of affairs in America.
Does anybody in the world know what "Evangelical" means,
in our current religious speech? The other day, a professedly
evangelical pastor, serving a church which is certainly committed by its formularies to an evangelical confession, having

[28] "Aus Wissenschaft und Leben," 1911, ii, pp. 213 ff.

occasion to report in one of our newspapers on a religious meeting composed practically entirely of Unitarians and Jews, remarked with enthusiasm upon the deeply evangelical character of its spirit and utterances.

But we need not stop with "Evangelical." Take an even greater word. Does the word "Christianity" any longer bear a definite meaning? Men are debating on all sides of us what Christianity really is. Auguste Sabatier makes it out to be just altruism; Josiah Royce identifies it with the sentiment of loyalty; D. C. Macintosh explains it as nothing but morality. We hear of Christianity without dogma, Christianity without miracle, Christianity without Christ. Since, however, Christianity is a historical religion, an undogmatic Christianity would be an absurdity; since it is through and through a supernatural religion, a non-miraculous Christianity would be a contradiction; since it is Christianity, a Christless Christianity would be — well, let us say lamely (but with a lameness which has perhaps its own emphasis), a misnomer. People set upon calling unchristian things Christian are simply washing all meaning out of the name. If everything that is called Christianity in these days is Christianity, then there is no such thing as Christianity. A name applied indiscriminately to everything, designates nothing.

The words "Redeem," "Redemption," "Redeemer" are going the same way. When we use these terms in so comprehensive a sense — we are following Kaftan's phraseology — that we understand by "Redemption" whatever benefit we suppose ourselves to receive through Christ, — no matter what we happen to think that benefit is — and call Him "Redeemer" merely in order to express the fact that we somehow or other relate this benefit to Him — no matter how loosely or unessentially — we have simply evacuated the terms of all meaning, and would do better to wipe them out of our vocabulary. Yet this is precisely how modern Liberalism uses these terms. Sabatier, who reduces Christianity to mere altruism, Royce who explains it in terms of loyalty, Macintosh who sees in it only morality — all still speak of it as a "Redemptive

Religion," and all are perfectly willing to call Jesus still by the title of "Redeemer,"— although some of them at least are quite free to allow that He seems to them quite unessential to Christianity, and Christianity would remain all that it is, and just as truly a "Redemptive Religion," even though He had never existed.

I think you will agree with me that it is a sad thing to see words like these die like this. And I hope you will determine that, God helping you, you will not let them die thus, if any care on your part can preserve them in life and vigor. But the dying of the words is not the saddest thing which we see here. The saddest thing is the dying out of the hearts of men of the things for which the words stand. As ministers of Christ it will be your function to keep the things alive. If you can do that, the words which express the things will take care of themselves. Either they will abide in vigor; or other good words and true will press in to take the place left vacant by them. The real thing for you to settle in your minds, therefore, is whether Christ is truly a Redeemer to you, and whether you find an actual Redemption in Him, — or are you ready to deny the Master that bought you, and to count His blood an unholy thing? Do you realize that Christ is your Ransomer and has actually shed His blood for you as your ransom? Do you realize that your salvation has been bought, bought at a tremendous price, at the price of nothing less precious than blood, and that the blood of Christ, the Holy One of God? Or, go a step further: do you realize that this Christ who has thus shed His blood for you is Himself your God? So the Scriptures teach: [29]

> The blood of God outpoured upon the tree!
> So reads the Book.   O mind, receive the thought,

[29] Acts xx. 28, "Feed the church of God which He hath purchased with His own blood." The reading "God" is, as F. J. A. Hort says, "assuredly genuine," and the emphasis upon the blood being His own is very strong. There is no justification for correcting the text conjecturally, as Hort does, to avoid this. If the reading "Lord" were genuine, the meaning would be precisely the same: "Lord" is not a lower title than "God." in such connections. I Cor. ii. 8, "They would not have crucified the Lord of Glory," is an exact parallel.

Nor helpless murmur thou hast vainly sought
Thought-room within thee for such mystery.
Thou foolish mindling! Do'st thou hope to see
   Undazed, untottering, all that God hath wrought?
   Before His mighty "shall," thy little "ought"
Be shamed to silence and humility!
Come mindling, I will show thee what 'twere meet
   That thou shouldst shrink from marvelling, and flee
   As unbelievable, — nay, wonderingly,
With dazed, but still with faithful praises, greet:
Draw near and listen to this sweetest sweet, —
   Thy God, O mindling, shed His blood for *thee!*

XI

CHRIST OUR SACRIFICE

CHRIST OUR SACRIFICE [1]

"ACCORDING to the New Testament, primitive Christianity, when it used the words 'Jesus redeems us by His blood,' was thinking of the ritual sacrifice, and this conception is diffused throughout the whole New Testament; it is a fundamental idea, universal in primitive Christianity, with respect to the significance of Jesus' death." So remarks Paul Fiebig; [2] and W. P. Paterson, summarizing Albrecht Ritschl, [3] emphasizes the assertion. "The interpretation of Christ's death as a sacrifice," says he, [4] "is imbedded in every important type of New Testament teaching." By the limitation implied in the words, "every important type," he means only to allow for the failure of allusions to this interpretation in the two brief letters, James and Jude, the silence of which, he rightly explains, "raises no presumption against the idea being part of the common stock of Apostolic doctrine." It was already given expression by Jesus Himself (Mt. xxvi. 28, Mk. xiv. 24, I Cor. xi. 25, Mt. xx. 28, Mk. x. 45), [5] and it is elaborated by the Apostles in a great variety of obviously spontaneous allusions. They not only expressly state that Christ was offered as a sacrifice. [6] They work out the correspondence between His death and the different forms of Old Testament sacrifice. [7] They show that the differ-

---

[1] From *The Princeton Theological Review*, v. xv, 1917, pp. 385–422.

[2] "Jesu Blut ein Geheimnis?" 1906, p. 27.

[3] "Die Christliche Lehre der Rechtfertigung und Versöhnung³," 1889, v. ii, pp. 161 ff.

[4] Hastings' "Dictionary of the Bible," v. iv, 1902, p. 343 b.

[5] Fiebig, as cited, p. 19, remarks on the connection in the Jewish mind of the idea of purchasing, ransoming, with sacrifice, — referring to F. Weber, "Jüdische Theologie," etc²., 1897, pp. 313, 324.

[6] E. g., προσφορά, Eph. v. 2, Heb. x. 10, 14 (for the meaning of προσφορά see Heb. x. 18), θυσία, Eph. v. 2, Heb. ix. 26; cf. Rom. iii. 25, ἱλαστήριον; viii. 3, περὶ ἁμαρτίας.

[7] Paterson (from whom we are taking this summary), as cited, notes: "esp. the Sin-offering (Rom. viii. 3, Heb. xiii. 11, I Pet. iii. 18), the Covenant-sacrifice

ent acts of the Old Testament sacrificial ritual were repeated in Christ's experience.[8] They ascribe the specific effects of sacrifice to his death.[9] They dwell particularly, in truly sacrificial wise, on the saving efficacy of His out-poured blood.[10] William Warburton did not speak a bit too strongly when he wrote, more than a hundred and fifty years ago: "One could hardly have thought it possible that any man who had read the Gospels with their best interpreters, the authors of the Epistles, should ever have entertained a doubt whether the death of Christ was a real sacrifice."[11]

(Heb. ix. 15–22), the sacrifices of the Day of Atonement (Heb. ii. 17, ix. 12 ff.), and of the Passover (I Cor. v. 7)." Cf. Sanday-Headlam, "Romans[1]," p. 92.

[8] Paterson enumerates: "the slaying of the immaculate victim (Rev. v. 6, xiii. 8), the sprinkling of the blood both in the sanctuary as in the Sin-offering (Heb. ix. 13 ff.), and on the people as in the Covenant-sacrifice (I Pet. i. 2), and the destruction of the victim, as in the Sin-offering, without the gate (Heb. xiii. 13)" — referring to Ritschl ii. 157 ff.; and Sanday-Headlam, "Romans," p. 91.

[9] E. g.: "Expiation, or pardon of sin," says Paterson. Sanday-Headl-m mention as examples of passages in which the death of Christ is directly connected with forgiveness of sin: Mt. xxvi. 28; Acts v. 30 f., apparently; I Cor. xv. 3; II Cor. v. 21; Eph. i. 7; Col. i. 14 and 20; Tit. ii. 14; Heb. i. 3, ix. 28, x. 12, al.; I Pet. ii. 24, iii. 18; I John ii. 2, iv. 10; Rev. i. 5.

[10] Paterson: "A saving efficacy is ascribed to the blood of the cross of Christ, and in these cases the thought clearly points to the forms of the altar (Rom. iii. 25, v. 9, I Cor. x. 16, Eph. i. 7, ii. 13, Col. i. 20, Heb. ix. 12, 14; I Pet. i. 2, 19; I John i. 7, v. 6, 8; Rev. i. 5)." Cf. Sanday-Headlam, "Romans," p. 91 f. The matter is very interestingly presented by Fiebig, as cited, pp. 11–27 under the title: "What, according to the New Testament, did primitive Christianity think in connection with the words, 'Jesus has redeemed us by His blood'?" He takes his start, for the survey of a conception which he says is diffused throughout the whole New Testament, from I Pet. i. 17–19, the only key to which he declares to be "sacrifice, and indeed sacrifice as it was known to every Jew (and in a corresponding way to every heathen) from his daily life and from the festivals and duties of his religion, that is ritual sacrifice." From this passage he then proceeds through the New Testament and shows that the blood of Christ is used throughout the volume in a sacrificial sense, so that whenever we meet with an allusion to the blood of Jesus we meet with a reference to His death as a sacrifice.

[11] "The Divine Legation of Moses," Book ix, chapter ii, quoted in a note at the end of his excellent chapter on "The New Testament Description of the Atoning Work of Christ as Sacrificial," by Alfred Cave, "The Scriptural Doctrine of Sacrifice and Atonement[2]," 1890, pp. 274–289. Cave himself says (p. 289): "Not only portions but the whole New Testament — not only the New Testament teaching but any type of that teaching — must be cast aside unless the work of Christ be in some sense or other regarded as a sacrifice."

It would be strange in these circumstances if, in attempting to determine the Biblical conception of the nature of the work of Christ, appeal were not made to the sacrificial system; and it were not argued that the nature of Christ's work is exhibited in the nature of the sacrificial act. Whatever a sacrifice is, that Christ's work is. It will be obvious, however, that we are liable to fall into a certain confusion here. Jesus Himself and the Apostles speak of Christ's work as sacrificial, and it is clear (as Paterson duly points out [12]) that this is on their lips no figure of speech or mere illustration, but is intended to declare the simple fact. It is quite plain, then, that His work was conceived by them to be of precisely that nature which a sacrifice was understood by them to be. But it is by no means so plain that they conceived His work to be of the nature which we may understand a sacrifice to be. Failure to regard this very simple distinction has brought untold confusion into the discussion. If we would comprehend the teaching of the writers of the New Testament when they call Christ a sacrifice, we must, of course, not assume out of hand that their idea of a sacrifice and ours

[12] As cited: "Nor for the apostolic age was the description of Christ's death as a sacrifice of the nature of a mere illustration. The apostles held it to be a sacrifice in the most literal sense of the word." Paterson goes on to assign reasons. George F. Moore, "Encyclopaedia Biblica," v. iv. 1903, col. 4232 f. interposes a caveat: "To begin with, it is necessary to say that in describing the death of Christ as a sacrifice the New Testament writers are using figurative language. Some modern theologians, indeed, still affirm that 'the apostles held it to be a sacrifice in the most literal sense of the word'; but such writers do not expect us to take their 'literal' literally. The author of the Epistle to the Hebrews, for example, regarded the death of Christ as the true sacrifice, because by it was really effected what the Old Testament sacrifices only prefigured; but he was too good an Alexandrian to identify 'true' with 'literal.'" What Moore maintains is that the death of Christ was not believed to be expiatory because it was known to be a sacrifice, but that it was spoken of as a sacrifice because it was recognized to be expiatory. He does not doubt that the death of Christ was believed actually to have wrought the expiation which the sacrifices were understood to figure. "The association of expiation with sacrifice in the law and in the common ideas of the time leads to the employment of sacrificial figures and terms in speaking of the work of Christ; and even in Hebrews, where the idea of the death of Christ as a sacrifice is most elaborately developed, it is plain that the premise of the whole is that Christ by His death made a real expiation for the sins of men, by which they are redeemed." We take it that it is just this that Paterson means by speaking of Christ's death as a "literal" sacrifice.

are identical. The investigation of the previous question of the notion they attached to a sacrifice must form our starting-point. So little is this mode of procedure always adopted, however, that it is even customary for writers on the subject to go so far afield at this point as to introduce a discussion not of the idea of sacrifice held by the founders of the Christian religion, or even current in the Judaism of their day, or even embodied in the Levitical system; but of the idea of sacrifice in general, conceived as a world-wide mode of worship. The several theories of the fundamental conception which underlies sacrificial worship in the general sense are set forth; a choice is made among them; and this theory is announced as ruling the usage of the term when applied to Christ. Christ is undoubtedly our sacrifice, it is said: but a sacrifice is a rite by which communion with God is established and maintained, or by which a complete surrender to God is symbolized, or by which recognition is made of the homage we owe to Him as our God, or by which God's suffering love is manifested. As if the question of importance were what we mean by a sacrifice, and not what the New Testament writers mean by it.

It is manifestly of the highest importance, therefore, that we should keep separate three very distinct questions, to each of which a great deal of interest attaches, although they have very different bearings on the determination of the nature of Christ's work. These three questions are: (1) What is the fundamental idea which underlies sacrificial worship as a world-phenomenon? (2) What is the essential implication of sacrifice in the Levitical system? (3) What is the conception of sacrifice which lay in the minds of the writers of the New Testament, when they represented Jesus as a sacrifice and ascribed to His work a sacrificial character, in its mode, its nature and its effects? The distinctness of these questions is strikingly illustrated by the circumstance that not infrequently a different response is given to each of them by the same investigator. It may be said in general that few doubt that the conception of sacrifice at least dominant among the Jews of Christ's time was distinctly piacular: and, although it is more frequently questioned whether all the writers of the New Testament were in agreement with this conception, it is practically undoubted that some of them were, and generally admitted that all were. The majority of scholars agree also that the piacular conception informs sacrificial worship in the Levitical system. On the other hand speculation has as yet found no common ground with respect to the fundamental conception which is supposed to underlie sacrificial worship in general, and in this field hypothesis still jostles with hypothesis in what seems an endless controversy.

Question may even very legitimately be raised whether the assumption can be justified which is commonly (but of course not universally) made that a single fundamental idea underlies all sacrificial worship the world over. There seems no reason in the nature of things why a similar mode of worship may not have grown up in various races of men, living in very different circumstances, to express differing conceptions; and it certainly cannot be doubted that very diverse conceptions, in the long practice of the rite by these various races in their constantly changing circumstances, attached themselves, from time to time and from place to place, to the sacrificial mode of worship common to all. The Biblical narrative may lead us to suppose, to be sure, that sacrificial worship began very early in the history of the human race: it may seem to be carried back, indeed, to the very dawn of history, and to be definitely assigned in its origin to no later period than the second generation of men. But at the same time we seem to be advertized that at the very inception of sacrificial worship different conceptions were embodied in it by its several practitioners. It is difficult to believe at least that we are expected to understand that the whole difference in the acceptability to Jehovah of the two offerings of Cain and Abel hung on the different characters of the two offerers: [13] we are told that Jehovah had respect not merely

---

[13] This nevertheless is the common view. Driver supposes that the different treatment of the sacrifices can hardly have had its ground in "anything except the different spirit and temper actuating the two brothers": but he recognizes (without comment) that there is "another view," namely, "that there underlies

unto Abel and not unto Cain, but also to Abel's offering and not to Cain's. The different characters of the two men seem rather to be represented as expressing themselves in differing conceptions of man's actual relation to God and of the conditions of approval by Him and the proper means of seeking His favor.

It can scarcely be reading too much between the lines to suppose that the narrative in the fourth chapter of Genesis is intended on the one hand to describe the origin of sacrificial worship, and on the other to distinguish between two conceptions of sacrifice and to indicate the preference of Jehovah for the one rather than the other. These two conceptions are briefly those which have come to be known respectively as the piacular theory and the symbolical, or perhaps we should rather call it the gift, theory. In this view we are not to suppose that Cain and Abel simply brought each a gift to the Lord from the increase which had been granted him, to acknowledge thereby the overlordship of Jehovah and to express subjection and obedience to Him: and that it is merely an accident that Cain's offering, as that of a husbandman, was of the fruit of the ground, while Abel's, as that of a shepherd, was of the firstlings of the flock. There is no reason apparent why Jehovah should prefer a lamb to a sheaf of wheat.[14] The difference surely goes deeper, for it was "by faith" that Abel offered under God a more excellent sacrifice than Cain — which seems to suggest that the supreme excellence of his sacrifice is to be sought not in the mere nature of the thing offered, but in the attitude of

the story some early struggle between two theories of sacrifice, which ended by the triumph of the theory that the right offering to be made consisted in the life of an animal." Dillmann says: "The reason must therefore lie in the dispositions presupposed in the offerings"; but quotes Hofmann, "Schriftbeweis²," i, p. 585 for the view that "Abel had in mind the expiation of sin, while Cain had not" — "of which," says Dillmann, "there is no indication whatever." Similar ground is taken, for example, by Kalisch, Keil, Delitzsch ("New Commentary"), Lange, W. P. Paterson (Articles "Abel" and "Cain" in Hastings' B.D.).

[14] Gunkel thinks there is: Jehovah is the God of nomads. The old narrator, he says, would be surprised that anyone should wonder why Jahve had respect to Abel's offering and not to Cain's: he means just that Jahve loved the shepherd and flesh-offerings but would have nothing to do with the cultivator and fruit-offerings. Similarly Tuch: the story comes from nomads.

the offerer.[15] What seems to be implied is that Cain's offering was an act of mere homage; Abel's embodied a sense of sin, an act of contrition, a cry for succor, a plea for pardon. In a word, Cain came to the Lord with an offering in his hand and the Homage theory of sacrifice in his mind: Abel with an offering in his hand and the Piacular theory of sacrifice in his heart. And it was therefore, that Jehovah had respect to Abel's offering and not to Cain's. If so, while we may say that sacrifice was invented by man, we must also say that by this act piacular sacrifice was instituted by God.[16] In other modes of conceiving it, sacrifice may represent the reaching out of man towards God: in its piacular conception it represents the stooping down of God to man. The fundamental difference is that in the one case sacrifice rests upon consciousness of sin and has its refer-

---

[15] The allusion in Heb. xii. 24 is taken by some commentators as a reference to Abel's offering rather than to his death. Bleek (p. 954) says: "It may be mentioned merely in a historical interest that with the Erasmian reading ($\tau\grave{o}$ Ἄβελ), by Hammond, Akersloot, and Snabel (*Amoenitatt theologiae emblematicae et typicae*, p. 109 ff.), the blood of Abel is understood of the blood of the sacrificial animal offered by him; and that the first, with the received reading ($\tau\grave{o}\nu$ Ἄβελ), wishes to refer the $\tau\acute{o}\nu$ to the ῥαντισμόν in order to obtain the same sense." This interpretation has had great vogue in America, owing to its advocacy by the popular commentaries of Albert Barnes, 1843, F. S. Sampson, 1856, George Junkin 1873. Its significance for the matter of the nature of Abel's sacrifice may be perceived from the comment of Joseph B. McCaul, 1871, p. 317 f., who combines the two views: "Abel, being dead, can speak only figuratively. He does so by his faith, manifested by his bringing a vicarious sacrifice according to the Divine will. He therefore speaks, not only by the blood of his martyrdom, but also by the blood of his sacrifice, which latter obtained testimony from God that it was acceptable and accepted. It was *then* that God openly expressed his Divine selection of blood, to the exclusion of all other means of ransom, for the redemption of the soul. In the term 'the blood of Abel,' therefore, may be included the blood of all vicarious victims afterwards offered, in accordance with God's appointment, until the sacrifice of the death of Christ superseded them."

[16] Here perhaps is to be found the reply to the representation made for example by J. K. Mozley, "The Doctrine of the Atonement," 1916, p. 13, note 2, to the effect that writers of the school "which ignores or rejects modern criticism of the Old Testament" — represented by P. Fairbairn, "Typology of the Scriptures," W. L. Alexander, "Biblical Theology," A. Cave, "Scriptural Doctrine of Sacrifice"— had to explain how it is that the first sacrifices mentioned (those of Cain and Abel) "are not said to have been in any way ordered by God." The question of the origin of sacrifice, human or divine, Mozley says is no longer discussed. For a hint as to its literature see Cave, p. 41, note 2.

ence to the restoration of a guilty human being to the favor of a condemning God: in the other it stands outside of all relation to sin and has its reference only to the expression of the proper attitude of deference which a creature should preserve towards his Maker and Ruler.[17]

[17] This explanation of the narrative of "the first sacrifices" is not popular with the critical commentators. Skinner (in accordance with the alternative view of the passage mentioned by Driver) thinks that "the whole manner of the narrative" suggests that we here have "the initiation of sacrifice," and that, if this be accepted, it follows "that the narrative proceeds on a *theory* of sacrifice; the idea, viz. that animal sacrifice alone is acceptable to Yahwe." Why this should be so, he does not say. Franz Delitzsch, who in his "New Commentary on Genesis," will not look further for the reason of the difference in the treatment of the offerings than the different dispositions of the offerers, in his earlier "Commentary on Genesis," amid much inconsistent matter, has this to say: "The unbloody offering of Cain, as such, was only the expression of a grateful present, or, taken in its deepest significance, a consecrated offering of self: but man needs, before all things, the expiation of his death-deserving sins, and for this, the blood obtained through the slaying of the victim serves as a symbol." J. C. K. Hofmann, "Schriftbeweis[2]," i, pp. 584–585 remarks that the cultivation of the soil and the keeping of beasts were employments alike open to men: but he who adopted the one, dealing with a soil which was *cursed*, had to thank God for the yield it made despite sin, while he who adopted the other, in view of the provision God had made for hiding man's nakedness, had before him God's grace in hiding sin. If, now, Cain was satisfied to bring of the fruit of the earth to God, he was thanking God only for a prolongation of this present life, which he had gained by his own labor: while Abel, bringing the best beasts of his flock, gave Him thanks for the forgiveness of sin, the abiding symbol of which was the clothing given by God. "A grateful attitude such as Abel's had as its presupposition, however, the penitent faith in the word of God which saw in this divine clothing of human nakedness an approach to the forgiveness of sins which rests on the gracious will of God to man." Because Abel's sacrifice embodied this idea, it was acceptable to God and he received the witness that he was righteous. J. J. Murphy comments: "The fruit of the soil offered to God is an acknowledgment that the means of this earthly life are due to Him. This expresses the barren faith of Cain, not the living faith of Abel. The latter had entered deeply into the thought that life itself is forfeited to God by transgression, and that only by an act of mercy can the Author of life restore it to the penitent, trusting, submissive, loving heart." The remarks of "C. H. M." on the passage are very clear and pointed to the same effect. See them cited by A. H. Strong, "Syst. Theol.," ed. 1907, p. 727. J. C. Jones, "Primeval Revelation," 1897, p. 313 ff. gives a glowing popular expression to the same view. J. S. Candlish, "The Christian Salvation," 1899, p. 15, thinks that Abel's sacrifice plainly involves the confession of sin and compares his worship with that of the Publican in the parable, and Cain's to that of the Pharisee. T. J. Crawford, "Doctrine of Holy Scripture Respecting the Atonement[2]," 1875, p. 280, says that Abel's faith may have had respect not to a revelation with regard to

The appearance of two such sharply differentiated conceptions side by side in the earliest Hebrew tradition does not encourage us to embark on ambitious speculations which would seek the origin of all sacrificial doctrines in a single primitive idea out of which they have gradually unfolded in the progress of time and through many stages of increasing culture. We have been made familiar with such genetic constructions by the writings especially of E. B. Tylor, W. Robertson Smith, and Smith's follower and improver, J. G. Frazer.[18] In Tylor's view the beginning of sacrifice is to be found in a gift made by a savage to some superior being from which he hoped to receive a benefit. The gods grew gradually greater and more distant; and the gift was correspondingly spiritualized, until it ended by becoming the gift of the worshipper's self. Thus out of the offer of a bribe there gradually evolved its opposite — an act of self-abnegation and renunciation. The start is taken, according to W. Robertson Smith, rather from a common meal in which the totem animal, which is also the god, is consumed with a view to the assimilation of it by the worshippers and their assimilation to it. When the animal eaten came to be thought of as provided by the worshipper, the idea of gift came in; as all totemistic meals had for their object the maintenance or renewal of the bond between the worshipper and the god, the conception of expiation lay near — for what is expiation but the restitution of a broken bond?[19] H. Hubert and M.

sacrificial worship, but with regard to a promised Redeemer; this sacrifice may have expressed that faith. If so, God's acceptance of it gave a divine warrant to future sacrifice.

[18] We are abstracting in this account the illuminating survey by MM. Hubert and Mauss in the "L'Année Sociologique," II, 1897–1898, pp. 29 ff. They tell us, that Robertson Smith has been followed by E. Sidney Hartland, "The Legend of Perseus," 1894–1896, and "with theological exaggeration" by F. B. Jevons, "Introduction to the History of Religion," 1896.

[19] After threatening to become the dominant theory, this theory has recently lost ground, chiefly on account of the totemistic elements connected with it. See the criticisms by B. Stade, "Biblische Theologie des Alten Testaments," v. i, pp. 156–159; and M. J. Lagrange, "Études sur les religions Sémitiques," pp. 246 ff. The "gift" theory accordingly holds the field. W. R. Inge, "Christian Mysticism," 1899, p. 355, appears to prefer to suppose that neither conception is the source of the other: "There have always been two ideas of sacrifice, alike

Mauss are certainly wise in eschewing this spurious geneticism, and contenting themselves with seeking merely to isolate the common element discoverable in all sacrificial acts. It must be confessed, however, that we are not much advanced even by their less ambitious labors. Sacrifices, they tell us, are, broadly, rites designed by the consecration of a victim, to modify the moral state, or, as they elsewhere express it, to affect the religious state, of the offerers.[20] This is assuredly the most formal of formal definitions. All that differentiates sacrifices from other religious acts, so far as appears from it, is that they, as the others do not, seek their common end "by the consecration of a victim." Nor are we carried much further, when, at the end of their essay, we are told [21] that what binds together all the divers forms of sacrifice into a unity, is that it is always one process which is employed for their varied ends. "This process," it is then said, "consists in establishing a connection between the sacred world and the profane world by the intervention of a victim, that is to say, by something destroyed in the course of the ceremony." Sacrifice, we thus learn, is just — sacrifice. But what this sacrifice is, in its fundamental meaning, we seem not to be very clearly told. An impression is left on the mind that the word "sacrifice" embraces so great a variety of differing transactions that only a very formal definition can include them all.

Our guides having left us thus in the lurch, perhaps we cannot do better than simply survey the chief theories which have been suggested as to the fundamental idea embodied in sacrificial worship, quite in the flat. In doing so, we may take a hint from the two forms of conception brought before us in the narrative of the sacrifices of Cain and Abel and derive from them our principle of division. The theories part into two broad classes, which look upon sacrifices respectively as designed and adapted to express the religious feelings of man con-

in savage and civilized cults, — the mystical in which it is a *communion*, the victim who is slain and eaten being himself the god, or a symbol of the god; and the *commercial*, in which something valuable is offered to the god in the hope of receiving some benefit in exchange." This is very likely true as a general proposition.

[20] As cited, pp. 41 and 89.　　　　　　　　　　[21] P. 133.

ceived merely as creature, or as intended to meet the needs of man as sinner. The theories of the first class are by far the more numerous, and, nowadays at least, by far the more popular. Perhaps, thinking of sacrifices as a world-wide usage as at this point we are, we may say also that these theories are very likely to embody the true account of the meaning of much of the sacrificial worship, at least, which has overspread the globe. For man, even in the formation of his religious rites is doubtless no more ready to remember that he is a sinner craving pardon than that he is a creature claiming protection. Deep-rooted as the sense of sin is in every normal human conscience, and sure as it is sporadically to express itself and to color all serious religious observances, the pride of man is no less ready to find manifestation even in his religious practices. Let us look at the chief varieties of these two great classes of theories in a rapid enumeration.

The chief theories of sacrifice which allow no place to sin in its essential implications, may perhaps be collected into three groups to which may be assigned the names of theories of Recognition, of Gift and of Communion.

The theories to which we have given the name of theories of Recognition are also known as Homage or Symbolical theories. Their common characteristic is that they conceive sacrifices to be at bottom symbolical rites by means of which the worshipper gives expression to his religious feelings or aspirations or needs: "acts go before words." At their highest level these theories represent the worshipper as expressing thus his recognition of the deity, his own relation of dependence upon Him and subjection to Him, and his readiness to act in accordance with this relation and to render the homage and obedience due from him. The name of William Warburton is connected with these theories in this general form.[22] A slightly different turn is given to the general conception by Albrecht Ritschl.[23] According to him, even in the case of the later sacrificial system of Israel, the sacrifices express (with no reference

---

[22] Cf. "The Divine Legation of Moses," etc. iv. 4.
[23] Cf. "Rechtfertigung und Versöhnung³," ii. 201–203.

whatever to sin in the symbolism) only the awe and religious fear which the creature in his inadequacy feels in the presence of deity: man seeks "to cover" his weakness in the face of the destroying glory of God (Gen. xxxii. 31, Judges vi. 23, xiii. 22). There are others, to be sure, who are not so careful to exclude a reference to sin and, in speaking of the sacrifices of Israel at least, suppose that what is symbolized includes a hatred of sin, as well as self-surrender to God: in their hands the theory passes therefore upward into the other main class. On the other hand, in their lowest forms, theories of this group tend to pass downward into conceptions which look upon sacrifices as merely magical rites. The thing symbolized may be supposed to be not a spiritual attitude at all but a physical need. Primitive worshippers only exhibited before the deity the object they required, and this was supposed to operate upon the deity (something after the fashion of sympathetic magic) as a specimen, securing from Him the thing desired. Theorists of this order do not scruple to point to the "shew-bread" displayed in the temple of Israel and the offering of first-fruits as instances in point.

The theories which look upon sacrifices as essentially gifts, presents, intended to please the deity,[24] and thus to gain favor with Him, part into two divisions according as the gifts are conceived more as bribes or more as fines, that is according as they are conceived as designed more to curry favor with the deity, or more to make amends for faults — or, from the point of view of the deity, as a sort of police regulation, to punish or check wrong doing. In either case the idea of sin may come into play and the theory pass upward into the other main class. The chief representative of this type of theory among the old writers is J. Spencer, who looks upon it as self-evident that this was the primitive view of sacrifice.[25] The anthropologists (E. B. Tylor, Herbert Spencer) have given it great vogue in

---

[24] J. Jeremias, "Encyclopaedia Biblica," v. iv. col. 4119 says, in a representative assertion: "Sacrifice rests ultimately on the idea that it gives pleasure to the deity (cf. Dillmann, "Leviticus," 376)." So A. Dillmann, "Exodus und Leviticus[3]," p. 416: "The characteristic of sacrifice is a gift; that which differentiates it from other gifts is that it is enjoyed by the divinity."

[25] J. Spencer, "De Legibus Hebraeorum Ritualibus," 1727, v. ii. p. 762.

our day; and it is doubtless the most commonly held theory of the fundamental nature of sacrifice at present (e. g., H. Schultz, B. Stade, A. B. Davidson, G. F. Moore).[26] In one of the lower forms of this general theory the gifts are conceived as food supplied to the deity — who is supposed to share in the human need of being fed.[27] It is an advance on the crudest form of this conception when it is the savour or odor of the sacrifice which is supposed to be pleasing to the deity, and the food is thought to be conveyed to Him through the medium of burning. When the food is supposed to be shared between the offerer and the deity, an advance is made to the next group of theories.

This group of theories looks upon sacrifices as essentially formal acts of communion with the deity — a common meal, say, partaken of by worshipper and worshipped, the fundamental motive being to gratify the deity by giving or sharing with Him a meal.[28] This general view is often improved upon by a reference to the custom of establishing covenants by common meals, and becomes thereby a "meal-covenant" or "table-bond" theory. In this form it was already suggested by A. A. Sykes who speaks of sacrifices as joint meals, which are, he says, "acts of engaging in covenants and leagues." [29] It is a further addition to this theory to say that it was conceived that a physical union was induced between the deity and the worshipper, by the medium of the common meal.[30] And the notion

---

[26] Hubert and Mauss, as cited, p. 30, remark that "it is certain that sacrifices were generally in some degree gifts, conferring on the believer rights upon his God." They add in a note: "See a somewhat superficial brochure by Nitzsch, 'Idee und Stufen des Opferkultus,' Kiel, 1889"; and then, that "at bottom" this theory is held by Wilken, "Over eene Nieuwe Theorie des Offers" in "De Gids," 1891, pp. 535 ff. and by L. Marillier in the *Revue d'Histoire des Religions*, 1897–1898. Marillier connects sacrifices, however, with magical rites by which the deity is bent to the worshipper's will by the liberation of a magical force through the effusion of the victim's blood. The idea of "gift" grew out of this, through the medium of the cult of the dead.

[27] E. G. Piepenbring, "Théologie de l'ancien Testament," p. 56.

[28] W. P. Paterson, Hastings' "Dictionary of the Bible," iv. p. 331 b.

[29] A. A. Sykes, "Essay on the Nature etc. of Sacrifices," 1748, p. 75.

[30] J. Wellhausen, "Skizzen und Vorarbeiten," 1897; W. R. Smith, "Religion of the Semites²," 1894; as applied to Israel, H. Schultz, *American Journal of Theology*, 1900, p. 269.

has reached its height when the meal is thought of as essentially a feeding on the God Himself whether by symbol, or through the medium of a totem animal, or by magical influence.[31] H. C. Trumbull actually utilizes this conception to explain the mode of action of the Lord's Supper.[32]

One of the things which strikes us very sharply as we review these three groups of theories is the little place given in them to the slaughter, or more broadly the destruction, of the victim, or, more broadly, the offering. This comes forward in them all as incidental to the rite, rather than as its essence. In the third group the sacrificial feast — which follows on the sacrifice itself — assumes the main place; in the second it is the oblation which is emphasized as of chief importance; even in the first the slaughter is not cardinal, — at the best it is a prerequisite that the blood may be obtained, which is represented as the valuable thing, to present to the deity. This cirsumstance alone is probably fatal to the validity of these theories as accounts whether of sacrifice in general or sacrifice in Israel; and very certainly as providing an explanation of the meaning of the New Testament writers when they speak of our Lord as a sacrifice. There is reason to believe that the slaughter of the victim or destruction of the offering constitutes the essential act of sacrifice; and certainly in the New Testament it is precisely in the blood of Christ or in His cross, symbols of His death, that the essence of His sacrificial character is found.[33]

When we turn to the theories of sacrifice in which a reference to sin is made fundamental, we meet first with that form of the Symbolical theory in which the sacrifice is supposed to be the vehicle for the expression of the worshipper's "confession, his regret, his petition for forgiveness," [34] — that is to say, in one word, his repentance and his engagement to give back

[31] J. G. Frazer, "The Golden Bough[2]," 1900.

[32] "The Blood Covenant," 1888, at the end; see also his "The Covenant of Salt," 1899.

[33] Hubert and Mauss, as cited, p. 74. On the usage of the Hebrew word Zebach as a generic term for sacrifice, see Cave, as cited, pp. 511 ff.

[34] H. Schultz, *American Journal of Theology*, 1900, p. 310.

his life to God. Influential advocates of this view are K. C. W. F. Bähr, G. F. Oehler and F. D. Maurice.[35] By its side we meet also that form of the Gift theory in which the sinning worshipper is supposed to approach his judge with (on the lower level) a bribe, or (on the higher level) the fine for his fault in his hand. The former view is appropriate only to lower stages of culture, in which justice is supposed to go by favor. Even in the higher heathen opinion, so to think of the gods was held to be degrading to them: "Even a good man," says Cicero, "will refuse to accept presents from the wicked." [36] When the gift is thought of as amends for a fault, however, we have entered upon more distinctly ethical ground. It is, nevertheless, only in the Piacular or Expiatory view that theories of sacrifice reach their ethical culmination. In this view the offerer is supposed to come before God burdened with a sense of sin and seeking to expiate its guilt. The victim which he offers is looked upon as his substitute, to which is transferred the punishment which is his due; and the penalty having been thus vicariously borne, the offerer may receive forgiveness for his sin. Among the older writers W. Outram is usually looked upon as the type of this view: he explains the death of the victim as "some evil inflicted on one party in order to expiate the guilt of another in the sense of delivering the guilty from punishment and procuring the forgiveness of sin." [37] The general view has been held not only by such writers as P. Fairbairn, J. H. Kurtz, E. W. Hengstenberg, but also by such others as W. Gesenius, W. M. L. de Wette and even Bruno Bauer. E. Westermarck himself defines "the original idea in sacrifice a piaculum, a substitute for the offerer." [38]

A matter of importance which it may be well to observe in passing is that in no one of these theories are sacrifices sup-

---

[35] See Paterson (as cited, p. 341 a), who gives this form of the Symbolical Theory the not very satisfactory name of The Prayer Theory.

[36] "De Leg.," ii. 16.

[37] "De Sacrificiis libri duo," 1677 (E. T., "Two Dissertations on Sacrifices" . . . 1828) p. 248.

[38] J. J. Reeve, in the "International Standard Bible Encyclopaedia," p. 2640 quoting from "The Origin and Development of Moral Ideas," 1906. For Westermarck's notions as to expiating sacrifice at large, see v. i. pp. 61–72.

posed to terminate immediately upon the offerer and to have
their direct effect upon him. The offerer offers them; but it is to
the deity that he offers them; and their direct effect, whatever
it may be, is naturally upon the deity. Of course the offerer
seeks a benefit for himself by his offerings, and in this sense
ultimately they terminate on him; and in some instances their
operation upon him is conceived quite mechanically.[39] Nevertheless it is always through their effect on the deity that they
are supposed to affect men, and their immediate effect is upon
the deity himself. The nearest to an exception to this is provided
by those theories in which the stress is laid on the sacrificial
feast, or rather, among these, by those theories in which the
worshipper is supposed to "eat the God" and thereby to become sharer in his divine qualities. Even this notion, however,
is an outgrowth of the general conception which rules all sacrificial worship, that the purpose of the sacrifice is so to affect
the deity as to secure its favorable regard for the worshipper
or its favorable action in his behalf or upon him. This conception is no doubt extended in this special case to a great
extreme, in representing the benefit hoped for, sought and obtained, to be the actual transfusion of the deity's powers into the

---

[39] Hubert and Mauss, as cited, p. 41, seeking a comprehensive definition,
fix on this: "Sacrifice is a religious act which, by the consecrating of a victim,
modifies the state of the moral person who offers it or of certain objects in which
that person is interested." The meaning of this is amplified in an earlier passage
(p. 37): "In sacrifice on the contrary" — as distinguished, that is, from such
acts, as, say, anointing — "the consecration extends beyond the thing consecrated; it extends among others, to the moral person who defrays the cost of the
ceremony. The believer who has supplied the victim, the object consecrated, is
not at the end of the operation what he was at its beginning. He has acquired a
religious character which he did not have, or he is relieved from an unfavorable
character by which he was afflicted: he is elevated to a state of grace, or he has
issued from a state of sin. In either case he is religiously transformed." In a note
on the same page, on the basis of certain Hindu texts, they add: "These *benefits*
from the sacrifice are, in our view, necessary reactions (*contrecoups*) of the rite.
They are not due to a free divine will which theology interpolates little by little
between the religious act and its sequences." On this view sacrifices are assimilated
to magical acts, and their effects are conceived somewhat on the analogy of what
is known as the reflex action of prayer. But if the deity is thought of merely as
the object from which the sacrifices rebound to the offerer, it is on it nevertheless
that they must first strike that they may rebound.

worshipper's person. Even so, however, the fundamental idea of sacrifices is retained — the securing of something from the deity for the worshipper; and this is something very different from a transaction intended directly to call out action on the part of the worshipper himself. It is in effect subversive of the whole principle of sacrificial worship to imagine that sacrifices are offered directly to affect the worshippers and to secure action from them: their purpose is to affect the deity and to secure beneficial action on its part. "The purpose of sacrifice," says J. Jeremias justly,[40] "is invariably to influence the deity in favour of the sacrificer." Every time the writers of the New Testament speak of the work of Christ under the rubric of a sacrifice, therefore, they bear witness — under any theory of sacrifice current among scholars — that they conceive of His work as directed Godward and as intended directly to affect God, not man.

It must be borne steadily in mind that the theories of sacrificial worship which we have been enumerating do not necessarily represent the judgment of their adherents on the nature and implications of sacrificial worship in the developed ritual of Israel, and much less in the decadence of Israelitish religion which is thought to have been in progress when the New Testament books were written. These theories are general theories and are put forward as attempts to determine the ideas which gave birth to and in this sense underlie all sacrificial worship. The adherents of these theories for the most part recognize that in the course of the history of sacrificial worship many changes of conception took place, here, there, and elsewhere; many new ideas were incorporated and many old ones lost. They are quite prepared to look for and to trace out in the history of sacrificial worship, therefore, at least a "development," and this "development" is not thought of as necessarily running on the same lines — certainly not *pari passu* — in every nation. Though these theorists are inclined, therefore, to conceive all sacrificial worship as rooting in one notion, they are ordinarily willing to recognize that the "development" of sacrificial worship may have taken, or actually did take, its own

[40] "Encyclopaedia Biblica," col. 4120.

direction in each region of the earth and among each people, as the conditions of its existence and modifying influences may have varied from time to time or from place to place. The history of sacrificial worship in Israel becomes thus a special subject of investigation; and scholars engaged upon it have wrought out their schemes of "development," beginning, each, with his own theory of the origin and essential presuppositions of sacrificial worship, and leading up through the stages recognized by him to the culmination of Israelitish sacrificial worship in the Levitical system. When we say that the sacrificial worship of Israel culminated in the Levitical system, this has a special significance for the investigations in question, seeing that they ordinarily proceed more or less completely on the assumption of the schematization of the development of religion in Israel which has been worked out by the Graf-Wellhausen school. This places the Levitical system at the end of the long development, and looks upon it as the final outcome of the actual religious effort of Israel. From this point of view we are apt to have, therefore, successively, discussions of sacrificial worship in the primitive Semitic ages, in the early Israelitish times, in the prophetic period, and in the prescriptions of the Levitical law. Thus a long course of development is interposed between the origin of sacrifices and the enactments of the Levitical legislation; and the theorists are free from all embarrassment when they find sacrifices bearing a very different meaning and charged with very different implications in the Levitical system from what they had conceived their fundamental, that is, speaking historically, their primitive meaning and implication to be. It is not surprising, therefore, that in point of fact, the theorizers do ordinarily find the conceptions expressed in the Levitical system different from the fundamental ideas which they suppose to have been originally embodied in sacrificial worship.

It is quite common for them to find this difference precisely in this, — that the Levitical system is the elaborate embodiment of the piacular idea, while in earlier times some one of the other conceptions of sacrifice prevailed. On this view it is customary to say that the idea of expiation is first elaborated in the post-exilic period, in which the sin-offering takes the first place among types of sacrifices, and that special expiatory sacrifices are mentioned first in Ezekiel (xl. 39, xlii. 13, xliii. 19). The assumptions in this construction, to be sure, are challenged on both sides.

It is pointed out, on the one side, that the rise of special expiatory sacrifices is not the same thing as the rise of the conception of expiation in connection with sacrifices. A. Kuenen notes,[41] for example, that the burnt-offering, which is thought the oldest of all sacrifices, was offered in earlier times in those cases for which, in the completed legislation, the expiatory sacrifices proper were required; and indeed it is clear that the whole burnt-offering can still be expiatory in the late document which is isolated as P (Lev. i. 4, xiv. 20, xvi. 24). And Robertson Smith does not hesitate to declare [42] that "the atoning function of sacrifice is not confined to a particular class of oblation, but belongs to all sacrifices." Of course this declaration is made from his own point of view; but it is not valid merely from his point of view. For him all sacrifices go back to a primitive form in which the object is to maintain or to reinstate communion with the God. Expiation is in his view only the re-establishment of the broken bond: the original totemistic sacrifice had all the effects of an expiatory rite; and in all the developments which have followed, this element in their significance has never been lost. All trace of totemism is effaced; but the sense of expiation always abides and thus becomes the constant feature of sacrifices. Hubert and Mauss arrive at the same result along another pathway.[43] In all sacrifices there is a thing offered — the victim, we may call it for brevity's sake. This victim is an intermediary. When we say intermediary, however, we say representative. And when we say representative, we say broadly, substitute. "This is why the offerer inserts between the religious forces and himself intermediaries, the chief of which is the victim. If he went through this rite to the

[41] "The Religion of Israel," ii. p. 263.
[42] "Religion of the Semites²," p. 237.   [43] As cited, p. 134.

end himself, he would find in it death and not life. The victim takes his place. It alone enters into the dangerous region of the sacrifice, it succumbs there, and it is there in order to succumb. The offerer remains under cover; the gods take the victim instead of taking him. *It ransoms him.*" "There is no sacrifice," they add emphatically, "in which there does not intervene some idea of ransom." We may take it to be sufficiently clear, then, that, whatever conceptions may have from time to time and from place to place dominated the minds of sacrificial worship, the one constant idea which has always been present in it is precisely that of piacular mediation. And it is very plain indeed that we cannot look upon the Levitical legislation as the introduction of the piacular conception into the sacrificial system of Israel.

The criticism directed from the other side against the assumptions of the theory in question cannot be held to be so successful. The general contention of this criticism is that, while it is to be admitted that the drift in Israel was towards the piacular conception, yet that drift had not reached its goal in the Levitical system, which thus at best marks only a stage in the progress towards it. There are some indeed who will not grant even so much as this. They see very definitely expressed in the Levitical system too some quite different conception of sacrificial worship, the Homage conception, say, or the Communion conception, according to which respectively the sacrifices are thought of as analogous to prayers or to sacraments. Others find it more convenient simply to deny that any definite conception whatever informs the Levitical system. The framers of this legislation were not clear in their own minds what was the real nature of sacrificial worship, but were content to practice it as an ordinance of God and to leave the mode of its operation in that mystery which probably enhanced rather than curtailed its influence upon the awe-stricken consciousness of the worshipper.[44] This extreme view has obtained a very considerable vogue, but need scarcely be taken seriously. It is plain

[44] R. Smend, "Lehrb. d. A. T. Religionsgeschichte," p. 324, cf. G. F. Moore, "Encyclopaedia Biblica," col. 4226. Compare also A. B. Davidson, "Theology

enough that the Levitical system is something more than a series of blind rites, the whole value of the performance of which lies in the manifestation of implicit obedience to God. And it is generally allowed that the sacrificial conception of Israel, one stage in the development of which is marked by the Levitical system, was moving towards the idea of expiation to which it ultimately attained. Rudolf Smend, for instance, who supposes that the earliest sacrificial ideas of Israel saw in the sacrifices only acts of homage, yet considers that these ideas were steadily modified in later ages until they had run through all the stages up to that of reparation of sin — although he thinks it doubtful if the Israelites ever attained to a truly substitutionary theory.[45] H. J. Holtzmann, while insisting that the penal interpretation is not that of the law, feels compelled to admit that it was nevertheless the popular doctrine of the Jews and that traces of it found their way into the code itself.[46] A. B. Davidson, who believes that the earliest idea connected with sacrifice in Israel was that of "a gift to placate God," considers that this idea still underlies the law, and yet "in later times the other side was more prominent, that the death of the creature was of the nature of penalty, by the exaction of which the righteousness of Jehovah was satisfied." [47] "This idea," he adds, "seems certainly expressed in Isa. liii; at least these two points appear to be stated there, that the sins of the people, *i.e.*, the penalties for them, were laid on the servant and borne by him; and secondly, that thus the people were relieved from the penalty, and their sins being borne were forgiven." That there was a substitution in the law itself is recognized, on the other

of the Old Testament," pp. 352–354, where he says that the author of Leviticus has contented himself with stating the fact that the offering of a life atones, suggesting no explanation of why or how it atones. But he proceeds to remark that we can scarcely agree with Riehm that the blood atones merely because it is ordained that it shall, but should no doubt assume that there was a reason for the ordination, understood or not by the worshipper but no doubt at least dimly felt.

[45] As cited, p. 128.

[46] "Lehrbuch der Neutestamentlichen Theologie¹," 1897, v. i, pp. 67-68.

[47] "Theology of the Old Testament," p. 355, cf. 353. The use made of Davidson by W. L. Walker, "The Gospel of Reconciliation," 1909, p. 21, seems scarcely justified.

hand, by A. Dillmann, although he insists that this was not a substitution in kind, but of something not itself sin-bearing.[48]

W. Robertson Smith is well known as the powerful advocate of one of the lowest possible theories of the meaning of the primitive sacrifices of the Semites — that which sees the origin of sacrifice in a meal in which the worshipper was supposed to become physically imbued with the God on whom he fed in symbol. But he did not imagine that the Semitic peoples continued permanently to be sunk in this crass notion. Following Robertson Smith's guidance, W. P. Paterson adopts the common-meal conception of primitive sacrifice — "the fundamental motive was to gratify God by giving or sharing with Him a meal" — but fully recognizes that such changes had taken place in the progress of time that the Levitical system was just an elaborate embodiment of the piacular idea. In his view the whole system — in all its elements, and that not merely of animal but even of vegetable offerings — "contemplated the community as being in a state of guilt, and requiring to be reconciled to God." In it, in short, sacrifices "have in fact become — not excepting the Peace-offering in its later interpretation — piacular sacrifices which dispose God to mercy, procure the forgiveness of sin and avert punishment."[49] Accordingly he expounds the matter thus: [50] "The expiation of guilt is the leading purpose of the Levitical sacrifices. Their office is to cover or make atonement for sin. The word employed to describe this specific effect is כִּפֶּר. This efficacy is connected with all four kinds of principal offerings; the objects of the covering are persons and sins; the covering takes place before God, and it stands in a specially close relation to the sprinkling of the blood and the burning of the sacrificial flesh (Lev. i. 4,

---

[48] "A. T. Theologie," pp. 488–489.

[49] Hastings' "Dictionary of the Bible," v. iv, p. 338 b: "The Meat-offering also covered from sin and delivered from its consequences."

[50] As cited, p. 339 a. Cf. p. 342 a, where he sums up: "More likely is it that the step deemed by Holtzmann inevitable at a later stage was already taken, and that the chaos of confused ideas resulting from the discredit of old views was averted by the assertion of the substitutionary idea — 'the most external indeed, but also the simplest, the most generally intelligible, and the readiest answer to the question as to the nature of expiation.'"

etc.)." It is not to be doubted, of course, that elements of adoration and of sacramental communion also enter into the sacrificial rites of the Levitical system: nothing could be clearer than that in the several sacrificial ordinances, a variety of religious motives find appropriate expression, and a variety of religious impressions are aimed at and produced. But it would seem quite impossible to erect these motives and impressions into the main, and certainly not into the sole, notion expressed or object sought in these ordinances. It may be confidently contended that, present as they undoubtedly are, they are present as subsidiary and ancillary to the fundamental function of the sacrifice, which is to propitiate the offended deity in behalf of sinful man. Any unbiased study of the Levitical system must issue, as it seems to us, in the conviction that this system is through and through, in its intention and effect, piacular.

It is, naturally, quite possible to contend that it is not of the first importance for the interpretation of the New Testament writers, when they represent our Lord as a sacrifice, to determine what the conception of sacrifice was which underlay the Levitical legislation. It may be urged that the ideas of the writers of the New Testament were not influenced so much by the Levitical system, as by the notion of sacrifice current in the Jewish thought of their time. As we have seen, however, there are very few who doubt that the Jews in the time when the New Testament was in writing held the doctrine of substitutive expiation in connection with the sacrificial system. George F. Moore is one of these few.[51] He is quite sure that the idea of *poena vicaria* is a pure importation into the Old Testament, the prevailing conception of sacrifice in which he conceives to be that of "gift." And he seems to imply that the later Jewish doctors were of a quite indefinite mind as to how the sacrifice operated in expiating sin. "The theory that the victim's life is put in place of the owner's," he remarks, "is nowhere hinted at"; and he adds that this is "perhaps because the Jewish doctors understood better than our theologians what sin-offerings and trespass offerings were, and what they were for." We

[51] "Encyclopaedia Biblica," v. iv, coll. 4223–4226.

must leave it to him to make clear to himself — he has not made it clear to us — how such offerings could have been understood to "atone" — to make expiation for sin and to propitiate the offended deity — by the interposition of a slain victim, without any idea of vicarious penalty creeping in.

Even G. B. Stevens will not go the lengths of this. He apparently agrees with Moore, indeed, that the idea of the *poena vicaria* is absent from Old Testament sacrifices. But he seems to allow it even a determining place in the later Judaism. His prime contention at this point is, indeed, that it was from this later Judaism that Paul, for example, derived this conception. For he admits that in Paul, at least, "we have here the idea of satisfaction by substitution"; [52] and the precise thing on which he insists is that "this legalistic scheme which Paul wrought out of the materials of current Jewish thought." [53] He never tires in fact of scoring this teaching of Paul's as a mere remnant of Phariseeism, [54] in which, therefore, Christians are not bound to follow him. He is clearly so far right in this that this conception was part of Pharisaic belief. There are two conceptions indeed which beyond question — and probably no one questions it — lay together in the minds of the men of the New Testament times, forming the presuppositions of their thought concerning sin and its forgiveness. The one is that atonement for sin was wrought by the sacrifices; the other that vicarious sufferings availed for atonement. The former conception is crisply expressed by Heinrich Weinel thus: "At that time almost the only thought connected with sacrifice was that of a propitiatory rite, accompanied by the shedding of blood." [55] With respect to the latter H. H. Wendt points out the currency in the time of Jesus of "the idea of the expiatory significance of sufferings for guilt, and of the substitutionary significance of the excessive sufferings of the righteous for the sins of others." [56]

[52] "The Christian Doctrine of Salvation," p. 62, cf. p. 65.
[53] As cited, p. 66.
[54] As cited, pp. 73–75.   [55] "Saint Paul," E. T., p. 302.
[56] "Teaching of Jesus," E. T., v. ii, p. 243. He refers in support to F. Weber, "Jüdische Theologie²," 1897, § 70, p. 326 ff. and to E. Schürer, "Geschichte des jüdischen Volkes," v. ii, p. 466 (E. T. Div. II. v. ii, p. 186).

Needless to say both facts thus expressed are fully recognized even by, say, G. F. Moore. He tells us that in the Palestinian schools of the first and second Christian centuries, "the effect of sacrifice is expressed as in the Pentateuch, by the verb *kipper*, 'make propitiation,' 'expiation,'" and that "the general principle is that all private sacrifices atone, except peace offerings (including thank offerings), with which no confession of sin is made." [57] And he tells us as explicitly not only that an expiatory character was attributed to suffering, but that "the suffering and death of righteous men" were held "to atone for the sins of others." [58] It would seem inconceivable that such relatable ideas could be kept apart in the mind which gave harborage to both: it is inhuman for us to imagine that men, merely because they lived a few hundred years ago, were incapable of putting even one and one together. And as we read over, say, the ceremonial for the Day of Atonement in the Mishnah tractate *Yoma* we can scarcely fail to see that this one and one were put together. Paul Fiebig occupies a general position very similar to that of G. F. Moore: he is eager to make it clear that the men of old time in their religious rites troubled themselves very little about ideas, and lived much more in usages and ceremonies carried out with painful exactness. Yet he cannot refuse to add: [59] "This is not to say that the ritual of the Day of Atonement did not suggest a variety of ideas, — this idea for example: 'You, a sinner, have really deserved death, but this sacrificial animal now bears the punishment of your sin.' Or this: 'The sacrificial animal now bears the sin away into the wilderness; so soon as the goat which is sent to Azazel (cf. Lev. xvi.) into the wilderness is gone, the sins have also disappeared.' Ideas of substitution and reparation, of bearing the curse of sin, — and also of a gift by means of which the deity is to be propitiated — are suggested here. The sacrificial animal might also be thought of as a purchase price, as ransom-money, and the whole sacrifice be placed under the point of view of ransoming. All these ideas were suggested

---

[57] As cited, col. 4223.　　　　[58] As cited, col. 4226, cf. col. 4232.
[59] "Jesu Blut ein Geheimnis?" 1906, p. 33.

and were simply and easily to be read out of the ritual." We think it necessary to say, not merely that such ideas as these might be suggested by the ceremonial of the Day of Atonement, and — each in its own measure — by the several varieties of sacrifice which were in use; but that they were inevitably suggested by them and, in point of fact, formed the circle of ideas which make up in their entirety what we may justly think of as the sacrificial conception of the time.[60]

Whether, then, we look to the Levitical system or to the conceptions current at the time when the New Testament was written as determining the sense of the writers of the New Testament when they spoke of Christ as a sacrifice, the most natural meaning that can be attached to the term on their lips is that of an expiatory offering propitiating God's favor and reconciling Him to guilty man. An attempt may be made, to be sure, to break the force of this finding by representing sacrificial worship to have fallen so much into the background in the time of our Lord that it no longer possessed importance for the religious thought of the day. Martin Brückner tells us

[60] It is by a misapprehension that J. K. Mozley, "The Doctrine of Atonement," 1916, p. 20, supporting himself on G. B. Stevens, seems to deny the sacrificial character of the scape-goat: "As to the ritual of the Day of Atonement, here also the old opinion is not as firmly established as might appear at first sight. The culminating point is the sending away of the goat 'for Azazel,' but we must remember that 'the flesh of this goat was not burned; atonement was not made by its blood; it was not a sacrifice at all.'" The quotation is from Stevens, as cited, p. 11. On the other hand Hugo Gressmann, "Der Ursprung der israelitisch-jüdischen Eschatologie," 1905, pp. 328–329 sees the sacrificial idea at its height represented in the scape-goat. He is speaking of the Ebed and adverting to the ascription of "a substitutive expiatory character" to his sufferings and death, and remarks: "The sacrificial idea stands in the background. We have materially an exact parallel in the goat of Azazel which was offered as an expiatory sacrifice on the great Day of Atonement. . . . The goat is burdened with the sin of the congregation and offered substitutionally for it. For the expulsion of the goat is only a specific form of sacrifice (Hubert et Mauss, "Essai sur la nature et la fonction du sacrifice" in L'Année Sociologique Second quar., Paris, 1898, p. 75). The expiatory significance which is attached to the death of the Ebed fully corresponds with the expiatory character which is ascribed here to the goat." At the place cited, supplemented at pp. 78f. and 92, Hubert and Mauss assign the scape-goat to its right category and expound convincingly its character as an expiatory sacrifice, thus supplying a corrective to the exposition of W. R. Smith on which Stevens supports himself.

that there is no exposition of the Jewish theory of sacrifice given in W. Bousset's book on the "Religion of Judaism" because "there wasn't any." [61] Supposing, however, the fact to be as stated — that the doctrine of sacrifice played so small a part in the religion of the later Judaism that it may be treated as negligible in a summary of the religious conceptions of the time, — that would only add significance to the employment of it by the New Testament writers as a paradigm into which to run their conception of the work of Christ. The further they must be supposed to have gone afield to find this rubric, the more importance they must be supposed to have attached to it as a vehicle of their doctrine. We are not inquiring into the abstract likelihood of the New Testament writers making use of a rare rubric: their use of it is not in dispute.[62] We are estimating the measure of significance which must be attributed to their use of a rubric which they actually employ. The less a mere matter-of-course their employment of it can be shown to be, the more it must be recognized that they had a distinct purpose in using it and the more weight must be assigned to its implications in their hands. Brückner's remark, therefore, that sacrificial worship had become in the time of Christ "without importance" for Jewish theology reacts injuriously upon his main contention in the passage where it occurs — namely that it was without importance for Paul.

It has become almost a fashion to speak minimizingly of Paul's employment of the category of sacrifice in his explanation of Christ's work, and it is interesting to observe how hard Nemesis treads on the heels of the attempt to do so. Brückner's instance affords a very good example. What he wishes to do is to lower the importance of the conception of sacrifice in Paul's system of thought concerning the work of Christ. He seeks to do this by suggesting that the sacrificial language served with Paul little further purpose than to express the notion of sub-

[61] "Die Entstehung des paulinischen Christologie," 1903, p. 231.

[62] Of course nothing is ever absolutely undisputed. Paterson, as cited, p. 343, b, very properly remarks: "It has been denied that Paul adopts the category (Schmidt, "Die paul. Christologie," p. 84) but the denial rests on dogmatic rather than on exegetical grounds (Ritschl, ii. p. 161)."

stitution. "The idea of a sacrifice," he remarks, "came into consideration for Paul only as an illustration of a conception: the thing which he intended lies in the theory of substitution" — a substitution which, he proceeds to show, includes in it the idea of "a substitutive punishment." Paul, in other words, calls Christ a sacrifice only with a view to showing that Christ too offered Himself as a substitutive expiation of our sins. What more could he be supposed to have intended? The contrast between the minimizing tone adopted and the effect of the facts adduced to support it, is perhaps even more striking in the remarks of A. E. J. Rawlinson, writing in the collection of Oxford essays published under the title of "Foundations." [63] With Paul, he tells us, Christ is spoken of as a sacrifice only by way of "an occasional illustration or a momentary point of comparison." He refers to Christ as "our Passover, sacrificed for us," as "making peace by his blood," as in some sense a "propitiation." "Apart from the three phrases quoted in the text," he adds in a note, "and the statement in Ephesians v. 2, 'Even as Christ also loved you and gave Himself up for us, an offering and a sacrifice to God, for an odour of a sweet smell' — where the self-oblation of Christ is compared not to a sin-offering, but to a burnt-offering, — there do not appear to be any passages in St. Paul which interpret the work of Christ in sacrificial terms." Not Gal. iii. 13 (Deut. xxi. 23), since "sacrificial victims were never regarded as 'accursed.'" Not in the idea of vicarious suffering — which is not a sacrificial idea — only the scape-goat being a sin-bearer (Lev. xvi.) and the scape-goat not being sacrificed. The reader will scarcely escape the impression that a great deal of unavailing trouble is being expended here in an effort to remove unwelcome facts out of the way. And it will not be strange if he wonders what advantage is supposed to be gained from insisting that Paul has made little use of the category of sacrifice for expounding his view of the nature of Christ's work, so long as it is recognized that he does employ it, and that therefore it must be understood to be a suitable expression of his view. "St. Paul does not appear to have made

[63] "Foundations," 1912, p. 194.

great use of Old Testament ideas of sacrifice," remarks J. K. Mozley:[64] "Ritschl indeed in the second volume of his great work, lays stress on the importance of the sacrificial system for Paul's doctrine, but we can hardly go beyond the balanced statement of Dr. Stevens ("Christian Doctrine of Salvation," p. 63): 'While Paul has made a less frequent and explicit use of sacrificial ideas than we should have expected, it is clear that the system supplied one of the forms of thought by which he interpreted Christ's death.'" That allowed, however, and all is allowed: agree that the rubric of sacrifice lent itself naturally to the expression of what Paul would convey concerning the death of Christ,[65] and we might as well say frankly with Paterson that to Paul, "the sacrifice of Christ had the significance of the death of an innocent victim in the room of the guilty," and add with him, with equal frankness: "It is vain to deny that St. Paul freely employs the category of substitution, involving the conception of the imputation or transference of moral qualities" — although it might perhaps be well to use some more exact phraseology in saying it than Paterson has managed to employ.

There is one book of the New Testament of which it has proved impossible for even the hardiest to deny that Christ's death is presented in it as a sacrifice. We refer, of course, to the Epistle to the Hebrews. In it not only is Christ's death directly described as a sacrifice, but all the sacrificial language is gathered about it in the repeated allusions which are made

[64] "The Doctrine of the Atonement," 1916, p. 79, note.

[65] Is perhaps part of the difficulty which so many writers feel on this matter due to approaching it from a wrong angle, and thinking not so much of Paul's expressing his convictions concerning Christ's death in terms of sacrifice as of his imposing on the death of Christ mechanically ideas derived from the sacrifices? Paul's conviction that Christ had died for our sins, bearing them in His own body on the tree, is the primary thing: the sacrificial language he applies to it is one of his modes of stating this fundamental fact. He begins always with the great fact of the expiatory death of Christ. "Ménégoz has admirably remarked," says Orello Cone justly in a parallel matter, "that Paul's faith in the expiatory sacrifice of Christ was not the conclusion of a process of reasoning on the relation between the mercy and justice of God, but, on the contrary, the apostle's ideas on the justice and mercy of God were founded on his faith in the expiatory death of Christ."

to it as such.[66] Nor is it doubtful that it is distinctly of expiatory
sacrifices that the author is thinking when he presents Christ
as dying a sacrificial death. He even uses of it "that characteristic term inseparably associated in the Old Testament with
these sacrifices" (ἱλάσκομαι, ii. 17) the absence of which from
the allusion to Christ's sacrifice in other parts of the New Testament has been made a matter of remark — although it is not
really absent from them, but is present in its derivatives
(ἱλαστήριον, Rom. iii. 25; ἱλασμός, I John ii. 2, iv. 10) justifying
fully Paterson's remark [67] that "the idea of cancelling guilt,
of which a vital moment is liability to punishment, is associated
with Christ's sacrifice in Heb. ii. 17, I John ii. 2 (ἱλάσκεσθαι
with ἁμαρτίας as object, and so 'to expiate')." The Epistle to
the Hebrews does not, however, really stand apart from the
rest of the New Testament in these things, as, indeed, we have
just incidentally pointed out with reference to the Levitical
term for sacrificial expiation, employed as it is by Paul and
John as well as by this author. It only has its own points to
make and distributes the emphasis to suit them. Even in such
a peculiar matter as the ascription to Christ at once of the functions of priest and sacrifice, it may possibly have a parallel in
Eph. v. 2.[68] The fact is, as Paterson broadly asserts in words

[66] B. F. Westcott, "Epistle to the Hebrews," p. 299, speaks of Christ's sacrifice as being presented in the Epistle to the Hebrews "in three distinct aspects,"
"(1) as a Sacrifice of Atonement (ix. 14, 15); (2) as a Covenant Sacrifice (ix.
15–17); and (3) as a Sacrifice which is the ground-work of a Feast (xiii. 10, 11)."
This is true; but it is possible to press analysis over-far. The "Sacrifice which is
the ground-work of a Feast" is the sacrifice of which we hear in the institution
of the Lord's Supper, and this is distinctly a "Covenant Sacrifice." The "Covenant Sacrifice" (ix. 15, 17) is a sacrifice for sin (ix. 12, 26), and is therefore fundamentally piacular and atoning, as indeed its relation to the passover-lamb
sufficiently intimates. In His sacrifice Christ fulfilled all the functions of sacrifice,
and thus there are varied aspects in which His sacrifice may be looked upon. But
above all else, He made expiation for the sins of His people by immolating Himself on the altar — thus putting away sin by the sacrifice of Himself.

[67] As cited, p. 344 a.

[68] Cf. J. K. Mozley, "The Doctrine of the Atonement," 1916, p. 82, note 1:
"Eph. 1, 7 also refutes Pfleiderer's statement (ii. 175) that in this Epistle Christ
is not the expiatory sacrifice, but the sacrificing priest. The latter idea is certainly
that of v. 2, but St. Paul may as easily have united the two conceptions as did
the writer to the Hebrews."

which were quoted from him at the opening of this discussion, that every important type of New Testament teaching, including the teaching of Christ Himself, concurs in representing Christ as a sacrifice, and in conceiving of the sacrifice which it represents Christ as being, as a substitutive expiation. We say, including Christ Himself; and we may say that with our eye exclusively on the Synoptic Gospels. The language of Mt. xx. 28, Mk. x. 45 is sacrificial language; and it is very distinctly substitutive language, — "In the place of many." That of Mt. xxvi. 28, Mk. xiv. 24, Lk. xxii. 20 (the critical questions which have been raised about these passages are negligible) is sacrificial language; and it is equally distinctly expiatory language — "Blood shed for many," "For the remission of sins." [69]

The possibility of underrating the wealth and importance of the allusions of the writers of the New Testament to the death of Christ as sacrificial, in the sense of expiatory, appears to depend upon a tendency to recognize such allusions only when express references to sacrifices are made in connection with it, if we should not even say only when didactic expositions of it as a sacrifice are developed. Nothing can be more certain, for example, than that the references to the "blood" of Jesus are one and all ascriptions of a sacrificial character and effect to His death.[70] Nevertheless, we meet with attempts to explain these ascriptions away. Thus, for example, G. F. Moore writes as follows, having more particularly in mind Paul's usage: [71] "Evidence of a more pervasive association of Christ's death with sacrifice has been sought in the references to his blood as the ground of the benefits conferred by his death (Rom. iii. 25, v. 9): the thought of sacrifice is so constantly associated with his death, it is said, that the one word suffices to suggest

[69] Cf. the discussion of these passages by Mozley, as cited, chapter ii.

[70] In general these references comprise: (1) certain general passages, Heb. ix. 14, 20, x. 29, xii. 24, I Pet. i. 19, I John i. 7; (2) certain eucharistic passages, Mt. xxvi. 28, Mk. xiv. 24, Luke xxii. 20, I Cor. xi. 25; John vi. 53, 54, 55, 56, I Cor. x. 16; (3) the formula, διὰ τῆς αἵματος (or its equivalent), Acts xx. 28, Eph. i. 7, Col. i. 20, Heb. ix. 12, xiii. 12 (I John v. 6), Rev. xii. 11; and (4) the formula ἐν τῇ αἵματι (or its equivalent) Rom. iii. 25, v. 9, I Cor. xi. 25 (27) Eph. ii. 13, Heb. x. 19 (xiii. 25), I John v. 6, Rev. i. 5, v. 9, vii. 14.

[71] "Encyclopaedia Biblica," coll. 4229–4230.

it. But in view of the infrequency, to say the least, of sacrificial
metaphors in the greater epistles, it is doubtful whether $α ἷμα$
is not used merely in allusion to Jesus' violent death. Nor is
the case clearer in Col. i. 20, Eph. i. 7, ii. 13; the really noteworthy thing is that the context contains no suggestion of sacrifice either in thought or phrase." Such argumentation seems to
us merely perverse. The discovery of allusions to the sacrificial
character of Christ's death in the reiterated mention of His
blood is not a mere assumption deriving color only from the
frequency of other references to His sacrificial death; it has its
independent ground in the nature of these allusions themselves.
In every instance mentioned, so far from the context containing no suggestion of sacrifice, it is steeped in sacrificial suggestions. Is there no sacrificial suggestion in such language as
this: "Whom God set forth as a propitiation, through faith, in
His blood"? Or in such language as this: "While we were yet
sinners Christ died for us: much more then having been now
justified by His blood, we shall be saved by Him from the
wrath"? Or as this: "And by Him to reconcile all things unto
Him, having made peace through the blood of His cross"? Or
as this: "In whom we have redemption through His blood, the
forgiveness of sins"? Or as this: "But now in Christ Jesus you
who once were far off have been made nigh in the blood of
Christ"? This is the very language of the altar: "propitiation,"
"reconciliation," "redemption," "forgiveness." It passes all
comprehension how it could be suggested that the word
"blood" could be employed in such connections "merely in
allusion to Jesus' violent death." And that particularly when
Jesus' death was not actually an especially bloody death.
"Another remarkable thing," says Paul Fiebig.[72] "is this: why
is precisely the 'blood' of Jesus so often spoken of? Why is the
redemption and the forgiveness of sins so often connected with
the 'blood' of Jesus? This is remarkable; for the death on the
cross was not so very bloody that it should be precisely the
blood of Jesus which so impressed the eye-witnesses and
the first Christians. The Evangelists moreover (except John xix.

[72] As cited, p. 11.

35 f.) say nothing about it. This special emphasis on the blood cannot be explained therefore from the kind of death Jesus died." If we really wish to know what the New Testament writers had in mind when they spoke of the blood of Jesus we have only to permit them to tell us themselves. They always adduce it in the sacrificial sense. In his survey of the passages Fiebig begins [73] not unnaturally with I Pet. i. 17–19. "Knowing that ye were redeemed, not with corruptible things, with silver or gold, from your vain manner of life handed down from your fathers: but with precious blood as of a lamb without blemish and without spot, Christ." His comment runs thus: "Here the clause 'as of a pure and unspotted lamb' makes quite clear what the popular and at that time wholly clear conception is which provides the key to the problem of the redemptive significance of the blood of Jesus. This conception is the sacrifice; and of course the sacrifice such as every Jew (and in corresponding fashion, every heathen) knew it from his daily life and from the festivals and duties of his religion." This is of course only one passage; but in this case the adage is true, *ab uno disce omnes*, — we may spare ourselves the survey of the whole series.

The theology of the writers of the New Testament is very distinctly a "blood theology." But their reiterated reference of the salvation of men to the blood of Christ is not the only way in which they represent the work of Christ as in its essential character sacrificial. In numerous other forms of allusion they show that they conceived the idea of sacrifice to supply a suitable explanation of its nature and effect. We may avail ourselves of words of James Denney to sum up the matter briefly, — words which are in certain respects over-cautious, but which contain the essence of the matter. "We have every reason to believe," says he,[74] "that sacrificial blood universally, and not only in special cases, was associated with propitiatory power. 'The atoning function of sacrifice,' as Robertson Smith put it, speaking of primitive times, 'is not confined to a par-

[73] P. 13.
[74] "The Death of Christ," ed. 1903, pp. 53–54.

ticular class of oblation, but belongs to all sacrifices.' [75] Dr. Driver has expressed the same opinion with regard to the Levitical legislation. . . . Criticizing Ritschl's explanation of sacrifice and its effect, he says,[76] it seems better to suppose that though the burnt-, peace- and meat-offerings were not offered *expressly*, like the sin- and guilt-offerings, for the forgiveness of sin, they nevertheless (in so far as *kipper* is predicated of them) were regarded as 'covering' or neutralizing, the offerer's unworthiness to appear before God and so, though in a much less degree than the sin- or guilt-offering, as effectively *Kappārā* in the sense ordinarily attached to the word, viz. 'propitiation.' Instead of saying 'in a much less degree' I should prefer to say 'with a less specific reference or application,' but the point is not material. What it concerns us to note is that the New Testament, while it abstains from interpreting Christ's death by any special prescriptions of the Levitical law, constantly uses sacrificial language to describe that death, and in doing so unequivocally recognizes in it a propitiatory character — in other words, a reference to sin and its forgiveness." What this fundamentally means is that the New Testament writers, in employing this language to describe the death of Christ, intended to represent that death as performing the functions of an expiatory sacrifice; wished to be understood as so representing it; and could not but be so understood by their first readers who were wonted to sacrificial worship.

An interesting proof that they were so understood is supplied by a remarkable fact emphasized in a striking passage by Adolf Harnack.[77] Wherever the Christian religion went, there blood-sacrifice ceased to be offered — just as the tapers go out when the sun rises. Christ's death was recognized everywhere where it became known as the reality of which they were the shadows. Having offered His own body once for all and by this one offering perfected forever them that are sanctified, it

[75] "Religion of the Semites," p. 219.

[76] Hastings' "Dictionary of the Bible," s.v. "Propitiation," p. 132.

[77] "Das Wesen des Christentums," ed. 1900, pp. 98–99: E. T., "What is Christianity?" 1901, pp. 157 ff.

was well understood that there remained no more offering for sin. "The death of Christ," says Harnack — "of this there can be no doubt — made an end to blood-sacrifices in the history of religion." "The instinct which led to them found its satisfaction and therefore its end in the death of Christ." "His death had the value of a sacrificial death; for otherwise it would not have had the power to penetrate into that inner world out of which the blood-sacrifices proceeded," — and, penetrating into it, to meet, and to satisfy all the needs which blood-sacrifices had been invented to meet and satisfy.

The whole world thus adds its testimony to the sacrificial character of Christ's death as it has received it, and as it rests upon it. As to the world's need of it, and as to the place it takes in the world, we shall let a sentence of C. Bigg's teach us. "The study of the great Greek and Roman moralists of the Empire," he tells us,[78] "leaves upon my own mind a strong conviction that the fundamental difference between heathenism of all shades and Christianity is to be discovered in the doctrine of Vicarious Sacrifice, that is to say, in the Passion of our Lord." This is as much as to say that not only is the doctrine of the sacrificial death of Christ embodied in Christianity as an essential element of the system, but in a very real sense it constitutes Christianity. It is this which differentiates Christianity from other religions. Christianity did not come into the world to proclaim a new morality and, sweeping away all the supernatural props by which men were wont to support their trembling, guilt-stricken souls, to throw them back on their own strong right arms to conquer a standing before God for themselves. It came to proclaim the real sacrifice for sin which God had provided in order to supersede all the poor fumbling efforts which men had made and were making to provide a sacrifice for sin for themselves; and, planting men's feet on this, to bid them go forward. It was in this sign that Christianity conquered, and it is in this sign alone that it continues to conquer. We may think what we will of such a religion. What cannot be denied is that Christianity is such a religion.

[78] "The Church's Task under the Roman Empire," pp. x.-xi.

XII

ON THE BIBLICAL NOTION OF "RENEWAL"

ON THE BIBLICAL NOTION OF "RENEWAL"[1]

The terms "renew," "renewing," are not of frequent occurrence in our English Bible. In the New Testament they do not occur at all in the Gospels, but only in the Epistles (Paul and Hebrews), where they stand, respectively, for the Greek terms ἀνακαινόω (II Cor. iv. 16, Col. iii. 10) with its cognates, ἀνακαινίζω (Heb. vi. 6) and ἀνανεόομαι (Eph. iv. 23), and ἀνακαίνωσις (Rom. xii. 2, Tit. iii. 5). If we leave to one side II Cor. iv. 16 and Heb. vi. 6, which are of somewhat doubtful interpretation, it becomes at once evident that a definite theological conception is embodied in these terms. This conception is that salvation in Christ involves a radical and complete transformation wrought in the soul (Rom. xii. 2, Eph. iv. 23) by God the Holy Spirit (Tit. iii. 5, Eph. iv. 24), by virtue of which we become "new men" (Eph. iv. 24, Col. iii. 10), no longer conformed to this world (Rom. xii. 2, Eph. iv. 22, Col. iii. 9), but in knowledge and holiness of the truth created after the image of God (Eph. iv. 24, Col. iii. 10, Rom. xii. 2). The conception, it will be seen, is a wide one, inclusive of all that is comprehended in what we now technically speak of as regeneration, renovation and sanctification. It embraces, in fact, the entire subjective side of salvation, which it represents as a work of God, issuing in a wholly new creation (II Cor. v. 17, Gal. vi. 15, Eph. ii. 10). What is indicated is, therefore, the need of such a subjective salvation by sinful man, and the provision for this need made in Christ (Eph. iv. 20, Col. iii. 11, Tit. iii. 6).

The absence of the terms in question from the Gospels does not in the least argue the absence from the teaching of the Gospels of the thing expressed by them. This thing is so of the essence of the religion of revelation that it could not be absent from any stage of its proclamation. That it should be

[1] From *The Princeton Theological Review*, v. ix, 1911, pp. 242–267.

absent would require that sin should be conceived to have wrought no subjective injury to man, so that he would need for his recovery from sin only an objective cancelling of his guilt and reinstatement in the favor of God. This is certainly not the conception of the Scriptures in any of their parts. It is uniformly taught in Scripture that by his sin man has not merely incurred the divine condemnation but also corrupted his own heart; that sin, in other words, is not merely guilt but depravity: and that there is needed for man's recovery from sin, therefore, not merely atonement but renewal; that salvation, that is to say, consists not merely in pardon but in purification. Great as is the stress laid in the Scriptures on the forgiveness of sins as the root of salvation, no less stress is laid throughout the Scriptures on the cleansing of the heart as the fruit of salvation. Nowhere is the sinner permitted to rest satisfied with pardon as the end of salvation; everywhere he is made poignantly to feel that salvation is realized only in a clean heart and a right spirit.

In the Old Testament, for example, sin is not set forth in its origin as a purely objective act with no subjective effects, or in its manifestation as a series of purely objective acts out of all relation to the subjective condition. On the contrary, the sin of our first parents is represented as no less corrupting than inculpating; shame is as immediate a fruit of it as fear (Gen. iii. 7). And, on the principle that no clean thing can come out of what is unclean (Job xiv. 4), all that are born of woman are declared "abominable and corrupt," to whose nature iniquity alone is attractive (Job xv. 14–16). Accordingly, to become sinful, men do not wait until the age of accountable action arrives. Rather, they are apostate from the womb, and as soon as they are born go astray, speaking lies (Ps. lviii. 3): they are even shapen in iniquity and conceived in sin (Ps. li. 5). The propensity (יֵצֶר) of their heart is evil from their youth (Gen. viii. 21), and it is out of the heart that all the issues of life proceed (Prov. iv. 23, xx. 11). Acts of sin are therefore but the expression of the natural heart, which is deceitful above all things and desperately sick (Jer. xvii. 9). The only hope of an amendment

of the life, lies accordingly in a change of heart; and this change
of heart is the desire of God for His people (Deut. v. 29) and
the passionate longing of the saints for themselves (Ps. li. 10).
It is, indeed, wholly beyond man's own power to achieve it.
As well might the Ethiopian hope to change his skin and the
leopard his spots as he who is wonted to evil to correct his ways
(Jer. xiii. 23); and when it is a matter of cleansing not of hands
but of heart — who can declare that he has made his heart
clean and is pure from sin (Prov. xx. 9)? Men may be exhorted
to circumcise their hearts (Deut. x. 16, Jer. iv. 4), and to make
themselves new hearts and new spirits (Ezek. xviii. 31); but
the background of such appeals is rather the promise of God
than the ability of man (Deut. v. 29, Ezek. xi. 19, cf. Keil *in
loc.*). It is God alone who can "turn" a man "a new heart"
(I Sam. x. 9), and the cry of the saint who has come to understand what his sin means, and therefore what cleansing from
it involves, is ever, "Create (בְּרָא) in me a new heart, O God,
and renew (חַדֵּשׁ) a steadfast spirit within me" (Ps. li. 10[12]).
The express warrant for so great a prayer is afforded by the
promise of God who, knowing the incapacity of the flesh, has
Himself engaged to perfect His people. He will circumcise their
hearts, that they may love the Lord their God with all their
heart and with all their soul; and so may live (Deut. xxx. 6).
He will give them a heart to know Him that He is the Lord;
that so they may really be His people and He their God (Jer.
xxiv. 7). He will put His law in their inward parts and write
it in their heart so that all shall know Him (Jer. xxxi. 33, cf.
xxxii. 39). He will take the stony heart out of their flesh and
give them a heart of flesh, that they may walk in His statutes
and keep his ordinances and do them, and so be His people and
He their God (Ezek. xi. 19). He will give them a new heart and
take away the stony heart out of their flesh; and put His Spirit
within them and cause them to walk in His statutes and keep
His judgments and do them: that so they may be His people and
He their God (Ezek. xxxvi. 26, cf. xxxvii. 14). Thus the expectation of a new heart was made a substantial part of the Messianic
promise, in which was embodied the whole hope of Israel.

It does not seem open to doubt that in these great declarations we have the proclamation of man's need of "renewal" and of the divine provision for it as an essential element in salvation.[2] We must not be misled by the emphasis placed in the Old Testament on the forgiveness of sins as the constitutive fact of salvation, into explaining away all allusions to the cleansing of the heart as but figurative expressions for pardon. Pardon is no doubt frequently set forth under the figure or symbol of washing or cleansing: but expressions such as those which have been adduced go beyond this. When, then, it is suggested[3] that Psalm li, for example, "contains only a single prayer, namely, that for forgiveness"; and that "the cry, 'Create in me a clean heart' is not a prayer for what we call renewal" but only for "forgiving grace," we cannot help thinking the contention an extravagance, — an extravagance, moreover, out of keeping with its author's language elsewhere, and indeed in this very context where he speaks quite simply of the pollution as well as the guilt of sin as included in the scope of the confession made in this psalm.[4] The word "create" is a strong one and appears to invoke from God the exertion of His almighty power for the production of a new subjective state of things: and it does not seem easy to confine the word "heart" to the signification "conscience" as if the prayer were merely that the conscience might be relieved from its sense of guilt. Moreover, the parallel clause, "Renew a steadfast spirit within me," does not readily lend itself to the purely objective inter-

[2] "The necessity of a change of disposition for the reception of salvation is indicated (Jer. xxxi. 33, Ezek. xxxvi. 35)"— König, "Offenbarungsbegriff d.A.T.," II, p. 398, note. "Indications are not wholly lacking that some of the prophets, at least, believed man unable to make himself acceptable before God . . . It is God who cleanses the heart and life by purging away the dross (Isa. i. 25, vi. 7, Jer. xxxi. 31–34, xxxiii. 8)"— J. M. P. Smith, "Biblical Ideas of Atonement," 1909, p. 28. "Ezekiel is even so bold as to declare that we amend our lives because God gives us a new heart and a new spirit (xi. 19)"— Expository Times, Feb. 1908, p. 240).

[3] Cf. A. B. Davidson, "Theology of the O. T.," p. 232.

[4] P. 234; cf. in general p. 244: There is, therefore, both guilt and pollution to be removed in the realization in Israel of the life of God. Similarly Delitzsch in loc.: "the prayer for justification is followed by the prayer for renewing."

pretation.[5] That the transformation of the heart promised in the great prophetic passages must also mean more than the production of a clear conscience, is equally undeniable and indeed is not denied. When Jeremiah (xxxi. 31–33), for example, represents God as declaring that what shall characterize the New Covenant which He will make with the House of Israel, is that He will put His law in the inward parts of His people and write it in their hearts, he surely means to say that God promises to work a subjective effect in the hearts of Israel, by virtue of which their very instincts and most intimate impulses shall be on the side of the law, obedience to which shall therefore be but the spontaneous expression of their own natures.[6]

It is equally important to guard against lowering the conception of the Divine holiness in the Old Testament until the demand of God that His people shall be holy as He is holy,[7] and the provisions of His Grace to make them holy by an inner creative act, are robbed of more or less of their deeper ethical meaning. Here, too, some recent writers are at fault, speaking at times almost as if holiness in God were merely a sort of fastidiousness, over against which is set not so much all sin as uncleanness, as all uncleanness, as in this sense sin.[8] The idea is that what

[5] Baethgen's comment on the verse runs: "The singer knows that for the steadfastness of heart sought in verse 8, there is needed a new creation, a rebirth. בָּרָא in the Kal is always used only of the divine production. The heart is the central organ of the whole religious moral life; the parallel רוּחַ is its synonym. Steadfast (נכון) the spirit is called so far as it does not hesitate between good and evil."

[6] Cf. e. g., A. B. Davidson, "Hastings' BD," i, pp. 514 *sq.*: "Jehovah will make a new covenant with Israel, that is, forgive their sins and write His law on their hearts — the one in His free grace, the other by His creative act"; also iv, p. 119 a, and the fine exposition of Ezek. xxxvi. 17–38 in the "Theology of the O. T.," p. 343. On the other hand Giesebrecht, "Handkom. Jer.," p. 171 thinks "Jeremiah has not yet advanced to the 'new heart' (Ezek. xi. 19, xxxvi. 26 *sq.*, Ps. li. 12); what he is thinking of is an inner influence on the heart by divine power, so that it attains a new attitude to the contents of the law." But this divine power is certainly conceived as creative. "The prophets," says Gunkel, "Die Wirkungen des heiligen Geistes," 1909, p. 77, "were convinced that God Himself must interfere in order to produce the ideal condition which He demands. The ideal kingdom in which dwell piety and righteousness cannot, therefore, be a result of the natural development of the people, but it can come into existence only by an act of God, by a miracle, by the outpouring of the divine Spirit."

[7] Cf. Dillmann, "Alttest. Theologie," pp. 421–422.

[8] E. g., A. B. Davidson, "Theology of O. T.," pp. 348 *sq.*

this somewhat squeamish God did not find agreeable those who served Him would discover it well to avoid; rather than that all sin is necessarily abominable to the holy God and He will not abide it in His servants. This lowered view is sometimes even pushed to the extreme of suggesting [9] that "it is nowhere intimated that there is any danger to the sinner because of his uncleanness;" if he is "cut off" that is solely on account of his disobedience in not cleansing himself, not on account of the uncleanness itself. The extremity of this contention is its sufficient refutation. When the sage declares that no one can say "I have made my heart clean, I am pure from sin" (Prov. xx. 9), he clearly means to intimate that an unclean heart is itself sinful. The Psalmist in bewailing his inborn sinfulness and expressing his longing for truth in the inward parts and wisdom in the hidden parts, certainly conceived his unclean heart as properly sinful in the sight of God (Ps. li). The prophet abject before the holy God (Isa. vi) beyond question looked upon his uncleanness as itself iniquity requiring to be taken away by expiatory purging. It would seem unquestionable that throughout the Old Testament the uncleanness which is offensive to Jehovah is sin considered as pollution, and that salvation from sin involves therefore a process of purification as well as expiation.

The agent by whom the cleansing of the heart is effected is in the Old Testament uniformly represented as God Himself, or, rarely, more specifically as the Spirit of God, which is the Old Testament name for God in His effective activity. It has, indeed, been denied that the Spirit of God is ever regarded in the Old Testament as the worker of holiness.[10] But this extreme position cannot be maintained.[11] It is true enough that the

[9] *Ibid.*, pp. 352–353, against Riehm.

[10] Cf. e. g., Beversluis, "De heilige Geest en zijne Werkingen," 1896, p. 38: "Although the spirit of God may, no doubt, be brought into connection with a moral renewing (in Ezek. xxxvi. 27) nevertheless an ethical operation of the Spirit of God is nowhere taught in the Old Testament."

[11] Cf. e. g., Swete, "Hastings' BD.," ii, pp. 403–404; and Davidson, *ibid.*, iv, p. 119 a: "Later prophets perceive that man's spirit must be determined by an operation of God who will write His law on it (Jer. xxxi. 33), or who will put His own Spirit within him as the impulsive principle of his life (Isa. xxxii. 15, Ezek. xxxvi. 26 ff.)."

Spirit of God comes before us in the Old Testament chiefly as the Theocratic Spirit endowing men as servants of the Kingdom, and after that as the Cosmical Spirit, the principle of all world-processes; and only occasionally as the creator of new ethical life in the individual soul.[12] But it can scarcely be doubted that in Ps. li. 11 [13] God's Holy Spirit, or the Spirit of God's holiness, is conceived in that precise manner, and the same is true of Psalm cxliii. 10 (cf. Isa. lxiii. 10, 11 and see Gen. vi. 3, Neh. ix. 20, I Sam. x. 6, 9).[13] It is chiefly, however, in promises of the future that this aspect of the Spirit's work is dwelt upon.[14] The recreative activity of the Spirit of God is even made the crowning Messianic blessing (Isa. xxxii. 15, xxxiv. 16, xliv. 3, on the latter of which see Giesebrecht, "Die Berufsbegabung," etc., p. 144, lix. 21, Ezek. xi. 19, xviii. 31, xxxvi. 27, xxxvii. 14, xxxix. 29, Zech. xii. 10); and this is as much as to say that the promised Messianic salvation included in it provision for the renewal of men's hearts as well as for the expiation of their guilt.[15]

It would be distinctly a retrogression from the Old Testament standpoint, therefore, if our Lord — Himself, in accordance with Old Testament prophecy (e. g., Isa. xi. 1, xlii. 1, lxi. 1), endowed with the Spirit (Mt. iii. 16, iv. 1, xii. 18, 28, Mk. i. 10, 12, Lk. iii. 22, iv. 1, 14, 18, x. 21, Jno. i. 32, 33) above

[12] Cf. *The Presbyterian and Reformed Review*, Oct. 1895, pp. 669 *sq.*

[13] As even Gunkel allows, "Die Wirkungen, &c².," p. 77: "On the other hand the Spirit appears as the principle of religion and morality in Ezek. xxxvi. 27; Isa. xxviii. 6; xxxii. 15 *sq.*, with which Zech. xii. 10 may be compared. To these may be added the passages, not cited by Wendt, Isa. xi. 2 and Ps. li. 13; cxliii. 10, the two last of which have far the most significance for our problem, because they present the doctrine of the Spirit in its relation to the life of pious individuals" (cf. pp. 78 and 79). Delitzsch, on Ps. li. 12, 13, thinks it nevertheless a mistake to take "the Holy Spirit" here as "the Spirit of grace" as distinct from the "Spirit of office." David, he says, is thinking of himself as king, as Israelite, and as man, without distinguishing between them: the Spirit in his mind is that with which he was anointed (I Sam. xvi. 13); and he speaks of His total effects without differentiation.

[14] Cf. Gunkel, as cited, p. 78, and Delitzsch on Ps. li. 12, 13; also Dalman, "Words of Jesus," p. 296: "Jeremiah and Ezekiel recognized a miraculous transformation in the heart of the people of the future."

[15] Cf. in general, *The Presbyterian and Reformed Review*, Oct. 1895, art. "The Spirit of God in the O. T.," pp. 679 ff.

measure (Jno. iii. 34) [16] — had neglected the Messianic promise
of spiritual renewal. In point of fact, He began His ministry as
the dispenser of the Spirit (Mt. iii. 11, Mk. i. 8, Lk. iii. 16, Jno.
i. 33). And the purpose for which He dispensed the Spirit is
unmistakably represented as the cleansing of the heart. The
distinction of Jesus is, indeed, made to lie precisely in this, —
that whereas John could baptise only with water, Jesus bap-
tised with the Holy Spirit: the repentance which was symbolized by the one was wrought by the other. And this repentance
(μετάνοια) was no mere vain regret for an ill-spent past (μεταμέλεια), or surface modification of conduct, but a radical transformation of the mind which issues indeed in "fruits worthy
of repentance" (Lk. iii. 8) but itself consists in an inward reversal of mental attitude.

There is little subsequent reference in the Synoptic Gospels,
to be sure, to the Holy Spirit as the renovator of hearts. It is
made clear, indeed, that He is the best of gifts and that the
Father will not withhold Him from those that ask Him (Lk.
xi. 13), and that He abides in the followers of Jesus and works
in and through them (Mt. x. 20, Mk. xiii. 11, Lk. xii. 12); and
it is made equally clear that He is the very principle of holiness,
so that to confuse His activity with that of unclean spirits
argues absolute perversion (Mt. xii. 31, Mk. iii. 29, Lk. xii. 10).
But these two things do not happen to be brought together in
these Gospels.[17]

In the Gospel of John, on the other hand, the testimony of
the Baptist is followed up by the record of the searching conversation of our Lord with Nicodemus, in which Nicodemus is
rebuked for not knowing — though "the teacher of Israel" —
that the Kingdom of God is not for the children of the flesh
but only for the children of the Spirit (cf. Mt. iii. 9). Nicodemus
had come to our Lord as to a teacher, widely recognized as
having a mission from God. Jesus repels this approach as falling
far below recognizing Him for what He really was and for
what he had really come to do. As a divinely sent teacher He

---

[16] For on the whole it seems best so to understand this verse.
[17] See in general, however, Bruce, "The Kingdom of God," p. 259.

solemnly assures Nicodemus that something much more effective than teaching is needed: "Verily, verily, I say unto thee,
except a man be born anew he cannot see the Kingdom of God"
(iii. 3). And then, when Nicodemus, oppressed by the sense of
the profundity of the change which must indeed be wrought in
man if he is to be fitted for the Kingdom of God, despairingly
inquires "How can this be?" our Lord explains equally solemnly that it is only by a sovereign, recreating work of the
Holy Spirit, that so great an effect can be wrought: "Verily,
verily, I say unto thee, except a man be born of water and
the Spirit he cannot enter into the Kingdom of God"(iii. 5).
Nor, he adds, ought such a declaration to cause surprise:
what is born of the flesh can be nothing but flesh; only what is
born of the Spirit is spirit. He closes the discussion with a
reference to the sovereignty of the action of the Spirit in regenerating men: as with the wind which blows where it lists,
we know nothing of the Spirit's coming except Lo, it is here!
(iii. 8). About the phrase, "Born of water and the Spirit"
much debate has been had; and various explanations of it
have been offered. The one thing which seems certain is that
there can be no reference to an external act, performed by men,
of their own will: for in that case the product would not be
spirit but flesh, neither would it come without observation. Is
it fanciful to see here a reference back to the Baptist's, "I indeed baptise with water; He baptises with the Holy Spirit"?
The meaning then would be that entrance into the Kingdom
of God requires, if we cannot quite say not only repentance
but also regeneration, yet at least we may say both repentance
and regeneration. In any event it is very pungently taught
here that the precondition of entrance into the Kingdom of
God is a radical transformation wrought by the Spirit of God
Himself.[18]

[18] Cf. Wendt, "The Teaching of Jesus," E. T., ii, 91: "Jesus here at the
outset declares, in the only passage in the Fourth Gospel where the conception
of the Kingdom of God is directly mentioned, that a complete new birth, taking
place from the commencement, and, indeed, a birth from the Spirit of God, is
indispensably necessary in order both to seeing (that is, experiencing) and to
entering the Kingdom of God (vss. 3 and 5)."

Beyond this fundamental passage there is little said in John's Gospel of the renovating activities of the Spirit. The communication of the Spirit of xx. 22 seems to be an official endowment; and although in vii. 39 the allusion appears to be to the gift of the Spirit to believers at large, the stress seems to fall rather on the blessing they bring to others by virtue of this endowment, than on that they receive themselves. There remains only the great promise of the Paraclete. It would probably be impossible to attribute more depth or breadth of meaning than rightfully belongs to them, to the passages which embody this promise (xiv. 16, 26, xv. 26, xvi. 7, 13). But the emphasis appears to be laid in them upon the illuminating (cf. also Lk. i. 15, 41, 67, ii. 25, 26; Mt. xxii. 43) more than upon the sanctifying influences of the Spirit, although assuredly the latter are not wholly absent (xvi. 7–11).

Elsewhere in John, although apart from any specific reference to the Spirit as the agent, repeated expression is given to the fundamental conception of renewal. Men lie dead in their sins and require to be raised from the dead if they are to live (xi. 25, 26); it is the prerogative of the Son to quicken whom He will (v. 21); it is impossible for men to come to the Son, unless they be drawn by the Father (vi. 44); being in the Son it is only of the Father that they can bear fruit (xv. 1). Similarly in the Synoptics there is lacking nothing to this teaching, except the specific reference of the effects to the Holy Spirit. What is required of men is nothing less than perfection even as the heavenly Father is perfect (Mt. v. 48 — the New Testament form of the Old Testament "Ye shall be holy for I am holy, Jehovah your God," Lev. xix. 2). And this perfection is not a matter of external conduct but of internal disposition. One of the objects of the "Sermon on the Mount" is to deepen the conception of righteousness and to carry back both sin and righteousness into the heart itself (Mt. v. 20). Accordingly, the external righteousness of the Scribes and Pharisees is pronounced just no righteousness at all; it is the cleansing merely of the outside of the cup and of the platter (Mt. xxiii. 25), and they are therefore but as whited sepulchres, which outwardly

appear beautiful but inwardly are full of dead men's bones
(Mt. xxiii. 27, 28). True cleansing must begin from within; and
this inward cleansing will cleanse the outside also (Mt. xxiii.
26, xv. 11). The fundamental principle is that every tree brings
forth fruit according to its nature, whether good or bad; and
therefore the tree must be made good and its fruit good, or
else the tree corrupt and its fruit corrupt (Mt. vii. 17, xii. 33,
xv. 11, Mk. vii. 15, Lk. vi. 43, xi. 34). So invariable and all-
inclusive is this principle in its working, that it applies even
to the idle words which men speak, by which they may therefore be justly judged: none that are evil can speak good things,
"for it is out of the abundance of the heart that the mouth
speaketh" (Mt. xii. 34). Half-measures are therefore unavailing
(Mt. vi. 21); a radical change alone will suffice — no mere
patching of the new on the old, no pouring of new wine into
old bottles (Mt. ix. 16, 17, Mk. ii. 21, 22, Lk. v. 36, 39). He
who has not a wedding-garment — the gift of the host — even
though he be called shall not be chosen (Mt. xxii. 11, 12).

Accordingly when — in the Synoptic parallel to the conversation with Nicodemus — the rich young ruler came to Jesus
with his heart set on purchase (as a rich man's heart is apt to
be set), pleading his morality, Jesus repelled him and took occasion to pronounce upon not the difficulty only but the impossibility of entrance into the Kingdom of heaven on such
terms (Mt. xix. 23, Mk. x. 23, Lk. xviii. 24). The possibility
of salvation, He explains, just because it involves something
far deeper than this, rests in the hands of God alone (Mt. xix.
26, Mk. x. 27, Lk. xviii. 27). Man himself brings nothing to it;
the Kingdom is received in naked helplessness (Mt. xix. 21 ||).
It is not without significance that, in all the Synoptics, the
conversation with the rich young ruler is made to follow immediately upon the incident of the blessing of the little children
(Mt. xix. 13 ||). When our Lord says, with reference to these
children (they were mere babies, Lk. xviii. 15),[19] that, "Of
such is the kingdom of heaven," he means just to say that the
kingdom of heaven is never purchased by any quality whatever,

[19] Cf. "Hastings' DCG.," art. "Children."

to say nothing now of deed: whosoever enters it enters it as a child enters the world, — he is born into it by the power of God. In these two incidents, of the child set in the midst and of the rich young ruler, we have, in effect, acted parables of the new birth; they exhibit to us how men enter the kingdom and set the declaration made to Nicodemus (Jno. iii. 1 *sq.*) before us in vivid object-lesson. And if the kingdom can be entered thus only in nakedness as a child comes into the world, all stand before it in like case and it can come only to those selected therefor by God Himself: where none have a claim upon it the law of its bestowment can only be the Divine will (Mt. xi. 27, xx. 15).[20]

The broad treatment characteristic of the Gospels only partly gives way as we pass to the Epistles. Discriminations of aspects and stages, however, begin to become evident; and with the increased material before us we easily perceive lines of demarcation which perhaps we should not have noted with the Gospels only in view. In particular we observe two groups of terms standing over against one another, describing, respectively, from the manward and from the Godward side, the great change experienced by him who is translated from the power of darkness into the kingdom of the Son of God's love (Col. i. 13). And within the limits of each of these groups, we observe also certain distinctions in the usage of the several terms which make it up. In the one group are such terms as $\mu\epsilon\tau\alpha\nu\text{oε}\hat{\iota}\nu$ with its substantive $\mu\epsilon\tau\acute{\alpha}\nu\text{oια}$, and its cognate $\mu\epsilon\tau\alpha\mu\acute{\epsilon}\lambda\epsilon\sigma\theta\alpha\iota$, and $\epsilon\pi\iota\sigma\tau\rho\acute{\epsilon}\phi\epsilon\iota\nu$ and its substantive $\epsilon\pi\iota\sigma\tau\rho\text{oφή}$. These tell us what part man takes in the change. The other group includes such terms as $\gamma\epsilon\nu\nu\eta\theta\hat{\eta}\nu\alpha\iota$ $\check{\alpha}\nu\omega\theta\epsilon\nu$ or $\epsilon\kappa$ $\tau\text{oῦ}$ $\theta\epsilon\text{oῦ}$ or $\epsilon\kappa$ $\tau\text{oῦ}$ $\pi\nu\epsilon\acute{\upsilon}\mu\alpha\tau\text{oς}$, $\pi\alpha\lambda\iota\nu\gamma\epsilon\nu\epsilon\sigma\acute{\iota}\alpha$, $\alpha\nu\alpha\gamma\epsilon\nu\nu\hat{\alpha}\nu$, $\alpha\pi\text{oκνε}\hat{\iota}\sigma\theta\alpha\iota$, $\alpha\nu\alpha\nu\epsilon\text{oῦσθαι}$, $\alpha\nu\alpha\kappa\alpha\iota\nu\text{oῦσθαι}$, $\alpha\nu\alpha\kappa\alpha\acute{\iota}\nu\omega\sigma\iota\varsigma$. These tell what part God takes in the change. Man repents, makes amendment, and turns to God. But it is by God that men are renewed, brought forth, born again into newness of life. The transformation which to human vision manifests itself as a change of life ($\epsilon\pi\iota\sigma\tau\rho\text{oφή}$) resting upon a radical change of mind ($\mu\epsilon\tau\acute{\alpha}\nu\text{oια}$), to Him who searches

[20] Cf. Wendt, as cited, p. 54–55 note.

the heart and understands all the movements of the human soul is known to be a creation (κτίζειν) of God, beginning in a new birth from the Spirit (γεννηθῆναι ἄνωθεν ἐκ τοῦ πνεύματος) and issuing in a new divine product (ποίημα), created in Christ Jesus, into good works prepared by God beforehand that they may be walked in (Eph. ii. 10).

There is certainly synergism here; but it is a synergism of such character that not only is the initiative taken by God (for "all things are of God," II Cor. v. 18, cf. Heb. vi. 6), but the Divine action is in the exceeding greatness of God's power, according to the working of the strength of His might which He wrought in Christ when He raised Him from the dead (Eph. i. 19). The "new man" which is the result of this change is therefore one who can be described no otherwise than as "created" (κτισθέντα) in righteousness and holiness of truth (Eph. iv. 24), after the image of God significantly described as "He who created him" (τοῦ κτίσαντος αὐτόν, Col. iii. 10), — that is not He who made him a man, but He who has made him by an equally creative efflux of power this new man which he has become.[21] The exhortation that we shall "put on" this new man (Eph. iv. 24, cf. iii. 9, 10), therefore does not imply that either the initiation or the completion of the process by which the "new creation" (καινὴ κτίσις; II Cor. v. 17, Gal. vi. 15) is wrought lies in our own power; but only urges us to that diligent coöperation with God in the work of our salvation, to which He calls us in all departments of life (I Cor. iii. 9), and the classical expression of which in this particular department is found in the great exhortation of Phil. ii. 12, 13 where we are encouraged to work out our own salvation thoroughly to the end, with fear and trembling, on the express ground that it is God who works in us both the willing and doing for His good pleasure. The express inclusion of "renewal" in the exhortation (Eph. iv. 23 ἀνανεοῦσθαι; Rom. xii. μεταμορφοῦσθε τῇ ἀνακαινώσει) is indication enough that this "renewal" is a process wide enough to include in itself the whole synergistic "working out" of salvation (κατεργάζεσθε, Phil. ii. 12). But it has no tendency

---

[21] Cf. Lightfoot *in loc.*

to throw doubt upon the underlying fact that this "working out" is both set in motion (τὸ θέλειν) and given effect (τὸ ἐνεργεῖν), only by the energizing of God (ὃ ἐνεργῶν ἐν ὑμῖν), so that all (τὰ πάντα) is from God (ἐκ τοῦ θεοῦ, II Cor. v. 18). Its effect is merely to bring "renewal" (ἀνακαίνωσις) into close parallelism with "repentance" (μετάνοια) — which itself is a gift of God (II Tim. ii. 25, cf. Acts v. 31, xi. 18) as well as a work of man — as two names for the same great transaction, viewed now from the Divine, and now from the human point of sight.

It will not be without interest to observe the development of μετανοεῖν, μετάνοια into the technical term to denote the great change by which man passes from death in sin into life in Christ.[22] Among the heathen writers, the two terms μεταμέλεσθαι, μεταμέλεια and μετανοεῖν, μετάνοια, although no doubt affected in their coloring by their differing etymological suggestions, and although μετανοεῖν, μετάνοια seems always to have been the nobler term, were practically synonymous. Both were used of the dissatisfaction which is felt in reviewing an unworthy deed; both of the amendment which may grow out of this dissatisfaction. Something of this undiscriminating usage extends into the New Testament. In the only three instances in which μεταμέλεσθαι occurs in the Gospels (Mt. xxi. 29, 32, xxvii. 3, cf. Heb. vii. 21 from Old Testament), it is used of a repentance which issued in the amended act; while in Lk. xvii. 3, 4 (but there only) μετανοεῖν may very well be understood of a repentance which expended itself in regret. Elsewhere in the New Testament μεταμέλεσθαι is used in a single instance only (except Heb. vii. 21 from Old Testament) and then it is brought into contrast with μετάνοια as the emotion of regret is contrasted with a revolution of mind (II Cor. vii. 8 sq.). The Apostle had grieved the Corinthians with a letter and had regretted it (μετεμελόμην); he had, however, ceased to regret it (μεταμέλομαι), because he had come to perceive that their grief had led the

[22] Cf. Trench, "Synonyms of the N. T.," § lxix. Also Effie Freeman Thompson, Ph.D., "ΜΕΤΑΝΟΕΩ and ΜΕΤΑΜΕΛΕΙ in Greek Literature until 100 A.D.," 1908, p. 29 especially the summary of New Testament usage pp. 28–29: μετανοεῖν is not used in the New Testament of the intellect or sensibilities but always of voluntative action; and prevailingly not of specific but of generic choice.

Corinthians to repent of their sin (μετάνοια), and certainly the salvation to which such a repentance tends is not to be regretted (ἀμεταμέλητον). Here μεταμέλεσθαι is the painful review of the past; but so little is μετάνοια this, that it is presented as a result of sorrow, — a total revolution of mind traced by the Apostle through the several stages of its formation in a delicate analysis remarkable for its insight into the working of a human soul under the influence of a strong revulsion (verse 11). Its roots were planted in godly sorrow, its issue was amendment of life, its essence consisted in a radical change of mind and heart towards sin. In this particular instance it was a particular sin which was in view; and in heathen writers the word is commonly employed of a specific repentance of a specific fault. In the New Testament this, however, is the rarer usage.[23] Here it prevailingly stands for that fundamental change of mind by which the back is turned not upon one sin or some sins, but upon all sin, and the face definitely turned to God and to His service, — of which therefore a transformed life (ἐπιστροφή) is the outworking.[24] It is not itself this transformed life, into which it issues, any more than it is the painful regret out of which it issues. No doubt, it may spread its skirts so widely as to include on this side the sorrow for sin and on that the amendment of life; but what it precisely is, and what in all cases it emphasises, is the inner change of mind which regret induces and which itself induces a reformed life. Godly sorrow works repentance (II Cor. vii. 10): when we "turn" to God we are doing works worthy of repentance (Acts iii. 19, xxvi. 20, cf. Lk. iii. 8).

It is in this, its deepest and broadest sense, that μετάνοια corresponds from the human side to what from the divine point of sight is called ἀνακαίνωσις; or, rather, to be more precise, that μετάνοια is the psychological manifestation of ἀνακαί-

[23] Lk. xvii. 3, 4, Acts viii. 22, II Cor. vii. 9, 10, xii. 21, Heb. xii. 17; cf. also Rev. ii. 5, 5, 16, 21, 22, iii. 3, 19.

[24] Mt. iii. 2, iv. 17, xi, 20, 21, xii. 41, Mk. i. 15, vi. 12, Lk. x. 13, xi. 32, xiii. 3, 5, xv. 7. 10, xvi. 30, Acts ii. 38, iii. 19, xvii. 30, xxvi. 20, Mt. iii. 8, 11, Mk. i. 4, Lk. iii. 3, 8, v. 32, xv. 7, xxiv. 47, Acts v. 31, xi. 18, xiii. 24, xix. 4, xxvi. 20, Rom. ii. 4, II Tim. ii. 25, Heb. vi. 1, 6, II Pet. iii. 9, Rev. ix. 20, 21, xvi. 9, 11, cf. ii. 5, 5, 16, 21, 22, iii. 3, 19.

νωσις. This "renewal" (ἀνακαινοῦσθαι, ἀνακαίνωσις, ἀνανεοῦσθαι) is the broad term of its own group. It may be, to be sure, that παλινγενεσία should take its place by its side in this respect. In one of the only two passages in which it occurs in the New Testament (Mt. xix. 28) it refers to the repristination not of the individual, but of the universe, which is to take place at "the end": and this usage tends to stamp upon the word the broad sense of a complete and thoroughgoing restoration. If in Tit. iii. 5 it is applied to the individual in such a broad sense, it would be closely coextensive in meaning with the ἀνακαίνωσις by the side of which it stands in that passage, and would differ from it only as a highly figurative differs from a more literal expression of the same idea.[25] Our salvation, the Apostle would in that case say, is not an attainment of our own, but is wrought by God in His great mercy, by means of a regenerating washing, to wit, a renewal by the Holy Spirit.

The difficulty we experience in confidently determining the scope of παλινγενεσία, arising from lack of a sufficiently copious usage to form the basis of our induction, attends us also with the other terms of its class. Nevertheless it seems tolerably clear that over against the broader "renewal" expressed by ἀνακαινοῦσθαι and its cognates and perhaps also by παλινγενεσία, ἀναγεννᾶν (I Pet. i. 23) and with it, its synonym ἀποκυεῖσθαι (James i. 18) are of narrower connotation. We have, says Peter, in God's great mercy been rebegotten, not of corruptible seed, but of incorruptible, by means of the Word of the living and abiding God. It is in accordance with His own determination, says James, that we have been brought forth by the Father of Lights, from whom every good gift and every perfect boon comes, by means of the Word of truth. We have here an effect, the efficient agent in working which is God in His unbounded mercy, while the instrument by means of which it is wrought is "the word of good-tidings which has been preached" to us, that is to say, briefly, the Gospel of Jesus Christ. The issue is, equally briefly, just salvation. This salvation is characteristically described by Peter as awaiting its consummation in the

[25] So e. g., Weiss *in loc.*

future, while yet it is entered upon here and now not only (verse 4 *sq.*) as a "living hope" which shall not be put to shame (because it is reserved in heaven for us, and we meanwhile are guarded through faith for it by the power of God), but also in an accordant life of purity as children of obedience who would fain be like their Father and as He is holy be also ourselves holy in all manner of living. James intimates that those who have been thus brought forth by the will of God may justly be called "first fruits of His creatures," where the reference assuredly is not to the first but to the second creation, that is to say, they who have already been brought forth by the word of truth are themselves the product of God's creative energy and are the promise of the completed new creation when all that is shall be delivered from the bondage of corruption into the liberty of the glory of the children of God (Rom. viii. 19 *sq.*, Mt. xix. 28).

The new birth thus brought before us is related to the broader idea of "renewal" (ἀνακαίνωσις) as the initial stage to the whole process. The conception is not far from that embodied by our old Divines in the term "effectual calling" which they explained to be "by the Word and Spirit"; it is nowadays perhaps more commonly but certainly both less Scripturally and less descriptively spoken of as "conversion." It finds its further explanation in the Scriptures accordingly not under the terms ἐπιστρέφειν, ἐπιστροφή, which describe to us that in which it issues, but under the terms καλέω, κλῆσις [26] which describe to us precisely what it is. By these terms, which are practically confined to Paul and Peter, the follower of Christ is said to owe his introduction into the new life to a "call" from God — a call distinguished from the call of mere invitation (Mt. xxii. 14), as "the call according to purpose" (Rom. viii. 28), a call which cannot fail of its appropriate effect, because there works in it the very power of God. The notion of the new birth is confined even more closely still to its initial step in our Lord's discourse to Nicodemus, recorded in the opening verses of the third chapter of John's Gospel. Here the whole emphasis is thrown upon

[26] Cf. "Hastings' B. D.," ıv, 57 b.

the necessity of the new birth and its provision by the Holy
Spirit. No one can see the Kingdom of God unless he be born
again; and this new birth is wrought by the Spirit. Its advent
into the soul is unobserved; its process is inscrutable; its reality
is altogether an inference from its effects. There is no question
here of means. That the ἐξ ὕδατος of verse 5 is to be taken as
presenting the external act of baptism as the proper means by
which the effect is brought about, is, as we have already
pointed out, very unlikely. The axiom announced in verse 6
that all that is born of flesh is flesh and only what is born of
the Spirit is spirit seems directly to negative such an interpretation by telling us flatly that we cannot obtain a spiritual
effect from a physical action. The explanation of verse 8 that
like the wind, the Spirit visits whom He will and we can only
observe the effect and say Lo, it is here! seems inconsistent
with supposing that it always attends the act of baptism and
therefore can always be controlled by the human will. The new
birth appears to be brought before us in this discussion in the
purity of its conception; and we are made to perceive that at
the root of the whole process of "renewal" there lies an immediate act of God the Holy Spirit upon the soul by virtue of
which it is that the renewed man bears the great name of Son
of God. Begotten not of blood, nor of the will of the flesh, nor
of the will of man, but of God (Jno. i. 13), his new life will
necessarily bear the lineaments of his new parentage (I Jno.
iii. 9, 10; v. 4, 18): kept by Him who was in an even higher
sense still begotten of God, he overcomes the world by faith,
defies the evil one (who cannot touch him), and manifests in
his righteousness and love the heritage which is his (I Jno. ii.
29, iv. 7, v. 1). Undoubtedly the Spirit is active throughout the
whole process of "renewal"; but it is doubtless the peculiarly
immediate and radical nature of his operation at this initial
point which gives to the product of His renewing activities its
best right to be called a new creation (II Cor. v. 17, Gal. vi.
15), a quickening (Jno. v. 21, Eph. ii. 5), a making alive from
the dead (Gal. iii. 21).

We perceive, then, that the Scriptural phraseology lays be-

fore us, as its account of the great change which the man experiences who is translated from what the Scriptures call
darkness to what they call God's marvellous light (Eph. v. 8,
Col. i. 13, I Pet. ii. 9, I Jno. ii. 8) a process; and a process which
has two sides. It is on the one side a change of the mind and
heart, issuing in a new life. It is on the other side a renewing
from on high issuing in a new creation. But the initiative is
taken by God: man is renewed unto repentance: he does not
repent that he may be renewed (cf. Heb. vi. 6). He can work
out his salvation with fear and trembling only because God
works in him both the willing and the doing. At the basis of
all there lies an enabling act from God, by virtue of which alone
the spiritual activities of man are liberated for their work
(Rom. vi. 22, viii. 2). From that moment of the first divine
contact the work of the Spirit never ceases: while man is
changing his mind and reforming his life, it is ever God who is
renewing him in true righteousness. Considered from man's
side the new dispositions of mind and heart manifest themselves
in a new course of life. Considered from God's side the renewal
of the Holy Spirit results in the production of a new creature,
God's workmanship, with new activities newly directed. We
obtain thus a regular series. At the root of all lies an act seen
by God alone, and mediated by nothing, a direct creative act
of the Spirit, the new birth. This new birth pushes itself into
man's own consciousness through the call of the Word, responded
to under the persuasive movements of the Spirit; his conscious
possession of it is thus mediated by the Word. It becomes
visible to his fellow-men only in a turning to God in external
obedience, under the constant leading of the indwelling Spirit
(Rom. viii. 14). A man must be born again by the Spirit to become God's son. He must be born again by the Spirit and Word
to become consciously God's son. He must manifest his new
spiritual life in Spirit-led activities accordant with the new
heart which he has received and which is ever renewed
afresh by the Spirit, to be recognized by his fellow-men as
God's son. It is the entirety of this process, viewed as the work
of God on the soul, which the Scriptures designate "renewal."

It must not be supposed that it is only in these semi-technical terms, however, that the process of "renewal" is spoken of in the Epistles of the New Testament any more than in the Gospels. There is, on the contrary, the richest and most varied employment of language, literal and figurative, to describe it in its source, or its nature, or its effects. It is sometimes suggested, for example, under the image of a change of vesture (Eph. iv. 24, Col. iii. 9, 10, cf. Gal iii. 27, Rom. xiii. 14): the old man is laid aside like soiled clothing, and the new man put on like clean raiment. Sometimes it is represented, in accordance with its nature, less figuratively, as a metamorphosis (Rom. xii. 2): by the renewing of our minds we become transformed beings, able to free ourselves from the fashion of this world and prove what is the will of God, good and acceptable and perfect. Sometimes it is more searchingly set forth as to its nature as a reanimation (Jno. v. 21, Eph. ii. 4–6, Col. ii. 12, 13, Rom. vi. 3, 4): we are dead through our trespasses and the uncircumcision of our flesh; God raises us from this death and makes us sit in the heavenly places with Christ. Sometimes with less of figure and with more distinct reference to the method of the divine working, it is spoken of as a recreation (Eph. ii. 10, iv. 24, Col. iii. 10), and its product, therefore, as a new creature (II Cor. v. 17, Gal. vi. 15): we emerge from it as the workmanship of God, created in Christ Jesus unto good works. Sometimes with more particular reference to the nature and effects of the transaction, it is defined rather as a sanctification, a making holy (ἁγιάζω, I Thess. v. 23, Rom. xv. 16, Rev. xxii. 11; ἁγνίζω, I Pet. i. 22; ἁγιασμός, I Thess. iv. 3, 7, Rom. vi. 19, 22, Heb. xii. 14, II Thess. ii. 13, I Pet. i. 2; cf. Ellicott, on I Thess. iv. 3, iii. 13): and those who are the subjects of the change are, therefore, called "saints" (ἅγιοι, e. g., Rom. viii. 27, I Cor. vi. 1, 2, Col. i. 12). Sometimes again, with more distinct reference to its sources, it is spoken of as the "living" (Gal. ii. 20, Rom. vi. 9, 10, Eph. iii. 17) or "forming" (Gal. iv. 19, cf. Eph. iii. 17, I Cor. ii. 16, II Cor. iii. 8) of Christ in us, or more significantly (Rom. viii. 9, 10, Gal. iv. 6) as the indwelling of Christ or the Spirit in us, or with greater precision as the leading of the Spirit (Rom. viii. 14, Gal. v. 18): and its subjects are accordingly signalized as Spiritual men, that is, Spirit-determined, Spirit-led men (πνευματικοί, I Cor. ii. 15, iii. 1, Gal. vi. 1, cf. I Pet. ii. 5), as distinguished from carnal men, that is, men under the dominance of their own weak, vicious selves (ψυχικοί, I Cor. ii. 14, Jude 19, σαρκικοί, I Cor. iii. 3). None of these modes of representation more clearly define the action than the last mentioned. For the essence of the New Testament representation certainly is that the renewal which is wrought upon him who is by faith in Christ, is the work of the Spirit of Christ, who dwells within His children as a power not themselves making for righteousness, and gradually but surely transforms after the image of God, not the stream of their activities merely, but themselves in the very centre of their being.

The process by which this great metamorphosis is accomplished is laid bare to our observation with wonderful clearness in Paul's poignant description of it, in the seventh chapter of Romans. We are there permitted to look in upon a heart into which the Spirit of God has intruded with His transforming power. Whatever peace it may have enjoyed is broken up. All its ingrained tendencies to evil are up in arms against the intruded power for good. The force of evil habit is so great that the Apostle, in its revelation to him, is almost tempted to despair. "O wretched man that I am," he cries, "who shall deliver me out of the body of this death?" Certainly not himself. None knows better than he that with man this is impossible. But he bethinks himself that the Spirit of the most high God is more powerful than even ingrained sin; and with a great revulsion of heart he turns at once to cry his thanks to God through Jesus Christ our Lord. This conflict he sees within him, he sees now to bear in it the promise and potency of victory; because it is the result of the Spirit's working within him, and where the Spirit works, there is emancipation from the law of sin and death. The process may be hard — a labor, a struggle, a fight; but the end is assured. No matter how far from perfect we yet may be, we are not in the flesh but in the

Spirit if the Spirit of God dwells in us; and we may take heart of faith from that circumstance to mortify the deeds of the body and to enter upon our heritage as children of God. Here in brief compass is the Apostle's whole doctrine of renewal. Without holiness we certainly shall not see the Lord: but he in whom the Holy Spirit dwells, is already potentially holy; and though we see not yet what we shall be, we know that the work that is begun within us shall be completed to the end. The very presence of strife within us is the sign of life and the promise of victory.

The church has retained, on the whole, with very considerable constancy the essential elements of this Biblical doctrine of "renewal." In the main stream of Christian thought, at all events, there has been little tendency to neglect, much less to deny it, at least theoretically. In all accredited types of Christian teaching it is largely insisted upon that salvation consists in its substance of a radical subjective change wrought by the Holy Spirit, by virtue of which the native tendencies to evil are progressively eradicated and holy dispositions are implanted, nourished and perfected.

The most direct contradiction which this teaching has received in the history of Christian thought was that given it by Pelagius at the opening of the fifth century. Under the stress of a one-sided doctrine of human freedom, in pursuance of which he passionately asserted the inalienable ability of the will to do all righteousness, Pelagius was led to deny the need and therefore the reality of subjective operations of God on the soul ("grace" in the inner sense) to secure its perfection; and this carried with it as its necessary presupposition the denial also of all subjective injury wrought on man by sin. The vigorous reassertion of the necessity of subjective grace by Augustine put pure Pelagianism once for all outside the pale of recognized Christian teaching; although in more or less modified or attentuated forms, it has remained as a widely spread tendency in the churches, conditioning the purity of the supernaturalism of salvation which is confessed.

The strong emphasis laid by the Reformers upon the objective side of salvation, in the enthusiasm of their rediscovery of the fundamental doctrine of justification, left its subjective side, which was not in dispute between them and their nearest opponents, in danger of falling temporarily somewhat out of sight. From the comparative infrequency with which it was in the first stress of conflict insisted on, occasion, if not given, was at least taken, to represent that it was neglected if not denied. Already in the first generation of the Reformation movement, men of mystical tendencies like Osiander arraigned the Protestant teaching as providing only for a purely external salvation. The reproach was eminently unjust, and although it continues to be repeated up to to-day, it remains eminently unjust. Only among a few Moravian enthusiasts, and still fewer Antinomians, and, in recent times, in the case of certain of the Neo-Kohlbrüggian party, can a genuine tendency to neglect the subjective side of salvation be detected. With all the emphasis which Protestant theology lays on justification by faith as the root of salvation, it has never failed to lay equal emphasis on sanctification by the Spirit as its substance. Least of all can the Reformed theology with its distinctive insistence upon "irresistible grace" — which is the very heart of the doctrine of "renewal" — be justly charged with failure to accord its rights to the great truth of supernatural sanctification. The debate at this point does not turn on the reality or necessity of sanctification, but on the relation of sanctification to justification. In clear accord with the teaching of Scripture, Protestant theology insists that justification underlies sanctification, and not *vice versa*. But it has never imagined that the sinner could get along with justification alone. It has rather ever insisted that sanctification is so involved in justification that the justification cannot be real unless it be followed by santification. There has never been a time when it could not recognize the truth in and (when taken out of its somewhat compromising context) make heartily its own such an admirable statement of the state of the case as the following: [27] — "However far off it may be from us or we from it, we cannot and ought not to think

[27] W. P. Du Bose, "The Gospel in the Gospels," p. 175.

of our salvation as anything less than our own perfected and completed sinlessness and holiness. We may be, to the depths of our souls, grateful and happy to be sinners pardoned and forgiven by divine grace. But surely God would not have us satisfied with that as the end and substance of the salvation He gives us in His Son. Jesus Christ is the power of God in us unto salvation. It does not require an exercise of divine power to extend pardon; it does require it to endow and enable us with all the qualities, energies, and activities that make for, and that make holiness and life. See how St. Paul speaks of it when he prays, That we may know the exceeding greatness of God's power to usward who believe, according to that working of the strength of His might which he wrought in Christ when He raised Him from the dead."

LITERATURE: — The literature of the subject is copious but also rather fragmentary. The best aid is afforded by the discussions of the terms employed in the Lexicons and of the passages which fall in review in the Commentaries: after that the appropriate sections in the larger treatises in Biblical Theology, and in the fuller Dogmatic treatises are most valuable. The articles of J. V. Bartlet in Hastings' B. D. on "Regeneration" and "Sanctification" should be consulted, — they also offer a suggestion of literature; as do also the articles, "Bekehrung," "Gnade," "Wiedergeburt" in the several editions of Herzog. There are three of the prize publications of the Hague Society which have a general bearing on the subject: G. W. Semler's and S. K. Theoden van Velzen's "Over de voortdurende Werking des H. G.," (1842) and E. I. Issel's "Der Begriff der Heiligkeit im N. T.," (1887). Augustine's Anti-Pelagian treatises are fundamental for the dogmatic treatment of the subject; and the Puritan literature is rich in searching discussions, — the most outstanding of which are possibly: Owen, "Discourse concerning the Holy Spirit" ("Works": Edinburgh, 1852, v. iii.); T. Goodwin, "The Work of the Holy Ghost in our Salvation" ("Works": Edinburgh, 1863, v. vi.); Charnock, "The Doctrine of Regeneration," Phil. 1840; Mar-

shall, "The Gospel Mystery of Sanctification," London [1692],
Edinburgh, 1815; Edwards, "The Religious Affections." Cf.
also Köberle, "Sünde und Gnade im relig. Leben des Volkes
Israel bis auf Christum," 1905; Vömel, "Der Begriff der Gnade
im N. T.," 1903; J. Kuhn: "Die christl. Lehre der göttlichen
Gnade" (Part I) 1868; A. Dieckmann, "Die christl. Lehre von
der Gnade," 1901; Storr, "De Spiritus Sancti in mentibus
nostris efficientia," 1779; J. P. Stricker, "Diss. Theol. de
Mutatione homini secundum Jesu et App. doct. subeunda,"
1845. — P. Gennrich, "Die Lehre von der Wiedergeburt: die
christl. Zentrallehre in dogmengeschichtlicher und religions-
geschichtlicher Beleuchtung," 1907; and "Wiedergeburt und
Heiligung mit Bezug auf die gegenwärtigen Strömungen des
religiösen Lebens," 1908; H. Bavinck, "Roeping en Weder-
geboorte," 1903; J. T. Marshall, art. "Regeneration" in
Hastings' *ERE* v. x.

XIII

THE BIBLICAL DOCTRINE OF FAITH

FAITH [1]

I. The Philological Expression of Faith

THE verb 'to believe' in the Authorized Version of the Old Testament uniformly represents the Hebrew הֶאֱמִין, Hiphil of אָמַן, except, of course, in Dan. vi. 23 where it represents the corresponding Aramaic form. The root, which is widely spread among the Semitic tongues, and which in the word 'Amen' has been adopted into every language spoken by Christian, Jew, or Mohammedan, seems everywhere to convey the fundamental ideas of 'fixedness, stability, steadfastness, reliability.' What the ultimate conception is which underlies these ideas remains somewhat doubtful, but it would appear to be rather that of 'holding' than that of 'supporting' (although this last is the sense adopted in " Oxf. Heb. Lex."). In the simple species the verb receives both transitive and intransitive vocalization. With intransitive vocalization it means 'to be firm,' 'to be secure,' 'to be faithful,' and occurs in biblical Hebrew only in the past participle, designating those who are 'faithful' (II Sam. xx. 19, Ps. xii. 1, xxxi. 23). With transitive vocalization it occurs in biblical Hebrew only in a very specialized application, conveying the idea, whether as participle or verbal noun, of 'caretaking' or 'nursing' (II Kings x. 1, 5, Est. ii. 7, Ru. iv. 16, II Sam. iv. 4, Num. xi. 12, Isa. xlix. 23, Lam. iv. 5; cf. II Kings xviii. 16 'pillars' and [the Niphal] Isa. lx. 4), the implication in which seems to be that of 'holding,' 'bearing,' 'carrying.' The Niphal occurs once as the passive of transitive Qal (Isa. lx. 4): elsewhere it is formed from intransitive Qal, and is used very much in the same sense. Whatever holds, is steady, or can be depended upon, whether a wall which securely

[1] Article "Faith," from "A Dictionary of the Bible," ed. by James Hastings, v. i, pp. 827–838. Pub. N. Y. 1905, by Charles Scribner's Sons.

holds a nail (Isa. xxii. 23, 25), or a brook which does not fail (Jer. xv. 18), or a kingdom which is firmly established (II Sam. vii. 16), or an assertion which has been verified (Gen. xlii. 20), or a covenant which endures for ever (Ps. lxxxix. 28), or a heart found faithful (Neh. ix. 8), or a man who can be trusted (Neh. xiii. 13), or God Himself who keeps covenant (Deut. vii. 9), is נֶאֱמָן. The Hiphil occurs in one passage in the primary physical sense of the root (Job xxxix. 24). Elsewhere it bears constantly the sense of 'to trust,' weakening down to the simple 'to believe' (Ex. iv. 31, Ps. cxvi. 10, Isa. vii. 9, xxviii. 16, Hab. i. 5). Obviously it is a subjective causative, and expresses the acquisition or exhibition of the firmness, security, reliability, faithfulness which lies in the root-meaning of the verb, in or with respect to its object. The מַאֲמִין is therefore one whose state of mind is free from faintheartedness (Isa. vii. 9) and anxious haste (Isa. xxviii. 16), and who stays himself upon the object of his contemplation with confidence and trust. The implication seems to be, not so much that of a passive dependence as of a vigorous active commitment. He who, in the Hebrew sense, exercises faith, is secure, assured, confident (Deut. xxviii. 66, Job xxiv. 22, Ps. xxvii. 13), and lays hold of the object of his confidence with firm trust.

The most common construction of הֶאֱמִין is with the preposition בְ, and in this construction its fundamental meaning seems to be most fully expressed. It is probably never safe to represent this phrase by the simple 'believe'; the preposition rather introduces the person or thing in which one believes, or on which one believingly rests as on firm ground. This is true even when the object of the affection is a thing, whether divine words, commandments, or works (Ps. cvi. 12, cxix. 66, lxxviii. 32), or some earthly force or good (Job xxxix. 12, xv. 31, xxiv. 22, Deut. xxviii. 66). It is no less true when the object is a person, human (I Sam. xxvii. 12, Prov. xxvi. 25, Jer. xii. 6, Mic. vii. 5) or superhuman (Job iv. 18, xv. 15), or the representative of God, in whom therefore men should place their confidence (Ex. xix. 9, II Chron. xx. 20). It is above all true, however, when the object of the affection is God Himself, and that indifferently whether or not the special exercise of faith adverted to is rooted in a specific occasion (Gen. xv. 6, Ex. xiv. 31, Num. xiv. 11, xx. 12, Deut. i. 32, II Kings xvii. 14, II Chron. xx. 20, Ps. lxxviii. 22, Jon. iii. 5). The weaker conception of 'believing' seems, on the other hand, to lie in the construction with the preposition לְ, which appears to introduce the person or thing, not on which one confidingly rests, but to the testimony of which one assentingly turns. This credence may be given by the simple to every untested word (Prov. xiv. 15); it may be withheld until seeing takes the place of believing (I Kings x. 7, II Chron. ix. 6); it is due to words of the Lord and of His messengers, as well as to the signs wrought by them (Ps. cvi. 24, Isa. liii. 1, Ex. iv. 8, 9). It may also be withheld from any human speaker (Gen. xlv. 26, Ex. iv. 1, 8, Jer. xl. 14, II Chron. xxxii. 15), but is the right of God when He bears witness to His majesty or makes promises to His people (Isa. xliii. 10, Deut. ix. 23). In this weakened sense of the word the proposition believed is sometimes attached to it by the conjunction כִּי (Ex. iv. 5, Job ix. 16, Lam. iv. 12). In its construction with the infinitive, however, its deeper meaning comes out more strongly (Judg. xi. 20, Job xv. 22, Ps. xxvii. 13), and the same is true when the verb is used absolutely (Ex. iv. 31, Isa. vii. 9, xxviii. 16, Ps. cxvi. 10, Job xxix. 24, Hab. i. 5). In these constructions faith is evidently the assurance of things hoped for, the conviction of things not seen.

No hiphilate noun from this root occurs in the Old Testament. This circumstance need not in itself possess significance; the notions of 'faith' and 'faithfulness' lie close to one another, and are not uncommonly expressed by a single term (so πίστις, fides, faith). As a matter of fact, however, 'faith,' in its active sense, can barely be accounted an Old Testament term. It occurs in the Authorized Version of the Old Testament only twice: Deut. xxxii. 20 where it represents the Hebrew אֵמֻן and Hab. ii. 4 where it stands for the Hebrew אֱמוּנָה; and it would seem to be really demanded in no passage but Hab. ii. 4. The very point of this passage, however, is the sharp contrast which is drawn between arrogant self-sufficiency and faithful dependence on God. The purpose of the verse is to give a reply to the prophet's inquiry as to God's righteous dealings with the Chaldæans. Since it is by faith that the righteous man lives, the arrogant Chaldæan, whose soul is puffed up and not straight within him, cannot but be destined to destruction. The whole drift of the broader context bears out this meaning; for throughout this prophecy the Chaldæan is ever exhibited as the type of insolent self-assertion (i. 7, 11, 16), in contrast with which the righteous appear, certainly not as men of integrity and steadfast faithfulness, but as men who look in faith to God and trustingly depend upon His arm. The obvious reminiscence of Gen. xv. 6 throws its weight into the same scale, to which may be added the consent of the Jewish expositors of the passage. Here we have, therefore, thrown into a clear light the contrasting characteristics of the wicked, typified by the Chaldæan, and of the righteous: of the one the fundamental trait is self-sufficiency; of the other, faith. This faith, which forms the distinctive feature of the righteous man, and by which he obtains life, is obviously no mere assent. It is a profound and abiding disposition, an ingrained attitude of mind and heart towards God which affects and gives character to all the activities. Here only the term occurs in the Old Testament; but on this its sole occurrence it rises to the full height of its most pregnant meaning.

The extreme rarity of the noun 'faith' in the Old Testament may prepare us to note that even the verb 'to believe' is far from common in it. In a religious application it occurs in only some thirteen Old Testament books, and less than a score and a half times. The thing believed is sometimes a specific word or work of God (Lam. iv. 12, Hab. i. 5), the fact of a divine revelation (Ex. iv. 5, Job ix. 16), or the words or commandments of God in general (with ב Ps. cvi. 12, cxix. 66). In Ex. xix. 9 and II Chron. xx. 20 God's prophets are the object of His people's confidence. God Himself is the object to which they believingly turn, or on whom they rest in assured trust, in some eleven cases. In two of these it is to Him as a faithful witness that faith believingly turns (Deut. ix. 23, Isa. xliii. 10).

In the remainder of them it is upon His very person that faith rests in assured confidence (Gen. xv. 6, Ex. xiv. 31, Num. xiv. 11, xx. 12, Deut. i. 32, II Kings xvii. 14, II Chron. xx. 20, Ps. lxxviii. 22, Jon. iii. 5). It is in these instances, in which the construction is with ‎ב, together with those in which the word is used absolutely (Ex. iv. 31, Isa. vii. 9, xxviii. 16, Ps. cxvi. 10), to which may be added Ps. xxvii. 13 where it is construed with the infinitive, that the conception of religious believing comes to its rights. The typical instance is, of course, the great word of Gen. xv. 6, 'And Abram believed in the LORD, and he counted it to him for righteousness'; in which all subsequent believers, Jewish and Christian alike, have found the primary example of faith. The object of Abram's faith, as here set forth, was not the promise which appears as the occasion of its exercise; what it rested on was God Himself, and that not merely as the giver of the promise here recorded, but as His servant's shield and exceeding great reward (xv. 1). It is therefore not the assentive but the fiducial element of faith which is here emphasized; in a word, the faith which Abram gave Jehovah when he 'put his trust in God' (ἐπίστευσεν τῷ θεῷ LXX), was the same faith which later He sought in vain at the hands of His people (Num. xiv. 11, cf. Deut. i. 32, II Kings xvii. 14), and the notion of which the Psalmist explains in the parallel, 'They believed not in God, and trusted not in his salvation' (Ps. lxxviii. 22). To believe in God, in the Old Testament sense, is thus not merely to assent to His word, but with firm and unwavering confidence to rest in security and trustfulness upon Him.

In the Greek of the Septuagint πιστεύειν takes its place as the regular rendering of הֶאֱמִין and is very rarely set aside in favour of another word expressing trust (Prov. xxvi. 25 πείθεσθαι). In a few cases, however, it is strengthened by composition with a preposition (Deut. i. 32, Judg. xi. 20, II Chron. xx. 20, cf. Sir. i. 15, ii. 10 etc., I Macc. i. 30, vii. 16 etc., ἐμπιστεύειν; Mic. vii. 5, καταπιστεύειν); and in a few others it is construed with prepositions (ἔν τινι, Jer. xii. 6, Ps. lxxviii. 22, Dan. vi. 23, I Sam. xxvii. 12, II Chron. xx. 20, Mic. vii. 5, Sir. xxxv. 21;

ἐπί τινα, Isa. xxviii. 16 (?), III Macc. ii. 7; ἐπί τινι, Wis. xii.
2; εἴς τινα, Sir. xxxviii. 31; κατά τινα, Job iv. 18, xv. 15,
xxiv. 22).

It was by being thus made the vehicle for expressing the
high religious faith of the Old Testament that the word was
prepared for its New Testament use. For it had the slightest
possible connection with religious faith in classical speech.
Resting ultimately on a root with the fundamental sense of
'binding,' and standing in classical Greek as the common term
for 'trusting,' 'putting faith in,' 'relying upon,' shading down
into 'believing,' it was rather too strong a term for ordinary
use of that ungenial relation to the gods which was characteristic of Greek thought, and which was substantively expressed
by πίστις — the proper acknowledgment in thought and act
of their existence and rights. For this νομίζειν was the usual
term, and the relative strength of the two terms may be observed in their use in the opening sections of Xenophon's
"Memorabilia" (I. i. 1 and 5), where Socrates is charged with
not believing in the gods whom the city owned (νομίζειν τοὺς
θεούς), but is affirmed to have stood in a much more intimate
relation to them, to have trusted in them (πιστεύειν τοῖς θεοῖς).
Something of the same depth of meaning may lurk in the exhortation of the Epinomis (980 C), Πιστεύσας τοῖς θεοῖς εὔχου.
But ordinarily πιστεύειν τοῖς θεοῖς appears as the synonym of
νομίζειν τοὺς θεούς, and imports merely the denial of atheism
(Plut. "de Superst.," ii.; Arist."Rhet.," ii.17).It was only by its
adoption by the writers of the Septuagint to express the faith
of the Old Testament that it was fitted to take its place in
the New Testament as the standing designation of the attitude
of the man of faith towards God.

This service the Septuagint could not perform for πίστις
also, owing to the almost complete absence of the noun 'faith'
in the active sense from the Old Testament; but it was due to a
Hellenistic development on the basis of the Old Testament
religion, and certainly not without influence from Gen. xv. 6
and Hab. ii. 4 that this term, too, was prepared for New
Testament use. In classical Greek πίστις is applied to belief in

the gods chiefly as implying that such belief rests rather on trust than on sight (Plut. "Mor.," 756 B). Though there is no suggestion in this of weakness of conviction (for πίστις expresses a strong conviction, and is therefore used in contrast with 'impressions'), yet the word, when referring to the gods, very rarely rises above intellectual conviction into its naturally more congenial region of moral trust (Soph. "Oed. Rex," 1445). That this, its fuller and more characteristic meaning, should come to its rights in the religious sphere, it was necessary that it should be transferred into a new religious atmosphere. The usage of Philo bears witness that it thus came to its rights on the lips of the Greek-speaking Jews. It is going too far, to be sure, to say that Philo's usage of 'faith' is scarcely distinguishable from that of New Testament writers. The gulf that separates the two is very wide, and has not been inaptly described by saying that with Philo, faith, as the queen of the virtues, is the righteousness of the righteous man, while with St. Paul, as the abnegation of all claim to virtue, it is the righteousness of the unrighteous. But it is of the utmost significance that, in the pages of Philo, the conception is filled with a content which far transcends any usage of the word in heathen Greek, and which is a refraction of the religious conceptions of the Old Testament. Fundamental to his idea of it as the crowning virtue of the godly man, to be attained only with the supremest difficulty, especially by creatures akin to mortal things, is his conception of it as essentially a changeless, unwavering 'standing by God' (Deut. v. 31), — binding us to God, to the exclusion of every other object of desire, and making us one with Him. It has lost that soteriological content which is the very heart of faith in the Old Testament; though there does not absolutely fail an occasional reference to God as Saviour, it is, with Philo, rather the Divinity, τὸ ὄν, upon which faith rests, than the God of grace and salvation; and it therefore stands with him, not at the beginning but at the end of the religious life. But we can perceive in the usage of Philo a development on Jewish ground of a use of the word πίστις to describe that complete detachment from earthly things, and that firm conviction of the reality and supreme significance of the things not seen, which underlies its whole New Testament use.

The disparity in the use of the terms 'faith' and 'believe' in the two Testaments is certainly in a formal aspect very great. In contrast with their extreme rarity in the Old Testament, they are both, though somewhat unevenly distributed and varying in relative frequency, distinctly characteristic of the whole New Testament language, and oddly enough occur about equally often (about 240 times each). The verb is lacking only in Col., Philem., II Pet., II and III Jn., and the Apocalypse; the noun only in the Gospel of John and II and III Jn.: both fail only in II and III Jn. The noun predominates not only in the epistles of St. Paul, where the proportion is about three to one, and in St. James (about five to one), but very markedly in the Epistle to the Hebrews (about sixteen to one). In St. John, on the other hand, the verb is very frequent, while the noun occurs only once in I Jn. and four times in the Apocalypse. In the other books the proportion between the two is less noteworthy, and may fairly be accounted accidental. In the Old Testament, again, 'faith' occurs in the active sense in but a single passage; in the New Testament it is the passive sense which is rare. In the Old Testament in only about half the instances of its occurrence is the verb 'to believe' used in a religious sense; in the New Testament it has become so clearly a technical religious term, that it occurs very rarely in any other sense. The transitive usage, in which it expresses entrusting something to someone, occurs a few times both in the active (Lk. xvi. 11, Jn. ii. 24) and the passive (I Cor. ix. 17, Gal. ii. 7, I Thess. ii. 4, I Tim. i. 11, Tit. i. 3); but besides this special case there are very few instances in which the word does not express religious believing, possibly only the following: Jn. ix. 18, Acts ix. 26, I Cor. xi. 18, Mt. xxiv. 23, 26, Mk. xiii. 21, II Thess. ii. 11, cf. Acts xiii. 41, xv. 11, Jn. iv. 21, I Jn. iv. 1. The classical construction with the simple dative which prevails in the Septuagint retires in the New Testament in favour of constructions with prepositions and the absolute use of the verb; the construction with the dative occurs about forty-five

times, while that with prepositions occurs some sixty-three
times, and the verb is used absolutely some ninety-three times.

When construed with the dative, πιστεύειν in the New Testament prevailingly expresses believing assent, though ordinarily
in a somewhat pregnant sense. When its object is a thing, it is
usually the spoken (Lk. i. 20, Jn. iv. 50, v. 47, xii. 38, Rom. x.
16, cf. II Thess. ii. 11) or written (Jn. ii. 22, v. 47, Acts xxiv.
14, xxvi. 27) word of God; once it is divine works which should
convince the onlooker of the divine mission of the worker (Jn.
x. 38). When its object is a person it is rarely another than God
or Jesus (Mt. xxi. 25, 32, Mk. xi. 31, Lk. xx. 5, Jn. v. 46, Acts
viii. 12, I Jn. iv. 1), and more rarely God (Jn. v. 24, Acts xvi.
34, xxvii. 25, Rom. iv. 3 (17), Gal. iii. 6, Tit. iii. 8, Jas. ii. 23,
I Jn. v. 10) than Jesus (Jn. iv. 21, v. 38, 46, vi. 30, viii. 31, 45,
46, x. 37, 38, xiv. 11, Acts xviii. 8, II Tim. i. 12). Among these
passages there are not lacking some, both when the object is a
person and when it is a thing, in which the higher sense of devoted, believing trust is conveyed. In I Jn. iii. 23, for example, we
are obviously to translate, not 'believe the name,' but 'believe
in the name of his Son, Jesus Christ,' for in this is summed up
the whole Godward side of Christian duty. So there is no reason
to question that the words of Gen. xv. 6 are adduced in Rom.
iv. 3, Gal. iii. 6, Jas. ii. 23 in the deep sense which they bear in
the Old Testament text; and this deeper religious faith can
scarcely be excluded from the belief in God adverted to in Acts
xvi. 34, Tit. iii. 8 (cf. Jn. v. 24), or from the belief in Jesus adverted to in II Tim. i. 12 (cf. Jn. v. 38, vi. 30), and is obviously
the prominent conception in the faith of Crispus declared in
Acts xviii. 8. The passive form of this construction occurs only
twice — once of believing assent (II Thess. i. 10), and once
with the highest implications of confiding trust (I Tim. iii. 16).
The few passages in which the construction is with the accusative (Jn. xi. 26, Acts xiii. 41, I Cor. xi. 18, xiii. 7, I Jn. iv. 16)
take their natural place along with the commoner usage with
the dative, and need not express more than crediting, although
over one or two of them there floats a shadow of a deeper implication. The same may be said of the cases of attraction in Rom.

iv. 17 and x. 14. And with these weaker constructions must be ranged also the passages, twenty in all (fourteen of which occur in the writings of St. John), in which what is believed is joined to the verb by the conjunction ὅτι. In a couple of these the matter believed scarcely rises into the religious sphere (Jn. ix. 18, Acts ix. 26); in a couple more there is specific reference to prayer (Mk. xi. 23, 24); in yet a couple more it is general faith in God which is in mind (Heb. xi. 6, Jas. ii. 19). In the rest, what is believed is of immediately soteriological import — now the possession by Jesus of a special power (Mt. ix. 28), now the central fact of His saving work (Rom. x. 9, I Thess. iv. 14), now the very hinge of the Christian hope (Rom. vi. 8), but prevailingly the divine mission and personality of Jesus Himself (Jn. vi. 69, viii. 24, xi. 27, 42, xiii. 19, xiv. 10, xvi. 27, 30, xvii. 8, 21, xx. 31, I Jn. v. 1, 5). By their side we may recall also the rare construction with the infinitive (Acts xv. 11, Rom. xiv. 2).

When we advance to the constructions with prepositions, we enter a region in which the deeper sense of the word — that of firm, trustful reliance — comes to its full rights. The construction with ἐν, which is the most frequent of the constructions with prepositions in the Septuagint, retires almost out of use in the New Testament; it occurs with certainty only in Mk. i. 15, where the object of faith is 'the gospel,' though Jn. iii. 15, Eph. i. 13 may also be instances of it, where the object would be Christ. The implication of this construction would seem to be firm fixedness of confidence in its object. Scarcely more common is the parallel construction of ἐπί with the dative, expressive of steady, resting repose, reliance upon the object. Besides the quotation from Isa. xxviii. 16, which appears alike in Rom. ix. 33, x. 11, I Pet. ii. 6, this construction occurs only twice: Lk. xxiv. 25, where Jesus rebukes His followers for not 'believing on,' relying implicitly upon, all that the prophets have spoken; and I Tim. i. 16, where we are declared to 'believe on' Jesus Christ unto salvation, i.e., to obtain salvation by relying upon Him for it. The constructions with prepositions governing the accusative, which involve an implication of 'moral motion, mental direction towards,' are more frequently used. That with ἐπί, indeed, occurs only seven times (four of which are in Acts). In two instances in Rom. iv. where the reminiscence of the faith of Abraham gives colour to the language, the object on which faith is thus said relyingly to lay hold is God, described, however, as savingly working through Christ — as He that justifies the ungodly, He that raised Jesus our Lord from the dead. Elsewhere its object is Christ Himself. In Mt. xxvii. 42 the Jewish leaders declare the terms on which they will become 'believers on' Jesus; in Acts xvi. 31 this is the form that is given to the proclamation of salvation by faith in Christ — 'turn with confident trust to Jesus Christ,' and appropriately, therefore, it is in this form of expression that those are designated who have savingly believed on Christ (Acts ix. 42, xi. 17, xxii. 19). The special New Testament construction, however, is that with εἰς, which occurs some forty-nine times, about four-fifths of which are Johannine and the remainder more or less Pauline. The object towards which faith is thus said to be reliantly directed is in one unique instance 'the witness which God hath witnessed concerning his Son' (I Jn. v. 10), where we may well believe that 'belief in the truth of the witness is carried on to personal belief in the object of the witness, that is, the Incarnate Son Himself.' Elsewhere the object believed on, in this construction, is always a person, and that very rarely God (Jn. xiv. 1, cf. I Jn. v. 10, and also I Pet. i. 21, where, however, the true reading is probably πιστοὺς εἰς θεόν), and most commonly Christ (Mt. xviii. 6, Jn. ii. 11, iii. 16, 18, 36, iv. 39, vi. 29, 35, 40, vii. 5, 31, 38, 39, 48, viii. 30, ix. 35, 36, x. 42, xi. 25, 26, 45, 48, xii. 11, 37, 42, 44, 44, 46, xiv. 1, 12, xvi. 9, xvii. 20, Acts x. 43, xiv. 23, xix. 4, Rom. x. 14, 14, Gal. ii. 16, Phil. i. 29, I Pet. i. 8, I Jn. v. 10, cf. Jn. xii. 36, i. 12, ii. 23, iii. 18, I Jn. v. 13). A glance over these passages will bring clearly out the pregnancy of the meaning conveyed. It may be more of a question wherein the pregnancy resides. It is probably sufficient to find it in the sense conveyed by the verb itself, while the preposition adjoins only the person towards whom the strong feeling expressed by the verb is directed. In any event, what these passages express is 'an absolute transference of trust from ourselves to another,' a complete self-surrender to Christ.

Some confirmation of this explanation of the strong meaning of the phrase πιστεύειν εἰς may be derived from the very rich use of the verb absolutely, in a sense in no way inferior. Its absolute use is pretty evenly distributed through the New Testament occurring 29 times in John, 23 times in Paul, 22 times in Acts, 15 times in the Synoptics, and once each in Hebrews, James, I Peter, and Jude; it is placed on the lips of Jesus some 18 times. In surprisingly few of these instances is it used of a non-religious act of crediting, — apparently only in our Lord's warning to His followers not to believe when men say '"Lo, here is the Christ," or "here"' (Mt. xxiv. 23, 26, Mk. xiii. 21). In equally surprisingly few instances is it used of specific acts of faith in the religious sphere. Once it is used of assent given to a specific doctrine — that of the unity of God (Jas. ii. 19). Once it is used of believing prayer (Mt. xxi. 22). Four times in a single chapter of John it is used of belief in a specific fact — the great fact central to Christianity of the resurrection of Christ (Jn. xx. 8, 25, 29, 29). It is used occasionally of belief in God's announced word (Lk. i. 45, Acts xxvi. 27), and occasionally also of the credit given to specific testimonies of Jesus, whether with reference to earthly or heavenly things (Jn. iii. 12, 12, i. 50, Lk. xxii. 67), passing thence to general faith in the word of salvation (Lk. viii. 12, 13). Twice it is used of general soteriological faith in God (Jude 5, Rom. iv. 18), and a few times, with the same pregnancy of implication, where the reference, whether to God or Christ, is more or less uncertain (Jn. i. 7, Rom. iv. 11, II Cor. iv. 13, 13). Ordinarily, however, it expresses soteriological faith directed to the person of Christ. In a few instances, to be sure, the immediate trust expressed is in the extraordinary power of Jesus for the performance of earthly effects (the so-called 'miracle faith'), as in Mt. viii. 13, Mk. v. 36, ix. 23, 24, Lk. viii. 50, Jn. iv. 48, xi. 40; but the essential relation in which this faith stands to 'saving faith' is clearly exhibited in Jn. iv. 48 compared with v. 53 and ix. 38, and Jn. xi. 40 compared with v. 15 and xii. 39; and, in any case,

these passages are insignificant in number when compared with
the great array in which the reference is distinctly to saving
faith in Christ (Mk. ix. 42, xv. 32 [Jn. iii. 15], Jn. iii. 18. iv. 41,
42, 53, v. 44, vi. 36, 47, 64, 64, ix. 38, x. 25, 26, xi. 15, xii. 39,
xiv. 29, xvi. 31, xix. 35, xx. 31, Acts ii. 44, iv. 4, 32, v. 14, viii.
13, xi. 21, xiii. 12, 39, 48, xiv. 1, xv. 5, 7, xvii. 12, 34, xviii. 8, 27,
xix. 2, 18, xxi. 20, 25, Rom. i. 16, iii. 22, x. 4, 10, xiii. 11, xv.
13, I Cor. i. 21, iii. 5, xiv. 22, xv. 2, 11, Gal. iii. 22, Eph. i. 13, 19,
I Thess. i. 7, ii. 10, 13, II Thess. i. 10, Heb. iv. 3, I Pet. ii. 7).
A survey of these passages will show very clearly that in the
New Testament 'to believe' is a technical term to express reliance on Christ for salvation. In a number of them, to be sure,
the object of the believing spoken of is sufficiently defined by
the context, but, without contextual indication of the object,
enough remain to bear out this suggestion. Accordingly, a tendency is betrayed to use the simple participle very much as a
verbal noun, with the meaning of 'Christian': in Mk. ix. 42,
Acts xi. 21, I Cor. i. 21, Eph. i. 13, 19, I Thess. i. 7, ii. 10, 13 the
participial construction is evident; it may be doubted, however,
whether οἱ πιστεύσαντες is not used as a noun in such passages as
Acts ii. 44, iv. 32, II Thess. i. 10, Heb. iv. 3; and in Acts v. 14 πιστεύοντες is perhaps generally recognized as used substantively.
Before the disciples were called 'Christians' (Acts xi. 26, cf.
xxvi. 28, I Pet. iv. 16) it would seem, then, that they were called
'believers,' — those who had turned to Christ in trusting reliance (οἱ πιστεύσαντες), or those who were resting on Christ in
trusting reliance (οἱ πιστεύοντες); and that the undefined 'to believe' had come to mean to become or to be a Christian, that
is, to turn to or rest on Christ in reliant trust. The occasional
use of οἱ πιστοί in an equivalent sense (Acts x. 45, Eph. i. 1,
I Tim. iv. 3, 12, I Pet. i. 21, Rev. xvii. 14), for which the way
was prepared by the comparatively frequent use of this adjective in the classically rare active sense (Jn. xx. 27, Acts xvi. 1,
I Cor. vii. 14, II Cor. vi. 15, Gal. iii. 9, I Tim. iv. 10, v. 16, vi. 2,
Tit. i. 6), adds weight to this conclusion; as do also the use of
ἄπιστοι of 'unbelievers,' whether in the simple (I Cor. vi. 6, vii.
12–15, x. 27, xiv. 22–24, I Tim. v. 8) or deepened sense (II Cor.

iv. 4, vi. 14 f., Tit. i. 15, cf. Jn. xx. 27, Mt. xvii. 17, Mk. ix. 19, Lk. ix. 41), and the related usage of the words ἀπιστία (Mk. ix. 24 (xvi. 14), Mt. xiii. 58, Mk. vi. 6, Rom. iv. 20, xi. 20, 23, I Tim. i. 13, Heb. iii. 12, 19), ἀπιστέω (Mk. xvi. 11 (16), Lk. xxiv. 11, 41, Acts xxviii. 24, I Pet. ii. 7), and ὀλιγόπιστος (Mt. vi. 30, viii. 26, xiv. 31, xvi. 8, Lk. xii. 28), ὀλιγοπιστία (Mt. xvii. 20).

The impression which is thus derived from the usage of πιστεύειν is only deepened by attending to that of πίστις. As already intimated, πίστις occurs in the New Testament very rarely in its passive sense of 'faithfulness,' 'integrity' (Rom. iii. 3 of God; Mt. xxiii. 23, Gal. v. 22, Tit. ii. 10, of men; cf. I Tim. v. 12 'a pledge'; Acts xvii. 31 'assurance'; others add I Tim. vi. 11, II Tim. ii. 22, iii. 10, Philem. 5). And nowhere in the multitude of its occurrences in its active sense is it applied to man's faith in man, but always to the religious trust that reposes on God, or Christ, or divine things. The specific object on which the trust rests is but seldom explicitly expressed. In some six of these instances it is a thing, but always something of the fullest soteriological significance — the gospel of Christ (Phil. i. 27), the saving truth of God (II Thess. ii. 13), the working of God who raised Jesus from the dead (Col. ii. 12, cf. Acts xiv. 9, iii. 16), the name of Jesus (Acts iii. 16), the blood of Jesus (Rom. iii. 25), the righteousness of Jesus (II Pet. i. 1). In as many more the object is God, and the conception is prevailingly that of general trust in God (Mk. xi. 22, Rom. xiv. 22, I Thess. i. 8, Heb. vi. 1, I Pet. i. 21, cf. Col. ii. 12). In most instances, however, the object is specified as Christ, and the faith is very pointedly soteriological (Acts xx. 21, xxiv. 24, xxvi. 18, Gal. ii. 16, 16, 20. Rom. iii. 22, 26, Gal. iii. 22, 26, Eph. i. 15, iii. 12, iv. 13, Phil. iii. 9, Col. i. 4, ii. 5, I Tim. i. 14, iii. 13, 15, II Tim. i. 13, iii. 15, Philem. 5, Jas. ii. 1, Rev. ii. 13, xiv. 12). Its object is most frequently joined to πίστις as an objective genitive, a construction occurring some seventeen times, twelve of which fall in the writings of Paul. In four of them the genitive is that of the thing, namely in Phil. i. 27 the gospel, in II Thess. ii. 13 the saving truth, in Col. ii. 12 the almighty working of God, and in Acts iii. 16 the name of Jesus. In one of them it is God (Mk. xi.

22). The certainty that the genitive is that of object in these cases is decisive with reference to its nature in the remaining cases, in which Jesus Christ is set forth as the object on which faith rests (Rom. iii. 22, 26, Gal. ii. 16, 16, 20, iii. 22, Eph. iii. 12, iv. 13, Phil. iii. 9, Jas. ii. 1, Rev. ii. 13, xiv. 12). Next most frequently its object is joined to faith by means of the preposition ἐν (9 times), by which it is set forth as the basis on which faith rests, or the sphere of its operation. In two of these instances the object is a thing — the blood or righteousness of Jesus (Rom. iii. 25, II Pet. i. 1); in the rest it is Christ Himself who is presented as the ground of faith (Gal. iii. 26, Eph. i. 15, Col. i. 4, I Tim. i. 14, iii. 13, II Tim. i. 13, iii. 15). Somewhat less frequently (5 times) its object is joined to πίστις by means of the preposition εἰς, designating, apparently, merely the object with reference to which faith is exercised (cf. especially Acts xx. 21); the object thus specified for faith is in one instance God (I Pet. i. 21), and in the others Christ (Acts xx. 21, xxiv. 24, xxvi. 18, Col. ii. 5). By the side of this construction should doubtless be placed the two instances in which the preposition πρός is used, by which faith is said to look and adhere to God (I Thess. i. 8) or to Christ (Philem. 5). And it is practically in the same sense that in a single instance God is joined to πίστις by means of the preposition ἐπί as the object to which it restingly turns. It would seem that the pregnant sense of πίστις as self-abandoning trust was so fixed in Christian speech that little was left to be expressed by the mode of its adjunction to its object.

Accordingly, the use of the word without specified object is vastly preponderant. In a few of such instances we may see a specific reference to the general confidence which informs believing prayer (Lk. xviii. 8, Jas. i. 6, v. 15). In a somewhat greater number there is special reference to faith in Jesus as a worker of wonders — the so-called 'miracle faith' (Mt. viii. 10, ix. 2, 22, 29, xv. 28 [xvii. 20] [xxi. 21], Mk. ii. 5, iv. 40, v. 34, x. 52, Lk. v. 20, vii. 9, viii. 25, 48, xvii. 19, xviii. 42, Acts iii. 16, xiv. 9) — although how little this faith can be regarded as non-soteriological the language of Mt. ix. 2, Mk. ii. 5, Lk. v. 20 shows, as well as the parallelism between Lk. vii. 50 (cf. viii.

48, xvii. 19) and Mt. ix. 22, Mk. v. 34. The immense mass of the passages in which the undefined πίστις occurs, however, are distinctly soteriological, and that indifferently whether its implied object be God or Christ. Its implied reference is indeed often extremely difficult to fix; though the passages in which it may, with some confidence, be referred to Christ are in number about double those in which it may, with like confidence, be referred to God. The degree of clearness with which an implied object is pointed to in the context varies, naturally, very greatly; but in a number of cases there is no direct hint of object in the context, but this is left to be supplied by the general knowledge of the reader. And this is as much as to say that πίστις is so used as to imply that it had already become a Christian technical term, which needed no further definition that it might convey its full sense of saving faith in Jesus Christ to the mind of every reader. This tendency to use it as practically a synonym for 'Christianity' comes out sharply in such a phrase as οἱ ἐκ πίστεως (Gal. iii. 7, 9), which is obviously a paraphrase for 'believers.' A transitional form of the phrase meets us in Rom. iii. 26, τὸν ἐκ πίστεως 'Ιησοῦ; that the 'Ιησοῦ could fall away and leave the simple οἱ ἐκ πίστεως standing for the whole idea, is full of implications as to the sense which the simple undefined πίστις had acquired in the circles which looked to Jesus for salvation. The same implications underlie the so-called objective use of πίστις in the New Testament. That in such passages as Acts vi. 7, Gal. i. 23, iii. 23, vi. 10, Phil. i. 25, Jude 3, 20 it conveys the idea of 'the Christian religion' appears plain on the face of the passages; and by their side can be placed such others as the following, which seem transitional to them, namely: Acts xvi. 5, I Cor. xvi. 13, Col. i. 23, I Tim. i. 19, iv. 1, 6, v. 8, Tit. i. 13, and, at a slightly further remove, such others as Acts xiii. 8, Rom. i. 5, xvi. 26, Phil. i. 25, I Tim. iii. 9, vi. 10, 12, II Tim. iii. 8, iv. 7, Tit. i. 4, iii. 15, I Pet. v. 9. It is not necessary to suppose that πίστις is used in any of these passages as *doctrina fidei;* it seems possible to carry through them all the conception of '*subjective* faith conceived of *objectively* as a power,' — even through those in Jude and I Timothy, which are more commonly than any others interpreted as meaning *doctrina fidei*. But this generally admitted objectivizing of subjective faith makes πίστις, as truly as if it were understood as *doctrina fidei*, on the verge of which it in any case trembles, a synonym for 'the Christian religion.' It is only a question whether 'the Christian religion' is designated in it from the side of doctrine or life; though it be from the point of view of life, still 'the faith' has become a synonym for 'Christianity,' 'believers' for 'Christians,' 'to believe' for 'to become a Christian,' and we may trace a development by means of which πίστις has come to mean the religion which is marked by and consists essentially in 'believing.' That this development so rapidly took place is significant of much, and supplies a ready explanation of such passages as Gal. iii. 23, 25, in which the phrases 'before the faith came' and 'now that faith is come' probably mean little more than before and after the advent of 'Christianity' into the world. On the ground of such a usage, we may at least re-affirm with increased confidence that the idea of 'faith' is conceived of in the New Testament as the characteristic idea of Christianity, and that it does not import mere 'belief' in an intellectual sense, but all that enters into an entire self-commitment of the soul to Jesus as the Son of God, the Saviour of the world.

II. The Historical Presentation of Faith

It lies on the very surface of the New Testament that its writers were not conscious of a chasm between the fundamental principle of the religious life of the saints of the old covenant and the faith by which they themselves lived. To them, too, Abraham is the typical example of a true believer (Rom. iv., Gal. iii., Heb. xi., Jas. ii.); and in their apprehension 'those who are of faith,' that is, 'Christians,' are by that very fact constituted Abraham's sons (Gal. iii. 7, Rom. iv. 16), and receive their blessing only along with that 'believer' (Gal. iii. 9) in the steps of whose faith it is that they are walking (Rom. iv. 12) when they believe on Him who raised Jesus our Lord from the dead (Rom. iv. 24). And not only Abraham, but the whole series of Old Testament heroes are conceived by them to be examples of the same faith which was required of them 'unto the gaining of the soul' (Heb. xi.). Wrought in them by the same Spirit (II Cor. iv. 13), it produced in them the same fruits, and constituted them a 'cloud of witnesses' by whose testimony we should be stimulated to run our own race with like patience in dependence on Jesus, 'the author and finisher of our faith' (Heb. xii. 2). Nowhere is the demand of faith treated as a novelty of the new covenant, or is there a distinction drawn between the faith of the two covenants; everywhere the sense of continuity is prominent (Jn. v. 24, 46, xii. 38, 39, 44, I Pet. ii. 6), and the 'proclamation of faith' (Gal. iii. 2, 5, Rom. x. 16) is conceived as essentially one in both dispensations, under both of which the law reigns that 'the just shall live by his faith' (Hab. ii. 4, Rom. i. 17, Gal. iii. 11, Heb. x. 38). Nor do we need to penetrate beneath the surface of the Old Testament to perceive the justice of this New Testament view. Despite the infrequency of the occurrence on its pages of the terms 'faith,' 'to believe,' the religion of the Old Testament is obviously as fundamentally a religion of faith as is that of the New Testament. There is a sense, to be sure, in which all religion presupposes faith (Heb. xi. 6), and in this broad sense the religion of Israel, too, necessarily rested on faith. But the religion of Israel was a religion of faith in a far more specific sense than this; and that not merely because faith was more consciously its foundation, but because its very essence consisted in faith, and this faith was the same radical self-commitment to God, not merely as the highest good of the holy soul, but as the gracious Saviour of the sinner, which meets us as the characteristic feature of the religion of the New Testament. Between the faith of the two Testaments there exists, indeed, no further difference than that which the progress of the historical working out of redemption brought with it.

The hinge of Old Testament religion from the very beginning turns on the facts of man's sin (Gen. iii.) and consequent unworthiness (Gen. iii. 2–10), and of God's grace (Gen. iii. 15) and consequent saving activity (Gen. iii. 4, iv. 5, vi. 8, 13 f.).

This saving activity presents itself from the very beginning also under the form of promise or covenant, the radical idea of which is naturally faithfulness on the part of the promising God with the answering attitude of faith on the part of the receptive people. Face to face with a holy God, the sinner has no hope except in the free mercy of God, and can be authorized to trust in that mercy only by express assurance. Accordingly, the only cause of salvation is from the first the pitying love of God (Gen. iii. 15, viii. 21), which freely grants benefits to man; while on man's part there is never question of merit or of a strength by which he may prevail (I Sam. ii. 9), but rather a constant sense of unworthiness (Gen. xxxii. 10), by virtue of which humility appears from the first as the keynote of Old Testament piety. In the earlier portions of the Old Testament, to be sure, there is little abstract statement of the ideas which ruled the hearts and lives of the servants of God. The essence of patriarchal religion is rather exhibited to us in action. But from the very beginning the distinctive feature of the life of the pious is that it is a life of faith, that its regulative principle is drawn, not from the earth but from above. Thus the first recorded human acts after the Fall — the naming of Eve, and the birth and naming of Cain — are expressive of trust in God's promise that, though men should die for their sins, yet man should not perish from the earth, but should triumph over the tempter; in a word, in the great promise of the Seed (Gen. iii. 15). Similarly, the whole story of the Flood is so ordered as to throw into relief, on the one hand, the free grace of God in His dealings with Noah (Gen. vi. 8, 18, viii. 1, 21, ix. 8), and, on the other, the determination of Noah's whole life by trust in God and His promises (Gen. vi. 22, vii. 5, ix. 20). The open declaration of the faith-principle of Abraham's life (Gen. xv. 6) only puts into words, in the case of him who stands at the root of Israel's whole national and religious existence, what not only might also be said of all the patriarchs, but what actually is most distinctly said both of Abraham and of them through the medium of their recorded history. The entire patriarchal narrative is set forth with the design and effect of exhibiting the life of the servants of God as a life of faith, and it is just by the fact of their implicit self-commitment to God that throughout the narrative the servants of God are differentiated from others. This does not mean, of course, that with them faith took the place of obedience: an entire self-commitment to God which did not show itself in obedience to Him would be self-contradictory, and the testing of faith by obedience is therefore a marked feature of the patriarchal narrative. But it does mean that faith was with them the precondition of all obedience. The patriarchal religion is essentially a religion, not of law but of promise, and therefore not primarily of obedience but of trust; the holy walk is characteristic of God's servants (Gen. v. 22, 24, vi. 9, xvii. 1, xxiv. 40, xlviii. 15), but it is characteristically described as a walk 'with God'; its peculiarity consisted precisely in the ordering of life by entire trust in God, and it expressed itself in conduct growing out of this trust (Gen. iii. 20, iv. 1, vi. 22, vii. 5, viii. 18, xii. 4, xvii. 23, xxi. 12, 16, xxii.). The righteousness of the patriarchal age was thus but the manifestation in life of an entire self-commitment to God, in unwavering trust in His promises.

The piety of the Old Testament thus began with faith. And though, when the stage of the law was reached, the emphasis might seem to be thrown rather on the obedience of faith, what has been called 'faith in action,' yet the giving of the law does not mark a fundamental change in the religion of Israel, but only a new stage in its orderly development. The law-giving was not a setting aside of the religion of promise, but an incident in its history; and the law given was not a code of jurisprudence for the world's government, but a body of household ordinances for the regulation of God's family. It is therefore itself grounded upon the promise, and it grounds the whole religious life of Israel in the grace of the covenant God (Ex. xx. 2). It is only because Israel are the children of God, and God has sanctified them unto Himself and chosen them to be a peculiar people unto Him (Deut. xiv. 1), that He proceeds to frame them by His law for His especial treasure (Ex. xix. 5; cf. Tit. ii. 14). Faith, therefore, does not appear as one of the precepts of the law, nor as a virtue superior to its precepts, nor yet as a substitute for keeping them; it rather lies behind the law as its presupposition. Accordingly, in the history of the giving of the law, faith is expressly emphasized as the presupposition of the whole relation existing between Israel and Jehovah. The signs by which Moses was accredited, and all Jehovah's deeds of power, had as their design (Ex. iii. 12, iv. 1, 5, 8, 9, xix. 4, 9) and their effect (Ex. iv. 31, xii. 28, 34, xiv. 31, xxiv. 3, 7, Ps. cvi. 12) the working of faith in the people; and their subsequent unbelief is treated as the deepest crime they could commit (Num. xiv. 11, Deut. i. 32, ix. 23, Ps. lxxviii. 22, 32, cvi. 24), as is even momentary failure of faith on the part of their leaders (Num. xx. 12). It is only as a consequent of the relation of the people to Him, instituted by grace on His part and by faith on theirs, that Jehovah proceeds to carry out His gracious purposes for them, delivering them from bondage, giving them a law for the regulation of their lives, and framing them in the promised land into a kingdom of priests and a holy nation. In other words, it is a precondition of the law that Israel's life is not of the earth, but is hid with God, and is therefore to be ordered by His precepts. Its design was, therefore, not to provide a means by which man might come into relation with Jehovah, but to publish the mode of life incumbent on those who stand in the relation of children to Jehovah; and it is therefore that the book of the law was commanded to be put by the side of the ark of the covenant of the LORD, that it might be a witness against the transgressions of Israel (Deut. xxxi. 26).

The effect of the law was consonant with its design. Many, no doubt, looked upon it in a purely legalistic spirit, and sought, by scrupulous fulfilment of it as a body of external precepts, to lay the foundation of a claim on God in behalf of the nation or the individual, or to realize through it, as a present possession, that salvation which was ever represented as something future. But, just in proportion as its spirituality and inwardness were felt, it operated to deepen in Israel the sense of shortcoming and sin, and to sharpen the conviction that from the grace of God alone could salvation be expected. This humble frame of conscious dependence on God was met by a twofold proclamation.

On the one hand, the eyes of God's people were directed more longingly towards the future, and, in contrast with the present failure of Israel to realize the ordinances of life which had been given it, a new dispensation of grace was promised in which the law of God's kingdom should be written upon the heart, and should become therefore the instinctive law of life of His people (Jer. xxiv. 7, xxxi. 11 f., Ezek. xxxvi 25 f.; cf. Ezek. xvi. 60, Joel iii., Jos. ii. 9 f.). It lay in the very nature of the Old Testament dispensation, in which the revelation of God was always incomplete, the still unsolved enigmas of life numerous, the work of redemption unfinished, and the consummation of the kingdom ever yet to come, that the eyes of the saints should be set upon the future; and these deficiencies were felt very early. But it also lay, in the nature of the case, that the sense of them should increase as time passed and the perfecting of Israel was delayed, and especially as the whole national and religious existence of Israel was more and more put in jeopardy by assaults from without and corruption from within. The essence of piety came thus to be ever more plainly proclaimed as consisting in such a confident trust in the God of salvation as could not be confounded either by the unrighteousness which reigned in Israel or by Jehovah's judgments on Israel's sins, — such a confidence as even in the face of the destruction of the theocracy itself, could preserve, in enduring hope, the assurance of the ultimate realization of God's purposes of good to Israel and the establishment of the everlasting kingdom. Thus hopeful waiting upon Jehovah became more and more the centre of Israelitish piety, and Jehovah became before all 'the Hope of Israel' (Jer. xiv. 8, xvii. 13, l. 7, cf. Ps. lxxi. 5). On the other hand, while thus waiting for the salvation of Israel, the saint must needs stay himself on God (Isa. xxvi. 3, l. 10), fixing his heart on Jehovah as the Rock of the heart (Ps. lxxiii. 26), His people's strength (Ps. xlvi. 1) and trust (Ps. xl. 4, lxv. 5, lxxi. 5, Jer. xvii. 7). Freed from all illusion of earthly help, and most of all from all self-confidence, he is meanwhile to live by faith (Hab. ii. 4). Thus, along with an ever more richly expressed corporate hope, there is found also an ever more richly expressed individual trust, which finds natural utterance through an ample body of synonyms bringing out severally the various sides of that perfect commitment to God that constitutes the essence of faith. Thus we read much of trusting in, on, to God, or in His word, His name, His mercy, His salvation (בָּטַח), of seeking and finding refuge in God or in the shadow of His wings (חָסָה), of committing ourselves to God (גָּלַל), setting confidence (בָּטַל) in Him, looking to Him (הִבִּיט), relying upon Him (נִשְׁעַן), staying upon Him (נִסְמַךְ), setting or fixing the heart upon Him (הֵכִין לֵב), binding our love on Him (חָשַׁק), cleaving to Him (דָּבַק). So, on the hopeful side of faith, we read much of hoping in God (קִוָּה), waiting on God (יָחַל), of longing for Him (חִכָּה), patiently waiting for Him (הִתְחוֹלֵל), and the like.

By the aid of such expressions, it becomes possible to form a somewhat clear notion of the attitude towards Him which was required by Jehovah of His believing people, and which is summed up in the term "faith." It is a reverential (Ex. xiv. 31, Num. xiv. 11, xx. 12) and loving faith, which rests on the strong basis of firm and unshaken conviction of the might and grace of the covenant God and of the trustworthiness of all His words, and exhibits itself in confident trust in Jehovah and unwavering expectation of the fulfilment of, no doubt, all His promises, but more especially of His promise of salvation, and in consequent faithful and exclusive adherence to Him. In one word, it consists in an utter commitment of oneself to Jehovah, with confident trust in Him as guide and saviour, and assured expectation of His promised salvation. It therefore stands in contrast, on the one hand, with trust in self or other human help, and on the other with doubt and unbelief, despondency and unfaithfulness. From Jehovah alone is salvation to be looked for, and it comes from His free grace alone (Deut. vii. 7, viii. 18, ix. 5, Amos iii. 2, Hos. xiii. 5, Ezek. xx. 6, Jer. xxxix. 18, Mal. i. 2), and to those only who look solely to Him for it (Isa. xxxi. 1, lvii. 13, xxviii. 16, xxx. 15, Jer. xvii. 5, xxxix. 18, Ps. cxviii. 8, cxlvi. 3, xx. 7, I Sam. xvii. 45, Job xxxi. 24, Ps. lii. 9). The reference of faith is accordingly in the Old Testament always distinctly soteriological; its end the Messianic salvation; and its essence a trusting, or rather an entrusting of oneself to the God of salvation, with full assurance of the fulfilment of His gracious purposes and the ultimate realization of His promise of salvation for the people and the individual. Such an attitude towards the God of salvation is identical with the faith of the New Testament, and is not essentially changed by the fuller revelation of God the Redeemer in the person of the promised Messiah. That it is comparatively seldom designated in the Old Testament by the names of 'faith,' 'believing,' seems to be due, as has been often pointed out, to the special place of the Old Testament in the history of revelation, and the adaptation of its whole contents and language to the particular task in the establishment of the kingdom of God which fell to its writers. This task turned on the special temptations and difficulties of the Old Testament stage of development, and required emphasis to be laid on the majesty and jealousy of Jehovah and on the duties of reverence, sincerity, and patience. Meanwhile, the faith in Him which underlies these duties is continually implied in their enforcement, and comes to open expression in frequent paraphrase and synonym, and as often in its own proper terms as is natural in the circumstances. Especially in the great crises of the history of redemption (Gen. xv., Ex. iv. 5, xix. 9, Isa. vii.) is the fundamental requirement of faith rendered explicit and prominent.

On the coming of God to His people in the person of His Son, the promised Messianic King, bringing the salvation, the hope of which had for so many ages been their support and stay, it naturally became the primary task of the vehicles of revelation to attract and attach God's people to the person of their Redeemer. And this task was the more pressing in proportion as the form of the fulfilment did not obviously correspond with the promise, and especially with the expectations which had grown up on the faith of the promise. This fundamental function dominates the whole New Testament, and accounts at once for the great prominence in its pages of the demand for faith, by which a gulf seems to be opened between it and the Old Testament. The demand for faith in Jesus as the Redeemer so long hoped for, did indeed create so wide a cleft in the consciousness of the times that the term faith came rapidly to be appropriated to Christianity and 'to believe' to mean to become a Christian; so that the old covenant and the new were discriminated from each other as the ages before and after the 'coming of faith' (Gal. iii. 23, 25). But all this does not imply that faith now for the first time became the foundation of the religion of Jehovah, but only suggests how fully, in the new circumstances induced by the coming of the promised Redeemer, the demand for faith absorbed the whole proclamation of the gospel. In this primary concern for faith the New Testament books all necessarily share; but, for the rest, they differ among themselves in the prominence given to it and in the aspects in which it is presented, in accordance with the place of each in the historical development of the new life; and that is as much as to say in accordance with the historical occasion out of which each arose and the special object to subserve which each was written.

Indeed, the word 'to believe' first appears on the pages of the New Testament in quite Old Testament conditions. We are conscious of no distinction even in atmosphere between the commendation of faith and rebuke of unbelief in Exodus or the Psalms and the same commendation and rebuke in the days just before the 'coming of faith' (Lk. i. 20, 45); these are but specific applications of the thesis of prophetism, expressed positively in II Chron. xx. 20 and negatively in Isa. vii. 9. Already, however, the dawn of the new day has coloured the proclamation of the Baptist, the essence of which Paul sums up for us as a demand for faith in the Coming One (Acts xix. 4), and which John reports to us (Jn. iii. 36). In the synoptic report of the teaching of Jesus, the same purpose is the dominant note. All that Jesus did and taught was directed to drawing faith to Himself. Up to the end, indeed, He repelled the unbelieving demand that He should 'declare plainly' the authority by which He acted and who He really was (Mt. xxi. 23, Lk. xxii. 67): but this was only that He might, in His own way, the more decidedly confound unbelief and assert His divine majesty. Even when He spoke of general faith in God (Mk. xi. 22), and that confident trust which becomes men approaching the Almighty in prayer (Mt. xxi.

22||Mk. ix. 24, Lk. xviii. 8), He did it in a way which inevitably directed attention to His own person as the representative of God on earth. And this accounts for the prevalence, in the synoptic report of His allusions to faith, of a reference to that exercise of faith which has sometimes been somewhat sharply divided from saving faith under the name of 'miracle faith' (Mt. viii. 10, 13 || Lk. vii. 9; Mt. ix. 2; Mt. ix. 22 || Mk. v. 34, Lk. viii. 48; Mt. ix. 28, 29; Mt. xv. 28; Mt. xvii. 20 || Mk. ix. 20; Mt. xxi. 21, 22, cf. Lk. xvii. 6; Mk. iv. 40; Mk. v. 36 || Lk. viii. 50; Mk. x. 52 || Lk. xviii. 42; Lk. vii. 9). That in these instances we have not a generically distinct order of faith, directed to its own peculiar end, but only a specific movement of that entire trust in Himself which Jesus would arouse in all, seems clear from the manner in which He dealt with it, — now praising its exercise as a specially great exhibition of faith quite generally spoken of (Lk. vii. 9), now pointing to it as a manifestation of that believing to which 'all things are possible' (Mk. ix. 23), now connecting with it not merely the healing of the body but the forgiveness of sins (Mt. ix. 2), and everywhere using it as a means of attaching the confidence of men to His person as the source of all good. Having come to His own, in other words, Jesus took men upon the plane on which He found them, and sought to lead them through the needs which they felt, and the relief of which they sought in Him, up to a recognition of their greater needs and of His ability to give relief to them also. That word of power, 'Thy faith hath saved thee,' spoken indifferently of bodily wants and of the deeper needs of the soul (Lk. vii. 50), not only resulted, but was intended to result, in focusing all eyes on Himself as the one physician of both body and soul (Mt. viii. 17). Explicit references to these higher results of faith are, to be sure, not very frequent in the synoptic discourses, but there are quite enough of them to exhibit Jesus' specific claim to be the proper object of faith for these effects also (Lk. viii. 12, 13, xxii. 32, Mt. xviii. 6 || Mk. ix. 42, Lk. vii. 50), and to prepare the way for His rebuke, after His resurrection, of the lagging minds of His followers, that they did not understand all these things (Lk. xxiv. 25, 45), and for His great commission to Paul to go and open men's eyes that they might receive 'remission of sins and an inheritance among the sanctified by faith in Him' (Acts xxvi. 18).

It is very natural that a much fuller account of Jesus' teaching as to faith should be given in the more intimate discourses which are preserved by John. But in these discourses, too, His primary task is to bind men to Him by faith. The chief difference is that here, consonantly with the nature of the discourses recorded, much more prevailing stress is laid upon the higher aspects of faith, and we see Jesus striving specially to attract to Himself a faith consciously set upon eternal good. In a number of instances we find ourselves in much the same atmosphere as in the Synoptics (iv. 21 *sq.*, 48 *sq.*, ix. 35); and the method of Jesus is the same throughout. Everywhere He offers Himself as the object of faith, and claims faith in Himself for the highest concerns of the soul. But everywhere He begins at the level at which He finds His hearers, and leads them upward to these higher things. It is so that He deals with Nathanael (i. 51) and Nicodemus (iii. 12); and it is so that He deals constantly with the Jews, everywhere requiring faith in Himself for eternal life (v. 24, 25, 38, vi. 35, 40, 47, vii. 38, viii. 24, x. 25, 36, xii. 44, 46), declaring that faith in Him is the certain outcome of faith in their own Scriptures (v. 46, 47), is demanded by the witness borne Him by God in His mighty works (x. 25, 36, 37), is involved in and is indeed identical with faith in God (v. 25, 38, vi. 40, 45, viii. 47, xii. 44), and is the one thing which God requires of them (vi. 29), and the failure of which will bring them eternal ruin (iii. 18, v. 38, vi. 64, viii. 24). When dealing with His followers, His primary care was to build up their faith in Him. Witness especially His solicitude for their faith in the last hours of His intercourse with them. For the faith they had reposed in Him He returns thanks to God (xvii. 8), but He is still nursing their faith (xvi. 31), preparing for its increase through the events to come (xiii. 19, xvi. 29), and with almost passionate eagerness claiming it at their hands (xiv. 1, 10, 11, 12). Even after His resurrection we find Him restoring the faith of the waverer (xx. 29) with words which pronounce a special blessing on those who should hereafter believe on less compelling evidence — words whose point is not fully caught until we realize that they contain an intimation of the work of the apostles as, like His own, summed up in bringing men to faith in Him (xvii. 20, 21).

The record in Acts of the apostolic proclamation testifies to the faithfulness with which this office was prosecuted by Jesus' delegates (Acts iii. 22, 23). The task undertaken by them was, by persuading men (Acts xvii. 4, xxviii. 24), to bring them unto obedience to the faith that is in Jesus (Acts vi. 7, Rom. i. 5, xvi. 26, cf. II Thess. i. 8, II Cor. x. 5). And by such 'testifying faith towards our Lord Jesus Christ' (Acts xx. 21, cf. x. 43) there was quickly gathered together a community of 'believers' (Acts ii. 44, iv. 4, 32), that is, of believers in the Lord Jesus Christ (Acts v. 14, ix. 42, xi. 17, xiv. 23), and that not only in Jerusalem but beyond (viii. 12, ix. 42, x. 45, xi. 21, xiii. 48, xiv. 1), and not only of Jews (x. 45, xv. 1, xxi. 20) but of Gentiles (xi. 21, xiii. 48, xiv. 1, xv. 7, xvii. 12, 34, xviii. 27, xix. 18, xxi. 25). The enucleation of this community of believers brought to the apostolic teachers the new task of preserving the idea of faith, which was the formative principle of the new community, and to propagate which in the world, pure and living and sound, was its chief office. It was inevitable that those who were called into the faith of Christ should bring into the infant Church with them many old tendencies of thinking, and that within the new community the fermentation of ideas should be very great. The task of instructing and disciplining the new community soon became unavoidably one of the heaviest of apostolic duties; and its progress is naturally reflected in their letters. Thus certain differences in their modes of dealing with faith emerge among New Testament writers, according as one lays stress on the deadness and profitlessness of a faith which produces no fruit in the life, and another on the valuelessness of a faith which does not emancipate from the bondage of the law; or as one lays stress on the perfection of the object of faith and the necessity of keeping the heart set upon it, and another on the necessity of preserving in its purity that subjective attitude towards the unseen and future which constitutes the very essence of faith; or as one lays stress on the reaching out of faith to the future in confident hope, and another on the present enjoyment by faith of all the blessings of salvation.

It was to James that it fell to rebuke the Jewish tendency to conceive of the faith which was pleasing to Jehovah as a mere intellectual acquiescence in His being and claims, when imported into the Church and made to do duty as 'the faith of our Lord Jesus Christ, the Glory' (ii. 1). He has sometimes been misread as if he were depreciating faith, or at least the place of faith in salvation. But it is perfectly clear that with James, as truly as with any other New Testament writer, a sound faith in the Lord Jesus Christ as the manifested God (ii. 1) lies at the very basis of the Christian life (i. 3), and is the condition of all acceptable approach to God (i. 6, v. 15). It is not faith as he conceives it which he depreciates, but that professed faith (λέγῃ, ii. 14) which cannot be shown to be real by appropriate works (ii. 18), and so differs by a whole diameter alike from the faith of Abraham that was reckoned unto him for righteousness (ii. 23), and from the faith of Christians as James understood it (ii. 1, i. 3, cf. i. 22). The impression which is easily taken from the last half of the second chapter of James, that his teaching and that of Paul stand in some polemic relation, is, nevertheless, a delusion, and arises from an insufficient realization of the place occupied by faith in the discussions of the Jewish schools, reflections of which have naturally found their way into the language of both Paul and James. And so far are we from needing to suppose some reference, direct or indirect, to Pauline teaching to account for James' entrance upon the question which he discusses, that this was a matter upon which an earnest teacher could not fail to touch in the presence of a tendency common among the Jews at the advent of Christianity (cf. Mt. iii. 9, vii. 21, xxiii. 3, Rom. ii. 17), and certain to pass over into Jewish-Christian circles: and James' treatment of it finds, indeed, its entire presupposition in the state of things underlying the exhortation of i. 22. When read from his own historical standpoint, James' teachings are free from any disaccord with those of Paul, who as strongly as James denies all value to a faith which does not work by love (Gal. v. 6, I Cor. xiii. 2, I Thess. i. 3). In short, James is not depreciating faith: with him, too, it is faith that is reckoned unto righteousness (ii. 23), though only such a faith as shows itself in works can be so reckoned, because a faith which does not come to fruitage in works is dead, non-existent. He is rather deepening the idea of faith, and insisting that it includes in its very conception something more than an otiose intellectual assent.

It was a far more serious task which was laid upon Paul. As apostle to the Gentiles he was called upon to make good in all its depth of meaning the fundamental principle of the religion of grace, that the righteous shall live by faith, as over-against what had come to be the ingrained legalism of Jewish thought now intruded into the Christian Church. It was not, indeed, doubted that faith was requisite for obtaining salvation. But he that had been born a Jew and was conscious of the privileges of the children of the promise, found it hard to think that faith was all that was requisite. What, then, was the advantage of the Jew? In defence of the rights of the Gentiles, Paul was forced in the most uncompromising way to validate the great proposition that, in the matter of salvation, there is no distinction between Jew and Gentile, — that the Jew has no other righteousness than that which comes through faith in Jesus Christ (Gal. ii. 15 *sq.*), and that the Gentile fully possesses this righteousness from faith alone (Gal. iii. 7 *sq.*); in a word, that the one God, who is God of the Gentiles also, 'shall justify the circumcision by faith, and the uncircumcision through faith' (Rom. iii. 30). Thus was it made clear not only that 'no man is justified by the law' (Gal. ii. 16, iii. 11, Rom. iii. 20), but also that a man is justified by faith apart from law-works (Rom. iii. 28). The splendid vigour and thoroughness of Paul's dialectic development of the absolute contrast between the ideas of faith and works, by virtue of which one peremptorily excludes the other, left no hiding-place for a work-righteousness of any kind or degree, but cast all men solely upon the righteousness of God, which is apart from the law and comes through faith unto all that believe (Rom. iii. 21, 22). Thus, in vindicating the place of faith as the only instrument of salvation, Paul necessarily dwelt much upon the object of faith, not as if he were formally teaching what the object is on which faith savingly lays hold, but as a natural result of his effort to show from its object the all-sufficiency of faith. It is because faith lays hold of Jesus Christ, who was delivered up for our trespasses and was raised for our justification (Rom. iv. 25), and makes us possessors of the righteousness provided by God through Him, that there is no room for any righteousness of our own in the ground of our salvation (Rom. x. 3, Eph. ii. 8). This is the reason of that full development of the object of faith in Paul's writings, and especially of the specific connexion between faith and the righteousness of God proclaimed in Christ, by which the doctrine of Paul is sometimes said to be distinguished from the more general conception of faith which is characteristic of the Epistle to the Hebrews. This more general conception of faith is not, however, the peculiar property of that epistle, but is the fundamental conception of the whole body of biblical writers in the Old Testament and in the New Testament (cf. Mt. vi. 25, xvi. 23, Jn. xx. 29, 31, I Pet. i. 8), including Paul himself (II Cor. iv. 18, v. 7, Rom. iv. 16–22, viii. 24); while, on the other hand, the Epistle to the Hebrews, no less than Paul, teaches that there is no righteousness except through faith (x. 38, xi. 7, cf. xi. 4).

That in the Epistle to the Hebrews it is the general idea of faith, or, to be more exact, the subjective nature of faith, that is dwelt upon, rather than its specific object, is not due to a peculiar conception of what faith lays hold upon, but to the particular task which fell to its writer in the work of planting Christianity in the world. With him, too, the person and work of Christ are the specific object of faith (xiii. 7, 8, iii. 14, x. 22). But the danger against which, in the providence of God, he was called upon to guard the infant flock, was not that it should fall away from faith to works, but that it should fall away from faith into despair. His readers were threatened not with legalism but with 'shrinking back' (x. 39), and he needed, therefore, to emphasize not so much the object of faith as the duty of faith. Accordingly, it is not so much on the righteousness of faith as on its perfecting that he insists; it is not so much its contrast with works as its contrast with impatience that he impresses on his readers' consciences; it is not so much to faith specifically in Christ and in Him alone that he exhorts them as to an attitude of faith — an attitude which could rise above the seen to the unseen, the present to the future, the temporal to the eternal, and which in the midst of sufferings could retain patience, in the midst of disappointments could preserve hope. This is the key to the whole treatment of faith in the Epistle to the Hebrews — its definition as the assurance of things hoped for, the conviction of things not seen (xi. 1); its illustration and enforcement by the example of the heroes of faith in the past, a list chosen and treated with the utmost skill for the end in view (xi.); its constant attachment to the promises (iv. 1, 2, vi. 12, x. 36, 38, xi. 9); its connexion with the faithfulness (xi. 11, cf. x. 23), almightiness (xi. 19), and the rewards of God (xi. 6, 26); and its association with such virtues as boldness (iii. 6, iv. 16, x. 19, 35), confidence (iii. 14, xi. 1), patience (x. 36, xii. 1), hope (iii. 6, vi. 11, 18, x. 23).

With much that is similar to the situation implied in Hebrews, that which underlies the Epistles of Peter differs from it in the essential particular that their prevailingly Gentile readers were not in imminent danger of falling back into Judaism. There is, accordingly, much in the aspect in which faith is presented in these epistles which reminds us of what we find in Hebrews, as, for example, the close connexion into which it is brought with obedience (I Pet. i. 2, 22, ii. 7, iii. 1, iv. 17), its prevailing reference to what is unseen and future (I Pet. i. 5, 7–10, 21), and its consequent demand for steadfastness (v. 9, cf. i. 7), and especially for hope (i. 21, cf. i. 3, 13, iii. 5, 15). Yet there is a noteworthy difference in the whole tone of the commendation of faith, which was rooted, no doubt, in the character of Peter, as the tone of his speeches recorded in Acts shows, but which also grew out of the nature of the task set before him in these letters. There is no hint of despair lying in the near background, but the buoyancy of assured hope rings throughout these epistles.

Having hearkened to the prophet like unto Moses (Deut. xviii. 15, 19, Acts iii. 22, 23), Christians are the children of obedience (I Pet. i. 14), and through their precious faith (I Pet. i. 7, II Pet. i. 1) possessors of the preciousness of the promises (I Pet. ii. 7). As they have obeyed the voice of God and kept His covenant, they have become His peculiar treasure, a kingdom of priests and a holy nation (Ex. xix. 5, I Pet. ii. 9). Naturally, the duty rests upon them of living, while here below, in accordance with their high hopes (I Pet. i. 13, II Pet. i. 5). But in any event they are but sojourners and pilgrims here (I Pet. ii. 11, i. 1, 17), and have a sure inheritance reserved for them in heaven (i. 4), unto which they are guarded through faith by the power of God (i. 5). The reference of faith in Peter is therefore characteristically to the completion rather than to the inception of salvation (i. 5, 9, ii. 6, cf. Acts xv. 11). Of course this does not imply that he does not share the common biblical conception of faith: he is conscious of no difference of view from that of the Old Testament (I Pet. ii. 6); and, no less than with James, with him faith is the fountain of all good works (I Pet. i. 7, 21, v. 9, II Pet. i. 5); and, no less than with Paul, with him faith lays hold of the righteousness of Christ (II Pet. i. 1). It only means that in the circumstances of his writing he is led to lay special emphasis on the reference of faith to the consummated salvation, in order to quicken in his readers that hope which would sustain them in their persecutions, and to keep their eyes set, not on their present trials, but, in accordance with faith's very nature, on the unseen and eternal glory.

In the entirely different circumstances in which he wrote, John wished to lay stress on the very opposite aspect of faith. For what is characteristic of John's treatment of faith is insistence not so much on the certainty and glory of the future inheritance which it secures, as on the fulness of the present enjoyment of salvation which it brings. There was pressing into the Church a false emphasis on knowledge, which affected to despise simple faith. This John met, on the one hand, by deepening the idea of knowledge to the knowledge of experience, and, on the other, by insisting upon the immediate entrance of every believer into the possession of salvation. It is not to be supposed, of course, that he was ready to neglect or deny that out-reaching of faith to the future on which Peter lays such stress: he is zealous that Christians shall know that they are children of God from the moment of believing, and from that instant possessors of the new life of the Spirit; but he does not forget the greater glory of the future, and he knows how to use this Christian hope also as an incitement to holy living (I Jn. iii. 2). Nor are we to suppose that, in his anti-Gnostic insistence on the element of conviction in faith, he would lose sight of that central element of surrendering trust which is the heart of faith in other portions of the Scriptures: he would indeed have believers know what they believe, and who He is in whom they put their trust, and what He has done for them, and is doing, and will do, in and through them; but this is not that they may know these things simply as intellectual propositions, but that they may rest on them in faith and know them in personal experience. Least of all the New Testament writers could John confine faith to a merely intellectual act: his whole doctrine of faith is rather a protest against the intellectualism of Gnosticism. His fundamental conception of faith differs in nothing from that of the other New Testament writers; with him, too, it is a trustful appropriation of Christ and surrender of self to His salvation. Eternal life has been manifested by Christ (Jn. i. 4, I Jn. i. 1, 2, v. 11), and he, and he only, who has the Son has the life (I Jn. v. 12). But in the conflict in which he was engaged he required to throw the strongest emphasis possible upon the immediate entrance of believers into this life. This insistence had manifold applications to the circumstances of his readers. It had, for example, a negative application to the antinomian tendency of Gnostic teaching, which John does not fail to press (I Jn. i. 5, ii. 4, 15, iii. 6): 'whosoever believeth that Jesus is the Christ is begotten of God' (I Jn. v. 1), and 'whosoever is begotten of God doeth no sin' (I Jn. iii. 9). It had also a positive application to their own encouragement: the simple believer was placed on a plane of life to which no knowledge could attain; the new life received by faith gave the victory over the world; and John boldly challenges experience to point to any who have overcome the world but he that believes that Jesus is the Son of God (I Jn. v. 4, 5). Accordingly, it is characteristic of John to announce that 'he that believeth hath eternal life' (Jn. iii. 36, v. 24, vi. 47, 54, I Jn. iii. 14, 15, v. 11, 12, 13). He even declares the purpose of his writing to be, in the Gospel, that his readers 'may believe that Jesus is the Christ, the Son of God, and that, believing, they may have life in his name' (xx. 31); and in the First Epistle, that they that believe in the name of the Son of God 'may know that they *have* eternal life' (I Jn. v. 13).

III. The Biblical Conception of Faith

By means of the providentially mediated diversity of emphasis of the New Testament writers on the several aspects of faith, the outlines of the biblical conception of faith are thrown into very high relief.

Of its *subjective nature* we have what is almost a formal definition in the description of it as an 'assurance of things hoped for, a conviction of things not seen' (Heb. xi. 1). It obviously contains in it, therefore, an element of knowledge (Heb. xi. 6), and it as obviously issues in conduct (Heb. xi. 8, cf. v. 9, I Pet. i. 22). But it consists neither in assent nor in obedience, but in a reliant trust in the invisible Author of all good (Heb. xi. 27), in which the mind is set upon the things that are above and not on the things that are upon the earth (Col. iii. 2, cf. II Cor. iv. 16–18, Mt. vi. 25. The examples cited in Heb. xi are themselves enough to show that the faith there commended is not a mere belief in God's existence and justice and goodness, or crediting of His word and promises, but a practical counting of Him faithful (xi. 11), with a trust so profound that no trial can shake it (xi. 35), and so absolute that it survives the loss of even its own pledge (xi. 17). So little is faith in its biblical conception merely a conviction of the understanding, that, when that is called faith, the true idea of faith needs to be built up above this word (Jas. ii. 14 ff.). It is a movement of the whole inner man (Rom. x. 9, 10), and is set in contrast with an unbelief that is akin, not to ignorance but to disobedience (Heb. iii. 18, 19, Jn. iii. 36, Rom. xi. 20, 30, xv. 31, I Thess. i. 8, Heb. iv. 2, 6, I Pet. i. 7, 8, iii. 1, 20, iv. 18, Acts xiv. 2, xix. 9), and that grows out of, not lack of information, but that aversion of the heart from God (Heb. iii. 12) which takes pleasure in unrighteousness (II Thess. ii. 12), and is so unsparingly exposed by our Lord (Jn. iii. 19, v. 44, viii. 47, x. 26). In the breadth of its idea, it is thus the going out of the heart from itself and its resting on God in confident trust for all good. But the scriptural revelation has to do with, and is directed to the needs of, not man in the abstract, but sinful man; and for sinful man this hearty reliance on God necessarily becomes humble trust in Him for the fundamental need of the sinner — forgiveness of sins and reception into favour. In response to the revelations of His grace and the provisions of His mercy, it commits itself without reserve and with abnegation of all self-dependence, to Him as its sole and sufficient Saviour, and thus, in one act, empties itself of all claim on God and casts itself upon His grace alone for salvation.

It is, accordingly, solely from its *object* that faith derives its value. This object is uniformly the God of grace, whether conceived of broadly as the source of all life, light, and blessing, on whom man in his creaturely weakness is entirely dependent, or, whenever sin and the eternal welfare of the soul are in view, as the Author of salvation in whom alone the hope of unworthy man can be placed. This one object of saving faith never varies from the beginning to the end of the scriptural revelation; though, naturally, there is an immense difference between its earlier and later stages in fulness of knowledge as to the nature of the redemptive work by which the salvation intrusted to God shall be accomplished; and as naturally there occurs a very great variety of forms of statement in which trust in the God of salvation receives expression. Already, however, at the gate of Eden, the God in whom the trust of our first parents is reposed is the God of the gracious promise of the retrieval of the injury inflicted by the serpent; and from that beginning of knowledge the progress is steady, until, what is implied in the primal promise having become express in the accomplished work of redemption, the trust of sinners is explicitly placed in the God who was in Christ reconciling the world unto Himself (II Cor. v. 19). Such a faith, again, could not fail to embrace with humble confidence all the gracious promises of the God of salvation, from which indeed it draws its life and strength; nor could it fail to lay hold with strong conviction on all those revealed truths concerning Him which constitute, indeed, in the varied circumstances in which it has been called upon to persist throughout the ages, the very grounds in view of which it has been able to rest upon Him with steadfast trust. These truths, in which the 'Gospel' or glad-tidings to God's people has been from time to time embodied, run all the way from such simple facts as that it was the very God of their fathers that had appeared unto Moses for their deliverance (Ex. iv. 5), to such stupendous facts, lying at the root of the very work of salvation itself, as that Jesus is the Christ, the Son of God sent of God to save the world (Jn. vi. 69, viii. 24, xi. 42, xiii. 19, xvi. 27, 30, xvii. 8, 21, xx. 31, I Jn. v. 15), that God has raised Him from the dead (Rom. x. 9, I Thess. iv. 14), and that as His children we shall live with Him (Rom. vi. 8). But in believing this variously presented Gospel, faith has ever terminated with trustful reliance, not on the promise but on the Promiser, — not on the propositions which declare God's grace and willingness to save, or Christ's divine nature and power, or the reality and perfection of His saving work, but on the Saviour upon whom, because of these great facts, it could securely rest as on One able to save to the uttermost. Jesus Christ, God the Redeemer, is accordingly the one object of saving faith, presented to its embrace at first implicitly and in promise, and ever more and more openly until at last it is entirely explicit and we read that 'a man is not justified save through faith in Jesus Christ' (Gal. ii. 16). If, with even greater explicitness still, faith is sometimes said to rest upon some element in the saving work of Christ, as, for example, upon His blood or His righteousness (Rom. iii. 25, II Pet. i. 1), obviously such a singling out of the very thing in His work on which faith takes hold, in no way derogates from its repose upon Him, and Him only, as the sole and sufficient Saviour.

The *saving power* of faith resides thus not in itself, but in the Almighty Saviour on whom it rests. It is never on account of its formal nature as a psychic act that faith is conceived in Scripture to be saving, — as if this frame of mind or attitude of heart were itself a virtue with claims on God for reward, or at least especially pleasing to Him (either in its nature or as an act of obedience) and thus predisposing Him to favour, or as if it brought the soul into an attitude of receptivity or of sympathy with God, or opened a channel of communication from Him. It is not faith that saves, but faith in Jesus Christ: faith in any other saviour, or in this or that philosophy or human conceit (Col. ii. 16, 18, I Tim. iv. 1), or in any other gospel than that of Jesus Christ and Him as crucified (Gal. i. 8, 9), brings not salvation but a curse. It is not, strictly speaking, even faith in Christ that ˈsaves, but Christ that saves through faith. The saving power resides exclusively, not in the act of faith or the attitude of faith or the nature of faith, but in the object of faith; and in this the whole biblical representation centres, so that we could not more radically misconceive it than by transferring to faith even the smallest fraction of that saving energy which is attributed in the Scriptures solely to Christ Himself. This purely mediatory function of faith is very clearly indicated in the regimens in which it stands, which ordinarily express simple instrumentality. It is most frequently joined to its verb as the dative of means or instrument (Acts xv. 9, xxvi. 18, Rom. iii. 28, iv. 20, v. 2, xi. 20, II Cor. i. 24, Heb. xi. 3, 4, 5, 7, 8, 9, 11, 17, 20, 21, 23, 24 || 27, 28, 29, 30, 31); and the relationship intended is further explained by the use to express it of the prepositions ἐκ (Rom. i. 17, 17, iii. 26, 30, iv. 16, 16, v. 1, ix. 30, 32, x. 6, xiv. 23, 23, Gal. ii. 16, iii. 7, 8, 9, 11, 12, 27, 28, v. 5, I Tim. i. 5, Heb. x. 38, Jas. ii. 24) and διά (with the genitive, never with the accusative, Rom. iii. 22, 25, 30, II Cor. v. 7, Gal. ii. 16, iii. 14, 26, II Tim. iii. 15, Heb. vi. 12, xi. 33, 39, I Pet. i. 5), — the fundamental idea of the former construction being that of source or origin, and of the latter that of mediation or instrumentality, though they are used together in the same context, apparently with no distinction of meaning (Rom. iii. 25, 26, 30, Gal. ii. 16). It is not necessary to discover an essentially different implication in the exceptional usage of the prepositions ἐπί (Acts iii. 16, Phil. iii. 9) and κατά (Heb. xi. 7, 13, cf. Mt. ix. 29) in this connexion: ἐπί is apparently to be taken in a quasi-temporal sense, 'on faith,' giving the occasion of the divine act, and κατά very similarly in the sense of conformability, 'in conformity with faith.' Not infrequently we meet also with a construction with the preposition ἐν which properly designates the sphere, but which in passages like Gal. ii. 20, Col. ii. 7, II Thess. ii. 13 appears to pass over into the conception of instrumentality.

So little indeed is faith conceived as containing in itself the energy or ground of salvation, that it is consistently represented as, in its *origin*, itself a gratuity from God in the prosecution of His saving work. It comes, not of one's own strength or virtue, but only to those who are chosen of God for its reception (II Thess. ii. 13), and hence is His gift (Eph. vi. 23, cf. ii. 8, 9, Phil. i. 29), through Christ (Acts iii. 16, Phil. i. 29, I Pet. i. 21, cf. Heb. xii. 2), by the Spirit (II Cor. iv. 13, Gal. v. 5), by means of the preached word (Rom. x. 17, Gal. iii. 2, 5); and as it is thus obtained from God (II Pet. i. 1, Jude 3, I Pet. i. 21), thanks are to be returned to God for it (Col. i. 4, II Thess. i. 3). Thus, even here all boasting is excluded, and salvation is conceived in all its elements as the pure product of unalloyed grace, issuing not from, but in, good works (Eph. ii. 8–12). The place of faith in the process of salvation, as biblically conceived, could scarcely, therefore, be better described than by the use of the scholastic term 'instrumental cause.' Not in one portion of the Scriptures alone, but throughout their whole extent, it is conceived as a boon from above which comes to men, no doubt through the channels of their own activities, but not as if it were an effect of their energies, but rather, as it has been finely phrased, as a gift which God lays in the lap of the soul. 'With the heart,' indeed, 'man believeth unto righteousness'; but this believing does not arise of itself out of any heart indifferently, nor is it

grounded in the heart's own potencies; it is grounded rather in
the freely-giving goodness of God, and comes to man as a bene-
faction out of heaven.

The *effects* of faith, not being the immediate product of faith
itself but of that energy of God which was exhibited in raising
Jesus from the dead and on which dependence is now placed
for raising us with Him into newness of life (Col. ii. 12), would
seem to depend directly only on the fact of faith, leaving questions of its strength, quality, and the like more or less to one
side. We find a proportion, indeed, suggested between faith and
its effects (Mt. ix. 29, viii. 13, cf. viii. 10, xv. 28, xvii. 20, Lk.
vii. 9, xvii. 6). Certainly there is a fatal doubt, which vitiates
with its double-mindedness every approach to God (Jas. i.
6–8, cf. iv. 8, Mt. xxi. 21, Mk. xi, 23, Rom. iv. 20, xiv. 23, Jude
22). But Jesus deals with notable tenderness with those of
'little faith,' and His apostles imitated Him in this (Mt. vi.
30 f., 20, xiv. 31, xvi. 8, xvii. 20, Lk. xii. 28, Mk. ix. 24, Lk. xvii.
5, cf. Rom. xiv. 1, 2, I Cor. viii. 7, and see Doubt). The effects
of faith may possibly vary also with the end for which the trust
is exercised (cf. Mk. x. 51 ἵνα ἀναβλέψω with Gal. ii. 16 ἐπιστεύ-
σαμεν ἵνα δικαιωθῶμεν). But he who humbly but confidently casts
himself on the God of salvation has the assurance that he shall
not be put to shame (Rom. xi. 11, ix. 33), but shall receive the
end of his faith, even the salvation of his soul (I Pet. i. 9). This
salvation is no doubt, in its idea, received all at once (Jn. iii.
36, I Jn. v. 12); but it is in its very nature a process, and its
stages come, each in its order. First of all, the believer, renounc-
ing by the very act of faith his own righteousness which is out
of the law, receives that 'righteousness which is through faith
in Christ, the righteousness which is from God on faith' (Phil.
iii. 9, cf. Rom. iii. 22, iv. 11, ix. 30, x. 3, 10, II Cor. v. 21, Gal.
v. 5, Heb. xi. 7, II Pet. i. 1). On the ground of this righteousness,
which in its origin is the 'righteous act' of Christ, constituted
by His 'obedience' (Rom. v. 18, 19), and comes to the believer
as a 'gift' (Rom. v. 17), being reckoned to him apart from works
(Rom. iv. 6), he that believes in Christ is justified in God's
sight, received into His favour, and made the recipient of the

Holy Spirit (Jn. vii. 39, cf. Acts ʾv. 32), by whose indwelling
men are constituted the sons of God (Rom. viii. 13). And if
children, then are they heirs (Rom. viii. 17), assured of an incorruptible, undefiled, and unfading inheritance, reserved in
heaven for them; and meanwhile they are guarded by the power
of God through faith unto this gloriously complete salvation
(I Pet. i. 4, 5). Thus, though the immediate effect of faith is only
to make the believer possessor before the judgment-seat of God
of the alien righteousness wrought out by Christ, through this
one effect it draws in its train the whole series of saving acts of
God, and of saving effects on the soul. Being justified by faith,
the enmity which has existed between the sinner and God has
been abolished, and he has been introduced into the very family
of God, and made sharer in all the blessings of His house (Eph.
ii. 13 f.). Being justified by faith, he has peace with God, and
rejoices in the hope of the glory of God, and is enabled to meet
the trials of life, not merely with patience but with joy (Rom.
v. 1 f.). Being justified by faith, he has already working within
him the life which the Son has brought into the world, and by
which, through the operations of the Spirit which those who
believe in Him receive (Jn. vii. 39), he is enabled to overcome
the world lying in the evil one, and, kept by God from the evil
one, to sin not (I Jn. v. 19). In a word, because we are justified
by faith, we are, through faith, endowed with all the privileges
and supplied with all the graces of the children of God.

LITERATURE. — Schlatter, "Der Glaube im NT" (includes
a section on "Der Glaube vor Jesus") is the most comprehensive
work on the biblical idea of faith. The general subject is also
treated by Lutz, "Biblische Dogmatik," p. 312; H. Schultz, "Ge-
rechtigkeit aus dem Glauben im A. u. NT" (in *JDTh*, 1862, p.
510); Hofmann, "Schriftbeweis," i, p. 381; Riehm, "Lehrbr. d.
Hebräerbr.," p. 700; Cremer, "Bib. Theol. Lex." s. πίστις, πισ-
τεύω; Hatch, "Essays in Biblical Greek," p. 83. For OT, cf. the
relevant sections in the treatises on "OT Theology," especially
those of Oehler, H. Schultz, Riehm, Dillmann; and the commentaries on the passages, especially Delitzsch on Genesis and Hab-

akkuk. For NT, cf. Huther, "ζωή und πιστεύειν im NT" (in
JBDTh, 1872, p. 182), and the relevant sections in the general
treatises on "NT Theology," especially those of Neander
("Pflanzung," etc.), Schmid, Reuss, Weiss, Beyschlag, Holtzmann, and in the treatises on the theology of the several NT
writers, such as Wendt, "The Teaching of Jesus"; Usteri, "Paul-
inischer Lehrbegr."; Pfleiderer, "Paulinism"; Stevens, "The
Pauline Theology"; Lipsins, "Paulinische Rechtfertigungs-
lehre"; Schnedermann, "De fidei ratione ethica Paulina"; Haus-
leiter, "Was versteht Paulus unter christlichem Glauben?" (in
"Greifswalder Studien," p. 159); Riehm, "Lehrbegr. d. Hebräerbr."; Reuss, "Die Johan. Theologie" (in "Beiträge zur d.
Theol. Wissenschaft," i, 56); Köstlin, "Lehrbegr. Johann.";
Weiss,"Der Johann. Lehrbegr."; Stevens, "The Johannine The-
ology"; Weiss, "Der Petrin. Lehrbegr.":also such commentaries
as Rückert on "Romans"; Sanday-Headlam on "Romans";
Lightfoot on "Galatians"; Haupt on "I John"; Mayor on
"James"; Spitta on "James." The whole body of doctrinal dis-
cussion may be reviewed in De Moor, "Commentarius in J.
Marckii Compendium," iv, p. 287 f.; cf. also John Ball, "A
Treatise of Faith" (3rd ed. London, 1637), Julius Köstlin, "Der
Glaube, sein Wesen, Grund und Gegenstand" (1889), and "Der
Glaube und seine Bedeutung für Erkentniss, Leben und Kirche"
(1891). For some interesting historical notes, see Harnack, "Die
Lehre von der Seligkeit allein durch den Glauben in der alten
Kirche" (in *Zeitschrift. f. Theol. u. Kirche*, 1895, p. 88); E.
König, "Der Glaubensact des Christen" (1891); and for a gen-
eral survey, Cunningham, "Historical Theology," ii, pp. 56 ff.

XIV

THE TERMINOLOGY OF LOVE IN THE NEW TESTAMENT

THE TERMINOLOGY OF LOVE IN THE NEW TESTAMENT [1]

I

Considered as a monument of the Greek language at a particular stage of its development, the New Testament is a very interesting document; and not least so in the terminology which it employs to express the emotion of love. The end-terms of this development, so far as it is open to our observation, are found — we are speaking in broad categories — in the literature which we know as "classical" on the one side, and in the speech of the modern Greek world on the other. In passing from one of these end-terms to the other, a complete revolution has been wrought in the terminology of love; a revolution so radical that the ordinary verb for "to love" in classical Greek has lost that sense altogether in modern Greek, its place being taken by a verb in comparatively infrequent use in the classics; while the ordinary substantive for "love" in modern Greek, formed from this latter verb, does not occur even once in the whole range of classical Greek literature. Coming in somewhere between these two end-terms, the New Testament, flanked on the one side by the Septuagint version of the Old Testament and its accompanying Apocrypha, and on the other by the Apostolic Fathers, forms a compact body of literature in which alone we can observe the revolution in progress; or, we should better say, in which this revolution suddenly appears to sight already nearly completed. Without any heralding in the secular literature, all at once in this religious literature the change presents itself to our view as in principle already an accomplished fact.

All the terms expressing the idea of love current either in classical or in modern Greek are found in this body of religious literature. But they are found in it in such distribution as to

[1] From *The Princeton Theological Review*, v. xvi, 1918, pp. 1–45, 153–203.

make it evident that we are witnessing the dying of one usage while the other has already reached its vigorous youth. This phenomenon is the more impressive because this body of literature stands out in this respect in a certain isolation. Neither in the secular literature of the early Christian centuries, nor even in the immediately succeeding religious literature — in the Greek of the Apologists and the early Church Fathers — is the change in usage anything like so manifest. We have an odd feeling that, with respect to the expression of the idea of love at least, the Greek of the New Testament (along with that of the Septuagint and the Apostolic Fathers) has run ahead of its time, and reflects a stage in the development of the language not yet by some centuries generally attained. This is due doubtless in part to the extremely popular character of these writings. They tap for us the Greek language of their day as it was actuaally spoken; and enable us to see how far the spoken Greek was outstripping in its development the language of "the prigs who write books." In the Apologists at any rate we have a partial return to the more literary usage, with the effect that the language of the New Testament (with the Septuagint and Apostolic Fathers) seems more modern than that of even the Christian writers that came after them.

There are four verbs which, with their accompanying nouns (of course there are also various derivatives), are employed by the classical writers to express the idea of love. Of these φιλεῖν (φιλία) is in universal use as the general term for love, though naturally it has its specific implication which on occasion comes sharply into sight. By its side stand its synonyms, ἐρᾶν, ἐρᾶσθαι (ἔρως), στέργειν (στοργή), ἀγαπᾶν (ἀγάπησις), each of which also is no doubt employed (with decreasing frequency in the order in which they are here set down) to express every kind of love, but each with a specific implication which comes clearly into evidence whenever there is occasion for it to do so. What we mean to say is that, as synonyms, these terms do not so much cover a common ground over the edge of which each extends at a particular place to occupy an additional field all its own; as that they are so used that, within the common ground which they all alike cover, each has a particular quality or aspect which it alone emphasizes, and which it alone is fitted to bring into sight. If we should endeavor to hit off the special implication of each with a single word, we might perhaps say that with στέργειν it is nature, with ἐρᾶν passion, with φιλεῖν pleasurableness, with ἀγαπᾶν preciousness. The idea of love includes all these things, and these terms come severally to mind, therefore, in speaking of love, whenever love is contemplated from the angle of the special implication of each. If it is a question of the constitutional efflux of natural affection στέργειν is the most expressive word to use. If, of the blind impulse of absorbing passion, ἐρᾶν. If, of the glow of heart kindled by the perception of that in the object which affords us pleasure, φιλεῖν. If, of an awakened sense of value in the object which causes us to prize it, ἀγαπᾶν. It is probable that no one of the terms is ever used wholly without some sense in the speaker's mind of its specific implication. Nevertheless each of them is actually employed of every kind and degree of love — because there is no object which is fitted to call out the emotion of love at all which cannot be approached from numerous angles and envisaged from distinct points of view. Not merely differences in the objects on which the affection terminates, but also differences in the mental attitude of its subjects, determine the appropriateness of one or another of the terms, when love is spoken of.

We may take στέργειν as an illustration.[2] We have no doubt that the characterization of it by J. H. Heinrich Schmidt is substantially right. "Στέργειν," he writes,[3] "does not denote a passionate love or disposition, not a longing after something that takes our heart captive and gives to our efforts a distinc-

---

[2] Στέργειν, στοργή are not found in Homer, but are in good Attic use, and, though not of such common occurrence as, say φιλεῖν, φιλία, yet remain in constant employment throughout the whole history of the language, and apparently survive in modern Greek. N. Contopoulos in his "Modern Greek and English Dictionary," at least, lists both, with the definitions, for στέργω, of "to consent, to agree, to comply, to answer; to embrace with natural affection; to love"; and for στοργή, "tenderness, affection." Its etymology seems to be obscure. W. Prellwitz, "Etym. Wörterb².," 1905, records only Keltic analogies, with a reference to Stokes, BB. 23. 58.

[3] "Synonymik der griechischen Sprache," iii, 1879, p. 480 (136. § 4).

tive goal; it designates rather the quiet and abiding feeling within us, which resting on an object as near to us, recognizes that we are closely bound up with it and takes satisfaction in this recognition." "Of this sort," he adds, "is love to parents, to wife and children, to our close relations particularly, and then to our country and our king. There is revealed in στέργειν, accordingly, the inner life of the heart which belongs to man by nature; while φιλεῖν shows the inclination which springs out of commerce with a person or thing, or is called out by qualities in a thing which are agreeable to us; and ἐρᾶν expresses a passion pressing outward and seeking satisfaction." Nevertheless we can understand that one who, rising from reading this characterization, should light upon a passage like Plutarch's description of Pericles' love for Aspasia, might feel some doubts of its adequacy. "The affection (ἀγάπησις) which Pericles had for Aspasia," he explains,[4] "seems to have been rather of a passionate (ἐρωτική) kind." Discarding his wife, "he took Aspasia and loved her exceedingly (ἔστερξε διαφερόντως). Twice a day, as they say, on going out and on coming in from the market place, he would salute her with a loving kiss (καταφιλεῖν)." Στέργειν is used here of a distinctly erotic love, such as we might expect to be expressed rather by ἐρᾶν, and seems to be described, as distinguished from ἀγάπησις, precisely by its quality as passion. And certainly it is not of "natural affection" in the ordinary sense of that phrase that Meleager expects us to think when he asks concerning Eros, "Is not Ares his mother's lover (στέργει)?"[5] So little is it always conceived as independent of attractive qualities in its object, moreover, that Xenophon, in a discussion of the transitoriness of love (he is speaking of sexual love), uses it, when raising the question whether under the best circumstance — when namely the love is not only warm but mutual (ἢν δὲ καὶ ἀμφότερα στέρξωσι) — it can survive the fading

<hr/>

[4] Plutarch, "Pericles," 24 (ed. B. Perrin, pp. 70–71).

[5] "The Greek Anthology," v, 180 (ed. W. R. Paton, I, p. 216). Other instances of the use of στέργειν, στοργή of illicit love are found in v, 8 (p. 132); v, 166 (p. 206); v, 191 (p. 222); vii, 476 (v. ii, p. 258). In v, 180 (p. 216) we have also an instance of the use of στέργει with object of thing in the sense of yearning: "And yearns for anger like the waves."

of the charms of one or the other party.[6] Passages like these show how widely the application of στέργειν, στοργή is extended; and how nearly out of sight its specific implication of love as a natural movement of the soul — as something almost like gravitation or some other force of blind nature — may retire. Yet it probably never retires quite out of sight: the use of the word doubtless always suggests that in some way or other the love in question is natural, even if we must add that it has become natural only by the acquisition of a second nature. Even the love of sense may be conceived of, from this point of view, as a constitutional action of mere nature.[7]

Other and more numerous passages present themselves in which the native meaning of the word is thrown up strongly to observation. When Euripides wishes to reproach a father who has contracted a second marriage with neglect of the children of his dead wife, he naturally uses στέργειν of the love for them that he has lost. The passage contains a contrast between φιλεῖ and στέργει which puts a sharper point upon the specific meaning of the latter. "Hast learned this only now, That no man loves (φιλεῖ) his neighbor as himself? Good cause have some; with most 'tis greed of gain — As here: their sire for a bride's sake loves (στέργει) not these," [8] The guilt and tragedy of the situation are greatly increased by the fact that it is a natural and constitutional movement of the human heart which is outraged. Accordingly ἄστοργος — it is worth while to note it in passing, for ἄστοργος is a New Testament word — is a word of terrible significance. "Especially, however," writes Schmidt,[9] "is the meaning of στέργειν and στοργή illustrated by ἄστοργος, 'loveless.' It designates the unfeeling and hard, whose heart is warmed by no noble sentiment; it is applied particularly to inhuman parents, but also to animals who do not love their young. . . . How sharply the meaning of the word is differentiated is shown by the fact that it is used of women who have

---

[6] Xenophon, "Symposium," viii, 14: cf. 21.

[7] Στέργειν, στοργή are comparatively rarely used of the love of mere sense.

[8] Euripides, "Medea," 80–88 (A. S. Way's translation).

[9] As cited, pp. 489–490.

many love-affairs and who therefore are very certainly not
ἀνέραστοι, but on the other hand lack the nobler love to their
husbands."

It is this that is the natural use of στέργειν, and it occurs in
it very frequently. An instructive instance is found in a passage
in Plato's "Laws." [10] "I maintain," he writes, "that this colony
of ours has a father and mother, which is no other than the
colonizing state. Well, I know that many colonies have been,
and will be, at enmity with their parents. But in early days the
child, as in a family, loves and is beloved; even if there come a
time later, when the tie is broken, still, while he is in want
of education, he naturally loves his parents and is beloved by
them, and flies to them for protection, and finds in them his
natural defense in time of need; and this parental feeling already exists in the Cnosians." Some other term for love could
no doubt have been employed in this passage. But the employment of the phrase στέργει τε καὶ στέργεται, which, in an effort
to convey its implication, Jowett renders, "*naturally* loves his
parents . . .," gives particular force to the remark; this is precisely what children and parents feel to one another.

Another instructive passage is found in the Ninth Book of
Aristotle's "Nicomachaeon Ethics." It will repay us to run
rapidly through it. Aristotle is remarking on the odd fact of experience that benefactors love (φιλεῖν) the benefited, rather than
the other way round. The explanation is, he suggests, that the
benefited stand to the benefactors in a relation somewhat like
that of their product. It is to be noted, he says, that those who
have conferred favors love and prize (φιλοῦσι καὶ ἀγαπῶσι, 'feel
affection for and value') those who receive them quite irrespec-
tive of any hope they may cherish of a return. This is a feeling
common to all artificers: each loves (ἀγαπᾷ) his own especial
product much more than he could possibly be loved (ἀγαπηθείη,
'prized') by it, could life be conferred upon it. The poets supply
the supreme illustration; their love for their poems is inordinate
(ὑπεραγαπῶσι, 'the value that they place upon them'), and has a

[10] Page 754 B. (Jowett's translation of the Dialogues, 1874 v. iv, p. 276):
καθάπερ παῖς . . . στέργει τε καὶ στέργεται ὑπὸ τῶν γεννησάντων.

truly parental quality (στέργοντες ὥσπερ τέκνα). It is a just simile: every workman lives in the product of his energy, for what is living but the expenditure of energy? We love (στέργειν) what we make, because what we make is the extension of ourselves, and to love it is to love our own being. It will be noted that in this passage στέργειν is raised so much above φιλεῖν and ἀγαπᾶν that it is called in to give the specific quality of a ὑπεραγαπᾶν. When our love becomes strong and tender like a parents' love for his children it is most naturally described by στέργειν.

It is not, however, precisely the strength or the tenderness of a love which qualifies it to be described by στέργειν. It is its obligatoriness — if we may use that term in a quasi-natural rather than an openly moral sense; its "necessity" under the circumstances; a necessity by virtue of which its absence becomes not merely distressing but also reprehensible.[11] This is the proper term for the love which constitutes the cement by which any natural or social unit is bound together, and which is due from one member of every such unit to another. Of course such a unit may be mentally created out of any relation, natural or artificial, permanent or temporary; and the use of στέργειν of the sentiment existing between individuals is evidence that they are, for the moment at least, thought of as constituting such a unit, — as "bound together in some bundle of life." Accordingly it is used of the love which binds friends together, and which a friend has the right to expect from his friend. "I do not love a friend who loves with words (λόγοις δ' ἐγὼ φιλοῦσαν οὐ στέργω φίλην)," says Antigone:[12] and what she means is that she does not look upon one whose professed affection expresses itself only in words as bound up in one bundle of life with her and so worthy of the name of friend. Similarly when Lichas

[11] For the note of necessity in στέργειν see Schmidt, as cited, p. 482. Schmidt even says that with στέργειν it is often not a matter of pleasure at all, and never a matter of sensuous pleasure: it often conveys the meaning of yielding quickly and with constant mind to the inevitable. He cites such passages as Sophocles, "Phil.," 538: I think that no other man would endure to look on such a sight, "but I have learned by hard necessity to στέργειν ills" — that is, to acquiesce in them, accept them, take them as belonging to me; so "Lys.," 33. 4: it was necessary to στέργειν this fortune. This sense of toleration — "to put up with" — is shared by it with αἰνεῖν and ἀγαπᾶν.

advises Deianeira to receive Iole, in the words στέργε τὴν γυ-
ναῖκα,[13] he means something more than is expressed in the several
current renderings: "bear this woman with patience," "suffer
this maiden gladly," "treat the girl kindly": he means, take
her into a recognized relation to yourself, involving a duty of
affectionate treatment. The isolation of Menon the Thracian
could not be more strongly expressed than by Xenophon's description: "He evidently had no affection (στέργεν) for anyone";[14] it is implied that he was lacking in all that goes to bind
a man to his fellows and them to him. When the sausage-vender
cries out to Demos in Aristophanes' play:[15] May I be minced up
into very small meat indeed, εἰ μὴ σε φιλῶ, καὶ μὴ στέργω, — he
quickly corrects the protestation of mere personal sentiment
for Demos to an assertion of such a love for him as implied
identification of himself with him. Demos here represents a
whole people whom the sausage-vender describes as his friends,
to whom he asserts himself to be bound by a — not merely class
but organic — affection. It is just as easy to think of the whole
world as such an organic unity, compacted together by mutual
φιλανθρωπία. The Christian Apologists, rising to this conception, naturally give expression to it in the forms of speech long
consecrated to such things. We are φιλανθρωπότατοι to such
an extent, says Athenagoras,[16] that we do not love (στέργειν)
merely our friends (φίλους), for 'if ye love (ἀγαπῶνται) those
that love you,' says He, 'what reward will ye have?'" And
Justin:[17] "But concerning our loving all (περὶ δὲ τοῦ στέργειν
ἅπαντας), He taught us, 'If ye love those that love you (ἀγα-
πᾶτε τοὺς ἀγαπῶντας ὑμᾶς), what new thing do ye do?'" It is
exceedingly instructive to observe these writers, in the act of
citing our Lord's great commandment of universal love, replacing His ἀγαπᾶν with στέργειν in the interests of their own
feeling for the solidarity of the human race. Στέργειν, we see,
is the love of solidarity.[18]

---

[12] Line 543.

[13] "Trach.," line 486.

[14] "Anabasis," ii, 6. 23.

[15] "Eq.," line 769 (al. 715 or 748).

[16] 12. D (Otto, p. 56).

[17] "Apol.," i, 15.

[18] Aristotle, "Nic. Ethics," viii. 4, discusses what happens to the lover and
his mistress (ἐραστῇ καὶ ἐρωμένῳ) when the grounds on which their love (φιλία) is

And if the Deity be solidary with men — as Plato and the Stoics taught? Why, then, of course, στέργειν could be used of the love that binds the Deity and men together. Even the gods many and lords many could be said so to love, each its votaries. "This is right, Mr. Busybody, right," we read in Aristophanes: [19] "for the Muses of the lyre love us well (ἐμὲ γὰρ ἔστερξαν εὔλυροί τε Μοῦσαι)." And on a higher plane Athene is made to declare that she loves (στέργειν), even as one that tends plants, the race that has taken graft from the righteous.[20] But gods many and lords many are divisive things. We must come at least to the recognition of τὸ θεῖον before we can effectively conceive the divine and the human as bound up in one bundle of life, the cement of which is love. It is not without its deep significance, therefore, that the Emperor Constantine begins the oration which he delivered to "the Assembly of the Saints" with an allusion to the love (στοργή) to the Deity implanted in men,[21] and closes it with an assertion of the love (στοργή) of God to man, which is manifested in His providence.[22]

What has been said of στέργειν may in substance be repeated of ἐρᾶν, mutatis mutandis. What ἐρᾶν conveys [23] is the idea of passion; and since all love is a passion ἐρᾶν is applicable to all

built fall away. Sometimes the love (φιλία) passes away too. Sometimes — if the two are alike in their natures — custom has inspired them with an abiding affection and it holds (ἐὰν ἐκ τῆς συνηθείας τὰ ἤθη στέρξωσιν ὁμοήθεις ὄντες). Their love is thought of as στοργή only when they are conceived as constituting together a unity by reason of their similar natures.

[19] "Frogs," line 229.

[20] Æschylus, "Eumenides," line 912. The passage is a difficult one. We have followed Verrall. E. H. Plumptre renders thus: "For I, like gardener shepherding his plants, This race of just men, freed from sorrow, love."

[21] C. 2: "Eusebius Werke," ed. I. A. Heikel, v. i, 1902, p. 155 (τὴν πρὸς τὸ θεῖον στοργὴν ἔμφυτον).

[22] C. 25: as above, p. 192 (τὴν τοῦ θεοῦ πρόνοιαν καὶ τὴν πρὸς τοὺς ἀνθρώπους στοργήν).

[23] The derivation of the word is uncertain. It is ordinarily referred to the primitive Aryan root RA (see for example Skeat, "Etymolog. Dict. of the English Language," no. 289; cf. LAS, no. 324 which is an expansion of RA), which is given the senses of "to rest, to be delighted, to love." W. Prellwitz connects with the Old-Indian aris, with the meaning of trustworthy; but notes that Uhlenbeck, "Kurzgef. etym. Wörterb. d. altind. Sprache" connects aris with Gothic aljam, Old High German ellen, with the sense of "ardor."

love; but since ἐρᾶν emphasizes the passion of love it is above all applicable to especially passionate forms of love. It is naturally used, therefore, frequently to express the sexual appetite. This is not because it is a base word: it is no more intrinsically base than any other word for love. It is because its very heart is passion, and it therefore lends itself especially to express a love which is nothing but passion. But it just as readily lends itself to express a passion which is all love, and it accordingly is also used in the very strongest sense in which a term for love can be employed. Its characteristic uses thus lie at the two extremes of low and high, although of course it may be applied to any kind or degree of love lying between, if only it be for the moment thought of as passion. Schmidt [24] has persuaded himself that the fundamental idea of the word is absorbing preöccupation with its object, complete engrossment with it, the setting of the whole mind upon it — in accordance with a passage in Aristotle's "Rhetoric" [25] which tells us that people in love (ἐρῶντες), no matter what they are doing — talking or writing or acting — are always brooding with delight on the beloved one τοῦ ἐρω- μένου). Aristotle, however, seems to be only noting here a famil- iar effect of the passion which ἐρᾶν really expresses.

It is one of the most characteristic applications of ἐρᾶν which is illustrated by a frequently quoted passage from Xeno- phon's "Cyropaedeia." [26] This passage is a part of a disquisition designed to prove the voluntariness of love, and runs as follows. "'Do you observe,' said he, 'how fire burns all alike? That is its nature. But of beautiful things, we love (ἐρῶσι) some and some we do not: and one [loves] one [person], another another; for it is a matter of free-will, and each loves (ἐρᾷ) what he

[24] Page 475 (136. 2).

[25] I. 11. ii, ed. E. M. Cope, 1877, v. i, p. 209; Cope, however, explains the passage as saying that lovers take pleasure in busying themselves with the be- loved object in his absence, talking about him and sketching his features, and doing everything they can think of to recall him to their memories.

[26] 5. 1. 10.–12. We use a version that lies at hand, but have enclosed in square brackets some of the words which have been inserted by the translator to give greater lucidity to the passage, in order that the reader may not be misled with respect to the frequency of the occurrence of ἐρᾶν, or with respect to apparent variations in the term used.

pleases. For example, a brother does not [fall in] love [with] (ἐρᾷ) his sister, but somebody else [falls in love with] her; neither does a father [fall in love with] his daughter, but someone else does; for fear of God and the law of the land are sufficient to prevent [such] love (ἔρωτα). But,' he went on, 'if a law should be passed forbidding those who did not eat to be hungry, those who did not drink to be thirsty, forbidding people to be cold in the winter or hot in summer, no such law could ever bring men to obey its provisions, for they are so constituted by nature as to be subject to the control of such circumstances. But love (ἐρᾶν) is a matter of free-will; at any rate every one loves (ἐρᾷ) what suits his taste as he does his clothes and shoes.'" And then the discussion proceeds to raise the question of slavery to the passion of this love, and deals with it lamely enough — on the theory that love is purely a matter of will. Here certainly it is said distinctly that "a brother οὐκ ἐρᾷ a sister — nor a father a daughter," and that assuredly means that ἐρᾶν designates distinctively sexual passion. So it does — in this passage: and this is one of the most characteristic applications of the term. It is not, however, its only application. In point of fact it may just as well be said of a given brother or father that he does ἐρᾷ his sister or daughter as that he does not. We read for example in a fragment of Euripides: [27] "There is nothing dearer (ἥδιον) to children than their mother: love (ἐρᾶτε) your mother, children. There is no other love (ἔρως) so sweet as this loving (ἐρᾶν)."

When ἐρᾶν is employed in this latter fashion, something much more, not less lofty than φιλεῖν is meant. Phrases in which it is brought into immediate contrast with φιλεῖν to express something better than it, occur not infrequently. Plutarch, for example, tells us [28] that Brutus was said to have been liked (φιλεῖσθαι) by the masses for his virtue, but loved (ἐρᾶσθαι) by his friends; and Xenophon transmits [29] an exhortation in identical terms — that we should seek not only to be liked (φιλεῖν)

---

[27] Eur., Frag. "Erecht.," 19 (Dind.) ap. Stob. 79, p. 454. (Teubner's ed. of Euripides' Works, ed. by A. Nauck, 1892, v. iii, p. 90, fragment 360).
[28] "Brutus," c. 29.   [29] "Hi.," xi. 11.

but loved (ἐρᾶν) by men. Dio Chrysostom draws the same contrast in a passage [30] which we may quote more at length for the sake of its discriminating use of the several terms for love. Cattle, says he, love (φιλεῖν, 'are fond of') their herdsmen, and horses their drivers — they love and exalt them; dogs love (ἀγαπᾶν, 'prize') the huntsmen — love and guard them; all irrational things recognize and love (φιλεῖν, 'are fond of') those that take care of them: how shall a king, then who is gentle and benevolent (ἥμερον καὶ φιλάνθρωπον) fail to be not only liked (φιλεῖν) but also loved (ἐρᾶν) by men? In passages like these ἐρᾶν is exalted above φιλεῖν not φιλεῖν depressed below ἐρᾶν. The contrasted renderings "like" and "love" do not do justice to either. Both words mean "love" and what is intended to be expressed by ἐρᾶν is that high love of exalted devotion which, from this point of view, soars above all other love.

The same essential contrast between the two notions — the contrast between a love of liking and a love of passion — may occur, no doubt, with the balance of approbation tipped the other way. Thus Plato can tell us of some lovers really loving (φιλεῖν) the objects of their passion (ἐρᾶν).[31] And Aristotle can speak similarly of lovers who really have affection for one another (φιλοῦσιν οἱ ἐρώμενοι).[32] It is possible also to draw quite a different contrast between the two words, a contrast turning on the fact that passion is blind while true affection can see.[33] Meanwhile we are effectually warned off from conceiving ἔρως as essentially a base word and confounding it with ἐπιθυμία[34]

---

[30] i. p. 4M.

[31] "Phaedr.," 231 C: τούτους μάλιστά φασι φιλεῖν ὥς ἂν ἐρῶσι: "regard with affection those for whom they have a passion" (Liddell and Scott, 8th ed. 1901); "feel the highest (moral) affections for those who have inspired them with the sensual passion" (E. M. Cope, "The Rhetoric of Aristotle," 1877, i, p. 293).

[32] "Anal. Pr.," 2.29.1.

[33] Apollon., "De Constr.," p. 292.1 cited by Stephanus, "Thesaurus," 1829–1863, v. 3, col. 1966.

[34] Cope, op. cit., i, 293 describes ἔρως shortly as "the sexual form of ἐπιθυμία or natural appetite," supporting himself on Plato, "Phaedrus," 237D: "It is evident to all that ἔρως is an ἐπιθυμία," and "Timaeus," 42A: "Love is a mixture of pleasure and pain," which, he adds, is "the characteristic of ἐπιθυμία." This applies to ἔρως, however, only in one of its uses.

in order that we may escape confounding it with φιλία. We may observe the close affinity and real distinction of the three notions in a passage of Plato's which is, perhaps, the more instructive because in it ἐρᾶν is used in its lower application and still is separated from ἐπιθυμεῖν as sharply as from φιλεῖν. "No one who desires (ἐπιθυμεῖ) or loves (ἐρᾷ) another," we read,[35] "could ever have desired (ἐπιθύμει) or loved (ἤρα) him or become his friend (ἐφίλει) had he not in some way been congenial to his beloved (τῷ ἐρωμένῳ)." In every stage of its progress, attraction implies inherent congeniality: but the stages of attraction — desire, love, abiding affection — are distinct. When this is true of ἐρᾶν at its lowest, what are we to say of it at its highest, when it passes above φιλεῖν itself and the series runs lust, affection, ardent love?

"Like our 'love' of which it is almost an exact equivalent," writes Charles Bigg,[36] "ἔρως may be applied to base uses, but it is not, like ἐπιθυμία, a base word. From the time of Parmenides, it had been capable of the most exalted signification." . . . We need not stay, however, to refer to the elevated doctrine of the Platonic Eros in detail. Through it, if no otherwise, an association of high things with ἔρως was formed, which penetrated wherever the influence of Platonic thought extended. It is not merely in Plotinus' great conception of the νοῦς ἐρῶν that this lofty usage is continued. That the world ἔρως was not felt to be a term of evil suggestion is abundantly certified by the readiness with which Jew and Christian alike, touched by the same influences, employed it of their divine love. With Philo, it is precisely the ἔρως οὐράνιος which leads to God, and brings all the virtues to their perfection.[37] He often cites with deep feeling the great declaration of Deut. xxx. 20: "This is thy life, and thy length of days, — to love (ἀγαπᾶν) the Lord thy God"; and he does not scruple to define its ἀγαπᾶν in terms of ἔρως. "This is the most admirable definition of immortal life," he comments on one occasion:[38] "to be occupied by a love and

[35] "Lysis," 221D, 222A (Jowett, i, p. 63).

[36] "The Christian Platonists of Alexandria²," 1913, p. 7.

[37] "De Praem. et Poen.," (Mangey, ii, 421).

[38] "De Profugis," § 11 (Mangey, i. 554–555). Cf. the remarks of W. Lütgert, "Die Liebe im Neuen Testament," 1905, p. 48.

affection (ἔρωτι καὶ φιλίᾳ) to God which has nothing to do with flesh and body." To Philo, thus, ἔρως (along with φιλία) is a constituent element of ἀγάπη (for Philo has ἀγάπη), when conceived in its highest stretches, as the very substance of immortal life. There is a famous passage in Ignatius' letter to the Romans [39] in which he gives, or has been misunderstood to give, Christ Himself the name of Ἔρως: "My Love has been crucified," he says. We need not go into the vexed question of the real meaning which Ignatius intends to convey by this phrase.[40] It affords as striking evidence that ἔρως was not felt to be an intrinsically base term, that such a phrase should have been facilely misunderstood by Christian writers as referring to Christ, as that it should have been actually applied to Him by Ignatius. It does not appear that Origen was aware of the currency of any other interpretation of the words than his own, when he cites them in the prologue to his commentary on the Song of Songs in support of his contention that ἔρως and ἀγάπη may be used indifferently of love in its highest sense. "It makes then no difference in the Sacred Scriptures," Rufinus renders him as writing,[41] "whether caritas is spoken of or amor or dilectio; except that the name of caritas is exalted so that God Himself is called Caritas. . . . Take accordingly whatever is written of caritas as said of amor, caring nothing for the names. For the same virtue is shared by each. . . . It makes no difference whether God is said amari or diligi. Neither do I think that, if any one should give God the name of Amor, as John does that of Caritas, he would be blameworthy. I remember, in fine, that one of the saints, Ignatius by name, said of Christ, 'My Amor is crucified,' and I do not think him reprehensible for this." Later writers, especially those of mystical tendencies, naturally

[39] Ch. vii.

[40] The two sides of the question have been well stated and argued respectively by J. B. Lightfoot in his comment on the passage ("My (earthly) passion has been crucified": he actually renders it in his version of the letter, "My lust has been crucified"), and by Charles Bigg in the preface to his Bampton Lectures on "The Christian Platonists of Alexandria" ("My (divine) Love has been crucified"). There is a third possible view: "My preference (for death) has been crucified."

[41] "Prologue to the Song of Songs," Lommatzsch, xiv, pp. 299, 301, 302.

follow Origen's reading of Ignatius. The Pseudo-Dionysius is even prepared to say that the name of Ἔρως was thought by some to be more divine than that of Ἀγάπη.[42] But instances of the employment of words of this stem in a high sense are of course not lacking in earlier Christian writers: Justin,[43] Clement,[44] and Origen himself [45] use ἔρως of divine love, and Clement calls our Lord ὁ ἐραστός.[46]

Clearly it is ardor not lasciviousness which gives its "form" to ἐρᾶν (ἔρως) as a designation of love. Our senses may be inflamed by passion, but the love of the seraphs "who of all love Godhead most" also burns with pure flame. Ἐρᾶν (ἔρως) is not the exclusive possession either of the one or of the other; by virtue of its fundamental implication of passion it is the appropriate designation of both. The prominent employment of it of these two end-terms of the series of varieties of love may leave the impression that the middle region is left uninvaded by it. Schmidt, endeavoring to explain its general usage in a word,[47] even says formally that, when the object is a person, then either sensuous love is to be understood by ἐρᾶν or the highest and more or less passionate love. The vacation of the middle space is, however, an illusion. Since ἐρᾶν imports passion, the most passionate love is prevailingly designated by it; but since all love is passion all love may be spoken of in its terms. Whether it is employed will be determined by whether the love spoken of is at the moment thought of as passion. Ἐρᾶν, says Aristotle,[48] is a kind of φιλία; when φιλία goes to excess, that is ἐρᾶν.

As it is over against φιλεῖν (φιλία) that ἐρᾶν (ἔρως) stands out as designating the love of passion, we are sometimes tempted to render φιλεῖν in contrast with it by "like"; and, indeed, because all love is passion, in doing so to define it below the concept of love altogether. But, although the words, because each has a

---

[42] Cited with other mystical writers by Lightfoot, as above.
[43] "Dial.," viii. 1.   [44] "Cohort.," 71.
[45] "In Joann.," I. 14. (11): ed. Preuschen, p. 14, line 29.
[46] "Strom.," vi. 9. (72).   [47] As cited, p. 475.
[48] "Eth. Nic.," ix. 10; 1171A. 12: ἐρᾶν . . . ὑπερβολὴ γάρ τις εἶναι βούλεται φιλίας. But as he is thinking of ἐρᾶν in its sensual application, he adds: τοῦτο δὲ πρὸς ἕνα.

specific implication, may be set in contrast with one another, they do not receive their specific implications as contrasts of one another, and they are not to be defined as contradictories. Because ἐρᾶν means passionate love, we are not to imagine that φιλεῖν expresses a love which is devoid of passion, — whatever kind of love that may be. It is true enough that φιλεῖν may be employed when no implication of passion is felt; and is the proper word to employ when relatively unimpassioned manifestations of love are described, as for example for what we may call "friendly love." But this is not because it excludes passion but because it describes love from a different angle and the presence or absence of passion is indifferent to it. It is just as appropriate for the strongest and most impassioned as it is for the quietest and least ardent love: no love lies outside its field. "Φιλεῖν," says T. D. Woolsey justly,[49] "we need not say, is as early as the earliest Greek literature itself, and as wide in its meaning as our verb to *love*, running through all kinds and degrees of the feeling, from the love of family and friend down to mere liking, and to *being wont* to do a thing; and passing over from the sphere of innocent to that of licentious love, whether passionate or merely sensual."

The approach of φιλεῖν to the idea of love is made through the sense of the agreeable.[50] It is the eudaimonistic term for love. Whatever in an object is adapted to give pleasure when perceived, tends to call out affection; and this affection is what φιλεῖν expresses. It may be quiet or it may be passionate; it may be strong or it may be weak; it may be noble or it may be base: all this depends on the quality in the object which calls out the response and the nature of the subject which responds to the appeal. "Of φιλεῖν," says Schmidt,[51] "it is first of all to be said that it is the general designation for our 'love,' and has for its peculiarity that it designates an inner predilection (*Neigung*) for persons, and has for its contradictories μισεῖν and ἐχθαίρειν;

[49] *The Andover Review*, August, 1885, p. 167.

[50] The etymology of φιλεῖν is not very clear. G. Heine, "Synonymik des Neutestamentlichen Griechisch," 1898, p. 154, suggests for φίλος (after Vaniček): "one's own, that to which one is accustomed, and on which he depends, dear, worthy."   [51] Pp. 476–477.

but, even when the presentation leaves no ambiguity, it can designate the love of sense. The notion of φιλεῖν can be traced back to the disposition which grows out of an inner community (*Gemeinschaft*). We find therefore in Homer the meaning of 'to be in a friendly way at one's side,' 'to interest oneself in him in a friendly manner.' This happens, for example, on the part of the gods when they assist men in battle, or qualify them for manifold things: on the part of men, when they offer hospitality. For these transactions Homer has exact expressions, and φιλεῖν is expressly distinguished from ξεινίζειν or δέξασθαι. The word designates, therefore, only generally the treatment of another as one that is dear (φίλος) to me, or my friend (again φίλος), and the context must show what kind of action is meant."

When Liddell and Scott say that "the ancients carefully distinguished between φιλεῖν and ἐρᾶν," that is formally right, though we should prefer to say "instinctively" rather than "carefully." When, however, they add: "But φιλεῖν sometimes comes very near in sense to ἐρᾶν," citing passages in which φιλεῖν is used for the love of sense, a certain misunderstanding seems involved. Φιλεῖν is used from the earliest dawn of Greek literature as clearly of the love of sense as of any other kind of love. But this is not to "come very near the sense of ἐρᾶν": it is only to describe the same love which ἐρᾶν describes as passion, from its own point of view as delight. Nor is it easy to understand what Schmidt means when he appears to suggest that φιλεῖν is applied to the love of sense only by a euphemism — "by way of insinuation": nor how the passage from Plato to which he appeals for the purpose can be thought to lend support to this opinion. What we read in this passage [52] is merely that it is said of lovers (τοὺς ἐρῶντας) that they show a very special affection (φιλεῖν) for those they are in love with (ἐρῶσι), because they are prepared to do hateful things for the pleasuring of their beloved ones (τοῖς ἐρωμένοις). Φιλεῖν here is certainly not used euphemistically for ἐρᾶν; it is simply the broad word for love used here in contrast with ἐρᾶν which is employed of a special variety of love. The employment of φιλεῖν for the love of sense is from the

[52] "Phaedr.," 231C.

beginning perfectly frank and outspoken. Take, for example, these frequentative imperfects from Homer: "a concubine whom he φιλέεσκεν";[53] "Melantho μισγέσκετο καὶ φιλέεσκεν Eurymachus."[54] They do not in any way differ from the frequentative imperfect in "Il.," vi, 15: "and he was loved (φίλος ἦν) by men, for, dwelling by the road, φιλέεσκεν all to his house," — except in the nature of the acts to which they are applied. The son of Teuthras showed himself a φίλος to men by keeping openhouse and welcoming all comers. The concubines of Amyntor and Melantho showed themselves φίλαι to their lovers by fulfilling the function of mistresses to them. The usage is as simple and direct in the one case as in the other. The constant use in Homer of φιλότης with μίγνυμι should dispel all doubt on this point. And what could be franker than the use of φιλεῖν in Herodotus iv, 176?

The Greeks were very much preoccupied with the topic of Friendship: Plato, Xenophon, Aristotle discuss it endlessly: "in the circles of the philosophical schools interest in it far surpassed that of the family life."[55] Φιλεῖν was an ideal word for the expression of this form of affection, and this became one of its chief applications. Not, however, to the exclusion of other applications in which it gave expression to every variety of love which sentient beings could experience. Even, pace Hermann Cremer,[56] the love of God to men and of men to God. Cremer has permitted himself the sweeping statement: "To attribute love at all to the Deity was utterly impossible to the Greek." He supports himself on two passages from Aristotle, neither of which supports him. In both passages Aristotle is (of course) discussing Friendship, — not the term φιλία but the "friendship" which φιλία is in these discussions employed to express. What he is suggesting is not that God can neither love nor be loved in any sense, but that there is a certain incongruity

---

[53] "Il.," ix, 450.   [54] "Odyss.," xviii, 325.

[55] W. Lütgert, "Die Liebe im N.T.," 1905, p. 37: he sends us to E. Curtius, "Altertum und Gegenwart," i, p. 183 ff. for the matter. Consult also the remarks of Paul Kleinert, "Th. S. K.," 86 (1913) i, pp. 16 f.

[56] "Supplement to Biblico-Theological Lexicon of New Testament" Greek 1886, p. 593 (sub voc. 'Αγάπη).

in speaking of God and man as united in the specific bond which we call "friendship." "Friendship" is a form of love which more properly obtains between equals: between superiors and inferiors the assertion of some other tie would be more appropriate. The matter is not of large intrinsic importance; but it is worth while to transcribe the passages somewhat at length for their illustrative value.

In them, as elsewhere,[57] Aristotle divides friendship (φιλία) into three kinds, based respectively on virtue (ἀρετή), utility (χρήσιμον) and pleasure (ἡδύ); and then he divides the whole again into the cases between equals and those between unequals. True friendship is mutual and is found among equals only; love between unequals is only in a modified sense "friendship." "First, then," he writes in the former of the two passages now before us,[58] "we must determine what kind of friendship (φιλία) we are in search of. For there is, people think, a friendship (φιλία) towards God (πρὸς θεόν) and towards things without life; but here they are wrong. For friendship (φιλία), we maintain, exists only where there can be a return of affection (ἀντιφιλεῖσθαι: why not say, "return of the friendship"?), but friendship (φιλία) toward God (πρὸς θεόν) does not admit of love being returned (ἀντιφιλεῖσθαι: why not say, "of the friendship being returned"?), nor at all of loving (τὸ φιλεῖν: why not say "of friendly feeling"?). For it would be strange if one were to say that he loved Zeus (φιλεῖν τὸν Δία: why not say "felt friendly to"?). Neither is it possible to have affection returned (ἀντιφιλεῖσθαι: why not say, "to have friendship returned"?) by lifeless objects, though there is a love (φιλία) for such things, for instance wine, or something else of that sort. Therefore, it is not love (φιλία) towards God of which we are in search, nor love towards things without life, but love towards things with life, that is, where there can be a return of affection (ἀντιφιλεῖν)." Aristotle is not arguing here that there can be no such thing as

[57] E. g.; "Eth. Nic.," viii, 2. 1: "For it appears that not everything is loved (φιλεῖσθαι) but [only] τὸ φιλητόν: this is good (ἀγαθόν) or pleasant (ἡδύ) or useful (χρήσιμον)."

[58] "Magna Moralia," II. 11: p. 1208 B. The translation of St. George Stock is used.

love on the part of God, or to God; or that this love may not be
properly expressed in either case by φιλεῖν, φιλία. He is busying
himself only with that mutual affection which we know as
friendship; and it is this that he says is impossible between man
and God because of the inequality between them. It is incongruous to say that Zeus and I are a pair of friends, — we might almost as well say we are a brace of good fellows or *par nobile
fratrum*. He is speaking here, in a word, only of love based on
mutual agreeability (ἡδύ) in which what is necessary is to be
agreeable (τὸ ἡδέσιν εἶναι).[59] If the love in question is based on
utility or virtue, on the other hand, the case is different.[60]

The other passage [61] takes up the case when love is based on
virtue. "These, then," writes Aristotle here, "are three kinds
of friendship (φιλία); and in all of them the word friendship
(φιλία) implies a kind of equality. For even those who are
friends (φίλοι) through virtue are mutually friends by a sort of
equality of virtue. But another variety is the friendship [say
rather 'love'] of superiority to inferiority, e. g. as the virtue of
a god is superior to that of a man (for this is another kind of
friendship [φιλία; say 'love']), and in general that of ruler
to subject; just as justice in this case is different, for here it is a
proportional equality — not numerical equality (κατ᾽ ἀναλογίαν;
κατ᾽ ἀριθμόν). Into this class falls the relation of father to son,
and of benefactor to beneficiary; and there are varieties of these
again, e. g. there is a difference between the relation of father to
son, and of husband to wife, the latter being that of ruler to
subject, the former that of benefactor to beneficiary. In these
varieties there is not at all, or at least not in equal degree, the
return of love for love (ἀντιφιλεῖσθαι: say 'mutual loving'). For
it would be ridiculous to accuse God because the love one receives in return from Him is not equal to the love given Him,
(τὸ ἀντιφιλεῖσθαι ὡς φιλεῖτε), or for the subject to make the same
complaint against his ruler. For the part of a ruler is to receive,

---

[59] "Magna Moralia," p. 1210 A.
[60] "Magna Moralia," p. 1210 A: "It is evident then that friendship (φιλία)
based on utility occurs among things the most opposite."
[61] "Ethica Eudemia," vii, 3 (p. 1238b). J. Solomon's version is used.

not to give, love (φιλεῖσθαι οὐ φιλεῖν) or at least to give love
(φιλεῖν) in a different way. And the pleasure (ἡδονή) is different,
and that of the man who needs nothing over his own possessions
or child, and that of him who lacks over what comes to him, are
not the same. Similarly also with those who are friends [say
rather 'who love one another'] through use or pleasure, some
are on an equal footing with each other, in others there is the
relation of superiority and inferiority. Therefore those who
think themselves to be on the former footing find fault if the
other is not equally useful to and a benefactor of them; and
similarly with regard to pleasure. This is obvious in the case of
lover and beloved (ἐν τοῖς ἐρωτικοῖς); for this is frequently a
cause of strife between them. The lover (ὁ ἐρῶν) does not perceive that the passion (προθυμίαν) in each has not the same reason; therefore Ænicus has said, 'a beloved (ὁ ἐρώμενος) not a
lover (ἐρῶν), would say such things.' But they think that there
is the same reason for the passion of each." We are here told
that although friendship, properly so called — that is, mutual
affection based on congeniality or reciprocal agreeability — can
scarcely exist between beings so unequal as God and man, yet
love can; as readily as it can exist between ruler and subject, or
father and son. The term "love" (φιλία) is wide enough to describe all such cases, as it is wide enough also, as we learn at the
end of the passage, to describe the mutual affection which binds
"lovers" together: ἐρᾶν is a species of φιλεῖν, because, no matter
with what passion, it also rests on something agreeable perceived in its object.

We have seen that from the beginning there was a natural
tendency to carry φιλεῖν over from the sentiment of love itself to
its expression in outward act. Thus in a passage from the Iliad
already quoted,[62] Teuthramides is represented as habitually
showing himself friendly by keeping open-house — πάντας γὰρ
φιλέεσκεν, "he made all welcome." Similarly Penelope is described in the Odyssey as receiving all visitors well and giving
them welcome (φιλέει):[63] a phrase matched by a similar one in
the Iliad: "I entertained (φίλησα) them." [64] Along this line of

<hr>

[62] "Il.," vi, 15.   [63] "Odyss.," xiv, 128.   [64] "Il.," iii, 207.

development φιλεῖν early began to acquire the specialized sense
of "to kiss." "Φιλεῖν," writes Schmidt,[65] "means directly, with
or without the addition of τῷ στόματι, to kiss, therefore that act
which sensibly and externally brings to expression the fellowship of lovers or friends and, in general of those connected by a
close bond (also of parents and children)." This usage does not
yet occur in Homer: he employs κυνέω, κύσαι for kissing. But it
made its appearance soon afterwards,[66] and ultimately completely superseded the richer and higher uses of the word. In
Modern Greek φιλῶ means nothing else but "to kiss." [67] In
odd contrast with this development, ἀγαπᾶν, the great rival of
φιλεῖν in the expression of the general idea of love — a rival
which finally drove it entirely from the field, — appears from
the first in an analogous usage and is thought by many to have
begun as a term to express the external manifestations of
affection and only afterward to have come to be applied to the
emotion itself. At least the external sense is predominant in
Homer, both for ἀγαπᾶν and for its more frequently occurring
doublet ἀγαπάζειν;[68] and it remained in occasional use throughout the whole history of Greek letters. The range of suggestion
of the word in this external sense is rather wide. The instances
in Homer may ordinarily be brought under the broad category
of "welcoming," with suggestions of "embracing," or other
signs of hearty welcome. Thus Penelope asks forgiveness for not
"welcoming" her husband properly on his first appearing,[69]
"or," explains T. D. Woolsey,[70] "treating him with affection,"
remarking that Eustathius glosses with ἐφιλοφρονησάμην. Again
we read:[71] "As a father, feeling kindly, welcomes his son
(φίλα φρονέων ἀγαπάζει)." And yet again,[72] bringing φιλεῖν and
ἀγαπᾶν together in this external sense: "Our people do not

[65] As cited, p. 477.

[66] Herodotus, Xenophon and Attic writers generally.

[67] E. A. Sophocles says ("Bibliotheca Sacra," July 1889, p. 525): "As to the
modern φιλῶ, it retains only the meaning, to kiss."

[68] It is the sense of all the instances in which ἀγαπᾶν or ἀγαπάζειν occurs in
Homer, except one — "Odyss.," xxi, 289, where it means "to acquiesce in," "be
content with." Cf. Cope, as cited, p. 295.

[69] "Odyss.," xxiii, 214.   [70] Andover Review, August 1885, p. 167.

[71] "Odyss.," xvi, 17.   [72] "Odyss.," vii, 33.

φιλοῦσι a stranger ἀγαπαζόμενοι — "do not receive him with signs of regard," as Liddell and Scott gloss it. In a very similar passage,[73] we read of the swineherd kissing (κύνεον) Odysseus' head and shoulders ἀγαπαζόμενος, that is to say with a display of affection. And we find in Pindar [74] a passage like this: "And with mild words they welcomed him," where the action through which the affection is shown is defined as kind speech. In Euripides, in whom ἀγαπᾶν, ἀγαπάζειν occur only three times (they do not occur at all in Æschylus or Sophocles), they "are only used in the sense of tender offices to the dead":[75] as, for example, "Suppliants," 764: "You would have said so had you seen when he *treated lovingly* (Woolsey glosses: "made much of") the dead." In the light of such passages it is probable that when Xenophon, speaking of the transports of delight with which the Greeks at first welcomed the Hyrcanians as friends, says [76] that they almost carried them about in their bosoms ἀγαπῶντες, the ἀγαπῶντες means something more definite than "affectionately" — say "fondlingly." In an interesting passage in Plutarch [77] the sense is certainly "fondle." "On seeing certain wealthy foreigners in Rome carrying puppies and young monkeys about in their bosoms and fondling them (ἀγαπώντων), Caesar asked," we are told, "if the women in their country did not bear children. Thus in right princely fashion he rebuked those who squander on animals that proneness to love (φιλητικόν) and loving affection (φιλόστοργον) which is ours by nature and which is due only to our fellow men." In this passage the native sentiment of "fondness" and the stirrings of "natural affection" are given expression through other forms of speech; ἀγαπᾶν is employed of the external acts in which these movements of soul are manifested.

The persistence of this external use of ἀγαπᾶν is illustrated by its appearance in the letters of Ignatius. A probable instance occurs in "Smyrn.," 9: "In my absence and in my presence ye

<hr>

[73] "Odyss.," xxi, 224. [74] "Pyth.," iv, 241.

[75] John U. Powell in his edition of the "Phoenissae," 1911, p. 206. The passages are "Phoeniss.," 1327; "Suppl.," 764; Helen.," 937. Cf. also Woolsey, as cited, p. 167.

[76] "Cyrop.," vii, v. 50: ed. Holden, 1890, p. 74. [77] "Pericles," 1.

ἠγαπήσατε me," where Lightfoot renders "cherished." The instance in "Magn.," 6 can scarcely be doubted. E. A. Abbott fills out the passage thus: [78] "Since then I beheld in faith and *embraced* (in the spirit) the whole multitude (of the Magnesian church) in the above-mentioned persons (of their deputation)." [79] But the most interesting passage is "Polyc.," 2: "In all things I am devoted to thee — I, and my bonds which you ἠγάπησας." "Kissing the chains" of the prisoners of Christ, it seems, was a current figure by which the early Christians expressed their ardent sympathy for their martyrs.[80] Bunsen, followed by Th. Zahn, therefore, translates here, "which thou didst kiss." [81] Lightfoot demurs to this as too specific, and points out that the precise sense of "kissing" is not elsewhere verifiable for ἀγαπᾶν, — although he is very willing to allow that the actual thing referred to by the broader term may well have been in this instance kissing the chains. He proposes the synonyms, "didst welcome, caress, fondle," and somewhat infelicitously translates in his version, "cherished." Interest in this discussion is increased by the suggestion that, when we read in Mk. x. 21 of the rich young ruler that "Jesus looked on him and ἠγάπησεν αὐτόν," we are to understand the ἠγάπησεν not of the sentiment of loving but of the act of caressing: Jesus, in a word, kissed the young man in greeting him. This suggestion was made by Frederick Field a third of a century ago,[82] and has often since been repeated.[83] It does not commend itself particularly from an exegetical point of view: [84] but the fact that, as

[78] "Johannine Vocabulary," 1905, p. 261, note (1744, iv, b).

[79] Lightfoot *in loc.* comments: "'*welcomed, embraced.*' The word here refers to external tokens of affection, according to its original meaning."

[80] "Acta Pauli et Thec.," 18: καταφιλούσης his chains: Tertullian, "Ad. Uxor.," ii, 4, *osculanda* the martyr's chains.

[81] See Zahn, "Ignatius von Antiochien," 1873, p. 415, and also his comment on the passage itself.

[82] "Otium Novicense," Pars Tertia, 1881., *ad loc.*

[83] See [J. Hastings], *Expository Times,* xviii, 99 (Hastings generalizes: "In any case the word is that word for loving which means manifesting love in action"); Edwin A. Abbott, "Johannine Vocabulary," 1905, pp. 257 ff.; J. H. Moulton and G. Milligan, "The Vocabulary of the New Testament," i, 1914, p. 12, *sub voc.* ἀγαπᾶν.

[84] Swete, for example, rejects it decisively.

Abbott points out, the phrase is rendered in one Latin MS.
"osculatus est eum" supports the supposition that ἀγαπᾶν was
in use in the sense of kissing during the early Christian centuries.
The collocation of the words in the comment of Clement of
Alexandria, likewise adduced by Abbott, suggests that he also
may have understood ἠγάπησεν here in the sense of an external
manifestation. "Accordingly Jesus," he writes, "does not convict him as one that had failed to fulfil all the words of the Law;
on the contrary He" — so Abbott paraphrases — "loves and
greets him with unusual courtesy." The Greek words are
ἀγαπᾷ καὶ ὑπερασπάζεται; and it would not be unnatural to give
them both an external meaning.[85]

This usage of ἀγαπᾶν of the manifestation of love in act, although possibly (we can scarcely say very probably) original,[86]
and certainly real, is yet, in any case too infrequent to be of
large importance for the explanation of the word. Unlike the
corresponding usage of φιλεῖν it was a waning instead of a wax-
ing usage; and therefore it exercised less and less influence on
the general usage of the word. After all said, the word stands in
Greek literature as a term for loving itself, not for external
manifestations of love, more or fewer. And like other terms for
love, it is applied to all kinds and degrees of love. This includes
also the love of sense. It is true it seems to have acquired this
application only slowly, and, one would think, with some difficulty. There is nothing in the native implication of the word to

[85] It would be easy to reply, it is true, that both might be given an internal
meaning, and perhaps the usage of ὑπερασπάζεται encourages this view.

[86] J. B. Lightfoot argues for the originality of the external sense in an article
published in the *Cambridge Journal of Classical Philology*, v. iii (1857), no. 7,
p.9 2; and again in his note on Ignatius "ad Polyc.," 2, where he states the case with
his accustomed compressed force. "The word," he says, "seems originally to have
referred to the *outward demonstration of affection*. . . . This original sense appears still more strongly in ἀγαπάζω. The application of the term to the *inward
feeling* of love is a later development, and the earlier meaning still appears occasionally." But after all it is difficult to believe that the word began with this
external sense, and Homer does not record an absolutely primitive usage. E. M.
Cope, *op. cit.*, pp. 295-296 properly therefore rejects this reading of the history
of the word. Liddell and Scott's article on ἀγαπάω exaggerates the externality
of the term and might even give the impression that the internal affection of
love scarcely falls within its range at all.

suggest such an application; and the conjecture lies close that it was not until it had become the general term for love in common use for the whole notion that it was applied to this variety of love also, — at first doubtless by way of pure euphemism. Such euphemistic applications to the sexual impulse of all words denoting love are inevitable; [87] and unhappily many good words, euphemistically applied to lower uses, end by losing their native senses and sinking permanently to the level to which they have thus stooped, — as, for example, our English words "libertine," "harlot." [88] Fortunately this did not happen to ἀγαπᾶν, although its extention to cover the love of sense also became a fixed part of its ordinary usage. Liddell and Scott remark that it is "used of sexual love like ἐρᾶν, only in late writers, as Lucian "Jup. Trag.," 2; [89] for in Xenophon, "Mem.," I. 5. 4. πόρνας ἀγαπᾶν is not = ἐρᾶν, but to be content, or satisfied with such gratifications." [90] This explanation of the passage in Xenophon is certainly right. But it is not quite exact to speak of the appearance of this usage in Lucian, say, as marking its beginning. It already occurs in Plato.[91] And in any event the Septuagint is three or four hundred years older than Lucian, and not only is ἀγαπᾶν — and also its substantive (not found in the classical writers)

[87] Cf. "The Oxford Dictionary of the English Language," sub voc. "Love, subst.," no. 6 (p. 464 med.): "the animal instinct between the sexes and its gratification." Maurice Hewlett, "The Fool Errant," 1905, p. 247: "We ate frugally, drank a little wine and water, loved temperately, and slept profoundly."

[88] Cf. on this subject the excellent remarks of R. C. Trench, "On the Study of Words," ed. N. Y. 1855, pp. 50 ff.

[89] Lucian, "Jup. Trag.," 2: Hera accused Zeus of having a love-affair (ἐρωτικόν) on hand and, plagued by love (ἔρωτος), of thinking of falling through some roof into the lap of his ἀγαπωμένης. So, "Vera Hist.," ii, 25: Cinyres had fallen in love (ἤρα) with Helen, and she was plainly also enamoured (ἀγαπῶσα) with him; so, driven by love and despair (ὑπ' ἔρωτος καὶ ἀμηχανίας), they ran off. A hundred years before Lucian, Plutarch has the usage: cf. the passages cited by Thayer under φιλέω.

[90] J. S. Watson translates: "Who could find pleasure in the company of such a man, who, he would be aware, felt more delight in eating and drinking than in intercourse with his friends, and preferred the company of harlots to that of his fellows?" This sense of "to be satisfied with," is a not infrequent one for ἀγαπᾶν.

[91] Cope, as cited, p. 296: "In Plato's "Symposium," 180 B, it takes the place of ἐρᾶν in the representation of the lowest and most sensual form of the passion or appetite of love, ὅταν ὁ ἐρώμενος τὸν ἐραστὴν ἀγαπᾷ, ἢ ὅταν ὁ ἐραστὴς τὰ παιδικά."

ἀγάπη — used in it of the love of sense, but so used of it as to make it plain that they had long been used of it, and had become the current terms for the expression of this form of love also. To be convinced of this we have only to read the thirteenth chapter of II Samuel, — the story of Amnon and Thamar — the whole shocking narrative of which is carried on with ἀγαπᾶν and ἀγάπη, culminating in verse 15: "And Amnon hated her with exceeding great hatred, because the hatred with which he hated her was greater than the love (ἀγάπην) wherewith he loved (ἠγάπησεν) her." This love was mere lust: and it is very apparent that ἀγαπᾶν and ἀγάπη are used of it with perfect simplicity, undisturbed by any intruding consciousness of incongruity. This phenomenon means, of course, that in the Greek of the Septuagint we tap a stratum of the language of more popular character than that which meets us in the literary monuments of the times; and we see changes not only preparing but already accomplished in it which the recognized literary mode of the times had not yet accepted. Meanwhile, for literary Greek, it remains generally true that ἀγαπᾶν had not yet acquired the breadth of usage which led to its frequent application to the love of sense also; and so far as appears it did not acquire it for two or three centuries to come.

In the monuments of classical literature, ἀγαπᾶν, although in use from the beginning and occupying a distinctive place of its own, is never a very common word. It, and its doublet ἀγαπάζειν, occur in Homer but ten times, in Euripides but three times, and not at all in Æschylus or Sophocles.[92] The substantive ἀγάπησις is rare before, say, Plutarch;[93] while ἀγάπη appears first in the Septuagint, and has not as yet turned up with certainty in any secular writing.[94] 'Αγαπᾶν owes its peculiarity

[92] According to T. D. Woolsey, as cited, the indices record ἀγαπάω, ἀγαπητός, ἀγαπητῶς for Demosthenes twenty-two times; for Plato eighteen; for Lysias and Isocrates, each three times. These figures are, however, misleading: in Isocrates, for example, the words are of much more frequent occurrence.

[93] Cf. Lobeck on Phrynicus, p. 352, and Stephanus sub voc. Thayer sub voc. ἀγάπη, seems to intimate that the word appears first in Aristotle: Liddell and Scott, in Plato.

[94] The facts are carefully stated by Moulton and Milligan, as cited, sub voc.

to its etymological associations, which could not fail to suggest themselves to every Greek ear. Connected with ἄγαμαι, it conveyed the ideas of astonishment, wonder, admiration, approbation.[95] It expresses thus, distinctively, the love of approbation, or, we might say, the love of esteem, as over against the love of pure delight which lies rather in the sphere of φιλεῖν. It is from the apprehension of the preciousness rather than of the pleasantness of its object that it derives its impulse, and its content thus lies closer to the notion of prizing than to that of liking.[96] It is beside the mark to speak of it as a "weaker,"[97] or as a "colder"[98] word than φιλεῖν: the distinction between the two lies in a different plane from these things. A love rooted in the perception in its object of something pleasing (that is, of the order of φιλεῖν), or of something valuable (that is, of the order of ἀγαπᾶν), may alike be very weak or very strong, very cold or very warm: these things are quite indifferent to the distinction and will be determined by other circumstances, which may be present or absent in either case.

It is even more wide of the mark to speak of ἀγαπᾶν as distinctively voluntary love, or reasonable love. The former is the position taken with great emphasis by Cremer (it is also the

[95] On this etymology see Cope, as cited, p. 294, also p. 296. Other etymological suggestions are made. Cremer, in his third edition, finds the fundamental notion to be, "to find one's satisfaction in something"; but in his tenth edition reverts to the simple suggestion of a connection with ἄγαμαι in the sense of admiring. W. Prellwitz traces the word back to an Old-Aryan root Pō (Old-Indian Pā) bearing the sense of "protecting"; hence ἀγα-πός, "protecting," and the denominative ἀγαπάω, "entertain," or, as in Homer, "welcome." This view of the etymology favors the external sense of the word as original.

[96] Cope, as cited, p. 294, remarks that, whatever be the true derivation of the word, "this notion of selection or affection, conceived, on the ground of admiration, respect, and esteem, certainly enters into its meaning. Xen. "Mem.," ii. 7.9 is decisive on this point." On p. 295 he surveys the copious material in Aristotle's "Nicomachaean Ethics" and concludes that in every instance the word may, and in many instances it must, carry the implication of esteem. It is the *worth* of the object of preference which underlies the affection expressed by it.

[97] So e. g., Schmidt.

[98] So e. g., Gildersleeve. Woolsey, as cited, p. 182, with Trench in his mind, says very appositely: "We naturally avoid or distrust attaching this quality of coldness to ἀγαπάω or ἀγάπη; and while we ascribe to these words the consent of the will and benevolent regard, we do not strip them of feeling."

view of Cope); the latter is strongly argued for by Schmidt. "We shall make no mistake," says Cremer,[99] "if we define the distinction thus — that φιλεῖν designates the love of the natural inclination, of the emotion (*Affects*), the so-to-say originally involuntary love — *amare*, — while ἀγαπᾶν designates love as an effect (*Richtung*) of the will, *diligere*." It may be suspected that those who speak thus have in part misled themselves by the Latin analogy. The parallel is, it is true, very close with respect to the usage of the two pairs of words; but it does not extend to the etymological implications on which in each case the usage rests.[100] The conception underlying *diligere* is that of selection; the word bears an implication of choice in it. There is no such underlying suggestion in ἀγαπᾶν, its place being taken by the emotion of admiration.[101] In point of fact, the rise in the heart of love for an object perceived to be precious, is just as "originally involuntary," just as much a matter of pure feeling, as the rise in it of love for an object perceived to be delightful. The distinction between these two varieties of love rests on the differing qualities of the object to which they are the reactions, not on the presence or absence of volition in their production. "There can but two things create love," says Jeremy Taylor:[102] "perfection and usefulness; to which answer on our part, first,

[99] These sentences stand in all the editions from the third (1883) to the tenth (1915). Under ἀγάπη he says (ed. 10, p. 14): "It designates *the love which chooses its object with decisive will.*"

[100] It may be worth noting that Liddell and Scott, in explaining the distinction between ἐρᾶν and φιλεῖν, say it is that between *amare* and *diligere;* and in explaining the distinction between φιλεῖν and ἀγαπᾶν, say that *this* is that between *amare* and *diligere*. That is to say, φιλεῖν appears now as *diligere* and now as *amare* to meet the needs of the case.

[101] There is no philological reason for supposing that the peculiarity of ἀγαπᾶν among the terms for loving was that it suggested that love is a voluntary emotion. There is also no trace of such a distinction having been made in usage by the Greeks. In arguing for it we are arguing without regard to the Greek consciousness. We have had occasion to observe Xenophon insisting that ἐρᾶν expresses a voluntary act. But it was not ἐρᾶν distinctively that he had in mind: what he was really arguing was that love as such, under any designation, is a voluntary act. It was a psychological, not a philological, question in which he was interested.

[102] "The Rule and Exercises of Holy Living," ch. IV, sec. 3 (p. 21 of v. ii, of the Temple Classics edition).

admiration, and secondly desire; and both these are centered
in love." This is a piece of good psychology.

The form of statement which Schmidt prefers is that ἀγαπᾶν
designates the love which arises by "rational reflection." [103]
Citing a passage from Aristotle's "Rhetoric"[104] where he speaks
of φιλεῖσθαι as being "ἀγαπᾶσθαι for one's own sake," Schmidt
argues that "it follows from this passage that ἀγαπᾶν is not, like
φιλεῖν, an inclination attached to the person himself, as called
into being by close companionship and fellowship in many
things, but a love for which we can give ourselves an account
with our understanding; less sentiment than reflection." [105] As a
result, he concludes that "the ἀγαπῶν holds the qualities of a
person in view, the φιλῶν the person himself; the former gives
itself a justification of its inclination, while to the latter it
arises immediately out of an intercourse which is agreeable to
oneself." This reasoning rests on a confusion between the production of an emotion by rational considerations, and the justification of it on rational grounds. Of course the love of ἀγαπᾶν is
more capable of justification on rational grounds than the love
of φιλεῖν. It is the product of the apprehension of valuable
qualities in the object, and may be defended by the exhibition
of the value of these qualities. The love of φιλεῖν, on the other
hand, as the product of the apprehension of agreeable qualities
in the object, may be able to give no better defence of itself
than the traditional dislike of Dr. Fell: "I do not like you, Dr.
Fell; the reason why I cannot tell." But this subsequent justification to reason of the love of ἀγαπᾶν affords no warrant for
declaring it the product of will acting on rational considerations.
The perception of those qualities constituting the object admirable is an act the same in kind as the perception of those
qualities constituting it agreeable; and the reaction of the subject in the emotion of love is an act of the same nature in both
cases. The reaction of the subject in the love of the order which
is expressed by ἀγαπᾶν is just as instinctive and just as immediate an affectional movement of the soul, as in the order of love

[103] As cited, p. 482.   [104] I. 11. 17.
[105] Trench and Cope hold much the same view.

expressed by φιλεῖν. The two differ not in their psychological nature but in the character of the apprehended qualities to which they are emotional responses. It is meaningless to say that the one terminates on the person himself and the other only on certain of his qualities: both terminate, of course, on the person whose quality as precious or agreeable as apprehended has called them into being.

It is only by an artificial explanation of it, furthermore, that Aristotle's phrase, — that "φιλεῖσθαι is ἀγαπᾶσθαι for our own sake" — can be made to suggest that ἀγαπᾶν expresses a love based on rational considerations. It only suggests that Aristotle saw in φιλεῖν a love which found its account in the agreeableness of the object. What Aristotle is saying in this passage is that it is pleasant alike to love and to be loved; for one loves only because he enjoys it; and if he is loved — that makes him happy because he fancies there must be something fine in him to call out the passion. He explains this by adding that φιλεῖσθαι is ἀγαπᾶσθαι for one's own sake. Here is a quasi-definition of φιλεῖν: φιλεῖν is a love founded on nothing outside the object. But the most that can be inferred about ἀγαπᾶν is that it is a love which has cognizable ground. To conclude that that ground is or may be outside the object, or must be of the nature of a rational consideration operating through acts of reflection, and judgment, and will, is sufficiently illegitimate to be absurd. The actual ground of the particular act of ἀγαπᾶν here spoken of is the total personality of the object conceived as good, and as therefore justifying his becoming the object of φιλεῖν. Φιλεῖν is subsumed under ἀγαπᾶν taken for the moment as a wider category; and the ἀγαπᾶν which includes the φιλεῖν in itself cannot have as such a ground of essentially different nature.[106]

[106] Cope, as cited, v. i, p. 214, paraphrases Aristotle's phrase thus: "And being liked or loved is to be valued, esteemed, for one's own sake and for nothing else." He remarks: "It is probable that little or no distinction is here intended to be made between φιλεῖν and ἀγαπᾶν, since it is the end and not the process that is here in question, and they seem to be used pretty nearly as synonyms. They represent two different aspects of love, as a natural affection or emotion, and as an acquired value, which we express by esteem." We probably get Aristotle's whole meaning when we say that when we are loved, there is implied in that that we are valued for our own sake.

We are not left by the ancients, however, without very clear intimation of how they conceived φιλεῖν and ἀγαπᾶν in relation to one another. There is, for example, what amounts to a direct definition of the two words in their distinctive meanings in an interesting passage in the "Memorabilia" of Xenophon, with which the commentators have rather fumbled.[107] B. L. Gildersleeve, in that unfortunate edition of Justin Martyr (1877) which brought only grief to his admirers, goes the length of saying,[108] with his eye on this passage, that "Xenophon uses ἀγαπᾶν and φιλεῖν as absolute synonyms"; and, what is even stranger, Moulton and Milligan repeat this judgment — for this special passage at least with the added emphasis of pronouncing it "undeniable." [109] These, however, are eccentric opinions. That a distinction is made between the two words lies on the face of the passage and is, of course, universally recognized.[110] The only question that is open is what precisely that distinction is. What has often been overlooked is that Xenophon actually defines the two terms in the clauses, which, because their relations to one another have not been accurately caught, have given the commentators all their trouble. Socrates,

---

[107] "Memorabilia," II, vii. 9 and 12. We give the text of the passage in the translation of J. A. Watson. Fourteen free women — his relatives — had been introduced into Aristarchus' house as dependents. Socrates' comment and advice was this: "Under present circumstances, as I should suppose, you neither feel attached (φιλεῖν) to your relatives nor they to you, for you find them burdensome to you, and they see that you are annoyed with their company. For such feelings there is danger that dislike may grow stronger and stronger, and that previous friendly inclination may be diminished. But if you take them under your direction so that they may be employed, you will love (φιλήσεις) them, when you see that they are serviceable to you, and they will grow attached to you (ἀγαπήσουσιν) when they find that you feel satisfaction in their society; and remembering past services with greater pleasure, you will increase the friendly feeling resulting from them, and consequently grow more attached and better disposed toward each other." Aristarchus took this advice and the result was: "they loved (ἐφίλον) Aristarchus as their protector, and he loved (ἠγάπα) them as being of use to him."

[108] P. 135.

[109] As cited, p. 2, sub voc. ἀγαπᾶν.

[110] J. H. H. Schmidt, as cited, p. 483, has a full and excellent discussion of the passage, which leaves no doubt of the general distinction that is drawn. Edward M. Cope, as cited, p. 294, pronounces it "decisive" in the matter. Cf. also T. D. Woolsey, as cited, p. 168; and E. A. Abbott, as cited, p. 240.

we are told, found Aristarchus peevish, because, owing to the civil disturbances of the time, he had had fourteen female relatives — sisters, nieces, cousins — dumped on him, and he did not see why he should be held responsible for their support. He did not like it; and the women, on their part, did not like the condition of affairs either. "Neither do you φιλεῖς them," says Socrates in diagnosing the situation, "nor they you": a settled mutual dislike threatened to be the outcome. The remedy which Socrates proposed was that Aristarchus should put the women to work at useful employment; and he promised that, on that being done, their indifference to each other would pass away: Aristarchus would acquire an affection for them arising out of a sense of their value to him; and they would come to prize him on perceiving his pleasure in them. "You will φιλήσεις them," says Socrates, "when you see that they are profitable to you; and they will ἀγαπήσουσιν you, when they perceive that you take pleasure in them." What is to be observed is that the clauses here are so balanced that the participial adjunct in each defines the verb in the other; so that what is said is equivalent to saying: "You will φιλήσεις them when you see that they ἀγάπουσιν you; and they will ἀγαπήσουσιν you when they perceive that you φιλεῖς them." Instead of mutual dislike, a mutual liking and esteem will supervene. To the φιλεῖν, then, in the first clause the "take pleasure in" of the other corresponds: and to the ἀγαπᾶν of the second clause the "being profitable to you" of the first corresponds: and thus we have in effect definitions of the two verbs — φιλεῖν is taking pleasure in, ἀγαπᾶν is ascribing value to. Now, Xenophon continues, Aristarchus tried it and it worked. He put the women to work and at once there was a change: "They ἐφίλουν him as a protector, and he ἠγάπα them as profitable." They came to take pleasure in his protection, and he came to value them for their profitable labor. The relation of protector of useless women, as barely tolerated dependents, with their natural resentment of a grudging bounty, passed, by the simple expedient of the introduction of productive employment, into a relation of mutual affection and esteem. They came to like the man who gave them back their self-respect; he came to prize the women whose labor brought him profit. The words in this last clause, so far from reversing their positions as compared with the former (this is the chief source of the difficulty the commentators find in the passage) are in their right places according to their definitions there. Φιλεῖν, defined there as delighting in, is properly used here to describe the attitude of the women towards their protector: ἀγαπᾶν, defined there as attaching value to, is properly employed here of the attitude of an employer to profitable workers.

The definition of ἀγαπᾶν which Xenophon here gives us — by which it expresses the love of prizing as over against the love of simple liking — verifies itself in a survey of the general usage of the word. This may be illustrated by attending to the other passages in which φιλεῖν and ἀγαπᾶν are brought together, that are cited by Abbott in connection with his discussion of this one. We see at once that it is Xenophon's distinction which is in the mind of Dio Cassius,[111] when he tells us that it was said to the Roman people at the death of Julius Caesar: Ye ἐφιλήσατε him as a father, and ἠγαπήσατε him as a benefactor — that is to say, they both felt true affection for him and greatly valued him. The case is equally simple with the passage from Plato's "Lysis"[112] with which Abbott deals with somewhat clumsy fingers, ascribing to ἀγαπᾶν the sense of "being drawn towards," and to φιλεῖν that of "drawing towards oneself." The passage is taken from a long discussion on friendship which is conducted throughout with φιλεῖν, φιλία, φιλοί, until, it having been concluded that only the good can be friends, the question is raised, How can those be valued (ἀγαπηθείη) by each other who can be of no use to one another, and how can one who is not valued (ἀγαπῷτο) be a friend? The good man being sufficient to himself — so far as he is good — stands in need of nothing; and therefore would not attach value (ἀγαπῷη) to anything; and because he cannot attach value (ἀγαπῷη) to anything, he cannot be fond (φιλοί) of anything. And yet they who do not make much of one another (μὴ περὶ πολλοῦ ποιούμενοι ἑαυτούς) cannot be friends. These last words, "make much of" define for us the

111 xliv, 48, p. 175.   112 P. 215B (cf. Jowett, p. 54).

sense in which ἀγαπᾶν has been used throughout; and we perhaps can hardly do better than render the crucial sentences: "He who lacks nothing will attach value to nothing (οὐδὲ τὶ ἀγαπῴη ἄν)": "what he does not attach value to, he cannot be fond of (ὃ δὲ μὴ ἀγαπῴη, οὐδ᾽ ἂν φιλοί)." A little later in the discussion [113] the two words are coupled in the reverse order from that in which they occur in Dio Cassius. We read: "For if there is nothing to hurt us any longer we should have no need of anything that would do us good. Thus would it be clearly seen that we did but ἠγαπῶμεν καὶ ἐφιλοῦμεν the good on account of the evil, and as the remedy of the evil which was the disease; but if there had been no disease there would have been no need of a remedy." Jowett renders the pair of verbs by "love and desire" which certainly is wrong. Woolsey renders much better by "highly judge and love"; adding the comment: "The latter word contains something more of feeling, while the former contains more of regard, and a higher degree of respect." We can scarcely do better than render: "And thus it would be clear that we attached value to the good and looked with affection on it, only on account of the evil." Abbott's last example is drawn from Ælian's description of Hiero's love for his brothers.[114] He lived on terms of great intimacy with them, we are told, "holding them in very high regard (πάνυ σφόδρα ἀγάπησις), and being loved (φιληθεῖς) by them in return." The meaning seems to be what we might express by saying that he valued his brothers and they repaid him by true affection.

It is not intended to suggest that the content of ἀγαπᾶν is exhausted by the concepts esteem, value, prize. The word expresses the notion of love. What is contended for is that the particular manner love which the word is adapted to express, is the love which is the product of the apprehension of value in its object, and which is therefore informed by a feeling of its preciousness, so that it moves in a region closely akin to that of esteeming, valuing, prizing. The region in which it moves is, indeed, so closely akin to that of these conceptions, that there

---

[113] P. 220D (cf. Jowett, p. 61).
[114] "Var. Hist.," ix, 1 (Tauchnitz ed. p. 124).

are occasions when the idea it expresses is scarcely distinguishable from them. Take for example these two instances from
Isocrates.[115] "The same opinion is also held concerning the
Lacedemonians; for in their case their defeat at Thermopylae
is more admired (ἄγωνται) than their other victories, and the
trophy erected over them by the barbarians is an object of esteem (ἀγαπῶσι) and frequent visits (θεωροῦσι), while those set
up by the Lacedemonians over others, far from being commended (ἐπαινοῦσι), are regarded with displeasure; for the
former is considered to be a sign of valor, the latter of a desire
for self-aggrandizement" (V. 148). "Now, I am surprised that
those who consider it impossible that any such policy should be
effected do not know from their own experience, or have not
heard from others, that there have been indeed many terrible
wars the parties to which have been reconciled and done each
other great service. What could exceed the enmity between
Xerxes and the Hellenes? Yet every one knows that both we
and the Lacedemonians were more pleased (ἀγαπήσοντες) with
the friendship (φιλία) of Xerxes than with that of those who
helped us to found our respective empires" (V. 42). In the
former passage ἀγαπῶσι καὶ θεωροῦσι are put in a sort of parallel
with οὐκ ἐπαινοῦσιν ἀλλ᾽ ἀηδῶς ὁρῶσιν, and may perhaps be not
inadequately represented by "prized and gazed at," as over
against "not praised but looked askance at." The idea conveyed by ἀγαπήσαντες in the latter passage lies very close to
that of "prized more," "valued more" "set more store by."
Nevertheless Isocrates preferred to employ a word which said
these things with a slight difference; a slight difference which
enhanced the effect. He preferred to say that the trophy at
Thermopylae was loved, and that the Greeks loved the friendship of Xerxes more than that of their allies — employing,
however, for "loved" a term through which sounded the notions of esteeming, valuing, prizing, rather than that of enjoying.

We see the same implications shining through the word

[115] V. 148; V. 42. We draw these passages from Schmidt (p. 485), who presents them as involving no question of real love, but only of an esteeming or
valuing.

when we read in Demosthenes such phrases as these: "Neither did I love (ἠγάπησα) Philip's gifts," for which Woolsey suggests, "neither did I value":[116] "These he loves (ἀγαπᾷ) and keeps around him," which Woolsey renders "these he makes much of."[117] Examples, however, need not be multiplied. The word designates love — "without reference to sensuousness, close-intercourse, or heart-inwardness" — from the distinct point of view of the recognition of worthiness in its object. It is, therefore, intrinsically a noble word for love; or, let us give to it its rights and say definitely it is the noble word for love. It is in its right company when Plutarch [118] joins it with τιμᾷν and σέβεσθαι in the declaration that "the people ought to love and honor and revere the gods according to righteousness." But like other noble words it was possible for it to lose the sharpness and force of its higher suggestions. It became ultimately, in the development of the language, the general word for love. And in proportion as it became the general word for love and was applied without thought to all kinds of love, it naturally lost more or less of the power to suggest its own specific implications. The time came when it could be applied to the basest forms of love without consciousness of incongruity. Its lofty implications remained, however, embedded in its very form, and could always be recalled to consciousness and observation by a simple emphasis. And as long as any other term for love was current, sharing the field with it, it was always possible to throw the high implications intrinsic to it up to sight by merely setting the two in contrast.

This, then, is the equipment of the Greek language for the expression of the idea of love, which is revealed to us in the monuments of classical Greek. There were, we see, four terms which served as vehicles of it. Φιλεῖν held the general field, though not without its distinctive implications which were on occasion thrown into clear emphasis, and which were always more or less felt coloring the conception of love as it expressed itself by its means in current speech. These implications repre-

---

[116] "De Corona," p. 263, 7 Reiske.   [117] "De Olynth.," ii, p. 23, 23.
[118] "Aristides," 6.3.

sented love as the response of the human spirit to what appealed to it as pleasurable; therefore at bottom as a delight. Φιλεῖν was supported on both sides, however, by other terms of other implications. There was στέργειν in which love was presented as a natural outflow of the heart to objects conceived as in one way or another bound up very closely with it and making, therefore, a claim upon it for affection. There was ἐρᾶν which conceived love as an overmastering passion, seizing upon and absorbing into itself the whole mind. And there was, on the other side, ἀγαπᾶν which presented love as the soul's sense of the value and preciousness of its object and its response to its recognized worth in admiring affection.[119]

During the classical period these terms did not so much encroach on the dominance of φιλεῖν in the literary expression of love as rather come to its aid, bringing into fuller expression the several sides and aspects of love. A change, however, was preparing beneath the surface, in the broad region of popular speech. How this change was inaugurated, through what stages it passed, what were the forces which drove it forward, we are left to conjecture to suggest. There is no direct evidence available. We only know that in that body of literature constituted by the New Testament, along with the Septuagint version of the Old Testament and the Apostolic Fathers, a body of literature the peculiarity of which is that it dips into the popular speech,

---

[119] How fully these synonyms covered the idea of love in its complete range is illustrated by the opening words of Deutsch's article on "Love (Jewish)" in Hastings' ERE. viii, p. 173b. In transcribing what he says we insert the Greek terms at appropriate places. "The dictionaries define love as 'a feeling of strong personal attachment, induced by that which delights (φιλεῖν) or commands admiration (ἀγαπᾶν).' The subdivisions of this sentiment comprise the impulses of attachment, due to sexual instinct, or the mutual affections of man and woman (?ἐρᾶν); the impulses which direct the mutual affections of members of one family, parents and children, brothers and other relatives (στέργειν); the attachment that springs from sympathetic sentiments of people with harmonious character, friendship (φιλία); and finally, the various metaphorical usages of the word, as the love for moral and intellectual ideals." He adds: "To the last class belongs the religious concept of love for God, while the particular Biblical conception of God's love for Israel is closely related to the idea of paternal affection." As we shall see when we come to speak of the usage of the Septuagint, these higher religious conceptions were brought under ἀγαπᾶν.

we suddenly see the change well on its way. The most outstanding feature of it is the retirement of φιλεῖν into the background and the substitution for it of ἀγαπᾶν as the general term for love. We must not permit to fall out of sight that this means the general adoption of the noblest word for love the language possessed as its common designation in every-day speech. One may well suppose that an ethical force was working in such a change.[120] Such a supposition would find support in the general deepening of the ethical life which, as we know, was taking place during the closing centuries of the old era. We may readily suppose that in the increasing seriousness of the times the current conception of love too may have grown more grave; and that it may have, therefore, seemed less and less appropriate to speak of it in any lighter than the highest available terms. Whatever may have been the cause, however, it is plain matter of fact that ἀγαπᾶν, a word of essential nobility in its native implications, did gradually through the years become the ordinary term for the expression of love in the most general sense. And this necessarily wrought a distinct ennoblement of the common speech with respect to love.

The effect of the change on ἀγαπᾶν itself naturally was not so happy. The application of it indiscriminately to every form and quality of love unavoidably reduced its current acceptation to the level of every form and quality of love. The native implications of the word could not, to be sure, be entirely eradicated. But they could be covered up and hidden so as not to be noted in the ordinary use of it, and only now and again brought back into view, when in one way or another they were thrown into emphasis. How thoroughly they were thus obscured we should not have been able to guess had we the witness of the New Testament alone in our hands. The Septuagint, however, reveals it to us. There ἀγαπᾶν appears as in such a sense the general term for love that it is readily applied to every form and quality of love, apparently in the case of the lower forms with-

---

[120] Woolsey's remark (as cited, p. 169): "Such a change . . . must have come from a higher condition of moral feeling," is sound in itself although made in a connexion not easily justified.

out any consciousness whatever of its higher connotations. This phenomenon occurs, it is true, occasionally also in classical Greek. It is incidental to the free use of any word that it should get its edges worn off in the process, and become more or less a mere symbol for the general idea connected with it, without regard to any specific modifications of that general idea which it may embody. But it becomes much more marked in the Septuagint. Because ἀγαπᾶν has become the general word for love, what was exceptional in the classics has here become the rule. In the Septuagint the word has lost the precision of its specific notion and become merely a general term to express a general idea. A much nobler term for love has come into general use for the expression of the broad idea of love; and this ennobles the whole speech concerning love. But the word itself has suffered loss in thus permitting itself to be applied indifferently to all kinds and conditions of love.

On another side, however, the employment of ἀγαπᾶν as the general term for love brought it a great elevation in its Septuagint usage. If there was no love too low to be spoken of in its terms, there was equally no love too high for its use of it. And the application of it to describe the higher aspects of love as presented in the Old Testament revelation added great stretches to its range upwards. We are in the presence here of a double movement through which ἀγαπᾶν was prepared for its use in the New Testament. By the obscure linguistic revolution wrought among the peoples of Greek speech, as a result of which ἀγαπᾶν superseded φιλεῖν as the general Greek term for the expression of the idea of love, intrinsically the noblest word for love the Greek language afforded, came naturally to the hands of the Septuagint translators for rendering the idea of love as it appeared in the pages of the Old Testament. By the rendering of the idea of love throughout the Old Testament by ἀγαπᾶν, the whole content of the Old Testament idea of love was poured into that term, expanding it in its suggestions upwards, and training it to speak in tones indefinitely exalted. The total effect of this double change was immensely to extend the range of the word. As it was the noblest word for love in Greek speech, its range could be extended, on its becoming the general word for love, only downward. It was extended also upwards only by becoming the vehicle for the deepened conception of love which has been given to the world by the self-revelation of God in the Scriptures. When we open the Septuagint, therefore, and see ἀγαπᾶν lying on its pages as the general term for love, we are in the presence of some very notable phenomena in the preparation of the terminology of love in the New Testament.

The story of the Septuagint usage of the terms for love is almost told by the simple statistics. The verb ἀγαπᾶν occurs in the Septuagint about two hundred and sixty-six times, φιλεῖν about thirty-six times, ἐρᾶσθαι only three times, and στέργειν just once. Even this does not give the whole state of the case, for in the majority of its occurrences φιλεῖν is used in the sense of "to kiss." It occurs only sixteen or seventeen times with the meaning of "love." That is to say, this word, the common word for love in the classics, is used in the Septuagint in only a little more than five per cent of the instances where love falls to be mentioned: in nearly ninety-five per cent ἀγαπᾶν is used. Here is a complete reversal of the relative positions of the two words.

In more than a third of the instances in which φιλεῖν is used of loving, moreover, it is used of things — food or drink, or the like (Gen. xxvii. 4, 9, 14, Prov. xxi. 17, Hos. iii. 1, Isa. lvi. 10), leaving only a half a score of instances in which it is employed of love of persons. In all these instances (except Tob. vi. 14, where it is a demon that is in question) it is a human being to whom the loving is ascribed. The love ascribed to him ranges from mere carnal love (Jer. xxii. 22 [paralleled with ἐρασταί], Lam. i. 2, Tob. vi. 14, cf. Tob. vi. 17), through the love of a father for his son (Gen. xxxvii. 4), to love for Wisdom (Prov. viii. 17, xxix. 3, Wisd. viii. 2). Cremer drops the remark: "In two passages only does φιλεῖν occur as perfectly synonymous with ἀγαπάω, Prov. viii. 17, xxix. 3." [121] This cannot mean that ἀγαπᾶν does not occur in the senses in which φιλεῖν is used

<hr />

[121] "Biblisch-Theologisches Wörterbuch der Neutestamentlichen Gräcität³," 1883, p. 11, near bottom: E. T., p. 592, bottom. The remark seems to have been omitted from 10th ed., 1915.

in the other passages: ἀγαπᾶν is used in all these senses. What
is really meant is that in these two passages alone φιλεῖν bears
a sense which Cremer is endeavoring to fix on ἀγαπᾶν as its distinctive meaning — the sense of high ethical love. In both passages it is love to Wisdom that is spoken of: "I (Wisdom)
ἀγαπῶ them that φιλοῦντας me" (viii. 17); "When a man loves
(φιλοῦντος) wisdom, his father rejoices" (xxix. 3); and they bear
witness that this high love could readily be expressed by φιλεῖν,
as well as by ἀγαπᾶν. It is not obvious, however, that φιλεῖν is
used in these passages as perfectly synonymous with ἀγαπᾶν.
On the face of Prov. viii. 17, there is a difference between the
love (ἀγαπᾶν) ascribed to Wisdom and that (φιλεῖν) ascribed to
her votaries, if the distribution of the words be allowed any
significance. Perhaps it may be conjectured that some flavor
clings to φιλεῖν which renders it less suitable for the graver affection proper to Wisdom herself.

Despite the fewness of the occurrences of φιλεῖν, there are
quite a number of instances in which it is brought into more or
less close conjunction with ἀγαπᾶν, and a glance over these may
help us to some notion of the relation which the two words bear
to one another. Gen. xxxvii. 3, 4: "And Jacob ἠγάπα Joseph
more than all his sons. . . . And his brothers, seeing that his
father φιλεῖ him above all his sons, hated him." Prov. viii. 17:
"I (Wisdom) ἀγαπῶ them that φιλοῦντας me." Prov. xxi. 17:
"A poor man ἀγαπᾷ mirth, φιλῶν wine and oil in abundance."
Isa. lvi. 6, 10: "The strangers that attach themselves unto the
Lord . . . to ἀγαπᾶν the name of the Lord. . . . Dumb dogs,
. . . φιλοῦντες to slumber." Lam. i. 2: "Weeping, she weeps in
the night and her tears are upon her cheeks; and there is none
of all that ἀγαπώντων her to comfort her; all those that φιλοῦντες
her have dealt treacherously with her." Hos. iii. 1: "And the
Lord said to me, Go yet and ἀγάπησον a woman that ἀγαπῶσαν
evil things and an adulteress, even as the Lord ἀγαπᾷ the children of Israel, and they have respect to strange gods, and
φιλοῦσι cakes and raisins." Wisdom viii. 2, 3: "Her (Wisdom)
I ἐφιλήσα, and sought out from my youth, and I desired to make
her my wife and was an ἐραστής of her beauty. . . . Yea, the

Lord of all things Himself ἠγάπησεν her" (and then immediately below, at verse 7: "If a man ἀγαπᾷ righteousness"). Perhaps we should add Prov. xix. 7, 8, in which the noun φιλία and the verb ἀγαπᾶν occur, in distinct clauses no doubt, which yet stand rather close together: "Every one who hates a poor brother is also far from φιλία. . . . He that procures wisdom ἀγαπᾷ himself."

To fill out the general picture we may adjoin a few passages in which other combinations of terms for love are made. In his praise of woman in I Esd. iv. 14 ff., Zorobabel brings together these two statements — that a man can look a lion in the face, and can plunder and rob in the darkness — all to bring his spoil to τῇ ἐρωμένῃ; "yea a man ἀγαπᾷ his own wife more than father or mother." In Jer. xxii. 22, we read: "The wind shall tend all thy shepherds and thy ἐρασταί shall go into captivity; for then shalt thou be ashamed and disgraced by all τῶν φιλούντων σε." In Prov. vii. 18: "Come, and let us enjoy φιλίας until the morning; come, and let us embrace ἔρωτι." And again, in Sir. xxvii. 17, 18: "Στέρξον a friend (φίλον) and be faithful unto him; but if thou betrayest his secrets . . . thou hast lost the φιλίαν of thy neighbor."

It cannot be pretended that it is an easy task to find one's way through these passages, assigning a distinctive sense to each term. By one thing we are struck, however, at the first glance. In all the combinations of ἀγαπᾶν and φιλεῖν, the higher rôle is assigned to ἀγαπᾶν. The historian tells us in Gen. xxxvii. 3 that Jacob ἠγάπα Joseph; but when he repeats what the envious brothers said, φιλεῖν is used, as if they would suggest that their father's special love for him was an ungrounded preference. It is Wisdom who ἀγαπᾷ her votaries (Prov. viii. 17); they, on their part, φιλοῦνται her; and the Lord ἠγάπησεν Wisdom, while her servant ἐφίλησε her (Wisd. viii. 2, 3). There is some appearance here that ἀγαπᾶν was felt to be in some way the more appropriate word with which to express love of a superhuman order. Only in the case of Lam. i. 2 does the variation from ἀγαπᾶν to φιλεῖν seem to be purely rhetorical; and there the variation imitates a variation in the underlying Hebrew, and

gives ἀγαπᾶν the place of honor.[122] Similarly, in the passages
in which ἀγαπᾶν does not occur there appears to be in mind always
some valid distinction between the terms that are used, although
it is not always easy clearly to grasp it. It must be confessed,
for example, that it is difficult to discover the precise reason
for the variation from ἐρασταί to φιλοῦντες in Jer. xxii. 22, or
from φιλία to ἔρως in Prov. vii. 18. In the former of these passages
it is obvious enough, of course, that the φιλοῦντες are intended
to embrace both the shepherds and the lovers, and doubtless
that is the reason that a broader word is chosen. In the latter
the variation in terms reflects a variation in the underlying
Hebrew, but it is not clear that it reflects it accurately, or what
is the exact distinction intended. The general impression left
by the series of passages is that the several terms for love were
used quite freely and with various natural interchanges, as
substantial synonyms; but that ἀγαπᾶν was felt to be in some
sense of the highest suggestion, and when they were brought
into contrast, the higher place was instinctively given to it.

Certainly ἀγαπᾶν is used with the utmost freedom for every
conceivable variety of love, from the love of mere lust on the one
hand (e. g., II Sam. xiii. 1, 4, 15, Isa. lvii. 8, Ezek. xvi. 37) up to
the purest earthly love on the other (Lev. xix. 18, 34, Deut. x.
19, I Sam. xviii. 1, xx. 17, II Sam. i. 23), and beyond that to
the highest love which man can feel, love to God (Ex. xx. 6,
Deut. v. 10, vi. 5, vii. 9, x. 12, xi. 1, 13, 22, xiii. 3, xix. 9, xxx.
6, 16, 20, Judges viii. 3, Jos. xxii. 5, xxiii. 11, I Kings iii. 3, Ps.
xvii. 1, xxx. 23, lxviii. 37, xcvi. 10, cxvi. 7), and even above that,
to the inexplicable love of God Himself to His people (Deut. iv.
37, vii. 8, 13, x. 15, xxiii. 5, II Sam. xii. 24, II Chron. ii. 11, ix. 8, Isa.
xliii. 4, xlviii. 14, lxiii. 9, Jer. xxxviii. 3, Mal. i. 2, Prov. iii. 12).
It is quite true that it is used for the higher reaches of love far
more frequently than for the lower-lying varieties. This was
the inevitable effect of the proportionate place occupied by the
higher and lower forms of love in the pages of the Old Testa-

---

[122] According to Gesenius, אֹהֵב means "a friend, loving and beloved, intimate,
different from רֵעַ, a companion": רֵעַ, he says, implies less than אֹהֵב. In the text,
ἀγαπᾶν represents אֹהֵב and φιλεῖν רֵעַ.

ment, and argues little as to the relative adaptability of the term for expressing them severally. The plain fact is that ἀγαπᾶν is the general term for love in the Greek Old Testament, employed in some ninety-five per cent of the instances in which love is mentioned; and therefore it is employed of the several varieties of love, not in accordance with its fitness to express one or another of them, but in accordance with the relative frequency of their occurrence in the Old Testament. The five per cent or so of occurrences which are left to be expressed by other terms seem not to be divided off from the rest on the ground of the intrinsic unfitness of ἀγαπᾶν to express them. They include next to no kinds of love which ἀγαπᾶν is not employed to express in other passages.[123] It is not to be supposed, of course, that pure caprice has determined the employment of these terms in these few instances. There is doubtless always a reason for the selection which is made; and ordinarily the appropriateness of the term actually employed can be more or less clearly felt. But it does not appear that the reason for passing over ἀγαπᾶν in these cases was ordinarily its intrinsic incapacity for the expression of the specific love that is spoken of. As the general word for love it no doubt could have been used without impropriety throughout.

It is possible, moreover, to overpress the intrinsic significance of the predominant use of ἀγαπᾶν for the higher varieties of love. Both φιλεῖν (Prov. viii. 17, xxix. 3) and ἐρᾶσθαι (Prov. iv. 6, Wisd. viii. 2), along with it (Prov. viii. 21), are used for love to Wisdom. But no other term except ἀγαπᾶν happens to be employed of God's love to man, or of man's love to God, or even of that love to our neighbor which with them constitutes the three conceptions in which is summed up the peculiarity of the teaching on love of the religion of revelation. This is a notable fact; and it had notable consequences. It did not, however, so much result from, as result in, that elevation of ἀγαπᾶν above other terms for love, which fits it alone to express these high forms. It is probable that had the Septuagint translators found φιλεῖν still in use as the general term for love, they would have

---

[123] But see below page 373.

employed it as their own general word, and it would have fallen
to it therefore to be used to express these higher forms of love.
Instead, they found ἀγαπᾶν, an intrinsically higher word than
φιλεῖν and more suitable for the purpose; and they trained it to
convey these still higher conceptions also. Thus they stamped
ἀγαπᾶν with a new quality, and prepared it for its use in the
New Testament. What is of importance to bear in mind, however, is that the elevation of ἀγαπᾶν to this new dignity was not
due to its greater intrinsic fitness to express these new conceptions (though it was intrinsically more fit to do so), but to the
circumstance that it happened to be the general term for love
in current use when the Septuagint was written. This is proved
by the fact that it was not employed by the Septuagint writers
as a special word for the expression of the loftier aspects of love
alone, but as a general word to express all kinds and conditions
of love. It is simply the common term for love in the Greek Old
Testament, and the new dignity which clothes it as it leaves the
Old Testament has been contributed to it by the Old Testament
itself.

The account given of ἀγαπᾶν by Hermann Cremer, while
in its central statement perfectly just, is deformed by some remarkable inaccuracies, arising from a fruitless attempt to establish certain stated exceptions to this central statement.
"The New Testament usage with reference to the words
ἀγαπᾶν, ἀγάπη, ἀγαπητός," he writes,[124] "is in a very special
manner a consistent and complete one. It was prepared for by
the use, presented by the Septuagint, of ἀγαπάω for the Hebrew
אהב in the whole range of its applications, with one or two characteristic exceptions. The Hebrew word includes in itself the
significance of all three Greek synonyms" [i. e., φιλεῖν, ἐρᾶν, and
ἀγαπᾶν]; "it is especially frequently used in an application in
which the Greeks do not speak of love, that is to say, of the
love enjoined for God and His will, as well as of the love ascribed to God Himself (Deut. vii. 13, x. 15, 18, xxiii. 6, II Sam.
xii. 24, Ps. lxxviii. 68, lxxxvii. 2, cxlvi. 8, Isa. xliii. 4, xlviii. 14,

---

[124] As cited. We are quoting from 10th ed., 1915, but the passage has remained substantially unaltered since the 3d ed., 1883.

lxiii. 9), particularly the last, which is a conception beyond the imagination of the Greeks.[125] Apart, now, from a few passages in which the rendering is only according to the sense (Mic. iii. 2 = ζητεῖν, Prov. xviii. 21 = κρατεῖν, xvii. 19 = χαίρειν), אהב is regularly translated by ἀγαπᾶν, with the exception of when it stands for sensual love (sixteen times in all), in which case ἐρᾶν, ἐραστής are constantly used (see above), and when it denotes a sensuous inclination or a natural affection (ten times), and then it is rendered by φιλεῖν and its compounds — Gen. xxvii. 4, 9, 14, Isa. lvi. 10, Ecc. iii. 8; cf. II Chron. xxvi. 10, φιλογεωργός, A, אֹהֵב אֲדָמָה, as also two passages where there is mention of an objectionable disposition, I Kings xi. 1 φιλογύναιος (φιλογύνης, B), and Prov. xvii. 19, φιλομαρτήμων." W. G. Ballantine, commenting on the latter half of this passage, remarks trenchantly, but we are afraid not unjustly:[126] "Cremer's assertions regarding the translation of אהב in the Septuagint are sheer misstatements, as anyone who has Trommius' Concordance in his hands can see. We have already referred to half a score of passages where ἀγαπάω, as the translation of אהב, expresses lustful love. Φιλέω, as we saw above, but once expresses a natural affection, and but four times a sensual inclination. Ἀγαπάω expresses a natural affection in Gen. xxii. 2, xxv. 28, xxxvii. 3, xliv. 20, Ruth iv. 15, Prov. iv. 3, xiii. 24. Ἐράω translates אהב but twice. Cremer says that ἀγαπάω 'never means to do anything willingly, to be wont to do'; yet we have it in Jer. xiv. 10, 'They have loved to move their feet,' and in Jer. v. 31, 'And my people loved to have it so.'"

Cremer's statement certainly conveys the impression that ἀγαπᾶν is never used in the canonical Septuagint (as a rendering of אהב) for sensual love, or for a sensuous inclination or natural affection, its place being taken in the former case (there being sixteen instances in all) by ἐρᾶν, ἐραστής, and in the latter (ten instances) by φιλεῖν and its compounds. For the sixteen cases of ἐρᾶν rendering אהב, used of sensual love, he refers us to a

[125] On these assertions see *The Princeton Theological Review*, January 1918, pp. 20ff.

[126] "Bibliotheca Sacra," July, 1889, p. 534.

list previously given — "see above," he says — and that list
proves to run as follows: " 'Εράν is found only in a few passages
in the Old Testament (Esth. ii. 17, Prov. iv. 6, = אהב; Wisd.
viii. 2; ἐραστής, Ez. xvi. 33, 36, 37, xxiii. 5, 9, 22, Jer. xxii. 20,
22, Lam. i. 19, Hos. ii. 7, 9, 12, 14, 15, the stated rendering of
the Hebrew מְאָהֵב in the sensual sense)." There are seventeen
passages enumerated here; but they are not seventeen passages
in which אהב and מאהב are used in a sensual sense and are rendered by ἐράν and ἐραστής; they profess to be passages rather
in which ἐράν and ἐραστής are found in the Old Testament —
Wisd. viii. 2, of course, having no Hebrew base. They do not,
to be sure, exhaust the list of occurrences of words of this
group· in the Old Testament: ἐράσθαι occurs three times, not
two as here (add I Esdr. iv. 24); ἔρως, not mentioned here,
occurs twice (Prov. vii. 18, xxiv. 51 [xxx. 16]); and ἐραστής
appears nineteen times, as against the fifteen here enumerated.
But much less do the sixteen of them which are renderings of אהב
justify the description of them given in the main passage. One
of the two passages cited for ἐράν, indeed — "Love (Wisdom),
and she shall keep thee" (Prov. iv. 6) — refers to high ethical
love; as does also indeed Wisd. viii. 2 (ἐραστής), "I was a lover
of her (Wisdom's) beauty." The other passage cited for ἐράν,
"And the king loved Esther and she found favor beyond all the
virgins; and he put on her the queen's crown" (Esth. ii. 17),
while certainly referring to sexual love, can scarcely be spoken
of as referring to dishonorable love, as neither, indeed, can
I Esd. iv. 24, the third passage in which ἐράν occurs (not mentioned by Cremer): "And when he hath stolen, spoiled, and
robbed, he bringeth it to his beloved (ἐρωμένη); wherefore a
man loveth (ἀγαπᾷ) his wife better than father and mother."

As it is thus clear that the words of the ἐράν group do not
always express lustful, and not even always sexual, love, it is even
more clear that sensual or even lustful love is not expressed exclusively by words of this group. We have seen the carnal love
of a demon for a mortal maid expressed by φιλεῖν (Tob. vi. 15),
and the wicked lovers of Zion, in parallelism with ἐρασταί, expressed by φιλοῦντες (Jer. xxii. 22). The Hebrew piel participle

מאהב, rendered in the fifteen passages enumerated by Cremer
by ἐρασταί, occurs also in Jer. xxx. 14, Zech. xiii. 6, the former of
which is certainly of the same class with its fellows, and the
latter not certainly of a different class (so Hengstenberg). In
Jer. xxx. 14, however, it is rendered by οἱ φιλοί, "All thy lovers
have forgotten thee," and in Zech. xiii. 6, taken as a singular,
by ὁ ἀγαπητός, "With these I was wounded in my beloved
house," or, as in the Alexandrian MS., "in the house of my
beloved." It has already been intimated that numerous passages exist in which sensual love is expressed by ἀγαπᾶν. If we
are to take sensual love in a sense broad enough to include
Cremer's examples, we may adduce such passages as Gen.
xxiv. 67, xxix. 30, 32, xxxiv. 3, Ex. xxi. 5, Deut. xxi. 15, 16,
Judges xiv. 16, xvi. 15, I Sam. i. 5, xviii. 28, II Chron. xi. 21,
Ecc. ix. 9, and perhaps even I Kings xi. 2. If dishonorable love
is to be insisted upon, we may refer to II Sam. xiii. 1, 4, 15,
Ezek. xvi. 37, Hos. iii. 1, or we may content ourselves with the
single passage Isa. lvii. 8: "Thou hast loved (ἠγάπησας) those
that lay with thee, and now hast multiplied thy whoredom
(πορνείαν) with them." It is beyond question that not ἐρᾶν but
ἀγαπᾶν is the regular word to express sexual love in the Septuagint, and this fact is not to be obscured by pointing to ἐραστής
as the standing word for "lover" — which is a different matter.

No assertion could be more unfortunate, then, than that
ἐρᾶν is the constant vehicle in the Septuagint for the expression
of sensual love; and it is no mitigation to confine the assertion
to the instances of renderings of אהב by ἐρᾶν. Unless, indeed, it
be held even more unfortunate to assert that φιλεῖν and its compounds supply the stated means of the expression of the love of
sensuous inclination or natural affection — connected with the
further implication that there are only ten instances in which
love of this kind comes to expression in the Old Testament. A
full list of the ten instances he has in mind is not given by
Cremer, and it would be difficult to fill out such a list with instances exactly like the half-dozen which he adduces. These
half-dozen instances do represent one side of the usage of φιλεῖν
and its compounds — a usage in which it perhaps holds a

unique position in Old Testament Greek. We are not sure that
ἀγαπᾶν is found in any precisely similar applications. There is
even an appearance that such applications are avoided for
ἀγαπᾶν. Look, for example, at Prov. xxi. 17: "A poor man
loveth (ἀγαπᾶν) mirth, loving (φιλῶν) wine and oil in abundance." There seems to be reflected here a distinction in the
usage of the two terms, according to which φιλεῖν and not
ἀγαπᾶν is preferred for loving food and drink, just as in English
we say we "like" but only abusively that we "love" articles
of diet. But this is only a pocket in the usage of φιλεῖν, and does
not justify the broad characterization formulated by Cremer.
The love expressed by φιλεῖν includes also the elevated love of
Wisdom by her votaries (Prov. viii. 17, xxix. 3); and if Ecc. iii.
8, "There is a time to love (φιλῆσαι) and a time to hate" shows
that natural affections are expressed by φιλεῖν, what does Sir.
xiii. 15, "Every beast loves (ἀγαπᾷ) his like, and every man his
neighbor" [127] show? The fundamental fault of Cremer's statement lies in a zeal to mark off a special region within which each
term — ἐρᾶν, φιλεῖν, and above all, ἀγαπᾶν — shall be confined.
Accordingly, he arbitrarily narrows the range of the usage of
each, and very especially of ἀγαπᾶν. In point of fact, the usage
of ἀγαπᾶν covers the whole field which אהב itself covers, and
there is no real variety of love for which it is not employed somewhere or other in the Septuagint. Even such a conspectus of the
kinds of love for which it is used as that drawn up by Ballantine
in the following summary is only generally complete, although
it will doubtless serve to bring home to us the very wide field
covered by the word. "It is the word," he says, [128] "in constant
use to express (1) God's love to man, (2) God's love for truth
and other virtues and worthy objects, (3) man's love for God,
(4) man's love for salvation and worthy objects, (5) man's conscientious love for man, (6) ordinary human friendship, (7)
parental and filial affection, (8) the love of husband and wife,

[127] Lütgert, "Die Liebe im Neuen Testament," 1905, p. 35, remarks: "Here
the commandment of love comes forward as a law of nature, and that because it
ought to be presented as a rational thing." He is presenting it as an instance of
the rationalization of Jewish thought under the influence of Hellenism.

[128] As cited, p. 527.

(9) impure sexual love, (10) man's love for cursing and other vices and sinful objects."

One of the most striking accompaniments of the appearance of ἀγαπᾶν in the Septuagint as the general term for love, is the appearance by its side of two abstract substantives formed from this stem — ἀγάπησις and ἀγάπη. The classical writers got along without these substantives. ᾿Αγάπησις has, it is true, been turned up in Aristotle. But it does not come into wide use in profane literature until Plutarch — after the opening of the Christian era. ᾿Αγάπη has not hitherto been discovered in any profane author at all, unless a somewhat conjectural reading in Philodemus, an Epicurean writer of the first century before Christ, be an exception.[129] In a true sense, then, both of these words make their first appearance in the Septuagint. ᾿Αγαπᾶν itself was in comparatively limited use among the classical writers; and, with στοργή, ἔρως and φιλία in their hand, they apparently felt no need of a substantive representing the peculiar quality of ἀγαπᾶν, in order to give expression to all their conceptions of love. When, however, ἀγαπᾶν became the general word for love, a need for corresponding substantives seems to have come to be felt, and they were supplied. Of course the Septuagint did not invent these substantives: not even ἀγάπη, which is not found in any earlier writing. It took them over with ἀγαπᾶν from the common usage of the people. This appears very clearly from the nature of their use in the Septuagint. They are used as general terms for love, covering the whole range of the conception, and with the utmost simplicity and directness. A very careless manner of speaking of ἀγάπη is current, as if it were in some way a gift of revealed religion to the world, not to say a direct product of divine inspiration. When Trench says that "It should never be forgotten that the substantive ἀγάπη is a

---

[129] The treatise is known from Herculaneum papyri alone, and the reading in question is restored thus: δι' ἀ[γ]άπης ἐ[ναρ]γοῦς. It is recorded in Crönert's revision of Passow's Lexicon, sub voc., who accompanies it with a note, "sicher (?)"; and it is reported from his record by Moulton and Milligan, sub voc. G. A. Deissmann, "Bible Studies," 1901, p. 200, points out a scholium to Thucydides II. 51, which reads "φιλανθρωπίας καὶ ἀγάπης." But there is no telling how late this scholium may be, or whether the glossator was a Christian or not.

purely Christian word, no example of its use occurring in any heathen writer whatever," he has no doubt by a mere slip of the pen said "Christian" when the historical revelation of God in its entirety was what was in his mind. That correction, however, will not save his remark from being misleading. It is not true that "the word was born within the bosom of revealed religion"; it is true only that it has hitherto been found in the use only of adherents of revealed religion. What Zezschwitz means by saying that it "first makes its appearance as a current term in the Song of Solomon" is not clear, unless it be that it occurs more frequently in the Song of Solomon than in any other Old Testament book (eleven times as over against eight in the whole Old Testament besides). The plain fact about the word is that, as it appears in the pages of the Septuagint, it bears all the marks of being already an old word with a settled general usage.

Additional evidence of its general currency is supplied by its appearance in Aristeas (second or first century B.C.) and Philo (early first century A.D.). Each uses it a single time, and both in a noble sense — as the content of true piety. Aristeas, positing the question, What is equal to beauty? answers: [130] "Piety (εὐσέβεια); for that is an excellent beauty. But its power consists in ἀγάπη; for this is a gift of God. And," he adds, to the king whose inquiry he is answering, "you possess this, embracing in it all that is good." [131] Philo writes more elaborately to much the same effect. "And therefore it is," says he,[132] "that it appears to me that with these two principal assertions above

---

[130] § 229; ed. Wendland, p. 63. Aristeas uses ἀγαπᾶν (§ 123), ἀγάπησις (§§ 44, 265, 270) and ἀγάπη (§ 229); apparently not ἐρᾶν, ἔρως, or στέργειν, στοργή, at all; nor even φιλεῖν, but φιλία, §§ 40, 44, 225, 228, 231, φίλος a half-dozen times and compounds of φιλ- including φιλανθρωπεῖν, φιλανθρωπία, φιλανθρωπότερον.

[131] 'Αγάπησις is used in a less exalted sense. In § 44 (p. 15), Eleazar writes to Ptolemy that he would endeavor to do all that the king had asked, "for this is a mark of φιλίας and ἀγαπήσεως." Here ἀγάπησις is used of national amity (Done: "confederation and amity"). In § 270 (p. 73) it is said that a king ought to trust men whose loyalty (εὔνοια) towards him is indisputable, "for this is a mark of ἀγαπήσεως rather than of ill-will and timeserving." For § 265 see note 22. The verb ἀγαπᾶν is used very distinctly in its native sense of valuing in § 123.

[132] "Quod Deus sit Immutabilis," § 14, near the end; ed. Mangey, p. 283; ed. Cohn, v. ii, p. 72: Yonge's translation is used.

mentioned, namely that God is as a man and that God is not as a man, are connected two other principles consequent upon and connected with them, namely that of fear and that of love (φόβον τε καὶ ἀγάπην); for I see that all the exhortations of the laws to piety (εὐσέβειαν) are referred either to the love (τὸ ἀγαπᾶν) or the fear of the living God. To those, therefore, who do not attribute either the parts or the passions of man to the living God, but who, as becomes the majesty of God, honor (τιμῶσι) Him in Himself, and by Himself alone, to love (τὸ ἀγαπᾶν) Him is most natural; but to the others it is most appropriate to fear Him." It would, of course, be possible to say that both Aristeas and Philo got the word from the Septuagint; but it would be very difficult to prove that, and it seems vastly unlikely. Their use of it is highly individual,[133] and their independence in employing it is supported by its appearance in other Greek versions of the Old Testament in passages in which it is not found in the Septuagint.

There is a superficial appearance that ἀγάπη and ἀγάπησις are used by the Septuagint far less freely than ἀγαπᾶν. The verb certainly occurs much more frequently than the substantives — it, about two hundred and sixty-six times; they, together, only thirty times — ἀγάπη twenty times and ἀγάπησις ten. The relatively small number of the occurrences of the substantives is accounted for in part, however, by the comparative infrequency of the noun אַהֲבָה in the Hebrew Old Testament, which the Septuagint translates. That substantive occurs only forty times, in sixteen of which it is rendered by ἀγάπη (which include all the occurrences of ἀγάπη in which it has a Hebrew base), six by ἀγάπησις (all its occurrences with a Hebrew base), and thirteen by some form of the verb ἀγαπᾶν,[134] while it is rendered in only five instances by φιλία (a little more than half of its occurrences with a Hebrew base). That is to say, it is rendered in nearly ninety per cent of its occurrences by some form of the

<hr />

[133] On Philo's independence of the Septuagint in his use of the word, see Deissmann, as cited, p. 199; and Moulton and Milligan, as cited, sub voc.

[134] In Gen. xxix. 20, I Sam. xviii. 3, the clause containing אהבה is omitted in the Septuagint as printed whether by Tischendorf or by Swete; but it is supplied in some MSS.

ἀγαπᾶν group, and in nearly half of these by ἀγάπη itself. The
question remains an open one naturally why the translators re-
sorted so frequently to a paraphrase of the verb to render the
Hebrew substantive, and did not in all instances employ the
substantive ἀγάπη; they paraphrase by the verb (thirteen times)
almost as often as they render by ἀγάπη (sixteen times). The
distribution of the several manners of rendering אהבה through
the Septuagint is also rather odd. The paraphrase by the verb
is fairly evenly distributed through the volume from the Pentateuch to the Prophets and Psalms (none in the Wisdom books).
No substantive for love occurs in the Greek Bible, on the other
hand, until II Samuel; practically none until the Poetical and
Prophetic books.[135] The use of these substantives belongs thus
almost entirely to the latter portion of the Septuagint. And even
there their distribution is somewhat notable. The use of ἀγάπη
centers in the Song of Solomon: it occurs in it no less than eleven
times, more than half of all its occurrences in the Septuagint;
it and its verb (ἀγαπᾶν) are the sole vehicles in this book of the
notion of love. Outside the Song of Solomon, it occurs only
eight times, widely scattered through the volume. 'Αγάπησις is
found in five of its ten occurrences in the Prophets, and in four
of the others in the Poetical books. Φιλία occurs only in two well-
marked groups: in the great Wisdom books, Proverbs, Wisdom,
and Sirach, and in I and II Maccabees. It is well to note this
last fact, because it contributes to the understanding of what
seems, at first sight, a preponderance in the use of φιλία over
ἀγάπη and ἀγάπησις. Φιλία occurs thirty-five times, and ἀγάπη
and ἀγάπησις together but thirty times. More than half of the
occurrences of φιλία, however, fall in I and II Maccabees, where
it is employed exclusively in the highly differentiated sense —
one might even say the technical sense — of political amity.[136]
Only sixteen instances remain (all in the Wisdom literature) for
the expression of love in the ordinary applications of the word.

---

[135] The exceptions to the last statement are ἀγάπη, II Sam. i. 26, xiii. 15, and
ἀγάπησις, II Sam. i. 26.

[136] I Macc. viii. 1, 12, 17; x. 54; xii. 1, 3, 8, 16; xiv. 18, 22; xv. 17; II Macc.
iv. 11; I Macc. xii. 10, with ἀδελφότητα; x. 20, 23, 26 paralleled with συνθήκη.

After all, therefore, the chief vehicle for the idea of love in the Septuagint, even in its substantival expression, is furnished by the terms of the ἀγαπᾶν group. Ἀγάπη, ἀγάπησις together occur thirty times, φιλία sixteen, ἔρως twice (Prov. vii. 18, xxiv. 51 [xxx. 16], and στοργή not at all in the Septuagint proper, but four times in III and IV Maccabees (III Macc. v. 32, IV Macc. xiv. 13, 14, 17).

In range of meaning, ἀγάπη is spread thinly over the whole field; necessarily thinly, because of the infrequency of its occurrence. Its preponderant sense is sexual love. That is secured for it by its eleven occurrences in the Song of Solomon. But outside the Song of Solomon it is used in II Sam. xiii. 15 of the merely lustful love of Amnon for Thamar, as well as in the figurative passage Jer. ii. 2. In II Sam. i. 26, it is used of "the love of women" to which Jonathan's love there spoken of as ἀγάπησις) is compared: "Thy ἀγάπησις to me was wonderful, beyond the ἀγάπη of women" — as if ἀγάπη had some special fitness for the expression of the "love of women." At the opposite extreme are the four passages in the Wisdom books which carry us up to the highest reaches to which human love can ascend. The transition is made by two passages in Ecclesiastes (ix. 1, 6) in which it is used quite generally of love, as a universal human emotion, in contrast with hate: "My heart hath seen how the righteous and the wise and their works are in the hands of God, and there is no man that knoweth whether (it is) love or hate": "But the dead know nothing . . . and their love and their hate and their envy have perished." In Wisdom vi. 18 we have a passage built up in a kind of sorites, which reminds us of the passage in Aristeas: "For the most unerring beginning of wisdom is desire of discipline, and heed to discipline is love, and love is the keeping of her laws, and attention to the laws is the assurance of incorruption, and incorruption bringeth near to God." Here the love of wisdom is the secret of law-keeping and a step on the stairs that lead up to God. The climax is reached, however, in Wisd. iii. 9 and Sir. xlviii. 11, where love to God is spoken of, and its exceeding great reward. In the former passage we read: "They that put their trust in

Him shall understand the truth, and they that are faithful in love" — that is, in love to Him — "shall abide with Him, because there is grace and mercy for His elect." In the latter, the "famous men, even our fathers that begat us," are praised in these great words: "Blessed are they that saw Thee, and they that have fallen asleep in love; for we too shall surely live." [137] The employment of the word in the other Greek versions of the Old Testament is remarkable chiefly for a tendency to invade with it the book of Proverbs, which in the Septuagint is the especial field of φιλία. Aquila and Theodotion both use it in vii. 18 of sexual love; Aquila and Symmachus in x. 12, where it stands in contrast with hate; and all three, Aquila, Symmachus, and Theodotion in xv. 17, where it is praised as the condition of all happiness in life. Besides, it is used by Symmachus, in addition to some passages in the Song of Solomon (Aquila also uses it in one of these), in Psalm xxxii. 5, and Ezekiel xvi. 8. Commenting on this usage, Moulton and Milligan remark that it shows that the word "retained in independent writers the connotations we find in Canticles and Ecclesiastes." [138] The evidence as a whole goes to show that it was in full popular use during the later pre-Christian centuries as a general word for love of all kinds and degrees; and that it was taken over by the Septuagint writers in this general sense, and employed by them indiscriminately to express the idea of love as it fell to their task to speak of it. The effect was, as in the case of ἀγαπᾶν, to add depth to the word, because it was employed to express, among other kinds of love, also that love to God which is characteristic of the Biblical revelation.

It remains somewhat of a puzzle why the Septuagint writers, in no less than thirteen instances of the occurrence of אהבה, preferred to translate it by forms of ἀγαπᾶν; and the occurrence of ἀγάπησις by the side of ἀγάπη in their pages is susceptible of the interpretation that ἀγάπη did not hold the whole field in the popular Greek of the time, but shared it with the

---

[137] In this passage ἀγάπησις is printed by both Tischendorf and Swete; ἀγάπη is read by א.

[138] As cited, sub voc. ἀγάπη, near end.

sister word. The instances in which אַהֲבָה is paraphrased by forms of the verb the more call for remark, because they move in the high places. There is no instance of sexual love among them except [Gen. xxix. 20] where this form of love is at its height; and but three [four] in which love from man to man is spoken of (Ps. cviii. 4, I Sam. xx. 17 *bis*, [xviii. 3]), and in two [three] of these it is the supreme type of human love which is celebrated, the love of David and Jonathan: "And Jonathan swore yet again unto David because he loved (ἠγάπησε) the life of him that loved (ἀγαπῶντος) him." After that, we have an instance in which the love of mercy is expressed by it (Micah vi. 8), and all the others speak of the supernal love of God to man (Deut. vii. 8, I Kings x. 9, II Chron. ii. 11, ix. 8, Isa. lxiii. 9, Hos. iii. 1, ix. 15). Why should the Septuagint writers refuse just these passages to ἀγάπη and paraphrase them? One of the results is that they render אהבה, in no instance in which it expresses either love to God or God's love, by ἀγάπη; the instances in which ἀγάπη is used to express love to God (Wisd. iii. 9, Sir. xlviii. 11) come from that portion of the Septuagint which has no Hebrew base, as does also the instance in which ἀγάπη is used of love to Wisdom. The general concept of love as distinguished from hate (Ecc. ix. 1, 6) is the highest to which ἀγάπη attains when rendering אהבה. The impression made by these facts is increased when we observe that the usage of ἀγάπησις in general also moves on a higher plane than that of ἀγάπη. In only one instance does it allude to sexual love (Jer. ii. 33). In three others it is the love of man to man that is in question — II Sam. i. 26, Ps. cviii. 5, and we add Prov. xxx. 15 (xxiv. 50), where the noun is used adverbially to strengthen the verb: "the horse-leech had three daughters ἀγαπώμεναι ἀγαπήσει, loved with love," i. e., dearly loved. In one instance (Sir. xl. 20) it expresses man's love to Wisdom, and in two (Hab. iii. 4, Sir. xlviii. 11) man's love to God. In three instances (Jer. xxxviii. 3, Hos. xi. 4, Zeph. iii. 17) it expresses the love of God to man. Certainly an appearance is created that ἀγάπη lent itself with less readiness to the expression of the higher than of the lower forms of love. Perhaps just because it was the most popular

word for love in circulation, though it was a perfectly general
term and was used for all forms of love alike, its chief associations were with those forms of love which fell to be most frequently mentioned in everyday speech. It was accordingly predominantly used for those forms of love in the Septuagint, and
owes the exaltation of meaning with which it comes out of its
hands less to its own usage in the Septuagint than to its association with ἀγαπᾶν. There is a sense, then, in which we may
speak — as Moulton and Milligan do — of "its redemption
from use as a mere successor to the archaic ἔρως," although
we should not ourselves make use of just this language. It was
the successor of the classical φιλία, not of ἔρως; ἔρως was scarcely
"archaic," as its continued use in much later Greek shows; and
we think it a mistake to speak of ἔρως as if it were exclusively a
designation of sexual love. Nor can we ascribe quite the rôle
which Moulton and Milligan do to "Alexandrian Jews of the
first century B.C." in the "redemption" of the word. We see this
redemption taking place in Aristeas and Philo, it is true; but
we do not see it in the Jewish translators of the Old Testament
(Aquila, Symmachus, Theodotion). After it leaves the Septuagint we get no full evidence of the usage of the word until we
reach the New Testament. We are chary of concluding from the
single instance of its use, each, in Aristeas and Philo, that it
was they and such as they who wrought the work. All that we
can be sure of is that the redemption of the word was the work
of those who had learned what love is from the Divine revelation. If the word was not "born in the bosom of revealed religion," it was apparently redeemed to its nobler uses under
the influences of that religion.[139]

[139] Naturally the daily use of the word in its lower senses was not inhibited
by its acquisition of its higher senses. It has continued up to the present day.
Witness the lines of Christopoulos: Εἰς βουνὸν ἐγὼ κι' ὁ Ἔρως Κ' ἡ ἀγάπη μου
μαζή . . . ; or those of Zalokostas: Ἀπὸ τὴ μέση μὲ ἅρπαξε, μὲ φίλησε στὸ στόμα
Καὶ μοῦπε· γιὰ ἀναστεναγμούς, Γιὰ τῆς ἀγάπης τοὺς καϋμοὺς Εἶσαι μικρὸς ἀκόμα. When
Clement of Alexandria ("Paed.," III. xi. 257) tells us that love is not to be
estimated by kissing, but by kind deeds (ἀγάπη δὲ οὐκ ἐν φιλήματι, ἀλλ' ἐν
εὐνοίᾳ κρίνεται), that involves the understanding that there was an ἀγάπη which
expressed itself in kissing; and a similar implication lies in Chrysostom's declaration (*Hom. vii. on Romans*) that ἀγάπη does not consist in empty words or mere

Of the other substantives used for love in the Septuagint, φιλία is, of course, the most important. We have already pointed out the odd division of its usage into two well-marked groups. We are concerned now only with the sixteen instances in which it occurs in the great Wisdom books — nine in Proverbs, two in Wisdom, and five in Sirach. Its usage here is a broad· one; but, although it starts at the same low level with ἀγάπη, it does not scale the same heights. It is used occasionally of purely sexual love, even when this appears as mere lust (Prov. v. 19; vii. 18, where it is parallel with ἔρως in the same sense; Sir. ix. 8). It is used once of love, or perhaps we may even say here, of friendship, to God: "For she (Wisdom) is an eternal treasure to men, those who possess which have prepared φιλίαν to God" (Wisd. vii. 14). And it is used once of love to Wisdom herself: "And great good is in φιλία of her" (Wisd. viii. 18). But in the majority of cases it expresses merely that love which binds men together in the friendly intercourse of life: Prov. x. 12, xv. 17, parallel with χάρις, xvii. 9, xix. 7, xxv. 10, parallel with χάρις, xxvii. 5, Sir. vi. 17, xxii. 20, xxv. 1, "harmony of brothers, and φιλία of neighbors, and a wife and husband who agree together," xxvii. 18, "·στέρξον a friend and be faithful with him; but if thou betray his secrets . . . thou hast destroyed the φιλίαν of thy neighbor." These are all natural uses of φιλίαν, quite in accordance with its previous history. The impression is conveyed that it has suffered less from the revolution which had been wrought in the common terms for love than its verb.

Φίλος has apparently suffered not at all. It occurs with extraordinary frequency (about a hundred and eighty-two times), and is used quite along classical lines, chiefly as a noun to designate those who are bound to one another by an affection which does not root in ties of kinship (consult such conjunctions as "friends and neighbors," Ps. xxxvii. 12, lxxxvii. 18, Prov. xiv.

substantives, but in care and works. Even in the horrible story told by Epiphanius ("Adv. Haer.," 1. ii. xxvi, 4; Migne 1. 337c) of the Gnostic orgies, where the man bade the woman, "arise, do τὴν ἀγάπην with your brother," using ἀγάπη, as Sophocles says, κακεμφάτως, — ποιεῖν τὴν ἀγάπην was the standing phrase for celebrating the Ἀγάπη — the current use of ἀγάπη of the sexual act is doubtless implied.

20, xviii. 25; "friends and kindred," Prov. xvii. 9). 'Αγαπητός (twenty-two times) occupies a different field, and can scarcely be said to encroach upon that appropriated to φίλος. It is used chiefly in the singular — often of an only child (Gen. xxii. 2, 12, 16 [Judg. xi. 34], Amos viii. 10, Zech. xii. 10) [140] — to designate one especially loved; and there is already a class which is called God's ἀγαπητοί, beloved ones, so that this phrase is here seen in the making (Ps. lix. 5, cvii. 6, cxxvi. 2). Of course, compounds in φιλ- abound; the Greek language has never lost them, and has never formed corresponding compounds in ἀγαπ- which might supersede them.[141] Of these we are particularly interested in such as φιλάδελφος (II Macc. xv. 14, IV Macc. xiii. 21, xv. 10); φιλαδελφία (IV Macc. xiii. 23, 26, xiv. 1); φιλανθρωπεῖν (II Macc. xiii. 23); φιλάνθρωπος (I Esd. viii. 10, Wisd. i. 6, vii. 23, xii. 19, II Macc. iv. 11, IV Macc. v. 12); φιλανθρώπως (II Macc. ix. 27, III Macc. iii. 20); φιλανθρωπία (II Macc. vi. 22, xiv. 9, III Macc. iii. 15, 18); φιλόστοργος (IV Macc. xv. 13); φιλοστόργως (II Macc. ix. 21); φιλοστοργία (II Macc. vi. 20, IV Macc. xv. 6, 9). By φιλαδελφία and its companions, love to one's people — in this case the Jews — or, in other words, patriotism is expressed. Φιλανθρωπία with its group is used as a general term for kindness, graciousness, such as that shown by superiors to inferiors, especially by monarchs to those having official dealings with them (consult the paralleling of the adverb with ἐπιεικῶς, "fairly," "moderately," in II Macc. ix. 27).[142] The fundamental sense

[140] Cf. Swete on Mk. i. 11: "'Αγαπητός in the LXX answers to יָחִיד (μονογενής unicus, cf. Hort, "Two Dissertations," pp. 49f.) in seven instances out of fifteen." Also Zahn on Mat. iii. 17 (ed. 3, 1910, p. 149, note 68). The usage is classical from Homer down: cf. e. g., W. W. Goodwin, "Demosthenes against Midias," 1906, p. 95; or more fully R. Whiston, "Demosthenes," 1868, 11, p. 324; and Holden, "Xenophon's Cyropaedia, iv. vi. 5; Fritzsche "Aristotle's Eth. Eud.," iii. 6, 1233 and in criticism E. M. Cope, "Aristotle's Rhetoric," 1897, p. 150, esp. note.

[141] An exception like the Homeric ἀγαπήνωρ only proves the rule.

[142] Similarly Aristeas, § 290, ed. Wendland, p. 77, says that Ptolemy's greatness consisted not in the glory of his power and wealth, but in his ἐπιεικία καὶ φιλανθρωπία, "moderation and graciousness." Similarly in § 208, φιλάνθρωπος is "humane," and in § 36, φιλανθρωπότερον is "very graciously." In § 265, p. 71, on the other hand it is said apparently that the most necessary thing for a king to have is the φιλανθρωπία καὶ ἀγάπησις, "good feeling and affection" of his subjects, "for with these will come an indissoluble bond of loyalty(εὐνοίας)."

of φιλοστοργία and its group comes out clearly in IV Macc. xv.
6, 9, 13, where it is used of mother-love; in other passages its
application is extended to any strong affection: "I would with
fitting affection have remembered your kindness" (II Macc. ix.
21); "there are things which it is not lawful to do even *for
natural love* of life" (II Macc. vi. 20). A great elevation of sense
awaited these words in the future as a new religious spirit was
breathed into them. "Be φιλόστοργοι to one another in φιλαδελφία," says Paul (Rom. xii. 10), plumbing the depths of the
feeling of brotherhood. "But when the φιλανθρωπία of our Savior, God, appeared," he writes again (Tit. iii. 4), soaring to the
heights of the divine "humanity." Or we may find our examples
of the heightened sense of the terms, if we prefer, in the φιλαδελφία which Clement of Rome (xlviii. 1) demands that the
Corinthian Christians should more fully manifest; or in the
φιλοστοργία which the writer of the Epistle to Diognetus (i. 1)
asserts to be the cement which binds the Christian brotherhood
together; or in the "great φιλανθρωπία καὶ ἀγάπη" for which
this latter writer celebrates his God (ix. 5).

It is worth while, perhaps, to turn directly from the Septuagint to the Apostolic Fathers, that we may observe how the
great revolution in the usage of the Greek terms for love, of
which we get our first glimpse in the Septuagint, looks, after
its complete adjustment to the high conceptions of divine revelation. The Greek of the Apostolic Fathers is, like the Greek of
the Septuagint, fundamentally the popular Greek of its day;
but, no doubt, it can scarcely be looked upon as simply the
same popular Greek upon which the writers of the Septuagint
draw, at a later stage of its development. The religious language
of the Apostolic Fathers has been profoundly influenced directly
by the usage of the Septuagint itself. From the Septuagint they
derive a large part of their religious inspiration, and upon it
they draw in great part for the vocabulary in which they express their religious conceptions. Still more profoundly the religious language of the Apostolic Fathers has been influenced
by the usage of the New Testament, itself deeply affected by
that of the Septuagint. The fundamental basis of the language

of the Apostolic Fathers nevertheless is the common Greek of
the day; and that, needless to say, is just the common Greek
which the Septuagint uses, at a stage of its development some
three centuries later. To say this, obviously, is to question the
propriety of describing the Greek of the Septuagint as in any
very distinctive sense Judaic or Alexandrian. In the matter of
the linguistic phenomena which are for the moment occupying
our attention — the supersession of φιλεῖν by ἀγαπᾶν as the
general term for loving, the coming of the substantive ἀγάπη
into employment — it happens, no doubt, that they meet us
first in the writings of Alexandrian Jews; and we may be
tempted to conjecture on that ground that they are peculiarities
of the speech of Alexandrian Jews. This conjecture loses its
plausibility, however, when the usages in question are observed
in an even more extreme form in the Apostolic Fathers. The
Apostolic Fathers were not Jews of Alexandria; they fairly ring
the Mediterranean basin in their provenience; and it is incredible that, great as is the influence of the Septuagint upon their
religious terminology, it has given them their fundamental language. Whenever a usage is common to the Septuagint, Philo,
and the Apostolic Fathers, it is safe to say not only that it was
familiar to the Greek-speaking Jews of Alexandria, but also
that it was not alien to the Greek-speaking world at the opening
of the Christian era.[143]

The compositions of the Apostolic Fathers differ very
greatly in general character and subject-matter from the series
of writings which the Septuagint translators rendered into
Greek. If we think of the Apostolic Fathers in their narrowest
compass, as including only the Epistles of Clement, Barnabas,
Ignatius, and Polycarp, they are merely a collection of hortatory letters, devoted to the enforcement of religious and ethical
duty. In such writings we may anticipate relatively more frequent mention of love as a religious and ethical conception on
the one hand, and much less mention of it as a mere fact of daily

[143] See some apposite remarks on the general matter in A. Thumb, "Die
griechische Sprache im Zeitalter des Hellenismus," 1901, pp. 182 f. and 185.
On the affinity of the Greek of Philo and Biblical Greek, cf. H. A. A. Kennedy,
"Sources of New Testament Greek," 1895, p. 67.

occurrence on the other, than was natural in a varied assemblage of historical, poetical, and prophetic writings such as we have in the Septuagint. The addition to these simple letters of the other compositions which it is the custom to class with them under the caption of Apostolic Fathers — the homily commonly called II Clement, the book of Church-order known as the Teaching of the Apostles, the lengthy Apocalypse which goes under the name of the Shepherd of Hermas, the anonymous apology called the Epistle to Diognetus — brings no great change into the linguistic character of the whole. So far as the usage of the terms denoting love is concerned, these books are all of a piece, a fact which gives us confidence in viewing them as mirroring the established usage in the Christian churches of the time.

The chief fact which attracts our attention is a negative one: that φιλεῖν, φιλία have practically no place in these writings. Each occurs but a single time; and both in sufficiently weak senses. Ignatius exhorts Polycarp (ii. 1) thus: "If to good scholars only thou dost feel kindly (φιλῆς), this is not thankworthy in thee; rather bring the pestilent to submission by gentleness." The content of φιλεῖν here lies close to πραΰτης: to love is not much more than being mild and gentle in behavior. Hermas ("Mand.," 10, 1, 4) reprobates being "mixed up in business affairs, and riches, and heathen entanglements (φιλίαις), and the many other concerns of this world." Even φίλος occurs only eight times; and the list of compounds of φιλ- is comparatively small. [144] It looks almost as if φιλεῖν was ready to vanish away. Even ἐρᾶν (Ign. "Pol.," iv. 3, "Rom.," ii. 1, vii. 2), ἔρως ("Rom.," vii. 2), and στέργειν (I Clem. i. 3; Polyc. "Philip.," iv. 2) occur more frequently. Στέργειν is used in its fundamental sense of natural affection—here of the love of wives for their husbands — and in one of the instances of its occurrence is brought into contrast with ἀγαπᾶν as a word of deeper intensity of significance: I Clem. i. 3: "Loving their own husbands as is meet";

[144] φιλαδελφία, φιλανθρωπία, φιλάνθρωπος, φιλαργυρεῶ, φιλαργυρία, φιλάργυρος, φιλοδέσποτος, φιλόζωος, φιλονεικία, φιλόνεικος, φιλοξενία, φιλόξενος, φιλοπονεῖν, φιλόσοφος, φιλοστοργία, φιλότεκνος, φιλοτιμία, φιλόϋλος: eighteen.

Polyc. "ad Philip.," iv. 2: "And, then, let us teach our wives also to walk in the faith that hath been given unto them, and in ἀγάπῃ and ἁγνείᾳ, στεργούσας their own husbands in all truth, and ἀγαπώσας all men equally in all chastity." Ἐρᾶν is in every instance used of "desiring" something or "desiring" to do something — in one case preparing the way for the famous exclamation, which has already been spoken of, "My Ἔρως has been crucified!"

Quite a different state of affairs meets the eye when we look at ἀγαπᾶν and its accompanying noun and verbal adjective. Ἀγαπᾶν occurs about seventy-nine times; ἀγάπη about ninety-four times; and ἀγαπητός about twenty-five times, of which seventeen are in the plural ἀγαπητοί. Ignatius (20, 40, 6) and I Clement (8, 27, 18) are the largest depositories of these terms; but ἀγαπᾶν and ἀγάπη at least are fairly well distributed through the whole series of writers.[145] Too much stress must not be laid upon the fact that no instances of the lower senses of ἀγαπᾶν, ἀγάπη occur; that, for example, in no single case is either term used of sexual love. There was little occasion to speak of sexual love in these writings. But it may be worth noting that it almost seems as if ἀγαπᾶν was felt as a contrast to sexual love. When the twelve virgins require Hermas to pass the night with them, at all events, they emphasize that it is to be as a brother and not as a husband; and they add, "Hereafter we will dwell with thee, for we ἀγαπῶμεν thee exceedingly" (Sim. ix. 11, 3; cf. Vis. i. 1, "I began to ἀγαπᾶν her as a sister"). This could scarcely have been said precisely thus, unless ἀγαπᾶν had been felt in the circles for which Hermas wrote as a word of higher than sexual suggestion. A somewhat similar impression may be made when we read in Polycarp ("Philip.," iv. 2) an exhortation to wives to walk in the faith that has been given them, στεργούσας their own husbands in all truth, and ἀγαπούσας all men equally in all chastity." The words could not easily change places, and ἀγαπᾶν appears to be contrasted with even the purest sexual

---

[145] Ἀγαπητός is found only in I Clement (18 times), Ignatius (6), and the Martyrium of Polycarp, Hermas, and the Didache (each once). Ἀγαπητοί is almost a *peculium* of I Clement (15 times to Ignatius' 2).

love. Saying this, however, is in any event saying too little for
these special writings. The usage of ἀγαπᾶν and ἀγάπη alike in
them is at the top of their applications. They are here very distinctly words of ethical and spiritual import. This too, no doubt,
finds its account less in the implications of the words themselves than in the subjects dealt with in these writings. But it
has this not unimportant significance with respect to the words
themselves, that, when these high ethical and spiritual aspects
of love were dealt with, it was, among the words for love, ἀγαπᾶν
and ἀγάπη which suggested themselves to express them; and
that with such inevitableness that only these terms were employed for the purpose. No doubt we must keep in consideration that ἀγαπᾶν and ἀγάπη were very distinctly the common
words for love and may have been the first terms to suggest
themselves for the expression of any kind of love. There were,
however, other terms still in use, and they would have been
employed had there been any unnaturalness in using ἀγαπᾶν,
ἀγάπη in these high senses.

There is an occasional use of ἀγαπᾶν with the infinitive, to
express what one "loves" or would "love" to do (e. g., Ign.
"Trall.," iv. 2: "I *desire* to suffer"). But what is almost uniformly
expressed by it is the love of the Christian proclamation in its
three great exemplifications of the love of God or of Christ to
man, the love of God's people to Him or to Christ, and the love
of the Christian brethren to one another. Polycarp accordingly
tells (iii. 3) the Philippians that Paul's letter to them had the
power to build them up into the faith given to them, "which is
the mother of us all, while hope followeth after, and love goeth
before — love," he proceeds to explain, "towards God and
Christ and towards our neighbor." Christians are "the children
of love," as Barnabas phrases it; or as Polycarp calls Ignatius
and his companions ("Philip.," i. *init.*) "the followers of the True
Love," that is to say, of Christ, here called by the great title of
Ἡ Ἀληθῆς Ἀγάπη; and if they are to be imitators of Him who so
loved us ("Diog.," x. 3), they must love," love in Christ," "love
according to Jesus Christ." "Faith is the beginning, and love
the end of life" (Ign. "Eph.," xiv. 1); "faith and love are all in all

and nothing is preferred before them" (Ign. "Smyr.," vi. 1). As a typical passage, exhibiting the lofty sense which these terms had acquired in the familiar speech of these Christians, we may take perhaps the encomium on love which Clement pens to the Corinthians, inciting them to practice it in their own lives. It is full, it is true, of echoes of Paul's great hymn to love in the thirteenth chapter of his own First Letter to the Corinthians; but it is not less representative of the speech of the Apostolic Fathers on that account. "Let him that hath love in Christ," we read (c. 49), "fulfil the commandments of Christ. Who can declare the bond of the love of God? Who is sufficient to tell the majesty of its beauty? The height whereunto love exalteth is unspeakable. Love joineth us with God; love endureth all things, is longsuffering in all things. There is nothing vulgar, nothing arrogant in love. Love hath no divisions, love maketh no seditions, love doeth all things in concord. In love were all God's elect made perfect; without love nothing is well-pleasing to God; in love the Master took us unto Himself; for the love which He had towards us, Jesus Christ our Lord hath given His blood for us by the will of God, and His flesh for our flesh, and His life for our lives. Ye see, dearly beloved, how great and marvelous a thing is love, and there is no declaring its perfection. Who is sufficient to be found therein save those to whom God shall vouchsafe it?" It is this kind of love which, in the Apostolic Fathers, ἀγαπᾶν and ἀγάπη are practically exclusively used to express. "Oh the exceeding great φιλανθρωπία καὶ ἀγάπη of God" ("Diog.," ix. 2): "How wilt thou ἀγαπήσας Him that so προαγαπήσαντα thee!" (x. 2–3): "Now He that raised Him from the dead will raise us also if ἀγαπῶμεν the things that He ἠγάπησεν" (Polyc. "Philip.," ii. 2). This is the circle through which the idea of love runs in them.

It ought perhaps to be mentioned before we leave the subject that in Ign. "Smyrn.," viii. 2 we have an instance of a usage of ἀγάπη created by Christianity and vocal with the significance which love had for Christianity. "It is not lawful," we read, "apart from the bishop either to baptize or ἀγάπην ποιεῖν" — that is to say, as the parallel with baptizing suggests, "celebrate

the Lord's Supper." [146] The Lord's Supper was the feast of love.
"I wish the bread of God," says Ignatius in another place
("Rom.," vii. 3), "which is the flesh of Christ, who was the seed
of David; and I wish for a draught of His blood, which is love
(ἀγάπη) incorruptible." And in yet another place ("Trall.," viii.
1): "Do ye, then, arm yourselves with gentleness and recover
yourselves in faith, which is the flesh of the Lord, and in love
(ἀγάπη) which is the blood of Jesus Christ." An extension of the
usage of ἀγάπη like this is vocal with the place which the conception and the word had taken in the Christian community.

The New Testament stands between the Septuagint and
the Apostolic Fathers, receiving from the one, giving to the
other, sharing the particular type of Greek common to both.
In this type of Greek, ἀγαπᾶν, ἀγάπη had become the general
terms for the expression of love; and the Greek of the New
Testament participates fully in this usage. 'Αγαπᾶν occurs
about a hundred and forty-one times in the New Testament,
ἀγάπη about a hundred and eighteen times, and ἀγαπητός about
sixty-one times, while φιλεῖν (excluding three instances in which
it means "to kiss": Mat. xxvi. 48, Mk. xiv. 44, Lk. xxii. 47) occurs only about twenty-two times, φιλία but once, and even
φίλος only about twenty-nine times. 'Ερᾶν, ἔρως, and στέργειν,
στοργή do not occur at all. It is perhaps worth while also to
observe the distribution of the several terms through the New
Testament. The book of Acts contains no one of them except
φίλος (x. 24, xix. 31, xxvii. 3) and ἀγαπητός (xv. 25).[147] Hebrews
has ἀγαπᾶν and ἀγάπη each twice; James ἀγαπᾶν three times
and φιλία once — the only occurrence of φιλία in the New Testament; I Peter ἀγαπᾶν four times and ἀγάπη three times; II
Peter ἀγαπᾶν twice and ἀγάπη twice; Jude ἀγαπᾶν once and
ἀγάπη three times. Φιλεῖν does not occur in Hebrews or any of
the Catholic Epistles; φιλία only in James. In the Synoptic
Gospels ἀγαπᾶν occurs twenty-three times (8, 6, 9), φιλεῖν
five times (4, 0, 1); ἀγάπη only twice (once each in Matthew

---

[146] See Jude 12 and II Peter ii. 13, and compare Lightfoot's note on the
passage.
[147] It contains besides only φιλανθρώπως, xxvii. 3.

and Luke). The great depository of ἀγαπᾶν is John: it occurs thirty-seven times in the Gospel, twenty-eight times in the First Epistle, and twice and once in II and III John respectively — making sixty-eight times in all, to which may be added four times in Revelation. Next to John comes Paul, with thirty-three occurrences, distributed through all the epistles except Philippians, Philemon, II Timothy, and Titus. Ephesians is the most copiously supplied of the Epistles (ten times), and Romans next (seven times). With ἀγάπη the tables are turned. It is predominately a Pauline term, being found in every epistle without exception (I Cor. fourteen, II Cor. ten, Eph. ten, showing the highest figures), and totaling seventy-eight occurrences. Over against this copious use by Paul, it is found in John only twenty-eight times (Gospel seven times, I John eighteen, II John two, III John one, to which Rev. adds two). Ἀγαπητός also is a Pauline term, its sixty-one occurrences being distributed thus: Synoptic Gospels nine times, Acts once, Paul twenty times, Hebrews once, James three times, Peter eight times, Jude three times, John's Epistles ten times. It is particularly in the Gospels that φιλεῖν is used: in John thirteen times, and in the Synoptics five (4, 0, 1). In all of Paul's epistles it occurs but twice, twice also in Revelation, and nowhere else in the New Testament. We may perhaps generalize by saying that ἀγαπᾶν is distributed fairly evenly through the New Testament with some accumulation in the Gospel and First Epistle of John; that ἀγάπη is predominantly a Pauline word with a secondary depository in I John; and that φιλεῖν belongs particularly to the Gospel of John and after that to the Synoptics.

The highly preponderating use of ἀγαπᾶν, ἀγάπη in the New Testament is not due primarily to the deliberate selection of these terms by the writers of the New Testament as the fittest to express the high idea of love to which they had to give expression, though they were the fittest of Greek words to express this high idea and had moreover been prepared to express it by their usage in the Septuagint.[148] It is due primarily to the cur-

---

[148] E. F. Gelpke, "Theolog. Studien und Kritiken," 1849, pp. 646 f., gives the following account of these words as they came to the hands of the writers of

rency of these terms in the Greek native to the New Testament writers as the general terms for love — for love at its highest, no doubt, but also for love at its lowest. There can be little doubt that, had the New Testament writers had occasion to speak at large of sexual love — to write, for example, a series of narratives like those of Genesis xxiv. and Judges xvi. and I Samuel xiii. — they would have employed ἀγαπᾶν and ἀγάπη in them just as the writers of the Septuagint have done. Ballantine is so far quite right, when, criticizing Trench's suggestion that the explanation of the absence of ἔρως, ἐρᾶν, ἐραστής from the New Testament is, no doubt, in part "that these words" by the corrupt use of the world "had become so steeped in earthly sensuous passion," carried such an atmosphere of this about with them, "that the truth of God abstained from the defiling contact with them," he declares [149] that "This family of words was not used for Christian love for the very same reason that ἐπιθυμέω and its family were not used, namely, because they were not the general words in Hellenistic Greek for *love*." When he proceeds to say that "they were not used in their own

the New Testament. "The older profane writers know only the verb and adjective, not, however, the noun, precisely in which it was that the Christian writers found the abstract expression, recurring on every page, of the sentiment which bound all believers together. The verb, moreover, is found already with profane writers in the purer sense of reverential love, although it was later interchanged also, when conceived sensuously, with φιλεῖν, *amare*, the expression for personal affection. This usage is not only recognized in the LXX, where the word, it must be confessed, is used even more sensuously, and nevertheless also of the more sacred affection (Gen. xxii. 2); and again in the New Testament; but also it receives, first in this connection, its full content, as this follows of itself from the most Christian of all Christian declarations, I John iv. 8, ὁ θεὸς ἀγάπη ἐστίν (the abstract term is used, with the sense that God is the personal Love, presenting Himself personally), and from the religion of the spirit freed from all particularism and all sensuous elements. The word acquired, however, an entirely new, peculiarly Christian, sense, still further in the new demonstration of love conditioned by the deepened sentiment of love. Accordingly the word is used (1) of the love of God for Jesus and of Jesus for God, and of the love of both for men, and then again of the love of men for God and Christ, derived from the love of God and Christ, and of the love of men for one another inseparable from this as its vital basis; and then (2) of the actual, powerfully arising manifestation of love, the loving conduct in word and deed, I John iii. 1, cf. James iv, 8."

[149] "Bibliotheca Sacra," July 1889, p. 533.

proper senses simply because there was no occasion to refer to those ideas by *any* words," he is right in the main affirmation, but wrong, as we have seen, in seeming to assign sexual love to ἐρᾶν, ἔρως as their "proper sense." The simple truth is that the New Testament writers use ἀγαπᾶν, ἀγάπη to express the idea of love because it was the word for love current in their circle and lying thus directly in their way. They do not use ἐρᾶν, ἔρως, στέργειν, στοργή because they had no such occasion, in speaking of love, to throw up into emphasis the peculiar implications of these words — of passion or of nature — as to demand their employment. So far as such occasion arose, they had no difficulty with the words (Rev. xii. 10, φιλόστοργος; Rom. i. 31, II Tim. iii. 3, ἄστοργος). They do not push φιλεῖν into the background; they found it in the background, — from which they do not draw it, not because they looked upon it as a base word, but because it had become too inexpressive a word to meet their needs, especially since the Septuagint had communicated to the ordinarily current word for love additional shades of suggestion which enlarged its range of application precisely on the side on which the New Testament writers desired to speak of love. When φιλεῖν served their purpose better than ἀγαπᾶν, they used φιλεῖν; but this use could not escape being exceptional just because ἀγαπᾶν had become the general word for love, and the Septuagint had prepared it for New Testament use by filling it with the content which the New Testament writers most needed to express.

In the actual use which the New Testament writers make of φιλεῖν it is made evident that its distinctive suggestions have not faded out of sight; it is because of these distinctive suggestions that the New Testament writers occasionally make use of it — as it was doubtless because of them that it maintained its shrunken, if we cannot yet say its precarious, existence in the current speech of the day. It is meaningless for Gildersleeve to say that "The larger use of ἀγαπᾶν in Christian writers is perhaps due to the avoidance of φιλεῖν in the sense of 'kissing,'" although Moulton and Milligan think it worth while to quote the remark. And we can hardly account for Woolsey's suggestion that "The increased use of ἀγάπη and its family in the Septuagint and in the Christian Scriptures is probably to be accounted for by the frequent use of φιλεῖν and its derivatives in denoting sensual love, and in covering up foul acts under the veil of words so common and important." 'Αγαπᾶν had itself been current from its earliest recorded usage in senses as external as "kissing"; and in the Septuagint itself it is employed in senses quite as foul as any for which φιλεῖν was ever used. Ballantine's remark is again quite apposite: "If husbands are commanded to ἀγαπᾶν their wives because the other verb would have suggested sensual passion, it is unaccountable that wives should be commanded to be φίλανδροι (Tit. ii. 4). If men are not commanded to φιλεῖν God, as being inappropriate, it is strange that they are condemned for not being φιλόθεοι (II Tim. iii. 4)." The plain fact is that φιλεῖν had come to be comparatively little used because, ἀγαπᾶν having superseded it as the general term for love in common use, there was very little need for it. It had shrunken from the general term for love to the designation of a particular aspect of love, and was called for only when this particular aspect of love required emphasizing.

It is only right, then, that we should look, in each instance of its employment, for the reason why φιλεῖν is preferred instead of the prevailing ἀγαπᾶν. That such a reason exists it is natural to assume. It is not easy to believe that a body of writers have deserted their habitual usage in a few instances without some reason for it. This reason may, no doubt, be found in merely grammatical or purely rhetorical considerations, or in personal habits of speech belonging to individual writers; but it may also be rooted in the underlying implications of the words themselves by which a rarer form is given the advantage in special circumstances. It may not be easy to trace it; but pure caprice is not to be lightly assumed; and ordinarily some special fitness in the language actually employed may at least be suggested, if not actually shown. We may take the usage of Paul as an example. It is sheerly incredible that he should desert his copious use of ἀγαπᾶν (ἀγάπη) in just two instances in favor of φιλεῖν without some reason for it. We may perhaps see that reason in the more pointed suggestion of personal predilection which φιλεῖν conveys. This appears fairly clear in the case of I Cor. xvi. 22, when we observe that οὐ φιλεῖ there, in accordance with a frequent usage of οὐ in conditional clauses, coalesce in a sharply positive notion, so that we are to read, not "If anyone falls short of really loving the Lord," but, "If anyone not-loves the Lord" — that is to say, "hates Him." Φιλεῖν rather than ἀγαπᾶν is the proper word to use, remarks T. C. Edwards, because it expresses a natural affection, in this negative statement a personal antipathy. Paul "is thinking of a deep-seated antipathy, a malignant hatred of Jesus Christ": "If anyone turns away from Jesus Christ with antipathy." It is not of failure to love Jesus Christ supremely of which Paul is speaking; it is of failure to love Him at all. It is more difficult to see our way in Tit. iii. 15, "Salute them that love us in faith"; but the same general influences may not improperly be assumed to have determined the language here too. As Huther remarks, φιλεῖν may here mark "the inner personal relation." In other words, Paul is sending greetings to certain personal friends in the Christian body. The addition of ἐν πίστει is not fatal to this assumption. It may mean no more than that these friends of Paul's were also fellow-Christians (cf. for the order of the words, Eph. vi. 1).

When we turn to the larger body of instances which confront us in the Synoptic Gospels, we find ourselves in the same atmosphere. Only in a single passage has φιλεῖν a personal object, Mat. x. 37: "He that loveth father or mother more than me is not worthy of me; and he that loveth son or daughter more than me is not worthy of me." Th. Zahn's comment seems to meet the case: "Jesus declares him unworthy of Him, who, in the case of the decision under consideration, permits love to parents and children to obtain the upper hand of love to Jesus (cf. viii. 21 ff.). Through the contrast with kindred, to whom we are bound by natural love, already prepared for in verse 25 (οἰκιακοί, as verse 36), it is brought about that Jesus here represents the right relation to His person by φιλεῖν, not by ἀγαπᾶν (v. 43–46, vi. 24), because only φιλεῖν clearly expresses the hearty affection (*Zuneigung*) which roots in affinity — whether bodily or elective." That is to say the love of Jesus' people for Him is expressed here by φιλεῖν because thus it is brought expressly into comparison with the love of affinity: this spiritual affinity is to take precedence of all other. What He is saying is, not that His people must give their supreme love to Him rather than others, but that they must manifest in their conduct that their fundamental inclination, "drawing," is to Him above others; He must be supremely attractive to them.

In the other Synoptic instances φιλεῖν is followed by the accusative of the thing (Mt. xxiii. 6, Lk. xx. 46), or in one case (Mt. vi. 5) construed in the same sense with the infinitive — the only passage in the New Testament in which either φιλεῖν or ἀγαπᾶν is construed with the infinitive. From the point of view of the classical usage, φιλεῖν is properly used in these passages; and it bears its ordinary classical sense in them [150] — which is not quite the sense that αγάπᾶν bears in similar constructions. In its best classical usage, ἀγαπᾶν with the accusative of the thing means not so much to like a thing, to be pleased with it, as to content oneself with it; with the infinitive not so much to be wont to do a thing, as to put up with it. Meyer is perfectly right, then, when he finds φιλεῖν the proper word at Mt. vi. 5, and comments: "*They have pleasure in it*, they *love* to do it — a usage frequently met with in the classical writers." We must note, however, that ἀγαπᾶν with the infinitive had already acquired this sense in the Septuagint (e. g., Ps. xxxiii. 13, Prov. xx. 16, Jer. v. 31, xiv. 10), and is repeatedly used in the New Testament with the accusative of the thing in the sense of liking, taking pleasure in,[151] not of contenting ourselves with, putting up with; and indeed we have merely to turn to Lk. xi.

---

[150] Schmidt remarks (p. 479): "Even when applied to things, φιλεῖν retains its ordinary meaning and designates therefore the satisfaction in things which are pleasing (φιλία) to us, the possession of which, or contact with which, is pleasant to us. Even evil or contemptible things are included, Aristotle, "Eth. Nic.," 8.2.1: 'For it appears that not everything is loved, but τὸ φιλητόν, and this is the good, or the pleasant, or the useful.'"

[151] Lk. xi. 43, Jno. iii. 19, xii. 43, II Thess. ii. 16, I Pet. iii. 10, II Pet. ii. 15, I Jno. ii. 15, Rev. xii. 11, 15.

43 to find ἀγαπᾶν instead of φιλεῖν in a passage which seems the exact parallel of Mt. xxiii. 6, although φιλεῖν is used at Lk. xx. 46. We are in the presence, here, apparently of an unsettled usage. It seems still to be more natural to use φιλεῖν in the sense of liking things, or of liking to do things; but ἀγαπᾶν is fast encroaching upon it in this usage also.

So long as φιλεῖν remained in use at all in this sense, one would think it would be inevitable in such a passage as Rev. xxii. 15: "Without are the dogs, and the sorcerers, and the fornicators, and the murderers, and the idolaters, and everyone that loveth and doeth a lie." It is a personal affinity with the false, inward kinship with it, leading to its outward practice, which is intimated; [152] and this is even more emphatically asserted if the other order of the words be adopted, and the progress of thought be from the mere doing of a lie to personal identification with it. The use of φιλεῖν in Rev. iii. 19 is probably determined by the contrast between the treatment described and the sentiment asserted. What our Lord is saying is that reproof and chastening from Him are proof, not of hatred but of love; and it was natural to employ in this assertion the most personal and therefore in such a connexion the most emotional term for love. The emphasis on the pronoun should not be neglected: "As for me, whomsoever *I* love, I reprove and chasten." The most intimate relations are suggested, and the most intimate feelings are naturally put forward: it is the love of a parent disciplining his child for its good which is pictured. And the use of φιλεῖν is all the more striking, that in the underlying passage, Prov. iii. 12, "For whom the Lord loves, He rebukes," ἀγαπᾶν is the word employed. There is an advance made even on this affecting passage of Proverbs in tenderness of expression.[153]

It is especially in the Gospel of John that φιλεῖν occurs

[152] Cf. Swete *in loc.*: "ὁ φιλῶν goes deeper than ὁ ποιῶν; he who loves falsehood is in his nature akin to it, and has through his love of it proved his affinity to Satan, who is ὁ πατὴρ αὐτοῦ (Jno. viii. 44)."

[153] Cf. Swete *in loc.*: φιλῶ (Bengel: Philadelphiensem ἠγάπησεν, Laodicensem φιλεῖ) is perhaps deliberately preferred to the less emotional and less human ἀγαπῶ (i. 5, iii. 9) notwithstanding the use of the latter in Prov. iii. 12 (LXX. ὃν γὰρ ἀγαπᾷ Κύριος ἐλέγχει), which supplies the groundwork of the thought."

(thirteen times), as indeed does ἀγαπᾶν also (thirty-seven times).[154] In about one out of every four instances of the occurrence of a verb for love in this Gospel, φιλεῖν is employed; the proportion is even greater for Revelation, no doubt (one out of three), and not very much less in the Synoptic Gospels, but the absolute number of occurrences in these cases is not large enough to be impressive. In all of its occurrences in John's Gospel, moreover, except one (xii. 25), φιλεῖν has a personal object. The single instance in which it is construed with the accusative of a thing (xii. 25) is altogether similar to the instances of like construction in the Synoptic Gospels and Revelation. Loving is brought in it into sharp contrast with hating: "He who loves his life shall lose it, and he who hates his life in this world shall preserve it unto eternal life." It is a proverbial saying of universal application, adduced here in support of the solemn declaration of the preceding verse that fruit-bearing comes through sacrifice. The loving of life spoken of, then, is such pleasure in it, such a fixing of the heart upon it and doting on it, that nothing else comes into consideration in comparison with it. Pure joy in living, says our Lord in effect, is a short-sighted policy, because there lies something beyond this living which is absorbing our attention. Undoubtedly φιλεῖν is the appropriate word to express this idea, and has a pungency when employed to express it which the more customary ἀγαπᾶν would lack.

In one of the instances in John in which the object is personal, the subject is "the world"; and those whom the world is said to love are described as "its own" (xv. 19): "If the world

---

[154] A fresh study of ἀγαπᾶν and φιλεῖν, especially in John, by Sally Neil Roach taking its point of departure from G. B. Stevens, "Johannine Theology," Ch. xi.; is printed in *The Review and Expositor*, 1913, x. pp. 531 ff. Her discrimination of terms is as follows (p. 533): "'Αγαπᾶν (and the same is true of the noun, ἀγάπη) carries with it *invariably* the idea of the rights or the good of the object, sought at the cost of the subject, while φιλεῖν as uniformly suggests the pleasure of the subject as associated with and derived from the object." She speaks of this as looking upon ἀγαπᾶν as the altruistic, and φιλεῖν as the egoistic term for love. Perhaps the same general idea might be better expressed by distinguishing the two as the love of benevolence and the love of complacency; and perhaps better still as the love of regard and the love of delight. All the Johannine passages in which φιλεῖν occurs are examined with a view to validating the suggested distinction.

hateth you, ye know that it hath hated me first: if ye were of the world, the world would love its own; but because ye are not of the world, but I have chosen you out of the world, therefore the world hateth you." The appropriateness of φιλεῖν here is striking: it is very especially adapted to express the love of inner affinity — the love that grows out of the perception of something in the object especially attractive to the subject; and inner affinity is precisely what is emphasized here. Had ἀγαπᾶν been used, the simple fact of the love would be stated, and the fitness, inevitableness, of the love and hatred spoken of would have remained unexpressed.[155]

In two other instances what is spoken of is the love of the man Jesus for a friend (xi. 3, 36, cf. xi. 11): "Behold, he whom Thou lovest is sick"; "Behold, how He loved him!" Here, too, the use of φιλεῖν is so obviously appropriate as to seem inevitable; the love of friendship might almost seem to be the special field of φιλεῖν. Ἀγαπᾶν of course, could have been employed in its stead. It is actually used in xi. 5, where the Evangelist states the simple objective fact, for the purpose of his narrative: "Now Jesus ἠγάπα Martha, and her sister, and Lazarus"; that is to say, Jesus felt sincere regard for them. Φιλεῖν is used when the words are taken off of the lips of the anxious sisters in their petition for aid, and of the Jews when they observed Jesus' tears. It emphasizes the personal intimacy of the affection, such personal intimacy as justified the appeal to Him for prompt aid, and His tears at the grave.[156] It is Jesus' human heart which is here unveiled to us.

Quite close to these instances lies the employment of φιλεῖν in xx. 2 to express the affection of Jesus for John and Peter. Mary Magdalene, we are told, when she saw the stone removed from the grave on the Resurrection morn, "runneth and cometh to Simon Peter and the other disciple whom Jesus loved

---

[155] Cf. Karl Horn, "Abfassung, Geschichtlichkeit und Zweck vom Evang. des Johannes, Kap. 21," 1904, p. 170: "In xv. 19, it is said very significantly: 'If ye were of the world, ὁ κόσμος would love its own'; therefore natural inclination (Zuneigung) to that which is of kindred nature and has sprung from the same root is what is expressed."

[156] This is excellently shown by Horn, as above.

($\dot{\epsilon}\phi i\lambda\epsilon\iota$)" — where it seems most natural to understand both disciples to be described as loved by Jesus.[157] "The disciple whom Jesus $\dot{\eta}\gamma\dot{\alpha}\pi\alpha$" is the standing description of John in the latter part of the Gospel (xiii. 23, xix. 26, xxi. 7, 20); and obviously $\dot{\eta}\gamma\dot{\alpha}\pi\alpha$ is used in this description of intimate personal affection, and not of what we may speak of as the official love of Jesus for His disciples or of the saving love of the Redeemer for His children. Woolsey does not go too far, when, having regard to the imperfect tense, he remarks: [158] "It was an intimacy between the Master and the disciple of no short acquaintance. . . . He loved him with a continuous love." It has disturbed the commentators, therefore, that in the one instance of xx. 2, $\dot{\epsilon}\phi i\lambda\epsilon\iota$ has displaced the $\dot{\eta}\gamma\dot{\alpha}\pi\alpha$. One has been tempted to say it is because Peter is included with John in this one instance, to which it has been added that Peter was now under a cloud. Another has gone a step further and suggested that it is because "the beloved disciple himself had temporarily fallen into unbelief and was for the moment not worthy of the higher love" expressed by $\dot{\alpha}\gamma\alpha\pi\hat{\alpha}\nu$.[159] These suggestions take for granted that $\dot{\alpha}\gamma\alpha\pi\hat{\alpha}\nu$, even in such a connexion, conveys a "higher" sense than $\phi\iota\lambda\epsilon\hat{\iota}\nu$. Such an assumption underlies Woolsey's description of Jesus' love for John, as expressed in the $\dot{\eta}\gamma\dot{\alpha}\pi\alpha$, not only in such terms as this: "He discerned in His disciple lovely traits. . . . His love for John was a tried, strong, personal love, such as the man Jesus could feel for some souls with especial endowments which few possessed"; but also in such as these: "And it was a religious love which no one could so correctly feel as He who had an intuitive knowledge of hearts. . . . It was an earthly love of a heavenly soul." [160] $\Phi\iota\lambda\epsilon\hat{\iota}\nu$, it is suggested, might be used to denote such love as this, but it could not express it; $\dot{\alpha}\gamma\alpha\pi\hat{\alpha}\nu$ alone could express it, and would be the only natural word to employ in order to express it. This seems to leave the question, Why, then, is $\dot{\eta}\gamma\dot{\alpha}\pi\alpha$ replaced by $\dot{\epsilon}\phi i\lambda\epsilon\iota$ in

[157] So Westcott *in loc.*: cf. what Woolsey says, *Andover Review*, August 1885, p. 166.
[158] As cited, p. 167.
[159] E. A. Abbott, "Johannine Vocabulary," p. 241, bottom (1728 p.).
[160] As cited, p. 167.

John xx. 2, more clamorous than ever. Woolsey's own explanation [161] is not very clear, and indeed does not profess to be. "It
is in this place," he says, "not altogether plain why ἐφίλει is
used instead of ἠγάπα. Meyer, in his remark on the passage, says
that ἐφίλει expresses the remembrance of Christ with a more
tender sensibility,[162] to which B. Weiss seems to assent. Westcott [163] in like manner thinks that a personal affection is more
strikingly shown than it would be by ἠγάπα. The Vulgate translates as elsewhere by *amabat*. All these explanations concur in
something like this: That Jesus was conceived of under the
power of a new affection." The meaning of this appears to be
that in the interval between the death of our Lord and their assurance that He had entered upon His heavenly dominion, the
disciples dropped into both thinking and speaking of Him from
the point of view of His humanity. This involves the assumptions that ἐφίλει is here employed from Mary Magdalene's
standpoint, or at least from the standpoint of the incident described, not from that of the Evangelist, writing after the
recovery of faith; and that ἠγάπα was a word of such high significance that it would be inappropriate to use it of a simple man's
affection for his friends. We transcribe, however, Woolsey's own
exposition of his not very clear meaning: "It was natural that,
when the Lord showed Himself again to His disciples, they
could not but feel a want of nearness and familiarity which
helped them in their earthly intercourse with Him. Until their
faith grew, and they believed more joyfully in their divine
Master, the human sight and presence were supports which
sustained them while away from Him. But ἀγαπῶ returns in
xxi. 15 and 20, as to the divine Saviour, as soon as the presence
of Jesus began to be apprehended again by the help of sight.

[161] P. 177.

[162] Meyer, E. T., ii, p. 367, says: "With ἐφίλει the recollection speaks with
more feeling." What he means is apparently that John, recording the events in
his Gospel, was at this point suffused with deeper feeling than he ordinarily felt
as the recollection rushed over him of the personal affection which Jesus showed
toward him "in the days of His flesh"; and this expressed itself in ἐφίλει.

[163] Westcott's actual phraseology is that ἐφίλει here "marks a personal affection."

Faith grew stronger, and the loss of Jesus' presence was an enlargement of the sway of the nobler principle, and was no more felt to be an absence."

Perhaps the difficulty we feel in accounting for ἐφίλει at John xx. 2 arises in large part from approaching the question from only one side. We begin with the ἠγάπα of xiii. 23, xix. 26, xxi. 7, 20, and ask why the alteration to ἐφίλει in xx. 2. Let us reverse the question, and ask why ἠγάπα is used in xiii. 23 and its companions. In itself considered, ἐφίλει is altogether in place in xx. 2; this is the proper word to express the love of friendship, however warm. What really needs accounting for is why in the parallel passages ἠγάπα is used instead. It is customary to think at once of the high connotations of ἀγαπᾶν, and to develop, as Woolsey does, the aspects of nobility which may be discovered in Jesus' love for John. It may be easier to say simply that, in the type of Greek employed in the New Testament, ἀγαπᾶν was the current word for love, and was consequently in place whenever love of any kind was spoken of; and that the only thing that is illustrated by the appearance of ἐφίλει in xx. 2 is the emergence on one occasion of the more exact term for the particular variety of love that is here in question. 'Εφίλει might have stood in xiii. 23 and its companions, and ἠγάπα might have stood in xx. 2; in the former case the more specific word would have been used in all the instances, in the latter the more general. We learn from the actual distribution of the usage nothing of the specific meaning of ἀγαπᾶν; but we do learn something of the specific meaning of φιλεῖν. If we demand that a reason shall be rendered for the replacing of the general by the specific term just at xx. 2 and nowhere else, we do not know that a satisfactory answer can be given. We can only say that such an explanation as Meyer's is not without plausibility — that the circumstances he was in the act of narrating flooded John's mind as he wrote with an especially tender reminiscence of his Master's human love for His disciples.

From a passage like John xxi. 15–17 we learn something of the specific meaning of both words. The two words appear here side by side in contrast with one another, with the inevitable result that what is distinctive of each is thrown into relief. That anyone should doubt that the words are used here in distinctive senses would seem incredible prior to experience. The list of those who have expressed such doubt, however, is neither short nor undistinguished, running as it does from Grotius to Gildersleeve.[164] It is, however, as Moulton and Milligan remark,[165] "in so severely simple a writer as John it is extremely hard to reconcile ourselves to a meaningless use of synonyms, where the point would seem to lie in the identity of the word employed." In point of fact, our Lord does not put to Peter three times over the same question. Altering the question progressively, He drives the probe into Peter's conscience deeper and deeper. On the first occasion Jesus asks him: "Simon, son of John, dost thou ἀγαπᾷς me more than these?" — have you a deeper devotion [166] to me than the rest of my disciples? In his answer, spoken in deep humility, the repentant Peter avoids all comparison with his fellows, and merely asseverates his personal love for his master: "Assuredly, Lord; thou knowest that I φιλῶ Thee." In His second question, Jesus accordingly omits the comparison, and asks of Peter only whether he himself has the requisite devotion to His person: "He saith to him again, a second time, Simon, son of John, ἀγαπᾷς me?" Again Peter responds in the same humble spirit as before, waiving the question of proper devotion, and asseverating only his personal affection: "Assuredly Lord; Thou knowest that I φιλῶ Thee." Then, the third time, Jesus pushes the probe to the bottom and demands of Peter with sharp directness and brevity whether he has any real affection for Him: "He saith to him the

---

[164] "Justin Martyr," 1877, p. 135. Among later writers of the same mind, cf. W. G. Ballantine, "Bibliotheca Sacra," July 1889, pp. 524 ff.; John A. Cross, *The Expositor*, 1893, iv, vii, pp. 312 ff.; Max Eberhardt, "Ev. Joh. c. 21: ein exegetischer Versuch," 1897, p. 52; cf. also G. B. Stevens, "The Johannine Theology," ch. xi.

[165] As cited, p. 2.

[166] Roach, as cited, p. 544, on her principle, paraphrases ἀγαπᾶν here, not inaptly: "Do you love Me so that you can surrender your life to My interests?"; and φιλεῖν, in Peter's response: "Yes, Lord, Thou knowest that my heart goes out to Thee and my pleasure is found in Thee." This is, clearly, what was really meant by the terms — however we arrive at it.

third time, Simon, son of John, dost thou φιλεῖς me?" "And Peter was grieved because He said to him this third time, Dost thou φιλεῖς me? and he saith to Him" (omitting this time the asseveration, "Assuredly," because the precise assertion he had to make had been called in question), "Lord, Thou knowest all things; Thou dost see" (surely, surely the Lord must see it!) "that I φιλῶ Thee."

Of course there is no question here of our Lord's question, "Dost thou ἀγαπᾷς me?" "sounding too cold to Peter," because all the pulses of his heart were beating with earnest affection toward his Lord.[167] It is "humility and a feeling of unworthiness which leads Peter to choose another expression."[168] He could not in his heart-broken penitence assert of himself the ἀγαπᾶν which he had not illustrated in his acts; but he could not be false to his deep sense of real affection. 'Αγαπᾶν and φιλεῖν emerge, therefore, as respectively the love of complete devotion and the love (as Meyer phrases it) "of personal heart emotion"; the love of surrendering obedience and the love (as Westcott phrases it) of "personal attachment," "the feeling of natural love." Th. Zahn supposes [169] that the question of our Lord to Peter had as one of its ends, "bringing him to the consciousness that the love of the Lord which is a mark of a right disciple and the spring of his duty-doing, is not a matter of natural temperament, but a fruit of victory over inborn nature."[170] Therefore he supposes Him, avoiding the term which expresses the product of the natural temperament, to ask Peter

---

[167] So Trench: so also Henry Burton, *The Expositor*, v, i. p. 462 (1895), who paraphrases ἀγαπᾶν here, as the broader and weaker word of the two, by, "Do you care for me?" and represents it as "too cold, too distant for Peter's passionate soul," who asserts that he does not merely "care for" but loves His Lord.

[168] So rightly Woolsey, as cited, p. 182.   [169] P. 684.

[170] Cf. A. Klöpper. *Zeitschrift für wiss. Theologie*, 1899, 42, p. 363, who supposes the contrast to be between the expression of a natural human inclination (φιλεῖν) and the efflux of such a love as might be expressed in Pauline phrase as ἀγάπη ἐν πνεύματι (Col. i. 8). In general he finds the distinction drawn by Schmidt from the classical writers valid for John also. 'Αγαπᾶν is, however, he says, almost always used in the higher, spiritual sense, iii. 35, x. 17, xiv. 21 (of God); xiii. 1, 23, xix. 26, xi. 5 (of Christ); viii. 42, xiii. 34, xiv. 15, 21 (of the disciples).

whether he loved Him in this way; whereas Peter clings to the simple asseveration of his natural personal love to Jesus — until our Lord is driven, in order to prove his heart fully, to challenge that also, and so to compel Peter to face the possibility that even this personal love for his master had failed. Whatever may be said of the details of this exposition, it is certainly sound so far as this: that in this conversation ἀγαπᾶν and φιλεῖν are brought into contrast as in a sense the higher and the lower love — although these terms are somewhat infelicitous and may be misleading; perhaps we would better say, as the love of reverent devotion and the love of emotional attachment. And what is of most importance to observe is that the term which bore in its bosom the implication of reverent devotion had become for the men of the New Testament age the general word for love, while the term which expressed in its native suggestion the love of emotional attachment was in process of passing out of use. It is difficult to overstate the importance of this fact for the ready expression of the new revelation of love which the New Testament brought, in terms of current speech. The term which it was most natural to use of love, and which was in most familiar use among the people for love, was a term of such native connotation that it readily received and intelligibly expressed the new revelation of love.

Three instances alone remain, in which φιλεῖν is used by John, and in these three instances it is used of love in its highest relations. In one of them it expresses the love of Christ's people for Him their divine Saviour (xvi. 27); in another, the love of the Father for His people (xvi. 27); in the last, the love of the Father for His Son (v. 20). Here we are scaling the heights, and are discovering that φιλεῖν is not too low a word to be applied to the love which God Himself feels, or the love to God's only Son, whether on the part of His people, or even on the part of His Father. It is quite clear that the intrinsic implication of φιλεῖν is not low, not to say evil. It is differentiated from ἀγαπᾶν fundamentally by the side from which it approaches love and the aspect in which it describes it. It is applicable to all love which can be approached from that side or viewed in that aspect. If it is prevailingly employed in the New Testament of the lower grades of love, that is only because these lower grades of love are more naturally approached from the point of view from which φιλεῖν approaches love, and the comparative rarity of its occurrences afforded few opportunities for its application to exercises of love of the higher order. We must bear in mind that ἀγαπᾶν is the general term for love in the New Testament, and the use of φιλεῖν is in any event exceptional. We could expect it to be employed for manifestations of love such as in their nature ἀγαπᾶν would naturally express, only in the few instances in which, for one reason or another, it was desirable to throw up into view the aspect which φιλεῖν naturally expresses.

An example is supplied by v. 20: "For the Father φιλεῖ the Son and showeth Him all that He doeth" — the only passage in the New Testament in which the love of the Father to the Son is described otherwise than by ἀγαπᾶν. As compared with iii. 35: "The Father ἀγαπᾷ the Son and hath given all things into His hand," this passage might, on a surface view, be taken as a mere repetition of that, with a meaningless change in the verb. Such is, however, not the case; the difference in the verbs corresponds with an important difference in the sense conveyed. The thought of iii. 35 is fixed on the greatness of the Son whom the Father honors by His love; in v. 20 it is fixed on the fatherly tenderness with which the Father loves the Son. Zahn very properly comments, therefore: "Φιλεῖν was more suitable here than the ἀγαπᾶν of the otherwise parallel sentence in iii. 35, because φιλεῖν recalls the natural affection of the human father to his son, or of a friend to a friend, in contrast, say, with the relation of the master to the servant (xv. 13–15)." [171]

A similar account may be given of the two instances in xvi. 27: "For the Father Himself loveth you, because ye have loved Me, and have believed that I have come forth from with the Father." This is the only place in the New Testament where

[171] Cf. Horn, as cited, p. 170: Φιλεῖν stands very suitably at v. 20: 'The Father loves the Son and shows Him all that He Himself does.' For here the more intimate relation of the filial relation of the Son to the Father is suggested, and at the same time, it is thought of as one wholly natural, resting on elective affinity. The Son 'can' nothing of Himself."

God is said to φιλεῖν man — though it would be better to say, His children, for that enters into the case (but see Rev. iii. 19). And this is also the only place where φιλεῖν is used "of the affection of the disciples for their Lord" (yet consult xxi. 17 and I Cor. xvi. 22). Horn comments: [172] "The ὁ πατὴρ φιλεῖ ὑμᾶς of xvi. 27 has a different meaning from iii. 16: οὕτως γὰρ ἠγάπησεν ὁ θεὸς τὸν κόσμον. The latter is pitying love to the as yet unredeemed world, alien to God; the former is the natural pleasure of the Father in His believers, approved as faithful." [173] He adds in a note: "ἀγαπᾶν could, of course, stand here, as in the similar passage, xvii. 23 'in order that the world may know that Thou didst send me and didst love them even as Thou didst love me'; but the sense would not be precisely the same." What the difference in the sense of the two passages is, Horn does not tell us — although that is the particular point under discussion. Commenting on xvii. 23, he says, indeed: "In xvii. 23 the love of *the Father to the disciples* is spoken of as ἀγαπᾶν, since it belongs to them (cf. 20) because of their faith in Jesus." If that, however, would require ἀγαπᾶν to be used, it surely would have been used in both passages. And it looks as if φιλεῖν as the expression of the love of affinities would be equally appropriate in both passages. Perhaps it is enough to say that ἀγαπᾶν is used as a matter of course in xvii. 23, as the general word for love in common use — it needs no accounting for; while φιλεῖν in xvi. 27 is used to emphasize the affinity between God and His believers.

The abstract substantive connected with φιλεῖν — φιλία — occurs only a single time in the New Testament, Jas. iv. 4, where we read the arraignment: "Adulteresses! know ye not that the φιλία of the world is enmity with God?" It is customary to render φιλία here by "friendship," a course which the φίλος of the next clause makes especially convenient. But it may be well to guard against attributing to it too specific a notion. The implication is that of finding one's pleasure, satisfaction, in

---

[172] As cited, p. 170.

[173] This is in effect the love of benevolence in distinction from the love of complacency. Compare note 154.

the world, with a suggestion that by this one's affinity with the world is betrayed. The notion is similar to that expressed in John xv. 19: "If ye were of the world, the world would love its own" — for φιλία intimates mutual affection. To be at friends with the world is to love and to be loved by the world, to be bound by mutual ties to it. 'Αγαπᾶν would scarcely have expressed so much.

It may fairly be claimed that a survey of the passages in which φιλεῖν, φιλία occur leaves an impression of the naturalness of their use in these cases. But what should be kept ever fresh in mind is that the employment of them is highly exceptional, and rests on a background of a very copious use of ἀγαπᾶν, ἀγάπη — chiefly to express the great conceptions of love which permeate the Christian revelation. The equipment of the New Testament to express the idea of love consists, thus, in the possession in ἀγαπᾶν, ἀγάπη, of a high general term the native suggestion of which was a worthy one, and which had already been trained by the writers of the Septuagint to receive the great conceptions of revealed religion; and the possession by its side, of a subsidiary term by which, when occasion offered, a special aspect of love could be thrown into view — that aspect, to wit, in which love appears as the response of the soul to the perception of something which pleases it, is congenial to it, in the object. This is, to be sure, not as rich an equipment as was possessed by the Greek of the classical writers. It possessed four terms φιλεῖν, φιλία; ἐρᾶν, ἔρως; στέργειν, στοργή; ἀγαπᾶν, ἀγάπησις. But the comparative poverty of its terminology is offset in the case of the New Testament by the intrinsic superiority of its general term for love, ἀγαπᾶν, and by the higher content which it had acquired by its employment to express the conceptions of love embodied in the divine revelation. We must guard also against supposing that the resources for its expression of loving activities were absolutely exhausted by these, its direct vehicles. There were other terms which it might call to its aid when it wished to speak of love in one or another of its active exercises. There were such terms, for example, as οἰκτείρω, ἐλεέω, σπλαγχνίζομαι, with their accompanying substantives, and above all there was χάρις. As it was this aspect of love — love in gracious action — that the New Testament writers had most occasion to celebrate, their vocabulary was not quite so restricted as it sounds, when we say that only ἀγαπᾶν, ἀγάπη, with an exceptional use of φιλεῖν, φιλία, lay at their disposal.

It does not fall within our present purpose, however, to discuss the number and variety, or the nature and use, of such a subsidiary vocabulary. Let it only be further noted that compounds in φιλ- are in the New Testament, as in the Greek literature of all ages, numerous,[174] and that some of these compounds were significant, on one side or another, for the expression of love. We may mention, for example, such as φιλαδελφία (five times), φιλάδελφος (once), φίλανδρος (once), φιλανθρωπία (twice), φιλανθρώπος (once), φιλόθεος (once), φιλοξενία (twice), φιλόξενος (three times), φιλόστοργος[175] (once), φιλοτέκνος (once). By the aid of such forms a number of modifications of the idea of love are given expression. After all said, however, it is not the variety of the vehicles for the expression of love for which the New Testament is notable, but the depth and height of the conception of love which it is able to express through its fundamental terms, ἀγαπᾶν and ἀγάπη. The great fact which comes to view is that, in the providence of God, the noblest word which the Greek language afforded for the expression of love came into its hands as the natural term for it to use to express its conception of love, and that, as already trained to express love at the height of its conception by its use for that purpose in the Septuagint version of the Old Testament.

LITERATURE. — J. H. Heinrich Schmidt, "Synonymik der griechischen Sprache," III, 1879, pp. 474–491 (= § 136: on ἐρᾶν, φιλεῖν, στέργειν, ἀγαπᾶν). Edward Meredith Cope, on στοργή, ἔρως, φιλεῖν, ἀγαπᾶν, in "The Rhetoric of Aristotle,

---

[174] Add to those mentioned in the text: φιλάγαθος, φιλαργυρία, φιλάργυρος, φιλήδονος, φιλονεικία, φιλόνεικος, φιλοπρωτεύω, φιλοσοφία, φιλόσοφος, φιλοτιμέομαι, φιλοφρόνως, φιλόφρων.

[175] Consult on φιλόστοργος in the New Testament, E. Hoehne, Zeitschrift f. k. Wissenschaft und k. Leben, 1882 (III.) p. 6.

with a Commentary," 1877, v. i, pp. 292–296 (printed also in the *Journal of Philology*, v. i, No. 1 (1868), pp. 88–93). J. B. Lightfoot, in *The Cambridge Journal of Classical and Sacred Philology*, v. iii, (1857), No. 7, pp. 92 ff. (see also Lightfoot's comment on Ignatius, "Rom.," vii, p. 222). R. C. Trench, "Synonyms of the New Testament," 9th ed., 1880, xii, on ἀγαπάω, φιλέω. J. A. H. Tittmann, "Remarks on the Synonyms of the N. T.," E. T. in "The Biblical Cabinet," v. iii, 1833, pp. 90–97. Hermann Cremer, "Biblisch-theologisches Wörterbuch der Neutestamentlichen Gräcität," 10th ed., 1915, *sub voc.* E. Buonaiuti, "I vocaboli d'amore nel Nuovo Testamento," in the "Rivista Storico-critica di Scienze Teologiche," v. v, 1909, pp. 257–264. E. Höhne, "Zum Neutestamentlichen Sprachgebrauch: 1. Ἀγαπᾶν, φιλεῖν, σπλαγχνίζεσθαι," in Luthardt's *Zeitschrift für k. Wissenschaft und k. Leben*, III, 1882, pp. 6–19. K. A. G. von Zezschwitz, "Profangräcität und biblischer Sprachgeist," 1859, p. 62. W. G. Ballantine, "Lovest Thou Me?" in "Bibliotheca Sacra," July 1889, v. xlvi, pp. 524–542. Sally Neil Roach, "Love in Its Relation to Service," in *The Review and Expositor*, 1913, v. x, pp. 531–553. T. D. Woolsey, "The Disciple Whom Jesus Loved," in *The Andover Review*, iv. 1885, August, pp. 163–185. G. A. Deissmann, "Bible Studies," E. T., 1901, pp. 198 ff. W. M. Ramsay, *The Expository Times*, ix. p. 568. Fr. Vermeil, "Étude sur le 21, Chap. de l'Évang. selon S. Jean," 1861. John A. Cross, "On St. John xxi. 15–17," in *The Expositor*, iv. vii., 1893, pp. 312–320. Henry Burton, "The Breakfast on the Shore," in *The Expositor* v. i, 1895, pp. 450–472. A. Klöpper, "Das 21. Kap. des 4. Evang. erläutert," in *Zeitschrift für wiss. Theologie*, 1899, pp. 337–381. Max Eberhardt, "Evang. Joh. c. 21; ein exeget. Versuch," 1897. K. Horn, "Abfassung, Geschichtlichkeit und Zweck vom Evang. des Johannes, Kap. 21.," 1904, pp. 167–171. R. H. Strachan, "The Appendix to the Fourth Gospel," in *The Expositor*, viii, vii, 1914, pp. 263 ff. H. W. Magoun, "The Bible Champion," Oct. and Nov. 1919, pp. 404 ff., 446 ff.

XV

THE PROPHECIES OF ST. PAUL

THE PROPHECIES OF ST. PAUL [1]

I. — I and II Thessalonians

The whole teaching, whether oral or written, of the Apostles of the New Testament, was essentially prophetic. St. Paul, in entire harmony with the Old Testament conception, defines a prophet to be one who "knows mysteries and knowledge" (I Cor. xiii. 2) and "speaks to men edification and exhortation and consolation" (I Cor. xiv. 3). This is a fair description of his own work; his Epistles are full of mysteries and knowledge, and speak to men edification, strengthening, and comfort. Among the mysteries which they declare — the word, we must remember, does not denote something inherently inscrutable, but only something as yet unknown and needing to be revealed — there are not lacking some that have to do with the future. We may properly speak, therefore, of Paul's prophecies, even in that narrow sense in which the word is popularly used, and which makes it synonymous with predictions. It is in this sense, indeed, although under a mild protest, that we use it in these papers. Our purpose is to study the predictions of Paul.

We begin with his earliest writings, the Epistles to the Thessalonians, which were written at Corinth in A.D. 52 and 53. As is well known to every careful reader of the New Testament, these Epistles are also the richest in predictions of all Paul's writings. It is not too much to say that their main burden is the Coming of the Lord. To explanations concerning this, their only didactic portions are given; and, in the first Epistle at least, a constant allusion to it is woven like a golden thread throughout its whole texture, and each section, whatever its subject, is sure to reach its climax in a reference to it (i. 10; ii. 19; iii. 13; v. 23). This seems strange to some. And it has been suggested, either that the Apostle in his early ministry made

[1] From *The Expositor*, 3d ser. v. iv, 1886, pp. 30–44, 131–148, 439–452.

more of the Second Advent in his teaching than growing wisdom
permitted him to do later; or else, that at this particular period,
amid the special trials of his work — the persecutions in Mace-
donia, the chill indifference at Athens, the discouragements
that met him at Corinth — he had his heart turned more than
was usual with him to the blessed consolation of a Christian's
expectation of the coming glory. Both of these explanations are
entirely gratuitous. A sufficient reason for this marked peculiarity lies at the hand of all in that other fact that distinguishes
these letters from all their fellows — they are the only letters
that have come down to us, which were addressed to an infant
community just emerged from heathenism.

For it is undeniable that the staple of Paul's preaching to
the Gentiles was God and the Judgment. When addressing
Jews he could appeal to prophecy, and he preached Jesus to
them as Him whom all the prophets pointed unto, the Messiah
whom God had graciously promised. But with Gentiles he could
appeal only to conscience; and he preached Jesus to them as
Him through whom God would judge the world in righteousness, whereof He hath given assurance to all men in that He
hath raised Him from the dead. The address on the Areopagus,
which was delivered only a few months before I Thessalonians
was written, admirably illustrates how the Apostle tried to
reach the consciences of his heathen hearers; and the totality
of the message delivered in it was God (Acts xvii. 24–29) and
the Judgment (Acts xvii. 30, 31). But if Christ coming for
judgment was thus the very centre and substance of Paul's
proclamation to the Gentiles, it would not be strange if he had
dwelt upon it to the Thessalonians also. And that he had
preached just in this strain to them, when, so shortly before
writing this letter, he was with them, he tells us himself (I
Thess. i. 9, 10). For, what he chiefly thanks God for in their
case is that they "turned unto God from idols" in order to do
two things: — "serve the living and true God," and "await
patiently His Son from the heavens, whom He raised from the
dead, Jesus, our deliverer from the coming wrath." The parallel
with the speech on Mars' Hill is precise; it almost looks as if

the Apostle had repeated at Athens the sermon that had been so effective at Thessalonica.

But we not only learn thus how it happens that Paul dwells so much on the Second Advent when writing to the Thessalonians, but we learn also what is much more important, — how he himself thought of the Advent and in what aspect he proclaimed it. Plainly to him it was above all things else the Judgment. It was the Judgment Day that he announced in its proclamation; and this was the lever with which he prized at Gentile consciences. "The day in which God will judge the world in righteousness" was what he proclaimed to the Athenians, and that it was just this that was in mind in I Thess. i. 10 is evident from the office assigned to the expected Jesus, — "the Deliverer from the coming wrath." In harmony with this, every passage in which the Second Advent is adverted to in these Epistles conceives of it pointedly as the Judgment Day. The Apostle's eager desire for the purity and sanctification of his readers is always referred to the Advent: he wishes to have them to boast of before the Lord Jesus at His coming (I Thess. ii. 19), — he prays that their hearts may be established unblameworthy in holiness before God at the coming of our Lord Jesus (I Thess. iii. 13), — he beseeches the God of peace to preserve them in their whole being and all their faculties blameless, at the coming of our Lord Jesus Christ (I Thess. v. 23), — he declares that the Day of the Lord will bring sudden destruction upon the wicked (I Thess. v. 3), and will draw a sharp line in justice between the good and bad (II Thess. i. 9). He speaks of the Advent freely as the "Day of the Lord" (I Thess. v. 2, 4; II Thess. i. 10), a term which from Joel down had stood in all prophecy as the synonym of the final judgment.

The most important passage in this point of view is II Thess. i. 6–10, where the matter is not only treated at large, but the statements are explicit. Here the declaration is distinctly made that "at the revelation of the Lord Jesus from heaven (ἐν τῇ ἀποκαλύψει) together with the angels of His power, in a fire of flame," God will justly recompense affliction to those who persecuted the Thessalonians, and rest or relief to them.

Both the statement of what is to occur and the definition of the time when it is to occur are to be here observed; and as the one can refer to nothing else than the distribution of rewards and punishments for the deeds done in the body, so the other can have no other reference than to the act of the coming of Christ. Both matters are made even plainer by what follows. The Apostle proceeds to declare broadly that this revelation of Jesus of which he is speaking is as one giving vengeance to those ignorant of God and those disobedient to the gospel — a vengeance that comes in the way of justice, and consists in eternal destruction away from the face of the Lord and from the glory of His might. And so closely and even carefully is the time defined, that to the exact statement that all this occurs at the revelation of Christ from heaven, it is added at the end, that this "eternal destruction" takes place whenever (ὅταν) the Lord gloriously comes, — "at that day." Unless the Apostle is here representing the persecutors of the Thessalonians as partakers in the horrors of the punitive side of the Second Advent because he expected and here asserts that the Advent was to come before that generation passed away — and this will not satisfy the general representation of verses 8 *seq.* — it is certain that he here thinks of the Advent, considered as an act and not as a state, as the last judgment itself, when

"Nil inultum remanebit."

In this case it would presuppose a general resurrection.

That Paul had a resurrection in mind as accompanying the Second Advent is certain from another important passage (I Thess. iv. 13–18). The Thessalonians did not doubt that Jesus had risen from the dead (v. 14); but they had not realized even in thought all the consequents of this great fact. Like certain at a somewhat later date at Corinth, they did not understand that all men that die rise again by virtue of Christ's conquest of death. And thus, as they saw one and another of their own number "fall on sleep," they sorrowed inordinately over them, like the rest that have no hope. It is not exactly clear what they thought of the state of the dead, — whether they conceived of

them as with Christ indeed, in Paradise, but condemned to an
eternity of shade existence, separated from the body for ever,
which seems to have been the case with their Corinthian fellow-
errorists, — or whether they fancied that with the cessation of
bodily activity, the whole life went out, as may be hinted in the
sad words that they sorrowed as the rest who have no hope (v.
13). In either case the Apostle brings them quick consolation
in the glad announcement that the resurrection of Christ implies that of those who have fallen asleep; and that, raised
through Jesus, God will bring them with Him at His coming (v.
14). With this assurance he makes Christ's coming doubly precious to them. Then proceeding to more minute details, he
declares that those who are alive and are left unto the coming of
the Lord shall in no wise be beforehand with those who have
fallen asleep; for the Lord will come with a shout, and with an
archangel's voice, and with a blast of the trumpet of God, which
will pierce even into the grave. Thus the rising of Christ's dead
is secured before He reaches the earth; and only after they have
joined the throng, are the living along with them to be caught
up in (or on) clouds unto His meeting, — into the air, to
"swell the triumph of His train." "So," adds the Apostle, "we
shall be always with the Lord" (v. 17). Dire, then, as the coming will be to those who know not God and who obey not the
gospel, it will be bliss unspeakable to those in Christ; and as
the results, on the one side, are "eternal destruction away from
the face of the Lord and from the glory of His might" (II
Thess. i. 9); so on the other they will be eternal dwelling with
the Lord (I Thess. iv. 17). It goes without saying that the
Apostle has the believing dead only in his mind in our present
passage (iv. 16). How could he in such a passage speak of any
other? But is not the parallel too close for us not to suspect
that, as in the one case both the living and dead in Christ shall
partake in the bliss and the living shall not precede the dead, so
in the other the living who are left unto the Coming shall not
precede those who have passed away, in receiving the terrible
doom, and that the blare of the trumpet of God veritably

"Coget omnes ante thronum"?

Or is it more probable that Paul believed and taught that the Lord would certainly come before that generation passed away? There is no room to doubt that the Thessalonians expected the Advent in their own time. Their feelings towards death (I Thess. iv. 13 *seq.*) would be otherwise inexplicable. And it is worthy of note that the Apostle does not correct them in this belief. He points out to them that to fall asleep was not to miss the glory of the Advent, but that whether they waked or slept they should live together with their Lord (I Thess. v. 10). But he says no word that would declare them mistaken in expecting to live until "that day." On the contrary, he expresses himself in terms that left the possibility open that the Lord might come while they were still alive and left on the earth (I Thess. iv. 15, 17). This was far from asserting that the Lord would come in that generation; but, in the connexion in which the words stand, they would have been impossible had the Apostle felt justified in asserting that He would not come. And this appears to be the exact difference between the attitude of the Thessalonians and that of Paul; they confidently expected the Lord in their own day — he was in complete uncertainty when He would come. That He would assuredly come, to bring sudden destruction (I Thess. v. 3) upon all appointed unto wrath (v. 9) and rest and salvation to those in Christ, he was sure; but the times and seasons he knew perfectly were hidden in the Father's power (I Thess. v. 1). He might come soon — when He did come, it would be, he knew, with the unexpectedness of a thief in the night (I Thess. v. 2). But meanwhile, whether it found him waking or sleeping was of no moment; and though it became him to watch (I Thess. v. 6), yet the watch was to be not a nervous expectancy, but a quiet and patient waiting (I Thess. i. 10, ἀναμένειν, cf. Judith viii. 17). But if, just because the "when" was unknown, the Apostle could not confidently expect the Lord in his own time, the categorical assertion that the Advent would bring "eternal destruction away from the face of the Lord" (II Thess. i. 9) to the special persecutors of the Thessalonians, rests on his view of the Advent as synchronous with the final judgment and presupposes a general resurrection.

The very moderation of the Apostle's attitude made it difficult for the excited Thessalonians to yield themselves to his leading. Certainly his first letter did not allay their fanaticism. Things went rather from bad to worse, and so certain were they that the Lord was coming at once, that they fell an easy prey to every one who should cry "Lo, here!" or "Lo, there!" and even, apparently from this cause, began to neglect their daily business and became mere busybodies, refusing to work, and eating the bread of others. The Apostle sternly rebukes their disorder, and commands that they work with quietness; and with a view to preserving them from sudden agitation whenever any one chose to declare "The day of the Lord is upon us!" he points out certain events that must come before the Lord. That this practical, ethical purpose was the occasion of the important revelation in II Thess. ii. 1–12, the Apostle tells us himself (ii. 2). And a simple glance at his words is enough to expose the almost ludicrous inappropriateness of the contention of some that the error of the Thessalonians was not feverish expectancy of the Lord's coming, but the belief that the day of the Lord had already come and had brought none of the blessings they had expected from it, — not the Lord Himself, nor their resurrected friends, — nothing of all that the Apostle had taught and they had hoped.[2] What the Apostle says is that he wishes to save them from being suddenly shaken from their senses or troubled by any statement from any quarter, as that the day of the Lord was upon them. The passage is parallel to and probably founded upon the words of our Lord in His

---

[2] This curious misinterpretation is founded on a pressure of the verb ἐνέστηκεν, ii. 2, in forgetfulness of three things. (1) That this verb is a compound of ἴστημι, not of εἰμί, and means, not "is in progress," but "is upon us," in the two senses of "to threaten," and "to be actual" (especially in the participle). While it *may* mean "to be present," therefore, it *need not* mean it, and is not likely to in such a case. (2) That the clause "either by spirit or by word, or by letter as if from us," is an essential part of the context, the omission of which falsifies the text. What the Apostle says is *not* "be not troubled — as that the day of the Lord," etc. *but* "be not troubled *by any statement* as that the day of the Lord is upon us!" — something essentially different, which excludes the above interpretation. (3) That the broad context renders this explanation impossible and meaningless.

warning to His disciples not to be led astray or deceived by any
"who should say, 'Lo, here is the Christ!' or 'Here!'" (Mt.
xxiv. 23), and is already a valuable indication that throughout
this whole section Paul has the great apocalyptic discourse of
Jesus in mind and is to be interpreted from it.

The impression has become very widespread that, owing to
the lack on our part of the previous information to which Paul
alludes as given by him on a former occasion to the Thessalonians (verses 5 and 6), the interpretation of this prophecy must
remain for all time a sealed riddle to us. That two important
events, called by Paul "the apostasy," and "the revelation of
the man of sin," the latter of which was at the time deterred
by something else mysteriously designated "the restraint," or
"the restrainer," were to take place before the coming of the
Lord — this, we are told, is all that we can know, and any
effort to obtain any defined outlines for the misty shapes thus
barely named to us only succeeds in bringing the dense darkness in which they are steeped into tangibility and visibility.
We find it difficult to believe the matter so hopeless. On the contrary, the broad outlines, at least, of the prophecy appear to us
sufficiently clear; and we believe that a sound method of study
will give the humble student who is willing to put a stern check
on his imagination and follow the leading of the exegetical hints
alone, an adequately exact understanding of its chief details.

First of all, we must try to keep fresh in our minds the great
principle that all prophecy is ethical in its purpose, and that
this ethical end controls not only what shall be revealed in
general, but also the details of it and the very form which it
takes. Next, we must not fail to observe that our present prophecy is not independent of previous ones, — that its roots are
in Daniel, and from beginning to end it is full of allusions to
our Lord's great apocalyptic discourse. Still again, we must
bear in mind that it comes from a hand which throughout these
Epistles preserves an attitude of uncertainty of the "times and
seasons," and so expresses himself as to imply that he believed
that the Lord might come, in despite of all these preliminary
events, in his own day.

If, holding fast to these principles, we approach the prophecy itself, we observe first of all, that although the three
things — the Apostasy, the Revelation of the Man of Sin, and
the Coming of the Lord — are brought together, they are not
declared to be closely connected, or immediately consecutive
to one another. The mere "and" of verse 3 reveals nothing beyond the simple fact that both of those events must come to
pass before the Lord comes. So too for all that the prophecy
tells us, both of these evil developments might come and pass
away, and be succeeded by ages on ages which in turn might
pass away, and yet men be able to say, "Where is the promise
of His coming?" To point to the declaration in verse 8, that
"the Lord Jesus shall destroy" the lawless one — almost,
"blow him away" — "with the breath of His mouth and abolish him with the manifestation of His presence," as proving
that he will still be lording it on earth when the Lord comes to
his destruction, is to neglect the apparent indications of the
context. For this assertion does not go, in either vividness or
literality of expression, beyond what is stated just before of the
generation then living (II Thess. i. 7, 9); and it is inserted here
not as a chronological detail — and is out of place (cf. verses 9,
seq.) if considered a chronological detail — but as part of the
description of the lawless one, and for the ethical purpose of
keeping in the mind of the reader his judgment by God and his
final fate. In a word, this statement only declares of the Man
of Sin what was just before declared of the lesser enemies of the
Gospel, and what was in I Thess. v. 3 seq. declared of all to
whom wrath is appointed — that he shall meet with destruction at the Second Coming of the Lord. The revelation of the
Man of Sin is not, then, necessarily to be sought at the end of
time: we know of it, only that it will succeed the removal of
the "restraint," and precede, by how much we are not told, the
coming of the Lord.

We cannot fail to observe, however, next, that in his description of the Man of Sin, the Apostle has a contemporary, or
nearly contemporary phenomenon in mind. The withholding
power is already present. Although the Man of Sin is not yet

revealed, as a mystery his essential "lawlessness" is already working — "only until the present restrainer be removed from the midst." He expects him to sit in "the temple of God," which perhaps most naturally refers to the literal temple in Jerusalem, although the Apostle knew that the out-pouring of God's wrath on the Jews was close at hand (I Thess. ii. 16). And if we compare the description which the Apostle gives of him with our Lord's address on the Mount of Olives (Mt. xxiv.), to which, as we have already hinted, Paul makes obvious allusion, it becomes at once in the highest degree probable that in the words, "he that exalteth himself against all that is called God, or is worshipped, so that he sitteth in the sanctuary of God showing himself that he is God," Paul can have nothing else in view than what our Lord described as "the abomination of desolation which was spoken of by Daniel the prophet, standing in the holy place" (Mt. xxiv. 15); and this our Lord connects immediately with the beleaguering of Jerusalem (cf. Luke xxi. 20). This obvious parallel, however, not only places the revelation of the Man of Sin in the near future, but goes far towards leading us to his exact identification. Our Lord's words not only connect him with the siege of Jerusalem, but place him distinctly among the besiegers; and, led by the implication of the original setting of the phrase (in Dan. xi. 36) which Paul uses, we cannot go far wrong in identifying him with the Roman emperor.

Whether a single emperor was thought of or the line of emperors, is a more difficult question. The latter hypothesis will best satisfy the conditions of the problem; and we believe that the line of emperors, considered as the embodiment of persecuting power, is the revelation of iniquity hidden under the name of the Man of Sin. With this is connected in the description certain other traits of Roman imperialism — more especially the rage for deification, which, in the person of Caligula, had already given a foretaste of what was to come. It was Nero, then, the first persecutor of the Church, — and Vespasian the miracle-worker,[3] — and Titus, who introduced his divine-

[3] Tac., "Hist.," iv. 82; Suet., "Vesp.," 7; Dio Cass., lxvi. 8.

self and his idolatrous insignia into the Holy of Holies, perhaps with a directly anti-Christian intent,[4] — and Domitian, — and the whole line of human monsters whom the world was worshipping as gods, on which, as a nerve-cord of evil, these hideous ganglia gathered, — these and such as these it was that Paul had in mind when he penned this hideous description of the son of perdition, every item of which was fulfilled in the terrible story of the emperors of Rome.

The restraining power, on this hypothesis, appears to be the Jewish state. For the continued existence of the Jewish state was both graciously and naturally a protection to Christianity, and hence a restraint on the revelation of the persecuting power. Graciously, it was God's plan to develop Christianity under the protection of Judaism for a short set time, with the double purpose of keeping the door of salvation open to the Jews until all of their elect of that generation should be gathered in and the apostasy of the nation should be rendered doubly and trebly without excuse, and of hiding the tender infancy of the Church within the canopy of a protecting sheath until it should grow strong enough to withstand all storms. Naturally, the effect of the continuance of Judaism was to conceal Christianity from notice through a confusion of it with Judaism — to save it thus from being declared an illicit religion — and to enable it to grow strong under the protection accorded to Jewish worship. So soon as the Jewish apostasy was complete and Jerusalem given over to the Gentiles — God deserting the temple which was no longer His temple to the fury of the enemies, of those who were now His enemies — the separation of Christianity from Judaism, which had already begun, became evident to every eye; the conflict between the new faith and heathenism culminating in and now alive almost only in the Emperor-worship, became intense; and the persecuting power of the empire was inevitably let loose. Thus the continued existence of Judaism was in the truest sense a restraint on the persecution of Christians, and its destruction gave the signal for the lawless one to be revealed in his time.

[4] Sulp. Sev., "Sacr. Hist.," ii. 30, §§ 6. 7.

If the masculine form of "the restrainer" in verse 7 demands interpretation as a person — which we more than doubt — it might possibly be referred without too great pressure to James of Jerusalem, God's chosen instrument in keeping the door of Christianity open for the Jews and by so doing continuing and completing their probation. Thus he may be said to have been the upholder of the restraining power, the savour of the salt that preserved the Christians from persecution, and so in a high sense the restrainer.

Finally, in this interpretation, the apostasy is obviously the great apostasy of the Jews, gradually filling up all these years and hastening to its completion in their destruction. That the Apostle certainly had this rapidly completing apostasy in his mind in the severe arraignment that he makes of the Jews in I Thess. ii. 14–16, which reached its climax in the declaration that they were continually filling up more and more full the measure of their sins, until already the measure of God's wrath was prematurely (ἔφθασεν) filled up against them and was hanging over them like some laden thunder-cloud ready to burst and overwhelm them, — adds an additional reason for supposing his reference to be to this apostasy — above all others, "the" apostasy — in this passage.

We venture to think that the core of this interpretation may be accounted very probable, — so much of it as this: that the Apostle had in view in this prophecy a development in the immediate future closely connected with the Jewish war and the destruction of Jerusalem, although not as if that were the coming of Christ for which he was patiently waiting, but rather in full recognition of its being only the culmination of the Jewish apostasy and the falling of God's wrath upon them to the uttermost. When he declares that these events must precede the coming of Christ, this no doubt was clear evidence that the Advent was not to be looked for immediately; but was in no wise inconsistent with uncertainty whether it would come during that generation or not. As a matter of mere fact the growing apostasy of the Jews was completed — the abomination of desolation had been set up in the sanctuary — Jerusalem and the temple, and the Jewish state were in ruins — Christianity stood naked before her enemies — and the persecuting sword of Divus Cæsar was unsheathed and Paul had himself felt its keenness: all the prophecy had been fulfilled before two decades had passed away.

Let us gather up for the close, in brief recapitulation, the events which Paul predicts in these two Epistles. First of all, and most persistently of all, he predicts the coming of the Lord from heaven unto judgment, with its glorious accompaniments of hosts of angels, the shout, the voice of the archangel and the blast of the trumpet of God that awake the dead. Thus, he predicts the resurrection of Christ's dead to partake in the glory of His coming. Then, he foretells the results of the judgment — eternal destruction from the face of God for the wicked, and everlasting presence with the Lord for His own. Of the time of the Advent the Apostle professes ignorance; he only knows that it will come unexpectedly. But he does know that before it the apostasy of the Jews must be completed, and the persecuting power of the Roman state be revealed. This apostasy and its punishment he sees is immediately ready for completion (I Thess. ii. 16). Finally, he mentions having previously foretold the persecutions under which the Thessalonians were already suffering (I Thess. iii. 4).

II. — The Epistles to the Galatians, Corinthians, and Romans

WHEN we pass from the Epistles to the Thessalonians to the next group of letters — those to the Galatians, Corinthians and Romans, all four of which were written in the course of a single year, some five years later (A.D. 57–58) — we are at once aware of a great diminution in the allusions to the future. Galatians contains rather more matter than both letters to the Thessalonians, but does not contain a single prediction; and the much longer letter to the Romans, while alluding now and then to what the future was to bring forth, contains no explicit mention of the Second Advent. The first letter to the Corinthians is three times as long as both letters to the Thessalonians, but contains rather less predictive matter. We should not be far wrong if we estimated that these four letters, in about nine times the space, give us about as much eschatological matter as the two letters to the Thessalonians.

The contrast exists in nothing else, however, except the mere matter of amount. The two groups of letters are thoroughly at one in their teaching as to the future — at one, but not mere repetitions of one another. This group is continually supplying what almost seems to be explanations and extensions of the revelations in Thessalonians, so that it exhibits as great an advance in what is revealed as decrease in the relative amount of space given to revelations. So clear is it that the Apostle's preaching to all heathen communities was in essence the same, and that all grew up to the stature of manhood in Christ through practically the same stages, that we may look upon the Thessalonian letters as if they had been addressed to the infancy of every Church, and treat those at present before us as if they were intended to supplement them. This is probably the true account of the very strong appearance of being supplementary and explanatory to those in the letters to Thessalonica, which the predictions in this group of letters are continually presenting.

In these as in those, the Second Advent is represented primarily and most prominently in the aspect of judgment — as the last judgment. Here, too, the desire for moral perfection is referred constantly to it, as for example in I Cor. i. 8 cf. 7, where the actual moment in mind is that of the revelation of the Lord Jesus Christ. The mutual glorying of the Apostle and his readers in each other is to be "in the day of our Lord Jesus" (I Cor. i. 8). This is the day of punishment also: the incestuous man is delivered now unto Satan to be punished in the flesh in order that his spirit may be saved in the day of the Lord (I Cor. v. 5); and in exactly similar wise, those who are visited with bodily ills for unworthy partaking of the Lord's Supper, receive this chastening that they may not be condemned with the world (I Cor. xi. 32). The sanction of the anathema pronounced against all who do not love the Lord is Maranatha — "the Lord cometh!" (I Cor. xvi. 22). His coming is indeed so sharply defined as the time of judging, in the mind of Paul, that he advises his readers to "judge nothing before the time, until the Lord come" (I Cor. iv. 5). The connotation of "the day of the Lord" was to him so entirely judgment, that the word "day" had come to mean judgment to him, and he actually uses it as its synonym, speaking of a "human day," for "human judgment" (I Cor. iv. 3). Of like import is the representation of the second coming as the great day of revelation of character. Of the builders on the edifice of God's Church it is declared that "each man's work shall be made manifest by 'the day.'" "For the day is revealed in fire, and each man's work, of what sort it is, — the fire itself shall test." "If any man's work abideth, he shall receive reward; if any man's work is burned up, he shall be mulcted, but himself shall be saved, but so as through fire" (I Cor. iii. 13–15). It is scarcely an extension of this teaching to declare openly that when the Lord comes, He "will both bring to light the hidden things of darkness, and make manifest the counsels of the hearts; and then shall his praise come to each from God" (I Cor. iv. 5).

In the light of this it is evident what time the Apostle has in mind when he declares that "all of us must needs be made manifest[5] before the judgment-seat of Christ, that each may receive the things [done] through the body according to what he practised, whether good or bad" (II Cor. v. 10); and which day to him was "the day when God shall judge the secrets of men according to my gospel, by Jesus Christ" — "the day of wrath and revelation of the righteous judgment of God" (Rom. ii. 16, 5). Yet, in this last passage it is beyond all question that the Apostle has in mind the final judgment, when God "will render to every man according to his works," and the two verses which have been adduced are respectively the opening and closing verse of the splendid passage in which Paul gives us his fullest description of the nature and standards of the awful trial to which all men, whether Jews or Gentiles, whether those

----

[5] φανερωθῆναι, cf. φανερόν, I Cor. iii. 13; φανερώσει, I Cor. iv. 5.

who have law or those who have no law, are summoned "in the day when God shall judge the secrets of men according to my gospel through Christ Jesus." Elsewhere in Romans, where judgment necessarily holds an important place in the general argument, the wrath of God is kept hanging over ungodliness and unrighteousness (i. 18; iii. 5; v. 9) and the coming judgment is held before the eyes of the reader (iii. 6; xiv. 10).

For the realization of such a judgment scene (Rom. ii. 5–16; II Cor. v. 10; Rom. xiv. 10), a resurrection is presupposed, and the reference of the Apostle is obvious when he expresses his confidence that "He who raised up Jesus shall raise up us also with Jesus, and shall present us with you" (II Cor. iv. 14; cf. v. 10; also I Cor. vi. 14). In this compressed sentence, there is pointed out the relation of our resurrection both to the judgment (παραστήσει, cf. Col. i. 22) as preceding and in order to it, and to the resurrection of Christ (σὺν Ἰησοῦ, cf. the use of συνεγείρω in Col. ii. 12; iii. 1) as included in it as a necessary result and part of it. The latter matter is made very plain by the remarkably simple way in which Jesus is declared in Rom. i. 4 to have been marked out as the Son of God "by the resurrection of the dead" — a phrase which has no meaning except on the presupposition that the raising of Jesus was the beginning of the resurrection of the dead and part and parcel of it (cf. also Rom. vi. 4; viii. 11, etc.).

At this point our attention is claimed by that magnificent combined argument and revelation contained in the 15th chapter of I Corinthians, which has been the instruction and consolation of the saints through all Christian ages. The occasion which called it forth was singularly like and singularly unlike that which gave rise to the parallel revelation in I Thessalonians. As in the one Church so in the other, there were those who failed to grasp the great truth of the Resurrection, and laid their dead away without hope of their rising again. But in Thessalonica this was due to sorrowing ignorance; in Corinth, to philosophizing pride of intellect. And in the one case, the Apostle meets it with loving instruction; in the other, with a brilliant refutation which confounds opposition, and which, although carrying a tender purpose buried in its bosom, as all the world has felt, yet flashes with argument and even here and there burns with sarcasm. The Corinthian errorists appear to have been spiritualistic philosophizers, perhaps of the Platonic school, who, convinced of the immortality of the soul, thought of the future life as a spiritual one in which men attained perfection apart from, perhaps largely because separate from, the body. They looked for and desired no resurrection; and their formula, perhaps somewhat scoffingly and certainly somewhat magisterially pronounced, was: "There is no rising again of dead men." It is instructive to observe how the Apostle meets their assertion. They did not deny the resurrection of Christ (I Cor. xv. 2, 11) — probably explaining it as a miracle like the reänimation of Lazarus. Yet the Apostle begins by laying firm the proofs of Christ's resurrection (xv. 1–11), and doing this in such a way as to suggest that they needed primary instruction. He "makes known to them," rather than reminds them of the Gospel which he and all the Apostles preached and all Christians believed. With this opening sarcasm, he closes the way of retreat through a denial of the resurrection of Christ, and then presses as his sole argument the admitted fact that Christ had risen. How could they deny that dead men rise, when Christ, who was a dead man, had risen? If there is no resurrection of dead men, then not even is Christ risen. It is plain that their whole position rested on the assertion of the impossibility of resurrection; to which it was a conclusive reply that they confessed it in one case. Having uncovered their logical inconsistency, Paul leaves at once the question of fact and presses at length the hideous corollaries that flow from their denial of the possibility of dead men rising, through its involved denial that Jesus, the dead man, had risen — aiming, no doubt, at arousing a revulsion against a doctrine fruitful of such consequences (xv. 14–34).

Having thus moved his readers to shame, he proceeds to meet squarely their real objection to the resurrection, by a full explanation of the nature of the resurrection-body (xv. 35–50), to which he adjoins a revelation concerning the occurrences of the last day (xv. 51–58). To each of these we should give a moment's attention.

The intimate connexion of our resurrection with that of Christ, which we have seen Paul everywhere insisting upon, would justify the inference that the nature of our resurrection-bodies was revealed to men in His resurrection-body, that was seen and handled of men for forty days. This is necessarily implied in the assumption that underlies the argument at I Cor. xv. 12 *sq.*, and is almost openly declared at verse 49; II Cor. iv. 14; Rom. viii. 11. In our present passage, however, the Apostle reserves this for the last, and begins by setting forth from natural analogies the possibility of a body being truly one's own body and yet differing largely from that which has hitherto been borne. This is an assertion of sameness and difference. At verse 42 he proceeds to explain the differences in detail. As the change in the form of expression advises us, the enumeration divides itself into two parts at the end of verse 43 — the former portion describing in threefold contrast, the physical, and the latter in a single pregnant phrase the moral difference. On the one hand the new bodies that God will give us will no longer be liable to corruption, dishonour or weakness. On the other, they will no longer be under the power of the only partially sanctified human nature, but rather will be wholly informed, determined and led by the Holy Ghost (verse 44). That this is the meaning of the much disputed phrase: "It is sown a natural (psychic) body, it is raised a spiritual (pneumatic) body," is demonstrable from the usage of the words employed. It is plain matter of fact that "psychic" in the New Testament naturally means and is uniformly used to express "self-led" in contrast to "God-led," and therefore, unconverted or unsanctified; while "pneumatic" never sinks in the New Testament so low in its connotation as the human spirit, but always (with the single exception of Eph. vi. 12, where superhuman evil spirits are in mind) refers to "Spirit" in its highest sense, — the Holy Ghost.[6] In this compressed phrase, thus, the Apostle declares

---

[6] This is gradually becoming recognized by the best expositors. Compare the satisfactory article on πνευματικός in the *third* edition of Cremer's "Biblico-

that in this life believers do not attain to complete sanctification
(Rom. vii. 14–viii. 11), but groan in spirit awaiting the redemption of the body (Rom. viii. 23, vii. 24); while in the heavenly
life even their bodies will no longer retain remainders of sin,
but will be framed by (Rom. viii. 11), filled with, and led by
the Holy Ghost. The incomparable importance of this moral
distinction over the merely physical ones is illustrated by the
Apostle's leaving them to devote the next five verses to the
justification of this, closing (verse 50) with a chiasmic recapitulation in which he pointedly puts the moral difference first:
"Now this I say, brethren, that flesh and blood cannot inherit
the kingdom of God, neither doth corruption inherit incorruption." For, that "flesh and blood" must here be understood
ethically and not physically is already evident from the preceding context and is put beyond question by the settled ethical
sense of the phrase — which is, of course, used in the New
Testament also only in its established ethical sense, and could
not be used otherwise without misleading the reader. All crass
inferences that have been drawn from it, therefore, in a physical
sense are illegitimate to start with, and are negatived to end
with by the analogy of Christ's resurrection-body, which we
have seen Paul to understand to be a case under the rule, and
which certainly had flesh and bones (Luke xxiv. 39). Paul does
not deny to our resurrection-body, therefore, materiality, which
would be a *contradictio in adjecto*; he does not deny "flesh" to
it, — which he hints, rather, will be its material, though of
"another" kind than we are used to (verse 39); he denies to it
Theological Lexicon of N. T. Greek," with the very unsatisfactory one in the
second edition. He now tells us that the word is used "in profane Greek only in a
physical or physiological sense, commonly the former; — in biblical Greek only
in a religious, that is religio- or soteriologico-psychological sense = belonging to
the Holy Ghost or determined by the Holy Ghost," p. 675, cf. p. 676. (The reader
needs to be warned that he will find no hint of Cremer's entire rewriting of this
article, in the *Supplement* to their edition of Cremer's Lexicon issued by T. & T.
Clark this year.) So Meyer's latest view (to which he did not correct the Commentary throughout) is given in his Com. on I Cor., E. T., p. 298, *note:* "Πνευματικός"
is nowhere "in the New Testament the opposite of *material*, but of *natural* (I
Pet. ii. 5 not excluded); and the πνεῦμα to which πνευματικός refers is always (except Eph. vi. 12, where it is the *diabolic* spirit-world that is spoken of) the *Divine*
πνεῦμα." The italics are his own.

"fleshliness" in any, even the smallest degree, and weakness of any and every sort. In a word, he leaves it human but makes it perfect.

After so full an explanation of the nature of the resurrection-body, it was inevitable that deeper questions should arise concerning the fate of those found by the advent still clothed in their bodies of humiliation. Hence a further revelation was necessary beyond what had been given to the Thessalonians, and the Apostle adds to that, that those found living shall be the subjects of an instantaneous change which will make them fit companions for the perfected saints that have slept. For when the trumpet sounds and the dead are raised incorruptible, they too in the twinkling of an eye shall be "changed." And the change is for them as for the dead a putting on of incorruption and of immortality. The spectacle of these multitudes, untouched by death, receiving their perfect and immortal bodies is the great pageant of the conquest of death, and the Apostle on witnessing it in spirit cannot restrain his shout of victory over that whilom enemy of the race, whose victory is now reversed and the sinews of whose fatal sting wherewith it had been wont to slay men are now cut. So complete is Christ's conquest that it looses its hold over its former victims and the men still living cannot die. The rapidity of action on "the great day" is also worth notice. The last trump sounds — the dead spring forth from the grave — the living in the twinkling of an eye are changed — and all together are caught up into the air to His meeting, — or ever the rushing train of angels that surround their Lord and ours can reach the confines of the earth. Truly events stay not, when the Lord comes.

Important as these revelations are, they become almost secondary when compared with the contents of that wonderful passage I Cor. xv. 20–28, the exceeding richness of which is partially accounted for by the occasion of its utterance. It comes in the midst of Paul's effort to move his readers by painting the terrible consequences of denial of the possibility of resurrection, involving denial of the fact that Christ has risen. He feels the revulsion he would beget in them, and relieves his overburdened heart by suddenly turning to rest a moment on the certainty of Christ's rising, and to sweep his eye over all the future, noting the effects of that precious fact up to the end. He begins by reasserting the inclusion of our resurrection in that of Christ, who was but the first-fruits of those asleep, and then justifies it by an appeal to the parallel of Adam's work of destruction, declaring, apparently, that as physical death came upon all men through Adam's sin, so all men shall be rescued from its bondage by Christ's work of redemption. The context apparently confines the word "death" in these verses to its simple physical sense, while on the contrary the "all" of both clauses seems unlimited, and the context appears to furnish nothing to narrow its meaning to a class. They thus assert the resurrection of all men without distinction as dependent on and the result of Christ's work, just as all men, even the redeemed, taste of death as the result of Adam's sin. "But" the Apostle adds, returning to the Christian dead, "this resurrection though certain, is not immediate; each rises in his own place in the ranks — Christ is the first-fruits, then His own rise at His coming; then is the end" (verses 23, 24). The interminable debates that have played around the meaning of this statement are the outgrowth of strange misconceptions. Because the resurrection of the wicked is not mentioned it does not at all follow that it is excluded; the whole section has nothing to do with the resurrection of the wicked (which is only incidentally included and not openly stated in the semi-parenthetic explanations of verses 21 and 22), but, like the parallel passage in I Thessalonians, confines itself to the Christian dead. Nor is it exegetically possible to read the resurrection of the wicked into the passage as a third event to take place at a different time from that of the good, as if the Apostle had said: "Each shall rise in his own order; Christ the first-fruits, — then Christ's dead at His coming, — then, the end of the resurrection, namely of the wicked." The term "the end," is a perfectly definite one with a set and distinct meaning, and from Matthew (e.g. xxiv. 6, cf. 14) throughout the New Testament, and in these very epistles (I Cor. i. 8; II Cor. i. 13, 14), is the standing designation of the

"end of the ages," or the "end of the world." It is illegitimate
to press it into any other groove here. Relief is not however got
by varying the third term, so as to make it say that "then
comes the end, accompanied by the resurrection of the wicked,"
for this is importing into the passage what there is absolutely
nothing in it to suggest. The word τάγμα does not in the least
imply succession; but means "order" only in the sense of that
word in such phrases as "orders of society." Neither does the
"they that are Christ's" prepare the mind to expect a statement as to "those who are not Christ's," any more than in
Rom. ix. 6, when we hear of "Israel," and "those of Israel,"
we expect immediately to hear of "those not of Israel." The
contrast is entirely absorbed by the "Christ" of the preceding
clause, and only the clumsiness of our English gives a different
impression. Not only, however, is there no exegetical basis for
this exposition in this passage; the whole theory of a resurrection of the wicked at a later time than the resurrection of
the just is excluded by this passage. Briefly, this follows from
the statement that after the coming of Christ, "then comes the
end" (verse 24). No doubt the mere word "then" (εἶτα) does
not assert immediateness, and for ought necessarily said in it,
"the end" might be only the next event mentioned by the
Apostle, although the intervening interval should be vast and
crowded with important events. But the context here necessarily limits *this* "then" to immediate subsequence.

Exegetically this follows, indeed, from the relation of verse
28 to 23 *b*, for the long delay asserted in which it assigns the
reason: Christ's children rise not with Him, because death is
the last enemy to be conquered by Him, and their release from
death cannot, therefore, come until all His conquests are completed. The matter can be reduced, however, to the stringency
of a syllogism. "The end" is declared to take place "whenever
Christ giveth over (the immediateness is asserted by the present) the kingdom to God"; and this occurs "whenever He shall
have conquered" all His enemies, the last of which to be conquered is death (verse 26). Shortly, then, the end comes so soon
as death is conquered. But death is already conquered when it

is forced to loose its hold on Christ's children; and that is at the Parousia (ver. 23). If any should think to escape this, as if it were an inference, it would be worth while to glance at verse 54, where it is, as we have seen, asserted that the victory over death is complete and his sting destroyed at the Second Advent, and that the rising of Christ's dead is a result of this completed conquest. The end then is synchronous with the victory over death, which itself is synchronous with the second coming, and if the wicked rise at all (which verses 21, 22 assert), it is all one whether we say they rise at the Advent or at the end, since these two are but two names for the same event. Of this, indeed, Paul's language elsewhere should have convinced us: "who shall also confirm you unto the end, unaccusable in the day of our Lord Jesus Christ" (I Cor. i. 8), "I hope ye will acknowledge unto the end, . . . that we are your glorying even as ye are also ours, in the day of our Lord Jesus" (II Cor. i. 14). So then, the Second Advent is represented to be itself "THE END."

With the emergence of this fact, the importance of our present passage is revealed. It is immediately seen to open to us the nature of the whole dispensation in which we are living, and which stretches from the First to the Second Advent, as a period of advancing conquest on the part of Christ. During its course He is to conquer "every rulership and every authority and power" (verse 24), and "to place all His enemies under His feet" (verse 25), and it ends when His conquests complete themselves by the subjugation of the "last enemy," death. We purposely say, period of "conquest," rather than of "conflict," for the essence of Paul's representation is not that Christ is striving against evil, but progressively (ἔσχατος, verse 26) overcoming evil, throughout this period. A precious passage in the Epistle to the Romans (xi. 25 *sq.*, cf. verse 15) draws the veil aside to gladden our eyes with a nearer view of some of these victories; telling us that "the fulness of the Gentiles shall be brought into" the Church, and after that "all Israel shall be saved," and by their salvation great blessings, — such a spiritual awakening as can only be compared to "life from the dead" — shall be brought to all God's people. There may be some doubt as to the exact meaning of these phrases. The "fulness of the Gentiles," however, in accordance with the usual sense of the genitive with "pleroma," and the almost compulsion of the context, should mean, not the Gentile contingent to the elect, but the whole body of the Gentiles.[7] And "Israel" almost certainly means not the true but the fleshly "Israel." In this case, the prophecy promises the universal Christianization of the world, — at least the nominal conversion of all the Gentiles and the real salvation of all the Jews. In any understanding of it, it promises the widest practicable extension of Christianity, and reveals to us Christ going forth to victory. But in this, which seems to us the true understanding, it gives us a glimpse of the completion of His conquest over spiritual wickedness, and allows us to see in the spirit the fulfilment of the prayer, "Thy kingdom come, Thy will be done in earth even as it is in heaven." It is natural to think that such a victory cannot be wrought until the end is hastening — that with its completion nothing will remain to be conquered but death itself. But the Apostle does not tell us this,[8] and we know not from him how long the converted earth is to await its coming Lord.

[7] The exegetical question really turns on the sense to be given to 'Ισραήλ in xi. 26. If τὸ πλήρωμα τῶν ἐθνῶν in verse 25, means "those of the Gentiles who go towards filling up the kingdom," then πᾶς 'Ισραήλ of verse 26, must of necessity be the spiritual Israel, distinguished from 'Ισραήλ of verse 25, by the inclusive πᾶς. Then the sense would be that "hardening has befallen Israel" temporarily — viz. until the Gentile contingent comes in, — and thus ("in this way," the most natural sense of οὕτως), ALL Israel shall be saved; — not part only, but all. So that the passage continues to justify the temporary rejection of Israel by its gracious purpose, viz. that thus the Gentiles receive their calling, and all God's children, out of every nation, are saved. On the other hand if, as is most natural and usual, τῶν ἐθνῶν is genitive of what is filled up, so that the phrase means, the whole body of the Gentiles, then there is no thought to carry over from it to condition πᾶς 'Ισραήλ in verse 26, and it naturally follows in sense the 'Ισραήλ of verse 25. The sense then is that which is suggested in the text. That 'Ισραήλ of verse 26 is the fleshly Israel seems to follow from the succeeding context, as well as from the difficulty of taking the words in two different senses in so narrow a context. But if so, this carries the meaning of the "fulness of the Gentiles" with it, and the interpretation given in the text is the only admissible one.

[8] I shall not deny that the ζωὴ ἐκ νεκρῶν of ver. 15 may mean the general resurrection, but it is an unexampled phrase for this conception and cannot be asserted to mean it. Nor in this context is it natural to so understand it.

An even more important fact faces us in the wonderful revelation we have been considering (I Cor. xv. 20–28): the period between the two advents is the period of Christ's kingdom, and when He comes again it is not to institute His kingdom, but to lay it down (verses 24, 28). The completion of His conquest, which is marked by conquering "the last enemy," death (verse 28), which in turn is manifest when the just arise and Christ comes (verses 54, 23), marks also the end of His reign (verse 25) and the delivery of the kingdom to God, even the Father (verse 24). This is indubitably Paul's assertion here, and it is in perfect harmony with the uniform representation of the New Testament, which everywhere places Christ's kingdom before and God's after the Second Advent. The contrast in Mt. xiii. 41 and 43 is not accidental. We cannot enter into the many deep questions that press for discussion when this ineffable prediction is even approached. Suffice it to say that when we are told that Jesus holds the kingship for a purpose (verse 25), namely the completion of His mediatorial work, and that when it is accomplished He will restore it to Him who gave it to Him (verse 28), and thus the Father will again become "all relations among all creations," — nothing is in the remotest way suggested inconsistent with the co-equal Deity of the Son with the Father and His eternal co-regnancy with Him over the universe. Manifestly we must distinguish between the mediatorial kingship which Jesus exercises by appointment of His Father, and the eternal kingship which is His by virtue of His nature, and which is one with God's own.

As to the duration of Christ's kingdom — or in other words the length of time that was to elapse before the Lord came — Paul says nothing in this passage. Nor does he anywhere in these Epistles speak more certainly about it than in those to the Thessalonians (I Cor. i. 7; xi. 26). He so expresses himself as to leave the possibility open that the Lord might come in his own time (I Cor. xv. 51); but he makes it a matter for experience to decide whether He will or not (II Cor. v. 1, ἐάν with the subjunctive, cf. verse 3 *sq.*). It is only through misunderstanding that passages have been adduced as asserting a brief life for the world. When (I Cor. x. 11) the "ends of the ages" are said to have already come, a technical term is used which declares that after this present inter-adventual period there remains no further earthly dispensation, but nothing is implied as to the duration of these "last times" (*acharith hayyamim*). So, when (I Cor. vii. 25–29) the Corinthians are advised to refrain from earthly entanglements because of "the impending distress," which should shortly tear asunder every human tie, there is nothing to show that the Apostle had the Second Advent in mind, and everthing in the Neronian persecution and the wars of succession and the succeeding trials to Christians to fully satisfy the prediction.[9] The very difficult passage at Rom. xiii. 11–14 appears also to have been misapplied to the advent by the modern exegesis. Its obvious parallels are Eph. v. 1–14 and I Thess. v. 1–11. The whole gist of the passage turns on moral awaking; and the word "salvation" appears to refer to the consummation of salvation in a subjective rather than objective sense (Rom. x. 10; II Thess. ii. 13); while the aorist, "When we believed," seems not easily to lend itself to furnishing a *terminus a quo* for the calculation of time, but rather to express the act by which their salvation was brought closer. So that the meaning of the passage would seem to be: "Fulfil the law of love, I say. I appeal to you for renewed efforts by your knowledge of the time: that it is high time for you at length to awake out of sleep. Long ago when you believed, you professed to have come out of darkness into light, and to have shaken yourselves free from the inertia as well as deeds of the night. Now salvation is closer to us than it was when we made that step. Having begun, we have advanced somewhat towards the goal. The night of sin in which the call for repentance found us is passing away. Let us take off at length our night-clothes, and buckle on the armour for the good fight — yea, let us rid our-

---

[9] The reference of the phrase, "for the fashion of this world passeth away" (verse 31) is not to the broad but the narrow context, justifying the immediately preceding statement, that those who use the world should be as those not using it. It is but equivalent to the line, "This world is all a fleeting show," and is parallel to I John ii. 17. Although it may have some reference to the Second Advent, as the day of renovation, it does not affect verses 20 and 29.

selves of all that belongs to the night, and put on the Lord Jesus Himself." If this understanding is correct, the Apostle does not count the days and assert that the time that had elapsed since his conversion had nearly run the sands of all time out, but rather appeals to his readers to renew their strenuous and hearty working out of their salvation by the encouragement that they had already progressed somewhat on the road, and could more easily and hopefully take a second step.

There remain two very interesting passages (II Cor. v. 1–10; Rom. viii. 18–25) which give us an insight as no others do into the Apostle's personal feelings towards this life, death, and the Advent. Nowhere else are the trials under which he suffered life so clearly revealed to us as in the opening chapters of II Corinthians. Amid them all, the very allusions to which, lightly touched as they are, appal us, the Apostle is upheld by the greatness of his ministry and the greatness of his hope. Though his outward man is worn away — what then? He need not faint, for his inward man is renewed day by day, and this affliction is light compared with the eternal weight of glory in store for him. He longs for the rest of the future life (cf. also Rom. vii. 25); but he shrinks from death. He could desire rather to be alive when the Lord comes, and that he might put on "the house from God, the dwelling not made with hands, eternal in the heavens," over this "earthly tent-dwelling" which he now inhabits. He only desires — does not expect this; he does not at all know whether he shall be found not naked when the putting-on time comes. But he longs for relief from the burdens of life, that somehow this mortality may be swallowed up of life. And when he bethinks him that to be at home in the body is to be abroad from the Lord, the other world is so glorious to him that he is not only willing but even desires ("rather," verse 8) to enter it even "naked" — he is well pleased to go abroad from the body and go home to the Lord. Like Bunyan and the sweet singer, Paul, looking beyond the confines of earth, can only say, "Would God that I were there!" This longing for relief from earthly life is repeated in Romans (vii. 25), and the groaning expectation of the consummation as the swallowing up of corruption in incorruption is attributed in the wonderful words of Romans viii. 18 *sq.* to the whole of the lower creation. All nature, says Paul, travails in the same longing. And the consummation brings not only relief to Christ's children, who have received the firstfruits of the Spirit, in the redemption of the body, but also deliverance and renovation to all nature as well. This noble conception was implied already in the teaching of the Old Testament, not only in its declaration that the world was cursed for man's sake (Rom. viii. 20), but in the prediction of a new heavens and a new earth (verse 21). Paul here simply takes his position in the company of the prophets.

The glories of the future world find comparative expression again in I Cor. xiii. 10–13 as not only spiritual but eternal and perfect. There are besides two rapid allusions to future glories which are so slightly touched on in contexts of stinging satire as not fully to explain themselves. The one reminds the saints that they shall judge the world and angels (I Cor. vi. 2, 3), and the other assumes that at some time or other, they are to come to a kingship (I Cor. iv. 8). Out of our present epistles alone the time and circumstances when these promises shall be fulfilled can scarcely be confidently asserted. We can only say that if the reigning of the saints refers to a co-reigning with Christ (cf. II Tim. ii. 12), it must be fulfilled before Christ lays down His kingdom. And in like manner the judging must come before the Advent, unless it refers only to the part the saints take in the last judgment scene (cf. Mt. xix. 28; xxv. 31). The Apostle expects his readers to understand his allusions out of knowledge obtained elsewhere than in these epistles. Perhaps he has in mind such "words of the Lord" as are recorded in Luke xxii. 29, 30. For us, the whole matter may rest for the present *sub judice*.

III. — The Later Epistles

The distribution of predictive passages through the letters written by St. Paul during his first imprisonment, — Ephesians,

Colossians, Philemon and Philippians (A.D. 62 and 63), — is analogous to what we have observed in the preceding group. In the more theological and polemical letters, as there, so here, such passages are few, while in the more practical and personal letters they are comparatively numerous. The Second Advent is not directly mentioned at all in Ephesians, and only once, and then very incidentally, in Colossians; while, although the brief and purely occasional letter to Philemon naturally enough contains no allusions to the future, the Epistle to the Philippians, which resembles in general manner and contents the letters to the Corinthians and Thessalonians, like them too is full of them. The nature of the eschatological matter which is found in each epistle is in striking harmony with its purpose and general character: in Ephesians and Colossians it is confined to allusions, sometimes somewhat obscure, to eschatological facts which are introduced usually with a theological or polemic object; in Philippians, where Paul pours out his heart, it is free and rich, and usually has a direct personal design of encouragement or consolation. In all these epistles alike, however, it is introduced only incidentally — no section has it as its chief end to record the future; but in Philippians it is more fully and lovingly dwelt upon, in Ephesians and Colossians more allusively touched. It is not surprising, under such circumstances, that very little is revealed to us concerning the future in these epistles beyond what was already contained in the earlier letters, the teaching of which most commonly furnishes the full statement of the facts here briefly referred to. Now and then, however, they cast a ray of light on points or sides of the truth which were not before fully illuminated, and thus enable us to count distinct gains from their possession. Nowhere are they out of harmony with what the earlier epistles have revealed.

The eschatological contents of the twin letters, Ephesians and Colossians, will illustrate all this very sharply. Much is made in them of an inheritance of hope laid up in heaven for the saints in light (Eph. i. 14, cf. ii. 7; Col. i. 12, i. 5: cf. iii. 24). The time of its realization is when Christ our life shall be manifested, at which time we also shall be manifested with Him in glory (Col. iii. 4). It is clearly presupposed that the reception of the inheritance is conditioned on a previous judgment. We must be made meet for it by the Father, by a deliverance from the power of darkness and translation into the kingdom of Him by whom we have redemption, the forgiveness of our sins (Col. i. 12). Whatsoever good thing each one does, the same he shall certainly receive from the Lord (Eph. vi. 8). The inheritance itself is thus a recompense for our service here (Col. iii. 24). Judgment again is implied in the constant undertone of allusion to a presentation of us by God or Christ, pure and blameless and unaccusable at once before Christ and in Christ (Eph. i. 22; Col. i. 22, 28). But if Christ is thus the judge, we naturally enough are to live our life here in His fear (Eph. v. 21). The resurrection of the saints is implied now and then (Col. ii. 12, 13; cf. Eph. v. 23), and once asserted in the declaration that Christ has become "the first-born from the dead, that in all things He might have the pre-eminence" (Col. i. 18). The nature of this inter-adventual period is explained with apparent reference to some such teaching as is given in I Cor. xv. 25, to be a period of conflict (Eph. vi. 12), and its opening days are hence said to be evil (Eph. v. 16), though, no doubt, the evil will decrease as conflict passes into victory. The enemies of the Lord are named as principalities and powers, and their subjugation was potentially completed at His death and resurrection (Col. ii. 15). The actual completion of the victory and subjection of all things to the Son is briefly re-stated in each epistle. In the one it is declared that God has purposed with reference to the dispensation of the fulness of the times (*i.e.* this present dispensation of the ends of the ages, I Cor. x. 11) to gather again all things as under one head in Christ, the things in the heavens and the things upon earth (Eph. i. 10). In the other it is said that it was the Father's good pleasure that all the fulness should dwell in the Son, and that through Him all things should be reconciled to Him, whether things upon the earth or things in the heavens, and that this reconciliation should be wrought by His blood outpoured on the cross (Col. i. 19). The only

difference between such statements and such a one as II Cor.
v. 19 is that these deal with the universe, while that treats only
of man, and hence these presuppose the full teaching implied
in I Cor. xv. 10–28 and Rom. viii. 18–25, and sum up in a single
pregnant sentence the full effects of the Saviour's work. The
method of Christ's attack on the principalities and powers and
world-rulers of this darkness and spiritual hosts of wickedness,
and the means by which He will work His victory, are declared
at Eph. vi. 12; from which we learn — as we might have guessed
from Rom. xi. 25, *sq.* — that Christians are His soldiers in this
holy war, and it is through our victory that His victory is
known. It is easy to see that there is nothing new in all this, and
yet there is much that has the appearance of being new. We see
everything from a different angle; the light drops upon it from
a new point, and the effect is to bring out new relations in the
old truths and give us a feeling of its substantialness. We become more conscious that we are looking at solid facts, with
fronts and backs and sides, standing each in due and fixed
relations to all.

The Epistle to the Philippians differs from the others of its
group only in dwelling more lingeringly on the matters it mentions, and thus transporting us back into the full atmosphere of
Corinthians and Thessalonians. Here, too, Paul thinks of the
advent chiefly in the aspect of the judgment at which we are
to receive our eternal approval and reward or disapproval and
rejection. He is sure that He who began a good work in His
readers will perfect it, until the day of Jesus Christ (i. 6); he
prays that they may be pure and void of offence against the day
of Christ (i. 10); he desires them to complete their Christian
life that he may have whereof to glory in the day of Christ that
he did not run in vain, neither labour in vain (ii. 16). These
sentences might have come from any of the earlier epistles. The
events of the day of the Lord are detailed quite in the spirit of
the earlier epistles in iii. 20, 21. Our real home, the common-
wealth in which is our citizenship, is heaven, from whence we
patiently await a Saviour, the Lord Jesus Christ, who shall
fashion anew the body of our humiliation so that it shall be

conformed to the body of His glory, according to the working whereby He is able to subdue all things unto Himself. These two verses compress within their narrow compass most of the essential features of Paul's eschatology: Christ's present enthronement as King of the state in which our citizenship is, in heaven, from whence we are to expect Him to return in due time; our resurrection and the nature of our new bodies on the one side as no longer bodies of humiliation, on the other as like Christ's resurrection body, and hence glorious; Christ's conquest of all things to Himself, and last of all of death, in our resurrection, of which, therefore, all His other conquests are a guerdon.

The description of our resurrection bodies as conformed to Christ's glorified body is important in itself, and all the more so as it helps us to catch the meaning of the almost immediately preceding statement (iii. 10 *sq.*) of Paul's deep desire "to know Christ and the power of His resurrection and the fellowship of His suffering, becoming conformed unto His death, if by any means he may attain to the resurrection of the dead." It has become somewhat common to see in this passage a hint that Paul knew only of a resurrection of the redeemed, and himself expected to rise only in case he was savingly united to Christ. This exposition receives, no doubt, some colour from the phraseology used; but when we observe the intensely moral nature of the longing, as expressed in the immediately subsequent context, we cannot help limiting the term "resurrection from the dead" here, by the added idea of resurrection to glory, and the full statement of verse 21 inevitably throws back its light upon it. It is not mere resurrection that Paul longs for; he gladly becomes conformed to Christ in His death that he may be conformed to Him in His resurrection also, and the gist of the whole passage is bound up in this idea of conformity to Christ, with which it opens (verse 10) and with which it closes (verse 21). To think of two separate resurrections here — of the just and the unjust — in the former of which Paul desires to rise, is to cut the knot, not untie it. Nothing in the language suggests it — the "resurrection from the dead" is as unlimited [10] as the

---

[10] On ἐξανάστασις, see Meyer *in loc.*

"death" that precedes it. Nothing in the context demands or even allows it. Nothing anywhere in Paul's writings justifies it. It is inconsistent with what we have found Paul saying about the Second Advent and its relation to the end, at I Cor. xv. 20–28. And finally it is contradicted by his explicit statements concerning the general resurrection, in the discourses in Acts which are closest in time to the date of these letters, and which ought to be considered along with them, especially Acts xxiv. 15, where in so many words the resurrection is made to include both the just and unjust (cf. xxiii. 6; xxvi. 8, 23; xxviii. 20). The limitation which the context supplies in our present passage is not that of class, much less that of time, but that of result; Paul longs to be conformed to Christ in resurrection as in death — he is glad to suffer with Him that he may be also glorified together with Him. Yea, he counts his sufferings but refuse, if he may gain Christ and *be found in Him*, clothed in the righteousness which is by faith. This is the ruling thought which conditions the statements of verse 11, and is openly returned to at verse 21.

The mention of the subjection of all things to Christ in verse 21, which recalls the teaching of I Cor. xv. 20–28 again, was already prepared for by the account of the glory which God gave the Son as a reward for His work of suffering, in ii. 9–11. There His supreme exaltation is stated to have been given Him of God for a purpose — that all creation should be subjected to Him, should bow the knee to His Name and confess Him to be Lord to the glory of God the Father. The completion of this purpose Paul here (iii. 21) asserts Christ to have the power to bring about, but nothing is implied in either passage as to the rapidity of its actual realization.

Some have thought, however, that in this epistle also Paul expresses his confidence that all should be fulfilled in his own time. Plainly, however, the reference of the completion of our moral probation, or of our victory over the present humiliation, to the Second Advent goes no further than to leave the possibility of its coming in our generation open (i. 6; iii. 21), and the latter at least is conditioned by the desire for a good resurrection, which is earnestly expressed immediately before. "The Lord is at hand" (iv. 5) would be more to the point, if its reference to time and the Second Advent were plainer. But although it was early so understood (e. g., by Barnabas), it can hardly be properly so taken. It is, indeed, scarcely congruous to speak of a person as near in time; we speak of events or actions, times or seasons as near, meaning it temporally; but when we say a person is near, we mean it inevitably of a space-relation. And the connexion of the present verse points even more strongly in the same direction. Whether we construe it with what goes before, or with what comes after — whether we read "Let your gentleness be known to all men, [for] the Lord is near," or "The Lord is near, [therefore] be anxious for nothing, but in everything . . . let your requests be made known unto God," — the reference to God's continual nearness to the soul for help is preferable to that to the Second Advent. And if, as seems likely, the latter connexion be the intended one, the contextual argument is pressing. The fact that the same phrase occurs in the Psalter in the space-sense, and must have been therefore in familiar use in this sense by Paul and his readers alike, while the asyndetic, proverbial way in which it is introduced here gives it the appearance of a quotation, adds all that was needed to render this interpretation of it here certain.

The Apostle's real feelings towards the future life are clearly exposed to us in the touching words of i. 21 *sq.*, the close resemblance of which to II Cor. v. 1–10 is patent. Here he does not refer in the remotest way to a hope of living to see the advent, but begins where he ended in II Corinthians, with the assertion of his personal preference for death rather than life, because death brought the gain of being with Christ, "which is far better." Even the "naked" intermediate state of the soul, between death and resurrection, is thus in Paul's view to be chosen rather than a life at home in the body but abroad from the Lord. Yet he does not therefore choose to die: "but what if to live in the flesh — this means fruit of my work?" he pauses to ask himself, and can but answer that he is in a strait betwixt the two, and finally that since to die is advantageous to himself

alone, while to live is more needful for his converts, he knows
he shall abide still a while in this world. To him, too, man here
is but

> "a hasty traveller
> Posting between the present and the future,
> That baits awhile in this dull fleshly tavern";

and yet, though this tent-dwelling is seen by him in all its
insufficiency and inefficiency, like the good Samaritan he is
willing to prolong his stay in even so humble a caravanserai
(iii. 21) for the succouring of his fellows — nay, like the Lord
Himself, he counts the glory of the heavenly life not a thing to
be graspingly seized, so long as by humbling himself to the form
of a tenant here he may save the more. The spirit that was in
Christ dwelt within him.

The eschatology of the Pastoral Epistles — I Timothy,
Titus, and II Timothy (A.D. 67, 68) — the richest depository
of which is the Second Epistle to Timothy, is indistinguishable
from that of the other Pauline letters. In these letters again the
Second Advent is primarily and most prominently conceived as
the closing act of the world, the final judgment of men, and
therefore the goal of all their moral endeavours. Timothy is
strenuously exhorted "to keep the commandment," that is, the
evangelical rule of life, "spotless and irreproachable until the
appearing of our Lord Jesus Christ" (I Tim. vi. 14). All of
Paul's confidence is based on his persuasion that Jesus Christ,
the abolisher of death and bringer of life and incorruption to
light through the Gospel, is able to guard his deposit [11] "against
that day" (II Tim. i. 12), and that there is laid up for him the
crown of righteousness which the Lord, the righteous Judge,
shall give him at that day (II Tim. iv. 8). "And not to me only,"
he adds, as if to guard against his confidence seeming one personal to himself, "but also to all them that have loved His
appearing." Though at that day the Lord will render to Alexander according to his works (II Tim. iv. 14), he will grant
mercy to Onesiphorus (II Tim. i. 16); and in general he will at-

[11] $\tau\grave{\eta}\nu$ $\pi\alpha\rho\alpha\theta\acute{\eta}\kappa\eta\nu$ $\mu\upsilon$ = "what I have entrusted to him."

tach to godliness the promise both of the life that now is and that which is to come (I Tim. iv. 8).

It follows, therefore, that for all those in Christ the Second Advent is a blessed hope to be waited for with patience, but also with loving desire and longing. Christians are described as those that love Christ's appearing (II Tim. iv. 8), and the hope of it is blessed (Titus ii. 13) because it is the epiphany of the glory of our great God and Saviour Jesus Christ, even as the former coming was the epiphany of His grace (Titus ii. 13, cf. 11). It is implied that as the grace so the glory is for Christ's children. What this glory consists in is not, however, very sharply defined. It is the deposit of life and incorruption that the Saviour holds in trust for His children (II Tim. i. 12). It is the crown of righteousness which the righteous Judge will bestow upon them (II Tim. iv. 8). It is freedom from all iniquity (Titus ii. 14). It is the actual inheritance of the eternal life now hoped for (Titus iii. 7). But all this is description rather than definition. Nothing is said of resurrection except that they gravely err who think it already past (II Tim. ii. 18), nothing of the new bodies to be given to the saints, or of any of the glories that accompany the final triumph. What is said describes only the full realization of what is already enjoyed in its first fruits here or what comes in some abundance in the imperfect intermediate state.

For the glories of the advent do not blind Paul to the bliss of a Christian's hope in "this world," whether in the body or out of the body. In the fervid music of a Christian hymn the Apostle assures his son Timothy of his own steadfast faith in the faithful saying (II Tim. ii. 11–13):—

> "If we died with Him, we shall also live with Him;
> If we endure we shall also reign with Him;
> If we shall deny Him, He will also deny us;
> If we are faithless — He abideth faithful,
> For He cannot deny Himself."

And death itself, he says, can but "save him into Christ's heavenly kingdom" (II Tim. iv. 18). The partaking in Christ's

death and life in this passage seems to be meant ethically; and
the co-regnancy with the Lord that is promised to the suffering
believer apparently concerns the being with Christ in the heavenly kingdom, — whether in the body or abroad from the body.
Thus the Apostle is not here contemplating the glories of the
advent, but comforting and strengthening himself with the
profitableness of godliness in its promise of the life that now is,
under the epiphany of God's grace, when we can be but looking
for the epiphany of His glory. That he expects death (for now
he was sure of death, II Tim. iv. 6) to introduce him into
Christ's heavenly kingdom advertises to us that that kingdom is now in progress, and II Tim. iv. 1 is in harmony with
this just because it tells us nothing at all of the time of the kingdom.[12]

About Christ's reign and work as king — in other words,
concerning the nature of this period in which we live — these
epistles are somewhat rich in teaching. These "latter times"
or "last days"[13] — for these are, according to the fixed usage
of the times, the designations under which the Apostle speaks
of the dispensation of the Spirit, — are not to be an age of idle-
ness or of sloth among Christians; but, in harmony with the
statements of the earlier letters, which represented it as a time
of conflict with and conquest of evil, it is here pictured as a time
in which apostasies shall occur (I Tim. iv. 1), and false doctrines
flourish along with evil practices (II Tim. iii. 1, sq.), when the
just shall suffer persecution, and evil men and impostors wax
worse and worse (II Tim. iii. 13), and, even in the Church, men
shall not endure sound doctrine, but shall introduce teachers
after their own lusts (II Tim. iv. 3 sq.). It would be manifestly
illegitimate to understand these descriptions as necessarily
covering the life of the whole dispensation on the earliest verge
of which the prophet was standing. Some of these evils had al-

---

[12] Notice that the correct translation is: "I charge thee before God and Christ
Jesus who shall judge the quick and the dead, and by His appearing and by His
kingdom." Each item is adduced entirely separately; the Apostle is accumulating
the incitements to action, not giving a chronological list, which, in any case, the
passage does not furnish.

[13] ἐν ὑστέροις καιροῖς, I Tim. iv. 1; ἐν ἐσχάταις ἡμέραις, II Tim. iii. 1.

ready broken out in his own times, others were pushing up the ground preparatory to appearing above it themselves. It is historically plain to us, no doubt, that they suitably describe the state of affairs up to at least our own day. But we must remember that all the indications are that Paul had the first stages of "the latter times" in mind, and actually says nothing to imply either that the evil should long predominate over the good, or that the whole period should be marked by such disorders.

When the Lord should come, he indeed keeps as uncertain in these epistles as in all his former ones. In II Timothy he expects his own death immediately, and he contemplates it with patience and even joy, no longer with the shrinking expressed in II Corinthians. It is all the more gratuitous to insist here that the natural reference of Timothy's keeping the faith to the advent as the judgment (I Tim. vi. 14), implies that he confidently expected that great closing event at once or very soon. On the contrary it is reiterated in the same context that God alone knows the times and seasons, in the assertion that God would show the epiphany of our Lord Jesus Christ "in His own times." Beyond this the Apostle never goes; and it is appropriate that in his earliest and latest epistles especially he should categorically assert the absolute uncertainty of the time of the consummation (I Thess. v. 1; I Tim. vi. 15). Surely an intense personal conviction that the times and seasons were entirely out of his knowledge can alone account for so consistent an attitude of complete uncertainty.

It appears to be legitimate to affirm in the light of the preceding pages that it is clear that there is such a thing as a Pauline eschatology; a consistent teaching on the last things which runs through the whole mass of his writings, not filling them, indeed, as some would have us believe, but appearing on their surface like daisies in a meadow — here in tolerable profusion, there in quite a mass, there scattered one by one at intervals of some distance — everywhere woven into it as constituent parts of the turf carpeting. The main outlines of this eschatology are repeated over and over again, and exhibited from many separate points of view, until we know them from every side and are confident of their contour and exact nature. Details are added to the general picture by nearly every letter; and each detail falls so readily into its place in the outline as to prove both that the Apostle held a developed scheme of truth on this subject, and that we are correctly understanding it. A general recapitulation of the broadest features of his doctrine will alone be necessary in closing.

Paul, then, teaches that as Jesus has once come in humiliation, bringing grace into the world, and God has raised Him to high exaltation and universal dominion in reward for His sufferings and in order to the completion of His work of redemption; so when He shall have put all His enemies under His feet, He shall come again to judgment in an epiphany of glory, to close the dispensation of grace and usher in the heavenly blessedness. The enemies to be conquered are principalities and powers and world-rulers of this darkness and spiritual hosts of wickedness; this whole period is the period of advancing conquest and will end with the victory over the last enemy, death, and the consequent resurrection of the dead. In this advancing conquest Christ's elect are His soldiers, and the conversion of the world — first of the Gentiles, then of the Jews — marks the culminating victory over the powers of evil. How long this conflict continues before it is crowned with complete victory, how long the supreme and sole kingship of Christ endures before He restores the restored realm to His father, the Apostle leaves in complete uncertainty. He predicts the evil days of the opening battle, the glad days of the victory; and leaves all questions of times and seasons to Him whose own times they are. At the end, however, are the general resurrection and the general judgment, when the eternal rewards and punishments are awarded by Christ as judge, and then, all things having been duly gathered together thus again under one head by Him, he subjects them all to God that He may once more become "all relations among all creations." That the blessed dead may be fitted to remain for ever with the Lord, He gives them each his own body, glorified and purified and rendered the willing organ of the Holy Ghost. Christ's living, though they die not, are "changed" to a like glory. Not only man, but all creation feels the renovation and shares in the revelation of the sons of God, and there is a new heaven and a new earth. And thus the work of the Redeemer is completed, the end has come, and it is visible to men and angels that through Him in whom it was His pleasure that all the fulness should dwell, God has at length reconciled all things unto Himself, having made peace through the blood of His cross — through Him, whether things upon the earth or things in the heavens — yea, even us, who were in times past alienated and enemies, hath He reconciled in the body of His flesh through death, to present us holy and without blemish and unreproachable before Him.

XVI

THE MILLENNIUM AND THE APOCALYPSE

THE MILLENNIUM AND THE APOCALYPSE [1]

Of the section of the Apocalypse which extends (according to his division of the book) from xx. 1 to xxi. 8, Kliefoth remarks, as he approaches its study, that "because the so-called millennium is included in its compass, it has been more than any other part of the book tortured by tendency-exposition into a variety of divergent senses." [2] This is undoubtedly true: but in reprobating it, we must not permit ourselves to forget that there is a sense in which it is proper to permit our understanding of so obscure a portion of Scripture to be affected by the clearer teaching of its more didactic parts. We must guard, no doubt, against carrying this too far and doing violence to the text before us in the interests of Bible-harmony. But within due limits, surely, the order of investigation should be from the clearer to the more obscure. And it is to be feared that there has been much less tendency-interpretation of Rev. xx in the interest of preconceived theory, than there has been tendency-interpretation of the rest of Scripture in the interest of conceptions derived from misunderstandings of this obscure passage.

Nothing, indeed, seems to have been more common in all ages of the Church than to frame an eschatological scheme from this passage, imperfectly understood, and then to impose this scheme on the rest of Scripture *vi et armis*. To realize this, we have but to recall the manifold influences which have wrought not only on eschatological dreaming, but on theological thought and on Christian life itself, out of the conception summed up in the term "the millennium." Yet not only the word, but, as Kliefoth has himself solidly shown,[3] the thing, is unknown to Scripture outside of this passage.[4] And not only so, but there

---

[1] From *The Princeton Theological Review*, v. 2, 1904, pp. 599–617.

[2] "Die Offenbarung des Johannes," 1874, III, 254.

[3] "Christliche Eschatologie," 1886, pp. 183 *sq.*

[4] "Once, and only once," says the "Encyc. Bibl.," 3095, "in the New Testament we hear of a millennium." W. A. Brown, in Hastings' "Bible Dict.," III,

are not a few passages of Scripture — as Kliefoth also has shown [5] — which seem definitely to exclude the whole conception, and which must be subjected to most unnatural exegetical manipulation to bring them into harmony with it at all. We need not raise the question whether Scripture can contradict Scripture: in our day, certainly, there is no lack of expositors who would feel little difficulty in expounding the eschatology of Revelation as definitely the *antipodes* of that, say, of Paul, not to say the eschatology of one section of Revelation as the precise contradictory of that of another. But surely, for those who look upon the Bible as something other than the chance driftage of the earliest age of Christianity, it is at least undesirable to assume such an antagonism beforehand; and on the emergence of apparent inconsistencies it certainly becomes in the first instance incumbent upon us to review our expositions under the impulse of at least the possibility that they may prove to be in error. We shall not proceed far in such an undertaking, as it seems to us, before we discover that the traditional interpretation of Revelation which yields the notion of a "millennium" is at fault; and that this book, when taken in its natural and self-indicated sense, needs no harmonizing with the eschatology of the rest of the New Testament, for the simple reason that its eschatology is precisely the same with that of its companion books.

In order to make this good, it will not be necessary to do more than pass in rapid review the series of visions which constitute the particular section of the Apocalypse of which the millennium-passage forms a part. The structure of the book,

371. The period of 1000 years seems to be applied to such a conception first in the Slavonic "Book of the Secrets of Enoch," 33: 1, 2 (see "Encyc. Bibl.," 1368; Hastings, I, 711a, III, 371a) which is dated by Charles in the first half of the first century. It is there based on the idea of a Sabbatical week: as the world was created in six days followed by a day of rest, so the world will last 6000 years followed by 1000 years of rest. The same idea seems to underlie Barnabas, c. 15, though Dr. Salmond, "Christian Doct. of Immort.," 1895, p. 438, does not think so. Cf. Gebhardt, "The Doctrine of the Apocalypse," E. T., pp. 277–278.

[5] *Ibid.*, pp. 187–188. Cf. Milligan, "Baird Lectures on the Revelation of St. John," 1886, pp. 205 *sq.*; and "Expositor's Bible: The Book of Revelation," 1889, pp. 345 *sq.*

made up as it is of seven parallel sections,[6] repeating with progressive clearness, fullness and richness the whole history of the
inter-adventual period, and thus advancing in a spiral fashion
to its climax, renders it possible to do this without drawing too
much on a knowledge of the whole book. We have only to bear
clearly in mind a few primary principles, apart from which no
portion of the book can be understood, and we need not despair
of unlocking the secrets of this section also.

These primary principles are, with the greatest possible
brevity, the following: 1. The principle of *recapitulation*.[7] That
is to say, the structure of the book is such that it returns at the
opening of each of its seven sections to the first advent, and
gives in the course of each section a picture of the whole inter-
adventual period — each successive portraiture, however, rising above the previous one in the stress laid on the issue of the
history being wrought out during its course. The present section, being the last, reaches, therefore, the climax, and all its
emphasis is thrown upon the triumph of Christ's kingdom.
2. The principle of *successive visions*. That is to say, the several
visions following one another within the limits of each section,
though bound to each other by innumerable links, yet are presented as separate visions, and are to be interpreted, each, as
a complete picture in itself. 3. The principle of *symbolism*. That
is to say — as is implied, indeed, in the simple fact that we are
brought face to face here with a series of visions significant of
events — we are to bear continually in mind that the whole
fabric of the book is compact of symbols. The descriptions are
descriptions not of the real occurrences themselves, but of symbols of the real occurrences; and are to be read strictly as such.
Even more than in the case of parables, we are to avoid pressing

[6] The plan of the book is, then, something like the following: Prologue, I:
1–8; seven parallel sections divided at III: 22, VIII: 1, XI: 19, XIV: 20, XVI:
21 and XIX: 20; Epilogue, XXII: 6–21. The subdivisions of the several sections
follow, each, its own course.

[7] This principle of *recapitulatio* was announced by Augustine, and perfected by Nicolas Colladon (1584) and David Pareus (1618), and especially by
Cocceius and Vitringa. A very large number of expositors have employed its
fundamental principle, as, among later ones, for instance, Hofmann, Hengstenberg, Ebrard, Kienlen; but with varying degrees of judiciousness.

details in our interpretation of symbols: most of the details are details of the symbol, designed purely to bring the symbol sharply and strongly before the mind's eye, and are not to be transferred by any method of interpretation whatever directly to the thing symbolized. The symbol as a whole symbolizes the real event: and the details of the picture belong primarily only to the symbol. Of course, now and then a hint is thrown out which may seem more or less to traverse this general rule: but, as a general rule, it is not only sound but absolutely necessary for any sane interpretation of the book. 4. The principle of *ethical purpose*. That is to say, here as in all prophecy it is the spiritual and ethical impression that rules the presentation and not an annalistic or chronological intent. The purpose of the seer is to make known indeed — to make wise — but not for knowledge's own sake, but for a further end: to make known unto action, to make wise unto salvation. He contents himself, therefore, with what is efficacious for his spiritual end and never loses himself in details which can have no other object than the satisfaction of the curiosity of the mind for historical or other knowledge.

One of the effects of the recognition of these primary principles — an effect the perception of which is no more interesting in itself than fruitful for the interpretation of the book — is the transference of the task of the interpreter from the region of minute philology to that of broad literary appreciation. The ascertainment of the meaning of the Apocalypse is a task, that is to say, not directly of verbal criticism but of sympathetic imagination: the teaching of the book lies not immediately in its words, but in the wide vistas its visions open to the fancy. It is the seeing eye, here, therefore, rather than the nice scales of linguistic science, that is needful more obviously than in most sections of Scripture.

If, now, we approach the study of the section at present before us under the guidance of these principles, it is probable that we shall not find it impossible to follow at least its main drift.

The section opens with a vision of the victory of the Word of God, the King of Kings and Lord of Lords over all His enemies. We see Him come forth from heaven girt for war, followed by the armies of heaven; the birds of the air are summoned to the feast of corpses that shall be prepared for them: the armies of the enemy — the beasts and the kings of the earth — are gathered against Him and are totally destroyed; and "all the birds are filled with their flesh" (xix. 11–21). It is a vivid picture of a complete victory, an entire conquest, that we have here; and all the imagery of war and battle is employed to give it life. This is the symbol. The thing symbolized is obviously the complete victory of the Son of God over all the hosts of wickedness. Only a single hint of this signification is afforded by the language of the description, but that is enough. On two occasions we are carefully told that the sword by which the victory is won proceeds *out of the mouth* of the conqueror (verses 15 and 21). We are not to think, as we read, of any literal war or manual fighting, therefore; the conquest is wrought by the spoken word — in short, by the preaching of the Gospel. In fine, we have before us here a picture of the victorious career of the Gospel of Christ in the world. All the imagery of the dread battle and its hideous details are but to give us the impression of the completeness of the victory. Christ's Gospel is to conquer the earth: He is to overcome all His enemies.

There is, of course, nothing new in this. The victory of the Gospel was predicted over and over again even in Old Testament times under the figure of a spiritual conquest. It is thus also that Paul pictures it. It is thus that John himself elsewhere portrays it: it is indeed the staple representation of this whole book. In particular we perceive that this splendid vision is, after all, only the expansion of the parallel vision given in the second verse of the sixth chapter. When the first seal was opened, "And I saw," says the seer, "and, behold, a white horse, and he that sat thereon had a bow; and there was given unto him a crown: and he came forth conquering, and to conquer." It is the same scene that is now before us, only strengthened and made more emphatic as befits its place near the end of the book. We recall now the principle of "recapitulation" which governs the structure of the book, and see that this first vision of the last section, in accordance with the general method of the book, returns to the beginning and portrays for us, as vi. 2 and xii. 1 do, the first coming of the Lord and the purpose and now, with more detail and stress, the issue of this coming. What we have here, in effect, is a picture of the whole period between the first and second advents, seen from the point of view of heaven. It is the period of the advancing victory of the Son of God over the world, emphasizing, in harmony with its place at the end of the book, the completeness of the victory. It is the eleventh chapter of Romans and the fifteenth of I Corinthians in symbolical form: and there is nothing in it that was not already in them — except that, perhaps, the completeness of the triumph of the Gospel is possibly somewhat more emphasized here.

With the opening of the twentieth chapter the scene changes (xx. 1–10). Here we are not smitten in the face with the flame and flare of war: it is a spectacle of utter peace rather that is presented to us. The peace is, however, it must be observed, thrown up against a background of war. The vision opens with a picture of the descent of an angel out of heaven who binds "the dragon, the old serpent, which is the Devil and Satan," for a thousand years. Then we see the saints of God reigning with their Lord, and we are invited to contemplate the blessedness of their estate. But when Satan is bound we are significantly told that after the thousand years "he must be loosed for a little time." The saints themselves, moreover, we are informed, have not attained their exaltation and blessedness save through tribulation. They have all passed through the stress of this beast-beset life — have all been "beheaded" for the testimony of Jesus. And at the end we learn of the renewed activity of Satan and his final destruction by fire out of heaven.

This thousand-year peace that is set before us is therefore a peace hedged around with war. It was won by war; the participants in it have come to it through war; it ends in war. What now is this thousand-year peace? It is certainly not what we have come traditionally to understand by the "millennium," as is made evident by many considerations, and sufficiently so by this one: that those who participate in it are spoken of as mere "souls" (ver. 4) — "the souls of them that had been beheaded for the testimony of Jesus and for the Word of God." It is not disembodied souls who are to constitute the Church during its state of highest development on earth, when the knowledge of the glory of God covers the earth as the waters cover the sea. Neither is it disembodied souls who are thought of as constituting the kingdom which Christ is intending to set up in the earth after His advent, that they may rule with Him over the nations. And when we have said this, we are surely following hard on the pathway that leads to the true understanding of the vision. The vision, in one word, is a vision of the peace of those who have died in the Lord; and its message to us is embodied in the words of xiv. 13: "Blessed are the dead which die in the Lord, from henceforth" — of which passage the present is indeed only an expansion.

The picture that is brought before us here is, in fine, the picture of the "intermediate state" — of the saints of God gathered in heaven away from the confused noise and garments bathed in blood that characterize the war upon earth, in order that they may securely await the end.[8] The thousand years, thus, is the whole of this present dispensation, which again is placed before us in its entirety, but looked at now relatively not to what is passing on earth but to what is enjoyed "in Paradise." This, in fact, is the meaning of the symbol of a thousand years. For, this period between the advents is, on earth, a broken time — three and a half years, a "little time" (ver. 3) [9]

---

[8] So far L. Kraussold ("Das tausendjährige Reich," u. s. w., 1863) is right: "The souls of the righteous live before God and with God — that is their first resurrection." But though he thus correctly interprets the "first resurrection" of the intermediate state, he does not see that the "millennium" is the intermediate period.

[9] Cf. Milligan, "Baird Lectures," pp. 213–214; "Expositor's Bible," pp. 340–341. The *term* 'three and a half years' does not occur in the Apocalypse, but its equivalents, forty-two months (xi. 2, xiii. 5) and 1260 days (xi. 3, xii. 6) do, as well as the corresponding phrase "a time and times and half a time" (xii. 14), which is derived of course from Daniel vii. 25, xii. 7. All these designations alike "express the whole time of the Church's militant and suffering condition in the

— which, amid turmoil and trouble, the saints are encouraged
to look upon as of short duration, soon to be over. To the saints
in bliss it is, on the contrary, a long and blessed period passing
slowly and peacefully by, while they reign with Christ and enjoy the blessedness of holy communion with Him — "a thousand years." [10]

Of course the passage (xx. 1–10) does not give us a direct
description of "the intermediate state." We must bear in mind
that the book we are reading is written in symbols and gives us
a direct description of nothing that it sets before us, but always
a direct description only of the symbol by which it is represented. In the preceding vision (xix. 11–21) we had no direct
description of the triumph and progress of the Gospel, but only
of a fierce and gruesome war: the single phrase that spoke of
the slaying sword as "proceeding out of the mouth" of the
conqueror alone indicated that it was a conquest by means of
persuading words. So here we are not to expect a direct description of the "intermediate state": were such a description
given, that would be evidence enough that the intermediate
state was not intended, but was rather the symbol of something
else. The single hint that it is of the condition of the "souls"
of those who have died in Christ and for Christ that the seer is
speaking, is enough here to direct our thoughts in the right
direction. What is described, or rather, to speak more exactly —
for it is a course of events that is brought before us — what is
narrated to us is the chaining of Satan "that he should deceive
the nations no more"; the consequent security and glory of
Christ's hitherto persecuted people; and the subsequent destruction of Satan. It is a description in the form of a narrative:

world, the whole time between the First and Second Coming of the Lord" (Milligan: Com. in Schaff's "Pop. Com. on N. T." on xi. 2, pp. 93, 94, where there is
a clear and full statement). For the equivalent phrase "a little time" the references at the head of this note will suffice.

[10] Cf. Lee ("Speaker's Com." on xx. 2, p. 792): "That the period of a 'thousand
years' is to be taken figuratively is in accordance with such texts as Ps. xc. 4,
. . . or II Peter iii. 8 . . . A space of time absolutely long is denoted. . . .
A very great although not a countless number is signified. . . . . We are to
understand a long though finite duration, beginning from the First Advent of
Christ (I Cor. xv. 24, 25)."

the element of time and chronological succession belongs to the symbol, not to the thing symbolized. The "binding of Satan" is, therefore, in reality, not for a season, but with reference to a sphere; and his "loosing" again is not after a period but in another sphere: it is not subsequence but exteriority that is suggested. There is, indeed, no literal "binding of Satan" to be thought of at all: what happens, happens not to Satan but to the saints, and is only represented as happening to Satan for the purposes of the symbolical picture. What actually happens is that the saints described are removed from the sphere of Satan's assaults. The saints described are free from all access of Satan — he is bound with respect to them: outside of their charmed circle his horrid work goes on. This is indicated, indeed, in the very employment of the two symbols "a thousand years" and "a little time." A "thousand years" is the symbol of heavenly completeness and blessedness; the "little time" of earthly turmoil and evil. Those in the "thousand years" are safe from Satan's assaults: those outside the thousand years are still enduring his attacks. And therefore he, though with respect to those in the thousand years bound, is not destroyed; and the vision accordingly requires to close with an account of his complete destruction, and of course this also must needs be presented in the narrative form of a release of Satan, the gathering of his hosts and their destruction from above.

We may perhaps profitably advert to some of the traits that go to show that it is the children of God gathered in Paradise that are in view in the description of the rest and security that occupies the central section of the vision (vers. 4–6). We are told that the seer saw "thrones, and those that sat upon them, and judgment was given to them." Our Lord, we will remember, is uniformly represented as having been given a Messianic kingship in reward for His redemptive death, in order that He might carry out His mediatorial work to the end.[11] Those who, being His, go away from the body and home to the Lord, are accordingly conceived by the seer as ascending the throne with Him to share His kingship — not forever, however, but for a

[11] E. g., Phil. ii. 10.

thousand years, *i.e.*, for the Messianic period. Then, when the last enemy has been conquered and He restores the kingdom to the Father,[12] their co-reign with Him ceases, because His Messianic kingdom itself ceases. These reigning saints, now, are described as "souls" — a term which carries us back irresistibly to vi. 9, where we read of "the souls of them that had been slain for the Word of God resting underneath the altar," a passage of which the present is an expanded version. Similarly here, too, we are told that these souls are "of them that had been beheaded for the testimony of Jesus and for the Word of God, and such as worshipped not the beast, neither his image and received not the mark upon their forehead and upon their hand." The description in the symbol is drawn from the fate of martyrs; but it is not literal martyrs that are meant in the thing symbolized. To the seer all of Christ's saints are martyrs of the world. "For in the eyes of John," as has been well said, "all the disciples of a martyred Lord are martyrs": "Christ's Church is a martyr Church, she dies in her Master's service and for the world's good."[13] These all, dying in Christ, die not but live — for Christ is not Lord, any more than God is God, of the dead but the living. We must catch here the idea that pervades the whole of Jewish thought — inculcated as it is with the most constant iteration by the whole Old Testament revelation — that death is the penalty of sin and that restoration from death, that is resurrection, is involved, therefore, in reception into the favor of God. It is this that underlies and gives its explanation to our Lord's famous argument for the resurrection to which we have just alluded. And it is this, doubtless, that underlies also the seer's designation in our passage of the state of the souls in Paradise with their Lord, saved in principle if not in complete fruition, as "the first resurrection." "This," he says, "is the first resurrection"; and he pronounces those blessed who have part in it, and declares that over them "the

---

[12] I Cor. xv. 54.

[13] Milligan, "The Expositor's Bible: the Book of Revelation," pp. 182, 344. Cf. his beautiful words in Schaff's "Popular Commentary, The Revelation," *in loc.* IV.

second death" has no power. Subsequently he identifies "the second death" with eternal destruction (ver. 14) in the lake of fire — the symbol throughout these visions of the final state of the wicked. To say that "the second death" has no power over the saints of whom he is here speaking is to say at once that they have already been subjected to the "first death," which can mean only that they have suffered bodily death, and that they are "saved souls" with their life hidden with Christ in God. That is to say, they are the blessed dead — the dwellers in the "intermediate state." The "first resurrection" is here, therefore, the symbolical description of what has befallen those who while dead yet live in the Lord; and it is set in contrast with the "second resurrection," which must mean the restoration of the bodily life. As partakers of this "first resurrection" they are set in contrast with "the rest of the dead" — who were to "live not" until "the thousand years should be finished." This phrase advertises us once more that those of whom the seer speaks are themselves in a sense "dead," and as they are declared repeatedly to be *living* — living and reigning with Christ — this cannot refer to spiritual death, but must find its reference to bodily death. Though dead, therefore, in this bodily sense, they were yet alive — alive in the paradise of God with Christ. The rest of the dead, on the other hand — those not alive with Christ — wait for the end to live again: they are in every sense dead — already suffering the penalty of sin and to be restored to even bodily life only to be plunged into the terrible "second death."

It seems scarcely possible to read over these three verses, however cursorily, without meeting thus with constant reminders that the peace and security pictured is the peace and security of the blessed dead, seated in the heavenly places, in their Lord, on the throne of the universe in company with Him. Any hesitancy we may feel to adopt this view appears to arise chiefly from the difficulty we naturally experience in reading this apparently historical narrative as a descriptive picture of a state — in translating, so to speak, the dynamic language of narrative into the static language of description. Does not the

very term "a thousand years" suggest the lapse of time? And
must we not, therefore, interpret what is represented as occurring before and after this thousand years as historical prece-
dents and subsequents to it? Natural as this feeling is, we are
persuaded it is grounded only on a certain not unnatural incapacity to enter fully into the seer's method and to give ourselves entirely to his guidance. If he elected to represent a state
of completeness and perfection by a symbol which suggested
lapse of time when taken in its literal meaning, he had no choice
but to represent what was outside this state as *before* or *after:*
that belonged to the very vehicle of representation. Now it is
quite certain that the number 1000 represents in Bible symbolism absolute perfection and completeness; and that the
symbolism of the Bible includes also the use of a period of time
in order to express the idea of greatness, in connection with
thoroughness and completeness.[14] It can scarcely be necessary
to insist here afresh on the symbolical use of numbers in the
Apocalypse and the necessity consequently laid upon the interpreter to treat them consistently not merely as symbols but
as symbols embodying definite ideas. They constitute a language, and like any other language they are misleading unless
intended and read as expressions of definite ideas. When the
seer says seven or four or three or ten, he does not name these
numbers at random but expresses by each a specific notion. The
sacred number seven in combination with the equally sacred
number three forms the number of holy perfection ten, and
when this ten is cubed into a thousand the seer has said all he
could say to convey to our minds the idea of absolute completeness. It is of more importance doubtless, however, to illustrate
the use of time-periods to convey the idea of completeness.
Ezek. xxxix. 9 provides an instance. There the completeness of
the conquest of Israel over its enemies is expressed by saying
that seven years shall be consumed in the burning up of the
débris of battle: they "shall go forth," we read, "and shall make
fires of the weapons and burn them, both the shields and the
bucklers, the bows and the arrows, and the hand-staves and

14 Dr. Milligan has shown this very convincingly.

the spears, and they shall *make fires of them seven years.*" It were absurd to suppose that it is intended that the fires shall actually endure seven years. We have here only a hyperbole to indicate the greatness of the mass to be consumed and the completeness of the consumption. A somewhat similar employment of the time-phrase to express the idea of greatness is found in the twelfth verse of the same chapter, where, after the defeat of Gog "and all his multitude," it is said, "And seven months shall the children of Israel be burying of them that they may cleanse the land." That is to say, the multitude of the dead is so great that by way of hyperbole their burial is said to consume seven months. The number seven employed by Ezekiel in these passages is replaced by the number a thousand in our present passage, with the effect of greatly enhancing the idea of greatness and of completeness conveyed. When the saints are said to live and reign with Christ a thousand years the idea intended is that of inconceivable exaltation, security and blessedness — a completeness of exaltation, security and blessedness beyond expression by ordinary language.

We can scarcely go the length of Dr. Milligan, nevertheless, and say that the time-element is wholly excluded from our passage. After all it is the intermediate state that is portrayed and the intermediate state has duration. But it is within the limits of sobriety to say that the time-element retires into the background and the stress is laid on the greatness and completeness of the security portrayed. This is, however, portrayed under a time-symbol: and the point now is that, this being so, the very necessity of the symbolism imposed on the writer the representation of the other elements of the symbol also by time-expressions. Accordingly in the picture which he draws for us the vision of the security of the saints is preceded and followed by scenes represented as occurring before and after it, but to be read as occurring merely outside it. The chaining of Satan is not in the event a preliminary transaction, on which the security of the saints follows: nor is the loosing of Satan a subsequent transaction, on which the security of the saints ceases. The saints rather escape entirely beyond the reach of Satan when they ascend to their Lord and take their seats on His throne by His side, and there they abide nevermore subject to his assaults. This is indeed suggested in the issue (verse 9b), where the destruction of Satan is compassed by a fire from heaven and not through the medium of a battle with the saints. But while the saints abide in their security Satan, though thus "bound" relatively to them, is loosed relatively to the world — and that is what is meant by the statement in verse 3c that "he must be loosed for a little time" — which is the symbol of the inter-adventual period, in the world; and not less in verses 7-10. We must here look on the time-element, we repeat, as belonging wholly to the symbol and read in the interpretation space-elements in its place. The intermediate state is in one word conceived of not out of relation to the "world," but as, so to speak, a safe haven of retreat in the midst of the world: the world is around it, and there Satan still works and deceives, but he who escapes through the one door of "beheading" for Christ's sake, rises not only to security but to a kingdom.

As we scrutinize the text closely with this scheme of interpretation in mind, the apparent difficulties that stand in its path give way one after another. One clause alone seems so recalcitrant as not to lend itself readily to the proposed interpretation. This occurs in the middle of verse 3. There it is affirmed that Satan is chained "that he should deceive the nations no more." Under Dr. Milligan's interpretation of the thousand years' security, which he applies not to the saints in glory with their Lord — the intermediate state — but to the saints in conflict on earth — the militant state — this clause seems no doubt hopeless. But if we are to understand that it is the intermediate state that is portrayed, the difficulty which it presents does not seem to be insuperable. In its general meaning the clause indeed is only the extreme point of the temporal-machinery in which the vision is cast. If what is *spacially* distinct, so to speak, in the reality, is to be represented in the figure as *temporally* distinct, there seems no way in which it can be done except by saying that Satan is first bound so as not to act, in order that he may be afterward loosed so as to act. The only real difficulty lies in the word "nations." Should we not expect "saints" instead — for is it not merely with reference to the saints that Satan is supposed to be bound? And is not the word "nations" the standing denomination in the Apocalypse of precisely the anti-Christian hosts? The only solution that readily suggests itself turns on the supposition that the word "nations" may be used here in its wider inclusive sense, and not of "those without" in contrast with God's people. The term "world" occurs in this double sense, and there seems no reason why "nations" should not also, especially since it is continually understood that the "nations" include God's people in the making (xxii. 2). Possibly little more is intended to be conveyed by the phrase in verse 3 than "to bring out and express that aspect of Satan by which he is specially distinguished in the Apocalypse" — that is to say, to declare simply that "Satan the deceiver" was bound,[15] and what is more than this belongs to the drapery of the symbolism. In verse 8 it appears to have a slightly different turn given it. There is a special propriety in its suggesting in this context "those without" indeed, but those without not so much the circle of Christ's people in general as Christ's people as gathered into the secure haven of the intermediate state. In a word, it seems that we may understand the "nations" here, not of the anti-Christian world in contrast with the Christian, but of the world on earth in contrast with the saints gathered in Paradise. As such the "nations" may include Christians also, but Christians not yet departed to their security — nay their monarchy — with their Lord. If these suggestions be allowed, something will certainly be gained towards a suitable interpretation of the clause. But it cannot be pretended that a real solution of its difficulties has been offered in any case; it remains a dark spot in an otherwise lucid paragraph and must be left for subsequent study to explain.

If the interpretation we have urged be adopted, this vision, therefore, as a whole (xx. 1–20), in sharp contrast with the pre-

[15] We are quoting here from Dr. Milligan's "Baird Lectures," first ed., pp. 223–225 note, which seems to us more suggestive than the note in "The Expositor's Bible" volume, pp. 350–351.

ceding one (xix. 11–21), which pictured the strife of God's people in the world, brings before us the spectacle of the peace of God's saints gathered in heaven. It, too, embraces the whole inter-adventual period, but that period as passed in the security and glory of the intermediate state. This is set forth, however, not out of relation to the militant Church on earth, but as, so to speak, its other side. It is as if the seer had said, Look on this picture and on that: neither alone, but the two in combination supply the true picture of the course of events between the first and second advents. The Church toiling and struggling here below is but half the story: the Church gathering above is the other half. And both speed them to the end. For the one it is a period of conflict, though of a conflict advancing to victory. For the other it is a period of restful security, nay of royal ruling. It is the conjunction of the two that constitutes this inter-adventual period; and, together, they pass onward to the end:

> Blesséd that flock safe penned in Paradise;
> Blesséd this flock which tramps in weary ways;
> All form one flock, God's flock; all yield Him praise
> By joy or pain, still tending towards the prize."

Accordingly this vision is followed by a third, in which is depicted the last judgment, in which all — both in earth and heaven — partake. That this is the *general* judgment seems to be obvious on the face of it. Those whom it concerns are described as "the dead, both great and small," which seems to be an inclusive designation. That it is not merely the wicked who are summoned to it appears from the fact that not only the "book of deeds," but also the "book of life" is employed in it, and it is only those whose names are not found written in the book of life that are cast into the lake of fire — whence it seems to follow that some are present whose names are written in the "book of life." The destruction of "death and Hades" does not imply that the judgment is over the enemies of God only, but merely that hereafter, as Paul, too, says, death shall be no more. There is, no doubt, the "second death," but this is the lake of fire, that is to say, the eternal torment. It is, thus, the great final assize that is here presented to our contemplation: implying the general resurrection and preparing the entrance into eternal destiny. The former fulfills the proleptic declaration in verse 5 that "the rest of the dead lived not until the thousand years should be finished": now they are finished and "the second resurrection," in which all — not Christ's people only — share, takes place: and accordingly they, too, are, in this reference, classed among "the dead" (ver. 12). The latter is adverted to, so far as the wicked are concerned, with the brevity consonant with this culminating part of the Apocalypse, in the concluding verse of the chapter: "And if any was not found written in the book of life, he was cast into the lake of fire." With respect to the destiny of God's saints, the things the seer has to say of them require new visions.

The scene, therefore, shifts at once and a new vision is presented to us (xxi. 1–8). It is the vision of the consummated kingdom of God. There is a new heaven and a new earth: and the new Jerusalem, the city of God, descends from heaven: and God makes His dwelling in its midst: and the happy inheritance of the saints is exhibited to us in all its richness and blessedness. To enhance the value and desirableness of this picture of holy bliss destined for God's people it is set between two declarations of the fate of the wicked (xx. 15, xxi. 8).

Nor is this all. For this vision is followed immediately by a symbolical description of the glorified people of God under the similitude of a city (xxi. 9–xxii. 5). It is the bride, the wife of the Lamb (verse 9) that is depicted: and she is described as a perfect and glorious city in which the Lord makes His abode, and which He Himself supplies with all that it can need. This is not a picture of heaven, be it observed: it is a picture of the heavenly estate of the Church — not merely of the ideal of the Church, but of the ideal of the Church as *realized*, after the turmoil of earth and the secluded waiting in Paradise alike are over. We quite agree with Dr. Milligan then when, in his latest exposition, he expounds the vision as a "detailed account of the true Church under the figure of a city," and remarks that

this "city is really a figure, not of a place but of a people: it is
not the final home of the redeemed: it is the redeemed themselves." But we cannot go with him when he adds that it is
"essentially a picture, not of the future, but of the present; of
the ideal condition of Christ's true people, of His 'little flock'
on earth, in every age." [16] True, it may be that "every blessing
limned in upon this canvas is *in principle* the believer's now,"
but the realization of these blessings for the Church, as a whole,
is surely reserved until the time when that Church shall at
length be presented to its Lord "a glorious Church, not having
spot or wrinkle or any such thing, but holy and without blemish." "And I saw," said the seer, when he was contemplating
the consummating glory (xxi. 2), "the holy city, new Jerusalem,
coming down out of heaven from God, made ready as a bride
adorned for her husband." But now, gazing in vision on the
consummated glory, he has even more to show us. "Come
hither," the angel said to him (xxi. 9), and "I will show thee
the bride, *the Lamb's wife.*" The marriage has now taken place,
it is no longer the bride preparing for her husband, or even the
bride adorned for her husband: it is the bride, "*the Lamb's
wife.*" "The Church," says Dr. Milligan himself in an earlier
and in this point, we belive, a better exposition, "is not only
espoused *but married to her Lord.*" Gazing on the beautiful
traits limned for us, we see not indeed what we are, but what
we shall be, and who can wonder if we cry with the sweet
singer, Would God we were there!

It is not our purpose to go into a detailed exegesis of these
visions. We content ourselves with this mere suggestion of their
essential contents, satisfied to draw out from them merely the
great features of the eschatology of the Apocalypse, culminating as it does in this section in which is summed up its entire
teaching. So far as serves this purpose, we venture to hope that
the exposition will commend itself as reasonable: and it will

---

[16] "Expositor's Bible" volume on "The Book of Revelation" (1889), pp.
364, 368, 373. In his earlier "Commentary" in Dr. Schaff's "Popular Com. on the
N. T.," Dr. Milligan had interpreted this vision of the consummated Church —
though not of the Church so much as of its "eternal home," *i.e.*, heaven.

be wise not to lose ourselves in doubtful details of exegesis which might cloud the light that shines on the more general outline. Our main hesitation turns upon the distribution of the several visions. As we have read the section, we have separated it into only five visions. The whole structure of the Apocalypse is, however, dominated by the number seven. With a prologue and an epilogue the book is compounded of seven parallel and yet climactically wrought-out main sections. Four of these are formally subdivided into seven subsections each. It seems probable that this sevenfold structure runs through the remaining sections also, although it is not formally announced in them, and is left, therefore, for the reader to trace. On this ground we should expect the section now engaging our attention — xix. 11–xxii. 5 — to offer us a series of seven visions. But only five have been signalized by us. The suspicion lies close that we have in subdividing the section into its constituent visions missed two of its division lines. We think it very likely we have done so, but we have not been able to put our finger on obvious lines of cleavage, and have preferred to let the material fall apart where it naturally falls apart and to attempt no artificial dissecting. Possibly the points of separation may present themselves more clearly to others. In any event, it seems probable that if two separate visions have been confused by us into one, it is because they are very closely related visions, from one of which to the other there is rather progress than transition. In that very probable case the main lines of exposition would not be affected: and the purpose of our present enterprise would be secured as fully as if we had succeeded in separating between them.

What, then, is the eschatological outline we have gained from a study of this section? Briefly stated it is as follows. Our Lord Jesus Christ came to conquer the world to H'mself, and this He does with a thoroughness and completeness which seems to go beyond even the intimations of Romans xi and I Cor. xv. Meanwhile, as the conquest of the world is going on below, the saints who die in the Lord are gathered in Paradise to reign with their Lord, who is also Lord of all, and who is from His throne directing the conquest of the world. When the victory is completely won there supervenes the last judgment and the final destruction of the wicked. At once there is a new heaven and a new earth and the consummation of the glory of the Church. And this Church abides forever (xxii. 5), in perfection of holiness and blessedness. In bare outline that is what our section teaches. It will be noted at once that it is precisely the teaching of the didactic epistles of Paul and of the whole New Testament with him. No attempts to harmonize as the several types of teaching are necessary, therefore, for their entire harmony lies on the surface. John knows no more of two resurrections — of the saints and of the wicked — than does Paul: and the whole theory of an intervening millennium — and indeed of a millennium of any kind on earth — goes up in smoke. We are forced, indeed, to add our assent to Kliefoth's conclusion, that "the doctrine of a thousand-year kingdom has no foundation in the prophecies of the New Testament, and is therefore not a dogma but merely a hypothesis lacking all Biblical ground." [17] The millennium of the Apocalypse is the blessedness of the saints who have gone away from the body to be at home with the Lord.

But this conclusion obviously does not carry with it the denial that a "golden age" yet lies before the Church, if we may use this designation in a purely spiritual sense. As emphatically as Paul, John teaches that the earthly history of the Church is not a history merely of conflict with evil, but of conquest over evil: and even more richly than Paul, John teaches that this conquest will be decisive and complete. The whole meaning of the vision of xix. 11–21 is that Christ Jesus comes forth not to war merely but to victory; and every detail of the picture is laid in with a view precisely to emphasizing the thoroughness of this victory. The Gospel of Christ is, John being witness, completely to conquer the world. He says nothing, any more than Paul does, of the period of the endurance of this conquered world. Whether the last judgment and the consummated kingdom are to follow immediately upon its conquest — his visions

[17] "Christl. Eschatol.," 1886, p. 188.

are as silent as Paul's teaching. But just on that account the possibility of an extended duration for the conquered earth lies open: and in any event a progressively advancing conquest of the earth by Christ's Gospel implies a coming age deserving at least the relative name of "golden." Perhaps a distinction may be made between a converted earth and a sanctified earth: such a distinction seems certainly more accordant with the tone of these visions than that more commonly suggested between a witnessed-to earth and a converted earth. The Gospel assuredly must be preached to the whole world as a witness, before the Lord comes. These visions seem to go farther and to teach that the earth — the whole world — must be won to Christ before He comes: and that it is precisely this conquest of it that He is accomplishing during the progress of this inter-adventual period.

Whether they go so far as to say that this winning of the world implies the complete elimination of evil from it may be more doubtful. In favor of the one view is the tremendous emphasis laid on the overthrow of all Christ's enemies, which must mean precisely his spiritual opponents — all that militates against the perfection of His rule over the hearts of men. In favor of the other is the analogy of the individual life, in which complete sanctification lags behind after the life has been in principle won to God. Perhaps it may even be said that a perfect life is not to be thought possible for sin-born men in the conditions of this sin-cursed world. Perhaps it may be affirmed that what is thus true of each individual must be true of the congeries of these individuals which we call the world. Perhaps it may be maintained on such grounds as these that as the perfecting of the individual waits for the next life, so the perfecting of the world must wait until the conquest is over — the last assize is held — and the New Jerusalem descends from heaven. In a word, that the perfected world — with all that means — is not to be discovered at xix. 21, but at xxi. 1, and that the description of it is to be read therefore in xxi. 9–xxii. 5, and at no previous point. No doubt there is an element of speculation in such suppositions, and we may well be content to leave the text to teach its own lessons, without additions from us. These lessons, however, at least include as much as this: that there is a "golden age" before the Church — at least an age relatively golden gradually ripening to higher and higher glories as the Church more and more fully conquers the world and all the evil of the world; and ultimately an age absolutely golden when the perfected Church is filled with the glory of the Lord in the new earth and under the new heavens. All the aspirations of the prophets, all the dreams of the seers, can surely find satisfaction in this great vision.

Meanwhile, the saints of God do not need to await the consummation of the ages before they enter into the joy of their Lord. Even "in this world" they receive their reward. The seer, in his vision, sees their accumulated hosts. But through all the years they are gathering, —

> "They are flocking from the East
> And the West,
> They are flocking from the North
> And the South,
> Every moment setting forth,
>
> * * * * .* *
>
> Palm in hand, and praise in mouth,
> They are flocking up the path
> To their rest."

This their "rest" is the "Millennium" of the Apocalypse.

LIST OF OTHER ARTICLES ON BIBLICAL DOCTRINES

I. Doubt. (Article in Hastings' "Dictionary of the Bible," v. i, pp. 618–619.)

II. Godhead. (Article in the "International Standard Bible Encyclopaedia," v. ii, pp. 1268–1270.)

III. Little Ones. (Article in Hastings' "Dictionary of Christ and the Gospels," v. ii, pp. 36–39.)

IV. New Testament Terms Descriptive of the Great Change. (*The Presb. Quarterly*, v. v, 1891, pp. 91–100.)

V. The Principle of the Incarnation. (*The Bible Student*, v. ii, 1900, pp. 315–323.)

VI. The Fundamental Significance of the Lord's Supper. (*The Bible Student*, v. iii, 1901, pp. 77–83.)

VII. God's Revelation of Himself to Israel. (*The Bible Student and Teacher*, v. vii, 1907, pp. 289–292.)

VIII. The Meaning of "Adam" in the Old Testament Hebrew. (*The Bible Student and Teacher*, v. viii, 1908, pp. 130–138.)

IX. On the Emotional Life of Our Lord. (Princeton Theol. Sem., "Biblical and Theol. Studies," 1912, pp. 35–90.)

X. The Importunate Widow and the Alleged Failure of Faith. (*The Exp. Times*, v. xxv, 1913–1914, pp. 69–72, 136–139.)

XI. The Gospel and the Second Coming. (*The Bible Magazine*, v. iii, 1915, pp. 300–309.)

XII. Are They Few That be Saved? (*Lutheran Ch. Rev.*, v. xxxiv, 1915, pp. 42–58.)

XIII. Election. 22 pp. Phila. 1918.

XIV. Jesus Christ the Propitiation for the Whole World. (*The Expositor*, 8th ser., v. xxi, 1921, pp. 241–253.)

XV. Antichrist. (*The Exp. Times*. v. xxxii, 1920–1921 pp. 358–360.)